JAZZ SCHOLARSHIP AND PEDAGOGY

Routledge Music Bibliographies

SERIES EDITOR: BRAD EDEN

COMPOSERS

Isaac Albéniz (1998)
Walter A. Clark

C. P. E. Bach (2002)
Doris Bosworth Powers

Samuel Barber (2001)
Wayne C. Wentzel

Béla Bartók, Second Edition (1997)
Elliott Antokoletz

Vincenzo Bellini (2002)
Stephen A. Willier

Alban Berg (1996)
Bryan R. Simms

Leonard Bernstein (2001)
Paul F. Laird

Johannes Brahms (2003)
Heather Platt

Benjamin Britten (1996)
Peter J. Hodgson

William Byrd, Second Edition (2005)
Richard Turbet

Elliott Carter (2000)
John L. Link

Carlos Chávez (1998)
Robert Parker

Frédéric Chopin (1999)
William Smialek

Aaron Copland (2001)
Marta Robertson and Robin Armstrong

Frederick Delius (2005)
Mary Christison Huismann

Gaetano Donizetti (2000)
James P. Cassaro

Edward Elgar (1993)
Christopher Kent

Gabriel Fauré (1999)
Edward R. Phillips

Christoph Willibald Gluck, Second Edition (2003)
Patricia Howard

G. F. Handel Second Edition (2005)
Mary Ann Parker

Paul Hindemith (2005)
Stephen Luttmann

Charles Ives (2002)
Gayle Sherwood

Scott Joplin (1998)
Nancy R. Ping-Robbins

Zoltán Kodály (1998)
Mícheál Houlahan and Philip Tacka

Franz Liszt, Second Edition (2003)
Michael Saffle

Guillaume de Machaut (1995)
Lawrence Earp

Felix Mendelssohn Bartholdy (2001)
John Michael Cooper

Giovanni Pierluigi da Palestrina (2001)
Clara Marvin

Giacomo Puccini (1999)
Linda B. Fairtile

Maurice Ravel (2004)
Stephen Zank

Gioachino Rossini (2002)
Denise P. Gallo

Camille Saint-Saëns (2003)
Timothy S. Flynn

Alessandro and Domenico Scarlatti (1993)
Carole F. Vidali

Heinrich Schenker (2003)
Benjamin Ayotte

Jean Sibelius (1998)
Glenda D. Goss

Giuseppe Verdi (1998)
Gregory Harwood

Tomás Luis de Victoria (1998)
Eugene Casjen Cramer

Richard Wagner (2002)
Michael Saffle

Adrian Willaert (2004)
David M. Kidger

GENRES

American Music Librarianship (2005)
Carol June Bradley

Central European Folk Music (1996)
Philip V. Bohlman

Chamber Music (2002)
John H. Baron

Choral Music (2001)
Avery T. Sharp and James Michael Floyd

Ethnomusicology (2003)
Jennifer C. Post

Jazz Scholarship and Pedagogy, Third Edition (2005)
Eddie S. Meadows

Music in Canada (1997)
Carl Morey

The Musical (2004)
William Everett

North American Indian Music (1997)
Richard Keeling

Opera, Second Edition (2001)
Guy Marco

The Recorder, Second Edition (2003)
Richard Griscom and David Lasocki

Serial Music and Serialism (2001)
John D. Vander Weg

String Quartets (2005)
Mara E. Parker

Women in Music (2005)
Karin Pendle

JAZZ SCHOLARSHIP
AND PEDAGOGY
THIRD EDITION

A RESEARCH AND INFORMATION GUIDE

EDDIE S. MEADOWS

ROUTLEDGE MUSIC BIBLIOGRAPHIES

Routledge
Taylor & Francis Group
New York   London

Published in 2006 by
Routledge
Taylor & Francis Group
711 Third Avenue
New York, NY 10017

Published in Great Britain by
Routledge
Taylor & Francis Group
2 Park Square
Milton Park, Abingdon
Oxon OX14 4RN

© 2006 by Taylor & Francis Group, LLC
Routledge is an imprint of Taylor & Francis Group

International Standard Book Number-10: 0-415-93965-8 (Hardcover)
International Standard Book Number-13: 978-0-415-93965-2 (Hardcover)
Library of Congress Card Number 2005013887

Library of Congress Cataloging-in-Publication Data

Meadows, Eddie S.
    Jazz scholarship and pedagogy : a research and information guide / Eddie S. Meadows.-- 3rd ed.
        p. cm. -- (Routledge music bibliographies)
    Includes index.
    ISBN 0-415-93965-8 (hardback : alk. paper)
    1. Jazz--Bibliography. I. Title. II. Series.

ML128.J3M34 2005
016.78165--dc22

2005013887

Taylor & Francis Group
is the Academic Division of Informa plc.

Visit the Taylor & Francis Web site at
http://www.taylorandfrancis.com

and the Routledge Web site at
http://www.routledge-ny.com

To J.J.
For your support and love.

Contents

Preface

The purpose of this bibliography is to provide the scholar, performer, and teacher with the most comprehensive annotated list of materials to date on jazz. Coverage is limited to books dating from the 1920s through late 2004, representing both domestic and foreign publishers. The annotations are divided into 15 major categories, and some categories are further subdivided.

This bibliography differs from those of Carner (1990), Gray (1988), Gregor (1969), Haselgrove and Kennington (1960), Horn (1977), Kennington and Read (1980), Meadows (1981), Meadows (1995), Merriam and Benford (1974), and Reisner (1959) in one or all of the following ways: (1) it is completely annotated; (2) it contains research, performance, and teaching materials; and (3) it contains categories such as "Theses and Dissertations," "Videos," "Journals," and "Collections" (recordings and the Harlequin Collection of Jazz and Hot Dance) not covered in any previously published jazz reference work. Although the 1995 bibliography differs from my first work, *Jazz Reference and Research Materials* (1981), in both the previously mentioned ways and because of its comprehensive coverage, a limited number of entries cited were retained for the 1995 reference work. In the 1995 work, overlap occurred in two broad areas and can be summarized as follows: identical annotations were indicated by including the year (1981) in the citation, and annotation revisions were indicated. However, this new reference book retains all entries from the 1995 book, and includes both books not cited in 1995 as well as a comprehensive sampling of books and pedagogical materials published since 1995. Although adding over 800 new entries and an essay to the 1995 book, this new reference book retains the organizational structure of the 1995 book with occasional expansions and revisions to individual categories. Also, in a few instances, an entry might be cited under two different categories if, in the author's opinion, it will aid the researcher or teacher.

This reference guide is limited to books and therefore should not be construed as the most comprehensive annotated listing of either jazz research or performance materials. Although the literature is permeated with scholarly articles, these were not included because of the difficulty in obtaining copies for annotation. Instead, this is, to date, the most comprehensive sampling of books and other materials devoted to jazz research, performance, and pedagogy. Finally, although the preponderance of entries are by American authors, the "Jazz in World Cultures" category includes a wide sampling of books published outside of America, many in foreign languages. The latter were chosen based upon their availability to the author.

The categories reflect an attempt to produce a comprehensive, user-friendly reference for performers, researchers, and teachers of jazz. The annotations are factual, descriptive, and in many cases, evaluative. They are limited to the writer's appraisal of the literature and are not meant to represent the conclusions of others.

References

Carl Gregor, Herzog zu Mecklenburg. *International Jazz Bibliography: Jazz Books from 1917 to 1969.* Graz: Universal Edition; 1969.

Carner, Gary, (compiler). *Jazz Performers: An Annotated Bibliography of Biographical Materials.* Foreword by John Chilton. New York, London, Westport, Conn.: Greenwood Press (Music Reference Collection, Number 26); 1990.

Gray, John. *Fire Music: A Bibliography of the New Jazz, 1959–1990.* Foreword by Val Wilmer. Westport, Conn.: Greenwood Press; 1991.

Haselgrove, J. R., and Donald Kennington (Editors). *Reader's Guide to Books of Jazz.* Two Volumes. London: Library Association, County Libraries Section; 1960.

Horn, David. *The Literature of American Music in Books and Folk Music Collections: A Fully Annotated Bibliography.* Metuchen, N.J.: Scarecrow; 1977.

Kennington, David, and Danny L. Read. *The Literature of Jazz: A Critical Guide.* Chicago: American Library Association; 1980.

Meadows, Eddie S. *Jazz Research and Performance Materials: A Select Annotated Bibliography.* Second Edition. New York and London: Garland Publishing; 1995.

_____. *Jazz Reference and Research Materials: A Bibliography.* New York: Garland Publishing; 1981.

Merriam, Alan P., and Robert J. Benford. *A Bibliography of Jazz.* Philadelphia: American Folklore Society; 1974.

Reisner, Robert George. *The Literature of Jazz: A Selective Bibliography.* Second Revised Edition. New York: New York Public Library; 1959.

Acknowledgments

This work is the culmination of a process that began after the publication of my first two jazz reference books, *Jazz Reference and Research Materials* (1981), and *Jazz Research and Performance Materials: A Select Annotated Bibliography* (1995). This new reference book is the result of long and arduous hours spent reading, annotating, and editing, and will, I hope, prove useful to scholars, performers, and teachers. Both individuals and publishers have assisted me, with contributions ranging from identifying and locating materials to general encouragement. Among the many individuals that should be recognized are Jacqueline DjeDje and Olly W. Wilson. I wish to thank the numerous nameless individuals who toil at publishing houses and helped to identify, secure, and route me to appropriate individuals or departments. In addition to the aforementioned, a special acknowledgment is due to the music librarians at UC Berkeley, UCLA, and San Diego State University, and to Rebecca Leyden of KPBS (San Diego State University). A special thanks to Richard Carlin, Shannon McLachlan, and Robert Sims of Taylor & Francis for their assistance in making this new reference book a reality.

I welcome any and all information on corrections, omissions, and revised editions. I accept full responsibility for the contents of this bibliography.

Affecting Presence: Horace Silver's Funky Style

Throughout its history, jazz research has focused primarily on autobiographical and biographical studies and on studies that deal with historical and stylistic assessments. However, in recent years, ethnomusicologists and others have expanded the scholarly research of jazz to include issues of gender, identity, representation, and social context. In addition, they have espoused research methodologies that include anthropological, literary, philosophical, and sociological paradigms, thereby expanding ways and means that scholars can appreciate and understand jazz as a cultural phenomenon inextricably linked to an ever-changing social context. In an attempt to illuminate the importance of attitudes, beliefs, and philosophy in composing and improvising jazz, I use the ideas of Robert Plant Armstrong to deconstruct selected funky compositions and improvisations of Horace Silver. My goal is to provide an understanding of both the affective and cognitive attributes that constitute his funky style.

Jazz Context

In the 1950s and 1960s, jazz styles were nurtured and developed in at least three stylistic directions. One direction was bebop, a style rooted in the harmonic inventions of Thelonious Monk, and the improvisations of Dizzy Gillespie, Fats Navarro, Charles Parker, Bud Powell, and others. Bebop featured melodies based on disjunct intervals, the use of harmonic changes based on "I Got Rhythm," ii–V–I, and I–Vi–ii–V–I progressions. Polyrhythmic drummers accented strategic musical situations and signaled both the ensemble and soloists, the pianist would comp, and the bass played walking lines to create a constant reference to the harmony, and more (Meadows 2003: 91–241). However, after Parker's death in 1955, the movement known as hard bop emerged in both a real and imagined form. The music of Clifford Brown, Miles Davis, Sonny Rollins, and others was, in reality, an outgrowth of bebop, the embryonic style of most of its practitioners. Whereas ii–V–I progressions and rhythm changes can still be heard, hard bop expanded its harmonic language to include more noncontrafact progressions, and repetitious and swinging rhythmic patterns were more common than the breaking up of the rhythm dogma of bebop drummers. In addition, the piano comping had more rhythmic and voicing variety. This also was the era during which Clifford Brown, Coleman Hawkins, and Sonny Rollins developed thematic improvisation to a high art, and the genius of Miles Davis and groups like the Modern Jazz Quartet (MJQ) and Art Blakey's Jazz Messengers became noticeable. Within this confluence of musical creativity, Miles Davis explored laid-back rhythms, soft dynamics, connected melodies, use of the Harmon mute, and a diminished use of his higher range in what became known as cool jazz (ibid.: 275–301). He also experimented with Gil Evans, and pointed the way to more use of modes as the basis for compositions and improvisations. Art Blakey's groups continued to set hard bop creative standards by featuring individual giants such as Clifford Brown, Joe Henderson, Jackie Mclean, Wayne Shorter, Horace Silver, and many other emerging stars of the era. Simultaneously, in cool and "third stream," a term coined by Gunther Schuller and championed by MJQ, one can discern a deliberate attempt to avoid the fast tempos of bebop and hard bop, a penchant toward soft dynamics, and use of instruments not common to jazz groups such as oboes, bassoons, and strings instruments. Third stream, music that lies between the classical and jazz polarity, composers often used classical musical forms and instruments in their compositions and generally deemphasized the importance of improvisation, in addition to compositions by Gunther Schuller and the many MJQ recordings, especially "Third Stream" and "Blues on Bach." Third stream influences can be heard in Milton Babbitt's "All Set for Jazz Ensemble" (1957), Leonard Bernstein's "Prelude and Fugue," and "Riffs for Orchestra" (1949), and "West Side Story" (1957), George Gershwin's "Rhapsody in Blue" (1924), and "Porgy and Bess" (1935) opera, William Grant Still's "Afro-American Symphony" (1930, revised in 1969), and Igor Stravinsky's "Ebony Concerto for Clarinet and Big Band" (written for Woody Herman in 1965), to name a few.

Whereas the big bands of Count Basie and Duke Ellington continued to espouse musical excellence, the 1950s and 1960s were dominated by small group creativity.

The aforementioned is a concise summary of the musical context that surrounded Horace Silver, a context that he both helped to create and to push into new musical directions.

Horace Silver was an insider in the bebop and hard bop movements, and at various times performed with artists such as Art Blakey and the Jazz Messengers, Miles Davis, and Sonny Rollins, as well as with Stan Getz, one of the shakers and movers of the cool movement. Silver formed his first quintet in 1956, a group that featured Blue Mitchell (trumpet) and Junior Cook (tenor saxophone). Thereafter, from 1956 to today, his quintets have featured some of the best musicians of the modern jazz era, including Joe Henderson, Branford Marsalis, Hank Mobley, Wayne Shorter, and Stanley Turrentine on tenor saxophone, Donald Byrd, Tom Harrell, Wynton Marsalis, and Woody Shaw on trumpet, Louis Hayes on drums, and Bob Cranshaw on bass, to name a few. Shaped by both the bebop stylings of Bud Powell, and the blues and gospel music he heard in his youth, Silver composed and performed freely between the two jazz worlds. The purpose of this essay is to focus on one area of his musical output, specifically his funky style works, a process that Armstrong describes as:

Concerned to discover those *critical* and *definitive* processes through which such a work produces [*sic*] in its ambient as a particular kind of phenomenon—indeed as a member of a most important class of man-made works which are characterized in a unique way by a special kind of subjectivity, a subjectivity as real and in fact as personable as that of man himself. (Armstrong 1977: 73)

In my research, funky style is the end result of how Silver uses earthy blues and gospel musical influences to create compositions and improvisations.

Affecting Presence

In this essay, I use humanistic and social anthropological theoretical concepts to explain affect in selected funky compositions and improvisations of Horace Silver. Humanistic anthropology, especially the ideas of Armstrong (1975: 1–8), is appropriate because it is concerned with the nature and value of things, and with elaborating on the "condition and experience of humans" and "the understanding and the appreciation of man" (Armstrong 1975: 2). When Armstrong discusses the "affecting presence," he transcends the physical and social study of culture to include the affective presence, which includes felt values, dreams, affecting symbols, natural objects, and events of which affect has accrued (Armstrong 1971: 43).

Furthermore, according to Armstrong:

The affective realm is the universe of man's interiority, and its mode of address is direct. As with the physical and mental areas of culture, it is characterized not only by universals but also by both cultural and idiosyncratic modifications of those universals. Thus, the experience of love, hate, loyalty, fear, and other such emotions are characteristically generated and the means of their expression are subject to cultural variables, while subscription to these norms and the intensity of feeling is obviously subject to individual variability. (Armstrong 1971: 43)

Therefore, what separates Silver's funky style from that of Jimmy Smith and Stanley Turrentine are the cultural and idiosyncratic modifications he applies to universals. Specifically, Silver's decorative features serve as a clear and distinctive separation of his style from other practitioners of the same style. In addition, a study of decorative features is important because they are directly related to the attitudes, beliefs, feelings, judgments, and values of Silver's human condition and experience. In turn, these behaviors are part of the social dimension and reflective of the affecting presence in a musical situation, a phenomenon that Armstrong describes as secondary relevancies or "attitudes toward the work, once it has been manufactured," "judgments about its quality and effectiveness," "theories, if any, about the nature and function of such works," and "the role of the work in ritual and belief" (Armstrong 1971: 41).

I treat Silver's funky style as a phenomenon that exists not solely as a musical structure but also as an entity that is imbued with affective, cognitive, and psychomotor components. By using Armstrong's paradigm and Silver's response to issues related to the realization of his music, I believe a deeper and more penetrating insight into his funky musicking is possible. In turn, the internalization and pontification of affective attitudes, beliefs, and feelings addresses the premise that funky style encompasses affective and cognitive attributes that can only be understood when individual roles and functions are fully explored. According to Armstrong, generalizations about a "physical work," "or the complete properties of a work, would differ from those arrived at through a proper and relevant study of the affecting presence. Therefore, a study that is limited to an assessment of physical properties presents an incomplete picture of Silver's compositions and improvisations. Thus, it is reasonable to assume that Silver's affective domain is operative whenever he composes and performs, and as such separates his musicking of funky style from that of other artists because:

> Affect is the interior condition of feeling related to the presence or absence of socially articulated values, or to the presence of felt, visceral values. (Armstrong 1971: 43–44)

Because an affective presence results only when its initiator is value-involved, and when the values that guide them are immediately presentable, an expression of attitudes, beliefs, and feelings toward composing and improvising jazz is the best way to gage the interiority of a musician. Silver believes his compositional philosophy might produce a greater understanding of his music; it is as follows:

A. Technical Conveyances
   1. Melodic Beauty
   2. Meaningful Simplicity
   3. Harmonic Beauty
   4. Rhythm
   5. Environmental, Hereditary, Regional, and Spiritual Influences.

B. Emotional Conveyances
   1. Happiness (to laugh, to sing, to dance, peace, beauty, love, tranquility, joy, etc.)
   2. Sadness (to cry, to be nostalgic, to be melancholy)
   3. Soulfulness or Inner Depth
   4. Emotion Intellectuality

Silver does not believe in anger, hatred, or politics in his musical composition. He believes musical composition "should give something to people not detract from them." It should give people an emotion that they have lost, or would like to recover, "if only for the moment." Also, "musical composition should bring happiness and joy to people," make them both forget and possibly overcome about their troubles (Silver 1968: Serenade to A Soul Sister from the album liner notes).

Within this context, Silver's affective comments are directly related to his knowledge and experience as a bandleader, composer, and pianist. They also constitute an important understanding and conceptualizing of the nature and values of his music and human experience.

Funky Style

Because funky style evokes a need for both inner an outer anthropological paradigms, the writer combines affective phenomenon with structural analysis to create a holistic assessment of Silver's funky style. However, before proceeding, it is important to identify and discuss affective guidelines that govern the composing and performance of Silver's Funky Style. The rules of formation can provide either a discursive or affective communication which, in turn, provides the schemata in which a composer or performer works. Although a composer or performer does not always form rules of formation, Horace Silver is an exception. In a 1989 interview, he expressed specific attitudes, beliefs, and feelings that were necessities rather than important, but not necessary, to composing and performing his music. It was evident in the interview that his attitudes and feelings reflected what Armstrong describes as a "metaphoric base," which categorizes his funky style as an affective system from which one cannot escape and within which one finds his meaning. Also, a cultural metaphoric base:

Asserts the totality of style, the cultural identity, the historical reality of a people, and it perpetuates their feelings, even after the creators have disappeared from earth. (Armstrong 1971: 65)

In my 1989 interview with Silver, both affecting substance and affecting content were addressed. Affecting substance means one's view of relationships between style and intention of the work, specifically the "intrinsic" rather then "extrinsic" attributes of a work. Affecting content means a context composed of attendant and related feelings, which, in turn, enriches the substance (Armstrong 1971: 52). In the interview, Silver provided information on the roots of his funky style, the "whatness" of the style, and attendant and related attitudes, beliefs, and feelings germane to understanding the intrinsic substance and affecting content of his funky style compositions and improvisation.

My questions and a synopsis of his responses are as follows:

Q.   When did you switch to funky style?
A.   Well, I never switched, it's always been my style. And I never made a
         switch to blues and gospel because that is what influenced me from the
         beginning.

Silver revealed that his mother was a member of the Methodist Church and
his father was Catholic, and in his youth he would attend both churches. However,
he admits that he was attracted to the earthiness of the gospel quartets and groups
he heard at his mother's church. He also noted that his godmother lived near a
storefront sanctified church in New York City and he loved to visit her when they
were having church services because "they were 'burnin'."

Q.   Where were some of the churches located?
A.   I used to stand out front and listen to the music, so I've always liked that
         kind of music. After I grew up I used to stop by some of those churches,
         I didn't go in but I stopped by some of the churches on 21st Street and listen
         to them cook. They had an organ, sometimes they had drums, tambourine,
         trumpet or saxophone; Father Devine's church on 125th Street, diagonally
         across from the Powell Theater. I used to listen while waiting for the bus
         when I lived in the Bronx.

Thus, Silver's attitudes, beliefs, and feelings about music were a direct result
of the music he was exposed to in his youth. He listened carefully, and internalized
both the affective and structural elements required to make his music real to
audiences and to emit the earthiness of blues and black gospel music. To Silver,
this music was great because it communicated, and because to him structural
phenomenon such as form, tempo, and chord changes should be subservient to
the affective feelings generated by a person or group.

Silver continued by expounding on the attendant and related feelings that
shaped his funky style:

A.   I've always loved gospel music. I've always loved the blues, I like the old
         folks from the South like Memphis Minney, Lightnin' Hopkins, Memphis
         Slim, and Muddy Waters. I can remember when I got older and started play-
         ing jazz with some hip cats, we had an intermission and I put some nickels
         and dimes in the juke box on people like Lightnin' Hopkins or someone like
         that, and one of the guys in the band said "man, why are you playing that
         stuff?" I said, "Well, I like it." I said, "They may not be technical maybe nor
         schooled musicians, but I dig the soul, the feeling, you know."

         So, I've always done that and that has always been a part of me; I never
         switched to the blues. I suppose it's always been a part of me, from the
         beginning.

In addition to the religious and musical forces that shaped his funky style. Silver provided insight into the intrinsic interiority that makes his music appealing.

A. I think it's the earthy quality, the earthy element within. The blues is very earthy, very elemental, and down to the nitty-gritty, and so is gospel. I think it's that quality in the music that gets to the people. Even some of the more sophisticated people hear that music and let their hair down, and get on down with it, you know.

In this observation, Silver describes both an affect that transcends the structural musical intangibles of his funky compositions, and underscores the importance he gives to affective behaviors. Furthermore, he is cognizant of both the extramusical attitudes and feelings that make his compositions appealing, and the interior affect of feeling in his funky style.

Q. How do you ensure that your players are playing funky?

A. Well, you don't ensure it because no matter how you might try to put it in there, if you don't have the right guys to play it, it want come out right. Blue Mitchell and Junior Cook, I mean that band was great for playing that kind of music. It came out, funky, you know. Then there are some guys that can't play funky, can't play bebop, or they are too hip. They are great soloist but when it comes to the funky things they are lacking. Blue Mitchell and Junior Cook are very rounded in that respect. That's why we had so much success. When they got with the funky stuff they played it like they liked it because they did like it. For some guys it would be a chore, they're so hip that it's beneath them, but we never though that way.

Q. Do you recruit musicians based on their ability to play funky?

A. I try. You never know exactly what you've got until you get out there with it. You can try them out in the studio and think this is what is best for the band. And, when you get out there it doesn't always work out that way.

Affecting Style

Because Silver's funky compositions and improvisations are the result of the affective and idiosyncratic attitudes, beliefs, feelings, and values in his musical formations, one can best identify them by analyzing features within and among different works. In addition, my purpose is to ascertain what Armstrong calls "affecting style," specifically the characteristic fashion in which structure is wrought. In this context, I will examine whether the works assert either a continuity or compromise of development, and whether structural musical elements stress extension or intension.

Several similarities exist between the six analyzed compositions. There is a fondness for either flat or minor key signatures, "Doodlin" is a blues in D♭ major, "Song for My Father" is a 24-bar tune in AAB in F minor, "Serenade to a Soul Sister" in E♭ minor, "Filthy McNasty" is a 12-bar blues in B♭ major, "Senor Blues" is a 48 (AA) bar modal blues in E♭ minor that substitutes a B7chord for the usual iv chord in the blues progression, and "Juicy Lucy" is a 32-bar AABA composition in F major. In addition, there is a penchant for two- and four-bar phrases, frequent us to of 9th and 13th chords; "Song for My Father" 9th., "Serenade to a Soul Sister" 9th and 13th,' "Filthy McNasty," 13th., "Senor Blues," 9th., and "Juicy Lucy," 7th. and 9th. Among the other similarities are each of the compositions should be played in a medium to moderate tempo, "Senor Blues" with a Latin tempo and feel, and "Song for My Father" with a bossa nova feel, and each has a bass ostinato. Three of three compositions contain an anacrusis, "Song for My Father" and "Filthy McNasty" on the and of the fourth beat; "Serenade to a Soul Sister" on the second beat in 3/4 meter; "Juicy Lucy" on the and of the third beat in 4/4 meter, and "Senor Blues" on the and of the fifth beat in 6/8 meter. "Song for My Father" has a four-bar introduction, and "Senor Blues" a 16-bar introduction; "Doodlin," "Filthy McNasty," and "Serenade to a Soul Sister" do not have introductions. Meter variations also exist, "Doodlin," "Song for My Father," "Filthy McNasty," and "Juicy Lucy" are in 4/4 meter, "Serenade to a Soul Sister" in 3/4, and "Senor Blues" in 6/8 meter.

Structural similarities also exit in interval use, use of melodic motifs, and harmonic rhythm. In the analyzed compositions, Silver's interval use can be summarized as a preference for the minor seconds, minor thirds, augmented and perfect fourths, perfect fifths, and minor sevenths (see Figure 1). His melodic structures are also permeated with the aforementioned intervals. In addition, one seldom hears a leap wider than a fifth, in fact the octave interval heard in the melody, measures 20–21 of "Juicy Lucy," an interval larger than a seventh occurs in the bass line of "Juicy Lucy," and the sharp ninths in the bass line of "Serenade to a Soul Sister" are exceptions in the analyzed compositions (see Figure 2).

FIGURE 1 "Juicy Lucy." Music by Horace Silver. © 1986 by Ecaroh Music, Inc. Renewed 1995.

FIGURE 2 "Serenade to a Soul Sister." Music by Morace Silver. © 1996 by Ecaroh Music, Inc.

As previously noted, intervals larger than a fifth were rare in the analyzed compositions. Other uses of intervals can be seen in the following compositions: minor seconds in "Doodlin" (see Figure 3), "Song for My Father," "Filthy McNasty," as well as "Juicy Lucy," and "Senor Blues."

FIGURE 3 "Doodlin." Music by Horace Silver. © 1984 by Ecaroh Music, Inc. Renewed 1995.

Minor thirds also appear in all but "Filthy McNasty." A perfect fourth and raised fourth appears in "Serenade to a Soul Sister," fourths and fifths in "Doodlin, and fifths in "Filthy McNasty," "Juicy Lucy," and "Doodlin." While the major and minor seconds occur as a result of conjunct melodic motion, Silver used them often enough to indicate an affective preference.

His affective preference also included altered intervals, specifically flat fives, flat sevenths, flat, sharp, and natural ninths, which are common in "Song For My Father," "Juicy Lucy," "Senor Blues," and "Serenade to a Soul Sister." The combinations of intervals, often part of the harmonic structure, produce a blues and gospel affect, an important affect within Silver's funky style.

In addition to his interval and harmonic preferences, Silver uses either the original or a retrograde version of the motif in four of the analyzed compositions.

Original/Retrograde Versions of the Motif

FIGURE 4 Both the original and retrograde versions of the motif appear in hundreds of jazz compositions.

The original version of one motif appears in "Song for My Father" (see Figure 5), and "Serenade to a Soul Sister," and the retrograde version appears in "Doodlin," "Senor Blues" (see Figures 3 and 6), and "Juicy Lucy."

FIGURE 5 "Song for My Father." Music by Horace Silver. © 1987 by Ecaroh Music, Inc. Renewed 1992.

Retrograde

FIGURE 6 "Senor Blues." Music by Horace Silver. © 1984 by Ecaroh Music, Inc. Renewed 1986.

"Filthy McNasty" was the only analyzed composition that did not contain the motif. Whereas the five analyzed compositions constitute only a small portion of Silver's overall repertoire, they are some of his best-known funky tunes. In addition to his generic use of the motif, his approach to and resolution of the motif was identical in three of the compositions. For example, he approached and resolved the motif with two eighth notes in "Song for My Father" and "Serenade to a Soul Sister." In two retrograde uses of the motif it was approached differently for both "Juicy Lucy" and "Senor Blues." He used an eighth rest, eighth, quarter, and dotted half notes to approach the motif in "Juicy Lucy," and a quarter note preceded the motif in "Senor Blues." He resolved the "Juicy Lucy" motif with eighth and quarter notes, and the "Senor Blues" with two eighth rests. The "Doodlin" and "Song For My Father" motifs were resolved on quarter notes. In addition to the use and function of the motif in the aforementioned compositions, a modified version was used in "Kiss Me Right," "Mellow D," and "Down and Out."

Silver also uses the ♩. ♪♪ harmonic rhythm as a unifying compositional device. The harmonic rhythm and its variants are as follows: ♩. ♪♩. ♪ in "Song for My Father (see Figure 7)," ♪♩. ♩ in "Serenade to a Soul Sister," ♩ ♪ ♪ in "Filthy McNasty," ♩♪ ♫ in "Senor Blues" (see Figure 8), and ♩. ♪♩. ♪ in "Juicy Lucy."

FIGURE 7 "Song for My Father." Music by Horace Silver. © 1987 by Ecaroh Music, Inc. Renewed 1992.

FIGURE 8 "Senor Blues." Music by Horace Silver. © 1984 by Ecaroh Music, Inc. Renewed 1986.

The one exception is the harmonic rhythm found in "Doodlin."

Concurrent with these structural similarities, Silver also used ostinati and sequences frequently in the analyzed compositions. Unison repetition of bass and piano lines can be heard in "Senor Blues," and "Song for My Father," and repetition and sequencing of lines can be heard in "Doodlin," "Filthy McNasty," and "Juicy Lucy" (see Figure 9).

FIGURE 9 "Juicy Lucy." Music by Horace Silver. © 1986 by Ecaroh Music, Inc. Renewed 1995.

Because similarities of musical elements exist in the analyzed compositions, one can speculate that Silver used these devices to ensure a specific mood or feel. If frequency of occurrence indicates preference, consciously or unconsciously, I believe Silver used the previously mentioned generic musical elements to achieve an earthy, funky feel. These devices include the beat/rhythm, closely related tempos, harmonic rhythm, repeated melodic, harmonic, and rhythmic motifs, and a group sound characterized by the tenor saxophonist and trumpet scored a fourth apart. By using the same elements constantly within and between compositions he achieves familiarity, which, in turn, is compounded when the same musical devices and soundscapes are repeated in a variety of musical contexts. By using continuity of elements and soundscapes, an audience or musical group develops a comfort zone, which frees them to concentrate on unfamiliar elements, or sounds that might occur within the performance of a composition. Instead of viewing them as a reworking of the same, recognition and familiarity become affective attributes because they are used to reinforce the earthy, funky sound of the composition. In turn, recognition and familiarity frees one to concentrate on new musical elements including a melody, harmony, or the idiosyncratic improvisational ideas used by a soloist.

Overall, Silver's attitudes, beliefs, and feelings about blending blues and gospel musical influences provide significant insight into his affective domain. He recruited musicians and instructed them in the subtle nuances of phrasing, articulations, and the feelings desired in a correct interpretation of his compositions. He also recruited musicians such as Blue Mitchell and Junior Cook to realize his funky compositions, thereby providing significant insight into the feelings and values essential to the interior domain of his funky style.

In summary, when the intrinsic feelings and values are combined with extrinsic analysis, a holistic assessment of Silver's funky style is revealed.

Silver on Improvisation

Silver's comments on affecting substance and affecting content also extend to his improvisations. In the interview, his responses to improvisation issues were a mirror image of his conceptual and creativity interiority. In addition, his comments on improvisation reveal the attitudes, beliefs, and feelings he deems important to realizing improvisations.

Q. Do you follow a specific model when improvising?

A. It depends on how I am feeling at the time. That's what it's all about. But, it always dictates the kind of solo you have to play, or you should play. The melody and the feeling of the tune dictate primarily the type of solo you should play. When somebody comes out and plays the melody of "Filthy McNasty," that melody don't say, play me a hip solo. That melody says, give me some down to earth, simple, funky, gut roots type of shake your behind solo, you know. If you come in playing bla bla bla on a melody like that, that's out of context. It's like you are playing some avant-garde tune, and you start playin' funky, you're out of context there.

Because Silver was proficient in both funky and hip playing, his recognition of the importance of structure and feeling as prerequisites for improvising is noteworthy. His synopsis applies pathetics to aesthemics, and his belief that melody and feeling should dictate the solo evokes both intrinsic and extrinsic behaviors. Whether cultural or idiosyncratic, Silver's belief is reflected in both his and his sidemen's improvisations.

He continued by expounding on the importance of musical context.

Q. Are today's young players as attune to musical context as their elders?

A. Well, again, it depends on the individual. Some do, and some don't. Most of the young guys are trying, sometimes they're not quite making it. Thinking back to the old days there were a few guys, extremely good players, who played everything hip. It was beneath them to play funky. When I played one of those funky tunes, they would still play bla bla bla, all those notes. And some guys who couldn't play as well as the hip player, would give me just what I wanted on a funky tune. It would fit, and it was in the context of what was suppose to happen there.

Within the context of funky style performing, Silver commented on the ability of African American musicians.

A. Most black musicians play funky, I won't say all because I know some black musicians who don't play funky and can't play worth a dam damn. But that's the minority. I am thinking back a few years when I was a young cat. There were some young cats around, hell of a great players, but so involved in the hip thing that they never played funky. Maybe they never had a gig with a rhythm and blues band, like Lou Donaldson or Julian Adderley had, or played with Willie Mayborn, or a blues band. But that's good training.

In addition to eschewing opportunities to perform in either a rhythm and blues, or blues band, Silver believes that lack of knowledge of harmony, ear training, and the ability to improvise plagues many of today's young musicians.

A. It's a difference, a hell of a difference because cats like Hank Mobley can run changes like drinking a glass of water. He's a bitch, put some changes in front of him and he just kick ass, and he is playing some slick and appropriate ideas. I mean, Joe Henderson, and Tom Harrell, playing man. Harrell is the last cat I had in my band that could really play the changes. You can rely on cats like Joe Henderson, Hank Mobley, Stanley Turrentine, and Freddie Hubbard to give you a good solo every time.

He continued by relating an experience he had when performing with Dizzy Gillespie.

A. You've got to study, practice it. Like Dizzy said on one of those television interviews. When Miles (Davis) first came to New York, he would hang out with Dizzy. And Miles used to ask, "Dizzy, that note you played in 'Hothouse,' what was that? Why did you play that? What chord is that? What is this and what is that." And Dizzy said, "Miles you got to get to the piano, man. Get to the piano and it's all in front of your eyes, you can see it and envision it." That's what these cats need to do, learn the piano. If you want to be a jazz musician, you've got to get with these chord changes because that what it's all about.

Q. Because you require your sidemen to adhere to strict musical discipline when performing your tunes, to perform funky and hip tunes, bossa nova, Latin, and rock rhythmic structures, and traditional and nontraditional forms, have you experienced trouble finding competent musicians to perform with?

A. As far as the arrangements are concerned, I want to play the way I want to play. When its your time to solo, say something, put some soul, fire, and drive into it, get to the people and say something exciting. When it comes to the arrangement, I want it played the way I wrote it or interpreted it. I want the little nuances that I wrote and don't want you messing around with it, changing it. I like people to know that I can play funky and hip. A few years back I was a little self-conscious, but grateful, that critics were focusing on my funky stuff. I want them to know that Horace Silver is well rounded, I love Latin music and Latin rhythms creep into my writing. A lot of our things are inspired by folk music, African, Indian, whatever. I like classical music and some rock, we have incorporated some of the rock rhythms into our music.

I have a hard time with bass players because some of my compositions have repetitious bass lines. A lot of them are written above the bass clef, and they go out of tune when they get up there. I have a problem with that because I am playing the same thing in my left hand, its sound terrible and I have a problem with that

Q.   How about drummers?

A.   Yes and no. In recent years it's been increasingly harder to get the caliber of musicianship that I had in the old days. You might get one or two, however I usually wound up with one guy who is lacking. I've been lucky with drummers, and Andy Bey is a hell of a singer, too.

Improvisation

In "Doodlin," one can hear Silver actualizing musical attitudes, beliefs, and values that are important to his funky style. The composition and improvisation is based on the 12-bar blues, and he uses flat thirds, fifths, sevenths, and the mixolydian mode throughout the composition. He uses a complimentary rhythm, across-the-barline concepts, and quarter-, eighth-, and occasional sixteenth-note triplets patterns to add rhythmic contrast. He also used silence, and occasional short followed by longer note to create an ebb and flow within the swing feel durations. The three-chorus solo includes implied chord changes in the bass line and melody but not necessarily by Silver's composing. The implied chord changes are consistent with the ii–V7–I changes found in bars 9–11. Another interesting reharmonization occurs in bars 18–20, when compared to the original in bars 6–8. Interpolation, a common occurrence in Silver's improvisations, can be heard in the quote from "When the Saint's Go Marching In," in bars 12 and 13, which is repeated in bars 17–20 (see Figure 10).

FIGURE 10 "Doodlin." Music by Horace Silver. © 1984 by Ecaroh Music, Inc. Renewed 1995.

Overall, the solo displays what Armstrong calls a rigorous "intension" rather that a synchronic approach. He evokes historical precedents that can be heard in his solos and those of others. The historical precedents include his use of blue notes, blues harmonies, mixolydian modal concepts, implied and reharmonization concepts, ii–V7–I harmonic concepts, and more. His use of the ♪♫ rhythmic figure is also rooted in history because Dizzy Gillespie, Thelonious Monk, and Charles Parker used it extensively. History is also evident in his use of interpolation, a device used by Charles Parker and others. By evoking historical precedents, Silver creates a continuity of musical elements that are generic to his funky style improvisations. In addition, when the historical precedents are combined with affective attitudes, beliefs, and feelings, we better understand the whole of Silver's funky style.

"Senor Blues"

In "Senor Blues," we hear both continuity and contrariwise with "Doodlin," and "Song for My Father." "Senor Blues" is a blues in E♭ minor with a bVi major chord instead of a iv minor chord in bar 5. In his solo, each of the four choruses has its own distinctive flavor; the first chorus is primarily diatonic and features several scale-chord relationships. In bar 4, he used the diminished scale; in bars 5 and 6, we hear a major pentatonic scale; and in bars 9 and 10, B♭ and A♭ mixolydian modes are implied (see Figure 11):

FIGURE 11 "Senor Blues." Music by Horace Silver. © 1984 by Ecaroh Music, Inc. Renewed 1986.

The second chorus (bars 13–24) is diatonic to E♭ blues, and we continue to hear the mix of B♭ and A♭ mixolydian modes in the turnaround of bars 21 and 22. In the third chorus, bars 25–36, we hear a bluesy sound that features lots of flat thirds, fifths, and sevenths. He builds tension by both rhythmic displacement and playing in the cracks of the beats. The B♭ and A♭ mixolydian mix is heard in the turnaround, and in the last chorus, beginning on bar 36, we hear a contrariwise with "Doodlin," and with his earlier choruses in this improvisation. In this chorus, he explore "outside" concepts by using the E♭ diminished scale in bars 36–40, and a E♭ diminished scale on the B chord in bar 41 and half of bar 42. In addition, he reintroduces and transforms the motif from bar four of the first chorus on beats 3 and 4 of bar 41 (see Figure 12), as well as the use of the natural 6th. on E♭ in bar 44 (same as bar 8). These quotes from earlier uses and functions within

FIGURE 12 "Senor Blues." Music by Horace Silver. © 1984 by Ecaroh Music, Inc. Renewed 1986.

the improvisation coupled with a return to a diatonic mixolydian mode in bars 45 and 46 complete the solo.

"Song for My Father"

In "Song for My Father," a 24-bar AAB composition in F minor, Silver evokes historical precedents in his use of blue notes, blues scale, and the use of mixolydian modal concepts on the dominant chord, and a swinging rhythm punctuated with silence. He also uses a blues scale on the dominant and tonic (F) chords, and flat thirds, fifths, and sevenths throughout the improvisation. We also hear contrariwise in the improvisation when Silver changes from harmony in thirds to harmony in fourths in the second chorus, beginning on bar 25. A bass and piano ostinato permeates the composition.

Whereas the sum total of the distinctive features of the three improvisations constitutes Silver's funky style, one also can find evidence of what Armstrong calls "decoration," an adjunctive property (part of Silver's affective finish) that according to Armstrong "tends to increase the affect of a piece" (Armstrong 1971: 52–55). Contrariwise or decorative features such as the reharmonization and interpolation in "Doodlin," original and retrograde use of a signature melodic motif, outside solo concepts in "Senor Blues," and reharmonizing from third to fourths in "Song for My Father" distinguishes Silver's improvisation from others on the same compositions.

In conclusion, Silver's use of contrariwise features in the three improvisations demonstrates his idiosyncratic stylistic concepts and the affective attitudes, beliefs, and feelings essential to conceptualizing, performing, and understanding his funky style improvisations.

References

Armstrong, Robert Plant. "The Affecting Presence in the Time-Space Ambient," in *Essays For A Humanist: An Offering for Klaus Wachsmann.* New York: The Town House Press; 1977: 73–83.

_____. *The Affecting Presence: An Essay in Humanistic Anthropology.* Urbana: University of Illinois Press; 1971.

_____. *Wellspring: On the Myth and Source of Culture.* Berkeley: University of California Press; 1975.

Meadows, Eddie S. *Bebop to Cool Context, Ideology, and Musical Identity.* Westport, Conn., Praeger Press; 2003.

Discography/Transcriptions

Blues on Bach. Atlantic Records SD-1652.

"Doodlin," "Filthy McNasty," and "Senor Blues," from *The Best of Horace Silver.* Blue Note Records: c. 1009.

"Serenade to a Soul Sister," from *Serenade to a Soul Sister, The Horace Silver Quintet Featuring Stanly Turrentine*. Blue Note: BST 84277.

"Song for My Father," from *Song for My Father.* Blue Note 99002.

Third Stream Music: The Modern Jazz Quartet and Guests: *Jimmy Giuffre Three and The Beaux Arts String Quartet.* Atlantic Records SD-1345.

I

Aesthetics, Appreciation, Criticism, Clubs and Festivals, Philosophy

1. Agostinelli, Anthony J. *The Newport Jazz Festival, Rhode Island, 1954–1971: A Bibliography, Discography, and Filmography.* Providence: The author; 1977.

    A selected bibliography of articles, books, and music in general presses. Also lists references in the *Providence Journal, Bulletin* (1954–75), and in the *New York Times* (1954–72). A comprehensive list of artists, performance dates, personnel, titles of recordings, and record release numbers is included in the discography. Additionally, a filmography (feature and general), with personnel for some, and a list of Voice of America radio broadcasts are included.

2. _____. *The Newport Jazz Festival, Rhode Island (1954–1971): A Significant Era in the Development of Jazz.* Providence: The author; 1978.

    An account of the history, role, and function of the festival. Covers the beginnings, tourist appeal, racism in Providence, and the riots that eventually lead to the cancellation of the festival. Reflections by George Wein, festival promoter/organizer, are also included.

3. Ake, David. *Jazz Cultures.* Berkeley: University of California Press; 2002.

    A revision and expansion of his doctoral dissertation in musicology at UCLA. He blends historical research with textual criticisms and cultural theory to enhance our appreciation and understanding of jazz. He approaches his topic from the viewpoint of a practicing musician who is simultaneously steeped in the theory and practice of cultural theory.

4.   Armitage, Andrew D., and Dean Tudor. *Popular Music Record Reviews.* Metuchen, N.J.: Scarecrow Press; 1973.

A compilation of jazz and popular recording reviews indexed into one publication. The jazz reviews were first published in journals such as *Coda, Different Drummer, Down Beat, Jazz Journal, Jazz New England,* and *Jazz Report.*

5.   Baker, David N. *New Perspectives on Jazz.* Foreword by Eunice Lockhart-Moss. Washington, D.C., London: Smithsonian Institution Press; 1990.

Several essays and responses commissioned by The National Jazz Service Organization for a conference held September 1986. Subjects include cultural, historical, and economic issues. Harold Horowitz, Gunther Schuller, Olly Wilson, Gary Giddins, Dan Morgenstern, Amiri Baraka, Stanley Crouch, Billy Taylor, Jimmy Lyons, George Butler, and Martin Williams gave the papers and responses. The Gunther Schuller-Olly Wilson (respondent) paper, "The Influence of Jazz on Concert Music," is enlightening. Appendices contain notes on the contributors, conference participants, and the conference planning committee.

6.   Baraka, Imanu Amir. *Reflections on Jazz and Blues;* with Amiri Baraka. New York: W.W. Morrow and Company; 1987.

A collection of jazz essays, drama, and poetry. The central theme is that of the capitalist exploitation of African American music (the works are permeated with references to both capitalism and racism). Baraka covers the genius of John Coltrane, Thelonious Monk, Charles Parker, Clifford Brown, Horace Silver, and the socio-political-musical message of Gil Scott-Heron. The essay "The Phenomenon of Soul in African American Music" provides insights into the return, by some artists, to the African American church for their musical elements and inspiration.

7.   Becker, Howard S. *Outsiders: Studies in the Sociology of Deviance.* New York: Free Press of Glencoe; London: Collier-Macmillan; 1963.

The author is a former jazz pianist and therefore lends insider credibility to this classic study. When performing, Becker observed and later documented the behavioral characteristics of a group of jazz musicians. Becker's insider experiences formed the basis of two chapters, "The Culture in a Deviant Group: The Dance Musician," and "Careers in a Deviant Occupation Group: The Dance Musician." The first chapter documents how the musicians view themselves as "outsiders" in music and in overall behavior, which tends to lead to self-segregation. In the second chapter, the author discusses the effects of choosing a career as a jazz musician, including problems encountered in family relationships.

8.   Bornemann, Ernest. *A Critic Looks at Jazz.* London: Jazz Music Books; 1946.

A collection of previously published articles (*Record Changer*), which uses both an anthropological and historical approach. Bornemann's anthropological approach deals with issues of continuity and change in instrumentation and tradition. His historical essay addresses prejazz issues/genres such as African roots, blues, spirituals, ring shouts, minstrelsy, and the emergence of jazz. He also addresses economic and sociological factors. The weakness of the book is the superficial way in which he treats the transformation from prejazz genres to jazz. Selected bibliography and reference notes.

9.   Brown, Charles T. *The Jazz Experience.* Dubuque, Iowa: William C. Brown Publishers; 1989.

The book is designed to provide a method by which nonskilled listeners might acquire an appreciation of jazz. Accordingly, the book does not contain musical examples other than the analyses, nor is there a thorough discussion of chord changes. Brown covers topics ranging from "Origin of Jazz," "Blues," "Ragtime," "Dixieland and Classic Jazz," "The Big Band Era," "Combo-Style Jazz" (bebop, cool, hard bop, free), "Fusion Jazz," and "An Overview of the Eighties: Players and Singers." In each case, the topics are treated succinctly. There are appendices of technological/electronic terms, definitions, analyses, a selected discography (including several listings drawn from the Smithsonian Collection of Classic Jazz), a bibliography, and an index.

10.   Buckner, Reginald T., and Steve Weiland (editors). *Jazz in Mind.* Detroit: Wayne State University Press; 1991.

A collection of essays on the history and meanings of jazz. The authors cover biographies of famous and not-so-famous artists, performance analysis, and descriptions of sociophilosophical issues in jazz. In the latter essays, they address issues such as whether jazz from Russia has affected American practices, the reliability of sociopsychological issues in jazz performance, and the contributions of James Reese Europe to jazz, and more. Unfortunately, these issues are not fully addressed in all cases. Still, the book raises some significant issues. Numerous reference citations and a selected bibliography.

11.   Carr, Roy, Brian Case, and Fred Dellar. *The Hip: Hipsters, Jazz, and the Beat Generation.* Boston: Faber and Faber; 1986.

A sociocultural commentary on the attitudes and values of cultural out-siders. Focuses on the beliefs about cultural change in American society.

12.   Carruth, Hayden. *Sitting In: Selected Writings on Jazz, Blues, and Related Topics.* Iowa City: University of Iowa Press; 1986.

Includes 25 essays and 13 poems written over a 38-year period that cover issues such as the African American culture in the larger North American context, the origin of the blues, the idea of jazz, and writings on musicians such as Pee Wee Russell, Ben Webster, and others. Poems are interspersed throughout the text that deals with jazz and jazz musicians, including The Chicagoans, Earl "Fatha" Hines, Maxine Sullivan, and Joe Turner. His essay, "Eleven Memoranda on the Culture of Jazz" is provocative. There are some nonprovocative essays as well.

13.   Ceoroy, André, and André Schaegger. *Le Jazz.* Paris; 1926.

In French. One of the first critical works of jazz. Contains useful and insightful remarks, particularly for its time.

14.   Cerulli, Dom, Burt Korall, and Mort L. Nasatir (editors). *The Jazz Word.* New York: Ballantine, 1960; London: Dobson, 1962; London: Jazz Book Club; 1963; New York: Da Capo; 1988.

Attempts to compile a list of the most provocative, authentic, and trail-blazing essays that have been previously published. The essays, taken from journals, record liner notes, press releases, books, and newspapers, cover various topics (critical assessments, fiction, and poetry), and individuals (including Louis Armstrong and Lester Young). More anecdotal than schol-arly. Index.

15.   Clayton, Peter, and Peter Gammond. *The Guinness Jazz Companion.* London: Guinness Publishing Ltd.; 1989.

The book contains entries on slang, programs, phonographs, terms and concepts, and maps. It is geared toward things more than to people; however, it is difficult to locate the information because of incomplete or misleading headings.

16.   Coker, Jerry. *Listening to Jazz.* Englewood Cliffs, N.J.: Prentice Hall; 1978.

This concise volume provides an introduction to the basic elements of jazz, particularly improvisation. The primary focus is to teach the user "how" and "what" to listen to in jazz, beginning with the medium, the chorus, the chord progressions, and the role and function of the instruments in the rhythm section.

17.   Collier, Graham. *Jazz: A Student's and Teacher's Guide.* Cambridge: Cambridge University Press; 1975.

This book is permeated with information designed to facilitate the learning, listening, and teaching of jazz. The author includes information for both insiders and outsiders, including understanding technical aspects (with musical examples); advice for listening; and additional references for reading. In part one, the author discusses and evaluates the music of Armstrong, Ellington, Brubeck, Davis, Hawkins, Parker, and Reinhardt. Part two is devoted to a discussion of arranging, blues improvisation, big bands, modes and scales, jazz composition, and contemporary trends.

18.   Collier, James Lincoln. *Inside Jazz.* New York: Four Winds; 1973.

Begins with a discussion of rhythm and improvisation and proceeds to a discussion of why music is considered to be jazz. This evolution is traced through blues and ragtime to contemporary jazz (early 1970s). Specific chapters deal with styles, blues, life of a jazz musician (drugs and alcohol addiction), and jazz today (early 1970s).

19.   _____. *Jazz: The American Theme Song.* New York: Oxford University Press; 1993.

Questions many previously held assumptions, origins, significant exponents, importance of improvisation and spontaneity/creativity in performance, and the jazz world. In 10 essays, Collier discusses the place of jazz in American culture, past, present, and future; trends and styles; and African and European influences on the evolution of jazz. He argues that jazz is not African American per se but the cultural heritage of all races and classes. Index.

20.   _____. *The Reception of Jazz in America: A New View.* New York: I.S.A.M.; 1988.

Refutes the thesis that Europeans were the first to accept jazz both critically and historically. Instead, Collier espouses that Americans were the first to accept jazz for several reasons, including its role and function in American culture. He focuses on early jazz and swing, and makes unorthodox conclusions regarding the public's attitudes toward jazz. Index.

21.   Cortex, Jayne. *Jazz Fan Looks Back.* Brooklyn, N.Y.: Hanging Loose Press; 2002.

A collection of poetry characterized by the author's imaging for times past. She is a preservationist and believes jazz history ended when bebop blended with fusion, R&B became funk, and whites began playing the blues. The author has performed her poetry with music on at least nine recordings.

22.   Crow, Bill. *Jazz Anecdotes*. New York: Oxford University Press; 1990.

Compiles data from biographies, autobiographies, oral histories, and interviews to produce an entertaining account of musician's travels, relationships, and situations. Also contains information on African American
bands.

23.   Dankworth, Avril. *Jazz: an Introduction to its Musical Basis*. London, New
York: Oxford University Press; 1968.

Focuses on the musical elements of jazz and their use in specific styles.
The book covers elements such as chords, forms, scales, rhythm, and tonal
effects in jazz styles dating from prejazz to the 1960s. The aforementioned
is supported with numerous musical examples. There are three indexes:
jazz tunes with composer, date of publication, key, and publisher, tunes,
and styles.

24.   Delaunay, Charles. *DeLaunay's Dilemma: De La Peinture ou Jazz*. Macon,
France: Editions W; 1985.

In French. The title, *Delaunay's Dilemma,* is from a composition by John
Lewis (a lead sheet is included). Includes several critical assessments of
styles, contributions, and people. Illustrated.

24a.   DeVeaux, Scott. *Jazz in America: Who's Listening? Research Division
Report: National Endowment of the Arts, No. 3*. Cabin John, Md.: Seven
Locks Press; 1995.

He addresses the question posed in the title and presents data that deals
with demographics, attendance at live concerts, media participation in jazz,
and listening to jazz recordings. In addition, he assesses trends during the
1982–92 decade, and compares participation in jazz with participation in
other selected art forms. His presentation is thorough and in-depth and
supplemented with figures and tables.

25.   Feather, Leonard. *The Jazz Years: Ear Witness to an Era*. London, New
York: Da Capo; 1988.

Permeated with anecdotes and recollections of selected artists concerning
their attitudes about change in jazz. Covers many topics. Index and illustrations.

26.   Feather, Leonard, and Jack Tracy. *Laughter From The Hip: The Lighter
Side of Jazz*. New York: Horizon, 1963; New York: Da Capo; 1979.

A collection of anecdotes, humorous quotations, and stories. The 1979
edition contains a new foreword by Feather. There are several musical
examples as well as drawings by A. Brinbaum.

27. Feinstein, Sascha, and Yusef Komunyakaa (editors). *The Jazz Poetry Anthology*. Bloomington: Indiana University Press; 1992.

Contains poems that run the gamut of social, political, and spiritual emotions. There are also poems that celebrate the musical achievements of significant artists. The contributors are organized alphabetically, with a biographical sketch and a statement of poetics, which details the characteristics of the individual poem. The appendix contains listings of individual artists, jazz musicians, blues musicians, vocalists, and more.

28. Ferstl, Erich. *Die Schule des Jazz*. Munich; Unknown Publisher; 1963.

In German. Geared to the concerns of jazz critics, historians, and the musically literate reader interested in performing jazz. This book is not concerned with stylistic subdivisions. The author covers musical elements and approaches. Informative for its time, although much better studies are available today (addition to 1981).

29. Filipacchi, Daniel, Frank Ténot, and Jean Wagner. *Mais Oui—Vous Comprenez le Jazz*. Paris: Jour; 1964.

In French. Contains biomusical portraits, essays on topical issues, and critical assessments. The coverage is diverse and insightful. Glossary, illustrations.

30. Finkelstein, Sidney. *Jazz: A People's Music;* illustrated by Jules Halfant. New York: Citadel Press, 1948; Secaucus, N.J.: Citadel Press, 1948; London: Jazz Book Club, 1964.

The objectives of this book are to recognize jazz as a significant contribution to world music and to mediate the schism that exists between classical and jazz musicians. Finkelstein also mediates the controversy between advocates of different jazz styles, arguing that jazz should be judged by both its musical characteristics and by an understanding of the relationship that exists between jazz and sociocultural issues. Future directions are also addressed. Selected discography and an index.

31. Fordham, John. *Jazz: The Essential Companion for Every Jazz Fan*. Foreword by Sonny Rollins. London, New York, Stuttgart: Elm Tree Press; 1993.

A potpourri of essays and excellent photographs on such subjects as "Improvisation," "Modal Jazz," and "Dance Roots." The book includes a history of jazz, anatomy of instruments, techniques, classic recordings, and coverage of jazz giants (Scott Joplin, Jelly Roll Morton, Louis Armstrong, Bix Beiderbecke, Sidney Bechet, Duke Ellington, Coleman Hawkins, Billie Holiday, Lester Young, Count Basie, Charles Mingus, Charlie Parker, Dizzy Gillespie, Miles Davis, Thelonious Monk, Art Blakey, Sonny Rollins, John

Coltrane, Ornette Coleman, and Keith Jarrett). None of the coverage is in-depth; however, significant viewpoints are presented. Index.

32. Frankenstein, Alfred V. *Syncopating Saxophones.* New York: R.O. Ballou; 1926.

The author, a clarinetist in the 1926 Chicago Civic Orchestra, gives his views on jazz, saxophones, and syncopation. Although the essays are read-able, the author was no expert on the topic: points are often introduced but not developed.

33. Gabbard, Krin (editor). *Representing Jazz.* Durham, N.C.: Duke University Press; 1995.

Contains a dozen essays that deal with jazz myth and culture as repre-sented in literature, cinema, dance, and art. He includes essays that exam-ine jazz in *Mo' Better Blues* (1990), *Jammin' the Blues* (1944), and *Cabin in the Sky* (1943). Jazz dance is examines in *A Day at the Races* (1937), and Mona Hadler and Michael Jarrett examine jazz as an abstract expres-sion for artists and Western tropes in Sonny Rollins's *Way Out West* album, respectively. In addition, Arthur Knight, Michael Curtis, and Spike Lee offer important and provocative insights into both jazz and American popular culture.

34. _____. *Jazz Among the Discourses.* Durham, N.C.: Duke University Press; 1995.

The author asserts that jazz studies are poised to become institutionalized within the academy. This book is a companion to his volume entitled *Representing Jazz.* Together there are 24 contributions to these antholo-gies; however, the volume has the most provocative and extended treat-ments of historiographical issues and problems. Of special note are the essays that deal with empirical research problems by William Howland Kenny and Burton W. Peretti.

35. Gioia, Ted. *The Imperfect Art: Reflections on Jazz and Modern Culture.* New York: Oxford University Press; 1988.

The author uses literary criticism, art history, sociology, and aesthetic phi-losophy to discuss jazz within the sociocultural context of the twentieth century. Within this matrix he provides concise portraits of several sig-nificant jazz artists and styles. The author believes jazz is destined to fail because of its dependence on improvisation. He also believes jazz is not subject to the controls inherent in other arts.

36. Gleason, Ralph J. (editor). *Jam Session: An Anthology of Jazz.* New York: Putnam, 1958; Toronto: Longmans, 1958; London: Davies, 1958; London: Jazz Book Club, 1961.

Essays and portraits that cover jazz and to a lesser degree blues (only one essay "The Blues" by Huddie Ledbetter is not strictly jazz). Among the other titles are "A New Orleans Funeral" by Jelly Roll Morton; "Chicago" by Art Hodes; "Young Man With a Horn" by Otis Ferguson; "Eddie Condon" by George Frazier; and "What is This Thing Called Jazz" by Henry Pleasants. Other than the author's description of the meshing of poetry and cool jazz in San Francisco's avant-garde community of the late 1950s, the most informative essays are by Ferguson.

37.   Goffin, Robert. *Aux Frontiéres du jazz;* preface by Pierre MacOrlan. Paris: Editions du Sagittaire; 1932.

In French. Imparts the author's views that jazz is both a significant art form and an important contribution to world music. He distinguishes between authentic and commercial jazz and champions Louis Armstrong, not Paul Whiteman, as the real king of jazz.

38.   Goldblatt, Burt. *Newport Jazz Festival: The Illustrated History.* New York: Dial Press; 1977.

Provides an in-depth history of the festival from its beginnings through its demise in Newport (1971) and move to New York (1972–76). The author draws on his personal experiences at each of the festivals, with over 140 interviews (audience, musicians, organizers, and local residents); festival reviews are also quoted extensively. Topics include: insightful comments on the performers, difficulties of presenting respective festivals, and problems evolving from racism. Both a chronological discography and a list of festival programs, 1954–76, are included.

39.   Goldman, Albert. *Freakshow: The Rock Soulbluesjazzsickjew blackhumorsexpoppsychgig and Other Scenes from the Counter-Culture.* New York: Athenaeum Publishers; 1970.

This collection contains over 50 essays covering comedians, jazz, novelists, rock, sex, psychosis, and psychedelics. The essays were originally published in periodicals such as the *New York Times, New York Magazine, Commentary, Life,* and *The New American Review.* His jazz contributions include John Coltrane and Charles Parker; however, he offers no new insights.

40.   Gordon, Max. *Live at the Village Vanguard.* Introduction by Nat Hentoff. New York: St. Martin's Press; 1980.

An eclectic account of life in the Greenwich Village Nightclub. The author, founder and owner, opened the club in 1934, which soon became a magnet for both audiences and musicians. In the 1940s, the club featured artists like Judy Holliday, Josh White, Leadbelly, and Woodie Guthrie. Thereafter, it became known as a venue for jazz musicians. The author includes jazz portraits (the last part of the book) of artists such as Miles Davis, Rashaan Roland Kirk, Coleman Hawkins, Charles Mingus, and Thelonious Monk.

41. Hartman, Charles G. *Jazz Text: Voice and Improvisation in Poetry, Jazz, and Song.* Princeton, N.J.: Princeton University Press; 1991.

Examines the ways and means "voice" can be symbolized or used to discuss poetry, jazz, and song. He discusses Lee Konitz, Ornette Coleman, Joni Mitchell, and "Jazz, Song, Poetry: Toward Speaking for Closure." Some musical analysis interspersed with cultural and literary theory.

42. Harvey, Charles (editor). *Jazz Parody: Anthology of Jazz Fiction.* London: Spearman Publishers, Ltd; 1948.

Foreword by Charles DeLaunay, this 110-page monograph features a series of 14 parodies on topics ranging from drinking, women, and black life in America. The essays are concise, and based on fiction.

43. Haskins, Jim. *The Cotton Club.* New York: Random House; 1977.

In the 1920s and 1930s, the Cotton Club functioned as a magnet for both white patrons and African American entertainers. For white patrons slumming in Harlem, it provided first-rate entertainment and satisfied some of their stereotypes. For the African American entertainer, it provided an artistic outlet, steady pay, and wide exposure. It is within this context that the author has touched on the African Americanization of Harlem, the opening of the Cotton Club in 1923 (Madden), the transfer of the club to Broadway in 1936, and its eventual closure in 1940. Many African American entertainers became stars after performing there, including Cab Calloway, Duke Ellington, Lena Horne, and Ethel Waters.

44. Hentoff, Nat. *American Music Is.* New York: Da Capo Press; 2004.

A collection of essays and columns written for the *Wall Street Journal* and *Jazz-Times Magazine,* primarily between 1995 and 2003 (a single entry is dated 1988). The book recalls his 1976 book *Jazz Is* by expanding the earlier work's perspective to include sections on "The Blues," "The Rainbow of Country Music," "The Farther Rainbow," and sections on "The Jazz Voice" and "Jazz Ahead." In the more than 60 entries, he writes intimately about Duke Ellington, Ralph Ellison, Dizzy Gillespie, Billie Holiday, Charles Mingus, Willie Nelson, and the Nitty Gritty Dirt Band. Offers many new insights into the musicians and the music they performed.

45. _____. *Jazz Is.* New York: Random House; 1976.

A selective tribute and guide to jazz performers, music, and life. Rather than a chronological or comprehensive history, the author presents a personal exploration, discussing the nature of changes that continued to occur through the mid-1970s. He examines the contributions of artists like Louis Armstrong, John Coltrane, Charles Parker, Cecil Taylor, and Charles Mingus. Some of the quotes are excerpted from *Hear Me Talkin' To Ya,* edited by Hentoff and Nat Shapiro.

46.   Hodier, André. *Les Mondes du Jazz.* Paris: Union Générale d'Editions, 1970; *The Worlds of Jazz;* Translated by Noel Burch. New York: Grove Press, 1972; New York: Random House, 1974.

Uses fiction to focus on stylistic developments. Hodier adapts a kind of blindfold format using fictionalized characters (archeologists, arrangers, a Finnish jazz composer, professors, and others), to assess the music of individual artists, arrangers, and composers. He believes the future of jazz lies with the creativity of jazz composers. In addition to mixing fiction and critical assessments, one additional weakness of the book is the author's rejection of post-bebop innovations.

47.   Jones, Leroi. *Black Music.* New York: Morrow; 1967.

The 28 pieces cover the performance approaches of selected artists as well as critical topics such as "Jazz and the White Critic." Jones advocates that African American music is an outgrowth of African American culture and should be assessed or viewed accordingly. His essays on John Coltrane, Thelonious Monk, Cecil Taylor, and others espouse that their musical approaches and output are directly related to sociocultural movements in African American culture. The articles and reviews were previously published in journals like *Down Beat* and *Liner Notes* between 1959 and 1967. Selected discography.

48.   Kernfeld, Barry. *What to Listen for in Jazz.* New Haven, Conn.: Yale University Press; 1995.

Organized around seven topics: rhythm, forms, arrangement, composition, improvisation, sound, and style. He uses musical examples from 21 recordings to illustrate his views. Also includes appendices on chordal notation, discography, and biographical sketches of selected musicians.

49.   Lambert, Constant. *Music Ho! A Study of Music in Decline.* London: Faber, 1934; revised edition. London: Faber, 1937; third edition with an introduction by Arthur Hutchings. London: Faber, 1966; New York: October House, 1967.

Connects music, including jazz, with life in the twentieth century. The book is interesting because it provides an account of Jewish and European elements in jazz. Film music and symphonic jazz are also covered.

50.   Lange, Art, and Nathaniel Mackey (editors). *Jazz in Poetry and Prose.*
New York: Coffee House Press; 1993.

Contains poems and stories by 59 writers from Langston Hughes to Xam
Cartier and Jessica Hagedorn. Although some of the poetry is abstract or
stentorian, the fact that the poetry is centered on jazz is interesting. Among
the most interesting essays are James Baldwin's "Sonny's Blues," Julio
Cortazar's report on a Louis Armstrong concert, and Jay Wright's "End
of an Ethnic Dream." The selections are also interesting because they
allow the reader to speculate on what musician(s) inspired the authors to
write their essays.

51.   Lees, Gene. *Cats of any Color: Jazz Black and White.* New York: Oxford
University Press; 1995.

Contains 10 essays based on interviews, and concludes that jazz in practice
has long been plagued by racism. The primary argument evolves in the
last essay, "Jazz Black and White," in which he details his own generalized
ideology and polemics to attack Stanley Crouch and Wynton Marsalis
while championing Louis Armstrong's belief that musicians of all colors
should be able to perform together. His ad hominem approach displays
an intolerance for the views of artists who disagree with his worldview
without addressing the deep issues and problems that shaped those views.

52.   Leonard, Neil. *Jazz and the White Americans: The Acceptance of a New
Art Form.* Chicago: University of Chicago Press, 1962; London: Jazz Book
Club, 1964.

Based on the author's doctoral dissertation at Harvard, *The Acceptance of
Jazz by Whites in the United States, 1918–1942* (History, 1960), the book
details "The rapid change of taste for jazz in America between the two
world wars" (p. 3). Inspired by Morroe Berger's article, "Jazz: Resistance
to the Diffusion of a Cultural Pattern," the author addresses five questions
raised by Berger: (1) Why did jazz evoke such intense opposition?; (2) Why
did jazz continue to spread in the face of this opposition?; (3) What kinds
of jazz were acceptable to whom?; (4) What changes did it undergo as
it gathered supporters?; and (5) What were the public's feelings about it
as it gained a relatively large audience? He synthesized these issues into
one central question, "acceptance of jazz among whites." (p. 3). The author
also addresses the nature of the artist-audience gap. Glossary, content
analysis of lyrics, chapter reference notes, selected bibliography, and an
index.

53.   Lopes, Paul Douglas. *The Rise of a Jazz Art World.* New York: Cambridge
University Press; 2002.

Explores the evolution of ideas about the nature and significance of jazz both as a music and as a cultural phenomenon in the twentieth century. Specifically, he is concerned with how jazz came to signify various contours of status, distinction and identity in American music when espoused by professional musicians and others. He is influenced primarily by the work of Pierre Bourdieu, and traces discourses on jazz since the 1910s. Although scholarly, he pays little attention to the major trend in jazz and American culture after approximately 1945.

54.   Lyons, Jimmy. *Dizzy, Duke. The Count and Me: The Story of the Monterey Jazz Festival;* with Ira Kamin; drawings by David Stone Martin; Photographs by Peter Breinig. San Francisco: California Living Books; 1978.

The author covers three topic areas; first, he relates anecdotal memories about the festival, musicians, and organization of the festival; second, he provides an indepth chronology of the festival 1958–77, with details on each program; and, third, he gives festival reviews and reminiscences by jazz reviewers such as Leonard Feather, Ralph Gleason, and Richard Hadlock. Index.

55.   Martin, Henry, and Keith Waters. *Jazz: The First 100 Years.* New York: Thomson/Schrimer; 2002.

Written for courses that focus on jazz history, appreciation, or as an introduction to jazz. He balances theory, biographies, and social history with listening activities/guides. The musical examples are contained on a two-CD set.

56.   Metzler, David (editor). *Reading Jazz.* San Francisco: Mercury House; 1993.

Examines the influence of jazz on other forms of modern cultural expression. There are criticisms, assessments, and analysis by authors like Simone de Beauvoir, Anatole Broyard, W.E.B. Du Bois, Ralph Ellison, Franz Fanon, Langston Hughes, Norman Mailer, Igor Stravinsky, Eileen Southern, and Ronald Takaki. In addition to its slant toward jazz, the writers use cultural criticism, history, and sociology to explain the role, function, and history of jazz in American culture.

57.   Miller, William Robert. *The World of Pop Music and Jazz.* St. Louis, London: Concordia; 1965.

Discusses cause, effect, and aesthetics of both popular music and jazz from a Christian viewpoint. Miller is concerned with the impact of these genres on contemporary society. Selected references and bibliography.

58. Morris, Ronald L. *Wait Until Dark: Jazz and the Underworld 1880–1940.* Bowling Green, Ohio: Bowling Green University Popular Press; 1980.

An illuminating account of the role of the underworld in the growth and dissemination of jazz from early New Orleans to the late 1930s. Using both historical and sociological methodologies, the author portrays the underworld as "sponsors," rather than egocentric individuals or groups, "culturally atavistic, materialistically mad, and terrifyingly destructive" (p. 7). He discusses Chicago and New York in the 1920s nightclub life before underworld involvement, life of a typical early jazz musician, and New Orleans jazz in the Italian community. In addition, he discusses the nature and decline of the underworld patronage system and the nature of the present (1980). Although the book contains important information on the relationship between jazz and the underworld, the author's methodology is questionable. Specifically, his informants did not provide much of the data eventually included in the book. Hence, much of his data is based either on secondary sources, or his interpretation(s) of jazz sources. Lists of Italian jazz figures and jazz clubs in New Orleans (around 1905) and of New York jazz clubs are listed in the appendix. Index.

59. Murray, Albert. *The Blue Devils of Nada: A Contemporary Approach to Aesthetic Statement.* New York: Pantheon Books; 1996.

Presents his artistic principles on African American musical literature, and visual arts. He discusses how artists such as Louis Armstrong, Count Basie, Duke Ellington, and painter and collagist Romare Bearden, and writer Ernest Hemingway. He writes about the lives and technical achievements of the artists, the affinities between Count Basie and Matisse, Ellington's performance as it relates to other music and more. Overall, he is concerned with the ongoing dialogue with tradition across cultures, countries, and races.

60. Nanry, Charles (editor). *American Music: From Storyville to Woodstock;* with a foreword by Irving Louis Horowitz. New York: Dutton, 1971; New Brunswick, N.J.: Transaction Books, 1972.

A collection of papers given at a scholarly conference devoted to "Jazz and All That Sociology" at Rutgers University. Both jazz and rock and roll are represented. The papers examine how jazz and rock represent continuity and change in American culture. To that end, mostly scholars who espouse a sociohistorical approach author the essays. These are Howard S. Becker, Morroe Berger, Nat Hentoff, Howard Junker, Jon Landau, Robert R. Faulkner, I. L. Horowitz, Neil Leonard, Richard A. Peterson, and Robert A. Stebbins. The essays offer important new insights into the connections between music and culture. Selected bibliography and reference notes.

61.   _____ and Edward Berger. *The Jazz Text.* New York: Van Nostrand; 1979.

This book is distinguished by its sociological approach, which focuses on sociocultural context rather than jazz styles and analysis. The book is organized into three sections; section one focuses on "An Introduction to Jazz" (head arrangement and theme and variations); section two focuses on "The Emergence and Development of Jazz" (blues, cities, and people); and section three focuses on "Jazz Research" (concise annotated survey materials and issues). A selected bibliography and index are included. The book is unique because it concentrates on the social context that influenced and shaped the music of artists such as W. C. Handy, Jelly Roll Morton, King Oliver, Louis Armstrong, Bix Beiderbecke, Benny Goodman, Duke Ellington, Count Basie, Lester Young, Benny Carter, Coleman Hawkins, Miles Davis, Thelonious Monk, Charles Parker, and John Coltrane. Although he includes a selected discography of each artist, the context and profiles are limited.

62.   Newton, Francis. *The Jazz Scene.* London: MacGibbon and Kee, 1959, 1989; Toronto: Ambassador, 1959; New York: Monthly Review, 1960; London: Jazz Book Club, 1960; Harmondsworth, England: Penguin, 1963; Roma: Riuniti, 1963; Paris: Flammarion, 1966; Praha: Supraphon, 1973; New York: Da Capo, 1975; Roma: Riuniti, 1982.

Details origins, development, stylistic developments and instrumentalist's contributions. Also covers sociocultural issues such as the role of jazz musicians, jazz as social protest, the jazz public, and the economics of jazz. Contains chapter reference notes, an appendix on jazz argot, recommended readings, and an index. The 1963 and 1982 Italian editions are entitled *Il Mondo del Jazz* and *Stori Sociale del Jazz,* respectively. The French edition is entitled *Sociologie du Jazz.*

63.   Ogden, Kathy J. *The Jazz Revolution: Twenties America and the Meaning of Jazz.* New York: Oxford University Press; 1989.

Debates the schism that existed between the Anglo and African American communities regarding jazz. By the 1920s, jazz was the dominant influence on American popular music. However, some whites railed against it, and some African Americans felt that jazz cast a negative light on their community. The author discusses this schism within the context of the 1920s. She states that those who accepted modernity embraced jazz, and those who resisted change shunned it. She covers topics such as prohibition, economics, and the phonograph record. Ogden offers new insights into the sociocultural matrix that nurtured the jazz revolution of the 1920s. Selected bibliography and an index.

64.   O'Meally, Robert G. (editor). *The Jazz Cadence of American Culture.* New York: Columbia University Press; 1998.

A collection of 35 essays divided into six sections. The sections are "What is Jazz," "One Nation Under Groove," "Visual Arts," "Dance," "African Arts," and "Jazz and Literature and Poetry." The collection is unique because it includes contributions by artists and scholars, and for its coverage of selected historical issues.

65.   Ostransky, Leroy. *Understanding Jazz.* Englewood Cliffs, N.J.: Prentice Hall; 1977.

The book is organized into two main sections. The first five chapters cover topics such as "Toward a Definition of Jazz," "Understanding Improvisation," "The Musical Elements of Jazz," and "Understanding Style." In the latter, he discusses what makes one artist different from another. The second half of the book is devoted to a chronological study of jazz. He outlines the musical contributions of significant practitioners, and discusses how jazz reflected the major events in history, from prohibition to the civil rights movement. This book is a revised edition of *Anatomy of Jazz;* three new chapters, "The Early Sixties," "Toward the Seventies," and "The Seventies" replaced the previous final chapter, "Toward the Future." Updated bibliography and Index.

66.   Palmer, Richard, and John White. *Larkin's Jazz: Essays and Reviews, 1940–1984.* New York: Bayou Press; 2001.

Philip Larkin was a poet and wrote for the *Daily Telegraph* (London) from 1961 to 1971. His previous work *All That Jazz* is a collection of 126 record-review columns he wrote while working for the newspaper. In addition, this collection contains essays that he wrote for several other journals/newspapers, including *The American Scholar, Guardian, New Statesman,* and *Observer.* Many of the essays focus on sympathy.

67.   Panassié, Hugues. *Real Jazz;* translated by Anne Sorelle Williams; adapted for American publication by Charles Edward Smith. New York: Smith and Durrell; 1943.

Advocates the idea that because jazz is of African American origin, it is difficult for outsiders to understand or interpret. He discusses blues, jazz, and swing, and evaluates selected artists (instrumentalists and vocalists, African American and Anglo-American). His musical analysis is solid. Appendix contains a selected discography arranged alphabetically by artist.

68.   Panish, Jon. *The Color of Jazz: Race and Representation in Postwar American Culture.* Jackson: University Press of Mississippi; 1997.

Focuses on America's attitudes toward jazz from the end of World War II to the beginning of the Black Power Movement. He uses literature, film, musical criticism, and television to reveal fundamental contrasts between blacks and whites regarding jazz. Covers topics such as racial politics, Greenwich Village, image of Charles Parker, cultural construction of jazz performance, and literature's imitation of jazz improvisation. Good insights and scholarly.

69.   Peretti, Burton. *The Creation of Jazz: Music, Race, and Culture in Urban America.* Urbana: University of Illinois Press; 1993.

An account of how the racial and cultural dynamics of American cities created jazz. He uses oral histories of more than 70 jazz artists, including Benny Carter, Bud Freeman, Alberta Hunter, and Teddy Wilson as well as newspaper articles covering 1890 to 1940 to forge a picture and social history of the music known as jazz. He also covers dress codes, argot, and the use of drugs. References and an index.

70.   Pleasants, Henry. *Death of a Music? The Decline of the European Tradition and the Rise of Jazz.* London: Gollancz, 1961; London: Jazz Book Club; 1992.

Promotes the thesis that jazz and serious music (classical) dominate the twentieth-century American musical landscape. He discusses both the status of jazz and the refusal of the classical musical community to accept it. Of particular significance is his discussion of the swing concept in relation to rhythm. He also believes a correlation exists between the musical characteristics of jazz and those of the musical and opera. This book and the subsequent volume accurately assess many of today's problems in the understanding and acceptance of jazz. Selected bibliography.

71.   _____. *Serious Music—and All That Jazz! An Adventure in Music Criticism.* Gollancz, New York: Simon and Schuster; 1969.

The author believes jazz and classical music dominate twentieth-century music. In this book, he compares jazz performers with serious music performers, and believes African American music to be the most important idiom of the day. He demonstrates that new jazz and serious musicians share many of the same problems and furthermore that African American vocal styles are bound to dominate in the future. The latter he identifies as blues, big band singers, gospel singers, and African American influenced country music and rock. He also discusses film music. A thought-provoking volume. Index.

72.   Porter, Eric. *What is This Thing Called Jazz: African American Musicians as Artists, Critics, and Activists.* Berkeley: University of California Press; 2002.

Traces the ways and means African American musicians have verbalized their accomplishments. Portrays musicians as creators, thinkers, and politically astute, and as artists who are simultaneously shaped by, and are shaping, their respective political and social environments. He analyzes and contextualizes the critical, historical, and aesthetical writings of some of the most important composer and performers of African American music.

73.   Postgate, John. *A Plain Man's Guide to Jazz.* London: Hanover Books; 1973.

An introduction to jazz that focuses on history, general concepts of jazz (improvisation, intonation, rhythm), and the characteristics of specific genres (from New Orleans to the early 1970s). He also comments on significant exponents of instrumental and vocal jazz. The book is geared to novices rather than scholars. There are no musical examples. Glossary and index.

74.   Ramsey, Frederic, and Charles E. Smith (editors). *Jazz hMen.* New York: Harcourt, Brace, 1939, 1959, 1972, 1977; Toronto: McLeod, 1939, 1957; New York: Armed Forces, 1942; Paris: Flammarion, 1949; New York, London: Sidgwick & Jackson, 1957; London: Jazz Book Club, 1958; St. Clair Shores, Michigan: Scholarly Press, 1972; New York: Limelight, 1985.

Includes 15 outstanding articles on analytical and historical topics. The book is divided into four basic style sections: New Orleans, Chicago, New York, and "Hot Jazz Today." The definition and development of these styles is told through the contributions and careers of outstanding jazz personalities. Among the writers contributing to this excellent volume are William Russell, E. Simms Campbell, Wilder Hobson, and the authors. Selected references, index, and illustrations (addition to 1981).

75.   Sinclair, John, and Robert Levin. *Music and Politics.* Foreword by Pauline Rivelli. New York: World; 1971.

Combines interviews, essays, and reviews previously published in *Jazz and Pop.* The articles cover Anthony Braxton (biographical portrait), Marion Brown (record review), Chick Corea (record review), Eric Dolphy (record review), Booker Little (interview), Jimmy Lyons (biographical portrait), and Sunny Murray (oral history). The record reviews tend to be subjective. Selected discography.

76.   Szwed, John. *Jazz 101: A Complete Guide to Learning and Loving Jazz.* New York: Hyperion; 2001.

An introduction to jazz that is geared to the casual listener and enthusiast. In addition to the concise history, he discusses the challenger inherent in improvisation and includes sidebars with recommended listening. Also, discusses people, the jazz scene in Europe, acid jazz, and neoswing, jazz on the Internet, jazz films, and more.

77. Tirro, Frank. *Living With Jazz: An Appreciation.* New York: Thomson/ Schrimer; 1996.

Intended for use as a primary text in jazz appreciation, or as a supplement to courses in music appreciation, the humanities, American studies, or American music. He introduces aural skill, and covers musicians, history, and the social forces that shaped jazz.

78. Traill, Sinclair (editor). *Concerning Jazz.* London: Jazz Book Club; 1958.

An anthology of essays, written by jazz historians and critics, covering a myriad of topics. The essays tend to be anecdotal, journalistic, and heavily laden with personal biases (especially the 1950s critics). The essays and their focus are as follows: Mezz Mezzrow's "In the Idiom" lacks focus and depth; Stanley Dance's "Evolution and Appreciation" is a broad attempt to delineate the relationship between jazz and audiences; Hugues Panassié's "A Soul and a Beat: The Essence of Jazz" is an attempt to discuss the basics of jazz; Gerald Lascelles does a good job in detailing people/trends/ influences in piano playing; Mike Butcher's "Modern Jazz" is a surface summary of salient elements/people of modern jazz from bebop to the late 1950s; and Douglas Hague's "The Jazz Scene in America" is concerned with the complex of events existing in a limited time span.

79. Ulanov, Barry. *A Handbook of Jazz.* New York: Viking Press, 1957; revised, with a foreword by Kingsley Amis, London: Hutchinson, 1958; London: Jazz Book Club, 1960.

Includes a myriad of approaches, including historical, stylistic, instrumental, linguistic, biographical, and critical. He also incorporates discography in his chapters, although most only contain cursory comments. The indexes include biographical portraits of 500 musicians, a comparative chronology of jazz and other arts, and an index.

80. Werner, Craig Hansen. *Playing the Changes: From Afro-Modernism to the Jazz Impulse.* Urbana: University of Illinois Press; 1994.

The book consists of several phrases that are focused on the relationship between Euro-American postmodernism and African American culture. The author uses the cross-cultural dialogues of writers such as Roland Barthes, Charles Chestnutt, T. S. Eliot, Toni Morrison, and Melvin B. Tolson to make his point. The book focuses on an eclectic mix of literary and musical texts but is centered primarily on how blues, jazz, and gospel have comprised African American cultural practice. He also creates a dialogue between black writers such as James Baldwin, Gwendolyn Brooks, W.E.B. Du Bois, Zora Neal Hurston, and August Wilson, and white writers such as T.S. Eliot and William Faulkner.

81.   Williams, Martin T. *Jazz in Its Time*. New York: Oxford University Press; 1989.

In this collection of previously published essays, Williams discusses the current state of jazz criticism, jazz artists, and the popular culture of jazz. The author believes there should be higher standards for jazz critics. He also criticizes jazz in academia, including Charles Hamm and the editors of *The New Grove Dictionary of American Music*. He has high praise for Ornette Coleman and Milt Jackson but disparages the contributions of Stan Kenton. Index.

82.   _____. *Where's the Melody? A Listener's Introduction to Jazz*. New York: Pantheon Books, 1966, 1968; New York: Minerva Press, 1967, revised edition, New York: Pantheon Books; 1969.

Divided into three parts, the book is designed to introduce listeners to jazz and jazz musicians. In part one, the author discusses the role of the composer-arranger, basic elements and practices, and provides a selected discography. He uses eight recordings to outline basic elements and practices. Four artists are detailed in part two: Thelonious Monk, Milt Jackson, Big Joe Williams, and Jimmy Guiffre. Finally, he comments on other artists, expands previous subjects, and addresses the avant-garde movement. No musical examples. Selected bibliography, discography, and an index.

83.   Zwerin, Michael (editor and translator). *Round About Close to Midnight: The Jazz Writings of Boris Vian*. London and New York: Quartet Books; 1988.

A selective and adapted collection that captures the syntax and prose of Vian's writings, many from his columns in *Jazz Hot* and *Combat* (French) in the 1940s and 1950s. The collection contains 63 essays, covering topics from artists and groups, criticism, and sociopolitical issues such as racism and dislike of jazz. Although the essays are short, they are permeated with humor, anecdotes, and insightful comments regarding the music of both individuals and ensembles (Dizzy Gillespie, Gene Krupa, Zoot Sims, Stan Kenton, Miles Davis, Charles Parker, Coleman Hawkins, Howard McGhee, and more). In addition to his writing skills, Vian was a trumpeter and composer. Contains some provocative insights and opinions. Index.

84.   _____. *Close Enough For Jazz*. London, New York, Melbourne: Quartet; 1983.

Twenty-two essays divided into three parts and several tags (Chet Baker, John Cage, Manfred Eicher, Jimmy Gibson, Elvin Jones, Jaco Pastorius, Adolphe Sax, and Sun Ra). The essays focus on anecdotes, criticism, and opinions. Portions were previously published in the *International Herald Tribune,* the *Village Voice, Mademoiselle,* the *Paris Metro, Jazz Forum, Passion Magazine, Jazz Hot,* and the *Holland Herald.* Insightful and witty. Index.

II

Reference Works: Bibliographies, Dictionaries, Encyclopedias

85. Allen, Daniel. *Bibliography of Discographies, 1935–1980, Volume 2: Jazz.* New York: R. R. Bowker; 1981.

Contains discographies of jazz, blues, gospel, ragtime, and rhythm and blues published between 1935 and 1980. Allen uses a single-letter prefix and numbers the alphabetical letters in a separate sequence. He covers artists as well as numerous other topics.

86. Asman, James, and Bill Finell. *Jazz Writings.* Nottingham, England: Jazz Appreciation Society; 1945.

Contains a listing of selected articles and books on jazz to the mid-1940s. Artists, history, criticism, and reference materials are covered.

87. Behncke, Bernhard H. *Storyville Index.* Hamburg: Unknown Publisher: 2002.

An index of issues 1 to 162 of *Storyville,* the scholarly journal that was published in England.

88. Bird, Christiane. *The Jazz and Blues Lover's Guide to the U.S.: With More Than 900 Hot Clubs, Cool Joints, Landmarks and Legends from Boogie-Woogie to Bop and Beyond.* Menlo Park, Calif.: Addison Wesley Publishing Company; 1991.

An attempt to chronicle the existence of numerous venues throughout the United States that feature blues and jazz. The information was compiled to assist travelers in locating these venues, but is also important to jazz scholars. Permeated with historical information about the venues, comprehensive and detailed.

89.   Bohlander, Von Carlo, and Karl Heinz Holler. *ReClams Jazzfuhrer.* Stuttgart: Phillip ReClam; 1977.

In German. Begins with an essay on what jazz is and covers biographies, musical instruments, concepts, terms, and compositions. The biographies cover jazz and a few blues musicians, American and other nationalities. The entries contain the instrument played, birth and death dates, classification as to swing, modern jazz, and so on, and details on the bands with which an individual artist has played. The compositions are especially interesting because the composer, publisher, form, performers that have recorded it and musical excerpts from each are cited. The tunes are organized alphabetically.

90.   Burley, Dan. *Dan Burley's Original Handbook of Harlem Jive.* New York: The author; 1964.

Primarily a glossary of the argot associated with bebop.

91.   Burns, Kristine H. (editor). *Women and Music in America Since 1900.* Westport, Conn.: Praeger Press; 2002.

A two-volume work that represents the first major effort to describe the role of women in all genres in the United States since 1900. Permeated with information on female artists in blues and jazz, and covers additional issues such as gender, education, musical genres, organizations, and professions.

92.   Calloway, Cab. *The New Cab Calloway's Hepsters Dictionary; Language of Jive.* New York: The author; 1944.

Parallels Dan Burley's *Original Handbook of Harlem Jive;* contains definitions of bebop argot, including terms like ax, cool, hip, and moldy figs.

93.   Item deleted.

94.   Carl Gregor, Herzog zu Mecklenburg. *International Jazz Bibliography: Jazz Books from 1919 to 1968.* Strasbourg: Baden-Baden; 1969.

The objective is "to serve the serious friend of jazz, the jazz musician, and musicologist." The 1,562 entries (limited to books) include bibliographies, dictionaries, encyclopedias, general literature, histories, instruction, musical theory, blues, ragtime, and literature related to pseudo-jazz musicians such as George Gershwin, Irving Berlin, and Richard Rogers. There are 11 indices including authors of forewords or epilogues, contributors and collaborators, countries, illustrators, persons, editors, subjects, second authors, translators, and series.

95. _____. *1970 Supplement to International Jazz Bibliography, and International Drum and Percussion Bibliography.* Graz: Universal Edition; 1971.

A supplement of 429 titles of books and monographs published between 1968 and 1970. The supplement is divided into 14 categories, covering topics such as biographies and monographs, bibliographies and reference works, discographies, blues, history, theory, and several more. The drum and percussion entries cover 358 books dealing with a myriad of approaches to drumming, including dance band, jazz, Latin American styles, and rock and roll. No indices.

96. _____. *1971/72/73 Supplement to International Jazz Bibliography, and Selective Bibliography of Some Jazz Background Literature, and Bibliography of Two Subjects Previously Excluded.* Graz: Universal Edition; 1975.

This second supplement contains books published between 1971 and 1973. There are 1,302 entries divided into 15 categories with no index. The represented subjects have been expanded to include books on rock and pop-related genres, and dissertations. Whereas the three volumes constitute an enormous addition to the literature, it is significant to note that many of the entries are incomplete, ostensibly because others supplied the information. There are no indices.

97. _____. *International Bibliography of Jazz Books.* Volume I: 1921–1949, Volume II: 1950–1959. Compiled with the assistance of Norbert Ruecker. Strasbourg: Baden-Baden, 1983 (Volume I), and 1988 (Volume II).

Revised and expanded from the original (1969), and its supplements (1971 and 1975). In addition to original editions, there are reprints, new editions, and translations. Over 400 entries in Volume I. Volume II follows the same format and contains 823 entries, a supplement to Volume I (up to 1944), an index of collaborators, an index of key words and persons named in the titles, indices of subjects, collections and series, countries, and a chronological survey of the years of publication.

98. Carles, Philippe, Andre Clergeat, and Jean-Louis Comolli. *Dictionnaire du Jazz.* Paris: Laffont; 1994.

New and augmented edition that contains the definitions to numerous terms and concepts.

99.   Carner, Gary. *Jazz Performers: An Annotated Bibliography of Biographical Materials.* Westport, Conn.: Greenwood Press; 1990.

Contains an alphabetical listing of numerous jazz artists and ensembles. Entries also include birth/death dates, instrument, and references (books and articles). The reference's sources contain authors, titles, page numbers, and concise annotations (not all entries are annotated). In addition, the references and entries include several foreign artists and numerous foreign publications. The comprehensive supplementary bibliography includes numerous entries, divided into collection books, general works, histories and textbooks, reference works, and both author and subject indices. Comprehensive.

100.   Carr, Ian, Digby Fairweather, and Brian Priestly. *Jazz: The Essential Companion.* London: Grafton Books, 1987; Englewood Cliffs, N.J.: Prentice Hall, 1987.

The first jazz dictionary written by musicians. Contains over 1,600 biographies (including the international scene) of musicians who have made either an international impact or a specific contribution to the music. Also included are concise essays on stylistic developments, concepts, and terms. The stylistic essays for the beginnings to the 1940s were written by Digby and Priestly and covered the 1940s and 1950s, and Carr 1960 to 1986. A list of representative recordings is cited at the end of each essay. Although North American musicians predominate, there are also entries from South America, Europe, Asia, Africa, and the Antipodes. The strength of this reference work is the insider perspectives that are offered on the process of music making, problems of creativity, and the cultural, financial, and physical conditions that shape the lives of musicians. Very few references are cited.

101.   Case, Brian, and Stan Britt. *The Illustrated Encyclopedia of Jazz.* New York: Harmony Books; London: Salamander Books; 1978.

More than an encyclopedia, this volume is a biographical and critical guide to musicians. Contains information on more than 400 musicians, covering all jazz periods; favors musicians from bebop and after. The entries emphasize biographical facts rather than career assessments. All entries include selected discographies, including American and European labels. Also included are numerous photographs by Valerie Wilmer. A name index is also included.

102.   _____. *The Harmony Illustrated Encyclopedia of Jazz;* revised and updated by Chrissie Murray, third edition. New York: Harmony Books; 1987.

A richly illustrated (color and B&W photographs) encyclopedia that contains entries on musicians and selected essays, each supplemented with a selective discography giving the record title followed by North American and British labels in brackets. Entries include titles such as "Afro-Jazz" and "British Jazz," and cover groups such as "Mezzoforte," "The Jazz Messengers," and the "Brecker Brothers." Good source for discographical references.

103. Cerri, Livio. *Il Mondo del Jazz*. Pisa: Nistri-Lischi; 1958.

In Italian. A comprehensive biographical dictionary that includes entries on Louis Armstrong, Count Basie's orchestra, Benny Carter, and Spike Hughes, Duke Ellington, Dizzy Gillespie, Benny Goodman, Fletcher Henderson's style 1922–38, Jimmy Lunceford (career overview), Charles Parker, and Ben Pollack. There are music examples, solo transcriptions, and a bibliography.

104. Chilton, John. *Who's Who of Jazz: Storyville to Swing Street;* foreword by Johnny Simmen. Radnor, Pa.: Chilton Book Company; 1972.

Provides biographical profiles of over 1,000 artists active in jazz before 1920. The focus is on the significant activities of the artists. He omits musicians born after 1920 and does not include reference notes; he acknowledges his debt to informants and periodical literature. Selected bibliography.

105. Claghorn, Charles Eugene. *Biographical Dictionary of Jazz*. Englewood Cliffs, N.J.: Prentice Hall; 1983.

Alphabetical listing of over 3,000 artists covering early artists to the 1980s. Each entry includes year and place of birth and death (if appropriate) and a biographical profile that details when and with whom the artist performed. Some of the entries contain comments or quotes from other musicians or critics. Recordings are often listed without full discographical information (like the label number(s) or dates). The Leonard Feather dictionaries are more complete.

106. Clayton, Peter, and Peter Gammond. *Jazz A–Z*. London: Guinness Books; 1986.

Atypical of most dictionaries, encyclopedias, or histories, this book focuses on the geography, places, venues, landmarks, shrines, monuments, artifacts, and language of jazz. The focus is on "what's what" instead of "who's who." The book is permeated with anomalies (Chu Berry is included and Miles Davis is not; Bix Beiderbecke is listed as "Bix Legends"). Dates are often missing for musicians; however, they are often included when a person's activities are linked to pursuit, movement, or a place being described in the entry. Because the primary focus is not on "who's who" there are obvious omissions. Selective list and index of "Jazz Musicians and Singers."

107. Clergeat, André. *Dictionnaire du Jazz.* Second edition cowritten by Philippe Carles and Jean Louis Camolli. Seghers, 1966; Paris: Laffont, 1988.

In French. A dictionary of musicians, organized alphabetically, which is current to the mid-1960s. Each entry contains instrument(s), career highlights, birth/death dates, personnel with whom the musician performed, and some references to compositions and recordings. Definitions of the primary jazz styles and some photographs. Selected bibliography, glossary, and illustrations.

108. Collier, Graham. *Jazz: A Student's and Teacher's Guide.* New York: Cambridge University Press; 1978.

Bibliography and discography. A selected list of entries that is not in-depth in any particular area.

109. Cooper, David E. *International Bibliography of Discographies: Classical and Jazz and Blues, 1962–1972: A Reference Book for Record Collectors, Dealers, and Libraries.* Littleton, Colorado: Libraries Unlimited; 1975.

Deals in the first section with classical music and in the second with blues and jazz. A carefully organized and categorized bibliography, complete with full discography details, including titles, dates, venue, and personnel (addition to 1981).

110. deLerma, Dominique-René. *Bibliography of Black Music.* Four volumes. Westport, Conn.: Greenwood; 1981–1984.

Volume 2 is devoted to jazz and lists numerous articles and some books. The entries are weighted heavily toward American jazz. There are selected jazz entries in the other volumes. Also contains a comprehensive list of domestic and foreign jazz journals.

111. DeMichael, Don (editor). *Down Beat's Music.* Chicago: Maher; 1962–1967.

A compilation of the seventh through twelfth annual yearbooks. The yearbooks include a summary of the contents published during a specific year. Illustrated.

112. Dorigne, Michel. *Jazz. Culture ET société:* suivi du "Dictionnaire du Jazz." Paris: Les Editions Ouvriéres; 1967.

In French. Contains several articles on the role, function, and historical evolution of jazz in American culture. The articles cover topics such as the sociology of jazz, jazz in American society, blues, spirituals, musical language, and a discussion of the elements of swing. In his discussion of swing, he compares the different definitions of several scholars, including Chase, Hodier, and Malson. Also included is a short, (11-page) essay on the situation of jazz in France. There is a concise discussion of the pedagogy of jazz, a selected biography (organized by alphabet), discography, a bibliography, filmography, and list of French jazz clubs.

113. Eckland, K. O. *Jazz West 1945–1985: The A–Z Guide to West Coast Jazz Music.* Photographs by Ed Lawless. Carmel-by-the Sea, Calif.: Cypress; 1986.

An alphabetically arranged list of West Coast musicians and groups that the author characterizes as "predominantly performers with traditional orientation" (p. 13). In addition to individual entries, there are lists of organizations and celebrations and a family album. Individual listings indicate, if known, full name, instrument(s), birth/death dates, place of birth, band affiliations, and other professions. Band listings include popular title of the group; personnel; periods of involvement; recording data; and more. Good reference for traditional West Coast musicians and bands.

114. Feather, Leonard. *The Encyclopedia of Jazz;* foreword by Duke Ellington. New York: Horizon Press, 1955; London: Barker, 1956; New edition revised and updated; appreciation by Duke Ellington, Benny Goodman, and John Hammond; New York: Horizon Press; New York: Bonanza Books, 1960; London: Barker, 1961; London: Jazz Book Club, 1963; New York: Da Capo, 1982.

Contains over 2,000 biographies spanning the evolution of jazz from its origins to 1959. The entries contain career details, date and place of birth and death, instrument played, and the contributions and significance of the person in jazz history. An assessment and musical outline of the evolution of jazz is also included. There is a provocative essay on jazz and classical music by Gunther Schuller as well as lists of booking agencies, birthdays and birthplaces, jazz organizations, record companies, and a selected bibliography.

115. Feather, Leonard, and Ira Gitler (editors). *The Biographical Encyclopedia of Jazz.* New York: Oxford University Press; 1999.

A comprehensive guide with contains more than 3,300 entries. Contains concise entries on famous and lesser known females and males associated with both blues and jazz.

116. _____. *The Encyclopedia of Jazz in the Sixties;* foreword by John Lewis. New York: Horizon Press; New York: Bonanza Books; 1966.

Expands on *The Encyclopedia of Jazz,* with emphasis on activities in the early 1960s, and several new names among the 1,100 biographies listed.

The listings include musical contributions in the 1960s, date and place of birth and death, and a selected assessment of an artist's style and influence(s). There is an essay on the blues and folk music by Pete Welding. Selected discography by artist and a selected bibliography of books published in the 1960s.

117.   _____. *The Encyclopedia of Jazz in the Seventies.* Introduction by Quincy Jones. New York: Horizon Press, 1976; London: Quartet Books, 1978.

Primarily a biographical dictionary containing information on approximately 1,300 musicians (arrangers, composers, singers), active in the 1970s. This is the third volume in Feather's encyclopedia series. Although this volume includes entries featured in his previous encyclopedias, Feather focuses primarily on their activities in the 1970s (with a concise summary of facts about their earlier accomplishments). Entries include instrument where warranted, birthdates, career achievements and importance, and a selected discography. Also included are several blindfold tests (originally published in *Down Beat*), a discography (recommended listing), and a selected bibliography (English language).

118.   Filmer, Vic. *Jive and Swing Dictionary.* Penzance, England: The author; 1947.

Like the books of Burley, Calloway, and Gold, this book is a glossary of the concepts and terms used by swing and bebop musicians. The author's coverage of jive language is not as in depth as that of Calloway. Index.

119.   Garfield, Jane. *Books and Periodicals: Articles on Jazz in America from 1926 to 1934.* New York: Columbia University School of Library Science; 1934.

Covers artists, criticism, life, and some musical assessments. The entries are not annotated; the manuscript is not published.

120.   Garraty, John, and Mark C. Carner (editors). *American National Biography.* New York: Oxford University Press; 1999.

Among the numerous biographies are some of jazz musicians, including Bunny Berigan, Tadd Dameron, Miles Davis, Duke Ellington, Louis Jordan, Blue Mitchell, Thelonious Monk, Jelly Roll Morton, Jaco Pastorius, Billy Strayhorn, and many more. The entries include information on their beginnings in jazz, accomplishments, and influences. Selected bibliography at the end of each entry.

121.   Gold, Robert S. *A Jazz Lexicon.* New York: Knopf; 1967.

Contains a discussion of words and phrases used in the jazz world. Included are entries on "parts of speech," origins, and definitions of each term. The author then chronologically lists passages quoting the terms in context and points out differences in meaning over time. Contains definitions of almost 700 slang words, including terms such as "ax," "jive," "pad," "stretch out," and many more. Before preparing the dictionary, the author interviewed musicians and consulted numerous publications (addition to 1981).

122.   _____. *Jazz Talk.* New York: Bobbs-Merrill Company; 1975.

Lists slang terms in jazz that date from the earliest forms to the 1970s. He provides a definition, a list of sources that use the term in conversation, and an etymology for each entry. Among the numerous terms cited are "ax," "changes," and "ghost notes."

123.   Gonzales, Babs. *Be-Bop Dictionary and History of Its Famous Stars.* New York: Arlan; 1947.

An alphabetical listing of concepts, terms, and artists significant in bebop.

124.   Gray, John. *Fire Music: A Bibliography of The New Jazz, 1959–1990;* foreword by Val Wilmer. Westport, Conn.: Greenwood Press; 1991.

There are more than 7,100 nonannotated entries, covering American and European works, including books, dissertations, periodicals, newspapers, films, videos, audiotapes, and more. Artist or group name arranges the section on biographical and critical studies alphabetically. Concert and record reviews are limited to major artists. The entries are cross-referenced. The appendices list references consulted, cite archives and research centers, and list the country and instrument of new jazz artists.

125.   Haselgrove, J. R., and D. Kennington (editors). *Reader's Guide to Books of Jazz.* 2 vols. London: Library Association, County Libraries Section; 1960.

Both editions cover general background, theory, biographies, criticism, discographies, and more. Second volume is more detailed than the first.

126.   Hefele, Bernhard. *Jazz Bibliography: International Literature on Jazz, Blues, Spirituals, Gospel and Ragtime Music with a Selected List of Works on the Social and Cultural Background from the Beginning to the Present.* New York, London, and Paris: K.G. Saur München; 1981.

Organized by reference areas and genres, this bibliography contains 6,576 entries covering books, monographs, and periodicals, none of which are annotated. The entries are international in scope; however, citations are either inaccurately described or incorrectly classified. Good sections on "Jazz by Country" and useful in compiling a comprehensive bibliography of African American musical, social, and cultural literature to 1981.

127.   Hine Darlene Clark (editor). *Black Women in America*. New York: Carlson
        Publishing Inc.; 1993.

        Profiles numerous jazz artists among the hundreds of biographies. Includes
        biographies on both stars and many under publicized artists. Among the
        biographies are entries on Dorothy Ashby, Ethel Ennis, Nina Simone,
        Dakota Staton, and Nancy Wilson. The entries cover their careers, accom-
        plishments, and influences. Selected bibliography at the end of each entry.

128.   Hippenmeyer, Jean-Roland. *Jazz sur-films, ou; 55 années de rapports
        jazz-cinema vus à Travers plus de 800 films tournés entre 1917 et 1972;
        Filmographie Critique*. Yverdon: Editions de la Thièle; 1973.

        In French. Filmography, organized chronologically. Contains both films
        with jazz scores and movies devoted to jazz subjects. Films with jazz
        scores but no specific performance of jazz are listed separately. Some
        entries contain critical assessments, including references to reviews. Both
        title and name indexes are included.

129.   Hoffman, Franz. *Jazz Advertised in the Negro Press: The Negro Newspapers
        of New England, 1910–1929*. Berlin: The author; 1980.

        Comprehensive presentation of the content and breadth of jazz writings
        in selected African American newspapers. The newspapers are the New
        York *Amsterdam News, New York Age,* and Baltimore *Afro-American,
        Chicago Defender*, the *New York Times,* and others. Extensive coverage.
        Index.

130.   Horn, David. *The Literature of American Music in Books and Folk Music
        Collections: A Fully Annotated Bibliography*. Metuchen, N.J.: Scarecrow;
        1977.

        A detailed listing of 1,696 books considered essential for a comprehensive
        library on American music: folk, country, blues, rock, musical stage, soul,
        and 243 entries on jazz. Excellent annotations.

131.   Jackson, Edgar. *The Literature of Jazz: A Critical Guide*. London: Library
        Association, 1970. Reprint. Chicago: American Library Association; 1972.

        Designed to promote the company's interest rather than promote scholar-
        ship on the topic. Contains a selected list of recordings of many different
        artists, including Count Basie, Duke Ellington, and Benny Goodman (addi-
        tion to 1981).

132.   Jackson, Edgar, and Leonard Hibbs. *Encyclopedia of Swing*. London:
        Decca, 1941; London: Decca, 1942.

        Focuses on swing artists and bands. Although limited, the major artists are
        included. Some topical essays.

133. Jørgensen, John, and Erik Wiedemann (editors). *JazzLexikon.* Hamburg: Mosiak Verlages; Gütersloh: Bertelsmann; Stuttgart: Europäischen Buch und PhonoKlub; Vienna: Buchgemeinschaft Donauland; 1991.

In German and English. Biographical portraits, jazz terminology, concise coverage of styles, and a selected bibliography. The portraits are concise, containing instrument, birth/death dates, and names of artists performed with. Entries are limited primarily to American artists. Also covers topical issues such as "Jim Crow" and a historical overview from New Orleans through a renaissance of bop. There are no new insights.

134. Kennington, David. *The Literature of Jazz: A Critical Guide.* London: Library Association, 1970. Reprint. Chicago: American Library Association, 1972.

Provides access to a cross section of jazz literature. Includes entries on jazz history, biographies, analysis and theory as well as reference and periodical literature. The author provides a short annotated bibliography at the end of each chapter. He also covers "Jazz in Novels, Poetry, Plays, and Films," "Jazz Education," and "Jazz Periodicals." Focuses on books published in English to 1979. There are some references to dissertations (addition to 1981).

135. Kennington, David, and Danny L. Read. *The Literature of Jazz: A Critical Guide.* Second edition. Chicago: American Library Association; 1980.

The bibliography is divided into chapters dealing with General Background, The Blues; The History of Jazz; The Lives of Jazz Musicians; Analysis, Theory and Criticism; Reference Sources; Jazz Education; Jazz in Novels, Poetry, Plays, and Films; and Jazz Periodicals. Each chapter contains a concise explanation of the criteria used to place books in the categories. The books are annotated. Name and subject indices.

136. Kernfeld, Barry (editor). *The New Grove Dictionary of Jazz.* Second edition. New York: Grove's Dictionary, Inc.; 2002. Three volumes.

This edition is divided into three volumes, contains 2,750 new entries, 3,000 revised essays, selected film and videos, and interviews of artists. Of the 2,750 new entries, 2,250 are new, and 1,500 cover musicians who became prominent in the 1980s and 1990s. Includes entries on international artists, jazz on a global basis, including in the Caribbean, Japan, and South Africa. There are extensive entries on blues, brass bands, soul music, ragtime, and rock music. In addition, the essays cover styles such as boogie woogie, blues, ragtime, Latin music, different instruments, clubs and festivals, jazz terms, and different styles of jazz. The essays are cross-referenced, and include bibliographies. A bibliography and list of contributors is included at the end of volume 3.

137.   _____. *The New Grove Dictionary of Jazz.* Two volumes. New York: Macmillan; 1988.

The two-volume dictionary is the most comprehensive compilation of biographies and articles on various topics in print. The entries are organized alphabetically and in addition to the numerous biographies, there are numerous articles covering topics such as Theory, Rhythm, Record Labels, Festivals, Films, Jazz Education, Improvisation, and Instruments. Each entry contains a selected bibliography and discography, and there are several appendices.

138.   Kinkle, Roger D. *The Complete Encyclopedia of Popular Music and Jazz, 1900–1950.* Four volumes. New Rochelle, New York: Arlington House; 1974.

The four volumes are organized as follows: Volume 1, Music Year by Year, 1900–1950; Volume 2, Biographies A–K; Volume 3, Biographies L–Z; and Volume 4, Indexes and Appendices. Volume 1 supplements the music lists with the names of the composers, lyricists, and performers as well as Broadway musicals, popular songs, movie musicals, and selected popular and jazz recordings. In volumes 2 and 3, careers and selected compositions of significant and lesser-known popular and jazz artists in concise critical biographies appear with selected compositions and recordings. Volume 4 contains *Down Beat* and *Metronome* poll winners (1937–72); annual release dates for 19 major recording labels (with record numbers), 1924–45; Academy Award winners and nominees for music, 1934–37, and indices of names, Broadway musicals, movie musicals, and popular and jazz composition titles.

139.   Kirchner, Bill (editor). *The Oxford Companion to Jazz.* New York: Oxford University Press; 2000.

The editor commissioned essays from 59 jazz critics, including Gene Lees, Dan Morgenstern, John McDonough, Gene Santoro, and Gunther Schuller. The essays cover historical trends and persons, discuss jazz in different countries, review the role of most instruments, and assess the place of jazz in dance, literature, and film. Except for Patricia Willard's essays on Ella Fitzgerald and Billie Holiday, female contributors to jazz are slighted.

140.   Kull, Percy, and Lars Resberg. *Jazzboken.* Stockholm: Forum; 1955.

In Swedish. A biographical dictionary with selected essays on history and evolution. Covers both American and foreign artists. Biographical entries include birth/death, career accomplishments and highlights, selected references to recordings, and musical associations. Also includes some musical examples. Selected bibliography and chronology of historical events.

141. Kunzler, Martin. *Jazz-Lexicon.* Hamburg: Rowohlt Taschenbuch Verlag GmbH; 1988.

In German. A comprehensive two-volume encyclopedia that covers musicians and topical areas. Volume 1 entries cover A–K and Volume 2 covers L–Z. In addition to birth/death dates (where warranted), the musician entries are replete with information on performing associations, important dates, achievements, and occasional quotes from other sources. Although thorough, some articles ("Afro-Americkanische Musik" and "Harmonik") are superficial. The entries contain several references to German and other non-American musicians (Joe Nay, Albert Mangelsdorff, Wolfgang Puschning), and references to lesser-known musicians such as Herb Flemming, Craig Harris, Walter Norris, and Barbara Thompson. Also included are in-depth entries on musicians such as Alberta Hunter, Clifford Jordan, Gunther Schuller, and Sun Ra. The strength of the encyclopedia is the coverage of non-American jazz musicians and the breadth and depth given to many lesser-known American musicians.

142. Kuzmich, John, Jr. *Survey of Teaching Materials for Jazz Improvisation.* Manhattan, Kans.: IAJE Publications; 2000.

Contains over 700 reviews of jazz improvisation books, and other jazz education materials. The entries cover generic approaches to improvisation, chord studies, materials on specific instruments and voice, and more. The entries were compiled from the author's column in past issues of both the *National Association of Educators Journal,* and its replacement the *Jazz Educator Journal.*

143. Kuyper, Ruud. *Jazz Enomstreken.* Amsterdam: Elmar; 1984.

In Dutch. A biographical dictionary that includes both American and foreign artists and includes information on birth/death dates, career highlights and accomplishments, and selected recordings. Index, illustrations.

144. Lee, Bill. *Bill Lee's Jazz Dictionary.* Foreword by Stan Kenton. New York: Shattinger International Music Corporation; 1979.

The dictionary is organized into three broad categories: terms dealing with performance, recording, and jazz study; colloquial or slang language; and technical terminology. The terms and their definitions appear to be a reflection of the author's experiences and wishes rather than a scientific survey of the argot used by jazz musicians. Although this volume is useful, Robert Gold's *A Jazz Lexicon* might be better. The dictionary also includes a chart of jazz periods and styles; outstanding jazz musicians 1900 to 1978, and the *Down Beat* Poll Winners, 1937 to 1978 (addition to 1981).

145.   _____. *People in Jazz: Jazz Keyboard Improvisers of the 19th and 20th Centuries.* Charlotte, N.C.: Columbia Lady Music, Inc.; 1984.

Chronicles numerous improvisers, covering preragtime, blues, folk and minstrel, early ragtime, ragtime-stride, blues-boogie woogie, as well as specific jazz genres. The title is misleading because many of the entries are not jazz musicians. The entries are organized as follows: Nineteenth Century Births; Births from 1900 through 1909; Births from 1910 through 1919; Births from 1920 through 1929; Births from 1930 through 1939; Births from 1940 through 1949, and Births from 1950 and beyond. No criteria for inclusion/exclusion were given. There are 876 entries, each containing birth/death dates (where warranted), and titles of compositions, career information, and relevant historical context information. He includes one, and for the 1940 through 1949 era, two transcriptions under each category. Recorded keyboard anthologies and collections, index, and bibliography are included. Excellent introduction to numerous keyboardists covering several genres from the nineteenth century to the early 1980s. Includes the music of eight compositions.

146.   Loade, Wolfgang. *Jazz Lexicon.* Stuttgart: G. Hatze; 1953.

Dictionary of jazz terms and phrases. Covers terms and phrases commonly used in the jazz community to the early 1950s. The dictionary is not as in depth as the works of Robert S. Gold (addition to 1981).

147.   Longstreet, Stephen. *Jazz From A to Z: A Graphic Dictionary.* Drawings and text by Stephen Longstreet. Highland Park, New Jersey: CatBird Press; 1989.

Covers jazz personalities, jazz terms, selected cities, dances, festivals, and ways of playing. Drawings cover a period ranging from the mid-1920s to the late 1980s. Each illustration is accompanied by text. He also includes "A List of Essential Recordings"; "A List of Basic Books"; "A List of Jazz Societies"; and a selected list of "The Clubs of New York, Chicago, Los Angeles, and New Orleans." In each case, the text is limited and is designed to present a capsule account of the drawing rather than a scholarly essay on a topic.

148.   _____. *The Real Jazz Old and New.* Baton Rouge: Louisiana State University; 1956.

Contains illustrations and text by the author that is more opinionated than critical or historical. The text is esoteric and is not connected to any specific goal or approach. No references or bibliography. Name index.

149. Longstreet, Stephen, and Alfons M. Dauer. *Knaurs Jazz-Lexikon.* München: Knaur, 1957; *Encyclopedie du jazz; adaption francaise de Jacques Bureau.* Paris: Somogy; 1958.

Contains precise definitions of dances, instruments, jazz styles, technical terms, individuals, and associated concepts and terms.

150. Lord, Tom. *Cadence All-Years Index: 1976–1991.* New York: Cadence; 1991.

An index of 27,600 entries covering 7,969 different artists and scholars. He also addresses 720 recordings. There are chapters on anthologies, books, calendars, interviews, journals, videos, and more.

151. Luciano, Danny. *Yesterday, Today and Tomorrow: The Musicians, Times and Places.* Upland, Pa.: Unknown Publisher; 1998.

Concise biographies of numerous musicians, and entries on venues and other pertinent information on jazz.

152. Lupi, Vladimiro. *Vocal Groups in Modern Jazz, Vocalese: Storia, Discographia, Biographie.* Ferrara, Italy: S.A.T.E.; 1986.

In Italian. Biographical and style portraits of several vocal groups, including Lambert, Hendricks, and Ross, The Swingle Singers, Double Six of Paris, Manhattan Transfer, and many more.

153. Markewich, Reese. *Bibliography of Jazz and Pop Tunes Showing the Chord Progressions of Other Compositions.* Riverdale, New York: Markewich; 1970.

An alphabetical list of tunes titles. Each title is followed by a list of other compositions based on the same chord progressions, the contrafact (1981).

154. _____. *The Definitive Bibliography of Harmonically Sophisticated Tonal Music.* Riverdale, N.Y.: Markevich; 1970.

Contains several listings of interest to serious jazz performers but is not a definitive listing of materials on the subject.

155. _____. *Jazz Publicity: Bibliography of Names and Addresses of International Critics and Magazines.* Riverdale, New York: Markewich; 1973; *Jazz Publicity II: Newly Revised and Expanded Bibliography of Names and Addresses of Hundreds of International Jazz Critics and Magazines.* Riverdale, N.Y.: Markevich; 1974.

Listing of organizations and their addresses as well as magazines devoted to jazz. Extensive and thorough. Volume 2 includes names of critics.

156.   _____. *The New Expanded Bibliography of Jazz Compositions Based on the Chord Progressions of Standard Tunes.* Riverdale, N.Y.: Markewich; 1974.

Includes the name of the composer, publisher, and recorder of numerous standard tunes. An expansion of *Bibliography of Jazz and Pop Tunes Sharing the Chord Progressions of Other Compositions.* The objective is to provide the titles of recorded jazz compositions based on the contrafact. Entries are arranged alphabetically by titles, and include the composer, publisher, and the names of movies or shows where the composition was performed. There are 150 total entries that are derived from the contrafact.

157.   Meadows, Eddie S. *Jazz Research and Performance Materials: A Select Annotated Bibliography.* Second edition. New York and London: Garland Publishers; 1995.

A comprehensive sampling of books and other materials devoted to jazz research, performance, and pedagogy. This reference tool differs from other jazz bibliographies because it is fully annotated, and because it contains books, theses and dissertations, videos, improvisation materials, and a detailed of scholarly journals and research libraries. The annotations are divided into 14 major categories, and are limited to books and other materials published between 1920 and 1995.

158.   _____. *Jazz Reference and Research Materials: A Bibliography.* New York: Garland Publishing; 1981.

The bibliography is divided into two sections: Jazz and Its Genres and Reference Materials. The first section lists books, articles, and theses and dissertations in the following categories: general, preswing, swing, bop, and modern. The annotated Reference Materials are divided into Research Tools, Biographies-Autobiographies, Discographies, Histories-Surveys, and Technical Materials. In addition, a list of record anthologies and a list of *Jazz Research Libraries* are provided. There is an index for each section.

159.   _____. *Theses and Dissertations on Black American Music.* Beverly Hills: Theodore Front Musical Literature; 1980.

The first and only monograph devoted to the topic, it is limited to North American entries. The bibliography is current to 1978 and is divided into categories: Practices Before 1900; Origins and Acculturation; and several genres, including blues, jazz, rhythm and blues, ragtime, gospel, and classical. The jazz entries constitute the largest single category.

160.   Merriam, Alan P., and Robert J. Benford. *A Bibliography of Jazz.* Philadelphia: American Folklore Society, 1954. Rev. Ed. New York: Da Capo; 1974.

This first book-length bibliography of jazz literature contains 3,324 entries, each coded to 1 of 32 subject categories, presenting a thorough listing that includes a subject index with jazz artist's names. The citations cover newspaper and periodical articles, portions of books, and contain two indices; subject, and an alphabetical listing of the periodicals from which the entries were taken. It is current to the mid-1940s. Includes a list of jazz periodicals (addition to 1981).

161. Miller, Paul Edvard. *Esquire's Jazz Book;* introduction by Arnold Gingrich. New York: Smith and Durrell, Inc., 1944; New York: Da Capo, 1987.

The first of three Esquire Jazz books, published consecutively in 1944, 1945, and 1946. The first book has three objectives; first, "to make available to the casual listener a short course in music appreciation; second, to preserve selected writings of the previous ten years that have imparted jazz appreciation and scholarship, and third, to provide a compendium of information in one volume, information that will make this book a valuable reference tool" (p. vii). Covers topics ranging from jazz appreciation, an historical chart of jazz influences, biodiscographies, and the Esquire All-American Band. Consists of mostly opinions and attitudes rather than scholarly discourse.

162. _____. *Esquire's 1945 Jazz Book;* introduction by Arnold Gingrich. New York: A.S. Barnes and Company; 1945.

Contains historical, discographical, and biodiscographical essays, and insights into 1945 jazz people and practices. Leonard Feather's essay, "A Survey of Jazz Today" is permeated with artists and activities, and the "Fifty Years of New Orleans Jazz" includes data pertinent to the evolution of New Orleans jazz. Factual and comprehensive.

163. _____. *Esquire's 1946 Jazz Book;* introduction by Arnold Gingrich. New York: A.S. Barnes and Company, 1946; New York: Da Capo, 1987.

Covers October 1944 to October 1945. Offers insights into Chicago style jazz, including a 1914–1928 map of Chicago. Also covers biographies of the Poll Winners, the Art in Jazz, the 1945 jazz scene, perspectives for jazz, and more. The essays on the history of Chicago jazz are permeated with names, dates, and activities.

164. Moon, Pete. *A Bibliography of Jazz Discographies Published Since 1960. Edited by Barry Witherden.* London: British Institute of Jazz Studies; 1969.

Devoted primarily to single artist discographies. The bibliography is arranged alphabetically by artist with details of compiler, source, and format (1981).

165. Morgenstern, Dan, Ira Gitler, and Jack Bradley. *Bird and Diz: A Bibliography.* New York: New York Jazz Museum; 1973.

Divided into sections on Gillespie and Parker, each with a list of articles, books, chapters in books, and selected discographies. The entries cover 1945–73 for Gillespie, and 1947–71 for Parker.

166. Oathout, Melvin C. *Bibliography of Jazz; An Unpublished Manuscript.* Washington, D.C.: Library of Congress; 1953.

A selected listing of articles and books covering the gamut of jazz: artists, criticism, history, and reference sources.

167. O'Meally, Robert (editor). *Encyclopedia of African American Culture and History.* New York: Simon and Schuster; 1996.

Included among the numerous biographies and essays are profiles of numerous jazz artists. Among the biographies are entries on Cannonball Adderley, Louis Armstrong, Clifford Brown, Harry Carney, Betty Carter, Eric Dolphy, Billy Eckstine, Coleman Hawkins, Wynton Marsalis, Bobby McFerrin, Charles Mingus, Sonny Rollins, Horace Silver, Billy Taylor, and many more. Covers their careers and contributions. Selected bibliography at the end of each entry.

168. Ortiz, Néstor R. *Diccionario del jazz.* Buenos Aires: Ricordi Americana; 1959.

In Spanish. Contains jazz terms and phrases.

169. Panassié, Hugues, and Madeleine Gautier. *Dictionnaire de jazz.* Paris: Laffont; 1954.

In French. Includes entries for bands, instruments, styles, and technical terms as well as such useful information as song titles (1981).

170. Polendnak, Ivan. *Kapitolky Ø Jazzu.* Praha: Statni hudenbi Vydavatelstvi; 1964.

In Czech. Contains a glossary of terms/concepts, followed by a discussion of blues, and modern jazz improvisation elements (form, rhythm, melodies, harmonies, and instrumentation). There are concise listings of artists by instruments and biomusical portraits of Jelly Roll Morton, Louis Armstrong, Duke Ellington, Count Basie, Benny Goodman, Lester Young, Charles Parker, Stan Kenton, Miles Davis, John Lewis, and Art Blakey. In each case, the information is limited. Selected literature of jazz, no index.

171. Polillo, Arrigo. *Conoscere il Jazz.* Milano: Mandadori, 1967; London: Hamlyn; 1969.

In Italian. Combines jazz history and evolution with a biographical dictionary. The historical coverage is current to the late 1960s, and the biographical entries cover basic details regarding life, career, and achievements. Also includes a glossary, selected bibliography, and index. The English edition is entitled *Jazz: A Guide to the History and Development of Jazz and Jazz Musicians,* and was translated from Italian by Peter Muccini.

172. Powell, Neil. *The Language of Jazz.* Manchester, England: Unknown Publisher 1997.

Permeated with explanations of some jazz terms, nicknames, and names of performance venues.

173. Reisner, Robert George. *The Literature of Jazz: A Selective Bibliography.* Second revised edition. New York: New York Public Library; 1959.

Arranged in four sections: books on jazz, background books, selective magazine references in nonjazz periodicals, and international magazines devoted to jazz. The entries are arranged alphabetically by author (1981).

174. Ruecker, Norbert. *Jazz Index, 1977–1980: Bibliography of Jazz Literature in Periodicals and Collections.* Frankfurt: Norbert Ruecker; 1980.

The purpose of this index, dating from the first edition in 1977, is to provide complete coverage of relevant articles and reviews published in jazz periodicals as well as a kaleidoscope of activities and results of jazz research. The 1977 (March) index contains the following headings: form, subject, geography, and names of bands. Thereafter, issues contain the following changes: (1) volume 1, no. 3 contains articles published in collections; (2) volume 2, no. 1 includes blues entries; (3) beginning with volume 3, the editor issued a triple number series due to the volume of material; (4) an attempt was made to index unpublished material, however this objective was not completed; and (5) English rather than German was the first language in a bilingual format. The entries contain full bibliographical information.

175. Sadie, Stanley, and John Tyrrell. *The New Grove of Music and Musicians.* New York: Oxford University Press; 2001.

176. Sandergren, Kåre, Sven Møller Kristensen, John Jørgensen, Erik Wiedemann, and Børge Roger Henrichsen. *Boken om Jazz.* Stavanger, Sweden: Dreyer; 1954.

In Swedish. Concise biographical portraits supplemented with an essay on the history of jazz. There are several musical examples and a tune index with publishers. The portraits cover life, career highlights, and some references to style and recordings. Glossary, selected bibliography, illustrations.

The 29 volumes in the second edition contain contains over 28,000 articles, including many expanded and revised articles from the first edition. In addition, neglected areas of music are also represented including jazz and other genres of world music. The jazz entries cover styles, music, theory, individual musicians, and groups.

177.   Shelly, Low. *Hepcats Jive Talk Dictionary.* Derby, England: T.W.O. Charles; 1945.

Details concepts and terms used primarily during the bebop era arranged alphabetically. Index.

178.   Simon, George T. *The Best of Music Makers.* Foreword by Dinah Shore. Garden City, N.Y.: Doubleday; 1979.

Biographical dictionary that contains both popular music and jazz artists. The jazz entries are extensive and contain birth/death dates, career highlights, some references to recordings, and musical associations. Illustrated.

179.   Skowronski, JoAnn. *Black Music in America: A Bibliography.* Metuchen, N.J.: The Scarecrow Press; 1981.

Although the bibliography covers entries in all African American genres, a significant number of entries are devoted to jazz musicians. The bibliography is divided into three major sections: Selected Musicians and Singers; General References, and Reference Works. The entries are arranged alphabetically and consist primarily of periodical literature and some books. Musical compositions, phonograph records, films, and most newspaper literatures are excluded; however, reviews of the aforementioned are cited. The entries are numbered consecutively to 14,319. Author index.

180.   Staffordshire County Library. *Jazz: A Selection of Books.* Stafford, England: Staffordshire County Library; 1963.

A limited collection of articles and books, covering artists, criticism, and history. Only 60 entries.

181.   Stechenson, Anne, and Anthony Stechenson. *The Stechenson Classified Song Directory.* New York: Criterion; 1986.

Classifies 100,000 song titles into 395 different categories. There is a supplement. Index.

182.   Stewart, S. Allen. *Stars of Swing: Swing Who's Who.* London: British Yearbooks; 1947.

Profiles numerous swing artists, includes birth/death dates (where warranted), career highlights, and references to recordings. Includes all major swing artists. Discography, illustrations.

183. Stratemann, Klaus. *Negro Bands on Film: An Exploratory Filmo-discography;* Volume 1: Big Bands 1928–1950. Lübbecke, Germany: Uhle and Kleimann; 1981.

Documents the appearances of African American big bands on film and includes dates, venues, nature of appearance, compositions performed, title of film, and more. Selected discography.

184. Summerfield, Maurice J. *The Jazz Guitar: Its Evolution and Its Players.* Foreword by Barney Kessel. Gateshead, England: Ashley Mark; 1978, 1979, 1980.

Contains pertinent details of the lives of 115 jazz guitarists. Each entry includes birth, death (if warranted), and concise details of the person's musical career. The entries are divided into two classifications: those with 100–250 words and those with 300–500 words. The former is limited to facts about the aforementioned, whereas the latter also contain some comments regarding the person's style/music. Artists covered include Charlie Christian, Django Reinhardt, Joe Pass, Kenny Burrell, Wes Montgomery, Eddie Durham, Rudolf Dasek, Eddie Condon, Charlie Byrd, George Benson, Billy Bauer, Danny Barker, Pat Martino, Mundell Lowe, Eddie Lang, Stanley Jordan, Grant Green, Freddie Green, and others. A concise history of the guitar in jazz is also included. Index and illustrations.

185. Ténot, Frank. *Dictionnaire du Jazz.* Paris, Kehl: Larousse, 1967, 1977. The 1977 edition is entitled *Le Jazz,* and is cowritten with Philippe Carles.

In French. Primarily an alphabetical listing of jazz musicians, with occasional blues, and related entries (bossa nova, cinema, clarinet, etc.). Each entry (when appropriate) contains birth/death dates, instrument performed, associations with other musicians, major appearances and achievements, and style characteristics. Some of the short essays on topics such as "bebop," "Swing," "Boogie Woogie," and "Discography" are limited in both breadth and depth.

186. Testoni, Gian Carlo, Arrigo Polillo, Giuseppi Barazzetta, Roberto Leydi, and Pino Maffei. *Enciclopedia del jazz.* Second edition. Milano: Messaggerie musicale, 1953, 1954, 1956.

In Italian. Contains brief biographies and detailed discographies of recordings issued in Italy from 1920 to 1950. The recordings are arranged alphabetically by artist, and contain full discographical information (date, venue, personnel, title, and matrix number). Also includes topical articles, some musical examples, and a general discography. Illustrated (addition to 1981).

187. Townley, Eric. *Tell Your Story: A Dictionary of Jazz and Blues Recordings 1917 to 1950.* Chigwell, England: Storyville, 1976; Volume 2: *A Dictionary* *of Mainstream Jazz and Blues Recordings, 1951–1975.* Chigwell, England: Storyville; 1976. Volumes 1 and 2.

Describes the meanings of 270 compositions from 1917 to 1950 in volume 1, and 2,000 titles in volume 2. The meanings are derived from the author's assessments and do not include feedback from the composers.

188. Tracy, Jack (editor). *Down Beat Record Reviews.* Chicago: Maher; 1956, 1957, 1958.

A compilation of group and individual record reviews, which include the text and rating of recordings. Some provide critical assessments whereas others are more descriptive.

189. Tudor, Dean, and Nancy Tudor. *Popular Music Periodicals Index, 1973.* Metuchen, N.J.: Scarecrow Press; 1974.

Included are several jazz periodicals, including *Coda, Down Beat, Jazz Journal,* and many more.

190. Unterbrink, Mary. *Jazz Women at the Keyboard.* Jefferson, N.C.: McFarland and Company; 1983.

Provides biographical portraits on several known and little-known pianists dating from the early jazz styles. Among the well-known artists covered are Lil Hardin Armstrong, Joanne Brackeen, Marian McPartland, and Mary Lou Williams. Lesser-known artists include Billie Pierce, Cleo Brown, Barbara Sutton Curtis, Jane Jarvis, and many more. The portraits include information on their introduction to jazz, family, musical associations, and career highlights. There are few insights into their styles, and little musical analysis (no transcriptions), or discographies. However, the book offers anecdotal information on several important but little-known women jazz pianists.

191. Voigt, John. *Jazz Music in Print. Second edition.* Boston: Hornpipe Music Publishing Company; 1978.

Designed as an index to the published work of significant jazz composers and performers. Included is sheet music, pedagogical materials (methods), transcriptions of solos, and arrangements for small ensembles and big bands. The entries include tune titles, publisher, price, and a designation of whether it is a "lead sheet" intended for combo or big band. Voigt does not list out-of-print materials, and the organization of the listings around musicians instead of publishers or composers presents some problems in locating materials. Selected bibliography and a list of publishers in the appendix.

192. _____. *Jazz Music in Print, by John Voigt and Randall Kane.* Winthrop, Mass.: Flat Nine Music, 1925; Second edition, Boston: Hornpipe Music, 1978; Third edition, Boston: Hornpipe Music, 1979.

Although he does not define "jazz," the author, nevertheless indexes "all published works of the most significant jazz composers and players." No definition of "significant" is given. In spite of these omissions, the author based his entries on performers rather than composers, editors, or publishers. Of special interest to jazz researchers is the list of publisher's addresses.

193.   Wassenberger, Igor. *Jazzovy slovnik.* Praha: Statni; 1966.

In Czech. Dictionary of jazz that includes biographical portraits of both individuals and groups and topical articles on styles, instruments, and some terms. Entries are arranged alphabetically and the biographical portraits include career highlights and some references to recordings.

194.   Wölfer, Jürgen. *Handbuch des Jazz.* Munich: Heyne; 1979.

In German. Emphasizes terms, places, styles, instruments, record companies, and similar information for the nonjazz specialist. Contains 400 entries, which are designed to introduce the terms and concepts encountered in jazz literature. There are no entries on individuals. Many of the entries contain concise bibliographical and discographical notes. A cross-reference system educates the user to the relationships that exist between some terms and concepts.

195.   Young, Bob, and Al Stankus. *Jazz Cooks: Portraits and Recipes of the Greats.* New York: Berkshire: Stewart, Tabor, and Chang; 1989.

Insider perspectives of 90 artists who discuss their beginnings in jazz, life on the road, and their culinary habits and food preferences. Among the interviewees are Harry Connick Jr., Dizzy Gillespie, Branford Marsalis, Carmen McRae, and Tito Puente. The artists suggest music to accompany their favorite foods. Index.

Music Business

196.   Curran, Mark W. *Sell Your Music: The Musician's Survival Guide to Direct Distribution on the Internet.* New York: NMD Books; 2001.

A thorough guide to independent music distribution over the Internet. Contains chapters on how to record and sell your music from home, how to design your own sales Web site, and how to market your music directly to the consumer. The author balances factual information with his views regarding marketing one's art on the Web. The book assumes computer literacy.

197.   Halloran, Mark. *The Musician's Business and Legal Guide.* New York: Pearson Education; 2001.

The product of entertainment lawyers who are active in settling intellectual property disputes. Covers a myriad of issues regarding copyright infringement, fair use, public domain, and intellectual property. Well-written and clear discussions.

198.   Hatschek, Keith. *How to Get a Job in the Music and Recording Industry.* Boston: Berklee Press (distributed by Hal Leonard); 2000.

Features advice on building a music business, networking, resume development, landing a profitable internship, and a discussion of careers in the new media.

199.   Smith, Regina. *Music Publishing 101.* New York: No Walls Press; 2001.

A crash course in music publishing covering issues from the origins of copyright law to intellectual property, public domain, fair use, and sampling. Uses case studies to discuss the aforementioned issues, and offers good and factual information on how musicians should protect themselves, their works, and their wallets in the music industry.

200.   Spellman, Peter. *The Self-Promoting Musician.* Boston: Berklee Press (Distributed by Hal Leonard); 2000.

Permeated with do-it-yourself strategies, tips for creating press kits, using the Internet for promotion, customizing demos, getting music played on college radio, and more.

III

Photographic Essays

201. Abe, K. *Jazz Giants: A Visual Retrospective.* New York: Billboard Publishers; 1988.

Compiled by a Japanese fan and photographer, this is one of the best available books on jazz photography. With the exception of the concise introduction by Abe and Nat Hentoff, the book contains no text. The mostly black-and-white photographs are arranged in a free-associative manner, and include the photographs of William Gottlieb, Jay Maisel, Bob Parent, and Charles Smith. Included are composers, arrangers, performers, vocalists, and behind-the-scenes personalities. Each of the 359 photographs is accompanied by an identification caption.

202. Balen, Noël, with collaboration from Frank Bergerot, Maurice Culloz, Jacques Lacava, Mario Roulman, Etienne de Saint-Marcel, Alain Tomas. *Jazz Hot: Les Grandes Voix du Jazz.* Paris: Editions de l'Instant/Jazz Hot; 1986.

In French and English. Contains numerous photographs accompanied by text. The text includes birth/death dates (where warranted), career highlights, and references to significant recordings. There are several shots of each artist of group. The photographs represent mostly jazz although some blues artists and curiously one gospel group, the Golden Gate Quartet, are included.

203. Berendt, Joachim Ernest. *Photo-Story des Jazz.* Frankfurt: Kruger, 1978. *Jazz: A Photo History* (translated by William Odom). London: Deutsch; New York: Schirmer; 1979.

Using photographs from the collections of the author, William Caxton, Guiseppe Pino, Duncan P. Scheidt, and others, Berendt attempts to communicate both the personality and music of the musicians. The collection consists of 370 black-and-white photographs, most previously unpublished. A section entitled "History" is misleading as it contains concise biographies of musicians (written to appeal to beginning jazz enthusiasts), which do not relate to the photographs.

204. Brask, Ole. *Jazz People;* photographs by Ole Brask; text by Dan Morgenstern; introduction by James Jones. New York: Abrams; 1976.

Presents portraits primarily from the 1960s and 1970s. The book follows a chronological format. Although the text is well written, the information on prejazz history is questionable. In addition, the photographic coverage is uneven: some significant musicians receive little attention (Parker, Coltrane) whereas others (Budd Johnson, Stuff Smith) receive more.

205. Condon, Eddie. *The Eddie Condon Scrapbook of Jazz;* with Hank O'Neal. New York: St. Martin's Press; 1972.

A pictorial essay of the jazz world that the author knew and performed in. Most of the numerous photographs are new as well as the accompanying anecdotes.

206. Dale, Rodney. *The World of Jazz.* Oxford: Phaidon Press; 1980.

Consists of a chronologically organized listing of photographic portraits of jazz musicians. The photographs were selected from several published and unpublished sources. Additionally, concise biographical notes, placement of the person in jazz historical context, and introductory comments regarding the music are provided. Index.

207. Demlinger, Sandor, and John Steiner. *Destination: Chicago Jazz.* Stroud, Gloucestershire, United Kingdom: Tempus; 2003.

A collection of nearly 300 photographs relating to the history of jazz in Chicago. Includes photographs of individuals, groups, and club scenes.

208. Driggs, Frank, and Harris Lewine. *Black Beauty, White Heat: A Pictorial History of Classic Jazz, 1920–1950.* New York: Da Capo Press; 1996.

Contains numerous photographs, covering people and venues from early jazz to 1950. The photographs cover artists such as Louis Armstrong, Duke Ellington, Thelonious Monk, Charles Parker, and many more.

209. Fontana, Luke. *New Orleans and Her Jazz Funeral Marching Bands: A Ten-Year Collection of Photography.* New Orleans: Jazz; 1980.

Photographs with text of many of the most famous funeral bands, including Eureka, Olympia, and many more.

210. Friedman, Carol. *A Moment's Notice: Portraits of American Jazz Musicians;* Text by Gary Giddins. New York: Schirmer Books; 1983.

Contains brief comments to accompany the portraits of several artists including Count Basie, Dexter Gordon, Lionel Hampton, Tony Bennett, Jim Hall, Art Blakey, Cecil Taylor, Charlie Haden, and many more. Index.

211. Goldblatt, Burt. *Jazz Gallery I.* New York: Newbold Publications; 1982.

Contains numerous photographs of jazz artists as they appeared away from the bandstand. The photos depict artists hanging-out backstage, getting out of taxis, playing with children, and toying with instruments other than their own. Among the photographed are John Coltrane, Miles Davis, Duke Ellington, Stan Getz, Billie Holiday, Max Roach, and many more.

212. Gottlieb, William P. *The Golden Age of Jazz.* New York: Simon and Schuster, 1979; New York: Da Capo; 1985.

A collection of photographs of jazz artists, over 200 including comments about the people, the music, or the times (1930s and 1940s). Gottlieb was a writer-photographer for both the *Washington Post* and *Down Beat.* The photographs capture a myriad of moods and musical performance shots, and are accompanied by anecdotes and stories. This might be the best overall collection of photographs covering this important period in the history of jazz.

213. Heerkens, Adrian. *Jazz: Picture Encyclopedia.* Alkmaar, Holland: Arti; 1954.

The photographs cover individuals as well as scenes and are accompanied by text written in English, Dutch, French, and German.

214. Lenormand, Herve. *Saint-Louis Jazz.* Paris: Nantes and the Association of Saint-Louis Jazz; 1996.

A pictorial history of jazz in St. Louis, Senegal that showcases both local artists and many of the prominent musicians who performed in St. Louis. Among the photographs are artists such as Count Basie, Duke Ellington, Jack DeJohnette, and McCoy Tyner. The text accompanying the photographs is in French.

215. Pino, Guiseppe. *From Spirituals to Swing;* photographs by Pino; text by Jean-Claude Arnavdon; English version by Fanni L. Jones and Willy Leiser. Montreux: International Booking Agency; 1979.

Parallel French and English text. The photographs are arranged by genre: spirituals, blues, and swing.

216.   Redfern, David. *David Redfern's Album.* London: Eel Pie; 1980.

Contains black-and-white photographs taken in the 1960s and 1970s in America and Europe. The photographs were taken at concerts, clubs, in the author's studio, on the road, and so on. The photographs display an eclectic array of expressions, moods, and postures. A professional photographer, Redfern has contributed to many albums and articles. Index.

217.   Schiedt, Duncan. *Jazz in Black and White: The Photographs of Duncan Schiedt.* Bloomingon: Indiana University Press; 2004.

A collection of his classic black-and-white photographs of many of the world's most famous jazz musicians. Among the numerous artists included are Louis Armstrong, Count Basie, John Coltrane, Dizzy Gillespie, Charles Mingus, Thelonious Monk, and Charles Parker.

218.   Smith, Michael P. *New Orleans Jazz Fest: A Pictorial History.* Gretna, La.: Pelican Publishing Company; 1991.

A documentation of over 400 photographs of the evolution of the New Orleans Jazz Festival. The book is divided into four sections of five-year periods. Captures crew scenes, and musicians like Miles Davis, Duke Ellington, Dizzy Gillespie, Mahalia Jackson, Irma Thomas, and Stevie Wonder. Also contains photos of performers like Como Fife and Drum Corps, the Meters, and Beausoleil.

219.   Stock, Dennis. *Jazz Street;* with an introduction by Nat Hentoff. New York: Doubleday; 1959.

A photographic exploration of selected significant exponents of jazz. There are 130 photographs of musicians including Louis Armstrong, Duke Ellington, Bud Powell, Charles Parker, Lester Young, and many more. The texts, which accompany the photographs, are grouped together at the back of the book, thereby creating an awkward arrangement between photographs and text. The photographs capture moods ranging from humor and sadness to happiness and vitality.

220.   Stockman, Hardy. *Cape Town Jazz 1959–1963.* Copenhagen: Gyldendal.; 2002.

Includes numerous photographs of individuals and groups representing various styles of South African music. The text was edited by Lars Rasmussen.

221.   Stokes, W. Royal. *Swing Era New York: The Jazz Photographs of Charles Peterson; Photographic Preparation by Don Peterson; Foreword by Stanley Dance.* Philadelphia: Temple University Press; 1994.

Peterson documents the New York jazz scene between 1935 and 1942. He captures artists such as Louis Armstrong, Sidney Bechet, Eddie Condon, Duke Ellington, Billie Holiday, and Art Tatum, to name a few. In addition, he captures Harlem at the peak of its renaissance, clubs on 52nd Street, and venues such as Nick's and the Village Vanguard. He also photographed jam sessions, recording sessions, and the world of the big band. Among the most interesting photographs are those depicting racial integration at the height of racial separatism in American society.

222.   Tanner, Lee. *Jazz Address Book;* photographs by Lee Tanner. Studio City, California: Pomegranate Art Books; 1991.

Contains 40 photographs of jazz greats such as Chet Baker, Art Blakey, John Coltrane, Larry Coryell, Miles Davis, Roy Eldridge, Dexter Gordon, Coleman Hawkins, Gerry Mulligan, Nina Simone, Zoot Sims, and Sony Stitt. Each photograph contains either a quote by or about the artist.

223.   Vail, Ken. *Jazz Milestones: A Pictorial Chronicle of Jazz 1900–1990.* New York: Omnigraphies; 1996.

An illustrated chronology of jazz from the turn-of-the-century to 1990. Jazz before 1920 is allotted half of one page, and only two pages are allotted to jazz beginning with 1920. For each year, the author lists births, deaths, significant events, films or books about jazz, and important compositions and recordings. An index of musicians contains the instrument played, birth and death dates. The chronicle contains inserts on Harlem, 52nd Street, Greenwich Village, and other venues, and maps locating famous clubs. The book was originally published in Great Britain in 1993.

224.   Weinberg, Barbara. *Jazz Space Detroit: Photographs of Black Music, Jazz and Dance;* text by Herb Boyd. Detroit: Jazz Research Institute; 1980.

Primarily a photo essay with text celebrating the Detroit musicians who remained during the exodus of the 1970s, though some attention is given to expatriate "stars." The book also celebrates the revitalized Detroit jazz scene of the 1970s. The commentary contains both historical and current information. No index.

225.   Wilmer, Valerie. *The Face of Black Music: Photographs by Valerie Wilmer;* introduction by Archie Shepp. New York: Da Capo; 1976.

An excellent collection of black-and-white photographs that capture a myriad of expressions and moods of both blues and jazz musicians. The photographs were taken in both America and Europe, 1963–75, and include the famous and not-so-famous, different genres (blues and jazz), and scenes from the road, home, and backstage. Also included are excerpts from interviews of several musicians made previously by Wilmer.

Jazz Cinema and Dance

226.   Dodge, Roger Pryor. *Hot Jazz and Jazz Dance: Roger Pryor Dodge Col-lected Writings, 1929–1964;* selected and edited by Pryor Dodge; New York: Oxford University Press.

The collected writings of the dancer, choreographer, and jazz critic. There are 45 essays, 33 on jazz, and the others with ballet and classical music. Whereas some of the essays are informative, others are controversial, misguided, and lack reference. Of specific importance to dance and jazz scholars are the sketches of several jazz and dance pioneers, reviews of early jazz recordings, and photographs shot by his father.

227.   Emery, Lynne Fauley, and Kathleen Dunham. *Black Dance: From 1619 to Today.* New York: Princeton Book Corporation; 1988.

Updated and corrected with a new chapter on black dance of the last 15 years before publication of the book. Covers dance in the slave and postslave eras, comprehensive and informative.

228.   Gabbard, Krin. *Jammin' at the Margins: Jazz and the American Cinema.* Chicago: University of Chicago Press; 1996.

Discusses the treatment of jazz music and musicians in the American cinema. The author focuses primarily on issues dealing with race and sex in films. His analysis is permeated with textual references and analysis, semiotics, and psychoanalysis. He refers to Miles Davis as "Post-Phallic," and Louis Armstrong as the "Phallic authority." He concludes that the solitary, intense nature of jazz precludes any accurate visual narrative. Well researched, written, and scholarly.

229.   Knowles, Mark. *Tap Roots: The Early History of Tap Dancing.* New York: McFarland and Company; 2002.

Discusses this art form in terms of three broad influences; primary, theatrical, and "other." His primary influences include African, Irish clog, English, West Indian, and plantation styles. Theatrical influences incor-porate the worlds of minstrels, vaudeville, and music halls. By "other," influences he means American country, German, Gypsy, Indian, and Native American.

230.   Kraines, Minda Goodman, and Esther Pryor. *Jump Into Jazz: The Basics and Beyond for Jazz Dance Students.* New York: McGraw-Hill; 2000.

Provides students with well-illustrated descriptions of all basic jazz steps, movements, and information on alignment, improvisation, history, and injury prevention.

231. Malone, Jacqui. *Steppin' on The Blues: The Visible Rhythms of African American Dance (Folklore and Society).* Urbana: University of Illinois Press; 1996.

Covers African American dance from the public dance contests of slave times, to the minstrel shows, Harlem cabaret scene of the 1920s to the stylized moves of Motown groups. She also covers the choreography of African American marching bands such as Florida A&M, Grambling, and Southern, and the step show routines of African American fraternities and sororities.

232. Miller, Norma, and Evette Jensen. *Swinging at The Savoy: The Memory of a Jazz Dancer.* Philadelphia: Temple University Press; 2001.

An autobiography and historical look at swing dancing through the eyes of a participant observer. Miller provides an insider perspective, and a sense of the personalities and places, She celebrates the Lindy Hop. Informative and humorous.

233. Stearns, Marshall Winslow. *Jazz Dance: The Story of American Vernacular Dance.* New York; Da Capo; 1994.

A history of jazz dance from its African roots to the date of this publication. The coverage ranges from voodoo of nineteenth-century New Orleans to the contemporary television productions of the day. He includes the accounts of Teddy Drayton, Ida Forsyne, and Rufus Greenlee who recall their contributions to the struggle for acceptance.

234. Therhorm, Dorte Wessel. *Jazz Dance Training.* New York and Frankfurt: Meyer and Meyer Fachverlag und Buchhandel GmbH; 1999.

In English. Covers basic training and the roots, origin, and development of jazz dance in America and its subsequent spread to Europe.

IV

Jazz in World Cultures

General

234a. Atkins, E. Taylor. *Jazz Planet.* Jackson: University Press of Mississippi; 2003.

An edited collection of essays by scholars such as Christopher G. Bakriges, Christopher Ballantine, Raul A. Fernandez, Johan Fornas, Benjamin Givan, Bruce Johnson, Warren R. Pickney, Jr., Frederick Starr, Linda Williams, Stefano Zenni, and others. The essays are informative, and the book is the first to document the evolution and dissemination of jazz into cultures outside of the United States.

African, Afro-Cuban, and Latin Influences

235. Ballantine, Christopher. *Marabi Nights: Early South African Jazz and Vaudeville.* Athens, Ohio: Ohio University Press (North American Distributor); 1994.

Focuses on the "black jazzing sub-culture" era(s) of development, inventing, and perfecting of its styles and dance. He details the music and contributions of Peter Rezant, "Zuluboy" Cele, The Jazz Revellers, The Merry Blackbirds, and The Pitch Black Follies. He also describes the social context, which gave birth to the music. The book is accompanied by a cassette tape of 25 tracks (vaudeville, jazz) recorded between 1930 and 1945.

236.   Boggs, Vernon W. *Salsiology: Afro-Cuban Music and the Evolution of Salsa in New York City.* Westport: Greenwood Press; 1992.

A history of salsa in New York City. The author demonstrates how Afro-Cuban music was embraced and how it has evolved into a popular genre in contemporary times. In addition to change in style, he documents the contributions of artists like Prez Prado, Eddie Palmieri, Machito, Chano Pozo, and the musical mixing between jazz artists like Dizzy Gillespie, Charles Parker, Stan Kenton, Howard McGhee, and musicians such as Machito, a movement coined Cubop. Also discusses venues, bandleaders, promoters, and includes interviews of performers of salsa. Selected bibliography, discography, and an index.

237.   Dauer, Alfons M. *Der Jazz: Seine Ursprünge und Entwicklung.* Kassel, Germany: Roth, 1958, 1962, and 1977.

In German. One of the best little-known studies on the origins and development of jazz. Perhaps this study has not been frequently cited because it has not, to my knowledge, been translated into English. The book contains 70 transcriptions representing African music, African music in America, Afro-American music in South America and the West Indies, Creole music, Afro-American music in North America (hollers and work songs), Afro-American religious music, blues, and early jazz. Concise comments are made on each transcription and the author makes numerous references to the transcriptions in the text. As with all studies on origins and retentions, this study does not demonstrate convincingly how jazz evolved from Africa through other African American genres finally to jazz. Selected bibliography, discography, and index.

238.   Davies, Rick. *Trompeta: Chappottin, Chocolate, and Afro-Cuban Trumpet Style.* Lanham, Md., and Institute of Jazz Studies (Rutgers University); 2003.

Provides a comprehensive history of mainstream Cuban music by examining the music of all eras from the perspective of trumpeters Felix Chappottin and Alfredo "Chocolate" Armenteros. The two artists were integral to and significant cogs in almost every stylistic development of Cuban music from its earliest days. He presents an overview of Afro-Cuban music, and provides an in-depth examination of both Chappottin's and Armenteros's styles.

239.   Figueroa, Rafael. *Salsa and Related Genres: A Bibliographical Guide.* Westport, Conn.: Greenwood Press; 1992.

This bibliography documents data about salsa and related genres in books, articles, dissertations, encyclopedia entries, videos, recordings, liner notes, and reviews. There is author, title, and subject indices.

240. Gerard, Charley, and Marty Sheller. *Salsa: The Rhythm of Latin Music.* Crown Point, N.Y.: White Cliffs Media Company; 1989.

Draws on the authors' practical musical experiences and interviews of insiders to provide an approach to understanding this genre. The authors attempt to draw an insider's perspective of the musical intangibles and to impart this information to novices who do not have the time to learn on their own. Focuses on rhythmic formulae, roles, techniques, and variations in the first half and related genres in the second half. The primary weakness is that they fail to document the importance of culture on the performance of salsa. A transcription of a Santeria religious ceremony (Sheller), a salsa arrangement, footnotes, a glossary, a selected annotated bibliography, and discography are included.

241. Kaufman, Frederick, and John P. Guckin. *The African Roots of Jazz.* Sherman Oaks, Calif.: Alfred Publishing Company; 1979.

A poor attempt to clarify the relationship that exists between jazz and West Africa. The authors took a tour-guide-like approach to their research by visiting selected West African societies, identifying musical elements like call and response, riffs, scales, and assuming these were the roots of jazz. The book draws heavily on the ideas espoused by Marshall Stearns in *The Story of Jazz,* and Gunther Schuller in *Early Jazz: Its Roots and Musical Development* (research venues, riffs, and blues scale ideas). The book is poorly researched because it does not adequately cover the literature dealing with the topic and because it fails to address issues such as transformation, adaptation, and reinterpretation. The bibliography and references reveal the authors' lack of expertise in their topic area.

242. Lenormand, Herve. *Saint-Louis Jazz.* Paris: Nantes and the Association of Saint-Louis Jazz; 1996.

A pictorial history of jazz in Saint-Louis, Senegal, that showcases both local artists and many of the prominent musicians who performed in Saint-Louis. Among the photographs are artists such as Count Basie, Duke Ellington, Jack DeJohnette, and McCoy Tyner. The text accompanying the photographs is in French.

243. Roberts, John Storm. *Latin Jazz: The First of the Fusions, 1880s to Today.* New York: Schirmer Books; 1999.

Roberts traces generic Latin influences including Brazilian, Cuban, Dominican, Haitian, and Puerto Rican influences in the music of prejazz New Orleans, ragtime, and the reemergence of the mambo, tango, and rumba in the United States in the 1920s and 1930s. He covers the music of artists such as Airto, Chick Corea, Paquito D'Rivera, Elaine Elias, Stan

Getz, Dizzy Gillespie, Stan Kenton, Jelly Roll Morton, Flora Purim, and Cal Tjader. The book is part historical and part discographical survey.

244.   _____. *The Latin Tinge: The Impact of Latin American Music on the United States*. New York: Oxford University Press, 1979; reprint, Tivoli, New York: Original Music, 1985.

The first assessment of the impact of Latin American genres on musical styles. The author documents the birth, growth, and maturity of North American-Latino traditions such as salsa and norteno; the Cuban and Mexican role in the birth of jazz; the acculturation processes that created Cubop, Latin rock, and impacted African American styles like R&B and funk; the popularization of the habanera, tango, mambo, rumba, chachachá, and bossa nova; and the Latin tinge in country music. The book focuses on transformation and reinterpretation and is replete with references to recordings, venues, dates, associations (bebop and musicians such as Machito, which led to Coop), and styles. There is a glossary, selected bibliography and discography, and an index.

245.   Stockman, Hardy. *Cape Town Jazz 1959–1963*. Copenhagen: Gyldendal; 2002.

Includes numerous photographs of individuals and groups representing various styles of South African music. Lars Rasmussen edited the text.

246.   Weinstein, Norman C. *A Night in Tunisia: Imaginings of Africa in Jazz*. Metuchen, N.J.: Scarecrow Press, Inc.; 1992.

Explores Africa as a motif in the recordings of numerous musicians. The focus is on the recordings rather than migrations of musicians to/from Africa or tours of Africa. The author explains that by "imagining" he means "an energetic force which constellates, in ever new and changeable con-figurations, ideas, and images surrounding notions of Africa" (p. viii). He uses an "Afro-centric" approach to his topic and focuses on individuals such as John Coltrane, George Russell, Count Basie, Randy Weston, Max Roach, Archie Shepp, Yusef Lateef, Sunny Murray, and Ronald Shannon Jackson. Although there are no musical examples, the book is permeated with insider quotes and references. There are chapter notes, two discog-raphies, selected play lists of the African theme, and an index.

Australia

247.   Bisset, Andrew. *Black Roots White Flowers: A History of Jazz in Australia*. Foreword by Don Burrows. Sydney: Golden; 1979.

Details the history of jazz in Australia, including North American influ-ences, dissemination, contact with foreign musicians, and the activities and careers of local musicians. There is some discussion of style, with musical examples. Selected bibliography, lead sheets, and transcriptions.

248. Clare, John, and Gail Brennan. *Bodgie Dada and the Cult of Cool.* Sidney, Australia: University of South Wales Press; 1995.

Details specific periods in Australian jazz, with emphasis on selected artists, why artists played a certain way, relationship of music to culture, and the degree that local musicians create their own music. Among the artists discussed are Norm Erskine, Sandy Evans, Roger Frampton, Tony Gorman, Cathy Harley, Craig Scott, and Lloyd Swanton

249. Hayes, Milehan, Ray Scribner, and Peter Magee. *The Encyclopedia of Australian Jazz.* Eight Mile Plains, Australia: The author; 1977.

Contains information on all aspects of jazz in Australia, including artists, history, recording, and information that chronicles the impact of jazz on the country. Index.

250. Johnson, Bruce. *The Oxford Companion to Australian Jazz.* New York: Oxford University Press; 1988.

This is the first comprehensive overview of the history of Australian jazz from 1917 to the late 1980s. The author combines over 300 entries that cover major and minor musicians, bands, venues, record labels, and a series of essays that detail change and historical context. The author begins with 1917 because that was the year of the first American jazz recording by ODJB and consequently, the beginning of the dissemination of American jazz. Bibliography, selected discography, and an index.

251. Williams, Mike. *The Australian Jazz Explosion.* London, Sydney, Singapore, Manila: Angus and Robertson; 1981.

Biographical dictionary with concise portraits of numerous past and present (1981) musicians. The portraits cover birth/death dates (when warranted), career highlights, and more. There are several photographs. Index.

Austria

252. Kraner, Dietrich Heinz, and Klaus Schulz. *Jazz in Austria: Historische Entwicklung und Diskographie des Jazz in Österreich.* Graz: Universal Edition; 1972.

In German. A discography of recordings made by Austrian jazz musicians in Austria. Begins with an overview of jazz in Austria, organized by years, with the focus on artist's recordings and activities, and visits by foreign artists, mostly Americans. The discography is organized by artist alphabetically, and includes several entries on Joe Zawinul (leader and sideman), and seven recordings by an American, Thurmond Young (Trumpet Young). List of catalogs used and name index.

Asian Americans

252a. Wong, Deborah Ann. *Speak It Louder: Asian Americans Making Music.* New York: Taylor and Francis Group; 2004.

Documents the myriad of musics—from traditional Asian genres through jazz, classical, and popular styles—that have been created by Asian Americans. The book focuses on Asian Americans making music rather than Asian American music. In addition to jazz, she tracks involvement in numerous additional styles, including Laotian Song, Cambodian music drama, karaoke, Vietnamese pop, Japanese American taiko, improvisational music that encompasses jazz and avant-garde classical styles, hip hop, and more. One of the first books to document Asian Americans making jazz.

Belgium

253. deGraef, Jack. *Jazz in Belgie: De Swing Period (1935–1947).* Antwerpen: Dageraad; 1980.

In French. Focuses on history, people, and activities of Belgian swing. Also included are a discussion of outside influences and the impact of jazz on Belgium. Permeated with names, accomplishments, references to activities, and some recordings.

254. Pernet, Robert. *Jazz in Little Belgium: Historique et Discographie de 1881 a 1966.* Bruxelles: Sigma; 1967.

In French. Covers the history and evolution of jazz to the mid-1960s. Contact with African American culture began in the late nineteenth century (minstrel acts, ragtime, and eventually jazz). The discography chronicles the history of recordings and includes artists/groups, dates, venues, labels, and matrix numbers. Selected bibliography and index.

Britain

255. Berg, Ivan, Ian Yeomans, and Nick Brittan. *Tradition: An A-Z Who's Who of the British Traditional Jazz Scene.* Foreword by Bill Carey. London: Foulsham; 1962.

Lists numerous artists, arrangers, and composers of jazz. Important because it provides insight into the pre-1962 British jazz scene, specifically 1947 to 1962. Portraits include birth/death dates (when warranted), career highlights, references to recordings, and occasional influences. Concise and informative. Illustrated.

256. Boulton, David. *Jazz in Britain.* Foreword by Chris Barber. London: Allen, Toronto: Smithers, 1958; London: Jazz Book Club, 1959, London: Allen, 1960.

A history of jazz in England to the late 1950s. Provides details of American influences, contact with American musicians, acceptance, and the names and career highlights of several British musicians. Not as comprehensive as Jim Godbolt's two-volume study, *A History of Jazz in Britain.* Bibliography and discography in the 1959 and 1960 editions. Index and some illustrations.

257. Carr, Ian. *Music Outside: Contemporary Jazz in Britain.* London: Latimer; 1973.

Portraits of several post–World War II British musicians. The portraits cover background and some stylistic points, as well as references to history and context. The portraits cover Ian Carr, Mike Gibbs, Jon Hiseman, Chris McGregor, Evan Parko, John Stevens, Trevor Watts, and Mike Westbrook. Bibliography, selected discography, and index. With illustrations.

258. Colin, Sid. *And the Bands Played On.* Foreword by George Chisholm. London: Elm Tree; 1977.

Chronicles and profiles British dance bands and their activities to the mid-1970s. Covers numerous bands, their contributions and recordings, and the role and function of dance bands in British culture. The impact of American bands on their British counterparts is also discussed. Selected discography. Illustrated.

259. Cotterrell, Roger. *Jazz Now: The Jazz Centre Society Guide.* Preface by Spike Milligan. London: Quartet; 1976.

A potpourri of biomusical portraits, essays, interviews, and a list of related guides devoted primarily to British jazz. Also includes a filmography, and list of record companies, dealers, and jazz societies. Selected bibliography, index, and illustrations.

260. Fordham, John. *Let's Join Hands and Contact the Living: Ronnie Scott and His Club.* London: Elm Tree; 1986.

A biography of one of the most enduring British nightclub owners and saxophonists. In addition to his life and musical career, the biography contains data on the numerous artists, including Americans, who performed at his club. Important on contact and dissemination of jazz in England. Selected discography, bibliography, illustrations.

261.   Godbolt, Jim. *All This and Many a Dog: Memoirs of a Pessimist/Loser.* (revision of *All This and 10%*). London: Quartet.

An autobiography that covers his achievements, trials, and tribulations. Focuses on his frustrations, though he includes anecdotes and recollections concerning other British artists. Illustrated.

262.   _____. *A History of Jazz in Britain, 1919–50.* London, Melbourne, N.Y.: Quartet Books; 1984.

A comprehensive examination of the first three decades of jazz in Britain. There are numerous references to artists, books and journals, discographers, and the transfer of jazz to England. Contact with American jazz musicians and their influence on British musicians is chronicled in "Jazz Comes to Britain by Stealth" (pp. 236–54). He quotes liberally; however, some of the quotes contain racially insensitive reference to African Americans. Selected discography and bibliography, index of tune titles, and general index.

263.   _____. *A History of Jazz in Britain, 1950–70.* London, Melbourne, New York: Quartet Books; 1989.

Proceeds from the end of his first book. He feels that the post-1950 British jazz scene was significantly different from the pre-1950 jazz scene. He ends his coverage at 1970 because, with the exception of the free-form movement, he believes British jazz was a continuation of earlier styles. Among the topics covered are the influence of traditional and bop styles, the influence of foreign musicians, the impact of literature and recordings, and the impact of the ban on foreign musicians imposed in 1934. Very thorough. Bibliography and discography by Alun Morgan.

264.   Goddard, Chris. *Jazz Away From Home.* New York: Paddington Press; 1979.

One of the few studies that discusses jazz outside of America. This is not a comprehensive study of jazz in England or France; still, it provides some insight into the transfer and adaptation of jazz in these countries. The author also touches on the reactions of the European (England and France) musical community to the transfer of jazz to their countries. He details the reception received by James Reese Europe, Will Marion Cook, Sidney Bechet, ODJB, and Paul Whiteman. The impact of jazz on composers such as Milhaud and Ravel and the development of European jazz criticism (Goffin, Lambert, and Panassié) are also discussed. The appendix contains a selected bibliography, discography, and transcripts of interviews of American and European musicians made 1976–78. Index.

265. Goddard, Jim. *A History of Jazz in Britain 1919–1950.* New York: Merrimack Publishers' Circle; 1984.

Deals with "Those English jazz musicians whose careers were contained within the confines of their nation." There are in-depth accounts of musicians, groups, clubs, recordings, and publications. He also includes quotes from *Melody Maker* that focus on anti-Semitism and racism. He chronicles jazz appreciation in England and mentions the significance of the Louis Armstrong and Duke Ellington visits in the early 1930s. Selected bibliography and an index.

266. Green, Benny. *Drums in My Ears; Jazz in Our Time.* New York: Horizon Press; 1972.

The author, a British journalist and critic, presents his view of jazz in London over the 15 years before the publication of this book. The essays are concise, opinionated, and spiced with anecdotes. His comments regarding American artists such as Dave Brubeck and John Lewis are unwarranted. No index.

267. Grime, Kitty. *Jazz at Ronnie Scott's;* photography by Val Wilmer. London: Robert Hale; 1979.

One of the world's most famous jazz clubs, this British club has long been a favorite of American jazz performers. This book is described as a "patchwork" of interviews organized and synthesized into subjects like life as a jazz musician, influences of musicians like Charles Parker, travel, and insider perspectives of jazz as a vocation. While the first portion was pieced together from comments made by both individual American and British musicians, a second focus of the book is the comments of instrumental groups. The interviews were conducted over several years and feature American artists such as Andrew Cyrille, Bud Freeman, Dizzy Gillespie, Woody Herman, Thad Jones, Charles Mingus, and Archie Shepp, to name a few. Name and title index.

268. Jenkins, Tricia, and Tony Doyle. *Let's Go Dancing: Dance Band Memories of 1930s Liverpool.* Liverpool: Institute of Popular Music; 1994.

Recalls the names and bands that performed in 1930s Liverpool. Also provides insight into venues, and the popularity of dance band music.

269. Rust, Brian. *The Dance Bands.* London: Ian Allan; 1972.

Lists mainly British bands from 1919 to 1944, with many rare photographs. Important because it chronicles the accomplishments of leaders like Ted Heath. Index.

270.   Scott, Ronnie. *Some of My Best Friends Are Blues.* London: Allen; 1979.

Focuses on the activities and management of his London jazz club. In the introduction, Benny Green addresses the history and significance of Scott and his club, which is complimented by Spike Milligan's Postscript. Mike Hennessey provided editorial assistance. Cartoons by Mel Calman.

271.   Tracy, Sheila. *Talking Swing: The British Big Bands.* Edinburgh: Trafalgar Square Publishing; 1997.

There are 24 pages of photographs in this comprehensive assessment of British big bands. In addition to discussing American influences, the book is replete with the names and deeds of performers, and performance venues.

272.   Walker, Edward S. *Don't Jazz—It's Music: or Some Notes on Popular Syncopated Music in England During the 20th Century.* Walsall, Staffs: The Author; 1979.

A history of growth and dissemination of jazz and dance music in England. The book is also important because it provides the names of numerous American musicians, Noble Sissle and Paul Whiteman, for example, who performed in England over the years.

273.   Whitehouse, Edmund. *The Book of British Dance Bands From The Twenties to the Fifties.* London: Cheltenham; 2001.

A comprehensive and illustrated assessment of British dance bands complete with the names of performers. The book is loaded with with names of performers that are little known outside of England.

274.   _____. *The Second Book of British Dance Bands: The Singers and Small Bands.* London: Cheltenham; 2001.

A second illustrated volume in this important topic that focuses on the names, roles, and functions of vocalists and small bands in British jazz history.

275.   Wickes, John B. *Innovations in British Jazz.* London: Chelmsford; 1999.

One of the first books to detail the reasons and procedures of modern, free, and jazz rock in British culture. His discussion is limited primarily to the 1960–1980 period and contains the names and accomplishments of performers and groups. The author also alludes to the reasons why different styles of jazz were acceptable in England.

Canada

276.   Gilmore, John. *Swinging in Paradise: The Story of Jazz in Montreal.* Montreal: Véhicule Press; 1988.

Chronicles jazz activity in Montreal from shortly after World War I to the late 1980s. In his discussion, it is apparent that Montreal jazz was a reflection of American events rather than a venue that fostered innovative change. He mentions many jazz artists and provides numerous photographs. The decline of jazz in Montreal is chronicled with the annual Alcan International Jazz Festival as one of the last legacies of a once-thriving jazz city.

277. Litchfield, Jack. *The Canadian Jazz Discography 1916–1980.* Toronto, Buffalo, and London: University of London Press; 1982.

Attempts to list all jazz recordings by Canadian artists, 1916–1980. Each entry contains a biographical sketch, plus standard discographical information on each recording (personnel, city and date of recording, label, serial number, title, and composer credits). Also included are piano rolls and motion pictures containing jazz, and recordings that contain "substantial jazz passages" although the overall style might not be jazz. He defines terms such as "jazz," "Canadian," and "record." A significant addition to jazz discography because it includes information not available in other discographies.

278. Miller, Mark. *Such Melodious Racket The Lost History of Jazz In Canada, 1914–1949.* Toronto, Canada: Mercury Press; 1997.

The author is concerned with discovering and retrieving details of Canada's past jazz history and piecing them together to produce an introduction, dissemination, and early development of jazz in Canada. He begins with the Canadian debut of the New Orleans Creole Band in 1914, and proceeds to the American debut of Montreal pianist Oscar Peterson in Carnegie Hall in 1949. The book is permeated with data on the appearance of American jazz artists appearing in Canada, material drawn from more than 70 interviews, and the subsequent influence of American jazz on Canadian jazz. Includes a 1914–1949 "Time Line," notes, bibliography, and excellent photographs.

279. _____. *Boogie, Pete and the Senator: Canadian Musicians in Jazz, the Eighties.* Toronto: Nightwood; 1987.

Contains numerous bio-musical portraits, augmented with interview material, that cover the breadth and depth of jazz activities in Canada in the 1980s. The portraits cover the nature of the activities as well as the role and function of selected individuals within the activity. Among the portraits are Ian Bargh, Kid Bastien, Jean Beaudet, Ed Bickert, Paul Bley, Terry Clarke, Tony Collacott, Jean Derome, Michel Donato, Dennis Elder, Roddy Ellis, Jane Fair, Hugh Fraser, Jim Galloway, Linton Garner, Boogie Gaudet, Sonny Greenwich, Lance Harrison, Oliver Jones, Fraser MacPherson, Rob McConnell, Guy Nadon, Phil Nimmons, Don Palmer,

66

Claude Ranger, Fred Stone, Neldon Symonds, John Tank, Mike Taylor, Don Thompson, Bob Tildesley, and Vic Vogel. Some portraits include a selected discography. Photographs and an index.

280. _____. *Jazz in Canada: Fourteen Lives*. Toronto: University of Toronto Press; 1982.

Biographies of trumpeters Trump Davidson and Herbie Spannier; saxophonists Teddy Davidson, Paul Perry, P. J. Perry, Brian Barley, and Ron Park; pianists Chris Gage and Wray Downes; drummers Larry Dubin, Guy Nadon, and Claude Ranger; and guitarists Nelson Symonds and Sonny Greenwich. The biographies contain anecdotes and comments from the musicians that are linked by the narrative voice of the author. When warranted, a selected discography is provided; however, one artist has no professional recordings to his credit. Miller's chronological arrangement demonstrates how performers and Canadian audiences have evolved from big bands to clubs, and from coffee houses to concert jazz venues.

281. Rosenthal, Ron. *Portrait d'un Festival; Festival International d Jazz de Montreal*. Montreal: Vehicule.; 1999.

A comprehensive account of the musicians and activities that have transpired at this famous jazz festival. Includes information on the many Canadian musicians like Oscar Peterson and George Shearing, and several American artists who have appeared at the festival.

Central and South America

282. Trueba, Fernando. *Calle 54*. Paris: Filippacchi; 2000.

This is a book about a film that features numerous Central and South American jazz musicians. The book also includes numerous color photographs and biographical sketches.

Czechoslovakia

283. Breda, Arie Van. *"100 Jaar" Jazz in Den Haag; het New Orleans Van de Lage Landen*. Praha: Den Haag; 2000.

A comprehensive illustrated history of jazz in the Hague, complete with names, contributions, and performance venues. The book includes local and international artists. Text in Dutch

284. Doruzka, Lubomír. *Fialová koule Jazzu*. Praha: Panton, 1970; Panton; 1990.

In Czech. The 17 interviews are permeated with information on influences, background, and styles. Of particular note are the attitudes about changes in jazz 1935–88 (the period covered). The interviews include Jan Beranek, Rudolf Dasek, Ondrej Ernyei, Ladislav Habart, Jan Hammer Sr., Vojtech Havel, Jaromir Anilicka, Jana Koubkova, Mirka Krivankova, Karel Ruzicka, Pavel Smetacek, Jiri Stivin, Milan Svoboda, Karel Velebny, Emil Viklicky, and Inka Zemankova. Good discussion of styles. There are several musical (score) examples. Illustrated.

285. Doruzka, Lubomír, and Ivan Polendnak. *Ceskoslovensky Jazz: Minulost a Prítomnost.* Praha: Supraphon; 1967.

In Czech with an English abstract. Details the history of Czech jazz to the late 1960s. Includes numerous references to artists, influences, and contact with outsiders, dissemination, and styles. Includes the activites and contributions of the musicians covered in *Fialová Koule Jazzu.* References to artists and recordings including Rudolf Dasek, Ladislav Habart, Jan Hammer Sr., Pavel Smetacek, and others. Discography, references, index, and illustrations.

286. Kotek, Josef. *Knonika ceské synkopy: Pulstoletí Ceského Jazzu a moderní populární hubby u obrazech a svedectuí soucasníku i: 1903–1938.* Praha: Supraphon; 1975.

In Czech. Discusses the first 30 years of Czech jazz and modern popular music in both films and contemporary documents. Permeated with names, accomplishments, and outside influences. Index.

Denmark

287. Gjedsted, Jens Jørn. *Montmartre Gennem 10 ÅR* Copenhaven Gyldendal; 1986.

In Danish. Chronicles the jazz activities of this club over a 10-year span, 1976–86. Covers artists, dates, and activities. Illustrations.

288. Malone, Leonard. *The Danish Radio Big Band, 1964–1984.* Copenhagen: Danmarks Radio; 1985.

Discusses the role and function of the Danish Radio Big Band in disseminating jazz and the impact of several African American artists in this dissemination; Thad Jones (conductor, composer, and soloist with the band), Miles Davis, Dizzy Gillespie, and several others. Musical examples (score facsimiles).

289. Wiedemann, Erik. *Jazz i Danmark, Tyverne, Trediverne og Fyrrene: En musikkulturel Underøgelse.* Three volumes. Copenhagen: Gyldendal; 1982.

In Danish. A comprehensive cultural-musical investigation of jazz in Denmark in the 1920s, 1930s, and 1940s. The text is derived from the author's dissertation written at the University of Copenhagen, 1981. Covers history, acceptance, artists and accomplishments, influences, dissemination, and style. Frequent references to recordings. Scholarly and thorough with an English summary. Bibliography, cassettes, discography, and index.

Estonia

290. Ojakaar, Walter. *Continuity of National Tradition in Estonia Jazz.* N.C.: Menden; c. 1989.

Although only 18 pages with illustrations, the author discusses how local musicians strive to incorporate nationalism into their jazz. Contains some names of performers.

Europe

291. Bausch, Armando. *Jazz in Europa.* Frankfurt: Echternach; 1985.

In addition to presenting a generic overview of the music and musicians, including local and visiting artists, the author also includes interviews with important exponents and supporters of the music. There are interviews with Carlo Bohlander, A. Mangelsdorff, Ronnie Scott, and others.

292. Boubet, Arnaud. *Cote du Jazz Europeen en Vinyl.* Paris: Filippacchi; 2003.

A comprehensive guide to the recordings and prices of albums recorded by European jazz artists.

293. Büchter-Römer, Ute. *New Vocal Jazz.* New York, Frankfurt, and Paris: Peter Lang; 1991.

In German. Includes an essay on the methodology used to collect and analyze the data, followed by an essay on improvisation (Jazz—John Cage—Johann Adolph Hasse), and a discussion of new music and jazz. These essays are supplemented with analysis using several musical examples. Also covered are the improvisational styles of Cathy Berberian, Lauren Newton, Jeanne Lee, Urszula Dudziak, Maria Joao, and Maria de Alvear. The analysis of styles and techniques is systematic and scholarly. The appendix contains several complete transcriptions by other scholars and a selected bibliography.

294. Canellas, Gerardo. *Jazz Voyeur.* Barcelona: Unknown Publisher; 2002.

The text is in Spanish and English in this collection of black-and-white photographs. The photographs depict jazz stars performing in European Jazz Festivals.

295. Cerri, Livio. *Jazz, Musica d'Øggi.* Milano: Malfasi; 1948.

In Italian. A chronological and historical discussion of European jazz soloists. The portraits focus on style, influences, and recordings. Significant because he discusses pre-1948 artists who are largely unknown in the West. References, index, and illustrations.

296. Desthomas, Daniel. *Quand le Jazz est 1.* Paris: Filippacchi; 2002.

Although only eight pages, he includes 20 oversized black-and-white leaves in a box of artists such as Louis Armstrong, Miles Davis, Ella Fitzgerald, Billie Holiday, and several more.

297. Jost, Ekkehard. *Europas Jazz: 1960–1980.* Frankfurt: Fischer Taschenbuch Verlag; 1987.

In German. Details the activities and style of selected individuals and ensembles in Germany, East Germany, England, the Netherlands, and France. Among the individuals/ensembles covered from Germany are the Globe Unity Orchester, Irère Schweizer, Gunter Hampel, Modern Jazz Quintett Karlsruhe, and Albert Mangelsdorff; from East Germany, Ulrich Gumpert, Gumpert-Sommer Duo, Manfred Schulze, and the Berliner Improvisations Quartett; from England, Tony Oxley, Paul Rutherford, Derek Bailey, Evan Parker, and John Surman; from the Netherlands, William Breuker, Misha Mengelberg, Mengelberg-Bennick Duo; and from France, the Expatriates, Jef Gilson, Francois Tusques, Michel Portal, and Bernhard Lubat. In addition to several essays that cover trends and issues, the biomusical portraits provide insight into careers, influences, and styles. There are no musical examples. Selected discography by artist, chapter notes, and name index.

298. Knauer, Wolfram. *Jazz in Europa.* Frankfurt: Hofheim; 1994.

Primarily concerned with a discussion of jazz in Europe, 1933–1945, and deals with performers and the role and function of performers in spreading the music. Provides names of local and visiting artists who performed. In German.

299. Lotz, Rainer E. *Black People: Entertainers of African Descent in Europe and Germany.* Bonn, Germany: Der Jazzfreund; 1997.

Profiles some of the many African American performers who performed in Europe in the early years of the twentieth century. Includes information on the Bohee Brothers, Black Diamonds, Black Troubadours, Belle Davis, Arabella Fields, Edgar Jones, Will Garland, Hampton and Bowman, Louisiana Troupes, Musical Spillers, and several more.

300.   McCarthy, Albert (editor). *The PL Yearbook of Jazz 1946.* London: PL Editions Poetry; 1946.

The 19 essays cover a myriad of topics, including history, appreciation, discography, literature, and aesthetics. The essays on jazz in England, Belgium, France, and Switzerland are concise and replete with names, accomplishments, and the transformation of jazz to those venues. Panassié's essay "Fats Waller in Paris," although mostly anecdotal, contains some important facts about his performance. A discography of year's recordings (Albert J. McCarthy) is included.

Finland

301.   Granholm, Ake (editor). *Finnish Jazz: History, Musicians, and Discography.* Helsinki: Finnish Music Information Center, 1974; revised in 1982 by M. Kontinnen, and in 1986 by J. P. Vvorela.

In Finnish. Covers the introduction, history and evolution, and dissemination of jazz to the early 1980s. Profiles numerous Finnish artists, arrangers, and composers, and list significant recordings. The influence of American jazz artists is also mentioned. The discography includes full details.

302.   Westerberg, Hans. Suomalaiset jazzlevytysket 1932–1976: *t: 45 Americans, 92 Europeans and Hundreds of Finns, A Finnish Jazz Discography 1932–1976.* Helsinki: Suomen Jazzliitto; 1977.

In English and Finnish. Includes jazz recordings by Finns in Finland, by Finns abroad (leaders and sidemen), by foreigners in Finland, and recordings by foreigners abroad if the recording was made for a Finnish record producer and first published in Finland. Also includes the listings of the Finnish Broadcasting Corporations (oy Yleisradio Ab) transcriptions of music. The entries include title, individual or group, recording sessions, dates, venues, master numbers, and more. Radio broadcasts are not listed. Index of musicians.

France

303.   Cotro, Vincent. *Chants Libres; Le Free Jazz en France 1960–1975.* Paris: Peter Lang; 1999.

In addition to providing the names and some background information on several free musicians, the author includes numerous musical examples to assist his assessment of the respective approaches and styles of free jazz.

304. Dupuy, Philippe-Gerard, and Serge Loupien. *Backstage: Jazz in Marciac.* Paris: Toulouse; 2002.

Includes black-and-white photographs by Dupuy, and text by Loupien of the Marciac Jazz Festival.

305. Harrison, Max. *A Jazz Retrospect.* New York: Crescendo Publishers; 1977.

A collection of articles previously published in jazz periodicals. The author addresses attitudes on improvisation, group attitudes toward the language of jazz, and cross-influences between jazz and other music. In addition, he discusses the widely differing styles of some of the greatest artists. An account of French and Czechoslovakian jazz, and a view of Sidney Finkelstein's *Jazz: A People's Music* are also included. Index.

306. Hélian, Jacques. *Les grandes Orchestres de music hall en France: Souvenirs and temoignages.* Preface by Frank Ténot. Paris: Filippacchi; 1984.

In French. A pictorial history of French jazz, 1920–49, with the emphasis on dance bands. Selected discography and index.

307. Hippenmeyer, Jean-Roland. *Le Jazz En Suisse, 1930–1970.* Averdon: Editions De La Thièle; 1971.

In French. Covers individuals and groups such as The Langiros, The Original Teddies/Teddy Stauffer, Eddie Brunner, Fred Böhler, Bob Huber, Rio de Gregori, Hazy Osterwald, The New Hot Peppers, Loys Choquart, The New Orleans Wild Cats, Henri Chanx, and The Old School Band. In addition to biomusical essays, Hippenmeyer includes dates, rosters of visiting North American bands, photographs, a discography, and bibliography. Good historical overview.

308. Jackson, Jeffrey H. *Making Jazz French: Music and Modern Life in Interwar Paris.* Durham, N.C.: Duke University Press; 2003.

Uses memoirs, press accounts, and cultural criticism to examine the wide popularity of jazz in Paris during the 1920s and 1930s. He also examines specifics ways and means that jazz became integrated into the French entertainment tradition, the disgust of some French persons about jazz, and the role and function that expatriate jazz musicians had on the acceptance and dissemination of the music in France.

309. Jamin, Jean, and Patrick Williams (editors). *Jazz et Anthropologie.* Paris: L'Homme, No. 158–159, April/September, 2001.

In French. A special edition of this important anthropology journal that focuses on a variety of topics, including style, anthropology and jazz, diffusion and reception, and other important issues and topics. Contains an insightful article on Thelonious Monk, and a glossary/index of musicians. Offers important and scholarly insights by numerous French scholars.

310. Laplace, Michel. *Portraits of French Jazz Musicians.* Paris: Menden; c. 1985.

A concise 44-page collection of biographical information on pre-1960 jazz musicians, includes American and some European jazz artists.

311. Latxague, Robert. *Jazz, la Photographie.* Paris: Chambery; 1996.

A documentation by 26 photographers of the 15 years of the French festival *Jazz Vienne.* Contains numerous photographs of artists and people attending the festival.

312. *Les Annees Jazz Magazine 1954–2000.* Paris: Levallois-Perret; 2000.

A comprehensive collection of articles and photographs from 45 years of the magazine's issues. The articles cover local and visiting artists, influence of jazz, and new directions. In French.

313. Loupien, Serge, and Philippe-Gerard Dupuy. *Backstage Jazz in Marciac.* Paris: Unknown Publisher; 2002.

Dupuy supplied the photographs and Loupien the text regarding the history of the Marciac Jazz Festival.

314. Regnier, Gerard. *Jazz au Havre and Caux, Depuis Les Annees 20.* La Havre: Luneray; 1997.

An illustrated history of jazz in La Havre, including accounts of local and visiting musicians. Text in French.

315. Shack, William A. *Harlem in Montmartre: A Paris Jazz Story Between The Great Wars.* Berkeley: University of California Press; 2001.

Focuses on the principle artists who played critical roles in shaping the jazz scene in Montmartre after the war. He uses "thick description" to discuss the social institutions, moving back and forth in time and space. He juxtaposes periods of ragtime, jazz, and swing that transformed African American popular music, however his approach is anthropological and not musical. Among the persons interviewed for his study were Maurice and Vonette Cullaz and Jacques Bureaux.

Germany

316. Budd, Michael (editor). *Jazz and The Germans: Essays on the Influence of Hot American Idioms on 20th-century German Music.* Westport, Conn.: Pendragon Press; 2002.

The essays are the outgrowth of a conference held at the University of Missouri in 1995. The essays and topics are: Alan Lareau examines jazz influences in Ernst Krenek's 1927 opera *Jonny Spielt Auf,* Frank Tirro explores how jazz traveled from the United States to Germany, E. Douglas Bomberger discusses ragtime compositions by Igor Stravinsky and Paul Hindemith, Dane Heuchemer traces jazz influences in the opera house, and David Snowball discusses the Germans dismissal of jazz. The authors do not reference much of the latest research in their respective topics.

317. Edelhagen, Viola, and Joachim Holzt-Edelhagen. *Die Big Band Story: Die Big-Bands nach 1945 in der BRD Verlag.* Buchhandlung and Antiquariat: Verlag; 1988.

In German. Divided into two parts. Part one contains essays on topics like Jazz in Germany, Big Bands of the Forties and Fifties, the Impact of Pop and Rock on Big Band Repertories, the general attitudes about and acceptance of the bands, as well as sociopolitical factors affecting the bands. In the second part, the bands of artists like Joe Wick, Kurt Edelhagen, Erwin Lehn, Werner Müller, Max Greger, Kurt Henkels, Walter Dobschinsk, Bert Kämpfert, James Last, Paul Kuhn, and Hugo Strasser are discussed. The entries are concise and limited primarily to origin, history, and some references to recordings. Selected bibliography and discography.

318. Hagen, Rochus A. M. *Jazz in der Kirchen: Zur Erneverung der Kirchenmusic.* Stuttgart: Kohlhammer; 1967.

In German. Discusses how German church music is undergoing change, specifically how and why jazz is being used in the church. Covers ideas relevant to cultural transformation and offers important insights into German religious identity in the 1960s. Selected bibliography and index.

319. Joehnk. Hans-Helmut. *Von den Goldenen Zwanzigern zum Trummerjazz; Jazz, Swing und Tanzmusik in Kiel 1923–1950.* Kiel: Unknown Publisher; 1998.

A history of jazz in Kiel from 1923 to 1950 complete with names of local and foreign performers, names of venues, and the impact of jazz on the city. There are 14 pages of photographs. In German.

320. Karl, Ingrid. *Let's Cool One: Chamber Jazz/Lektorat.* Frankfurt: Wien; 1996.

In German An eight-page program book of a concert series that featured Franz Koglmann, Joe Maneri, Myra Melford, and Hannes Zerbe. The program contains background information on the artists and a synopsis of their compositions.

321.   Kater, Michael H. *Different Drummer: Jazz in the Culture of Nazi Germany.* New York: Oxford University Press; 1992.

Explores the underground history of jazz in Hitler's Germany. Kater details that for the Nazis, jazz was perceived as a threatening form of expression. By using archival records and eyewitnesses of the Third Reich, the author demonstrates how the expression of jazz became a powerful symbol of social and political protest in Germany. His research was also situated within a period of increased investigations into the social and cultural history of Nazi Germany. An important contribution to the literature. Selected bibliography. The book is a scholarly compliment to Michael Zwerin's first person version in *La Tristesse de Saint Louis: Jazz Under the Nazis.*

322.   Lange, Horst Heinz. *Jazz in Deutschland: Die deutsche Jazz-Chronik 1900–1960.* Berlin: Colloquium Verlag; 1966.

In German. A history of jazz in Germany, tracing influences from cakewalks and ragtime and the dissemination of American recordings to the 1960s. The book is permeated with references to names, recordings, and criticism. The chronology is divided into years and contains important information on the fate of jazz during Hitler's reign. This work is also important because it contains information regarding the diffusion and criticism of jazz as well as the names and deeds of several German individuals and groups. Bibliography, discography (ragtime and jazz recordings from 1900 to 1960), list of cited instruments, and a name index.

323.   Lauth, Wolfgang. *These Foolish Things; Jazztime in Deutschland, ein Swingender Ruckblick.* Mannheim: Unknown Publisher; 1999.

A concise account of the uses and functions of jazz in Germany. Mentions names of performers and the overall reaction to jazz within German culture. In German.

324.   Lotz, Rainer E. *Hot Dance Bands in Germany: A Photo Album. Volume I: Pre-History up to 1920.* Bonn: Rainer E. Lotz, and Menden: der JazzFreund, 1979(?). *Volume II: The 1920's.* Bonn: Rainer E. Lotz, and Menden: der JazzFreund, 1982. *Volume III: The 1930's.* Bonn: Rainer E. Lotz, and Menden: der JazzFreund, 1983 (?).

Volume II. In German and English. A collection of photographs presented in chronological order accompanied by text covering the 1920s. The text focuses on the bands' origin, personnel, occasional birth dates, and some historical information. Rare photographs of some African American musicians and bands, including an African American drummer in the Orchestre Magnery and Yardaz Band (Belgian origin), Revue Negre (which included Sidney Bechet), The Original Fred Joe Jazz Band (an African musician who settled in Germany), and a reference to Arthur Briggs. Some musicians in the photographs are not identified. Index.

325. Neumeister, Klaus. *And Our Hearts in New Orleans: die Geschichte des Hot Jazz in Hamburg.* Hamburg: Schacht-Audorf; 1998.

Details the rich history of jazz in Hamburg. Traces the popularity and transmission of jazz to the city, and names both local and foreign performers who have performed in the city. Also provides insight into why jazz became popular in Hamburg. In German.

326. Noglik, Bert. *Klangspuren: Wege Improvisierter Musik.* Frankfurt: Transit.; 1992.

Illustrations of Jeanne Lee, Harry Miller, and others and a discussion of the philosophy and procedures used in improvised music. Includes lots of names, and accomplishments of performers.

327. _____. *Jazzwerkstatt International.* Berlin: The author, 1981; 1983.

In German. Interviews of several European avant-garde musicians including Willem Breuker, Albert Mangelsdorff, Evan Parker, Aladar Pege, Paul Rutherford, Alex Schlippenbach, and John Tchicai. The interviews are permeated with information on background, careers, aesthetics, influences, and the acceptance-rejection of their music. Also included is a discussion of their respective styles. Good insights into the European avant-garde jazz community.

328. Noglik, Bert, and Heinz-Jürgen Lindner. *Jazz Im Gespräch.* Berlin: Verlag Neue Music; 1978.

In German. Interviews covering the life and music of Conrad Bauer, Günther Fischer, Hans-Joachim Graswurm, Ulrich Gumpert, Manfred Hering, Hubert Katzenbeier, Hermann Keller, Klaus Koch, Ernst-Ludwig Petrowsky, Friedhelm Schönfeld, Manfred Schulze, and Günter Sommer. Permeated with historical and philosophical information and musical details.

329. Polster, Bernd. *Swing Heil: Jazz im Nationalsozialismus.* Berlin: Transit; 1989.

In German. Concerned with German attitudes about jazz, from around 1933 to 1945. Includes official condemnations of jazz, accounts of jazz activities, and documentation of German racial associations with jazz. Also includes interviews with Hans Blüthner, Walter Dobschinsky, Walter Kwiecinsky, Albert Joost, Margit Symo, Emil Mangelsdorff, Ernst Jandl, Walter Jens, Günter Discher, and Günter Lust. Contains a list of American music films shown in Germany, 1933 to 1944, and chapter references.

330.   Prinssen, Gerrit. *Hannover: Momente in einer Weltstadt des Jazz.* Hanover: Dedenhausen; 1999.

In German. The title translates as "Moments in a Metropolis of Jazz," and includes a CD of unreleased live performances by several artists who visited the city. The CD includes live tracks by Chet Baker, Harry Colyer, Lionel Hampton, and Major Holly.

331.   Rosenhain, Sigurd, and Karlheinz Drechsel. *Fascination Jazz: Jazz in der DDR.* Berlin: VEB Lied der Zeit Musikverlag; 1974.

In German and English. Photographs by Rosenhain and text by Drechsel of the fascination with jazz. The photographs capture the moods, peculiarities, and atmosphere of jazz sessions of amateur and professional groups as well as selected foreigners.

332.   Schestag, Ruediger, and Werner Stiefele. *Jazz in Stuttgart.* Stuttgart: Esslingen; 2000.

The photographs by Schestag are accompanied by text from Stiefele, and depict the long and successful acceptance of jazz in Stuttgart. The photographs and text are accompanied by a CD of 20 tracks of live performances by either local or visiting musicians. In German.

333.   Stephens, Harry. *Swing Threatens Third Reich.* Suffolk: Unknown Publisher; 1991.

The author describes the sociopolitical conditions and reactions to American jazz when he was growing up in Hamburg, Germany. Of particular interest is his discussion of the threat that swing posed to the Third Reich.

334.   Zwerin, Michael. *La Tristesse de Saint Louis: Jazz Under the Nazis.* New York: W.W. Morrow and Company; 1987.

Uses interviews of surviving musicians and jazz enthusiasts to address the question "What happened to jazz in Nazi Germany and in countries occupied during the war?" Although the book suffers from a lack of solid scholarship, his discussion of a Jewish band in Theresienstadt (The Ghetto Swingers), Viennese musicians who reinterpreted the St. Louis blues into "Sauerkraut," and Django Reinhardt, are both informative and provocative.

Holland

335. Whitehead, Kevin (editor). *Bimhuis 25: Stories of Twenty Five Years at the Bimhuis.* Amsterdam: Spectrum; 1999.

A collection of photographs and reminiscences of 25 years of concerts at the Bimhuis club in Amsterdam, Holland. The photographs feature many American jazz artists. Text in English.

Hungary

336. Gábor, Turi. *Azt Mondom: Jazz.* Budapest: Zenemükiado; 1983.

In Hungarian. Biomusical portraits of 19 Hungarian artists. The artists are Gyula Babos, Jeno Beamter, Sandor Benko, Tamas Berki, Karoly Binder, Laszlo Dés, Csaba Deseo, Karoly Friedrich, Attila Garay, Janos Gonda, Kornél Kertesz, Imre Koszegi, Gyula Kovacs, Antal Lakatos, Aladar Pege, Gyorgy Szabados, Bela Szakcsi Lakatos, Rudolf Tomsits, and Gyorgy Vukan. The portraits cover background, careers, influences, and attitudes, and provide penetrating insights into the music and musicians. Illustrated.

337. Simon, Geza Glbor. *Magyar Jazztortenet.* Budapest: Zenemukiado; 1999.

In Hungarian. A thorough examination of events, musicians, and other factors that have shaped the history of jazz in Hungary. The book is permeated with names of local and visiting artists who have helped to transmit the music to this former Communist country. In addition, two CDs accompany the book and contain rare and unissued recordings 1906–1948 and 1958–1998.

Italy

338. Cogno, Enrico. *Jazz Inchiesta Italia: Il Jazz Negli ammi 70.* Foreword by Massimo Mila. Bologna: Cappelli Editore; 1971.

In Italian. Concerned with jazz and jazz research in Italy in the 1970s. Discusses artists, their influences, and impact on the local jazz scene. Also alludes to the role of foreign influences on shaping Italian jazz. Selected bibliography, illustrations.

339. Giardina, Nardo, and Luigi Nasalvi. *Bologna; la citt del jazz.* Bologna: Cappelli Editore; 2002.

A collection of photographs by Nasalvi and text by Nardo that focus on the history of jazz in Bologna. The text is in both English and Italian.

340.   Marti, Jacky. *Venti di Estival.* Rome: Pregassona-Lugano; 1998.

A photographic history of the 20-year history of this festival. Includes photographs with accompanying text in English and Italian of the numerous local and foreign musicians who have performed at the festival.

341.   Tarabelli, Massimo. *Il Gomito del Jazzista; Vent' Anni di Ancona Jazz.* Anacona: Unknown Publisher; 1998.

An illustrated guide to the 20-year history of this festival. The photographs are accompanied by Italian text.

Japan

342.   Atkins, E. Taylor. *Blue Nippon: Authenticating Jazz in Japan.* Durham: Duke University Press; 2001.

Explores the true and legitimate nature of Japanese jazz though the voices of its practitioners. He discusses the 1920s dance halls to examine the Japanese Jazz Age, and the role and function that urban modernisms has had on jazz in Japan. In addition, he discusses how jazz became a troubling symbol of Japan's intimacy with the West, and how Japanese artists sought validation from their American counterparts in the face of criticism that Japanese jazz musicians can't swing. A good mixture of cultural history and strong scholarship.

343.   Iwanami, Yozo. *Nihon no Jazumen.* Tokyo: Tairiku; 1982.

In Japanese. Biomusical portraits of numerous Japanese instrumentalists and vocalists, male and female. Contains career accomplishments and highlights, references to style, influences, and associations with artists such as Herbie Hancock, Lionel Hampton, Wes Montgomery, Sonny Rollins, and others.

344.   Minor, William. *Jazz Journey to Japan: The Heart Within.* Ann Arbor: University of Michigan Press; 2004.

He discusses his Japanese jazz journey from its inception in the United States through his extended stay in Japan. The book is permeated with observations on Japanese culture, music, and topics like jazz restoration in Japan and the Tokyo jazz scene. He also provides personal assessments of artists/bands like Akira Tana, Makoto Ozone, and The Albatross Swing Orchestra. Includes a bibliography, discography, and index.

Netherlands

345.   Koopmans, Rudy (editor). *Jazz: Improvisatie en Organisatie Van een Groeiende Minderheid.* Amsterdam: SUA; 1977.

In Dutch. A collection of essays that cover both the improvisation and organization of selected Dutch artists and groups. The essays also cover their growing influence, stature, and ability to unite for a common cause. Illustrated.

346. Van Eyle, Wim. *Jazz and Geimproviseerde Muziek in Nederland.* Utrecht, Antwerpen: Spectrum; 1978.

In Dutch. Traces the history of jazz and improvised music in the Netherlands and is a biographical dictionary. The biographical entries include career highlights and accomplishments and references to recordings. Limited to Netherlands' artists. Selected bibliography, discography, and index.

347. Zwartenkot, Henk Wim Van Eyle, Gerard Bielderman, Jan Mulder, Rien Wisse, and Herman Openneer. *The Dutch Jazz and Blues Discography 1916–1980.* Amsterdam, Holland: Spectrum; 1981.

A compilation of all jazz and blues records of Dutch origin up to January 1, 1980. They also list big band swing, contemporary improvised music, hot dance music, modern jazz, Dixieland, ragtime, small combo swing, live concert recordings, some nonjazz groups, for example, Hawaiian ensembles, and selected Latin American recordings. Foreign musicians who recorded in the Netherlands are also included as are recordings made on Glass and Lacquer Records and the Decca Dutch Supplies. Entries include artist or group, personnel, title, label, matrix numbers, date, and venue. A list of sources (musicians and companies), collections, and a preface in Dutch and English are included.

Norway

348. Angell, Olav, Jan Erik Vold, and Einar Økland (editors). *Jazz i Norge.* Oslo: Møller; 1975.

In Norwegian. Covers activities, history, and people to the early 1970s; the role and function of jazz in Norway; and the influence and dissemination of American jazz. Includes a discography by Johs Bergh. Index and illustrations.

349. Stendahl, Bjorn. *Jazz Hot and Swing: Jazz i Norge 1920–1940.* Olso: Norsk Jazzarkiv; 1987.

In Norwegian. An important addition to the history of Norwegian jazz, contact with American musicians, and the study of musical diffusion. Covers the activities and contributions of several Norwegian musicians and profiles details of several American artists in Norway, including Jimmy Lunceford (1937), Edgar Hayes and His Blue Rhythm Band (1938), Duke

Ellington (1939), and others. Includes several photographs, an 1897 arrangement (Oscar Borg) of "Georgia Cake Walk," a chronology of events (including contact with Blackface Minstrels, 1840–1860, and The Fisk Jubilee
Singers in 1871), several Norwegian biographical portraits, an English
summary of "The Pioneering Years—before 1923," and an index.

350.   Stendahl, Bjorn, and Johs Bergh. *Cool and Dixie: Jazz i Norge 1950–1960.*
         Oslo: Moller.; 1997.

         An illustrated and comprehensive assessment of the Dixieland and cool
         styles of the 1950–1960 period in Norway. Includes the names and accom-
         plishments of local performers, and the influence of American jazz artists.
         Also includes a discography of Norwegian musicians.

Poland

351.   Brodacki, Krystian (editor). *Polskie sciez kido Jazz u.* Warszawa: Polskie;
         1983.

         In Polish. Focuses on the history, development, acceptance, influences,
         people, activities, and role and function of Polish jazz between 1945 and
         1960. Index and illustrations.

352.   Lyttleton, Humphrey. *Why No Beethoven?* London: Robson; 1984.

         Chronicles the author's visits to Poland and the Middle East. He details
         jazz activities and people associated with jazz. This is a diary, not a history
         or study of jazz in either locale. Illustrated.

353.   Panek, Waclaw (editor). *Z Polskie krytyki Jazzoweg: Eseje, dyskusje, repor-
         taze, recenzje, felietony, wywiady, 1956–1976.* Krakow: Krajowa; 1978.

         In Polish. A potpourri of essays that cover criticism, discussions, reports,
         and interviews. Covers both American and Polish artists including Louis
         Armstrong, Dave Brubeck, Benny Goodman, Krzysztof Komeda (violin),
         Zbigniew Nmyslowski (alto sax), Tomasz Stanko (trumpet), and Ben Web-
         ster. The Polish musicians provide insight into their careers and influences,
         whereas the Americans provide no new insights.

354.   Poprowa, Jan. *Jazz w Krakowie.* Kraków: Krajowa; 1975.

         In Polish. A concise, but excellent coverage of jazz activities, developments,
         and acceptance in Cracow (Poland) since 1945. Mentions artists and con-
         tact with foreign musicians. Illustrated.

Portugal

355.   Duarte, Jose. *Jazz-escute e olhe, Portugal 1971–2001.* Lisbon: Coimbra;
         2001.

A collection of 150 photographs by 12 Portuguese photographers that document the musical activities of local and visiting artists on the Portugal musical scene.

Soviet Union

356. Batashev, Alexey. *Soviet Jazz: An Historical Survey.* Moscow: Musica State Publishers; 1972.

Covers the history of jazz and pseudo-jazz music in the USSR since 1922 (date of the first jazz concert in Moscow). Special attention is given to the events of the prewar period, activities of the national jazz bands and artists during World War II, contemporary developments, and the USSR jazz scene 1955–1970. In addition, special chapters are devoted to the tours made by African Americans in the 1920s, including Sidney Bechet, Tommy Ladnier, Frank Witters, and Sam Wooding. Also covers several Soviet artists, bandleaders, and composers, including Leonid Utysov, Victor Knushevitski, Eddie Rozner, Alexander Tstasman, and Oleg Lundstrem. Many top Soviet artists of the 1920s and 1930s are discussed. The author is considered to be the foremost authority on Soviet jazz. Comprehensive and thorough.

357. Feigin, Leo (editor). *Russian Jazz: New Identity.* New York: Quartet Books; 1985.

According to the editor, this is an "anthology of essays, reviews, interviews, and travel accounts on the state of free or avant-garde jazz in Russia today (mid-eighties)." Includes travelogues, by Graham King, Hans Kumpf, and Larry Ochs that are permeated with insights into Soviet life. Essays by Bert Noglik (Arkhangelsk, Arkhangelsk), which detail the music/life of several contemporary artists, and "A 1984 Panorama of Soviet Jazz," which are informative. The essays are more lavish accounts than they are critical assessments.

358. Koren V. *Rozhdenie Dzhaza.* Moscow: Sovetskii Konpozitor; 1984.

In Russian. The first fundamental Soviet work dedicated to the development of jazz, its musical-expressive system (muzykal'no-vyrazitel'naia sistema), and its aesthetics. Against a broad historical-cultural background, the author examines the process of the origin of new musical views and genres so different from traditional European ones. It is shown that the birth of jazz in the USSR was determined by the preconditions/prerequisites of the development of music in the United States, sharply distinguished from European conditions. This is in turn intimately connected with the synthesis of African and European cultures and with the peculiarities of

America's social history. At the heart of the book is the question, why music, arising in a provincial, exclusively Negro medium, assumed such a visible place not only in the United States but also in the life of other countries.

359.   Minor, William. *Unzipped Souls: A Jazz Journey Through the Soviet Union.* Philadelphia: Temple University Press; 1995.

The author recounts his 1990 jazz-and-culture tour through the former Soviet Union where he attended jazz festivals, and interviewed musicians. He attended the first Moscow International Jazz Festival, the Georgian city of Tbilisi, and others. Among the many musicians who discussed their music were pianist Sergei Kuryokhin and composer Germann Lukianov. The primary focus is to determine what is distinctive about Russian Jazz. The book is permeated with references on literature and painting. A good update to Frederick Starr's *Red and Hot: The Face of Jazz in the Soviet Union* and Leo Feigin's *Russian Jazz: New Identity.*

360.   Starr, Frederick. *Red and Hot: The Fate of Jazz in the Soviet Union.* New York: Oxford University Press; 1983.

Provides an assessment of the history, performers, composers, and producers of Russian jazz. He details Soviet jazz history through mass culture touching on public opinion, popular values, the limits of authority, and the overall impact of U.S. culture on the Soviet Union. Some of his comments on the reception and development of jazz in other European countries are questionable.

Sweden

361.   Bergner, Roger. *Den Gyllene Cirkeln: Jazzen pa 1960-Talent.* Stockholm: Redaktor; 2002.

An illustrated book in Swedish and a CD of nine tracks of mostly unissued live music from the 1960s. The music was recorded at a famous Stockholm jazz club. The CD includes performances by Don Cherry, Bill Evans, Kenny Dorham, Dexter Gordon, Lars Gullin, George Russell, Ben Webster, and others.

362.   Eklund, Hans, and Lars Lindström. *Jazzen i Stockholm, 1920–1960.* Stockholm: Svensk; 1983.

In Swedish. This Concise book is permeated with people, events, and musical references regarding jazz in Stockholm. Mentions artists and contributions, and the influence of American artists on the history and dissemination of jazz in Stockholm. Illustrations.

363. Kjellberg, Erik. *Svensk Jazzhistoria: En Oversikt.* Stockholm: Norstedt; 1985.

In Swedish. An overview of Swedish jazz from its beginnings to the early 1980s. Covers the impact of American jazz on Sweden, including expatriates, and the music of selected Swedish artists including Lars Gullin and Bengt Hallberg. References, index, and solo transcriptions of Gullin and Hallberg. Illustrations.

364. Knox, Keith, and Gunnar Lindqvist. *Jazz Amour Affair: En Bok Om Lars Gullin.* Stockholm: Svensk; 1986.

In Swedish. A biography of Lars Gullin, Swedish baritone saxophonist. In addition to his life, musical influences, and accomplishments, there is a comprehensive analysis of his style. The analytical section includes transcriptions by Pelle Broberg and Lars Sjösten, and several compositions by Gullin including "Danny's Dream," "For F.J. Fans Only," "Portrait of My Pals," and "The Aching Heart of Oak." Very thorough analysis. Discography by Pär Rittsel, illustrated.

Yugoslavia

365. Mazur, Mladen M. *100 Names of Yugoslav Jazz: A Short Who's Who in Yugoslavian Jazz.* Zagreb: n.1.; 1969.

Documents the careers, accomplishments, selected recordings, and musical associations of 100 Yugoslav musicians. Selected discography.

V

Biographies and Autobiographies of Individuals

Sylvester Ahola

366. Hall, Dick. *Sylvester Ahola: The Gloucester Gabriel.* Lanham, Maryland: Scarecrow Press, and Institute of Jazz Studies (Rutgers University); 1993.

Provides insight into the life and music of this largely unknown trumpet player. Ahola played on 2,000 recordings and was a sideman in about 50 orchestras. Charts his musical career from the growth of jazz through the Depression to the development of commercial radio. Comprehensive discography of all his known recordings.

Don Albert

367. Wilkinson, Christopher. *Jazz on the Road: Don Albert's Musical Life.* Berkeley: University of California Press; 2001.

Born Albert Dominique in New Orleans in 1908, the author covers his name change, musical education in the Creole community, fusion of New Orleans jazz and Texas blues styles in the 1920s during his tenure with Troy Floyd's Orchestra of Gold, and the founding of his band in 1930. Also covers his role as a bandleader, influence of his band, role as a San Antonio nightclub owner in the 1940s and 1950s, and the role that race played in his life. Provides important insights into the evolution of both New Orleans and San Antonio jazz.

Henry "Red" Allen

368. Chilton, John. *Ride Red Ride: The Life of Henry "Red" Allen*. London and New York: Continuum; 1999.

Cover his life from his early years in Algiers, Louisiana (now West New Orleans), to his final years in New York. Chilton Chronicles his personality, analyzes his recordings, and recognizes him as a legitimate rival of Louis Armstrong. Equally important is the author's contrasting Allen's showmanship on stage with his off-stage reticence. Contains interesting and fascinating details of his early New Orleans years, and experiences on Mississippi riverboats.

Louis Armstrong

369. Armstrong, Louis. *Swing That Music*. London: Longmans, Green; 1937.

Covers the first 36 years of Armstrong's life in this first autobiography of a black jazz musician. An interesting music section contains 10 musical examples, an original song ("Swing That Music"), and individual improvisations by several swing musicians (e.g., Benny Goodman, Tommy Dorsey, Bud Freeman, Red Norvo, and Louis Armstrong). This section also contains a discussion of Armstrong's style. Introduction by Rudy Vallee, music section edited by Horace Gerlach. Selected discography (addition to 1981).

370. _____. *Louis Armstrong, A Self-Portrait*. New York: Eakins Press; 1971.

In this interview with Richard Meryman, Armstrong describes his life up until he left Chicago for New York in 1928. He discusses his New Orleans childhood, the Chicago jazz scene with King Oliver, and his experiences with Fletcher Henderson. In addition, he talks about an entertainer's life and his survival in the music world. Some of the interview was previously published in *Life* magazine (April 1966) (addition to 1981).

371. _____. *Satchmo: My Life in New Orleans*. Paris: Julliard, 1952; Hamburg: Rowohlt, 1953; New York: Prentice-Hall, New York: New American Library, 1954; London: Davies, 1954, 1955, 1956; Kobenhavn: Gyldendal, 1955; Oslo: Aschehoug, 1955; Stockholm: Bonnier, 1955; New York: Signet, 1955, 1961; Milano: Garzanti, 1956; London: Ace, 1957, 1965; London: Jazz Book Club, 1957; Zeist, Neth.: Den Haag, 1958; Antwerpen: Standard, 1958; Stockholm: Aldus & Bonnier, 1960; Helsinki: Otava, 1961;

Hamburg: Towohlt, 1962; Bucaresti: Muzicala, 1966; Berlin: Henschel, 1967; Praha: Mladá, 1968; Tokyo: Ongaku, 1970; Kraków: Wyd, 1974; Zurich: n.1., 1977, 1985; New York: Da Capo, 1986.

Portrays the early life and music of Louis Armstrong. Takes his career through his New Orleans stage to the time he joined King Oliver (Chicago in 1922). Acceptance, experiences, and problems encountered by Armstrong and other New Orleans musicians are also discussed (addition to 1981).

372. Berrett, Joshua. *The Louis Armstrong Companion: Eight Decades of Commentary.* New York: Schirmer Books; 1999.

Included are Armstrong's autobiographical writings, letters to friends and family (some previously not published), and writings on his life and music from the 1920s to today. Includes insights from Lil Hardin Armstrong, Dizzy Gillespie, Lewis Porter, and Ron Welburn.

373. Biamonte, Salvatore. *L. Armstrong: L'Ambasciatore del Jazz.* Milano, Italy: Mursia; 1973.

In Italian. Traces the background, career, and accomplishments of Armstrong. Details his New Orleans and Chicago years and his contributions as a film star and ambassador of jazz. Interesting insights into the Hot Five and Hot Seven and his association with Earl "Fatha" Hines.

374. Boujut, Michel. *Pour Armstrong.* Paris: Jazz Magazine, 1975; Paris: Filipacchi, 1976.

In French. Contains biographical material and several photographs. The biographical data includes information on his background, career, and accomplishments. There are several musical examples. Selected bibliography (Daniel Nevers), filmography, and an index.

375. Brooks, Edward. *The Young Louis Armstrong on Records: A Critical Survey of the Early Recordings, 1923–1928.* Lanham, Maryland, and Institute of Jazz Studies (Rutgers University); 2002.

A comprehensive chronological survey and analysis of all recordings Armstrong made during the 1923 to 1928 period. The book is important because it provides insight into Armstrong's style before he became a jazz icon.

376. Brothers, Thomas (editor). *Louis Armstrong, In His Own Words: Selected Writings.* New York: Oxford University Press; 2001.

The letters and writings provide a penetrating glimpse into Armstrong's early musical influences, rise to fame, life on the road, role in the civil rights movement, and his final years. He discusses Armstrong's idiosyncratic style, and orthographic peculiarities. Includes several previously unpublished photographs.

377.   Collier, James Lincoln. *Louis Armstrong: An American Genius.* New York: Galaxy Book (Oxford University Press); 1983.

Covers his life and music in venues such as New Orleans, Chicago, and New York. Details are provided on Armstrong's rise as a musician, changing musical style, innovative contributions to jazz, and effect on other musical genres (rock, pop). His portrayal of Armstrong's need for approval, occasional jealousy, and quest for commercial success is often questionable as is his discussion of topics like "Jazz is born in New Orleans" (pp. 46–56). Chapter notes and an index.

378.   _____. *Louis Armstrong: An American Genius.* New York: Oxford University Press, 1983, 1985; London: Joseph, 1984; Paris: n.a., 1987; Bergisch-Glubbach, Germany: Lübbe, 1987; Moskva: Raduga, 1987; Barcelona, Buenos Aires: Vergara, 1987.

A version of the original that is geared to young adults. The material is condensed and summarized into language, concepts, and metaphors that are more easily read and understood. Selected discography, annotated bibliography, and index.

379.   Cornell, Jean Gay. *Louis Armstrong: Ambassador Satchmo.* Champaign, Illinois: Garrard Publishing Company; 1968.

This is one of the books that was published in the *American All* series, which focuses on biographies of people that have contributed to American life. This book is permeated with anecdotes and stories detailing Armstrong's life and musical contributions. The book is geared to children in grades 3–6, written at a fourth grade reading level. Armstrong's life is chronicled from New Orleans, with his adult life presented by recounting successful performance engagements.

380.   Eaton, Jeanette. *Trumpeter's Tale: The Story of Young Louis Armstrong.* New York: William Morrow; 1955.

Appeals particularly to young jazz fans. Follows a story format about his life and musical achievements to the mid-1950s.

381.   Giddins, Gary. *Satchmo.* New York: Dolphin; 1988.

Photographs supplemented with biographical data. Selected bibliography, discography, with some illustrations.

382.   Goffin, Robert. *Horn of Plenty: The Story of Louis Armstrong.* Translated by James Bezov. Paris: Seghers; Toronto: McLeod; New York: Allen,

Towne, and Heath, 1947; Budapest: Gondolat, 1974; New York: Da Capo, 1977; and Westport, Conn.: Greenwood Press, 1978.

Details the life and musical career of Armstrong up to 1946. Contains information on early musical influences on Armstrong, his life in New Orleans, associations with King Oliver, and the Hot Five and Hot Seven groups. There are also French, Hungarian, and Belgian editions (addition to 1981).

383. Hoskins, Robert. *Louis Armstrong: Biography of a Musician.* Los Angeles: Holloway House; 1979.

Focuses on his early career, especially his background in New Orleans, the Hot Five and Hot Seven groups, his role in films, and his association with Earl "Fatha" Hines. No new insights. Filmography.

384. Iverson, Genie. *Louis Armstrong.* New York: Thomas Y. Crowell; 1976.

Another story on Armstrong written for children. Details Armstrong's life and musical successes. Not for scholars.

385. Jones, Max, and John Chilton. *Louis: The Louis Armstrong, 1900–1971.* London: Studio Vista; Boston, Toronto: Little, Brown, 1971; St. Albans, England: Mayflower, 1975; New York: Da Capo, 1988.

An outgrowth of *Salute to Satchmo,* the 1988 edition contains a new preface by Dan Morgenstern. Draws heavily on Armstrong's account of his musical evolution from New Orleans to success in both Chicago and New York. Armstrong discusses the evolution of his musical style and chronicles his lifestyle and the effects of racism. There is a chapter on Armstrong's recordings, which contains additional information on his style. Only superficial comments on his later life. In addition to the biographical material there is an excellent discographical essay by John Chilton, a chronology of events, filmography, and an index. Several photographs.

386. Jones, Max, John Chilton, and Leonard Feather. *Salute to Satchmo.* London: Specialist and Professional, London: Melody Maker; 1970.

Contains a tribute by Feather and other musicians to Armstrong on his 70th birthday. The main text is concerned with Louis the man—his public relations, his personality, and his life. A good book for learning how and why people admired Armstrong. Contains an introductory letter from Armstrong. Selected discography, filmography, chronology, and an index.

387. Mauro, Walter. *Louis Armstrong: Il Rei del Jazz.* Milano: Rusconi; 1974.

In Italian. Armstrong's life and music, including his early career in New Orleans, his Hot Five and Hot Seven groups, achievements, and associations in Chicago and other venues. Armstrong's role as an ambassador of jazz, a film star, and his musical style are also explored.

388. McCarthy, Albert J. *Louis Armstrong.* London: Cassell, 1960; New York: Barnes, 1961.

Covers Armstrong's career to 1959 with special attention given to the middle years. He briefly chronicles his early years in New Orleans, the 1930–35 and 1935–47 years. The characteristics of his style are delineated from recordings with special attention to, in the author's opinion, his virtuoso years, 1930–35. A chapter on the "All Stars" is permeated with anecdotes from his peers. Selected discography.

389. Meckna, Michael. *Satchmo: The Louis Armstrong Encyclopedia.* Westport, Conn., Praeger Press; 2004.

An authoritative reference on Armstrong. The alphabetically arranged entries give detailed information on many aspects of Armstrong's life and music. There are several appendices, including one of CD releases, a chronology of movies, and a resource guide to "Satchmo on the Web," and a selected list of black-and-white photographs completes the volume.

390. Meryman, Richard. *Louis Armstrong: A Self-Portrait.* New York: Eakins; 1971.

An interview with Armstrong that focuses on his background, career, achievements, and opinions. The interview was previously published in *Life* magazine.

391. Millender, Dharathula H. *Louis Armstrong: Young Music Maker.* Indianapolis: Bobbs-Merrill; 1972.

A children's biography that covers his life from New Orleans through his career and achievements in jazz and films.

392. O'Brien, Ralph. *Louis Armstrong.* Zurich: Sanssouci; 1960.

A concise account of his life and musical accomplishments, from New Orleans to leader of the Hot Five and Hot Seven, and film star. No new information.

393. Panassié, Hugues. *Louis Armstrong.* Paris: Belvédère, 1947; Paris: Nouvelles Editions Latines, 1969; New York: Scribner, 1971; Louisville: American, 1973, and New York: Da Capo, 1979, 1980, 1985.

The biography is divided into three chapters: life of Armstrong, a general description of Armstrong's jazz styles, and a chronological survey and discography of Armstrong's recordings from 1923 to 1968. The author considers all periods of Armstrong's musical life including the Hot Five and Hot Seven recordings and his later years. Included are 38 photographs and a discography covering 1923 to 1968. The text is permeated with anecdotes.

394. Pinfold, Mike. *Louis Armstrong: His Life and Times.* Turnbridge, England: Spellmount, N.Y.: Universe; 1987.

Focuses on Armstrong's distinguishing attributes. Includes a discographical essay centered on some of Armstrong's most important recordings. Index and illustrations.

395. Richards, Kenneth G. *People of Destiny: Louis Armstrong.* Chicago: Children; 1967.

A children's biography that is limited to Armstrong's early career. Selected bibliography, index, and illustrations.

396. Sanders, Roby. *Jazz Ambassador: Louis Armstrong.* Chicago: Children's Press; 1973.

Written for children, complete with his life and musical successes. The author uses stories and associations consistently throughout the book. Not for jazz scholars.

397. Slawe, Jan. *Louis Armstrong: Zehn Monographische Studien.* Basel: Papillon; 1953.

In German. A biography of Armstrong's life and musical achievements to the early 1950s. Rehashes known material about his early life, musical associations, and style.

398. Tanehaus, Sam. *Louis Armstrong: Musician.* New York: Chelsea; 1989.

One of several children's biographies of Armstrong, with emphasis on his life, career, and significance. Introduction by Coretta Scott King. Chronology of events, index, and illustrations.

399. Winkler, Hans-Jürgen. *Louis Armstrong: Ein Porträt.* Wetzlar, Germany: Pegasus; 1962.

In German. Covers his life and musical achievements in a succinct manner. This is an overview of Armstrong's life to the early 1960s; the coverage is superficial. Lacks in-depth detail of his Hot Five and Hot Seven contributions, compositions, and more.

David Amram

400. Amram, David. *Vibrations.* New York, Toronto: Macmillan; 1968; 1971.

An autobiography that focuses on his background, career, philosophy, contributions, associations, and attitudes about several significant jazz musicians, including Charles Parker.

Billy Amstell

401.   Amstell, Billy, and R. T. Deal. *Don't Fuss, Mr. Ambrose: Memoirs of a Life Spent in Popular Music.* Turnbridge, England: Spellmount; 1986.

Both an autobiography and a history of jazz bands in England. Amstell's background, career, associations, and influences are covered. In addition, names and selected details (accomplishments and significance) of several dance bands are given. Important data on the impact of dance bands in England.

Svend Asmussen

402.   Henius, Bent. *Svend Asmussen.* Foreword by Erik Moseholm. København: Erichsen; 1963.

In Danish. Biography of an important Danish jazz violinist. Covers his background, introduction to jazz, influences, and accomplishments. Also offers significant insights into the acceptance and diffusion of jazz in Denmark. Selected discography, illustrated.

Alice Babbs

403.   Hedman, Frank. *Alice Babs: Berättelsen om Artisten Alice "Babbs."* Nilson Sjöblom: Stockholm; Raben and Sjögren; ISBN: 1975.

In Swedish. Biography of the singer best known for her work with Duke Ellington (Sacred Concerts). Her background and accomplishments in her jazz career. Selected discography.

Chet Baker

404.   Baker, Chet. *As Though I Had Wings: The Lost Memoir.* New York: St. Martin's Griffin; 1997.

Concise but factual autobiography that include details of West Coast jazz in the 1950s. He details his spiral into cocaine and heroin, relationships, ventures in and out of jail, army service, travels, and views on Gerry Mulligan, Charles Parker, Bob Zieff, Serge Chaloff, and others. Includes some handwritten notes, and provides insights into his music making.

405.   de Valk, Jeroen. *Chet Baker: His Life and Music.* Berkeley: Berkeley Hills Books; 2001.

The author interviewed dozens of Baker's colleagues, friends, musicians, as well as his wife, Carol Baker, to research this book. He blends details of his life with an account of Baker's recordings career. In addition to details regarding drug abuse, army career, prison stays, and relationship with other musicians, insight into Baker's intuitive artistry and music making is provided. He corrects many half-truths and misconceptions, and provides a complete discography.

406. Gavin, James. *Deep in a Dream: The Long Night* of *Chet Baker*. New York: Alfred A. Knopf; 2002.

Meticulously researched and provides new insights into Baker's life, relationship with his wife and other women, drug addiction, musical associations with Gerry Mulligan and others. Also, covers the facts surrounding his death.

407. Lewien, Lothar. *Chet Baker Blue Notes*. Hannibal-Verlag: Robert Azderball; 1991.

In German. Focuses on his musical associations, performances, relationships, and travels. No new insights. Contains a discography.

Josephine Baker

408. Rose, Phyllis. *Jazz Cleopatra: Josephine Baker in Her Time*. New York: Doubleday; 1989.

Biography of the American dancer from her birth into poverty in St. Louis to her death in Paris. Covers her dancing in the 1920s and 1930s, her undercover activities for France in World War II, and assent into a cultural icon. However, the book gives only scant attention to her early life, two marriages, and denigrates her dancing.

Gato Barbieri

409. Gullo, Lillo, and Angelo Leonardi. *Visintin: Gato Barbieri*. Milano: Ottaviano; 1979.

In Italian. Covers the life and music of Gato Barbieri, including his introduction to jazz, musical associations, influences, and contributions. Informative and penetrating.

Danny Barker

410. Barker, Danny, and Alyn Shipton. *A Life in Jazz*. London: Macmillan, New York: Oxford University Press, 1986; 1988.

Offers significant insights into the early New Orleans music scene and encounters with racism. Musical associations, including New Orleans musicians and others such as Benny Carter, Cab Calloway, Dizzy Gillespie, Jelly Roll Morton, and Lucky Millinder, are discussed. Excellent sociomusical, insider perspectives. Selected discography, index, and illustrations.

Charlie Barnet

411.   Dance, Stanley. *Those Swing Years: The Autobiography of Charlie Barnet;* foreword by Billy May. New York: Da Capo Press; 1991.

Barnet is best known as a tenor saxophonist and popular bandleader. Includes perceptive comments about his marriages, drinking, smoking marijuana, visits to houses of ill repute, and musical contributions. His theme song, "Cherokee," became a standard in the jazz repertoire. Barnet was also one of the first white band leaders to desegregate his band; among his African American musicians were Roy Eldridge, Lena Horn, and Clark Terry. Selected bibliography, discography, and an index.

Count Basie

412.   Basie, Count, and Albert Murray. *Good Morning Blues: The Autobiography of Count Basie.* New York: Random House, 1985; New York: Fine, 1987.

Covers Basie to 1950 and includes significant data on the history and context of both the Harlem and Kansas City jazz scenes of the 1920s and 1930s. Also included is an account of Basie's rise to fame, the role of vaudeville, and the trials and tribulations of performing on the T.O.B.A. circuit. Index and illustrations.

413.   Dance, Stanley. *The World of Count Basie.* New York: Scribner's; London: Sidgwick and Jackson, 1980; New York: Da Capo, 1985.

Thirty-four interviews with Count Basie and Jay McShann, the pivotal figures in this study. In addition to musical attributes, the book contains information on the networking between musicians on both musical and social levels. The book is well researched and is an important contribution as the author viewed both Basie and McShann as members of a musical community. The appendix contains Basie itineraries and selected discographies of Basie and 27 additional Kansas City musicians, including Buck Clayton, Jimmy Rushing, Buddy Tate, and Lester Young as well as a selected bibliography.

414. Horricks, Raymond. *Count Basie and His Orchestra: Its Music and Musicians.* New York: Citadel Press; London: Gollancz, 1957; London: Jazz Book Club, 1958; Westport, Conn.: Negro University Press, 1971.

Presents a penetrating view of Basie as a bandleader and musician as well as discussing musicians who made up the band from 1936 to 1950. After opening with a portrait of Basie as a leader, the author gives an illuminating account of the evolution and development of the band's musical style in its first 20 years. Horricks also comments on Basie as a pianist and on the style and contribution of some of his most famous sidemen— Buck Clayton, Dickie Wells, Lester Young, Jimmy Rushing, and several more from the 1950s. There are 36 biographical portraits, 22 from the 1936–50 period, and 14 from post-1950. Includes a discography of recordings on which Basie performs and a selected listing of recordings made by sidemen without Basie performing.

415. Morgan, Alun. *Count Basie.* Turnbridge, England: Spellmount, New York: Hippocrene; 1984.

A biodiscography focusing on the Benny Moten and Kansas City years, Basie's assent to fame, and the role and function of selected musicians. The significance of Basie's band is also explored. The selected discography contains venue, dates, personnel, matrix numbers, and titles. Selected bibliography, illustrated.

416. Schiozzi, Bruno. *Count Basie.* Milano: Ricordi; 1961.

Divided into two parts, biography and selected discography. The biography traces his career and assent to fame from the Benny Moten band, through his association with John Hammond. The roles that some musicians played in the evolution of the band are discussed. Illustrated.

417. Vail, Ken. *Count Basie: Swingin' the Blues 1936–1950.* Lanham, Md.: Scarecrow Press; 2003.

Number three in the series, he chronicles Basie's musical career from his Kansas City years. Discovery by John Hammond, triumph in New York, his unique rhythm section, the role of Lester Young, and the eventual demise of his band. He also cites some club and concert appearances, and recording sessions, and includes some interesting photographs.

Sidney Bechet

418. Bechet, Sidney. *Treat It Gentle: An Autobiography.* London: Cassell; New York: Hill and Wang, 1960; London: Jazz Book Club, 1962, and London:

Transworld, 1964. Reprint with a new preface by Rudi Blesh. New York: Da Capo; 1978.

An insider perspective of his musical career and the role and function that New Orleans culture and musicians had on his life. Bechet recorded his reminiscences in the early 1950s in Paris, after which Joan Reid, Desmond Flower, and John Ciardi edited the material. In addition to his salient references to "Omar" (his paternal grandfather, a slave who was murdered), the book is more than a tribute to his ancestors. Bechet outlines his life from New Orleans to Europe (with Will Marion Cook's Southern Syncopated Orchestra), through the 1920s and 1930s, until he finally settled in Paris (1950). Within the context of his life and New Orleans he offers important insights into musicians like Louis Armstrong, Buddy Bolden, Bunk Johnson, Freddie Keppard, Tommy Ladnier, Manuel Perez, Noble Sissel, and Clarence Williams. Overall, Bechet appears to be searching for a way to mediate his past with his present, to give meaning to both his music and existence. Includes a chronological discography with record numbers but no personnel or bibliography.

419.   Chilton, John. *Sidney Bechet: The Wizard of Jazz.* New York: Oxford University Press; 1987.

Follows Bechet's life and musical career from his childhood in New Orleans to his experiences in Europe. The material is derived from interviews and published materials (articles and chapters). Also included are anecdotal reminiscences of Bechet by other musicians, comprised of mostly laudatory comments accepted without validation by the author. Overall, this is a comprehensive documentation of Bechet's musical accomplishments as well as his frustrations. Included are detailed discussions of recordings at selected places in the chronology, an insight into early New Orleans, post–World War I recollections, and discussions of his European experiences. Selected bibliography, discography, and an index.

420.   Hippenmeyer, Jean-Roland. *Sidney Bechet, ou l'extraordinaire odyssée d'un musicien de jazz.* Geneva: Tribune Editions; 1980.

In French. Rather than a biographical portrait, this book is organized as an in-depth account of his life and musical career. Included is detailed information on dates, names, places, and titles. The book is also interesting because it contains reminiscences from Bechet's peers and insightful anecdotes on his career by people that knew him. In short, the book is approached more like a diary than a biography. A filmography, discography of reissues, and a selected bibliography are included. No index.

421.   Kunst, Peter. *Sidney Bechet: Ein Porträt.* Wetzlar, Germany: Pegasus; 1959.

In German. A concise biography and selected discography. Includes information on his New Orleans years, recording experiences, and expatriate years. Selected discography, illustrated.

422. Mouly, R. *Sidney Bechet, Notre Ami.* Paris: La Table Ronde; 1954.

In French. Contains some details of Bechet's life from New Orleans to Paris. The book contains anecdotes and recollections about travel, associations with other musicians, and his musical style. Comprehensive discography with some inaccuracies.

Bix Beiderbecke

423. Baker, Dorothy. *Young Man with a Horn.* Boston: Houghton Mifflin, 1938; London: Gollancz, 1938; New York: Reader's Club, 1943; New York: Dial Press, 1944; Cleveland: World, 1946; London: Jazz Book Club, 1957; London: Transworld, 1962.

Follows Beiderbecke's life and musical career from Davenport, Iowa, to his eventual success as a cornetist with Paul Whiteman, and leader of the Wolverines. His association with Frank Trumbauer is also chronicled.

424. Burton, Ralph. *Remembering Bix: A Memoir of the Jazz Age.* New York: Harper and Row; 1974.

Written by the brother of Vic Berton, the drummer who recorded with the Wolverines in 1924 and 1927, this book is more concerned with spotlighting Berton's contribution than with Beiderbecke himself. The book contains angry utterances by the author concerning, in the author's opinion, the denial of Vic Berton's immense contributions as a drummer. Offers no new information on Bix. Selected bibliography and reference notes.

425. James, Burnett. *Bix Beiderbecke.* London: Cassell, 1959. Reprint. New York: Barnes; 1961.

Primarily a biomusical study that gives a short but insightful account of Bix's life, style, and contributions (with reference to his recordings). Contains references to the Wolverines and other Chicago musicians of the 1920s. A selected, fully detailed discography that lists all the Microgroove collections released in Britain is also provided. The discography contains personnel and dates of recordings.

426. Scheuer, Klaus. *Bix Beiderbecke: Sein Leben, Seine Musik, Seine Schallplatten.* Verlag: Oreos; 1995.

In German. Begins with his early years in Davenport, Iowa, followed by his Chicago experiences with the Wolverines, and performances with Jean

Goldkette and Paul Whiteman. Also discusses his relationship with Nick LaRocca, Emmett Louis Hardy, Paul Mares, King Oliver, Louis Armstrong, Freddie Keppard, Jimmy McPartland, Red Nichols, Bubber Miles, and others. Also included is a discussion of his recordings.

427.   Sudhalter, Richard M., and Philip R. Evans. *Bix: Man and Legend.* New Rochelle, N.Y.: Arlington House; London: Quarter Books; 1974.

Perhaps the best-written and best-researched biography to date on Beiderbecke. The authors, with William Deun-Myatt, separate fact from fiction in assessing the achievements of Beiderbecke. Including much information gathered from Beiderbecke's friends and colleagues as well as anecdotes from other sources, they cover his life, the formation and recordings of the Wolverines, his membership in the Goldkette and Whiteman bands, his fascination with the piano and the music of the European tradition, and his physical and psychological problems. The book also features a unique "diary" of Bix's life and a 78-rpm discography with music notations to differentiate takes (1981).

428.   Waring, Charles, and George Garlick. *Bugles for Beiderbecke.* London: Sidgwick & Jackson, 1958; London: Jazz Book Club, 1960.

Offers a study of Beiderbecke that is arranged in three parts: his life and career; his musical expertise, compositions, and contributions; and a comprehensive, fully detailed discography. Concerning his life and career, there are details of his evolution from Davenport, Iowa, to his arrival in Chicago. The second part addresses his influences (on and from), musical compositions, and relationship with Frank Trumbauer (addition to 1981). Selected bibliography.

Bunny Berigan

429.   Danca, Vince. *Bunny: A Bio-discography of Jazz Trumpeter Bunny Berigan.* Rockford, Illinois: The author; 1978.

Contains a biographical profile and a comprehensive list of his recordings. Each record listing contains complete discography details.

430.   DuPris, Robert. *Bunny Berigan: Elusive Legend of Jazz.* Baton Rouge and London: Louisiana State University Press; 1993.

The author provides a penetrating assessment of Berigan's life and musical accomplishments. In addition to his musical influences and the bands he performed with, the author parallels the styles of Bix Beiderbecke and Bunny Berigan in the chapter "In a Mist." The impact of the bands of Tommy and Jimmy Dorsey, Benny Goodman, and Glenn Miller is also discussed in "Night Song." The author interviewed Donna Berigan (Bunny's widow), and his two daughters (Patricia Berigan Slavin and Joyce Berigan), and used both quotations and paraphrases of interviews with musicians conducted by Bozy White and Tom Cullen. There are six appendices, including "List of Guests on Saturday Night Swing Club during Its First Year," "Schedules of the Berigan Band," "A Partial Berigan Genealogy," and "Berigan's Recorded Legacy." A selected bibliography, discography, and an index are included.

Clyde E. B. Bernhardt

431. Harris, Sheldon. *I Remember, Eighty Years of Black Entertainment, Big Bands, and the Blues; Clyde E. B. Bernhardt as told to the Author.* Philadelphia: University of Pennsylvania Press; 1986.

Contains the recollections of Clyde E. B. Bernhardt, trombonist and blues singer. Bernhardt played in several bands, including Jay McShann, King Oliver, and Fats Waller. He was the organizer and leader of the Harlem Blues and Jazz Band (1972). The book is permeated with anecdotes and reminiscences and provides important insights into the life of a sideman, bandleader, and vocalist. The comprehensive discography contains information on other musicians that worked with Bernhardt. Selected bibliography.

Barney Bigard

432. Bigard, Barney, and Barry Martyn. *With Louis and the Duke.* New York: Oxford University Press; 1986.

Details his experiences as a sideman with two giants of jazz. He provides anecdotes and stories about both, covering topics ranging from repertoire to travel, all in a very positive tone. Bigard also provides critical comments about some of his fellow musicians: he considered Bunk Johnson to be "pathetic" (p. 87); he felt the Yerba Buena Jazz Band "plays out of key" (p. 89); and he comments on the behavior of Billie Holiday when shooting a film in 1946. He also had warm praise for Sid Catlett and Jack Teagarden. This book provides honest assessments of Bigard and his musical associates. Selected bibliography, discography, and an index.

Art Blakey

433. Giese, Hannes. *Art Blakey: Sein Leben, Seine Musik, Seine Schallplatten.* Verlag: Oreos; 1990.

In German. Cover details of his life as a sideman with artists such as Billy Eckstine, as a leader of the Jazz Messengers with sidemen like Curtis Fuller, Freddie Hubbard, Lee Morgan, and Wayne Shorter. Includes comments on several recordings, transcription and analysis of several solos, and the influence of Africa on his drumming.

434.   Goldsher, Alan. *Hard Bop Academy: The Sidemen of Art Blakey and The Jazz Messengers.* Milwaukee: Hal Leonard Publications; 2002.

Contains a biographical assessment of Blakey's sidemen divided into categories. He discusses bassists, trumpeters, saxophonists, pianists, and the musical philosophy of Blakey. Among the numerous musicians discussed are Clifford Brown, Branford and Wynton Marsalis, Lee Morgan, Freddie Hubbard, Horace Silver, Donald Williams, Wayne Shorter, and many more.

Terence Blanchard

435.   Margo, Anthony. *Contemporary Cat: Terence Blanchard with Special Guests.* Lanham, Md., and Institute of Jazz Studies (Rutgers University Press); 2003.

A thorough examination of his life and work through interviews with musical colleagues, and other artists. The author connects jazz to the civil rights movement, to film, and to southern African American ideologies. He includes the views of Spike Lee, Branford and Wynton Marsalis, Nicholas Payton, and others.

Paul Bley

436.   Bley, Paul, and David Lee. *Stopping Time: Paul Bley and The Transformation of Jazz.* Montreal: Vehicule Press; 1999.

In addition to his musical beginnings and childhood experiences, musical achievements are also discussed. Bley is portrayed as an innovator and creative artist who was not afraid to implement new ideas. Bibliographical references, a discography, and an index are included.

Johnny Blowers

437.   Vache, Warren W. *Back Beats and Rim Shots: The Johnny Blowers Story.* Lanham, Md.: The Scarecrow Press, and Institute of Jazz Studies (Rutgers University); 1997.

Chronicles his adventures, dedication, disillusion, elations, and other human emotions. A discussion of his musical associations with artists like Bunny Berigan, Eddie Fisher, Frank Sinatra, and Mel Torme is also included. Presents Blowers as a highly regarded musician with a multi-faceted career.

Buddy Bolden

438. Barker, Danny. *Buddy Bolden and the Last Days of Storyville.* New York: Continuum; 2001.

Edited by Alyn Shipton, Barker discusses how the social mores of the South contributed to Bolden's insanity. He encapsulates Bolden via folklore and stories told to him by other musicians, including Bunk Johnson and Jelly Roll Morton. Also included are Barker's recollections about the last days of Storyville, his work with big bands, life on the road with Cab Calloway, and information from the "Jazzland Research Guide," an organization founded by Barker in the 1940s to research the musical backgrounds of his New Orleans colleagues.

439. Marquis, Donald M. *Finding Buddy Bolden, First Man of Jazz: The Journal of a Search.* Goshen, Ind.: Pinch-Penny Press (Goshen Press); 1978.

Details the methods and procedures used to collect, organize, and synthesize the data used in his biography, *In Search of Buddy Bolden: First Man of Jazz.* Recommended for teaching research methods.

440. _____. *In Search of Buddy Bolden: First Man of Jazz.* Baton Rouge: Louisiana State University Press, 1978; Reprint, New York: Da Capo Press, 1983.

A thorough documentation of Bolden's (1877–1931) family life, school and early life, musical influences, musical life in New Orleans, eventual decline and institutionalization (1907), and death. While the author contradicts some assumptions, he agrees that Bolden was a significant early New Orleans pioneer. In addition, the musical context in which Bolden performed is fully explored. Bibliography includes both references and interviews conducted. Index.

Anthony Braxton

441. Lock, Graham. *Forces in Motion: The Music and Thoughts of Anthony Braxton;* foreword by Anthony Braxton; photographs by Nick White. New York: Da Capo; 1988.

Using both journalistic and musical analysis, the author provides a perceptive insight into the man and the role and function of his music. The
author focuses on Braxton's perceptions of Duke Ellington, John Coltrane,
Chick Corea, and Charles Parker as well as issues like poverty and racism.
The book was the outgrowth of Braxton's 1985 tour of England and also
covers his views of astrology, acid rain, Egypt, feminism, and hamburgers.
Locke also provides a thorough analysis of Braxton's music. Selected
discography, bibliography, and an index.

442.   Radano, Ronald. *New Musical Figurations: Anthony Braxton's Cultural
Critique.* Chicago: University of Chicago Press; 1994.

Focuses on Braxton's aesthetics, philosophy, and music, as well as his
role as a seminal figure in modern music. In probing the aesthetics of
Braxton's music, the author clarifies both his acceptance and contributions
as an innovative musician. Braxton is discussed not solely as a jazz
musician but as an innovator at the juncture of jazz and classical music.
A scholarly account, Radano provides a probing critique of the misrepresentations made by some journalists and scholars. His deconstruction
of "musical assertions of Black Identity," in particular, AACM's Pan-
African musical ideas are insightful, and provide the ideological basis
necessary to understand Braxton's musical journey. Of particular note is
the author's ability to relate ideas regarding ideology and racism within
a discussion of contemporary musical culture in the United States.
Includes a music index, general index, recording citations, pictures, and
titles of compositions citations.

443.   Wilson, Peter Niklas. *Anthony Brazton: Sein Leben, Seine Musik, Seine
Schallplatten.* Verlag: Oreos; 1993.

In German. A thorough assessment of his life, music, and philosophy.
Includes notes on Braxton's recordings, musical analysis, and a systematic
depiction of his musical structures, philosophy, and recordings.

Clifford Brown

444.   Catalano, Nick. *Clifford Brown: The Life and Art of the Legendary Jazz
Trumpeter.* New York: Oxford University Press; 2001.

Traces his life and musical beginnings from his middle-class and cultivated roots in Wilmington, Delaware, to his assent as one of the most
important trumpet players in jazz history. Discusses his virtuoso style,
marriage, stints in rhythm and blues bands, the Max Roach-Clifford Brown
quintet years in Los Angeles, and influence on contemporary jazz

trumpeters. Also covers his performance on numerous recordings. Contains a discography and chapter notes.

445. Gerber, Alain. *Clifford Brown.* Paris: Librairie Fayard; 2001.

In French. Begins with his early years and musical experiences in Wilmington, Delaware, and recognizes the importance of the area during and after the Emancipation Proclamation in 1863. Thereafter, he discusses Brown and Miles Davis, Fats Navarro, Max Roach, Lionel Hampton, and others. He also discusses Brown's Paris and Stockholm, Sweden, experiences.

Marion Brown

446. Brown, Marion. *Recollections: Essays, Drawings, Miscellanea.* Frankfurt: Schmitt; 1984.

An autobiography tracing his influences, experiences, and feelings and opinions on a myriad of topics. Contains important insights into his avant-garde jazz experiences. Illustrated.

Sandy Brown

447. Brown, Sandy. *The McJazz Manuscripts: A Collection of the Writings of Sandy Brown;* compiled and introduced by David Binns. London: Faber and Faber; 1979.

Brown was born in India, the offspring of a Scottish father and a Hindu mother. He led itinerant bands in Denmark, Paris, and Scotland. He is not listed in any American reference books on jazz. The book is divided into two sections: an unfinished, esoteric, rambling autobiography that Brown was working on when he died in 1975, and a collection of 15 essays written by Brown for *The Listener,* 1968–1973, along with correspondence he conducted with colleagues, friends, and public figures. His writing contains some interesting comments about jazz, though he does not break any new ground.

Garvin Bushell

448. Bushell, Garvin, as told to Mark Tucker. *Jazz From the Beginning;* introduction by Lawrence Gushee. Ann Arbor: University of Michigan Press; 1988.

A compendium of life on the road, insights into musicians, and honest appraisals of topics ranging from jazz as a business to racism. Bushell comes across as an honest, no-nonsense person who tells-it-like-it-is. His anecdotes and recollections are blunt and equally laudatory and critical. He asserts that Chick Webb couldn't hold a tempo and wanted his band to sound like a white band; he did not respect Cab Calloway as a band-leader; and was unflattering to Fletcher Henderson. On the other hand, he had high praise for Louis Armstrong, Billie Holiday, Ethel Waters, and others. The strength of the book is Tucker's ability to allow Bushell to tell his story as he saw it. References after each chapter, a complete discography with comments and identification of soloists, and a glossary of musician and performers.

Red Callendar

449. Callender, Red, and Elaine Dohen. *Unfinished Dream: The Musical World of Red Callender.* London: Quartet Books; 1985.

An integral member of the Los Angeles jazz scene for the past five decades, Callender details jazz from Central Avenue venues to bebop and recording studios. He also provides insights into the music business, the entertainment world, and his associations with musicians such as Louis Armstrong, Erroll Garner, Art Tatum, and Lester Young. Callender also arranged for R&B artists such as Jesse Belvin and the Platters, taught Charles Mingus, and helped to desegregate the Los Angeles Musicians Union. A significant addition to jazz literature because it provides insights into people, venues, and life-of-the-time in the under researched Los Angeles jazz world.

Cab Calloway

450. Calloway, Cab, and Bryant Rollins. *Of Minnie and Moocher and Me;* with illustrations selected and edited by John Shearer. New York: Crowell; 1976.

Titled after his famous theme song, the book contains Calloway's account of his musical career from his childhood in Rochester and Baltimore. Beginning in the aforementioned cities, he also spent some time in Chicago and New York in a career-enhancing tenure at the Cotton Club in 1930, and continued his overall career as bandleader, vocalist, and musical-theater actor. Surprisingly, the account is both laudatory and critical. Recollections of Calloway by other musicians and his family enrich the book. Although he was not a significant jazz innovator, Calloway should be respected for his musical versatility, entertainment professionalism, and jazz argot. In fact, his 1944 book, *The New Cab Calloway's Hepsters*

Dictionary (argot), and *Prof. Cab Calloway's Swing Formation Bureau* (quiz), published in 1939, are included at the back of the book. No index.

Hoagy Carmichael

451. Carmichael, Hoagy. *The Stardust Road.* New York: Rinehart, 1946; London: Musician's Press; 1947.

Details the spirit of the 1920s with humorous anecdotes and fits his life within that period. Carmichael's life is covered to the death of Beiderbecke. Focuses on his stay at Indiana University.

452. _____. *Sometime I Wonder: The Story of Hoagy Carmichael;* with Stephen Longstreet. New York: Farrar, Straus and Giroux, 1965; London: Redmen, 1966; New York: Da Capo, 1981.

Continues his life story into the 1950s with accounts of associations and encounters he made with exponents of film, jazz, and popular music. He includes coverage from his Midwestern roots to his contact with the lifestyle of Harlem and New York. He also repeats some information on his relationship with Bix Beiderbecke, which he covered in his previous autobiography. Several photographs.

Benny Carter

453. Berger, Morroe, Edward Berger, and James Patrick. *Benny Carter: A Life in American Music.* Foreword by Benny Carter. Introduction by Dan Morgenstern. Two volumes. Newark and Metuchen, N.J.: Institute of Jazz Studies (Rutgers University). Lanham, Md.: Scarecrow Press; 1982.

A mammoth account of Carter's immense contributions as composer, performer, and bandleader. The authors chronicle his musical evolution from its beginnings to his tenure as a sideman with Fletcher Henderson, McKinney's Cotton Pickers, Chick Webb, Duke Ellington, and many more. His success as a jazz arranger-composer and scorer of films, as well as his lectureship at Princeton University are also covered. The biography is also important because it covers his associations with other artists and includes anecdotes and recollections from numerous musicians on Benny Carter's importance. Volume 2 contains a chronology, discography, list of arrangements and compositions, list of LPs, filmography, and bibliography. Also covers details of Benny Carter's formation and dissolution of big bands from 1928 to 1946, and the dates and locations of all engagements, and route listings of his bands. An important addition to jazz scholarship.

Betty Carter

454. Bauer, William R. *Open the Door: The Life and Music of Betty Carter.* Ann Arbor, The University of Michigan Press; 2002.

Discusses Carter's musical accomplishments within the context of her personal aesthetics and approaches. Unlike other vocalists, Bauer correctly champions Carter's superb musicianship and respect from her peers. The author translates 15 performances into musical notation and uses phonetic transcriptions to illustrate her approach to singing lyrics, scat singing, phrasing and articulations. Scholarly and thorough.

Serge Chaloff

455. Simosko, Vladimir. *Serge Chaloff: A Musical Biography and Discography.* Lanham, Md.: Scarecrow Press, and Institute of Jazz Studies (Rutgers University); 1998.

Begins with a biographical portrait of the life, musical associates, and influences of this composer-performer. Includes details of his association with bandleaders such as Woody Herman, and a musical analysis of his style. Includes a comprehensive discography

Buck Clayton

456. Clayton, Buck, with Nancy Miller Elliott. *Buck Clayton's Jazz World.* New York: Oxford University Press; 1987.

Includes anecdotes and reminiscences about his life, music, and peers. The anecdotes and reminiscences are often concise, less than probing, and seem to indicate that Clayton was reluctant to provide more than laudatory insights, especially regarding his peers. He performed with and was a friend of Count Basie, Billie Holiday, and Lester Young, to name a few. Selected bibliography, discography, and an index.

Nat King Cole

457. Cole, Marie Ellington, and Louie Robinson. *Nat King Cole: An Intimate Biography.* New York: Morrow, 1971; London: Allen, 1973; New York: Da Capo, 1987.

Permeated with remembrances and recollections about his life, family, career, and associations. Includes information about his transition from performing as jazz pianist to pop singer and his encounters with racism. Selected discography. Illustrated.

458. Haskins, James, and Kathleen Benson. *Nat King Cole: A Personal and Professional Biography*. Chelsea, Mich.: Scarborough House Publishers; 1984, 1990.

Traces his life, achievements, and experiences with racism from his birth in 1919 until his death in 1965. Discusses his trios, fame as a vocalist, problems with the IRS, and his marriage to Maria Hawkins. Also includes a discussion of "Nature Boy" and other recordings. Includes a discography.

Bill Coleman

459. Coleman, Bill. *Trumpet Story*. London: Macmillan Press Ltd., 1990, Boston: Northeastern University Press; 1991.

Coleman chronicles his musical experiences from his debut at the Harlem Savoy Ballroom in 1927 to his recording sessions of the 1970s. He also discusses the racism that he experienced and eventual acceptance as an expatriate artist in France. Coleman was a sideman with numerous artists, including Benny Carter, Fats Waller, and Teddy Wilson. He immigrated to France in 1948 and gained immediate popularity, primarily because his work with Fats Waller had become popular in France. His discussion of clubs, concert dates, and musicians is very informative.

Ornette Coleman

460. Litweiler, John. *Ornette Coleman: A Harmolodic Life*. New York: William Morrow; 1993.

Updates and expands his analysis of Ornette Coleman presented in an earlier book *The Freedom Principle*. The coverage includes Coleman's postbop recordings, free jazz experiments, and his recent film soundtrack *Naked Lunch* (1992). He combines an analysis of Coleman's music with details about his relationship with his son (Denardo), criticism of his music, and encounters with racism. The role of interpretation in harmolodic theory is also explored.

461. McRae, Barry. *Ornette Coleman*. London: Apollo; 1988.

A biography that traces his career, beginning with his experiences as a rhythm and blues saxophonist in Fort Worth, Texas, through his recognition as an original artist. Has references to recordings and some references to his sidemen. Selected discography, bibliography, filmography. Illustrated.

462. Wilson, Peter Niklas. *Ornette Coleman: His Life and Music*. Berkeley: Berkeley Hills Books; 2001.

In addition to his early years in Fort Worth, Texas, musical associations, and eventual elevation to controversy and stardom, the author also explains "Harmolodics." His explanation is lucid and clear. A discussion of Prime Time, his group, and associations with artists like Jerry Garcia and Pat Metheny is also included. Contains reviews of several recordings and includes references.

Buddy Collette

463. Collette, Buddy, and Steven Isoardi. *Jazz Generations: A Life in American Music and Society*. New York: Continuum; 2000.

Introductions by Isoardi and Gerald Wilson, the book chronicles Collette's life and music from his early years in Los Angeles to 2000. Includes factual insights to the Central Avenue musical scene, and to artists such as Eric Dolphy and Charles Mingus. The amalgamation of Local 767 and Local 47, studio scene, and his stint with the Chico Hamilton Quintet is also covered. Contains photographs and a discography.

Lee Collins

464. Collins, Lee. *Oh, Didn't He Ramble: The Life Story of Lee Collins as Told to Mary Collins;* edited by Frank J. Gillis and John W. Miner; foreword by Max Jones. Urbana: University of Illinois Press; 1989.

Details the evolution of jazz in New Orleans and Chicago from 1900 to 1960. The Collins story illuminates his role in this evolution and sheds light on many musicians with whom he associated, venues in which he performed, and the difficulties he/they encountered. Details on his life from 1929 when he settled in Chicago to around 1954 are chronicled. Collins replaced Armstrong in King Oliver's band in Chicago in 1924. The manuscript was completed by Frank Gillis. Selected bibliography, discography, and notes.

John Coltrane

465. Cole, Bill. *John Coltrane: A Musical Biography*. New York: Schirmer; London: Collier Macmillan; 1976.

One of the earliest musical biographies of this giant. This book is an outgrowth of the author's 1975 doctoral dissertation at Wesleyan University. The author focuses on style (he analyzes numerous recordings), sound, and the role and function of Coltrane's philosophy in shaping his music. Cole believes the key to understanding Coltrane's music is in understanding "the way of life of the traditional African" (p. 13). To substantiate his theory, Cole draws heavily from Fele Sowande's *The Role of Music in African Society* (Sowande was one of Cole's teachers at the University of Pittsburgh). Unfortunately, Cole does not demonstrate the transformation and adaptation of Sowande's ideas by Coltrane. In fact, there is no proof that Coltrane was aware of Sowande. In addition to this flaw, there are occasional mistakes in the citing of personnel. Contains musical examples (transcriptions by the imminent Coltrane scholar and tenor saxophonist Andrew White). Selected bibliography and discography.

466.   Filtgen, Gerd, and Michael Ausserbauer. *John Coltrane: Seine Leben, seine Musik, seine Schallplatten.* Waakirchen, Germany: Oreos; 1983.

In German. The biography covers his career, acceptance, and impact on jazz. Includes references and discussion of several recordings. Among the highlights are discussions of his stints with Miles Davis and Thelonious Monk and his role as a group leader and jazz innovator. Illustrated.

467.   Fraim, John. *Spirit Catcher: The Life and Art of John Coltrane.* West Liberty, Ohio: The Greathouse Company; 1996.

A biography of Coltrane's spiritual quest, and his evolution from backing up a Polka player in the 1950s to dominating the jazz world in the 1960s. Also covers the interim before his ascent to fame, associations, and influences such as Eric Dolphy, John Gilmore, and Sun Ra. Coltrane's connection to Eastern mysticism and spiritual transformation are also discussed.

468.   Fujioka, Yasuhiro, Lewis Porter, and Yoh-Ichi Hamada. *John Coltrane: A Discography and Musical Biography.* Lanham, Maryland: Scarecrow Press, and Institute of Jazz Studies (Rutgers University); 1994.

A comprehensive guide to his recordings and professional career. He lists all known recordings, including 30 live sessions not previously cited, and the details of the unissued sessions that Coltrane recorded with Miles Davis. Includes a listing of every issue worldwide through 1993, including CD, cassette, video, and LP, with standard discographical information.

469.   Gerber, Alain. *Le cas Coltrane;* foreword by Francis Marmande. Marseille: Parenthèses; 1985.

In French. This is not a biography. Instead, the author focuses on his personality and creativity by analyzing four recordings ("Giant Steps,"

"My Favorite Things," "Plays the Blues," and "Olé"). Some of the material was previously published in *Jazz Magazine.*

470. Nisenson, Eric. *Ascension: John Coltrane and His Quest.* New York: St. Martin's Press; 1993.

Explores the spiritual, psychological, philosophical, and social forces that influenced Coltrane and his music. The author focuses on the inner quest that led Coltrane from his role as an R&B tenor saxophonist to his attempt to reach God through his music. He chronicles the impact of both Eastern and Western religions, the civil rights movement, and the black liberation movement. The narrative also refers to selected recordings within the context of his inner spirituality. Offers important insights into the forces that shaped Coltrane and his music.

471. Priestley, Brian. *John Coltrane.* London: Apollo; 1987.

Details the frustrations of his early career stints with Thelonious Monk and Miles Davis, and contributions as a bandleader and proponent of avant-garde jazz. He also discusses how Coltrane's later style mirrowed the sociocultural context and uncertainty of America in the 1960s. Includes a discussion of his evolution from bebop and a discography. Concise, only 96 pages, but informative.

472. Putschögl, Gerhard. *John Coltrane und die AfroAmerikanische Graltradition.* Graz, Austria: Akademische Druck—. Verlagsanstalt (Jazz Forschung 25); 1993.

In German. A comprehensive and scholarly assessment of John Coltrane's music as a product of African American aesthetics, value systems, and cultural and social reality. He combines a detailed investigation of transcriptions with a deep structural assessment of cultural roots and musical context. Before analyzing Coltrane's modal and postmodal periods, he presents a survey of stylistic concepts that were used in the previous period of functional harmonic improvisation. In the modal period, the author focuses on Coltrane's structural and expressive stylistic concepts. There are numerous musical examples. One of a limited number of jazz studies that assesses jazz as an expressive phenomenon within African American culture. English summary, bibliography, reference notes, and several transcriptions.

473. Simpkins, Cuthbert Ormond. *Coltrane: A Biography.* Perth Amboy, New Jersey: Herndon House; 1975.

Written by a medical doctor and passionate jazz fan, especially of Coltrane, the biography portrays its subject in both musical and nonmusical roles. Information was gleaned from numerous oral sources and published accounts, including reviews. The author covers the gamut of Coltrane's career (before, during, and after musical success) as well as his spirituality. There are some informal references to his music, and transcriptions by Zita Carno are included in the index. Reprints of selected pages from Coltrane's workbook are also included. No index.

474. Thomas, J. C. *Chasin' the Trane: The Music and Mystique of John Coltrane.* Garden City: Doubleday, 1975; London: Elm Tree, 1976; New York: Da Capo, 1976, 1977, 1979; Wien: Hannibal, 1986.

Includes biographical information along with comments and recollections of musicians who knew and admired Coltrane. The book is interesting for the insight it provides into Coltrane as a person and musical innovator as well as the opinions of him that other musicians held. Although there are penetrating comments about the man and his music, unlike Bill Cole's *John Coltrane: A Musical Biography,* there are no transcriptions or musical analysis. Contains photographs, a selected discography, compositions by Coltrane, selected bibliography, and an index.

475. White, Andrew. *Trane 'n Me: A Treatise on the Music of John Coltrane.* Washington, D.C.: Andrew's Music; 1981.

Personal insights on his infatuation with Coltrane, stylistic analysis, a concise summary of four Coltrane periods, and a selected discography according to periods.

476. Woideck, Carl (editor). *The John Coltrane Companion: Five Decades of Commentary.* New York: Schirmer Books; 1998.

The essays cover his life and playing from his early years with Miles Davis and Thelonious Monk through his pioneering groups of the 1960s. Included are articles, interviews, and performance and record reviews that characterize both the man and his music. The collection includes eight interviews, 23 other articles, a chronology, discography, and a select bibliography.

477. Yasuhiro, Fujioka, Lewis Porter, and Yoh-ichi Hamada. *John Coltrane: A Discography and Musical Biography.* Lanham, Maryland: Scarecrow Press, and Institute of Jazz Studies (Rutgers); 1995.

A thoroughly researched, well-written, and scholarly document. Corrects mistakes in other works on Coltrane, and offers a definitive account of his life and music. Contains numerous photographs, song titles, and recording company indices are also included.

Eddie Condon

478. Condon, Eddie. *We Called It Music: A Generation of Jazz.* Narration by Thomas Sugrue. New York: Holt, Toronto: Oxford; 1947; London: Davies,

1948, 1956, 1961; London: Jazz Book Club, 1956; London: Corgi, 1962; München: Nymphenburger, 1964; Westport, Conn.: Greenwood, 1970, 1974; New York: Da Capo, 1988.

Draws a vivid picture of the events and personalities in Chicago and New York jazz in the 1920s and 1930s. Numerous musicians give first-hand accounts of jazz during this era, including some interesting and insightful anecdotes about Condon. An extensive discography of Condon is also presented (1981).

479.   Condon, Eddie, and Hank O'Neal. *The Eddie Condon Scrapbook of Jazz.* New York: St. Martin's, 1973; London: Hale, 1974.

Primarily an album of Condon's recollections, clippings, posters, and letters, rather than a detailed biomusical study. Permeated with anecdotes, humorous stories, and information on musicians of the 1920s and 1930s (addition to 1981).

Carlton A. Coon, Sr., and Joe L. Sanders

480.   Edmiston, Fred W. *The Coon-Sanders Nighthawks: The Band That Made Radio Famous.* Jefferson, N.C.: McFarland and Company; 2003.

The complete history of how Carlton A. Coon, Sr., and Joe L. Sanders formed the Coon-Sanders Orchestra in 1919 in Kansas City, Missouri. He covers their different personalities, various band members association with Jules Cesar Stein who later established Music Corporation of America (MCA), and the band broadcasting on WDAF in Kansas City.

Bob Crosby

481.   Chilton, John. *Stomp Off, Let's Go! The Story of Bob Crosby's Bob Cats and Big Band.* London: Jazz Book; 1983.

A biography and history of his bands including references to personnel, travel, accomplishments, and acceptance. A biographical dictionary of his sidemen is included. Illustrated.

Bill Crow

482.   Crow, Bill. *From Birdland to Broadway: Scenes from a Jazz Life.* New York: Oxford University Press; 1992.

Insider account of four decades of an artist's life in jazz. The author, a jazz bassist, provides anecdotes of several significant pioneers of modern jazz with whom he either performed or befriended. These include Benny Goodman, Stan Getz, Dizzy Gillespie, Slim Gaillard, Terry Gibbs, Benny Goodman, Billie Holiday, Judy Holliday, Dave Lambert, Thelonious Monk, Gerry Mulligan, Claude Thornhill, and more. His personal stories cover topics such as "Birdland," "Seattle," "jam sessions," and "scuffling." The anecdotes transpired in venues like Birdland, the Half Note, the Playboy Club, and on Broadway. Although most of the personal insights are previously unpublished, some appeared in a different form in Gene Lees's *Jazzletter,* and in the author's column entitled "The Band Room," in *Allegro,* the monthly newspaper of New York's Local 802 of the American Federation of Musicians.

Mike Daniels

483. Bowen, Michael. *Mike Daniels and the Delta Jazzmen.* Melton, England: Houseman; 1980, 1982.

A comprehensive biodiscography of the leader and his group. Included is information on Daniels' introduction, influences, and career, combined with the names and contributions of selected sidemen. Illustrated.

Cleo Laine and John Dankworth

484. Collier, Graham. *Cleo and John: A Biography of the Dankworths.* London: Quartet Books; 1976.

The life and music of John Dankworth and Cleo Laine. Includes important information on the British jazz scene.

Michael Danzi

485. Lotz, Rainer E. *Michael Danzi: American Musician in Germany 1924–1939—Memoirs of the Jazz, Entertainment, and Movie World of Berlin During the Weimar Republic and the Nazi Era—and in the United States.* Schmitten: Norbert Rücker; 1986.

Autobiography of the banjoist, acoustic guitarist, electric Hawaiian guitarist, and mandolinist. Danzi transplanted American popular genres to Berlin in the 1920s. The text is permeated with anecdotes as well as historical facts regarding music during the Weimar Republic and Nazi eras. Although he did not limit his musical activities to jazz, his account of both American and European music and show business activities of the 1920s, 1930s, and 1940s is important for jazz scholars. Several appendices: memorable items from the Danzi repertoire, listing of bands and orchestra leaders in chronological order, Danzi's own recording sessions (Rainer E. Lotz), listing of films (Rainer E. Lotz), selected bibliography and further reading, compiled and annotated (Rainer E. Lotz), and index. Sixteen-page section of photos.

Joe Darensbourg

486.   Darensbourg, Joe. *Jazz Odyssey: The Autobiography of Joe Darensbourg as told to Peter Vacher;* supplementary material compiled by Peter Vacher. Baton Rouge: Louisiana State University Press; 1988.

Darensbourg, a jazz clarinetist and saxophonist, chronicles his life, his role with The Original Dixieland Jazz Band, his appearance with Kid Ory on the "This Is Jazz Broadcast" (1947), the television show "Stars of Jazz," and more. He also details being shot in a Prohibition-era gang war. There is a discography of 103 recordings, a supplementary discography of tapes, a list of his compositions and film appearances, and a chronology of his career, 1916 through 1985.

Charlie Davis

487.   Davis, Charlie, and Lewis Turco. *That Band from Indiana.* Osego, New York: Mathom; 1982.

Autobiography that chronicles the career, accomplishments, and significance of an Indianapolis bandleader of the 1920s and 1930s. Permeated with references of historical importance. Also includes a transcription of Bix Beiderbecke's "Cloudy." Illustrated.

Joe Davis

488.   Bastin, Bruce. *Never Sell A Copyright: Joe Davis and His Role in the New York Music Scene 1916–1978.* London: Chigwell; 1990.

In addition to his life and role in music, the book contains important information on the history and evolution of jazz in New York. Discusses how some musicians sold the rights to their compositions and the affect that ownership of copyrights had on the New York music scene.

Miles Davis

489.   Carr, Ian. *Miles Davis: A Critical Biography.* London, Melbourne, New York: Quartet, 1982; New York: Morrow, 1982, 1984; London: Paladin, 1984; Baden, Baden: Unknown Publisher, 1985.

The 18 chapters cover topics ranging from his childhood and initiation into jazz to "The Birth of the Cool," "Miles Ahead," "Porgy and Bess," "After Coltrane," "Miles Run the Voodoo Down," and more. Details regarding specific recordings and personnel permeate the book and contain musical and personal insights. The book is significant because the author includes insights from several jazz artists and critics including musicians Jimmy Cobb, Dave Holland, Herbie Hancock, Red Rodney, Horace Silver, Keith Jarrett, Dave Liebman, and critics Leonard Feather, Ralph Gleason, Michael James, and LeRoi Jones. There are chapter references, a bibliography, nine transcriptions, a comprehensive discography, and an index.

490. Chambers, Jack. *Milestones: The Music and Times of Miles Davis.* New York: Quill; 1989.

A combining of two books originally published separately; *Milestones I: The Music and Times of Miles Davis to 1960,* and *Milestones 2: The Music and Times of Miles Davis Since 1960.* The book is divided into two parts: part one: Boplicity, and part two: Miles Ahead. Part one is organized by both topics and years: Tune Up 1926–44; 52nd Street Theme 1945–6; Ornithology 1947–8; and Move 1948–50. Part two is also organized by topics and years covering 1950 to 1959: Down 1950–4; Walkin' 1954–5; Cookin' 1955–7; and Fran Dance 1958–9. Each chapter is permeated with anecdotal and historical references to personnel, and occasional general remarks about the music. Book two covers roughly 1960 to the early 1980s, with the following topics/years: Pfrancing 1960–2; So Near, So Far 1963–4; Circle 1964–8; Miles Runs the Voodoo Down 1968–9; Funky Tonk 1969–71; Sivad Selim 1972–5; Shhh 1975–81; and It Gets Better: 1981 and After. The afterword is entitled So What. As in book one, this book is a reservoir of anecdotal and historical information with references to personnel and general remarks about selected sessions and music. The strength of the book is that the background material is very thorough, well written and researched. The book lacks scholarly analysis of the music. An index and a bibliography are included in each book.

491. Cole, Bill. *Miles Davis: A Musical Biography.* New York: William Morrow; 1974. Retitled reprint, *Miles Davis: The Early Years.* New York: Da Capo; 1994.

Provides an interesting study of the musical career of Miles Davis. The author discusses Davis's musical influences and style as well as the rejection of that style in the late 1960s. He also comments on the succession of musicians who performed with Davis, although there are occasional mistakes—for example, in the personnel listed for the *Bitches Brew* album. The 13 transcriptions cover compositions ranging from "Jeru" (*Birth of the Cool,* 1949), to "Sanctuary (*In a Silent Way,* 1969). Cole also addresses the issue of commercialization that confronted Miles when he changed to fusion in the late 1960s. Comprehensive bibliography, list of recording sessions to 1972, and an index. The 1994 reprint includes discography and personnel corrections.

492.   Crisp, George. *Miles Davis.* New York: Franklin Watts (A division of Grolier Publishing); 1997.

Divided into 11 chapters, the author traces Davis's career from his early years to his death. Mostly anecdotal, no new insights. However, the book contains a photograph of Miles Dewey Davis, II, Miles's father, at his Northwestern University Dental School graduation.

493.   Cugny, Laurent. *Electrique Miles Davis, 1968–1975.* Marseille: Andre' Dimanche Editeur; 1993.

In French. Discusses Miles Davis's use of electronic instruments, musical analysis of concepts, and his innovations with Chick Corea, Dave Holland, Keith Jarrett, John Mclaughlin, Wayne Shorter, and Joe Zawinul. His discussion is divided into years, and provides unique insights into the music.

494.   Davis, Miles, with Quincy Troupe. *Miles: The Autobiography.* New York: Simon and Schuster; 1989.

A vivid and forceful narration of Davis's career, associations, and perspectives on many issues. Miles speaks in a frank and honest voice, which is captured without sacrificing content and meaning by the excellent writing of Quincy Troupe. The book is permeated with anecdotes, stories, and impulsive comments on situations, for example, his visit to the White House, and his impression of why Bill Evans left his band (pp. 231–32). The book is significant because the narrative is Miles Davis's rather than an outsider's interpretation of Miles.

495.   James, Michael. *Miles Davis.* New York: Barnes; London: Cassell; 1961.

Studies Davis's musical development from about 1945 with Charles Parker to 1959 as demonstrated in selected recordings. The author elaborates on Davis's strengths and weaknesses. A selected bibliography is included but no index.

496.   Kerschbaumer, Franz. *Miles Davis: Stilkritische Untersuchungen zur musikalischen Entwicklung Seines Personalstils.* Two Volumes. Graz: Akademische Druck U. Verlagsanstalt; 1978.

In German. Focuses on Miles Davis's style 1945–68, using a musicological approach. Five styles (periods), are addressed: bebop, cool, mainstream (East Coast), hard bop, and modal style. He concludes with a concise discussion of the 1968–75 period. The author's approach is consistent throughout; each chapter contains a concise historical summary of the style; music of Davis during the period; musical analysis of performances (form, themes, arrangements, instrumentation, sound, rhythm sections, tonality, structure, comparison of improvisations, and influences [of and on other musicians]). The 55 transcriptions are found in the appendix. In addition, the author used a sonagraphic analysis of rhythmic devices to determine approaches to rhythm in the previously mentioned styles. A largely unknown but excellent work. Selected bibliography, and the discography is an appendix to J. G. Jepsen's 1969 discography.

497. Kirchner, Bill (editor). *A Miles Davis Reader.* Washington and London: Smithsonian Institution Press; 1997.

The anthology contains 24 interviews, reviews, record liner notes, and critical essays that trace the evolution of Davis's career from his early years with Charles Parker through the 1949–50 *Birth of the Cool* recordings. Also covers his 1950s and 1960s groups, the 1969 *Bitches Brew* album, and his reemergence in 1981 after a six-year hiatus. Provides good insight into Miles's cool style.

498. Murphy, Chris. *Miles To Go: Remembering Miles Davis.* New York: Thunder's Mouth Press; 2002.

The author worked for Miles from 1973 to 1983, with a four-year hiatus from 1976 to 1980, as a technician, road manager, and personal assistant. He covers many of Miles artistic, emotional, and physical struggles from an insider perspective. In addition, he discusses image and celebrity, music, and racism.

499. Nisenson, Eric. *'Round About Midnight: A Portrait of Miles Davis.* New York: Dial, 1980; Paris: Denoël, 1983; Wien: Hannibal, 1985.

A biography that covers his career from his East St. Louis roots to associations with Charles Parker, Gil Evans, and numerous other artists. His role as a bandleader and proponent of change, and contributions to jazz are also chronicled. Selected discography, index, and illustrations.

500. ____. *'Round About Midnight: A Portrait of Miles Davis* (Updated edition). New York: Da Capo Press; 1996.

The updated edition features a new preface, new material on Miles in the 1980s, and a recommended listening section.

501. ____. *The Making of* Kind of Blue: *Miles Davis and his Masterpiece.* New York: St. Martin's Press; 2000.

Recounts the story behind the creation of the album, *Kind of Blue.* He focuses on the period and overall milieu in which it was recorded, events and musical ideas that led to the period, individual musicians biographies and contributions to the album. He also covers the musical evolution and contributions of Miles Davis.

502. Tingen, Paul. *Miles Beyond: The Electric Explorations of Miles Davis, 1967–1991.* New York: Billboard Books; 2001.

The books cover the music Miles produced in his "electric period." This is not a comparison or discussion of Miles prefusion and fusion recordings; rather, it is to delineate the different emphasis, interpretation, language, and misinterpretations that are used in his fusion recordings. Provides insight into the role and function of personnel, includes a list of his 1963–91 personnel, and a 1967–91 discography and sessionography by Enrico Merlin.

503. Troupe, Quincy. *Miles and Me.* Berkeley: University of California Press; 2000.

A candid account of his friendship with Miles Davis since their St. Louis days, and describes the processes of Davis's creativity. Discusses how Miles influenced both musicians and nonmusicians, and his singular resistance to being an "unreconstructed black man." Intimate portrayal, and shows both the human and artistic side of Miles Davis.

504. Weissmüller, Peter. *Miles Davis: Sein Leben, seine Musik, seine Schall-platten.* Waakirchen, Germany: Oreos; 1984.

In German. Covers his life, career, accomplishments, associations, and contributions. Numerous references to recordings and contains a discussion of his style. No new insights. Illustrated.

505. Williams, Richard. *Miles Davis: The Man in the Green Shirt.* New York: Holt; 1993.

The title is a reference to the shirt that Davis wore on his 1958 *Milestones* album. Although the book is permeated with provocative photographs covering his entire career, the text is often marred by factual errors and bizarre comparisons. The latter can be seen in the attempt to convey the idea that the shirt in the picture on the cover was as important as the music. Rehashes known facts, no new insights. Selected bibliography and discography.

Buddy DeFranco

506. Kuehn, John, and Arne Astrup. *Buddy DeFranco: A Biographical Portrait and Discography;* foreword by Leonard Feather. Metuchen, N.J.: The Scarecrow Press and The Institute of Jazz Studies (Rutgers); 1993.

Covers DeFranco's life from childhood and musical training to his stints with numerous bands. His musical career is divided into yearly intervals and includes his time with Gene Krupa, Ted Fio Rito, Charlie Barnet, Tommy Dorsey, The Count Basie Sextet/Septet, Nelson Riddle, Glenn Miller, his solo career, and more. An extended interview with DeFranco, comprehensive discography, bibliography, and subject and song index are included.

507. Zammarchi, Fabrice, and Sulvie Mas. *A Life in The Golden Age of Jazz: A Biography of Buddy DeFranco*. Seattle: University of Washington Press.; 2002.

The biography is autographed by DeFranco, and covers his musical career as a bandleader and sideman. Includes information on his years with Charlie Barnett, Count Basie, Gene Krupa, Tommy Dorsey, Ted Fio Rito, Glenn Miller, and more. Also covers his solo career, and contains numerous photographs. The publication is limited to 1,000 copies.

Johnny Dodds

508. Lambert, G. E. *Johnny Dodds*. New York: Barnes; London: Cassell; 1971.

In addition to biographical information, includes a good discussion of Dodd's role in his recordings with King Oliver, Louis Armstrong's Hot Five and Hot Seven, his own Washboard Band, and his contributions at other sessions. His contributions to jazz are also discussed. The selected discography lists 78s and Microgroove recordings (1981).

509. Riesco, Jose Francisco. *El Jazz clasico y Johnny Dodds: Su Rei Sin Corona*. Santiago: Reisco; 1972.

In Spanish. Covers the history and culture of New Orleans jazz with special attention given to the career and achievements of Johnny Dodds. In addition, there are career overviews of Louis Armstrong, Jelly Roll Morton, and King Oliver. Index and illustrations.

510. Gara, Larry. *The Baby Dodds Story*. Los Angeles: Contemporary Press, 1959; Baton Rouge and London: Louisiana State University, 1992.

The first edition describes Dodd's life in New Orleans as well as the revival of New Orleans jazz in the 1940s. The author discusses Dodds's association with Louis Armstrong, King Oliver, Jelly Roll Morton, and Bunk Johnson. The information on the styles and the role of the drummer in New Orleans jazz makes this a particularly useful autobiography. The book is based on taped interviews made in 1953. In the revised edition, Gara provides more insight into his interviews with Dodds and expands his "additional recordings" and discography. He also replaces several photographs from the 1959 version.

Eric Dolphy

511.   Horricks, Raymond. *The Importance of Being Eric Dolphy.* Turnbridge, England: Spellmount; 1988.

Traces Dolphy's career from his Los Angeles roots through his associations with Booker Little and John Coltrane and his recognition as a virtuoso bass clarinetist, flutist, and alto saxophonist. Also chronicles Dolphy's significance as an innovator and leader of avant-garde jazz. Selected discography, illustrated.

512.   Simasko, Vladimir, and Barry Tepperman. *Eric Dolphy: A Musical Biography and Discography.* Foreword by Martin Williams. Washington: Smithsonian Institution Press, 1974, 1986; New York: Da Capo, 1979.

Evaluates Dolphy's contributions to jazz and analyzes his musical development as demonstrated in his recordings. In this short but valuable study the author also codes each composition to indicate whether or not Dolphy performs a solo and includes a list of composer credits. The discography is organized chronologically with details on date, venue, personnel, and release numbers. This biography is devoted to both assessing Dolphy's music and determining his contributions to jazz. Selected bibliography (addition to 1981).

Jimmy Dorsey

513.   Stockdale, Robert L. *Jimmy Dorsey: A Study in Contrasts.* Lantham, Md.: Scarecrow Press, and Institute of Jazz Studies (Rutgers); 1999.

A comprehensive biography of the man and his music. Covers the details of his life, relationship with his brother, Tommy Dorsey, success as a big band leader, and influence on other musicians. Contains a discography with specific details regarding titles, dates venues, and more. Comprehensive and thoroughly researched.

Tommy and Jimmy Dorsey

514.   Sanford, Herb. *Tommy and Jimmy: The Dorsey Years.* New Rochelle, New York: Arlington House; London: Ian Allan; 1972.

Presents a detailed account of the separate and combined careers of the Dorsey brothers, from the Goldkette and Whitman Orchestras through the swing era. With information compiled from anecdotes, personal recollections, and other research, the author reflects on the Dorsey brothers' accomplishments and critical reception. A 1935 itinerary, index, and list of musicians who worked with the Dorseys are also included. The biography contains few critical comments on either their music or their contributions to jazz (addition to 1981).

George Duvivier

515. Berger, Edward. *Basically Speaking: An Oral History of George Duvivier;* musical analysis by David Chevan; foreword by Benny Carter. Newark and Metuchen, N.J.: Institute of Jazz Studies Rutgers—The State University of New Jersey and The Scarecrow Press; 1993.

A self-portrait of George Duvivier (1920–85), as given to Edward Berger. Contains a thorough account of Duvivier's musical career (much of it in nonjazz venues), interfaced with comments by other musicians. Among his colleagues who contributed are Benny Carter, Louis Bellson, Ron Carter, Todd Coolman, Milt Hinton, Hank Jones, Ed Shaughnessy, and Arthur Taylor. Chevan's analysis offers insights into his use of chord tones, rhythm, solo techniques, phrasing, and walking bass lines. A discography/solography, discography of compositions and arrangements, 1940s compositions by Duvivier, bibliography, and index are included.

Edward Kennedy "Duke" Ellington

516. Arnaud, Noel. *Duke Ellington.* Paris: Messenger Boetus; 1950.

Discusses Ellington's early life, music, and rise to fame. The book also comments on some of Ellington's musicians and his relationship with artists like Billy Strayhorn and Paul Gonzales (1981).

517. Billiard, Francois, and Gilles Tordjman. *Duke Ellington.* Paris: Editions du Seuil, Auril; 1994.

In French. Covers his life, musical achievements, some travels, and relationship with artists like Sidney Bechet, Dizzy Gillespie, Fletcher Henderson, Charles Mingus, Don Redman, and Cootie Williams. Includes comments on many recordings, and the views of writers/musicians such as Stanley Dance, Derek Jewell, and Gunther Schuller.

518. Collier, James Lincoln. *Duke Ellington.* New York: Oxford University Press; 1987.

Parallels the author's biography on Louis Armstrong. Collier presents a perceptive portrait of this giant of jazz. He begins by tracing Ellington's childhood, environment, and musical influence from Washington, D.C., through his tenure and maturation at the Cotton Club, to his immense success as a bandleader and composer. Collier does not treat Ellington solely as an icon, rather, he presents both laudatory and critical assessments of Ellington's life and music. He also incorporates Ellington into the sociocultural context of the times. Some of his comments regarding Ellington are condescending, for instance, he believes that Duke's use of augmented chords was more accidental than logically derived; specifically, he believes that the chords evolved as a result of Ellington's fingers slipping on the piano keys. He also wonders why Ellington did not hire Bobby Hackett, Jack Teagarden, or Lee Wiley. The book contains some questionable interval and chord analyses. Selected bibliography, chapter notes, and an index.

519.   Dance, Stanley. *The World of Duke Ellington.* New York: Scribner's, 1970; London: Macmillan, 1971; New York: Da Capo, 1982.

Presents an excellent insight into Ellington, the man and his music, through interviews with Duke and his musicians. Among the 26 musicians interviewed are Billy Strayhorn, Mercer Ellington, and Thomas L. Whaley. The interviews are supplemented by the author's assessment of their musicianship. Of particular importance to some researchers will be Mercer Ellington's attitude toward his father. The book also contains descriptions of five important events in the musical career of Ellington: the Monterey Festival of 1961, the Sacred Concerts of 1965 and 1968, the Latin American Tour of 1968, and Duke's 70th birthday celebration at the White House in 1969. Also included is a chronology of Ellington's life, a limited discography, and an index (1981).

520.   Darrell, R. D. *Black Beauty.* Philadelphia: Unknown; 1933.

A chronicle of Ellington's music to the early 1930s. Includes his embryonic musical experiences, early acquaintances, and experiences in Washington, D.C.

521.   deTrazegnies, Jean. *Duke Ellington: Harlem Aristocrat of Jazz.* Bruxelles: Hot Club; 1946.

522.   Dietrich, Kurt. *Duke's Bones: Ellington's Great Trombonists.* Rottenburg, Germany: Advance Music; 1995.

A scholarly assessment of the role and function that Joe "Tricky Sam" Nanton, Juan Tizol, Lawrence Brown, and trombone sections from the late 1940s to his final years played in Ellington's bands. The author listened to and analyzed numerous recordings, critiques other writer's opinions, and used musical analysis and transcriptions to prove his conclusions. An excellent addition to Duke Ellington scholarship.

523. Ellington, Edward Kennedy. *Music is My Mistress.* Garden City, New York: Doubleday, 1973; London: Allen, 1974; München: List, 1974; New York: Da Capo, 1976; London: Quartet, 1977; Milano: Emme, 1981.

Presents musician's views of Ellington as well as Ellington's views of himself. The book contains excellent information on Ellington's life, early childhood in Washington, D.C., and foreign tours. A major portion of the book is devoted to recollections of numerous musical peers. The book does not contain a critical assessment of Ellington's musical contributions. A list of his honors and a catalog of his compositions in copyright order are also included. Selected bibliography and discography (1981).

524. _____. *The Great Music of Duke Ellington.* New York: Belwin Mills; 1974.

Contains several lead sheets and a concise profile of Ellington's life by Leonard Feather.

525. Ellington, Mercer. *Duke Ellington in Person: An Intimate Memoir;* with Stanley Dance. Boston: Houghton Mifflin, London: Hutchinson, 1978; New York: Da Capo, 1979; Stuttgart, Vienna: Kohlhammer, U.P., 1980.

A comprehensive coverage of the man, his music, female relationships, and relationships with musicians and family. The biography is important because Mercer Ellington (son of Duke) provides both personal observations and insights as a band member. Although anecdotal in many respects, Mercer's portrait is more factual than most because of his closeness and long tenure with his father. It is, however, important to be cognizant of the love-hate relationship that Mercer had with his father. Scholars should compare this book with Ellington's *Music is My Mistress.* A list of compositions not cited in the aforementioned book is included in the appendix.

526. Frankl, Ron. *Duke Ellington: Band Leader and Composer.* New York: Chelsea; 1988.

A concise biography written for children—covers his career, contributions, and significance. Numerous references to sidemen and compositions. A chronology of his musical career is included. Selected bibliography, discography, and an index. Illustrated.

527. Gammond, Peter (editor). *Duke Ellington: His Life and Music.* New York: Roy; London: Phoenix House, 1958; London: Jazz Book Club, 1959; Reprint. New York: Da Capo; 1977.

Offers contributions by 15 authors on Ellington. Among the areas covered are his musical style (piano playing and composition); an analysis of his recordings; and biographical sketches of most of his musicians. A fully detailed, chronological discography is included (1981).

528. George, Don. *Sweet Man: The Real Duke Ellington.* New York: Putnam, London: Robson, 1982; New York: Perigee, 1983.

A comprehensive history of the Ellington bands, including the achievements, personnel changes, and ability to withstand musical change. Selected discography, index, illustrated.

529. Greene, Robert (editor). *Duke Ellington.* Zürich: Sanssouci; 1961.

Biographical portrait that covers his career from his earliest days in Washington, D.C., to his migration and eventual success in New York and the world. His success at the Cotton Club and ability to survive jazz change is also alluded to. No new information.

530. Gutman, Bill. *Duke: The Musical Life of Duke Ellington.* New York: Random House; 1977.

Focused on young readers, the biography draws on interviews and chronicles Ellington's life and music. Selected bibliography and an index.

531. Hasse, John Edward. *Beyond Category: The Life and Genius of Duke Ellington;* foreword by Wynton Marsalis. New York: Simon and Schuster; 1993.

Uses the Duke Ellington archives (business records, letters, musical manuscripts, photographs, and scrapbooks) at the Smithsonian Institution to chronicle Ellington's musical achievements. There is new information on his personality, business affairs (especially dealings with Irving Mills), relationships with jazz and political leaders, and his ability to cultivate the talents of individual musicians in his band. Also included are comments on selected recordings covering different periods of Ellington's career. Hasse also comments on Ellington's ability to realize "an African American aesthetic that calls for, rather than replicating exactly what is given you, finding your own voice as a means of expressing your individuality" (p. 401). A profound point that has escaped many exponents of jazz. In addition to chapter notes, the following lists are included: Ellington's key musicians; most essential Ellington recordings; selected films and videos; Ellington songbooks and folios; selected reading; index, and a list of illustration credits. An impressive addition to Ellington scholarship.

532. Jewell, Derek. *Duke: A Portrait of Duke Ellington.* London: Elm Tree Books, 1977; New York: Norton, 1977, 1980; London: Sphere, 1978; London: Pavilion, 1986.

Although this biography lacks the authentic insights provided by Mercer Ellington in *Duke Ellington in Person: An Intimate Member* and Duke Ellington's *Music Is My Mistress,* it does contain some important assessments of Ellington's career, ideas, and life. Specifically, the years 1960 to 1974 (Ellington's death), are especially good. Also, insights into the shaping of his ideas are informative. However, coverage of Ellington's early career to 1960 and excessive reliance on secondary sources undercut the overall quality of this book. A bibliography of six books and a selected discography is included. Index.

533. Lambert, Eddie. *Duke Ellington: A Listener' Guide.* Lanham, Md.: Scarecrow Press, and Institute of Jazz Studies (Rutgers University Press); 1998.

Presents an analysis of many Ellington recordings, and includes lots of illustrations. Good insights into the music, and analytical concepts that enable one to understand Ellington's music from a conceptual viewpoint.

534. Lambert, George E. *Duke Ellington.* London: Cassell, 1959; Stockholm: Hörsta, 1959; New York: Barnes, Milano: Ricordi; 1961.

Assesses Ellington and describes his recordings, many in detail, to 1958. The author suggests ways Ellington tailored his talents to fit the personnel in his band instead of making the band adjust to his arranging and compositional skills. Some of the recordings are assessed critically. Selected discography of 78s, EPs, and LPs, and a bibliography. Italian edition has a discography by Roberto Capasso (addition to 1981).

535. Lavezzzoli, Peter. *The King of All, Sir Duke: Ellington and the Artistic Revolution.* New York: Bayou Press; 2001.

Concerned with Ellington's direct and profound influence on an eclectic group of jazz and popular musical artists. Traces his influence on James Brown, George Clinton, Miles Davis, Charles Mingus, Steely Dan, Prince, Sly Stone, Ravi Shankar, Sun Ra, Stevie Wonder, Frank Zappa, and others. This is the first study to chronicle Ellington's influence on musicians outside jazz.

536. Lawrence, A. H. *Duke Ellington and His World.* New York: Routledge; 2000.

Draws on lengthy interviews with Ellington's band personnel and family and friends, this is the first biography of Ellington written by a fellow musician, African American, and friend of the genius composer. Traces his life from his early years in Washington, D.C., to his death in New York in 1974. Also discusses Ellington's musical career in terms of the cultural, economic, political, and social realities of the time.

537.   Montgomery, Elizabeth Rider. *Duke Ellington "King of Jazz."* Champaign, Ill.: Garrard Publishing Company; 1972.

Another of the *American All* series of biographies that are geared to children, grades 3–6, and is written for a fourth grade reading level. She highlights Ellington's life by citing important events, associations, and achievements. Montgomery cites his first known composition "Soda Fountain Rag," the help he received from Will Marion Cook, and more. Although elementary students might be able to follow the story like "Syncopated," "Afterbeat" and "Harmony" might be confusing to them.

538.   Nicholson, Stuart. *Reminiscing in Tempo: A Portrait of Duke Ellington.* Evanston, Ill.: Northwestern University; 1999.

A portrait of the composer constructed out of what people who knew him reported publicly about him. Ellington is portrayed as a private man, a showman, manager of brilliant but somewhat disorderly bandsmen, conductor of international tours, and a composer of unique music. Contains a bibliography and discography.

539.   Peress, Maurice. *Dvorak to Ellington: A Conductor Explores America's Music and Its African American Roots.* New York: Oxford University Press; 2004.

The writer/conductor worked with Duke Ellington on the suite from *Black, Brown, and Beige,* and has reconstructed concerts of James Reese Europe's Clef Club band and more. He begins by recounting Dvorak's three-year residency as Director of the National Conservatory of Music in New York (1892–95), and the impact of some of his students including Will Marion Cook and Rubin Goldmark who, in turn, became the teachers of Duke Ellington, George Gershwin, and Aaron Copland. He concludes with a look at Ellington and his music, and overall offers a penetrating look at Dvorak, American music, and the inestimable African American influence on it.

540.   Rattenbury, Ken. *Duke Ellington, Jazz Composer.* New Haven, Conn.: Yale University Press; 1991.

Draws from the observations of Ellington himself and of members of his orchestra. The author documents the extent that Ellington drew from African American musical traditions like blues, ragtime, and the music of Tin Pan Alley, and further demonstrates how he merged these practices with Euro-American classical music. The book contains numerous examples/ transcriptions, as well as important insights into the interpretations of some of his soloists. He discusses Ellington's criteria for selecting sidemen, technical accomplishments, the "Ellington sound," and his gift as a melodist and songwriter. He transcribes and analyzes "Ko Ko," "Mr. J.B. Blues,"

"Concerto for Cootie," "Junior Hop," and "Subtle Slough." This book compliments the scholarly works of Gunther Schuller and Mark Tucker. There are five appendices, notes, a selected bibliography and discography, and an index.

541. Ruland, Hans. *Duke Ellington: Seine Leben, seine Musik, seine Schallplatten.* Waakirchen, Germany: Oreos; 1983.

In German. Covers his life from initial musical experiences in Washington, D.C., through his Cotton Club tenure, to world-renowned artist stature. Includes a good discussion of numerous recordings.

542. Schaaf, Martha. *Duke Ellington: Young Music Master.* Indianapolis: Bobbs-Merrill; 1975.

A children's biography that covers his life and musical achievements from Washington, D.C., through his rise to fame in New York. Includes a chronology and glossary. Illustrated by Fred M. Irvin.

543. Steed, Janna Tull. *Duke Ellington: A Spiritual Biography.* New York: The Crossroad Publishing Company; 1999.

Although Ellington's life is covered, this 192-page book is more concerned with his achievements, obstacles, the reactions of others, and his ability to achieve greatness in a somewhat hostile world. Situates Ellington within the sociocultural milieu of his time.

544. Stratemann, Klaus. *Duke Ellington Day-by-Day and Film-by-Film.* Copenhagen, Denmark: Jazz Media; 1992.

Chronicles the professional activities of Ellington from his first film in 1929 to his death in 1974. A factual, comprehensive, and well-documented account of Ellington and his bands, travels, recording activities, public performances, radio broadcasts, television appearances, and film work. Some appraisals are subjective, however most are based on second- or third-hand sources.

545. Timmer, W. E. *Ellingtonia: The Recorded Music of Duke Ellington and His Sidemen.* Fourth edition. Lanham, Md.: Scarecrow Press, and Institute of Jazz Studies (Rutgers); 1996.

A monumental collection of the recorded music of Ellington and his sidemen, including concerts, studio recordings, soundtracks, radio broadcasts, and private recordings. Also includes the recordings Ellington made with other bands.

Focuses on his early music and sidemen, including the crafting of his style, recordings, and experiments with popular songs. References, illustrated.

546.   Tucker, Mark. *Ellington: The Early Years.* Urbana and Chicago: University of Illinois Press; 1991.

Follows Ellington from his youth in Washington, D.C., to his emergence as a significant bandleader and composer in New York during the 1920s. Tucker uses newspaper accounts, interviews of people that knew him, and Ellington's own writings to compile a definitive study of his early years. He sheds new light on the conflicting musical influences that existed in the Washington of Ellington's youth (Southern and Northern jazz, blues, and a strong classical music tradition). Tucker also provides information on the function of jazz in the African American community. The book is based on the author's doctoral dissertation at the University of Michigan; it is well researched and permeated with musical examples. An important addition to Ellington scholarship because it illuminates his pre-1928 growth and development. Selected bibliography, discography, and reference notes.

547.   ____. (editor). *The Duke Ellington Reader.* New York: Oxford University Press; 1993.

The 101 essays profile Ellington as a person, bandleader, musician, and philosopher. Also, there are critical assessments of Ellington's music, positions on social issues, productivity, and position in American musical culture. The essays offer a holistic assessment of Ellington rather than a singular effusive laudatory overview. There are numerous musical examples and a bibliography.

548.   Ulanov, Barry. *Duke Ellington.* New York: Creative Age Press, 1946; Buenos Aires: Estuardo, 1946; London: Jazz Book Club, London: Musician, 1947; New York: Da Capo, 1975, 1976.

Accounts for Duke's life and music to about 1945. The book is particularly informative on the sociological conditions surrounding the development of jazz to this date, especially as it related to Ellington. Brief comments on several of Ellington's more popular recordings are also included. This was the first book-length biography of Ellington, and other Ellington biographers have used the subsequent materials on Harlem of the 1920s, swing, and the effects of bebop on his music. Covers his career to 1944. Selected discography limited to the 1925–1944 years. Index, illustrated (addition to 1981).

549.   Vail, Ken. *Duke; Diary: Part I: The Life of Duke Ellington, 1927–1950; Part II: The Life of Duke Ellington, 1950–1974.* Lanham, Maryland, and Institute of Jazz Studies (Rutgers University Press); 2002.

The author uses advertisements, contemporary photographs, newspaper reports, narratives, and reviews to chronicle Ellington's life, performance, and recording sessions. Volume one covers the first 21 years of his life, including daily and monthly activities and performing engagements. Also includes numerous rare photographs, reprints of news articles, and illustrations of posters from many of his performance venues; volume 2 begins with Ellington's return from his band's European tour in June of 1950, and covers his life until his death in 1974. He includes all known club, concert, film, jam session, television, theater, and the Ellington orchestras complete itinerary. A selected list of Ellington's recordings is also included.

Ethel Ennis

550. Kravetz, Sallie. *Ethel Ennis: The Reluctant Jazz Star.* Baltimore: Hughes; 1984.

Biography of the bandleader, vocalist, and pianist that traces her career from Baltimore through rhythm and blues influences and her jazz achievements. The impact of Billie Holiday, Sarah Vaughan, and Dinah Washington in shaping her style and her participation on the Arthur Godfrey Show are also discussed.

Pee Wee Erwin

551. Erwin, Pee Wee, and Warren W. Vaché, Sr. *Pee Wee Erwin: This Horn for Hire.* Foreword by William M. Weinberg. Metuchen, New Jersey, London: Scarecrow; 1987.

Comprehensive and detailed autobiography of the author's life, musical associations, and achievements, laden with discussions of his music. Much of the text is based on Erwin's recollections, although it was published in 1987, seven years after his death. Discography, index, illustrations.

James Reese Europe

552. Badger, Reid. *A Life in Ragtime: A Biography of James Reese Europe.* New York: Oxford University Press; 1995.

Details the life of the ragtime composer and conductor from his birth in Alabama in 1880 to his murder in 1919. Includes details of his activities with the Clef Club Orchestra, the diffusion of ragtime to Europe, his cultural and educational work in the African American community, and his achievements as the first African American officer to lead a World War I combat unit. Also important for jazz-related activities.

Gil Evans

553. Crease, Stephanie Stein. *Gil Evans Out of the Cool: His Life and Music.* Chicago: A Cappella Books; 2002.

Chronicles the pathos of his life, associations, and achievements. Portrays Evans as more than Miles Davis's arranger and friend, and focuses on his artistic philosophy, problems with record companies and promoters, and the refusal of many to acknowledge and appreciate his newer musical creations. Also covers his family life, enduring friendships with artists such as Miles Davis, Steve Lacy, and Gerry Mulligan, and resolute determination to remain true to his creative ideas.

554. Horricks, Raymond. *Svengali, or the Orchestra Called Gil Evans.* Turnbridge Wells, England: Spellmount, 1984; New York: Hippocrene Books, 1984.

Biodiscography of Evans, detailing his orchestrating style and musical associations with excellent insights into his association with Miles Davis. As Horricks stated, "He has put together sounds with combinations of instruments which for decades the academic colleges have told us just won't work" (p. 13). The biography provides details of how this was accomplished. Selected discography by Tony Middleton (recordings of his bands and with others).

Ella Fitzgerald

555. Colin, Sid. *Ella: The Life and Times of Ella Fitzgerald.* London: Elm Tree Books; 1986.

Covers her career from an amateur night performance at the Harlem Opera House through her associations with Louis Armstrong, Ray Brown, Duke Ellington, Oscar Peterson, and several more. The book is permeated with details of performances, important dates and events, and details of her honors and awards. Selected discography and an index.

556. David, Norman. *The Ella Fitzgerald Companion.* Westport, Conn: Praeger Press; 2004.

A celebration of her recordings and contributions to jazz. The guide includes information on her recordings, important influences, and collaborators. Also included is an overview of American popular singing as viewed through the accomplishments of Fitzgerald. The volume concludes with a comprehensive discography of reissued albums that are now on compact disc. Foreword by Tad Hershorn.

557. Gourse, Leslie (editor). *The Ella Fitzgerald Companion.* New York: Schirmer Books; 1998.

A collection of articles that race Fitzgerald's career from the winning of a talent contest at the Apollo to a celebration of her success as a leading jazz vocalist. Includes information on her style and influences.

558. Jungermann, Jimmy. *Ella Fitzgerald: Ein Porträt.* Wetzlar, Germany: Pegasus; 1960.

In German. A concise biography that covers her life, musical achievements, early influences, and associations to the late 1950s. Selected bibliography and discography. Illustrated.

559. Kliment, Bud. *Ella Fitzgerald.* Foreword by Coretta Scott King. New York: Chelsea; 1988.

Children's biography, which covers her life and musical achievements. Chronology, selected bibliography, discography, and an index.

560. Nicholson, Ella. *Ella Fitzgerald.* New York: Da Capo Press; 1993.

Chronicles the story of her rise from poverty to becoming one of the greatest jazz vocalists of all time. Covers her association with numerous musicians including Duke Ellington and Chick Webb, and highlights her unique style, accomplishments, and influences.

561. Nolden, Rainer. *Ella Fitzgerald: Seine Leben, seine Musik, seine Schallplatten.* Waakirchen, Germany: Oreos; 1986.

In German. Covers her musical beginnings, associations, influences, early piano experiences, and eventual transformation into a significant scat singer. Comprehensive discussion of her recordings. Illustrated.

562. Reginald, Oscar. *Ella Fitzgerald Story.* New York: Stein & Day; 1971.

Discusses Fitzgerald's life and musical career, including information on musicians with whom she performed or was associated. The biography is positive and informative not only for its account of her career but also for its insight into the music of several other prominent artists. Fitzgerald's associations with Chick Webb and Duke Ellington as well as her role as leader of her own bands are also chronicled. Selected bibliography and discography (addition to 1981).

563. Vail, Ken. *Ella Fitzgerald: The Chick Webb Years and Beyond.* Lanham, Md.: Scarecrow Press; 2003.

Like others in the series, this 96-page book chronicles her musical career from the time she was discovered by Chick Webb, the shock of Webb's early death, her years as a bandleader, success as a soloist, marriage to Ray Brown, and her first tour of England.

Herb Fleming

564. Biagioni, Egino. *Herb Fleming: A Jazz Pioneer Around the World.* Alphen aan de Rijn: Micrography; 1977.

The only publication to date on this important musician. Although he was not a jazz pioneer, he was important because he traveled and performed extensively in Europe; his performing/recording career spanned from 1919 to 1969. He traveled with Sam Wooding and recorded with Duke Ellington, Fats Waller, and several additional African American musicians. In addition, Flemming's (1898–1976) contact with African American musicians provided penetrating insights into the role and status of these musicians; Biagioni used unpublished material left by Flemming as the source for this biography. Flemming was also one of the limited number of jazz musicians of foreign descent (Tunisian and Egyptian parents) active in jazz, 1919–69. Selected discography.

Pops Foster

565. Foster, Pops. *Pops Foster: The Autobiography of a New Orleans Jazzman,* as told to Tom Stoppard. Berkeley: University of California Press; 1971.

Presents an accurate picture of the music and musicians of New Orleans from 1899 to 1919. Details of Foster's life and music are presented from his early New Orleans beginnings through his life in New York and his travels with Louis Armstrong. The introduction by Bertram Turetzky contains some information on his bass technique. A chronological list of the groups that he performed with, a discography by Ross Russell, and an index are also included (1981).

Pete Fountain

566. Fountain, Pete. *A Closer Walk: The Pete Fountain Story;* with Bill Neely. Chicago: Regnery; 1972.

Autobiography, ghosted by Bill Neely, that details the clarinetist's life and music. Included is information on Fountain's successful tenure with

Lawrence Welk, his role as a combo leader, and his successful return to New Orleans. Selected discography.

Bud Freeman

567. Freeman, Bud. *You Don't Look Like a Musician.* Detroit: BaLamp Publishing; 1974.

Anecdotal commentaries and recollections of fellow musicians. Contains numerous stories; useful for insider perspectives of musicians active during Freeman's career (mostly Chicago). Index.

568. _____. *If You Know of a Better Life! Please Tell Me.* Dublin: Bashall Eaves; 1975.

Continuation of the anecdotal commentaries, recollections, and stories presented in *You Don't Look Like a Musician.* Covers his musical associations in Chicago; less comprehensive (61 pages), than his first book (125 pages). No index.

569. _____. *Crazeology: The Autobiography of a Chicago Jazzman;* told to Robert Wolf, with a foreword by Studs Terkel. Urbana: University of Illinois Press; 1989.

Insider perspective of his musical career and achievements in Chicago, New York, and Europe. He provides information on history, musical peers, venues, and the life of the times.

Errol Garner

570. Doran, James M. *Errol Garner: The Most Happy Piano.* Foreword by Dan Morgenstern. Metuchen, N.J., and London: Scarecrow; 1985.

Based on oral history, the biography is permeated with historical references to his life and musical achievements and provides important data on his popular and jazz credentials. Chronology of musical achievements, bibliography, discography, filmography, index, and illustrations.

Stan Getz

571. Palmer, Richard. *Stan Getz.* London: Apollo; 1989.

Covers his life from his breakthrough performance on Woody Herman's *Summer Sequence Part IV* in 1947 to and through his years as an icon of cool jazz. Also covers his associations with Norman Granz's Verve label, with cool jazz, debt to Lester Young, and his bold foray into bossa nova jazz in the 1960s. Includes a selected discography and references.

Terry Gibbs

572.   Gibbs, Terry, and Gary Ginell. *Good Times: A Life in Jazz.* Lanham, Maryland, and Institute of Jazz Studies (Rutgers University); 2003.

An autobiography that traces the evolution of jazz from the post-war years to the rise of bebop. He includes anecdotes, attributes, and quirks of musicians such as Steve Allen, Benny Goodman, Billie Holiday, Chubby Jackson, Buddy Rich, Frank Sinatra, and many more. Also, he acknowledges the influence of bebop pioneers Dizzy Gillespie, Charles Parker, and Bud Powell.

Dizzy Gillespie

573.   Gourse, Leslie. *Dizzy Gillespie and the Birth of Bebop.* New York: Atheneum Publishers; 1994.

Written for students in grades 6 to 10, Gourse traces the life of Gillespie by focusing on his musical development, personal relationships, and bands. She portrays Gillespie as an innovator, committed to the development of progressive jazz, contributions to the birth of bebop, revulsion of alcohol and drugs, and contributions to the civil rights movement in the United States. The sources of some quotes are missing.

574.   Gillespie, Dizzy. *To Be or Not—To Bop: Memoirs,* with Al Fraser. Garden City: Doubleday, 1979; retitled, *Dizzy: The Autobiography of Dizzy Gillespie;* with Al Fraser. London: W. H. Allen; 1980.

A comprehensive account of Gillespie's life and musical career, the autobiography is based on the detailed recollections and reminiscences of Gillespie and 150 people, including family members, friends, and especially musicians. Of particular importance are Gillespie's recollections of music changes, context, and culture. Among the musicians cited are Milt Hinton, Budd Johnson, and Max Roach. A chronology of his life to the time of his White House concert in 1978, a discography of his developments and innovations, a filmography, and an index are included.

575.   Horricks, Raymond. *Dizzy Gillespie and the Be-Bop Revolution.* Turnbridge Wells, England: Spellmount, 1984; New York: Hippocrene Books, 1984.

Biodiscography of this giant. The biographical portion chronicles Gillespie's life and musical career to the early 1980s. Included are anecdotes and recollections of other musicians and information on his musical associations, personnel, tours. Selected references to compositions. Selected discography by Tony Middleton.

576. James, Michael. *Dizzy Gillespie.* London: Cassell, 1959; New York: Barnes, 1961.

A biomusical assessment of the life and music of Gillespie to 1957. The author analyzes the evolution of his style and notes Gillespie's importance in the development of modern jazz. James addresses Gillespie's role as a catalyst for change in the 1940s and offers comments on his recordings. A selected discography of 1939–57 is included (addition to 1981).

577. Shipton, Alyn. *Groovin' High: The Life of Dizzy Gillespie.* New York: Oxford University Press; 1999.

Traces his life and music from his early years in Cheraw, South Carolina, to his death in 1993. The author discusses Gillespie's fear of his father, move to New York, associations with numerous musicians, and role in developing bebop. Includes coverage of his years with Cab Calloway, Earl Hines, Billy Eckstine, and role as director of big bands. Important insights into his relationship with Louis Armstrong, Miles Davis, Thelonious Monk, Charles Parker, and love of Afro-Cuban music are included.

578. Tanner, Lee (compiler and editor). *Dizzy;* introduction by Jeff Kaliss and essay by Gene Lees. San Francisco: Pomegranate Art Books; 1991.

Pays homage to Gillespie on his 75th birthday by examining his career from the 1940s to the early 1990s. The book includes numerous photographs with quotations by and about Gillespie. Lee's essay is permeated with anecdotes and remembrances of encounters with Gillespie. This is not a history or scholarly analysis of his music.

579. Vail, Ken. *Dizzy Gillespie: The Bebop Years 1937–1952.* Lanham, Md.: Scarecrow Press; 2003.

One of the books written in *Ken Vail's Jazz Itineraries* series. In this book, only 96 pages, he chronicles Gillespie's life from his early struggles and childhood years in South Carolina, role in the birth and performance of bebop, the demise of his big bands, relationship with Thelonious Monk, Charles Parker, and others, and his departure to France in 1952.

580. Wölfer, Jürgen. *Dizzy Gillespie: Sein Leben, seine Musik, seine Schallplatten.* Waakirchen, Germany: Oreos; 1987.

In German. A thorough discussion of his life and recordings with special emphasis on the bebop years and his association with Charles Parker. His roles as bebop innovator, postbebop survivor, and father figure are also covered. Numerous recordings are cited and discussed. Illustrated.

Babs Gonzales

581.   Gonzales, Babs. *I Paid My Dues: Good Time ... No Bread.* East Orange, N.J.: Expubidence Publishing Corporation; 1967.

Deals primarily with Gonzales's extramusical activities with little information on his musical style. The book does provide insight into some followers of bebop. Only surface attention is given to other musicians of the 1940s and 1950s (addition to 1981).

582.   _____. *Movin' On Down de Line.* Newark, N.J.: Expubidence Publishing Corporation; 1975.

Continuation of issues and concerns covered in *I Paid My Dues: Good Time ... No Bread.* Covers critical appraisals of the drug scene, music business, racism, and unscrupulous characters.

Benny Goodman

583.   Collier, James Lincoln. *Benny Goodman and the Swing Era.* New York: Oxford University Press; 1989.

The third in a trilogy of biographies by the author (the others were on Armstrong and Ellington). In this book, Collier presents a warm appraisal of the man and his music. Collier reveals that it was Goodman's music that catapulted him toward a career in music. He speculates whether he would have been a good trumpeter; uses the insights of James T. Maher to delineate the contributions of Art Hickman and Ferdé Grofé; speculates on why Goodman favored specific chord progressions; how he compared to other clarinetists, and more. The author, however, does not address the relationship between Artie Shaw and Goodman, nor does he mention that Leonard Ware preceded Charlie Christian as the guitarist in Goodman's sextet. He covers figures like Ann Graham, Adrian Rollini, and Arthur Schutt. The chapter on "Marriage and Family" contains important insights into Goodman's personal life. Chapter notes, selected discography, and an index.

584.   Connor, Donald Russell. *Benny Goodman: Wrappin' It Up.* Lanham, Md.: Scarecrow Press, and Institute of Jazz Studies (Rutgers University); 1996.

Meticulously researched and inclusive of historical and personal facts regarding the man, his music, associations, and significance. Portrays

Goodman as both a serious and significant artist, inclusion of African American artists into his band, relationship with John Hammond, and humorous anecdotes regarding some of his experiences.

585. _____. *The Record of a Legend: Benny Goodman.* New York: Let's Dance, 1984; Westport, Conn.: Greenwood Press, 1985.

An unauthorized biodiscography that details Goodman's early life and musical influences, his rise to stardom, his penchant to include African Americans in his band, and his association with John Hammond. Index, illustrated.

586. Connor, Donald Russell, and Warren W. Hicks. *B. G. on the Record: A Bio-Discography of Benny Goodman.* New Rochelle, N.Y.: Arlington House; 1969.

Extends and revises *B. G. Off the Record,* with biomusical information on Goodman to 1968. The chronology of Goodman's musical life begins with his joining Ben Pollack's band and continues through his immense success in the 1930s, 1940s, 1950s, and 1960s. Particularly interesting are the author's critical comments on some of Goodman's recordings. A chronological, fully detailed discography of all Goodman's recordings is included along with tune titles and indices to radio and television programs and films.

587. Crowther, Bruce. *Benny Goodman.* London: Apollo; 1988.

A musical biography, which includes references to many recordings covering both his big band trio/quartet as well as the role and function of selected sidemen. Selected bibliography, discography, and filmography.

588. Firestone, Ross. *Swing, Swing, Swing: The Life and Times of Benny Goodman.* New York: W. W. Norton and Company; 1993.

Covers his life and experiences as seen through the eyes of his fans, managers, and players. The book is permeated with anecdotes and recollections and contains information on Goodman's associations with African American musicians, especially Fletcher Henderson. Overall, the author chronicles Goodman's position as an influential musician in twentieth-century popular music. Selected bibliography, chapter notes, and an index.

589. Goodman, Benny, and Stanley Baron. *Benny: King of Swing: A Pictorial Biography based on Benny Goodman's Personal Archives.* London: Thames and Hudson, 1979; New York: Morrow, 1979; New York: Da Capo, 1987.

Pictorial biography with text. The photographs cover several performance situations and the text includes information pertinent to context and history. Includes 212 photographs covering his sidemen, friends, and family.

The photographs also include his travels abroad and interaction with musicians from other cultures.

590.   Goodman, Benny, and Irving Kolodin. *The Kingdom of Swing.* New York: Stackpole; London: Allen, 1939; Reprint, New York: Ungar, 1961.

Discusses the life and music of Goodman to 1939, including details on his bands, travels, and musical associations. The characteristics of swing are discussed in a chapter entitled "Swing Is Here." Also included is information on the acceptance of Goodman by other musicians and his associations with John Hammond and African American musicians, especially Fletcher Henderson.

591.   Wachler, Ingolf. *Benny Goodman: Ein Porträt.* Foreword by Hans Reinfeldt. Wetzlar, Germany: Pegasus; 1961.

In German. A concise portrait that covers his early life in Chicago, entry into jazz, rise to stardom, musical associations, and influences. Selected discography, illustrated.

Dexter Gordon

592.   Britt, Stan. *Long Tall Dexter.* London, New York: Quartet Books; 1989.

Provides insights into his beginning in Los Angeles and evolution into a world-class tenor saxophonist from his years on Central Avenue (Los Angeles), his time in New York, and his expatriate experiences. Comments from other musicians regarding his recordings, gigs, and associations punctuate the biography. A bibliography, index, and discography by Don Tarrant are included.

593.   _____. *Dexter Gordon: A Musical Biography.* New York: Da Capo; 1989.

A retitled edition of *Long Tall Dexter,* this rendition is based on numerous interviews with Gordon's peers as well as with Gordon himself. The format was to focus on Gordon's music and contributions within the context of an overall jazz picture. Contains anecdotes and stories, details of the development of his style. His belief that being able to interpret song texts was crucial to instrumental jazz is noteworthy. Selected bibliography, comprehensive discography, and an index.

Stéphane Grappelli

594. Horricks, Raymond. *Stéphane Grappelli, or Violin with Wings.* Turnbridge, England, and Midas, N.Y.: Hippocrene, 1983; New York: Da Capo, 1985.

Details his life as a jazz violinist from the 1930s to the 1990s. Covers his tenure with Louis Vola, Django Reinhardt and the quintet, the deterioration of his relationship with Reinhardt, the impact of the war on his career, and his eventual travel and rise to fame in America. Selected discography by Tony Middleton, index, illustrated.

595. Smith, Geoffrey. *Stéphane Grappelli: A Biography.* London: Joseph; 1987.

Covers his entry into jazz, the Paris years, his associations with Louis Vola and Django Reinhardt, career accomplishments, and analysis of his style, contributions, and significance. Also, there is a discussion of the use of the violin in jazz. Discography by Brian Rust, index, and illustrations.

Grant Green

596. Green, Sharony Andrews. *Grant Green: Rediscovering the Forgotten Genius of Jazz Guitar.* San Francisco: Miller Freeman Books; 1999.

Because critics often dismissed the bulk of Green's output from the late 1960s and 1970s, the author concentrates on presenting a more inclusive perspective on the man and his music. The author believes Green's music is enjoying a revival because hip-hop groups and acid jazz fans have discovered him through the sampling of others. In addition, the author espouses that Green's "earthy feel was an important contribution to jazz." Selected reviews, discography, and references.

Lars Gullin

597. Knox, Keith, and Gunnar Lindqvist. *Jazz Amour Affair: En Bok om Lars Gullin.* Stockholm: Svensk; 1986.

In Swedish. A biography of Lars Gullin, Swedish baritone saxophonist. In addition to his life, musical influences, and accomplishments, there is a comprehensive analysis of his style. The analytical section includes transcriptions by Pelle Broberg and Lars Sjösten of several compositions by Gullin including "Danny's Dream," "For F.J. Fans Only," "Portrait of

My Pals," and "The Aching Heart of Oak." Very thorough analysis. Discography by Pär Rittsel, illustrated.

Connie Haines

598.   Haines, Connie. *For Once in My Life;* as told to Robert B. Stone. New York: Warner Books; 1976.

Covers the former jazz vocalist's life and career from her associations with the Tommy Dorsey and Harry James bands and her radio broadcasts to her ordination as a minister in the Unity Church. Also included are references to her gospel singing. Few references to musical style, concentrates on the "story" of her life.

John Hammond

599.   Hammond, John. *John Hammond on Record: An Autobiography;* with Irving Townsend. New York: Ridge Press, 1977. Reprint, Harmondsworth: Penguin Books, 1981.

A pioneer in the discovery and promotion of African American musicians in jazz, Hammond is one of the most significant disseminators of jazz of the 1930s and 1940s. The former brother-in-law of Benny Goodman was an active foe of racism; he was a member of the NAACP dating to the Scottsboro trials of the 1930s. Hammond believed "to bring recognition to the Negro's supremacy in jazz was the most effective and constructive form of social protest I could think of" (p. 68). He was significant in promoting the careers of numerous musicians—Count Basie, Charlie Christian, Benny Goodman, Billie Holiday (her first recording opportunity), Teddy Wilson—and eventually rock stars such as Bob Dylan and Bruce Springsteen, to name a few.

Lionel Hampton

600.   Hampton, Lionel, with James Haskins. *Hamp: An Autobiography.* New York: Warner Publications; 1989.

Chronicles the life and music of Hampton, however, the book contains several contradictions and lacks proper documentation in some cases. For example: "In the spring of 1944 I signed on with a label called Black Jack and I did my first LP with my own band" (p. 80). He later contradicts this statement by stating "In May-June 1944, I did an LP for the Joyce label" (p. 80). The controversy over the death of Bessie Smith ensues because of Richard Morgan's description (Lionel Hampton's uncle) compared to Haskin's account. Even though proper documentation is lacking in some cases, there are some important revelations in this autobiography. Index and "The Complete Commodore Jazz Recordings," by Vincent Pelote.

Hampton Hawes

601. Hawes, Hampton, and Don Asher. *Raise Up Off Me: A Portrait of Hampton Hawes.* New York: Coward, McCann, and Geohegan; 1974; reprint with new introduction by Gary Giddins. New York: Da Capo; 1979.

A penetrating account of this excellent bebop pianist's life, musical associations, and musical context. Although Hawes spent part of his life incarcerated (he was pardoned by President Kennedy), he was one of the best pianists of the bebop era. He provides insightful assessments of Thelonious Monk, Billie Holiday, and Charles Parker. Hawkes also provides a critical view of the bebop era, especially the cultural context.

Coleman Hawkins

602. Chilton, John. *The Song of the Hawk: The Life and Recordings of Coleman Hawkins.* Ann Arbor: University of Michigan Press; 1990.

A comprehensive account of Hawkins's life and music based on detailed documentation and quotes. In addition to his meticulous research, what is interesting about this book is the author's balanced approach. He details Hawkins's musical contributions, including his approach to improvisation and his influence on other jazz musicians, in a chronological manner. Only selected recordings are discussed. Selected bibliography and discography.

603. James, David Burnett. *Coleman Hawkins.* Turnbridge, England and Spellmount, New York: Hippocrene; 1984.

Covers his musical life, achievements, and the scope of his influence. Also covers his tenure with Fletcher Henderson (1923–34) and alludes to his influence on Sonny Rollins and John Coltrane. His significance as a harmonic improviser and impact beyond swing are also discussed. Selected discography by Tony Middleton. Annotated bibliography. Illustrations.

604. McCarthy, Albert J. *Coleman Hawkins.* London: Cassell; 1963.

Provides biographical information and analyzes Hawkins's recordings in three sections (1924–39; 1939–49; and 1949–62) to illustrate the development of his saxophone style. Comments on style, title of compositions, and personnel are contained in the author's assessment of Hawkins's recordings. A selected discography is included (addition to 1981).

Ted Heath

605.   Heath, Ted. *Listen to My Music: An Autobiography.* London: Muller; 1957.

Life of the British jazz band director whose band included many of the leading British jazz musicians in the 1940s and 1950s. Also contains information on his contacts with American jazz artists and their influence on him. Selected discography (addition to 1981).

Fletcher Henderson

606.   Allen, Walter C. *Hendersonia: The Music of Fletcher Henderson and His Musicians: A Bio-Discography.* Highland Park, New Jersey: Author; 1973.

Details Henderson's musical career with biographical and discographical materials. The discographies include all known recordings featuring Henderson as a performer or conductor as well as all known sessions recorded with Henderson musicians. The author also offers a chronological list of Henderson's compositions, a catalog of his arrangements, biographical rosters of his musicians and vocalists, tune titles, and more. An excellent portrait of the life and music of Fletcher Henderson. Selected bibliography and a comprehensive discography that details date of recording, venue, title, arranger, vocalist if applicable, soloists, tempo, matrix, and take number (addition to 1981).

607.   Audibert, M. *Fletcher Henderson ET son orchestre, 1924–1951: Sa place dans L'histoire du Jazz.* Bayonne, France: U.P.; 1983.

In French. Details his career, role in establishing swing, and subsequent influence on Benny Goodman. Also discusses his associations with Don Redman, Coleman Hawkins, and significance as a composer-arranger. No new insights. Selected bibliography.

Woody Herman

608.   Clancy, William D., with Audree Coke Kenton. *Woody Herman: Chronicles of the Herds.* New York: Schirmer Books; 1995.

Contains factual information and insightful comments about Herman and his bands. The author solicited quotes and reminiscences from Herman's personnel since his band was first organized in 1936. Among the numerous musicians who contributed information were Bill Byrne, Chubby Jackson,

Nat Pierce, and Shorty Rogers. Among the most interesting chapters is "Road Father—The Fusion Era: 1968–1979." Notes and bibliography.

609. Herman, Woody, with Stuart Troup. *The Woodchopper's Ball: The Autobiography of Woody Herman.* New York: Dutton; 1990.

Covers Herman's "Herds" bands from the mid-1940s to the "Four Brothers" and subsequent groups. There are numerous anecdotes and reminiscences from his former band members, including Billy Bauer, Chubby Jackson, Don Lamond, and Nat Pierce. These insights focus on the music, personnel, travel, and related issues. Unfortunately, the accounts of his sidemen dominate, and we are not treated to enough insights from Herman himself. Selected bibliography, discography, and an index.

610. Kriebel, Robert C. *Blue Flame: Woody Herman's Life in Music.* West Lafayette, Ind.: Purdue University Press; 1995.

Considers Count Basie, Duke Ellington, and Woody Herman as three of the best and most important proponents of big band jazz. His nearly 60-year career is covered from its beginnings, and includes information on his penchant for the blues, the Herds, Four Brothers, and the painful years of personnel loss, financial distress, and physical pain of the late 1970s. Includes reference notes, some quotes, selected discography, and a bibliography.

611. Lees, Gene. *Leader of the Band: The Life of Woody Herman.* New York: Oxford University Press; 1995.

The book is based on the author's personal friendship with Herman, and presents a humorous and likeable musician. He draws upon interviews with other artists/people, exchanging of stories, and his knowledge of big bands to place Herman within the context of the big band era. He also touches on the respect that both he and other musicians had for Herman.

612. Voce, Steve. *Woody Herman.* London: Apollo; 1986.

Chronicles the history of Herman's groups, especially the First and Second Herd, The Four Brothers, and his various mid-1960s groups. Focuses on his significance as a bop-oriented big band leader. Also covers intimate details of his early life, marriage to Charlotte Neste, and relationship with artists such as Ralph Burns, Serge Chaloff, Flip Phillips, Stan Getz, Zoot Sims, Al Cohn, and Don Lamond. Selected discography by Tony Shoppee, bibliography, and illustrations.

Earl "Fatha" Hines

613. Dance, Stanley. *The World of Earl Hines.* New York: Scribner's, 1977; New York: Da Capo, 1985.

Discusses the career of Fatha Hines drawing on personal interviews and the author's friendship with Hines. The book contains some important information on the people who performed with Hines but has few in-depth references to his style. Dance allows other musicians to provide their assessments of Hines as a man and musician, thereby confirming, clarifying, and occasionally contradicting each other. In this sense, Dance allows the reader to elicit the truth from this morass. Among the most informative stories is that of Hines' associations with Louis Armstrong and Charles Parker. Biographies of the personnel of the 1946 band, selected discography, and an index (addition to 1981).

Milt Hinton

614.   Hinton, Milt, and David G. Berger. *Bass Line: The Stories and Photographs of Milt Hinton.* Philadelphia: Temple University Press; 1988.

Details Hinton's life and musical achievements from his childhood in Vicksburg, Mississippi; embryonic musical experiences in Chicago in the 1920s; life on the road with Cab Calloway; experiences in New York, and other performances and travels. The book is permeated with his encounters with, and reactions to, racism, as experienced in the aforementioned contexts. These experiences are represented in both text and graphic photographs, for example, ones showing African American musicians such as Chu Berry, Doc Cheatham, and Tyree Glenn standing next to signs stating "For Colored Only," "Colored Entrance," and others. There are also photographs of major concerts, festivals, and recording sessions. Selected reference notes, discography, and an index.

Art Hodes

615.   Hodes, Art, and Chadwick Hansen. *Hot Man: The Life of Art Hodes.* Urbana: University of Illinois Press; 1992.

Details the musical experiences of Art Hodes in Chicago and New York. Hodes describes his early years in Chicago clubs, his New York years, his involvement in jazz of the 1940s, his affinity for blues and his "Chicago style," his associations with African American and white musicians, including Louis Armstrong, Bix Beiderbecke, Sidney Bechet, Pops Foster, Baby Dodds, Chippie Hill, Mama Yancey, and his efforts to educate people about jazz. Selected bibliography, and discography by Howard Rye.

Allan Holdsworth

616.   Holdsworth, Allan, and Christopher Hoard. *Allan Holdsworth: Reaching for the Uncommon Chord.* London: Twenty First Century; 1988.

Autobiography of the British guitarist's career, achievements, influences, associations, and role in British jazz. Contains four transcriptions by Fred Amendola ("Home", "Three Sheets to the Wind", "Tokyo Dream", and "White Line") with analysis. Offers insights into British jazz history.

Billie Holiday

617. Chilton, John. *Billie's Blues: A Survey of Billie Holiday's Career, 1933–1959.* New York: Stein & Day; London: Quarter Books; 1975.

    Approaches Holiday's life without sentimentality. In this well-researched study, the author comments on Holiday's musical style and how Holiday incorporated her life experiences into her style. Buck Clayton wrote the foreword. Chilton comments on both her vocal style and how her music reflected her life. A comprehensive bibliography covering 1933–74, list of acknowledgments, and a discography organized chronologically (addition to 1981).

618. Clarke, Donald. *Wishing on The Moon.* New York: Viking; 1994.

    A discussion of her early years in Baltimore, her musical relationships with Count Basie, Artie Shaw, Lester Young, and others. Offers insight into her drug addiction, career highlights and lowlights, and influence on other jazz vocalist.

619. DeVeaux, Alexis. *Don't Explain: A Song of Billie Holiday.* New York: Harper and Row Publishers; 1980.

    A biography that recounts Holiday's life, joys, and sorrows. Much of the book is taken from *Lady Sings the Blues* (William Dufty and Billie Holiday), and *Billie's Blues: The Story of Billie Holiday* (John Chilton). Includes two musical excerpts, but no discussion. No new insights.

620. Gourse, Leslie (editor). *The Billie Holiday Companion.* New York: Schirmer Books; 1997.

    The collection of essays focus on her beginnings in Baltimore, drug addiction, relationship with Lester Young, career, and more. Her associations with Count Basie, Benny Goodman, and Artie Shaw are also discussed.

621. Holiday, Billie. *Lady Sings the Blues.* Garden City, New York: Doubleday, 1956; New York: Lancer, 1956, 1965, 1969, 1972; Stockholm: Rabén & Sjögren, 1956; Hamburg: Hoffman & Campe, 1957; København: Gyldendal, 1957; Oslo: Mortensen, 1957; Tokyo: Seiwa, 1957; New York: Popular Library, 1958; London: Barrie & Jenkins, 1958, 1973; Milano: Londanesi, 1959; Paris: Plon, 1960; London: Harborough, 1960; London: Jazz Book Club, 1960; Paris: Club de Meilleur, 1960; Tokyo: Chikuma, 1963, 1968;

Hamburg: Rowohlt, 1964; London: Deutsch, 1966; London: Sphere, 1973; London: Abacus, 1975; New York: Avon, 1976; Marseille: Parenthèses, c.1980; Hamburg: n.1., 1983; New York: Penguin; 1984.

Stresses Holiday's life and the problems in her musical career rather than her musical style. The book deals with her start in jazz, her experiences with the Artie Shaw and Count Basie bands, and the so-called true account of her problem with drugs. Albert McCarthy contributed the comprehensive discography in the Barrie and Jenkins edition (1973) (addition to 1981).

622.   James, Burnett. *Billie Holiday.* Turnbridge, England and Spellmount, New York: Hippocrene Books; 1984.

Details her childhood in Baltimore, her drug addiction, and eventual fall from grace. He discusses her first recording in 1933, and her associations with Benny Goodman, Count Basie, Lester Young, and Artie Shaw. Holiday's role as a jazz innovator is also chronicled. Tony Middleton contributes a selective discography, which provides personnel, title, venue, and album number for each citation.

623.   Kuell, Linda, and Ellie Schokert. *Billie Holiday Remembered.* New York: New York Jazz Museum; 1973.

A 20-page booklet that is permeated with anecdotes and recollections of six people who either knew or performed with Holiday. Anecdotes and recollections cover her music and life, especially the impact of drugs on her career.

624.   Nabe, Marc-Edouard. *L'ame de Billie Holiday.* Paris: Denoel; 1986.

In French. Discusses how 34 songs performed by Holiday relate to her life experiences. Among the songs included are "Don't Explain," "God Bless the Child," "Strange Fruit," "No Regrets," "Gloomy Sunday," "Billie's Blues," and "Fine and Mellow." Covers her experiences with drugs, men, and racism.

625.   Nicholson, Stuart. *Billie Holiday.* Boston: Northeastern University Press; 1995.

Divided into 13 chapters, the author attempts to correct misrepresentations and factual errors found in the six biographies of Holiday published before 1995. Because many of the pre-1995 biographies relied on John Chilton's *Billie's Blues: The Story of Billie Holiday,* and that work was plagued by flaws and omissions, the author's major contribution was to correct existing factual and historical errors regarding her life. Among the corrections are the facts regarding her relationship with attorney Earle Warren Zaidins.

626. O'Meally, Robert. *Lady Day: The Many Faces of Billie Holiday.* New York: Arcade Publishing; 1993.

Deciphers Holiday's approach to singing by using word, image, and critical analysis to affirm her stature as the quintessential jazz chanteuse. He uses analysis to detail her career from her discovery of her singing ability to the triumphs and failures of her career. In addition, he treats Holiday as a serious musician and tracks her vocal approaches through several changes. Selected bibliography.

627. White, John. *Billie Holiday.* Turnbridge Wells, Kent: Spellmount Ltd.; New York: Universe Books; 1987.

Provides new and informative insights into her early years in Baltimore, Maryland. Holiday's problems as the first African American female to sing with an all-white band (Artie Shaw) are also covered. Bibliography and a selected discography.

Claude Hopkins

628. Vaché, Warren W. *Crazy Fingers, Claude Hopkins' Life in Jazz.* Washington, D.C.: Smithsonian Institution Press; 1992.

Covers the career of one of the most successful bandleaders of the 1920s and 1930s. He was the music director of Josephine Baker's first European tour, leader of house bands at the Savoy and Roseland ballrooms, and played some jobs as a sideman. The author used Hopkins own journal, and interviewed several musicians who knew him to complete the biography. Important because it sheds light on the 1920s to 1970s jazz world, and because it chronicles his struggles to find work in the Prohibition era.

Paul Horn

629. Horn, Paul, with Lee Underwood. *Inside Paul Horn: The Spiritual Odyssey of a Universal Traveler.* San Francisco: Harper San Francisco; 1990.

Permeated with insider perspectives by one of the most creative and innovative musicians of recent years. He covers his life and times, through his belief in one creator, one humanity, one world, and of music as a potent force for change evolved. His work with Duke Ellington, Miles Davis, Chico Hamilton, Buddy Rich, Ravi Shankar, Tony Bennett, Frank Sinatra, and the Beatles is chronicled. The book is about musical creativity and transformation, psychological evolution, and spiritual transformation. Selected discography.

Milt Jackson

630.   Wilbraham, Roy. *Milt Jackson: A Discography and Biography including Recordings Made with MJQ*. London: Frognal Bookshop; 1968.

Life and musical recordings with complete discography details. Covers his musical life before MJQ, his role and function within MJQ, and issues that led to the break-up of MJQ. Includes information on both his contributions to and influences of other jazz artists.

Harry James

631.   Levinson, Peter J. *Trumpet Blues: The Life of Harry James*. New York: Oxford University Press; 1999.

Copious details regarding his life, music, relationships, travel, and contributions to jazz. Includes references to recordings, his infatuation with bebop, and his accomplishments as a bandleader. The coverage begins in the early 1930s and continues for five decades. The author believes James's tender ballads helped to allay the loneliness and anxiety Americans were experiencing during the war years. In addition, he reveals that James attempted to build his band in the mold of Count Basie, and the respect artists such as Louis Armstrong, Miles Davis, Roy Eldridge, Dizzy Gillespie, and others had for James. Thoroughly researched with notes and a bibliography.

632.   Stacy, Frank. *Harry James' Pin-Up Life Story*. New York: Arco; 1944.

Chronicles his life and musical beginnings to his immense success as a band leader/trumpeter. Also offers important insights into swing as well as his musical influences. Index.

Keith Jarrett

633.   Andersen, Uwe. *Keith Jarrett: Seine Leben, seine Musik, seine Schallplatten*. Waakirchen, Germany: Oreos; 1985.

In German. The biography traces his early musical experiences, influences, and interest in classical music and jazz. Covers his stints with Miles Davis, Art Blakey, his time as a leader of his own quartet (1971–76), and his role as an innovative solo pianist. Also includes coverage of his recordings to the mid-1980s. Illustrated.

634.   Carr, Ian. *Keith Jarrett, the Man and His Music*. London: Grafton Books, 1991; New York: Da Capo Press, 1992.

Jarrett is one of the most influential jazz pianists performing today. Carr follows his life and musical career from his first solo performance at the age of seven to his 1960s stints with the Jazz Messengers and Charles Lloyd, and his tenure with Miles Davis on electric keyboards in the 1970s before becoming a band leader and soloist. The book delineates his musical eclecticism; he performs both classical and jazz. His skill as a solo pianist is especially noteworthy. Selected bibliography, discography, reference notes, and an index.

James P. Johnson

635. Brown, Scott, and Robert Hilbert. *A Case of Mistaken Identity: The Life and Music of James P. Johnson.* Metuchen, N.J.: Scarecrow Press; 1986.

The biography focuses on Johnson's life, music, and contributions. Specifically, the authors place Johnson's contributions as composer and performer in proper perspective. Misconceptions of Johnson are also discussed, corrected, or refuted. Index.

636. Brown, Scott, and Robert Hilbert. *James P. Johnson: A Case of Mistaken Identity,* and *A James P. Johnson Discography 1917–1950.* Metuhen, N.J.: Scarecrow Press, and Institute of Jazz Studies (Rutgers); 1986.

Covers his life, musical career, compositions, and recording legacy. In the discography, Hilbert clarifies many of the obscure and misleading facts about Johnson's 1920s recordings. An important contribution because Johnson was proficient in several genres, and because he was a pivotal figure in the history and development of jazz.

637. Trolle, Frank H. *James P. Johnson: Father of Stride Piano.* Two volumes. Alphan, Netherlands: Micrography; 1981.

The biography covers his life from the early years in New Jersey and New York, his infatuation with both classical music and African American genres, especially ragtime and jazz, and ascent to prominence. His influence as a composer, membership in the Clef Club, and style are also discussed. The discography is comprehensive including both piano and sideman recordings.

J. J. Johnson

638. Baker, David N. *J. J. Johnson, Trombone.* New York: Hansen House; 1979.

Written by a prolific jazz scholar, performer (trombone and cello), composer (classical and jazz), and educator (Chairman of Jazz, Indiana University).

This is one of several monograms written by Baker, covering Clifford Brown and Charles Parker among others. The monogram contains a concise biographical sketch, genealogy, improvisation tendencies, and several transcriptions. Worksheets designed to equate various aspects of improvisation (harmony patterns, cycles, scales, etc.) are also included.

639. Berrett, Joshua, and Louis G. Bourgois. *The Musical World of J.J. Johnson.* Lanham, Md.: Scarecrow Press and Institute of Jazz Studies (Rutgers); 1999.

Produced with the cooperation of Johnson, this is the first full-length study of the composer and trombonist. They interviewed Johnson and present details of his early years in Indianapolis, 1924–42, and include insights from musical associates, family members, and a stylistic analysis of his compositions and improvisations. Includes a catalog of compositions, filmography, discography, and bibliography. An excellent addition to the literature.

Willie Greary "Bunk" Johnson

640. Hillman, Christopher. *Bunk Johnson.* Turnbridge, England, and Spellmount, N.Y.: Universe; 1988.

Discusses his career from his early days in New Orleans and his associations with Buddy Bolden, Sidney Bechet, and brass bands (Excelsior, Superior Orchestra, etc.). He also covers Johnson's Chicago years, musical decline, and his role and function as one of the New Orleans revivalists of the 1940s. No new insights. Bibliography, index, and illustrations.

641. Sonnier, Austin M. *Willie Greary "Bunk" Johnson: The New Iberia Years.* New York: Crescendo Publishing; 1977.

The book is divided into two parts; first, a concise biography and discography of his 1940s recordings, and second, musicians of the 1900–30 New Iberia (Louisiana) years. When Johnson dropped out of jazz in the 1920s he lived and worked as a fieldhand in New Iberia. He remained living there after his rediscovery by two jazz scholars in the 1940s (rebirth of his career). The book is also significant because it contains the personnel of 16 bands and biographical portraits of 47 musicians. Transcriptions of Johnson's "Milenberg Joys" and "I Can't Escape from You" end the book. No bibliography or index, selected discography.

Quincy Jones

642. Horricks, Raymond. *Quincy Jones.* Turnbridge, England, and Spellmount, N.Y.: Hippocrene; 1988.

Discusses his career in both jazz and popular music. Begins with his early years in Chicago and Seattle, his short career as a jazz trumpeter, stay at Berklee College of Music, and rise to fame as a composer/arranger. Offers insights into his significance as a composer/arranger for artists/bands such as Count Basie, Michael Jackson, and other special musical projects. Selected discography by Tony Middleton, filmography, list of awards, illustrations.

Louis Jordan

643. Chilton, John. *Let the Good Times Roll: The Story of Louis Jordan and His Music.* Ann Arbor: University of Michigan Press; 1994.

This entry is included because Jordan's roots are in jazz before he became an internationally renowned star in rhythm and blues. The book is based on interviews of Jordan's peers, employers, lovers, and recordings, and argues that Jordan anticipated rock and roll and rhythm and blues. The biography covers Jordan's personnel, evolution of his style, and insight into the difficulty of touring the segregated South.

Max Kaminsky

644. Kaminsky, Max. *My Life in Jazz;* with V. E. Hughes. New York: Harper and Row, 1963; London: Deutsch, 1964; New York: Da Capo, 1984.

Contains penetrating accounts of the trials and tribulations of musicians living in Chicago as well as the life and music of Kaminsky. The author also presents several portraits of musicians that he performed with, including Louis Armstrong, Tommy and Jimmy Dorsey, Artie Shaw, Bix Beiderbecke, Billie Holiday, Eddie Condon, Gene Krupa, Benny Goodman, and Pee Wee Russell. The recollections and anecdotes reveal information on the behind-the-scenes activities of the aforementioned musicians. Index.

Stan Kenton

645. Agostinelli, Anthony J. *Stan Kenton: The Many Musical Moods of His Orchestra.* Providence: privately printed; 1986.

Covers his career from the early California years through his swing years, progressive jazz, experiments with Afro-Cuban music and instrumentation, neophonic sounds, and more. The role of arranger/composers such as Johnny Richards is also discussed as is influence. Bibliography and discography.

646.   Arganian, Lillian. *The Man and His Music.* New York: Artistry Press; 1989.

Concern with his life and musical accomplishments. Also discusses the influence of his neophonic bands and style, and many of his alumni including Stan Getz, Lee Konitz, and others.

647.   Easton, Carol. *Straight Ahead: The Story of Stan Kenton.* New York: Morrow, 1973; reprint: Da Capo.

An account of the bandleader's musical life and contributions. Explores his years on the road, his bands, and private life. Also included are the recollections of his children, wives (3), and musicians. Only scant attention is given to Kenton's reactionary socioracial views. The book contains significant historical information on the forming-touring-dismantling of many of his bands.

648.   Lee, William F. *Stan Kenton: Artistry in Rhythm;* edited by Audree Coke with a foreword by Mort Sahl. Los Angeles: Creative Press; 1980.

Using extensive interviews of Kenton's family, band members, and associates as well as articles and newspaper clippings, the author outlines the life, music, and influences of this big band leader. The book contains anecdotes, stories, and reminiscences of musical associations. Also included are the impact of Afro-Cuban music on Kenton and the importance of some of his arrangers/composers, such as Johnny Richards. The five appendices contain personnel, appearances in films, a detailed listing of his arrangements and compositions, all recordings made on the Creative World record label, and a chronological listing of recordings made throughout the world.

649.   Pirie, Christopher A., and Siegfried Müller. *Artistry in Kenton: A Bio-discography of Stan Kenton and His Music.* Two volumes. Vienna: privately printed, 1969, 1973.

The biography focuses on his career, achievements, bands (swing, progressive, Afro-Cuban, etc.), sidemen, and contributions to jazz education. Kenton's ability to change and his impact upon the careers of artists like Lee Konitz, Art Pepper, Bud Shank, Lennie Niehaus, Stan Getz, and Zoot Sims is also alluded to. Discography of recordings from 1937 to 1953, the 1940–53 itinerary, index. Volume 2 includes a chronology and itinerary since 1953 and an index.

650.   Schulz-Kohn, Dietrich. *Stan Kenton: Ein Porträt.* Wetzlar, Germany: Pegasus; 1960.

In German. A concise biography to the late 1950s covering his musical career from his early swing band years through the Afro-Cuban and progressive years. Mentions some of his sidemen. No new insights. Selected discography, illustrated.

Andy Kirk

651. Kirk, Andy, with Amy Lee. *Twenty Years on Wheels;* as told to Amy Lee. Ann Arbor: University of Michigan Press; 1989.

An affectionate recollection of his life and music complete with details on travel, personnel, and racism. In regards to the latter, Kirk is portrayed as a moderate African American who reveals, "The thing I remember so strangely is not the prejudice—I had a taste of that—but of people extending themselves to help me. All of this stayed with me. And I realized that color has nothing to do with anyone's personality, either black or white. In my time of growing up and in my experience I found that to be true" (p. 34). The book also contains an account of why Mary Lou Williams left the band; however, treatment of both her contributions and those of Dick Wilson is extremely disappointing. Index and selected discography.

Rahsaan Roland Kirk

652. Kruth, John. *Bright Moments: The Life and Legacy of Rahsaan Roland Kirk.* New York: Welcome Rain Publishers; 2000.

Covers his life from his humble beginnings in Columbus, Ohio, to his last concert with the Vibration Society on December 4, 1977, at Indiana University in Bloomington. Details his problems with critics, association with Jack Tracy of Argo Records, Chicago years, and quest to be understood and appreciated. Primarily journalistic in style, but permeated with quotes and insights from others. Contains a discography, guide to Kirk's musical instruments, and a bibliography.

Gene Krupa

653. Crowther, Bruce. *Gene Krupa: His Life and Times.* Turnbridge, England, and Spellmount, N.Y.: Universe; 1987.

Appraisal of his career and importance with special emphasis on his years with Benny Goodman. Also covers his character and influences. Selected discography, bibliography, index, and illustrations.

654. Klauber, Bruce H. *World of Gene Krupa: Legendary Drummin' Man.* Ventura, California: PathFinder Publishing; 1990.

The author collates Krupa's published interviews and organizes them according to the questions posed. He also incorporates anecdotes and comments from musicians who knew or performed with Krupa along with record reviews to formulate a complete picture of Krupa's life, music, and associations. The appendices contain Krupa's chronology, awards, personnel, filmography, and a selected discography.

John La Porta

655.   La Porta, John. *Playing It By Ear.* Redwood, New York: Cadence Jazz Books; 2001.

An autobiography of his life and musical career that focuses on the Woody Herman Orchestra and the New York jazz scene of the 1940s and 1950s. Includes information on his compositions, recordings, performances, and educational activities.

Nick LaRocca

656.   Lange, Horst H. *Nick LaRocca: Ein Porträt.* Wetzlar, Germany: Pegasus; 1960.

In German. A portrait of his life from his early experiences in "kid" bands to his role as business manager, star cornetist, and musical leader of The Original Dixieland Jazz Band. Also includes a selected discography. Illustrated.

George Lewis

657.   Bethell, Tom. *George Lewis: A Jazzman from New Orleans.* Berkeley: University of California Press; 1977.

Significant biography of the life and music of this New Orleans giant. Information was collected from several sources, including six taped interviews with Lewis, diaries and notebooks (1942–49) of William Russell's unpublished materials, materials housed in the Tulane University archives, and collections of other New Orleans musicians including Baby Dodds, Bunk Johnson, Lawrence Marrero, and Slow Drag Davageau. One of the questionable aspects about the book is the author's belief that jazz is not an African American art form. In fact, he rejects the notion that African Americans have retained any African cultural concepts. Rather, he believes African Americans pursued jazz because it was one of a limited number of pursuits not denied them. He does not offer reliable or valid proof to support his revisionist theories. Selected bibliography and discography.

658. Kraut, Eberhard. *George Lewis: Streifzug durch ein Musikerleben.* Menden, Germany: JazzFreund; 1980.

In German. A concise biography and discography of his musical career from the early New Orleans years to his national-international acclaim. Covers his years with Bunk Johnson both as a sideman and eventual leader of the band. No new insights. Selected discography.

659. Stuart, Jay Allison. *Call Him George.* London: Peter Davies, 1961; London: Jazz Book Club, 1963; revised edition, Ann Fairbairn, New York: Crown, 1969.

Compiled mostly from information provided by George Lewis, a New Orleans clarinetist. In addition to his life and his musical associations with people such as Louis Armstrong, a significant part of this biography is Lewis's account of the role of jazz in New Orleans. The 1969 addition traces his life through his death (1900–1968).

Guy Lombardo

660. Cline, Beverly Fink. *The Lombardo Story.* Don Mills, Ont.: Musson; 1979.

A well-researched biography that draws its information from written sources and interviews. Included in the interviews is one with Bill Lombardo (conductor of the band after Guy Lombardo's death in 1977). Provides insight into the beginning and cultivation of the Lombardo style. A list of Carmen and Guy Lombardo compositions and a selected discography in the appendix.

661. Herndon, B. *The Sweetest Music This Side of Heaven.* New York: McGraw-Hill; 1964.

Provides a penetrating look into the music and musical career of Guy Lombardo. Included is information on his family, his bands, and his music. This book is more functional than critical and does not treat in any significant detail an answer to whether Lombardo was a jazz or popular musician. Selected bibliography and discography.

662. Lombardo, Guy. *Auld Acquaintance;* with Jack Altschul: introduction by Jules Stein. Garden City, N.Y.: Doubleday; 1975.

Details his career from his debut in Cleveland in 1924 and eventual success in Chicago in 1927 until his death in 1977. Few details on his musical style.

Humphrey Lyttleton

663. Lyttleton, Humphrey. *I Play as I Please: The Memories of an Old Estonian Trumpeter.* London: MacGibbon and Kee, 1954; London: Jazz Book Club, 1957; London: Pan Books, 1959.

Anecdotes and recollections on the British jazz scene, 1945–1954. Important for the insider perspectives that it provides on British jazz history.

Wingy Manone

664. Manone, Wingy, and Paul Vandervoort. *Trumpet on the Wing.* Garden City, New York: Doubleday, 1948. Reprint. London: Jazz Book Club; 1964.

Covers Manone's career from his early life in New Orleans, St. Louis, New York, and Chicago, to his comedian/musician life in Hollywood. The foreword is by Bing Crosby.

Ellis Louis Marsalis, Jr.

665. Handy, D. Antoinette. *Jazz's Man's Journey: A Biography of Ellis Louis Marsalis, Jr.* Lanham, Md.: Scarecrow Press, and Institute of Jazz Studies (Rutgers University); 1999.

Covers the Marsalis family with emphasis on the father. Focuses on his work ethic, family values, and role as both an outstanding father, pianist, and educator. Details his educational and performance achievements, and contains reminiscences from friends and professional associates.

Wynton Marsalis

666. Gourse, Leslie. *Wynton Marsalis: Skain's Domain, a Biography.* New York: Schirmer Books; 1999.

Begins with his child prodigy days in New Orleans and follows his ascent to fame and becoming Artistic Director of Classic Jazz at Lincoln Center in 1987. Reveals his attitude regarding elevating jazz to its rightful status as an art form created by African Americans. Also discusses his respect and reverence for his father and family, and his contributions to jazz at Lincoln Center. Permeated with insights into his aesthetics and philosophy. The appendix contains the history of jazz at Lincoln Center, a discography, awards, nominations, videography, audio documentaries on cassette, and a bibliography.

667. Marsalis, Wynton, and Carl Vigeland. *Jazz in the Bittersweet Blues of Life.* New York: Da Capo Press; 2001.

Captures the world of Marsalis's septet on its last extended tour. Vigeland witnessed the septet's art, relationship with their audiences and among themselves. Draws on Marsalis's views on jazz, intimate meditations on home, family, creation and performance. Overall, the book captures the world of the group on several different and important levels.

668. Marsalis, Wynton. *Sweet Swing Blues on the Road;* photographs by Frank Stewart. New York: W. W. Norton and Company; 1994.

Examines the lives of jazz musicians on the road, with special emphasis on the experiences of Wynton Marsalis and his band. He argues for a return to a 1950s value system for African Americans, and reveals his admiration for Stanley Crouch. In addition, he pays homage to his predecessors, especially those who remained rooted in traditional jazz when the economic conditions were not propitious. An excellent insight into the man, his music, and philosophy.

Warne Marsh

669. Chamberlain, Safford. *An Unsung Cat: The Life and Music of Warne Marsh.* Lanham, Md., and Institute of Jazz Studies (Rutgers University); 2000.

Addresses reasons why Marsh is not better known, covers his family history, and analyzes his music. His associations with artists such as Lee Konitz, Lennie Tristano, and Lester Young are discussed. Excellent insights into Marsh's improvisations, and includes an extensive discography, photographs of Marsh in public performances and private settings, and a list of 220 persons interviewed; however, no index. Foreword by Gary Foster, well-written and scholarly.

McKinney's Cotton Pickers

670. Chilton, John. *McKinney's Music: A Bio-Discography of McKinney's Cotton Pickers.* London: Bloomsbury; 1978.

Chronicles the personnel and activities of this excellent band, including the role and function of Fletcher Henderson. Includes a biographical dictionary of the band members, including Chu Berry, Coleman Hawkins, Ben Webster, Lester Young, J. C. Higginbotham, Sandy Williams, and Don Redman. Reference notes, illustrated.

John McLaughlin

671. Stump, Paul. *Go Ahead John: The Music of John McLaughlin.* London: SAF Publishing LTD; 1999.

Discusses a myriad of musical related issues from the drug scene of the 1960s, fusion of the 1960s and 1970s, and his accomplishments of the 1990s. Also covers his involvement in the mid-1960s British blues boom, tenure with Miles Davis, and collaborations with artists such as Larry Coryell, Al Dimeola, Paco DeLucia, and Carlos Santana. The role that the Mahavishnu Orchestra played in linking jazz and rock is also discussed. Contains a bibliography and discography.

Milton "Mezz" Mezzrow

672. Mezzrow, Milton "Mezz," and Bernard Wolfe. *Really the Blues.* New York, Toronto: Random House, 1946; London: Secker and Warburg, 1946, 1957; New York: Dell, 1946; London: Musician, 1947; London: Jazz Book Club, 1959; London: Omnibook, 1947; Milano: Longanesi, 1949, 1956; Paris: Corréa, 1950, 1951; Stockholm: Rabén & Sjögren, 1953, 1955; Paris: Buchet-Corréa, Meilleur, 1957; London: Transworld, 1961; New York: Signet, 1964; Paris: Poche, 1964; Milano: Longanesi, 1968; Garden City, N.Y.: Doubleday, 1972; Stockholm: Sjogren, 1982; Berlin: Verlag Neune, 1986.

Contains many interesting details on jazz practices in both Chicago and New York of the 1920s and 1930s. He also covers his music, musical associations, and subsequent problems with drugs and time spent in prison. The autobiography is written in a colloquial style and includes a jazz slang glossary. There are appendices on the characteristics of New Orleans and Chicago styles, a selected discography of Mezzrow recordings that were supervised under Hugues Panassié, and an index.

673. Panassié, Hugues. *Quand Mezzrow Enregistar. Preface by Mezz Mezzrow.* Paris: Laffont; 1952.

In French. A chronology of Mezzrow's and Tommy Ladnier's recordings. Ladnier's recordings include dates with Ida Cox, Sidney Bechet, Louis Austin, and Fletcher Henderson. The Mezzrow recordings cover both his Chicago and European years. Illustrated.

Glenn Miller

674. Butcher, Geoffrey. *Next to a Letter from Home: Major Glenn Miller's Wartime Band.* Edinburgh: Mainstream, 1986; London: Sphere, 1987.

Concerned with the band's activities, personnel, and repertoire during World War II. Also focuses on the band's popularity and impact at home and abroad within the context of the war. Discography, chronology, index, and illustrations.

675. Flower, John. *Moonlight Serenade: A Bio-Discography of the Glenn Miller Civilian Band.* New Rochelle, N.Y.: Arlington House; 1972.

Combines biographical and discographical materials in an informative, well-researched portrait of Miller's life and music. The author provides a diary of the Miller band schedule from 1935 to 1963 with full discographical and broadcast detail. The broadcast details include date, venue, announcer, title of tunes, type of show, and in the case of a recording, matrix and release numbers (addition to 1981).

676. Green, Jonathan. *Glenn Miller and the Age of Swing.* London: Dempsey and Spurrier; 1974.

Details Miller's life, music, and tragic death. There is information on performances, personnel, travel, and the impact that success had on his band. Index.

677. Polic, Edward F. *The Glenn Miller Army Air Force Band: Sustineo Alas I Sustain the Wings.* Lanham, Md.: Scarecrow Press, and Institute of Jazz Studies (Rutgers University); 1989. Two volumes.

An historical approach, replete with details about everything that happen to and within the Miller band. He focuses on how the band began, developed, travels, personnel, and specific details regarding what they played, where, and who actually performed. Copious details, thorough, and scholarly.

678. Simon, George T. *Glenn Miller and His Orchestra.* New York: Crowell; London: W.H. Allen, 1974; New York: Da Capo, 1985.

Presents a positive and detailed view of Miller with material drawn from personal association with him as well as from material gathered from interviews. The author, Miller's first drummer, divided Miller's life into four stages: The Early Years, 1904 to 1935; The Band that Failed, 1935 to 1938; The Band that Made It, 1938 to 1942; and The Armed Forces Band, 1942 to 1944. Little information on the musical style of Miller is offered. Introduction by Bing Crosby. Selected discography and bibliography, and numerous photographs (addition to 1981).

679. Snow, George, and Jonathan Green. *Glenn Miller and the Age of Swing.* London: Dempsey and Squires; 1976.

A balanced assessment of Miller's successes and failures. The book devotes equal time to his life, including his personal and professional deficiencies, and his considerable success as an arranger and crowd pleaser. In addition, a concise discussion of swing style music is included. Selected discography.

Charles Mingus

680.   Béthune, Christian. *Charles Mingus*. Montpellier, France: Limon; 1989.

In French. Covers his life, musical career, associations, and achievements. Discusses his role as a bassist, bandleader, innovator in third stream, association with Teo Macero, and his overall contributions. Very informative.

681.   Coleman, Janet, and Al Young. *Mingus/Mingus: Two Memoirs*. Berkeley: Creative Arts Book Company; 1989.

Two personal portraits of Mingus that focus on their friendships and recount numerous experiences. The portrait by Young refers to Mingus' recordings and his experiences while touring with a trio. The focus of the book is to recount their experiences with Mingus not to provide details of his life or music.

682.   Luzzi, Mario. *Charlie Mingus*. Rome: Lato; 1983.

In Italian. A penetrating account of his musical career, achievements, associations, and frustrations, supplemented by an interview with Sue Mingus. His role as a bassist, bandleader, and innovator are covered as is his disdain of racism. References, selected discography, illustrated.

683.   Mingus, Charles. *Beneath the Underdog: His World as Composed by Mingus;* edited by Nel King. New York: Knopf, London: Weidenfeld and Nicholson, Toronto: Random House, 1971; New York: Bantam, 1972; Tokyo: Shobun, 1973; New York: St. Martin, 1975; Harmondsworth, England, New York: Penguin, 1975, 1980, 1981; Hamburg: Nautilus, 1980, 1986; Stockholm: Gidlund, 1981; Paris: Parenthèses, 1982.

Assesses Mingus's life and music from his beginnings in Watts (Los Angeles) to his successful career as both a sideman and bandleader. Within this account, he also mentions many of the great musicians of the bebop era, including Thelonious Monk, Dizzy Gillespie, Charles Parker, and Bud Powell. One of his most significant influences was Fats Navarro. An account of his voluntary commitment for psychiatric treatment at Bellevue Hospital (New York) is given as well as the impact of racism on his life.

684.   Priestley, Brian. *Mingus: A Critical Biography*. London, Melbourne, New York: Quartet, 1982; New York: Da Capo, 1983; London: Paladin, 1985.

Parallels *Beneath the Underdog: His World as Composed by Mingus,* by providing a penetrating assessment of his personality and music. Permeated with transcriptions, musical examples, and analysis and includes a structural analysis of "The Black Saint and Sinner Lady." Also includes a table that delineates the atypical form of compositions discussed in the text. Reference notes, discography, index, and illustrations.

Thelonious Monk

685. Bliek, Rob Van Der (editor). *The Thelonious Monk Reader.* New York: Oxford University Press; 2001.

A collection of essays, interviews, reviews, liner notes, and musical analysis. The 39 essays range in date from 1947 to 1999, and feature the views of writers like Leonard Feather, Ira Gitler, Nat Hentoff, Andre' Hodeir, Gunther Schuller, Martin Williams, and others. Among the topics covered are "Minton's and Before," "Blue Note," "The Music," and Monk's lifestyle, piano technique, the influence of artists such as Duke Ellington, Earl Hines, Art Tatum, and Fats Waller, his collaborations with John Coltrane, and creative use of style.

686. Buin, Yves. *Thelonious Monk.* Paris: D.O.L; 1988.

In French. Follows a chronological order in discussing his career, collaborations, and recordings. Includes comments on the music and recordings, personnel, and insights from musicians and scholars such as Andre Hodeir.

687. De Wilde, Laurent. *Monk.* Translated by Jonathan Dickinson. New York: Marlowe and Company; 1996.

Originally published in French, his portrait focuses on the women, producers, recording company (Columbia), businessmen, and musicians in his life. Provides new insights into his personal life and producers, and his pioneering experiments with big bands.

688. Fitterling, Thomas. *Thelonious Monk: Seine Leben, seine Musik, seine Schallplatten.* Waakirchen, Germany: Oreos; 1987.

In German. A comprehensive discussion of Monk's commercial recordings, both as leader and sideman, including ones made with Charlie Christian, Miles Davis, John Coltrane, and Sonny Rollins, covering style, personnel, and significance. Includes Jim Aikin's transcription of Monk's improvised solo on "Bag's Groove." Bibliography, list of compositions, discography, illustrations.

689. _____. *Thelonious Monk: His Life and Music.* Berkeley: Berkeley Hills Books; 1997.

Translated by Robert Dobbin, foreword by Steve Lacy. The author covers Monk's musical odyssey from his early years in North Carolina, through his success as a composer/bandleader, to the twilight of his career. Includes word analysis of Monk's recording legacy from his first dates with Coleman Hawkins in 1944 to the 1971 London sessions with Art Blakey and Al McKibbon. Also covers his influence on other musicians.

690.   Gourse, Leslie. *Straight, No Chaser: The Life and Genius of Thelonious Monk.* New York: Schirmer Books; 1997.

Tells the story of Monk's life, and covers both his genius and unique sound. Although no musical examples are included, she includes word analysis from historical sources, critical appraisals, and explanations by musicians who played the music.

691.   Houston, Bob (editor). *Thelonious Monk.* London, New York, Sidney: Wise; 1989.

Covers his musical life from his ragtime-influenced style to his assent to fame as a bebop composer and pianist. Also includes an analysis of Monk's music by Dave Gelly and comments on several Monk arrangements by Brian Priestley. Factual insights into his music.

692.   Santoro, Gene. *Myself When I am Real: The Life and Music of Charles Mingus.* New York: Oxford University Press; 2001.

Uses new interviews, archival materials, and previously unknown letters to portray Mingus's personal life, temperament, and artistic aspirations. Traces his life and musical development from Watts, and the teaching of Sam Brown to his postwar musical creativity in Greenwich Village. Also includes information on his battles with the music business, himself, and racism.

Wes Montgomery

693.   Ingram, Adrian. *Wes Montgomery.* Foreword by Joe Pass. Gateshead, England: Mark; 1985.

Biographical portrait of his early years in Indianapolis, relationship with his brothers, self-taught guitar technique, and style. Contains a discussion of his style, supplemented with oral history and interview materials. Includes the lead sheet to "West Coast Blues." Good analysis of style. Bibliography, list of compositions, and discography.

Jelly Roll Morton

694.   Lomax, Alan. *Mister Jelly Roll: The Fortunes of Jelly Roll Morton, New Orleans Creole and "Inventor of Jazz."* New York: Duell, Sloan &

Pearce, 1950, 1956; New York: Grosset & Dunlap, Toronto: Collins,1950; New York: Grove, 1950, 1956; New York, London: Cassell, 1952, 1955; Stockholm: Rabén & Sjogren, 1954; London: Jazz Book Club, 1956; København: Gyldendal, 1958; London: Pan, 1959; Zürich: Sanssouci, 1960; Zürich: Ex, 1964; Paris: Flammarion, 1964; Berkeley: University of California, 1973; Grénoble: Universitaires, 1980.

Based on interviews with Morton at the Library of Congress in 1938, this biography is particularly interesting for Jelly Roll's own assessment of his life and for Mabel Morton's comments on Jelly Roll and their life together. An appendix lists Morton's compositions, recordings, and tunes.

695. _____. *Mister Jelly Roll: The Fortunes of Jelly Roll Morton, New Orleans Creole and "Inventor" of Jazz.* Berkeley: University of California Press; 2001.

The biography first appeared in 1950; however, Lawrence Gushee has updated the new edition with a new afterword. This edition includes scores of Morton's arrangements, a discography, updated bibliography, a chronology of his compositions, and a new genealogical tree. The afterword provides new factual information and explains the importance of this work to jazz scholarship.

696. Pastras, Phil. *Dead Man Blues: Jelly Roll Morton Way Out West.* Berkeley: University of California Press; 2001.

Presents a well-researched and thorough discussion of two periods, 1917–22 and 1940–41, when Morton was on the West Coast. He rechecked sources, corrected mistakes in other published studies on Morton, and situated eyewitness narratives within the history of New Orleans and Los Angeles jazz. He also draws on a previously unknown collection of Morton memorabilia, including a 58-page scrapbook compiled by Morton, to complete the story of Morton's West Coast activities. Important addition to Morton scholarship.

697. Williams, Martin. *Jelly Roll Morton.* London: Cassell, 1962; New York: Barnes, 1963.

Analyzes Morton's piano solos, pre-Pepper and Red Hot Pepper recordings, duets, trios, and quartets, primarily through word analysis rather than detailed transcriptional analysis. The author also discusses the roots of and influences on Morton's style.

698. Wright, Laurie. *Mr. Jelly Lord.* Chigwell, England: Storyville; 1980.

Revised edition of John R. T. Davies and Laurie Wright's *Morton's Music.* Concise but factual, covers his travels, musical career in New Orleans and

Los Angeles, coping with change in the jazz world, and contributions to jazz. Includes a biography, bibliography, index, and illustrations.

Gerry Mulligan

699.   Horricks, Raymond. *Gerry Mulligan's Ark.* London: Apollo; 1986.

Biography supplemented with a selected discography by Tony Middleton. Although concise, the biography contains information on his compositions/ arrangements, concert jazz band, quartet, and style. His associations with significant artists and the influence of Lester Young are also covered. Associations, recordings with musicians like Claude Thornhill and Miles Davis, and his role in the 1949 *Birth of the Cool* album (Miles Davis) are discussed as is his extended stay in Denmark. Bibliography, illustrations.

700.   Klinkowitz, Jerome. *Listen: Gerry Mulligan (An Aural Narrative in Jazz).* New York: Schirmer Books; 1991.

The primary focus of this biography is a critical assessment of Mulligan's recordings. Biographical information is provided only as it relates to specific recordings. A good addition to jazz discography and stylistic analysis.

Turk Murphy

701.   Goggin, Jim. *Turk Murphy: Just for the Record.* San Leandro, California: San Francisco Traditional Jazz; 1982.

A biodiscography that not only provides insights into his musical career but also provides insight into his role and function as a 1940s New Orleans revivalist. Includes a comprehensive discography. Illustrated.

Nicholas Brothers

702.   Hill, Constance Valis. *Brotherhood in Rhythm: The Jazz Tap Dancing of the Nicholas Brothers.* New York: Oxford University Press; 2000.

Chronicles the lives of Fayard and Harold Nicholas, examines their eclectic talents, and their immense contributions to American dance and culture. Contains information on their early years, beginnings in dance, and dance influences. Also discusses their role in popularizing jazz tap dance.

Red Nichols

703.   Evans, Philip R., Stanley Hester, Stephen Hester, and Linda Evans. *The Red Nichols Story: After Intermission, 1942–1965.* Lanham, Md.: Scarecrow Press, and Institute of Jazz Studies (Rutgers University Press); 1997.

A comprehensive account of his later life, complete with facts about his musical associations, performances, and recordings. Covers facts not previously discussed, and provides information on his importance in jazz history

704.   Johnson, George. *The Five Pennies: The Biography of Jazz Band Leader Red Nichols.* New York: Dell; 1959.

Details Nichols's career, including groups he led and musicians with whom he associated (1981).

705.   Lange, Horst H. *Loring "Red" Nichols: Ein Porträt.* Wetzlar, Germany: Pegasus; 1960.

In German. Biography that covers his beginnings, influences, and musical achievements. Includes excellent insight into his role as leader of the Five Pennies, association with Benny Goodman, and stay in Europe. The influence of his recordings in Europe is also discussed. Selected discography, illustrated.

706.   Stroff, Stephen. *Red Head: A Chronological Survey of "Red" Nichols and His Five Pennies.* Lanham, Md.: Scarecrow Press, and Institute of Jazz Studies (Rutgers University); 1996.

Presents personal details, a biography, discography, and the organization and success of his group. He analyzes Nichol's work, associations with other artists, and the recordings made between 1925 and 1932. Includes information not previously published, thereby placing Nichols in a new light.

Anita O'Day

707.   O'Day, Anita, and George Eells. *High Time, Hard Times.* Foreword by Harry Reasoner. New York: Berkeley, 1982; London: Corgi, 1983; New York: Limelight, 1989.

A vivid insight into her drug encounters, romantic interludes, and musical associations with artists such as Roy Eldridge, Gene Krupa, and Stan Kenton. Begins with her show business years in the 1920s, the hip sophistication of the 1930s, performances with big bands, and postbebop experiments in the 1950s and after. Includes information on her singing with Count Basie, and bebop stint with Tadd Dameron. and comparison with June Christy and Chris Conner. Robert A. Sixsmith and Alan Eichler compiled the discography.

King Oliver

708.   Williams, Martin. *King Oliver.* London: Cassell, 1960; New York: Barnes, 1961.

Approaches Oliver's life in two sections: the first deals with his experiences from New Orleans to New York; the second assesses his "Creole Jazz Band," "Dixie Syncopators," and his 1929–30 Victory recordings orchestra by analyzing selected recordings. Additionally, he surveys both Oliver's improvisational style and role as a sideman.

Original Dixieland Jazz Band

709.   Brunn. H. O. *The Story of the Original Dixieland Jazz Band.* Baton Rouge: Louisiana State University Press, 1960; London: Sidgwick & Jackson; London: Jazz Book Club, 1963.

Attempts to prove that the Original Dixieland Jazz Band created jazz. In a rather biased approach and based primarily on material from LaRocca, the author does not mention how musicians such as LaRocca listened to and copied the style of African American musicians such as King Oliver. Because it fails to detail the black influence on the Original Dixieland Jazz Band, this book should not be taken as an accurate assessment of the band's music and influence. Appendix contains a chronological arrangement of ODJB's personnel, 1915–1938. Index (addition to 1981).

Drew Page

710.   Page, Drew. *Drew's Blues: A Sideman's Life with the Big Bands.* Baton Rouge: Louisiana State University Press; 1980.

An interesting portrait of a life-long sideman of Southwest bands in the late 1920s and early 1930s, dance bands in Chicago, and touring big bands. The book is significant because it provides information on life in the trenches. In addition to Page, references to other sidemen are also included. Harry James is the only "star" that contributes to this volume. It is significant that Drew Page appears to have encountered African Americans very rarely, and there is no discussion or comparison of the life of these musicians as compared to their Anglo counterparts. Index.

Charlie Parker

711.   Baker, David N. *Charlie Parker.* New York: Charles Hansen; 1978.

A monograph devoted to a biomusical assessment of Parker. Baker begins with a biographical sketch, outlined by year, of Parker's musical achievements. He follows with an assessment of his innovations, characteristics of bebop, a Parker genealogy, and a concise outline of Parker's tempos, rhythmic patterns, dramatic devices, key preferences, scale preferences, ii–V7 patterns, turnbacks and cycles, and substitutions. There is a list of Parker's original compositions as well as transcribed improvisations of "Out of Nowhere," "Now's the Time," "Hot House," and "Perdido," and a synopsis of his ii–V7 patterns. Selected bibliography.

712. Giddins, Gary. *Celebrating Bird: The Triumph of Charlie Parker.* New York: Beech Tree/William Morrow; 1987.

Chronicles Parker's life from his early years in Kansas City until his death in New York in 1955. Of particular note is Giddins's treatment of Parker's early years in the chapters "Youth" and "Apprenticeship," in which he draws on information provided by Rebecca Parker Davis, Parker's childhood sweetheart and first wife. The two chapters "Mastery" and "Bird Lives" also offer new insights into the man and his music. Specifically, Parker is portrayed as a witty, intelligent, curious musician who has eclectic musical tastes and is generous to aspiring younger musicians. This biography offers new perspectives on both the life and musical contributions of this great artist. Index and selected discography.

713. Harrison, Max. *Charlie Parker.* London: Cassell, 1960; New York: Barnes, 1961.

A short biomusical portrait of Parker's life that includes a critical assessment of both his musical contributions and life. The author succinctly addresses the polarity of Parker's unpredictable lifestyle with the genius of his musical productivity. Selected discography with personnel.

714. Koch, Lawrence O. *Yardbird Suite: A Compendium of the Music and Life of Charlie Parker.* Bowling Green, Ohio: Bowling Green State University Press; 1988.

This book should be retitled as a biomusical profile of Charles Parker. In addition to a presentation of his life covering his Kansas City years to 52nd Street, he presents a thorough analysis of the music. Koch addresses such concepts as melodic structure, rhythmic devices, harmony, intervals, and phrase structures. There are numerous examples and six appendices: a numerical listing of Charlie Parker's recordings; suggested Verve take listings for future reference; alphabetical listing of Parker record titles; a guide to SuperSax harmonizations; Parker as a composer; labelology; a selected bibliography; copyright information; analysis section; and chapter notes.

715. _____. *Yardbird Suite: A Compendium of the Music and Life of Charles Parker.* Revised edition. Boston: Northeastern University Press; 1999.

The revised edition includes newly discovered recordings and CD reissues among the numerous works analyzed for this edition. Includes four appendices and a bibliography.

716. Martin, Henry. *Charlie Parker and Thematic Improvisation.* Lanham, Md.: Scarecrow Press, and Institute of Jazz Studies (Rutgers University); 1996.

A scholarly discussion of Parker's thematic approach to improvisation. This treatment compliments the studies of Koch, Owens, and Woideck, and is permeated with new musical insights and analyses. The book is geared to serious scholars and performers of Charles Parkers's musical approaches to improvisation, and requires knowledge of musical notation and theory.

717. Miller, Mark. *Cool Blues: Charlie Parker in Canada, 1953.* Toronto: Nightwood; 1989.

Discography with details of performances, dates, venues, personnel, labels, and matrix numbers. Includes a bibliography, index, and illustrations.

718. Parker, Chan. *To Bird with Love.* Poitiers, France: Wizlov; 1981.

In French. A compilation of photographs with letters and contracts presenting important insights into Parker's career and personal life. Includes information not previously published. French text by Frances Paudras.

719. Priestley, Brian. *Charlie Parker.* Turnbridge, England, Spellmount, N.Y.: Hippocrene; 1984.

Biographical portrait that covers his life and musical transformation from his Kansas City influences (Buster Smith, Jay McShann, Lester Young) to his associations with musicians like Earl "Fatha" Hines, Dizzy Gillespie, and Miles Davis. His drug addiction is also chronicled. Also contains photographs of telegrams that Parker sent to Chan Parker and analysis of his style. Bibliography, selected discography.

720. Reisner, Robert George. *Bird: The Legend of Charlie Parker.* New York: Bonanza Books; New York: Citadel Press, 1962; London: MacGibbon and Eke, 1963; London: Jazz Book Club, 1965; New York: Da Capo: 1977, 1979, 1982, 1985, 1987, 1989, 1991.

Compiles anecdotes and recollections of Parker from 80 people, including Harold Baker, Walter Bishop Jr., Art Blakey, Rudi Blesh, Miles Davis, Kenny Dorham, Billy Eckstine, Art Farmer, Dizzy Gillespie, Earl "Fatha" Hines, Lawrence Keys, Howard McGhee, Jay McShann, Charles Mingus,

Adieu Parker, Gene Ramey, Buster Smith, Lennie Tristano, and Edgar Varies. There are some informative insights about his music (especially the recollections provided by his musical peers), although the book is mostly concerned with his life and personality; the author contributes his own recollections of Parker. Appendix includes a chronology of important events, a comprehensive discography, numerous photographs, and an index.

721. Russell, Ross. *Bird Lives: The High Life and Hard Times of Charlie (Yardbird) Parker.* New York: Charterhouse, 1973; Stockholm: Gidlunds, 1974, 1977; London: McKay, 1975; London: Quartet, 1976; Milano: Milano, 1978; Oslo: Gyldendal, 1978; Helsinki: Sölderström, 1979; Paris: Filipacchi, 1980; Wien: Hannibal, 1985; London, New York: Quartet, 1988.

Considered by many the best biography on Parker to date, this book is rich with material on Parker as a man and musician. Russell (who was the owner of Dial Records) conducted painstaking research into Parker's life and so provides a vivid picture of Parker from his beginnings as a Kansas City musician and his infatuation with Lester Young to his many experiences in New York. Russell also offers some musical examples as well as commenting on several of Parker's performances and the influence of the blues on his musical style. Selected bibliography and discography (1981).

722. Woideck, Carl. *The Charlie Parker Companion: Six Decades of Commentary.* New York: Schirmer Books; 1998.

Contains all the interviews given by Parker, early reviews, memoirs, and essays that focus on his life and music. Includes essays by Stanley Crouch, Gary Giddins, Dizzy Gillespie, Jack Kerouac, and many more. Also contains a chronology, discography, and selected bibliography. Important addition to Parker scholarship.

723. _____. *Charlie Parker: His Music and Life.* Ann Arbor: University of Michigan Press; 1996.

Begins with Parker's biography by outlining important events from his early years in Kansas City, learning period, stints with Big Jay McShann and Billy Eckstine, and relationship with artists like Dizzy Gillespie. In addition, he includes a detailed analysis of Parker's improvisations, samples some of his most important works to discuss repertoire, compositional style, rhythmic properties, accents and syncopation, harmonic vocabulary, and more. Permeated with insider perspectives, notes, and includes four transcriptions, numerous musical examples, a selected discography, and references.

Art Pepper

724.   Pepper, Art, and Laurie Pepper. *Straight Life: The Story of Art Pepper;* discography by Todd Selbert. New York: Schirmer; London: Collier Macmillan; 1979.

A penetrating account of this former alto saxophonist's life and musical career. Based on edited tapes, Pepper presents some revealing facts about his drug addiction, incarceration in San Quentin (1961–66), and eventual downfall. Recollections by family, friends, and musicians provide a glimpse into his music. Pepper was also unique because he was one of a few white musicians who played with African American musicians on Central Avenue (Los Angeles in the 1940s and 1950s); he also performed extensively with Stan Kenton. The discography contains numerous recordings (dates, personnel, titles, venues, record release numbers), of his Kenton tenure, 1943 to the late 1970s. Index.

Oscar Peterson

725.   Lees, Gene. *Oscar Peterson, The Will to Swing.* New York: Macmillan Publishers; 1991.

Covers the life, motivation, and quest for excellence of this outstanding pianist, beginning with his early years in Montreal to the 1980s. The author discusses his enforced practice sessions and his eventual success as one of the world's greatest pianists. His association with artists like Ray Brown, Nat King Cole, Dizzy Gillespie, Charles Parker, and Joe Pass, and promoter/record producer Norman Granz is also discussed. Includes quotes from several writers, sources, and musical associations. Contains a bibliography, discography, and index.

726.   Palmer, Richard. *Oscar Peterson.* Turnbridge, England, Spellmount, New York: Hippocrene; 1984.

Traces his life from his beginnings in Canada and forced piano practice to his musical achievements, associations, and recordings. His career as a soloist and bandleader, and role as an accompanist are also discussed. His work with Ella Fitzgerald, Stan Getz, Dizzy Gillespie, Sonny Stitt, and Ben Webster is covered. The biography is supplemented with British radio and television interview material. Especially noteworthy is the material on the Ray Brown, Joe Pass, and Oscar Peterson trio, and the importance of Norman Granz to his career. Reference notes, selected discography, and illustrations.

727.   Peterson, Oscar. *A Jazz Odyssey: The Life of Oscar Peterson.* New York: Continuum; 2002.

An autobiography in which the author provides vivid assessments about racism against black Canadians. He recalls how he broke the color lines in many whites-only clubs, and his experiences as the only black in a band lead by Maynard Ferguson's brother. His relationship with his father, early years in music, travels, and relationship with both his sidemen and other musicians are also discussed.

Pony Poindexter

728.   Poindexter, Pony, and Juergen A. Schmitt. *The Pony Express: Memoirs of a Jazz Musician.* Frankfurt: Jas; 1985.

The clarinetist/saxophonist recounts his career by describing his entry into jazz and his musical encounters. He also discusses his style, musical change, and issues related to context and history. Discography by John Hammond, Jr., illustrated.

Roy Porter

729.   Porter, Roy. *There and Back: The Roy Porter Story;* with David Keller. Baton Rouge: Louisiana State University; 1991.

Autobiography of his life, musical career, and his view of jazz in America. Porter is best known for the recordings that he made, as a drummer, with Charles Parker in 1946. The strength of the book is the insight that he provides regarding post–World War II Los Angeles jazz. He also chronicles encounters with racism and his views on the jazz business. Selected bibliography and an index.

Bud Powell

730.   Groves, Alan, and Alyn Shipton. *The Glass Enclosure: The Life of Bud Powell.* New York: Bayou Press; 2001.

Shipton supplemented Groves's text, and together they trace the highs and lows of Powell's life and musical career. Touches on his association with Charles Parker and other beboppers, contributors to bebop, drug abuse, and the uniqueness of his piano playing. Places Powell's life and music within the overall context of bebop.

731.   Paudras, Francis. *Dance of the Infidels: A Portrait of Bud Powell.* New York: Da Capo Press; 1998.

Written by a man who befriended Powell, and developed a personal trust and friendship with the pianist. His portrait is heartfelt and deeply moving because he provides insights not previously reveled. He discusses a brutal beating by the police, mental and physical abuse, electroshock therapy in the psychiatric institution, malnutrition, and more. His years in Paris, associations with other artists, and influence on modern jazz is also discussed.

Sam Price

732.   Price, Sam, and Caroline Richmond. *What Do They Want?* Urbana: University of Illinois Press; 1990.

An honest and penetrating assessment of his music, musical peers, managers, travel, and much more. Among his frank and honest assessments is an appraisal of the *Theater Owner's Booking Association* (TOBA), better known as Tough on Black Asses; fellow musicians Jonah Jones, Mezz Mezzrow, Jimmy Rushing, and Lester Young, as well as his managers. Although the book contains frank and honest assessments, there are misspelled names and factual errors; David "Fathead" Newman (a tenor player active in the 1970s and 1980s) is confused with George "Fathead" Thomas (vocalist with McKinney's Cotton Pickers), and the assumption that Sidney DeParis was a performer with the Cotton Pickers. Selected bibliography and an index.

Tito Puente

733.   Loza, Steven. *Tito Puente and the Making of Latin Music.* Urbana: University of Illinois Press; 1999.

Offers an analytical view of the historical, stylistic, and social progression of Latin music as embodied in the life and music of Puente. The framework is predicated on historical data, musical repertoire ethnographic interviews, and cultural theories and concepts. Also includes musical analysis, and a discography.

Flora Purim

734.   Bunker, Edward, and Flora Purim. *Freedom Song: The Story of Flora Purim.* New York: Berkeley; 1982.

Covers her life from her beginnings in Brazil to her success as a jazz vocalist in North America. Highlights many musical associations including those with Chick Corea and her husband Airto Moreira. She also discusses her jazz influences and approach to singing.

Teddy Reig

735. Reig, Teddy, and Edward Berger. *Reminiscing in Tempo: The Life and Times of a Jazz Hustler.* Lanham, Md., and Institute of Jazz Studies (Rutgers University); 1990.

Reig (1917–84) was a self-described hustler who was active in the music world from the 1940s to the 1970s. He was a respected record producer who was very active in Harlem, and highly respected by musicians such as Benny Carter and Dizzy Gillespie. Offers good insights into the recording business and his associations with African American musicians.

Django Reinhardt

736. Abrams, Max (editor). *The Book of Django.* Los Angeles: Privately printed; 1973.

A biodiscography tracing his life from his Belgian roots, stay in France, impact on North American guitarists (Eddie Lang and Charlie Christian), his role in the Quintet of Hot Club of France, and association with Stéphane Grappelli. Contains a separate list of recorded titles.

737. Delaunay, Charles. *Django Reinhardt, Souvenirs: Précedés d'un inédit de Jean Cocteau.* Paris: Editions Jazz'hot, 1954; Lausanne: Unknown publisher: 1954; London: Cassell, 1961, 1982; London: Jazz Book Club, 1963; Paris: Losfeld, 1968; Gateshead, Eng.: Mark, 1981; New York: Da Capo, 1981, 1982.

In French. Details his musical career from his beginnings and influences to his numerous associations with some of the giants of jazz. Reinhardt was one of the first non-Americans to be accepted by the American jazz community. Contains a discography.

738. Schmitz, Alexander, and Peter Maier. *Django Reinhardt: Seine Leben, seine Musik, seine Schallplatten.* Waakirchen, Germany: Oreos; 1985.

In German. A biography and discussion of Reinhardt's recordings. The biography details his life and musical achievements, stay in Paris, influence on American jazz musicians, and association with Stephane Grappelli, the Quintet of Hot Club of France, and others. The discussion of recordings centers on personnel and style. Illustrated.

739. Schulz-Köhn, Dietrich. *Django Reinhardt: Ein Porträt.* Wetzlar, Germany: Pegasus; 1960.

In German. Concise biography (48 pages) that presents an overview of his life, especially the Paris years, associations, and some influences. Selected discography.

740. Spautz, Roger. *Django, Reinhardt: Mythos and Realitität.* Luxembourg: Unknown Publisher; 1983, 1984.

A biographical portrait that focuses on his life and musical achievements as well as myths and realities. Covers his Paris years, membership in the Quintet of Hot Club of France, association with Stéphane Grappelli, musical influences, and people he influenced. Reinhardt's acceptance, rejection, and idiosyncrasies are also explored. Discography of all known recordings, illustrated.

The International Sweethearts of Rhythm

741. Handy, D. Antoniette. *The International Sweethearts of Rhythm:* Metuchen, N.J.: Scarecrow Press; 1983.

Chronicles the organization, accomplishments, and music of this all-female big band. The author covers the trials and tribulations of this African American female big band as well as their musical style and background. Selected bibliographies and an index.

742. _____. *The International Sweethearts of Rhythm: The Ladies' Jazz Band From Piney Woods Country Life School.* Lanham, Md., and Institute of Jazz Studies (Rutgers University); 1998. Revised edition.

The revised edition contains more historical facts, updates, and details regarding the musicians' travels and personal lives.

Buddy Rich

743. Balliett, Whitney. *Super Drummer: A Profile of Buddy Rich.* Indianapolis: Bobbs-Merrill; 1968.

This profile was first published in the *New Yorker* and results from the author's friendship with Rich. The profile focuses on his life, music, and associations, gleaned from Rich as well as the author's perspective. Contains several photographs.

744. Meriwether, Doug Jr. *We Don't Play Requests: A Musical Biography/ Discography of Buddy Rich.* Chicago: KAR; 1984.

Originally published as *The Buddy Rich Orchestra and Small Groups* in 1974, the biography covers his career and achievements as both leader and sideman. Covers his bands, styles, and recordings with several musicians including Tommy Dorsey, Dizzy Gillespie, and Charles Parker. Numerous references to recordings. Discographical research aided by Charence

Hintze and Joe Harvey. Includes a filmography of Rich's "Tonight Show" appearances and an index. Illustrated.

745. Nesbitt, Jim. *Inside Buddy Rich: A Study of The Master Drummer's Style and Technique.* Delevan, N.Y.: Kendor; 1984.

Explores his approaches to drumming in different contexts (large and small groups) and styles. Explores his foot pedal, cymbal, high-hat, wire brushes, swing playing, and other concepts. Concise, informative analysis.

746. Tormé, Mel. *Traps, The Drum Wonder: The Life of Buddy Rich.* New York: Oxford University Press; 1991.

Written by the jazz vocalist and author, this book covers Rich's early fame to his rise to stardom with the swing era Artie Shaw and Tommy Dorsey bands. He also covers Rich's abrasive personality, his friendship with Frank Sinatra, and his success as a bandleader. The book is even in its coverage of Rich's attributes and faults.

Sonny Rollins

747. Baker, David N. *Sonny Rollins.* Hialeah, Fla.: Studio 224; 1980.

Provides a biographical sketch of important musical achievements, outlined by years, a genealogy chart, and an outline of Rollins's musical preferences (preferred tunes, types, tempos, rhythmic characteristics, keys, scales, melodic characteristics, harmonic characteristics, and performance practice characteristics). There are transcriptions of "Vierd Blues," "Doxy," "Slow Boat to China," "Tenor Madness," "Newk's Fadeaway," "Tune Up," "Airegin," "Hold 'em Joe," and "Keep Hold of Yourself." Each transcription is followed by an outline of ii–V7 patterns and work sheets that are designed to test a student's knowledge of the aforementioned musical elements. Selected bibliography and discography.

748. Blancq, Charles. *Sonny Rollins: The Journey of a Jazzman.* Boston: G.K. Hall; 1983.

An outgrowth of the author's doctoral dissertation, "Melodic Improvisation in American Jazz: The Style of Theodore 'Sonny' Rollins, 1951–1962" (Tulane University). This book is both a biography and musicological study. There are 24 solo transcriptions, and a scholarly discussion of harmonic, melodic, rhythmic, and scalar devices. The biographical overview covers his life and associations with numerous giants of jazz. Also, there is a selected discussion of the improvisational styles of Louis Armstrong, Miles Davis, Coleman Hawkins, and Charles Parker. The discography is limited to the 1951–62 years. Bibliography.

749. Nisenson, Eric. *Open Sky: Sonny Rollins and His World of Improvisation.* New York: St. Martin's Press; 2000.

Although the author interviewed Rollins for this biography, he admits this is not a definitive work. Whereas he includes many facts of Rollins's life, the primary focus is on the evolution of his jazz sensibilities, musical life, and how his life meshed with his art. He emphasizes the middle years of his development, includes comments about his development, but no musical analysis.

750. Wilson, Peter. *Sonny Rollins: The Definitive Musical Guide.* Berkeley: Berkeley Hills Books; 2001.

An objective and musically knowledgeable account of the saxophonist life and career, written to coincide with Rollins's 70th birthday. The coverage enables readers to understand the musical context of Rollins's recordings. In each case, the author presents intelligent comments, and includes information regarding the significance of specific recordings. Includes a 140-page discography, which covers Rollins's 50-plus years of recordings. Excellent addition to the literature.

Marshall Royal

751. Royal, Marshall, with Claire P. Gordon. *Marshall Royal: Jazz Survivor.* London and New York: Cassell; 1996.

In addition to Royal's life in Los Angeles from the age of five, the book is permeated with historical and contextual information regarding the evolution of jazz in Los Angeles. Contains information on his associations with Lionel Hampton, his brother Ernie Royal, Count Basie, Duke Ellington, and numerous other local and visiting musicians. Also includes information on his travels and performances in Los Angeles venues. Contains a recording chronology by Howard Rye.

Willie Ruff

752. Ruff, Willie. *A Call to Assembly: The Autobiography of a Musical Storyteller.* New York: Penguin Group; 1991.

Chronicles his roots in north Alabama to his successful tenure as a professor at Yale University. The book details his life in narrative form and contains anecdotes on his associations with numerous jazz musicians. His association and success with his musical partner Dwike Mitchell is chronicled in detail. The book includes five major topics: "Home," "Army," "New Haven,"

"Performing," and "International Relations." Contains an index but no bibliography or discography.

Bill Russell

753. Kukla, Jon, et al. *Jazz Scrapbook: Bill Russell and Some Highly Musical Friends.* New Orleans: Historical New Orleans Collection; 1998.

A potpourri of photographs, recollections, and perspectives on Russell and some of his friends. He recalls his associations with artists like Louis Armstrong, Baby Dodds, Bunk Johnson, Jelly Roll Morton, Natty Dominique, Mahalia Jackson, and others. Several authors who are connected with the Historical New Orleans Collection pen the concise essays. Loaded with historical and musical information, and includes some previously unpublished photographs.

Pee Wee Russell

754. Hilbert, Robert. *Pee Wee Russell: The Life of a Jazzman.* New York: Oxford University Press; 1993.

Chronicles Russell's musical career through club dates, recordings, his image, and marriage. The author uses an unfinished biography by George Hoefer, Russell's letters, and remembrances from Buck Clayton, Eddie Condon, and Bud Freeman to provide an assessment of his life and musical contributions, including his associations with Thelonious Monk and Gerry Mulligan. He analyzes numerous recordings, and provides an idiosyncratic summary of his unique clarinet style. This is the first book-length study of Pee Wee Russell.

Bob Scobey

755. Scobey, Jan. *He Rambled: 'Til Cancer Cut Him Down: Bob Scobey, Dixieland Band Musician and Band Leader, 1916–1963.* Northridge, Calif.: Pal Publishing; 1976.

A tribute to an early jazz trumpeter featuring anecdotes, stories, and reminiscences from friends and musicians. Among the quoted musicians are Art Hodes, Clancy Hayes, Lizzy Miles, and Bill Napier. The supplied information is laudatory in focus; however, there is no critical assessment of either Scobey's contributions or significance in early jazz. A sympathetic account of the last months of his life, after being diagnosed with cancer, occupies a significant portion of the book. Selected discography and index.

Artie Shaw

756. Blandford, Edmund L. *Artie Shaw: The Man and His Music.* Foreword by Frank Jacobs. Hasting, England: privately printed; 1974, 1989.

Covers his personality, bands, successes and failures, associations with Roy Eldridge, Billie Holiday, Hot Lips Page, and others. Organized by years, the biography is more an overview rather than an in-depth treatment of Shaw's life and music. The Artie Shaw-Benny Goodman competition is also chronicled. The discography covers the 1936–54 years. Filmography, illustrated.

757. _____. *Artie Shaw: A Bio-discography.* Hastings, Sussex: Castle Books; 1973.

Compiles a portrait of Shaw drawn from *Down Beat, Melody Maker,* and *Metronome,* as well as from Shaw's autobiography, *The Trouble with Cinderella: An Outline of Identity.* The focus is biographical and discographical. There is no analysis of the music. Comprehensive discography of all Shaw recordings as a bandleader and sideman, 1928 to 1954.

758. Shaw, Artie. *The Trouble with Cinderella: An Outline of Identity.* New York: Farrar, Straus and Young, 1952; London: Jarrolds, 1955; New York: Collier. 1963; New York: Da Capo, 1984.

Outlines both the attitudes and personality of one of the most significant clarinetists and bandleaders of the swing era. Specifically, he covers his career from childhood name (Arthur Arshawsky) to his immense success as icon of the swing era. Seventeen photographs.

759. Simosko, Vladimir. *Artie Shaw: A Musical Biography and Discography.* Lanham, Md.: Scarecrow Press, and Institute of Jazz Studies (Rutgers); 2000.

A thorough and definitive survey of Shaw's musical career and recording legacy. The author is the first to provide a detailed listing of what Shaw played and recorded, including solos, before he became a bandleader. In addition, he covers Shaw's leadership of big bands, combos, classical musical activities, and importance as an arranger. Includes an appendix of tune titles. Discography, and an annotated selected bibliography.

Frank Sinatra

760. Barnes, Kim. *Sinatra and the Great Song Stylists.* London: Ian Allen; 1972.

Details the life and musical career of Sinatra, including his beginnings in the swing era and his subsequent recordings and movie appearances. There are also comments on Louis Armstrong, Mildred Bailey, Pearl Bailey, Nat Cole, Lena Horn, Mel Tormé, Jimmy Rushing, Dinah Washington, and many more.

761.   Goldstein, Norma. *Frank Sinatra: Ol 'Blue Eyes.* New York: Holt, Rinehart and Winston; 1982.

Traces the evolution of his musical career from his early years in Hoboken, New Jersey, to the early 1980s. Contains lots of photographs, including some with Ronald Reagan. Also notes his strong Republican affiliation, and contains comments about selected recordings. No new insights. Filmorgraphy and Discography.

762.   Kahn, Ely J. *The Voice.* New York: Harper; 1947.

Includes a series of articles that were previously published in the *New Yorker.* The articles cover Sinatra's life, musical career, movie successes, and his impact as a jazz stylist to the late 1940s. Index.

763.   Kelley, Kitty. *His Way: The Unauthorized Biography of Frank Sinatra.* New York and Toronto: Bantam Books; 1986.

This unauthorized biography led Sinatra to sue to stop publication. The author used materials by other researchers, including unpublished interviews, Ovid Demaris's interview of Bobby Garcia, David Horowitz's interview of Milt Ebbins, Michael Thornton's interview of Ava Gardner, and others. In addition, she interviewed numerous people in Hoboken, New Jersey (Sinatra's birthplace), and a myriad of others to produce a balanced and thorough portrait of Sinatra. The biography is permeated with insider quotes, and contains information on his relationship with Sammy Davis, Jr., and African Americans.

764.   Munn, Michael. *Sinatra: The Untold Story.* London: Allen; 2002.

The book was first published in 2001, and this new edition includes lots of photographs of Sinatra with friends and other musicians. One of the most interesting aspects of this book is the discussion of Sinatra's alleged Mafia connections.

765.   Mustazza, Leonard (editor). *Frank Sinatra and Popular Culture: Essays on an American icon.* Westport, Conn.: Praeger Publishers; 1998.

The essays are designed to provide an eclectic and provocative perspective on what Sinatra meant to popular culture. The writers are varied, including university scholars, personal friends, business associates, and famous personalities. One of the most interesting essays is Sinatra's "What's this about Race," another provocative essay is Will Friedwald's "Sinatra and Jazz.' The appendix contains "Career Highlights." Selected bibliography.

766.   _____. *Ol' Blue Eyes: A Frank Sinatra Encyclopedia.* Westport, Conn.: Greenwood Press; 1998.

Covers his artistic accomplishments, activities, and recognitions. This is not a biographical work, and the work is limited to details about his musical life. The book is divided into three parts, a survey of his music, appearances in film, on radio, video, and the Internet, and his work as a concert performer and world citizen. Contains appendices on studio recordings, V-Discs, and Sinatra on CD. Selected bibliography.

767.   Peykov, Steven, and Leonard Mustazza (editors). *The Frank Sinatra Reader.* New York: Oxford University Press; 1995.

The selections represent some of the best assessments of Sinatra's long and productive career. Organized chronologically, the essays by authors such as Henry Pleasants, Derek Jewell, Murray Kempton, Leonard Feather, Ralph Gleason, Mikal Gilmore, Harry Connick, Jr., and numerous other writers. The essays cover Sinatra's career from 1939 through the Capitol years (1953–61), until the early 1990s. Most of the essays are concerned with his work as a musician and the subsequent impact it had on popular culture. Very little of his film work; however, a filmorgraphy is included. Selected bibliography and discography.

768.   Ridgeway, John. *The Sinatra File.* Birmingham, England: John Ridgeway Books; 1977.

A collection of anecdotes and recollections about his life and musical career. Index.

769.   Shaw, Arnold. *Sinatra: Twentieth-Century Romantic.* New York: Holt, Reinhart and Winston; 1968.

Details Sinatra's musical career within the context of both jazz and popular music. Sinatra is portrayed as a vocal stylist who possesses the talent to function as both a big band vocalist and a soloist with small ensembles. His ability to interpret and phrase a song is highlighted. Index.

770.   Wilson, Earl. *Sinatra: An Unauthorized Biography.* New York: Macmillan; 1976.

Explores Sinatra from both laudatory and critical viewpoints. He is covered as a musical giant as well as a person with talents and interests that expand beyond music. His musical activities, movie acting, and extramusical activities are covered. Index and selected bibliography.

Stuff Smith

771.   Smith, Stuff. *Pure at Heart.* New York: Lewes; 2002.

Concise but factual account of his life from the early years to his acceptance as a great jazz artist. Covers bands he played with, associations, and influences. Also contains reminiscences by Timme Rosenkrantz and an interview with Val Wilmer

Willie "The Lion" Smith

772. Smith, Willie "The Lion." *Music on My Mind: The Memoirs of an American Pianist;* with George Hoefer; foreword by Duke Ellington. Garden City: Doubleday, 1964; London: MacGibbon and Kee, 1965; London: Jazz Book Club, 1966; New York: Da Capo, 1975.

Details the life and musical career of this piano giant, especially in New York. Smith was one of the pioneers of the "Harlem stride piano" movement of the 1920s; his role and influence on Duke Ellington, Thelonious Monk, and Fats Waller are covered. There are numerous anecdotes from his musical peers and acquaintances. Hoefer contributes four interludes to the biographical and historical section; the 1975 edition contains a new introduction by John S. Wilson. There is a European itinerary of 1949–50, a list of his compositions, and a discography covering 1920–61. Index.

Jess Stacy

773. Keller, Keith. *Oh, Jess: A Jazz Life.* Copenhagen: Jazz Media; 1989.

Covers his life from his Missouri beginnings through his eventual success as a jazz pianist. Also provides information on his associations with artists like Benny Goodman, Bob Crosby, Tommy Dorsey, Pee Wee Russell, and others, and his postswing career as a soloist. Discography, filmography, illustrations.

Harry Stephens

774. Stephens, Harry. *Swing Threatens Third Reich.* Suffolk: Unknown Publisher; 1991.

The author describes the sociopolitical conditions and reactions to American jazz when he was growing up in Hamburg, Germany. Of particular interest is his discussion of the threat that swing posed to the Third Reich.

Rex Stewart

775. Stewart, Rex William. *Boy Meets Horn,* edited by Claire P. Gordon. Ann Arbor: University of Michigan Press; 1991.

Stewart covers his musical career from his debut at the age of 14 with Ollie Blackwell's Clowns, to the bands of Billy Fowler, Billy Paige, Elmer Snowden, Fletcher Henderson, and Duke Ellington. The autobiography is also important because it covers his relationship with numerous jazz giants of the 1920s and 1930s including Louis Armstrong, Jimmy Harrison, Bubber Miley, King Oliver, Fletcher Henderson, Duke Ellington, Louis Russell, and McKinney's Cotton Pickers. Claire P. Gordon edited the book from his manuscripts.

Billy Strayhorn

776.   Hajdu, David. *Lush Life*. New York: North Point Press; 1996.

In this meticulously researched, objective, and engaging biography, the author discusses Strayhorn's life and musical accomplishments. He begins with his child prodigy years in Pittsburgh, first meeting with Duke Ellington, and proceeds to his musical relationship with Ellington. He discusses Strayhorn's role and function as an arranger and composer for Ellington, his brief departure from Ellington, his bibulous lifestyle in New York and Paris, Strayhorn's homosexuality, Ellington's threat to replace him with Luther Henderson, and more.

777.   Van de Leur, Walter. *Something to Live For: The Music of Billy Strayhorn*. New York: Oxford University Press; 2002.

The author argues that Strayhorn was more than Ellington's alter ego; rather, he introduced a radically new and visionary way of composing to the Ellington Orchestra. He surveys over 3,000 autographed scores to separate Ellington from Strayhorn, to establish who wrote what, and to make clear and distinct differences between the respective styles. He identifies differences between their harmonic, melodic, and structural designs. He uses "Something to Live For" to illustrate the characteristic features of Strayhorn's compositions and arrangements. Contains over 70 musical examples, detailed and scholarly.

Ralph Sutton

778.   Shacter, James D. *Piano Man: The Story of Ralph Sutton*. Chicago: Jaynar Press; 1975.

Details Sutton's musical career from the influence of Fats Waller to stints with Jack Teagarden at Condon's (1948–56), and the World's Greatest Jazz Band beginning in 1969. The biography is based on interviews with family and friends and includes information on both his successes and failures. Selected discography.

Tom Talbert

779. Talbot, Bruce. *Tom Talbert: His Life and Times: Voices From a Vanished World of Jazz.* Lanham, Md.: Scarecrow Press, and Institute of Jazz Studies (Rutgers University); 2004.

A composer, arranger, bandleader, and pianist, the book is permeated with memories of Los Angeles in the 1940s, road tours of the Midwest with Territory bands, life on the road with Johnny Richards, insights into the Minneapolis–St. Paul jazz scene during World War II, and a portrait of the 1950s jazz scene in New York City. Lots of anecdotes and memories of musicians he played with.

Art Tatum

780. Laubich, Arnold, and Ray Spencer. *Art Tatum: A Guide to His Recorded Music.* Metuchen, N.J.: Scarecrow Press and the Institute of Jazz Studies (Rutgers University); 1982.

Contains a chronological discography that lists domestic and foreign recordings both issued and unissued. V-discs, radio and television transcriptions, and tapes are also listed. Included are an index of personnel that performed with Tatum as a sideman or leader and data on his published music and piano rolls. There are some minor flaws: the "Shout" was composed by Joe Turner and Kirby Walker, not Tatum, and the authors fail to list John Arpin's imitation of Tatum's "Jade" in their section on "Imitations of Disc." The appendix contains a list of other discographies consulted, information on cross references, and matrix numbers.

781. Lester, James. *Too Marvelous for Words: The Life and Genius of Art Tatum.* New York, Oxford: Oxford University Press; 1994.

A full-length biography covering his origins, teachers and influences, entry into jazz, role in developing other artists, and his persona when not performing. His stints in Toledo, Chicago, New York, and California are chronicled, as are his bebop years. No musical examples, limited references to stylistic analysis. Selected references, notes, and index.

Jack Teagarden

782. Mückenberger, Heiner. *Meet Me Where They Play the Blues: Jack Teagarden und seine Musik.* Waakirchen, Germany: Oreos; 1986.

In German. Provides details of his life and recordings, including his role as a sideman, bandleader, trombonist, and influence in both America and

Europe. Also discusses his role in the New Orleans revival of the 1940s and associations/recordings with numerous artists. The discussion of recordings includes information on personnel and style. Illustrated.

783.   Smith, James D., and Len Guttridge. *Jack Teagarden: The Story of a Jazz Maverick.* London: Cassell, 1960; London: Jazz Book Club; New York: Da Capo, 1983.

A positive portrayal of his life and music including his rise to fame in Harlem night clubs, performances with Louis Armstrong, and significant contributions to the Chicago style of jazz of the 1920s and 1930s.

784.   Waters, Jr., Howard J. *Jack Teagarden's Music: His Career and Recordings.* Stanhope, N.J.: Allen; 1960.

A biodiscography that covers his life, musical achievements, associations, and contributions. The majority of the book is devoted to an exhaustive discography covering recordings as both sideman and leader. Bibliography and index.

Leslie Thompson

785.   Thompson, Leslie, and Jeffrey P. Green. *Leslie Thompson: An Autobiography.* Sussex, England: Rabbit; 1985.

Autobiography of a little known (Jamaican, 1901–87) but significant trumpeter who spent many years performing in London. Thompson's musical training in Jamaica, early visits to England (1929–20), and permanent stay in London (1929–40), is discussed. His work with Louis Armstrong, Benny Carter, Duke Ellington, Fats Waller, and other American and British musicians is also discussed. Bibliography, index, and illustrations.

Mel Tormé

786.   Tormé, Mel. *It Wasn't All Velvet.* New York: Viking; 1988.

An autobiography that covers his musical beginnings, struggles, and successes. Includes his stint with the Mel-Tones and his eventual successes as a leading interpreter of jazz lyrics. Also chronicles his associations with other artists, his ability to compose and arrange, and his influence on other artists. Comprehensive. Index. Illustrations.

Lennie Tristano

787.   Billard, Francois. *Lennie Tristano.* Montpellier, France: Limon; 1989.

Chronicles his beginning in Chicago to his role as pianist and leader of a group of progressive jazz musicians. His associations with Billy Bauer, Lee Konitz, Warne Marsh, Charles Mingus, and Miles Davis are covered. Tristano's style change, influences, compositions, and role as a proponent of change are also discussed.

Frankie Trumbauer

788. Evans, Philip R., and Larry F. Kiner with Frank Trumbauer. *Tram: The Frank Trumbauer Story, A Bio-Discography.* Metuchen, N.J.: Scarecrow Press, and Institute of Jazz Studies (Rutgers University); 1994.

Based on information supplied by former friends and associates, and memos written by Trumbauer in 1953 to produce a thorough book on the man, his music, and his associates. The biography includes information on his relationships with Bix Beiderbecke, Jean Goldkette, Miff Mole, Paul Whiteman, and Paul Zenter. Also covers both his early and final years in Chicago. The discography includes several entries on the Wolverines, featuring Trumbauer and Bix Beiderbecke.

Bruce Turner

789. Turner, Bruce. *Hot Air, Cool Music.* London: Quartet Books; 1986.

An autobiography of the British saxophonist-clarinetist. In addition to his life and musical accomplishments, the author argues that British jazz should be accepted as equal to American jazz. He mentions several British jazz musicians, however, he disdains the avant-garde jazz of the 1970s.

Sarah Vaughan

790. Leydi, Roberto. *Sarah Vaughan.* Milano: Ricordi; 1961.

Traces Vaughan's life and embryonic musical experiences from Newark, New Jersey, to the late 1950s. Includes information on her experience as an organist at Mount Zion Baptist Church, amateur night contest winner at the Apollo Theater, and associations with Earl "Fatha" Hines, Billy Eckstine, and John Kirby. Also discusses her marriage to George Treadwell. No new insights. Selected discography, illustrated.

Thomas "Fats" Waller

791. Fox, Charles. *Fats Waller.* London: Cassell, 1960; New York: Barnes; 1961.

A concise biographical sketch that includes critical comments on performance techniques and musical style. The assessments are derived from selected recordings. The biographical sketch covers his life from Harlem childhood through his relationship with James P. Johnson and Willie "The Lion" Smith. Selected discography, bibliography, and reference notes.

792. Kirkeby, W. T. *Ain't Misbehavin': The Story of Fats Waller;* in collaboration with Duncan P. Schiedt and Sinclair Traill. London: Davies, New York: Dodd, Mead, 1966; London: Jazz Book Club, 1967; New York: Da Capo, 1975, 1978, 1985; Ravensburg, Germany: Oreos, 1981.

A narrative account of Waller's life by Waller's manager from 1937 to his death. There are important accounts of his friends and musical peers and important information on the New York jazz scene of the 1920s and 1930s. His friendships with musicians from the "Harlem stride piano" school as well as Andy Razak are also covered. Compositions are referred to but not analyzed. Selected discography.

793. Machlin, Paul S. *Stride: The Music of Fats Waller.* Boston: G.K. Hall, London: Macmillan; 1985.

Details his life and music. There is coverage of his compositions and references to his stride piano style. The analysis covers many of his most significant compositions, including "Ain't Misbehavin'," "Honeysuckle Rose," "Jitterbug Waltz," and "The Joint is Jumpin'." His role as an innovative and creative composer of popular songs, his lifestyle, and his personality are also covered. Several musical examples. Bibliography, discography, chronology, index, and illustrations.

794. Shipton, Alyn. *Fats Waller.* New York: Universe; 1988.

The biography covers his early musical training, impact of stride piano on his style, his compositions, significance, lifestyle, and personality. His public image, tours, and associations with numerous musicians are also detailed. Bibliography, index, illustrations.

795. Vance, Joel. *Fats Waller: His Life and Times.* Chicago: Contemporary Books; 1977.

A warm and effusive account of Waller's life and musical career. The author asserts that Waller as an adult continued to live with the innocence of a child. He applauds his personality and acknowledges his musical greatness as both composer and pianist. He also lauds his ability to "entertain." In addition, Vance provides some perceptive comments on Waller's compositions and performances. There is no discussion of cultural context or of the sociocultural factors that enabled Waller to both exist and prosper. Selected bibliography and index.

796. Waller, Maurice, and Anthony Calabrese. *Fats Waller;* foreword by Michael Lipskin. New York: Schirmer Books; 1977.

An effusive account of Waller's experiences as a theater organist, house-rent party pianist, piano-roll recorder, and radio broadcaster as well as his achievements as accompanist, soloist, and composer. The narrative is permeated with anecdotes and stories, some of which focus on Waller's extramusical activities. Among the most interesting stories are his first encounter with African American music and his first contact with James P. Johnson and Luckey Roberts. Both his successes and sorrows are revealed, the book presents meticulous research, and it benefits from the insights of Maurice Waller, Fats's son. Contains an annotated list of recording dates, a list of piano-roll recordings, a list of published and unpublished compositions, three compositions, and a complete index.

Dinah Washington

797. Haskins, Jim. *Queen of the Blues: A Biography of Dinah Washington.* New York: Morrow; 1987.

Discusses her early years in Chicago, participation in the first all-female gospel group (Sallie Martin Colored Ladies Quartet), switch to secular music, and recordings. In addition, her switch from Mercury to Roulette records, marriages, personality, and influence on vocalists like Della Reese are chronicled, as is her assistance in building the careers of artists like Patti Austin, Johnny Mathis, Redd Foxx, and Quincy Jones. Discography, index, illustrations.

Ben Webster

798. De Valk, Jeroen. *Ben Webster: His Life and Music.* Berkeley: Berkeley Hills Books; 2001.

Details his life, influences, career as a sideman and leader, and contribu-tion to jazz. Discusses why Webster was respected, and how he compared to other tenor saxophonists. Also discusses his tenure with Duke Ellington and associations with other musicians.

Dicky Wells

799. Wells, Dicky. *The Night People: Reminiscences of a Jazzman;* as told to Stanley Dance. Boston: Crescendo; London: Hale; 1971.

Contains details of his life and musical tenure with bands like Count Basie, Ray Charles, and Fletcher Henderson. He presents his material in a series of anecdotes and recollections covering both significant and lesser-known musicians. In addition to the aforementioned, Wells comments on the impact of drinking on his later playing. Glossary and index.

Dick Wellstood

800.   Meyer, Edward N. *Giant Strides: The Legacy of Dick Wellstood.* Lanham, Md.: Scarecrow Press, and Institute of Jazz Studies (Rutgers University); 1999.

Chronicles the life and music of this important but little-known artist. Includes information on the evolution of his career, influences, and experiences

Paul Whiteman

801.   DeLong, Thomas A. *Pops: Paul Whiteman, King of Jazz.* Piscataway, N.J.: New Century; 1983.

Traces his life through his days as a symphonic violinist with both the Denver and San Francisco Symphony orchestras through his leadership of a dance band. Provides insight into his associations with Bix Beiderbecke, Bill Challis, Jack Teagarden, and Frankie Trumbauer. Also discusses his pseudo-jazz style and the acceptance of his music. Selected bibliography, chronology, index, and illustrations.

802.   Johnson, Carl. *A Paul Whiteman Chronology (1890–1967).* Williamstown, Mass.: Williams College, 1977; revised edition, 1979.

A chronological approach to the most significant events in Whiteman's musical career. All events are grouped by year, and the Whiteman chronology is compared with other popular musical events of the time. Selected discography and concise accounts of the Whiteman Collection at Williams College, lists of his personnel, radio shows, appearances in motion pictures, concert programs, and the availability of Whiteman recordings.

803.   Rayno, Don. *Paul Whiteman: Pioneer in American Music, Volume I: 1890–1930.* Lanham, Md.: Scarecrow Press, and Institute of Jazz Studies (Rutgers University); 2003.

The first of a proposed two-volume set that will serve as the definitive work on the life and music of the bandleader. Covers his early years from

1890 to 1930, with rich details and coverage of the life of the times. He provides a glimpse of life in the Roaring Twenties, a day-by-day chronology of the 1890 to 1930 years, an alphabetical listing of his 1918 to 1930 band members, biographical sketches of famous people, a comprehensive discography of his 1920s to 1930s recordings, extensive notes, references, bibliography, and an index. Also contains nearly 60 rare black-and-white photographs of Whiteman, his band members, and others.

804.   Whiteman, Paul, and Mary Margaret McBride. *Jazz.* New York: Sears, 1926. Reprint, New York: Arno Press; 1974.

A pseudo-jazzman's account that focuses primarily on his assessments of the characteristics of jazz. Although Whiteman (1890–1967) was crowned the "King of Jazz," his music should not be considered jazz, as he emphasized composition and arrangement rather than improvisation. He covers topics such as the social effects of the music, roles and functions of the instruments (orchestration, recording), and his belief that symphony musicians are preferred over others (including jazz). In that sense, it is insightful, however, the authors comments should be kept in context, as Whiteman was not a jazz musician.

Bob Wilbur

805.   Wilber, Bob. *Music Was Not Enough;* assisted by Derek Webster. New York: Oxford University Press; 1988.

Details the author's career as a jazz musician in both America and Europe. The author was a protégé of Sidney Bechet (a clarinetist and saxophonist) and has performed with several significant groups during his career. In this book, he discusses his studies with Bechet and other early jazzmen, his recovery from drug addiction, problems of surviving as a jazz musician in the 1950s and 1960s, and his return to stardom in the 1970s. The book won the 1989 ASCAP-Deems Taylor award. Index.

Alec Wilder

806.   Balliett, Whitney. *Alec Wilder and His Friends.* Boston: Houghton Mifflin, 1974; New York: Da Capo, 1977.

In addition to Wilder, provides portraits of Ruby Braff, Bobby Hackett, Marian McPartland, Mabel Mercer, and Blossom Dearie. The essays are biomusical and draw from both his acquaintances with and interviews of these musicians.

Clarence Williams

807.   Lord, Tom. *Clarence Williams*. London: Storyville; 1976.

A massive biodiscography, which includes musical analysis of several performances. Also discusses his group, the Blue Five, his role as musical director of OKEH race records (1923–28), and contributions as an accompanist on many recordings, including female blues-jazz artists. Includes musical examples, bibliography, index, and illustrations.

Joe Williams

808.   Gourse, Leslie. *Every Day: The Story of Joe Williams*. New York, Melbourne: Quartet, 1985, New York: Da Capo, 1986.

Chronicles his life from early musical experiences in the South and especially in Chicago with groups such as Red Saunders and at the Club Delisa to his long and successful tenures with Count Basie and Thad Jones. His career as a soloist, associations with numerous musicians, and his influences and significance are also discussed. Bibliography, discography, chronology, index, illustrations.

Mary Lou Williams

809.   Dahl, Linda. *Morning Glory: A Biography of Mary Lou Williams*. New York: Pantheon Books; 1999.

Covers her career from the early years in Pittsburgh, marriage to John Williams and Shorty Baker, Kansas City years with Walter Page, and her contributions to jazz from 1940 to her death in 1981. Discusses her stint at the Café Society, religious conversion, composing of religious compositions, and mentoring of artists such as Dizzy Gillespie, Thelonious Monk, Bud Powell, and many artists associated with the bebop and postbebop jazz styles. Also covers her travails in jazz, capacity to absorb new sounds, and teaching at Duke University.

810.   Kernodle, Tammy L. *Anything You Are Shows up in Your Music: Mary Lou Williams and the Sanctification of Jazz*. Boston: Northeastern University Press; 2003.

A biography of the jazz pianist, arranger, and composer (1910–81). Covers her musical career from her first public performance at the age of six, touring the black vaudeville circuit at the age of twelve, through her conversion and dedication to religious based compositions. Also covers her depression and withdrawal from jazz, relationship with artists like Walter

Page and Duke Ellington, stay in Paris, relationship with Father O'Brien, and contributions to early bebop.

Teddy Wilson

811. Leo, Humphrey Van, and Arie Ligthart (editors). *Teddy Wilson Talks Jazz.* Foreword by Benny Goodman. Ann Arbor: University of Michigan Press; 1993.

A vivid account of Wilson's life and musical career. Among the many personal insights are his recollections of Al Capone, respect for musicians like Jelly Roll Morton, account of Billie Holiday's recording career, and a very penetrating account of working with Benny Goodman. Of significant interest are the comparisons of the piano techniques of Earl "Fatha" Hines, Art Tatum, and "Fats" Waller. Overall, this autobiography offers a penetrating account of both Wilson's life and music, as well as the life and music of the 1930s, 1940s, and 1950s. Selected bibliography and discography.

Al Young

812. Young, Al. *Kinds of Blue.* San Francisco: Creative Arts; 1984.

Includes an assessment of Pepper Adams and Donald Byrd at the World Stage (Detroit, 1955); a biographical profile and memoir of John Coltrane; and an appreciation of the contributions and styles of Kenny Dorham and Charles Mingus. The approach is both descriptive and laudatory rather than critical.

Lester Young

813. Büchmann-Møller, Frank. *You Got To Be Original Man: The Music of Lester Young.* Foreword by Lewis Porter. New York and Westport, Conn.: Greenwood Press; 1990.

A complete "solography" of Young's recordings, including a critical assessment of his solos on records (private and unissued). Includes approximately 80 transcribed solos and numerous additional musical excerpts. The author expands the work of Lewis Porter and others by including newly discovered items and adding previously unknown recording dates and personnel to incomplete discographical citations in previous studies. The comments offer critical insights into the musical structure of the solos. Song index, index of transcribed solos, and name index. Excellent resource.

814.   _____. *Lester Young, You Just Fight for Your Life.* Westport, Conn.: Greenwood Publishers; 1990.

Focuses on the many bands that Young performed with prior to joining Count Basie in 1936. The author provides information on his beginning musical experiences with the Young family circus band, his military experience, and his years as a bandleader and soloist. His association with Billie Holiday and problems with drugs and racism are also detailed. Selected bibliography, reference notes, a discography, and an index.

815.   Burkhardt, Werner, and Joachim Gerth. *Lester Young: Ein Porträt.* Wetzlar, Germany: Pegasus; 1959.

In German. A concise overview of his life, early years with Basie and in Kansas City, and rise to fame as a tenor saxophonist. Also discusses his relationship with Billie Holiday and influence on other artists. No new insights. Discography, illustrations.

816.   Daniels, Douglass Henry. *Lester Leaps in: The Life and Times of Lester "Pres" Young.* Boston: Beacon Press; 2002.

A detailed biography of the man and his music from his early years in Woodville, Mississippi, until his death in 1958. Well-researched and written, the author covers Young's relationship with artists/topics such as Count Basie, Billie Holiday, Coleman Hawkins, his Mississippi and Los Angeles years, encounters with racism, and religious beliefs. The biography is permeated with new insights and interpretations, and includes extensive notes. Contains a selected discography and a list of persons interviewed.

817.   DeLannoy, Luc; translated from French by Elena B. Odio. *Pres: The Story of Lester Young.* Fayetteville: University of Arkansas; 1993.

Chronicles the story of Lester Young from his beginnings in his father's circus band to his death in 1959. Young's tenure with Count Basie, recordings with Billie Holiday, and impact on jazz are covered in detail. His encounter with racism in the army and bouts with depression are also chronicled.

818.   Franchini, Vittorio. *Lester Young.* Milan: Ricordi; 1961.

In Italian. Concise portrait of his life from his years with the family circus band and Count Basie to his short tenure with Fletcher Henderson. Young's contributions as a soloist and innovator, influence on other artists, and his style are discussed. Rehashes known material. Selected discography.

819.   Gelly, Dave. *Lester Young.* Turnbridge, England, and Spellmount, N.Y.: Hippocrene; 1984.

Biographical portrait with a discography by Tony Middleton. Covers his early experiences with his father's circus band, his years with Count Basie, and associations with artists such as Billie Holiday and Fletcher Henderson. No new insights.

820. Gerth, Joachim. *Lester Young: Ein Porträt.* Wetzlar, Germany: Pegasus; 1959.

In German. Biographical portrait that covers known facts about his life, associations, and significance as a soloist. The coverage is condensed (48 pages) and includes references to recordings. Bibliography, selected discography.

821. McDonough, John. *Lester Young;* notes on the music by Richard M. Sudhalter. Alexandria, Virginia: Time-Life Records; 1980.

A biographical portrait that was written to accompany the Time-Life "Giants of Jazz" series. Included are biographical details and comments on musical style. Since the publication of this booklet, other scholarly studies on Young have appeared, including Robert A. Luckey's *A Study of Lester Young and His Influence Upon Contemporaries* (Ph.D. dissertation, University of Pittsburgh); Lewis Porter's *Lester Young* (Boston: Twayne, 1985), also based on his doctoral dissertation. Although the author's biographical and musical comments are thorough, there is minimum discussion of cultural context.

822. Porter, Lewis. *Lester Young.* Boston: Twayne Publishers; 1985.

A scholarly study of his life and music. Porter's overall purpose is to expose his readers to the musical intangibles that made Young a great saxophonist. He begins with a biographical profile divided by years, after which in chapters 2 through 6 he examines selected improvisations in detail. Specifically, he examines melody, rhythm, harmony, glissandi, contour, dynamics and expression, and much more. There are 34 transcriptions, a note on the musical examples (diacritical markings), a chronology of important events in Young's life, and chapter notes. There is a comprehensive discography of Young as a sideman and bandleader, selected discography of LPs (LPs listed in the *Catalog of Recorded Works*), and an index.

823. _____(editor). *A Lester Young Reader.* Washington, D.C.: Smithsonian Press; 1991.

A compilation of 36 essays covering biographical pieces, musical studies, and interviews that cover the life and music of this giant. The essays are divided into three categories: biographical, interviews, and performance style analysis. Contributors include Douglas Daniels, John Hammond,

Nat Hentoff, Dan Morgenstern, and Martin Williams. No bibliography or discography, however both can be found in Porter's biography on Lester Young.

Collective Biographies, Portraits, Essays

824. Amery, Jean. *Im Banne des Jazz: Bildnisse grosser Jazz-Musiker.* Zürich, Stuttgart, Wien: Müller; 1961.

In German. Biomusical portraits that focus on background, career, styles, and influences. The artists covered are Louis Armstrong, Sidney Bechet, Bix Beiderbecke, Miles Davis, Duke Ellington, Ella Fitzgerald, Dizzy Gillespie, Lionel Hampton, Billie Holiday, Gene Krupa, John Lewis, Mezz Mezzrow, Kid Ory, Charles Parker, Django Reinhardt, Lennie Tristano, Sarah Vaughan, and Lester Young. No new insights.

825. Arnaud, Gerald, and Jacques Chesnel. *Masters of Jazz.* New York: Chambers; 1992.

A translation of *Les Grande Cre'ateurs du Jazz* and lists musicians by instrument or voice. Covers the majority of artists from throughout history condensed into concise biographical portraits of four or fewer pages. Topical essays, boxed sidebar and quotations, and some black-and-white photographs are also included.

826. Balliett, Whitney. *Collected Works: A Journal of Jazz 1954–2000.* New York: St. Martin's Press; 2001.

Captures the full range and register of the jazz scene, from the Newport Jazz Festival in 1954 to recent performances by a new generation of musicians. Includes portraits of Louis Armstrong, Duke Ellington, Dizzy Gillespie, Charles Mingus, Billie Holiday, Earl Hines, Django Reinhardt, Bessie Smith, Art Tatum, and more.

827. _____. *Barney, Bradley, and Max: Sixteen Portraits in Jazz.* New York: Oxford University Press; 1989.

A compilation of profiles that originally appeared in the author's jazz column in the *New Yorker.* The title refers to three jazz club owners: Barney Josephson, Bradley Cunningham, and Max Gordon. He includes lengthy monologues by the artists, personality traits, physical appearance, and pseudo-musical analysis. Covers artists such as Louis Bellson, Rudy Braff, Buddy DeFranco, Benny Goodman, Harvey Phillips, Mel Powell, Jimmy Rowles, George Shearing, Claude Thornhill, and Lester Young. Also includes information on club owners and operators such as Max Gordon.

828. _____. *American Singers: Twenty-Seven Portraits in Song.* New York: Oxford University Press; 1988.

A collection of essays that, with one exception, first appeared in the *New Yorker.* Each artist is introduced by several paragraphs and thereafter in their own words provides anecdotes and details regarding their musical careers. Includes portraits of artists such as Tony Bennett, Ray Charles, Nellie Lucher, Julius LaRossa, Alberta Hunter, Mabel Mercer, and Big Joe Turner. Several of the essays were previously published in other books by the author.

829. _____. *American Musicians: 56 Portraits in Jazz.* New York: Oxford University Press; 1986.

Combines portraits with interviews to cover sociomusical issues, careers, and attitudes toward change as expressed by insiders. Among the numerous artists profiled are Gene Bertoncini, Joe Bushkin, Betty Carter, Roy Eldridge, Coleman Hawkins, Art Hodes, Helen Humes, Warne Marsh, Jimmy McPartland, Django Reinhardt in the Stéphane Grappelli profile (reprinted from *Improvising: Sixteen Jazz Musicians and Their Art*), George Shearing, Milt Jackson, Connie Kay, John Lewis, Modern Jazz Quartet (histories of Kay, Heath, Lewis, Jackson, reprinted in *American Musicians),* and King Oliver. Additional reprints from the *New Yorker, Night Creature, Ecstasy at the Onion, Alec Wilder and His Friends,* and *Jelly Roll, Jabbo and Fats.*

830. _____. *American Musicians II: Seventy-Two Portraits in Jazz.* Second edition. New York: Oxford University Press; 1996.

Expands his *American Musicians* (1986) from 56 to 72 portraits of jazz musicians. The essays include critical, historical, and personal information and reflect the author's interest rather than an attempt to be comprehensive. He adds essays on Dizzy Gillespie, Charles Parker, and several other artists to fill the void in the first edition. Also, like the first edition there are no publication dates on the essays, nor is there a name index.

831. _____. *Good Byes and Other Messages: A Journal of Jazz, 1981–1990.* New York: Oxford University Press; 1991.

Contains many of the concise essays the author wrote for the *New Yorker.* The essays date from 1981 to 1990, and include only limited attention to the avant-garde, hard bop, and none on the fusion artists or the movement. The essays offer insightful historical and musical observations on artists such as Bunny Berigan, Duke Ellington, Dizzy Gillespie, Max Gordon Bill Coleman, Miles Davis, Roy Eldridge, Bill Evans, Otis Ferguson, John Hammond, and Thelonious Monk.

832.   _____. *Jelly Roll, Jabbo and Fats: 19 Portraits in Jazz.* New York: Oxford University Press; 1983, 1984.

Biomusical portraits and appreciations previously published in 1975–82 in the *New Yorker.* The portraits include Sidney Bechet, Tommy Ben Ford, Doc Cheatham, Ornette Coleman, Vic Dickenson, Erroll Garner, Sonny Greer, Lee Konitz, Ellis Larkins, Dave McKenna, Freddie Moore, Michael Moore, Jelly Roll Morton, Jabbo Smith, Fats Waller, Dick Wellstood, and Lester Young. The portraits cover sociomusical issues, although they lack transcriptions or musical examples.

833.   _____. *Night Creature: A Journal of Jazz, 1975–1980.* New York: Oxford University Press; 1981.

A collection of the author's essays that appeared in the *New Yorker* over a five-year period. The essays cover musical practices, performers, and analysis of several compositions. There are anecdotes and personal insights on some of the many jazz musicians performing in New York, including Doc Cheatham and Jimmy Knepper.

834.   _____. *Improvising: Sixteen Jazz Musicians and Their Art.* New York: Oxford University Press; 1966, 1977.

Several portraits, some previously published in the *New Yorker,* and in the author's *Such Sweet Thunder, Ecstasy at the Onion,* and *Super Drummer: A Profile of Buddy Rich.* There are portraits of Sid Catlett (which includes quotes from Helen Humes, Earl Hines, Dicky Wells, and Ray Eldridge), Kenny Clarke (revised in *American Musicians*), Stephen Grappled (reprinted in *American Musicians,* also includes information on Django Reinhardt), Jim Hall (reprinted in *American Musicians*). Percy Heath (revised in *American Musicians*), Earl "Fatha" Hines, Milt Jackson, Connie Fay, John Lewis, Modern Jazz Quartet (histories of Fay, Heath, Lewis, and Jackson reprinted in *American Musicians),* and King Oliver. The essays focus on the personalities and phobias of the men and women behind the music rather than detailed musical analysis. Practitioners of postbop and the avant-garde of the 1960s and 1970s are for the most part omitted.

835.   _____. *Ecstasy at the Onion: Thirty-One Pieces on Jazz.* New York: Bobbs-Merrill; 1971.

A collection of appreciations and reviews previously published in the *New Yorker.* Included are biomusical portraits of John Coltrane, Duke Ellington, Bobby Hackett, Elvin Jones, Charles Mingus, Red Norvo, and Art Tatum.

836.   _____. *Such Sweet Thunder.* Indianapolis: Bobbs-Merrill; 1966.

Continuation of the author's penchant to group previously published essays into one collection. These essays were originally published in the *New*

Yorker between 1962 and 1966. The essays cover a myriad of topics including reviews of festivals, selected performances and recordings. The portraits include Red Allen, Louis Armstrong, Count Basie, Sidney Bechet, Louis Bellson, Lou Black, Benny Carter, Ornette Coleman, Ray Eldridge, Duke Ellington, Bill Evans, Jimmy Giuffre, Bobby Hackett, Coleman Hawkins, Woody Herman, Earl "Fatha" Hines, James P. Johnson, Gene Krupa, Charles Mingus, Charles Parker, Bud Powell, Pee Wee Russell, Zutty Singleton, Jeremy Steig, Buddy Tate, Lucky Thompson, and Mary Lou Williams.

837.   _____. *Dinosaurs in the Morning.* Philadelphia: Lippincott, 1962, Toronto: McClelland, 1962, 1964; London: Phoenix, 1964: London: Jazz Book Club, 1965.

Several previously published appreciations, biographical portraits, concert, and record reviews from the *New Yorker.* Among the represented artists are Toshiko Akiyoshi, Buck Clayton, Ornette Coleman, Bix Beiderbecke, Emmett Berry, Miles Davis, Duke Ellington, Erroll Garner, Dizzy Gillespie, Coleman Hawkins, Fletcher Henderson, Johnny Hodges, Billie Holiday, Jo Jones, Humphrey Lyttelton, Charles Mingus, Modern Jazz Quartet, Thelonious Monk, Django Reinhardt, Buddy Rich, Max Roach, Sonny Rollins, Cecil Taylor, Jack Teagarden, Dick Wellstood, and Lester Young.

838.   _____. *The Sound of Surprise.* New York: Dutton, 1959, 1961; Toronto: Smithers, 1960; London: Kimber, 1960; Toronto: Clarke, Irwin, 1961; London: Jazz Book Club, 1961; Harmondsworth, England: Penguin, 1963; New York: Da Capo Press, 1978.

An eclectic collection of essays, appreciations, concert, and record reviews previously published in the *New Yorker* and *Saturday Review,* 1954–59. The profiles include Louis Armstrong, Sidney Bechet, Art Blakey, Sid Catlett, Teddy Charles, Miles Davis, Vic Dickenson, Duke Ellington, Art Farmer, Tommy Flanagan, Dave Frishberg, Erroll Garner, Jimmy Giuffre, Philly Joe Jones, Charles Mingus, Modern Jazz Quartet, Thelonious Monk, Joe Morello, Jelly Roll Morton, Max Roach, Pee Wee Russell, Art Tatum, Ben Webster, and Cootie Williams. Topics include career, recordings, change, and racism. Index.

839.   Bennett, Betty. *The Ladies Who Sing with the Band.* Lanham, Md., and Institute of Jazz Studies (Rutgers University); 2000.

Permeated with anecdotes and musical insights into many jazz and popular music icons. Among the persons covered are George Auld, Charlie Barnet, Nat "King" Cole, Dizzy Gillespie, Benny Goodman, and more. She addresses her marriage to André Previn and relationship with her current husband, Mundell Lowe. She also discusses black/white professional and personal interactions. females traveling with all-male bands, and insights into her singing style and philosophy.

840.   Blesh, Rudi. *Eight Lives in Jazz Combo: U.S.A.* New York: Hayden Book Company, 1971; Toronto: Nelson; Philadelphia, London: Chilton, 1971; New York: Da Capo, 1979.

Biomusical portraits of Louis Armstrong, Sidney Bechet, Jack Teagarden, Lester Young, Billie Holiday, Gene Krupa, Charlie Christian, and Eubie Blake. The portraits are supplemented with both insider and outsider perspectives, and cover their lives and music. Selected chapter reference notes, bibliography, discography, and an index.

841.   Brackett, David. *Interpreting Popular Music.* Berkeley: University of California Press; 2000.

Explores several genres of music, including jazz, through the recordings of artists such as James Brown, Bing Crosby, Billie Holiday, and Hank Williams. He examines both the cultural and musical dimensions of the music.

842.   Carr, Ian. *Jazz: The Rough Guide: Written by Ian Carr, Digby Fairweather and Brian Priestley;* with contributions from Chris Parker, et al; photographs by Jake Kilby, et al. New York: Rough Guides; 1995.

Contains the biographies of nearly 2,000 individual musicians and groups from early jazz to the mid-1990s. The entries include recommendations for purchase of the "best and representative recordings of a specific artist or group". They provide balance coverage of music and history, and include many British and Continental musicians. The guide includes a 30-page glossary that defines styles, techniques, and terms.

843.   Carver, Reginald, and Lenny Bernstein. *Jazz Profiles: The Spirit of the Nineties.* New York: Billboard Books; 1998.

Profiles the life and music of 40 musicians divided into bassists, drummers, guitarists, pianists/organists, trumpeters, trombonists, saxophonists/clarinetist, and vocalists. The biographical sketches were based on interviews, and include a photograph and concise discography.

844.   Collier, James Lincoln. *The Great Jazz Artists;* monoprints by Robert Andrew Parker. New York: Four Winds; 1977.

Profiles many leading artists in a mixture of tragedy and triumph. He accentuates the musical contributions as well as the impact of alcoholism and drugs on each artist. Among the artists covered are Ornette Coleman, Louis Armstrong, Benny Goodman, Leadbelly, Bessie Smith, Charles

Parker, and several more. The weakness of the book is that artists such as Stan Getz, Sonny Rollins, and Oscar Peterson are virtually ignored.

845. Crowther, Bruce, and Mike Pinfold. *Singing Jazz: The Singers and Their Styles.* San Francisco: Miller Freeman Books; 1997.

Provides profiles of legendary artists such as Louis Armstrong, Ella Fitzgerald, Billie Holiday, Carmen McRae, Sarah Vaughan, and many more. Explores lines, words, and music of vocalists past and present, examines career highs and lows learning processes, building a repertoire, finding work, traveling, and struggling for recognition. The A–Z reference section provides concise biographies and essential recordings for over 200 vocalists.

846. Davis, Francis. *In the Moment; Jazz in the 1980s.* New York: Oxford University Press; 1986.

Comprises a collection of artists' profiles and reviews from 1982 to 1985 that were previously published in several magazines and newspapers, including the *Philadelphia Inquirer* for which Davis is a jazz critic. He divides the essays into "New Faces," like the Marsalis brothers, David Murray, and Anthony Davis, and "Practiced Hands," like Ornette Coleman, Roscoe Mitchell, and Sonny Rollins. He mixes interview with overview, and is a strong advocate for his concepts and views. In "Judgment Calls," he reassesses the Modern Jazz Quartet in light of their 1980s comeback, and contributes an essay on Miles Davis's return in 1981. Good insights and understanding of 1980s jazz musicians and issues.

847. Dahl, Linda. *Stormy Weather: The Music and Lives of a Century of Jazz Women.* New York: Pantheon Books; 1984.

Presents a history of women in jazz from the 1890s to the early 1980s. She profiles female artists and demonstrates that women have been bandleaders, arrangers, composers, and instrumentalists. Among the numerous artists cited are Ella Fitzgerald, Sarah Vaughan, Marian McPartland, Lil Hardin, Dottie Dogion, Melba Liston, Ethel Ennis, Betty Carter, and Ethel Waters. Selected bibliography and discography of individual artists, and an index.

848. Deffa, Chip. *Traditionalist and Revivalists in Jazz.* Lanham, Md.: Scarecrow Press, and Institute of Jazz Studies I (Rutgers University); 1993.

Profiles 14 musicians who are dedicated to the performing and retention of early jazz styles. The profiles are simultaneously anecdotal, factual, and critical, and with the exception of Marty Gross none have been previously profiled in a book.

849.   _____. *In the Mainstream: 18 Portraits in Jazz.* Metuchen: Scarecrow Press; 1992.

The author, jazz critic of the *New York Post,* records the anecdotes and stories of 18 jazz artists. The interviewed artists are Ray McKinney, Andy Kirk, Erskine Hawkins, Johnny Mince, Bob Haggart, Doc Cheatam, Bill Challis, Bill Dillard, George Kelly, Sonny Igoe, Dick Hyman, Jack Hanna, Buddy Morrow, Oliver Jackson, Mahlon Clark, Joe Wilder, Bucky and John Pizzarelli, and Ken Peplowski. The anecdotes and stories cover bands, changes in jazz, styles, travel, and musical associations. The interviews cover artists from a wide range of jazz styles.

850.   _____. *Voice of the Jazz Age: Profiles of Eight Vintage Jazzmen.* Urbana: University of Illinois Press; 1990.

A collection of profiles of eight jazzmen who performed in the 1920s, including Sam Wooding, Bix Beiderbecke, Joe Tarto, Bud Freeman, Jimmy McPartland, Freddie Moore, and Jabbo Smith. The interviews are permeated with anecdotes and recollections, which, in turn, create a penetrating view of jazz of that period. He covers the arch of their musical careers. Chapter notes, selected bibliography, and an index.

851.   DeToledano, Ralph (editor). *Frontiers of Jazz;* foreword by Milton Gabler. New York: Durrell, 1947; London: Jazz Book Club, 1966; Second edition, New York: Ungar, 1962.

Sixteen articles previously published between 1926 and 1947 on forms and styles, includes essays by Abbe Niles on blues, Bill Russell on boogie-woogie, and Jean-Paul Sartre on the state of jazz in America. Part two contains essays on musicians such as Sidney Bechet, Bix Beiderbecke, Duke Ellington, Benny Goodman, James P. Johnson, Bunk Johnson, King Oliver, and Jelly Roll Morton. The latter essays are short and break no new ground. Index, bibliography, and reference notes.

852.   Enstice, Wayne, and Paul Rubin. *Jazz Spoken Here.* Baton Rouge: Louisiana State University Press; 1992.

Presents vivid assessments from 22 leading jazz artists about jazz life. The interviews cover aesthetics, innovation, travel, and approaches to jazz. Among the interviewed musicians are Art Blakey, Bill Evans, Larry Coryell, Gil Evans, Duke Ellington, Dizzy Gillespie, Charles Mingus, Joe Pass, Sonny Stitt, Clark Terry, and Henry Threadgill. The guest producers and hosts of "Just Jazz," which was broadcast on KVAT-FM, Tucson, Arizona, conducted the interviews. The interviews are preceded by a concise biographical profile of the artist, followed by a question-answer format. Index.

853. Erlewine, Michael (editor). *I All Music Guide to Jazz.* Second edition. San Francisco: Miller Freeman; 1994.

Provides profiles of 1,150 artists and 9,000 recordings. The biographies are arranged alphabetically, with the author's list of best recordings listed after the citation. Among the other features is a concise history of jazz, overview of jazz styles, a beginner's guide to jazz recordings, and several maps depicting the historical development of instruments most common in jazz.

854. _____. *All Music Guide to Jazz.* Second edition. San Francisco: Miller Freeman; 1996.

In this edition, he expands the number of artistic entries from 1,150 to 1,440, and the number of recordings from 9,000 to 13,200.

855. Fayenz, Franco. *Il Jazz dal mito all' avanguardia.* Milano: Sapere; 1970.

In Italian. The primary focus is the biomusical portraits of 15 artists, covering jazz from its earliest styles to the late 1960s. The portraits cover Louis Armstrong, Sidney Bechet, Bix Beiderbecke, Duke Ellington, Benny Goodman, Fletcher Henderson, Billie Holiday, Jelly Roll Morton, Charles Parker, Bud Powell, Archie Shepp, Art Tatum, Lennie Tristano, Fats Waller, and Lester Young. The portraits cover career and musical style/ achievements. There is some discussion of styles; however, no new information. Selected discography, references, index, and illustrations.

856. _____. *Grandi del Jazz.* Milano: Academia; 1961.

In Italian. Biomusical portraits and essays on several artists including Louis Armstrong, Bix Beiderbecke, Duke Ellington, Benny Goodman, Jelly Roll Morton, and Charles Parker. The portraits and essays focus on their careers and music. Selected discography, bibliography, and index.

857. Feather, Leonard. *The Jazz Years: Earwitness to an Era.* London, New York: Da Capo; 1987.

Recollections of selected artists, including Toshiko Akiyoshi, Benny Carter, Duke Ellington, Billie Holiday, Mezz Mezzrow, George Shearing, Dinah Washington, and Leo Watson. The essays reflect on the contributions and importance of the artists; no new insights. Index.

858. _____. *The Passion for Jazz.* New York, Wellington: Horizon Press; 1980.

Contains around 39 short essays, written between 1975 and 1980, originally published in the *Los Angeles Times, Jazz Times, Down Beat,* and *Gallery* (the author is a jazz reviewer). The essays are journalistic, focusing on portraits of musicians, and break no new ground. There is no significant discussion of style or social context. Artists covered include Toshiko Akiyoshi, Art Blakey, Carla Bley, Joanne Brackeen, Dollar Brand, Donald Byrd, Benny Goodman, Lionel Hampton, Albert, Jimmy, Percy Heath, Thad Jones, Stan Kenton, Mel Lewis, Pat Methany, Charles Mingus, Sonny Rollins, Howard Rumsey, George Shearing, Lew Tabackin, McCoy Tyner, and Phil Woods. Illustrated. No index.

859.		_____. *The Pleasures of Jazz: Leading Performers on Their Lives, Their Music, Their Contemporaries;* introduction by Benny Carter. New York: Horizon Press; 1976.

Establishes a context for mid-1970s jazz preferences and trends. Specifically, Feather relates jazz to European and American musical trends and influences over the 20 preceding years. He focuses on the careers and activities of 42 artists covering most aspects of jazz to the 1970s. He does not cover the jazz-rock/soul/fusion of that period.

860.		Fell, John L., and Terkild Vinding. *Fats, Jimmy, Lion, Lamb, and All the Other Tickllers.* Lanham, Md.: Scarecrow Press, and Institute of Jazz Studies (Rutgers University); 1999.

Chronicles the lives, musical contributions, and influences of selected pianists who bridged the gap between ragtime and swing. They discuss Fats Waller, James P. Johnson, Jimmy "The Lion" Smith, John Lamb, and several others.

861.		Friedwald, Will. *Jazz Singing: America's Great Voices from Bessie Smith to Bebop and Beyond.* New York: Scribner; 1990.

According to the author, his book is "about jazz's effects on popular singing." His insights into the relationship between jazz performers and the record industry are informative. He champions the achievements of performers such as Al Bowlly, Bob Eberle, and Helen Forrest; however, his coverage of artists such as Cab Calloway, Helen Merrill, and Dinah Washington are lacking. Some of his labels are also racially offensive, for example he labels African American female vocalists "colored canaries," and "colored chorines." His knowledge of music appears to be limited.

862.		Gebhardt, Nicholas. *Going for Jazz: Musical Practices and American Ideology.* Chicago University of Chicago Press; 2001.

Combines intellectual history, musical analyses, and philosophy to examine the social and ideological formation of jazz in the twentieth century. He discusses Sidney Bechet, Charles Parker, Ornette Coleman, and includes an epilogue, "A Tune Beyond Ourselves." The book is more than a series of biographical portraits, rather the portraits are situated within the sociopolitical milieu of modern America.

863. Gelly, Dave. *Masters of Jazz Saxophone: The Story of the Players and Their Music.* London: Balaphon; 2000.

He divides the use and function of the saxophone into categories like "Saxophone Breaks Through," "Still Swinging," "The Cool Sound," "Hard Boppers," "Post-bop Individualists," "Crossover/smooth," and more. Among the many saxophonists discussed are Coleman Hawkins, Lester Young, Charles Parker, Stan Getz, Sonny Rollins, John Coltrane, Ornette Coleman, Michael Brecker, and more. Also includes a chapter on European saxophonists.

864. Giddins, Gary. *Visions of Jazz: The First Century.* New York: Oxford University Press; 1998.

Enfolds numerous artists who have been discounted, patronized, or relegated to minor roles and functions in the literature. He presents a canvas or historical mapping of the music in a tableau of innovators, journeymen, precursors, and what he labels "sidesteppers." He believes each artist generates a distinct musical vision that is matchless, and in turn mirrors the essence of jazz. Detailed and scholarly.

865. _____. *Rhythm-a-ning: Jazz Tradition and Innovation in the 80's.* New York: Oxford University Press; 1985.

The author borrowed his title from the Thelonious Monk composition. This book is a collection of essays written, with three exceptions, for the *Village Voice,* 1980–84; all were revised. The essays that precede 1980 are discussions with Jaki Byard (1978), Cecil Taylor (1979), and a review of a Sarah Vaughan record. Most of the essays are concerned with eclectic neoclassicism in jazz; however, a few are only remotely concerned with either jazz in the 1980s or jazz itself. The essays average around three pages each, contain no musical examples, and offer the author's opinion about compositions either recorded or performed live. Among the numerous musicians cited are Jaki Byard, Jack DeJohnette, Miles Davis, Andrew Cyrille, Joe Turner, Woody Herman, Sonny Stitt, Tony Bennett, Lester Young, Teddy Wilson, Roy Eldridge, and Sarah Vaughan. There are no insider perspectives. Index.

866. Gottlieb, Robert (editor). *Reading Jazz: A Gathering of Autobiographical Reportage, and Criticism from 1919 to Now.* New York: Pantheon Books; 1996.

An anthology of jazz music and musicians with over 150 excerpts from the literature. Excellent autobiographical essays from artists such as Louis Armstrong, Sidney Bechet, Cab Calloway, Miles Davis, Charles Mingus, and Mary Lou Williams. The anthology also includes criticism from writers like Stanley Crouch, Gene Lees, Gary Giddins, and Dan Morgenstern.

One of the most interesting pieces is a Billie Holiday blindfold test from a 1950 issue of *Metronome*. In the test, she identifies musicians by listening to their recordings.

867.   Gourse, Leslie. *Time Keepers: The Great Jazz Drummers.* New York: Franklin Watts (a division of Grolier Publishing); 1999.

Discusses the lines and musical careers of numerous drummers from Baby Dodds and Zutty Singleton to Terri Lyne Carrington. The breath and depth of information is limited: the book is primarily an introduction to the artists and their careers, and does not contain a technical analysis of the respective styles. Includes suggested listening and some references.

868.   _____. *Fancy Fretwork: The Great Jazz Guitarists.* New York: Franklin Watts; 1999.

A companion to *Time Keepers: The Great Jazz Drummers,* covers the lives of jazz and some pop guitarists like Les Paul. Includes information on Kenny Burrell, Charlie Byrd, Eddie Condon, Wes Montgomery, Django Reinhardt, James "Blood" Ulmer, and many more. The coverage is concise and serves as an introduction to the artist, rather than an in-depth analysis of their styles.

869.   _____. *Madam Jazz: Contemporary Women Instrumentalists.* New York: Oxford University Press; 1995.

The book is divided into three sections, and focuses on female jazz instrumentalists. In the first third, she examines musicians currently prominent in the United States with descriptions of the bands and clubs they performed in. The second third focuses on profiles and interviews with artists discussing their thoughts about both the "unladylike" instruments they perform on, and the endemic discriminations they have experienced in their respective careers. In the final third, she provides a directory of women in jazz. Among the dozens of interviews of both rising and seasoned veterans are pianists Renee Rosnes and Rachel Z, trumpeters Rebecca Coupe Frank, saxophonist Virginia Mayhew, bassist Tracy Wormworth, and drummer Terri Lynne Carrington. In addition, veterans such as Dorothy Donegan, Shirley Horn, and Marian McPartland were also interviewed. The women are honest about career aspirations, being on the road, being female jazz artists, and in a separate chapter she discusses the stress of combining love, marriage, and motherhood with a life in jazz. She also provides information on additional female bassists, drummers, guitarists, and horn players.

870.   _____. *Louis' Children: American Jazz Singers.* New York: W.W. Morrow and Company; 1984.

The author believes that Louis Armstrong invented jazz singing. She provides a limited chronology of vocalists ranging from the New Orleans bluesman Cousin Joe, a contemporary of Louis Armstrong, to Betty Carter, Bing Crosby, Annie Ross, Joe Turner, Sarah Vaughan, Mel Tormé, the Brazilian artist Tania Maria, and more. In addition to the biographical portraits, she focuses on the struggle for financial success and artistic recognition in a highly demanding and competitive field. The book is permeated with generalizations about both African Americans and musicians; however, her descriptions of the lyric interpretations of selected vocalists are informative. Index.

871.　　Grime, Kitty. *Jazz Voices.* New York: Quartet Books; 1984.

Uses oral history techniques to profile 80 jazz artists. Among the artists are Mose Allison, Chet Baker, Jackie Cain, Betty Carter, Rosemary Clooney, Dave Frishberg, Billy Eckstine, Slim Gaillard, Helen Humes, Abbey Lincoln, Helen Merrill, Annie Ross, Jimmy Rowles, Joe Williams, Jimmy Witherspoon, and Trummy Young. Twenty-three of the interviews were previously published (articles, books, album notes). The chapter entitled "Lady" is devoted to Billie Holiday. There are 37 photographs in addition to a glossary and an index.

872.　　Harrison, Max. *A Jazz Retrospect.* London, Vancouver: David and Charles, Boston: Crescendo; 1976.

Several portraits, essays, and book and record reviews on selected artists representing several periods. The portraits include Serge Chaloff, Teddy Charles, Ornette Coleman, Tadd Dameron, Johnny Dankworth, Duke Ellington, Gil Evans, Dizzy Gillespie, Lionel Hampton, Bunk Johnson, James P. Johnson, Jimmie Lunceford, Hal McKusick, Miff Mole, Thelonious Monk, Jelly Roll Morton, Lennie Niehaus, Charles Parker, Martial Solal, and Fats Waller.

873.　　Haydon, Geoff. *Quintet of The Year.* London: U.P.; 2002.

An important book that describes the story behind the famous Jazz at Massey Hall concert in Toronto in 1953. He discusses Charles Parker, Dizzy Gillespie, Bud Powell, Charles Mingus, and Max Roach.

874.　　Hendrikse, Dick. *Twintig Reuzen Van de Jazz.* Haarlem: Spaarnestad; 1961.

Twenty-one biomusical portraits, each with a selected discography that covers background, career, influences, and styles. The artists covered are Louis Armstrong, Count Basie, Sidney Bechet, Dave Brubeck, Eddie Condon, Duke Ellington, Ella Fitzgerald, Erroll Garner, Dizzy Gillespie, Benny Goodman, Coleman Hawkins, Budd Johnson, Stan Kenton, John Lewis, Jelly Roll Morton, Charles Parker, Oscar Peterson, Jack Teagarden,

Lennie Tristano, Sarah Vaughan, and Fats Waller. The portraits are concise consisting of known materials.

875.   Hentoff, Nat. *American Music Is.* New York: Da Capo Press; 2004.

A collection of essays and columns written for the *Wall Street Journal* and *Jazz Times,* primarily between 1995 and 2003 (a single entry is dated 1988). The book recalls his 1976 book *Jazz Is* by expanding the earlier work's perspective to include sections on "The Blues," "The Rainbow of Country Music," "The Farther Rainbow," and sections on "The Jazz Voice" and "Jazz Ahead." In the more than 60 entries, he writes intimately about Duke Ellington, Ralph Ellison, Dizzy Gillespie, Billie Holiday, Charles Mingus, Willie Nelson, and the Nitty Gritty Dirt Band. Offers many new insights into the musicians and the music they performed.

876.   _____. *Listen to the Stories: Nat Hentoff on Jazz and Country Music.* New York: Harper Collins Publishers; 1995.

Opinionated and insightful, this collection of essays is divided into nine sections. He writes about the early years of Roy Eldridge, and the last years of Billie Holiday and Charles Parker. In addition, other essays focus on artists such as Danny Barker, Joan Baez, Count Basie, Duke Ellington, Dizzy Gillespie, Billie Holiday, Wynton Marsalis, Charles Mingus, Thelonious Monk, The Stanley Brothers, and Bob Wills. Especially noteworthy are the interviews with Dizzy Gillespie and Merle Haggard. The essays are concise, rarely more than three pages, and give the author's opinion without documentation.

877.   _____. *The Jazz Life.* New York: Dial Press, 1961; London: Panther, 1964; London: Davies, 1972.

Delineates the world in which jazz musicians live and work. The book is divided into two parts: the first part focuses on sociocultural issues such as drugs, attempts to expand the genres appeal, and the reasons for and against the nonacceptance of white musicians; the second part focuses on aspects of the musical experience, including the lifestyles of selected musicians (Basie, Hawkins, Davis, Lewis, and Mingus). This section details the musicians as individuals rather than as a monolithic community. Insights into recording are also covered.

878.   Hodes, Art, and Chadwick Hansen (editors). *Jazz Portraits from "The Jazz Record."* Berkeley: University of California Press; 1977.

A series of essays first published in *The Jazz Record.* The essays are categorized into five parts: part one, "The Facts of Life (Art Hodes)," focuses on the life and musical career of Hodes; part two is devoted to the

"Beginnings—Blues, Boogie-Woogie and Ragtime"; part three is entitled "New Orleans and All That Jazz"; part four is entitled "The Second Line"; and in part five, "Lest We Forget," the focus is nostalgic and reminiscent. The essays are short, mostly three pages, and replete with career highlights and historical data.

879. Item deleted.

880. Hodier, André. *Toward Jazz;* translated by Noel Burch. New York: Grove Press, 1962; London: Jazz Book Club, 1965.

This volume is based on articles that the author wrote between 1953 and 1959. In this volume, the author addresses the individual musician and his role and function within the group. The essay on "group relations" is insightful. There are essays on Count Basie, Benny Carter, Duke Ellington, Gil Evans, Milt Jackson, Thelonious Monk, and Charlie Parker. Some musical examples and an index.

881. Holmes, Lowell D., and John W. Thomson. *Jazz Greats: Getting Better With Age.* New York: and London: Holmes and Meir; 1986.

Concerned with the relationship between age and creativity, specifically whether a person's creative powers inevitably decline as one ages. In addition, they also research whether it is possible to maintain or to continue to develop creativity by taking advantage of the accumulated experiences that are a by-product of the aging process. They use interviews, attend concerts to ascertain audience response, listen to recent recordings, and read critics reviews. They evaluated Eddie Barefield, Lawrence Brown, Johnny Guarnieri, Milt Hinton, Andy Kirk, Eddie Miller, Marshall Royal, Howard Rumsey, Jess Stacy, Walter Thomas, and Mary Lou Williams. They concluded the artists maintained a high level of musical accomplishments throughout their careers.

882. Hultin, Randi. *Born Under the Sign of Jazz.* English translation by Tim Challman. London: Sanctuary Publishing Limited; 1998.

Permeated with anecdotes, memories, associations, and personal perspectives about numerous musicians who visited Oslo, Norway. Includes a foreword by Sonny Rollins, lots of previously unpublished photographs, and notes from musicians. Good for personal insight into the lives of musicians when they are not performing. Includes perspectives on Josephine Baker, Ray Brown, Dave Brubeck, Ray Charles, Roy Eldridge, Stan Getz, Coleman Hawkins, Rahsaan Roland Kirk, Sonny Rollins, Cecil Taylor, and many more. In addition, many of the artists allowed Hultin to use some of their performances in Gartnervein to make a CD.

883.   James, David Burnett. *Essays on Jazz.* London: Jazz Book Club, 1962, New York: Da Capo, 1988.

Biomusical portraits and essays that focus on the life, careers, and styles of selected musicians after bebop. The essays and profiles were previously published in *Jazz Monthly*. Artists covered are Bix Beiderbecke, Duke Ellington, Johnny Hodges, Billie Holiday, King Oliver, Oscar Peterson, and Lester Young. The essays on Beiderbecke, Ellington (compares to selected European artists), Hodges, Holiday, and Young are replete with assessments of style and significance. Good appraisal of career, significance, and styles.

884.   James, Michael. *Ten Modern Jazzmen: An Appraisal of the Recorded Work of Ten Modern Jazzmen.* London: Cassell; 1960.

Ten critical analyses of selected recordings of Miles Davis, Stan Getz, Dizzy Gillespie, Wardell Gray, John Lewis, Lee Konitz, Thelonious Monk, Gerry Mulligan, Charles Parker, and Bud Powell. The essays offer important insights into style and the changes and approaches that evolved in individual styles from recording to recording.

885.   Jepsen, David A. *Black Bottom Stomp: Eight Masters of Ragtime and Early Jazz.* New York: Rutledge; 2001.

Profiles Louis Armstrong, Eubie Blake, James P. Johnson, Scott Joplin, Jelly Roll Morton, Lucky Roberts, Willie "The Lion" Smith, and Fats Waller. The profiles are informative, well-written, and permeated with insights into their music, social backgrounds, and personalities. He views the eight as shrewd entertainers and always mindful of public tastes.

886.   Jones, Max. *Talking Jazz.* New York: W.W. Norton; 1988.

A collection of around 60 of his previously published articles for *Melody Maker.* The author conducted numerous interviews of jazz artists dating back to World War II. The essays cover numerous musicians divided by instrument, including vocalists, into five chapters. Among the profiles are Lee Collins, Billy Eckstine, Preston Jackson, Coleman Hawkins, Jimmy McPartland, Billie Holiday, Mary Lou Williams, Wingy Malone, Sarah Vaughan, Zoot Sims, Teddy Wilson, and several more. The essays on Holiday, McPartland, and Williams are more probing than the others. There are few new insights or perspectives not previously cited. Index.

887.   Jost, Ekkehard. *Jazzmusiker: Mateerialien zur Soziologie der Afro-Amerikanichen Musik.* Frankfurt, Wien: Ullstein; 1982.

In German. Essays and biomusical portraits covering issues ranging from background, career highlights, influences to styles, and racism. Among the portraits are Muhal Richard Abrams, Pepper Adams, Fred Anderson, Karl Berger, Louis Cottrell, Jr., Stanley Crouch, James DuBoise, Von Freeman, Bunky Green, David Holland, Oliver Lake, Jimmy Owens, Teddy Riley, Cy Touff, Monty Waters, Chris White, Oljan Fellin, Steve McCall, Willie Metcalf, Rufus Reid, and Charles Tyler. There are several musical examples and a selected discography. Both the essays and portraits offer important insights into sociomusical issues. Bibliography and index.

888. Keepnews, Orrin. *The View from Within: Jazz Writings, 1948–1987.* New York: Oxford University Press; 1988.

A collection of personal writings that cover critical assessments, opinions, and specific artists. There is no musical analysis. Many of the author's essays and liner notes were previously published in *Record Changer* or during his tenure with *Fantasy Records.* There are also essay excerpts from other writers, "Lady Sings the Blues," by William Duffy and Billie Holiday; "The Horn," by John Clellan Holmes; "Beware of Sparrows," by Ethel Waters with Charles Samuels, and more. The author's essays on Jelly Roll Morton, Art Tatum, Charles Parker, three separate views of Thelonious Monk, and the Riverside recording sessions of Cannonball Adderley, Bill Evans, and McCoy Tyner are noteworthy. The essays are very informative, well-written, and offer unique perspectives into history, recordings, styles, and personal observations.

889. Kienzle, Richard. *Great Guitarist: The Most Influential Players in Jazz, Country, Blues, and Rock.* New York: Facts on File; 1985.

Includes biographies of several jazz artists, including Charlie Christian, Django Reinhardt, Larry Coryell, Wes Montgomery, George Benson, and many more. Each portrait includes career details and contributions. Selected discographies and an index.

890. Kirchner, Bill (editor). *The Oxford Companion to Jazz.* New York: Oxford University Press; 2000.

A comprehensive collection of 60 essays that cover biographies, genres, and analyses. Includes contributions by Bill Crow, Gerald Early, Samuel A. Floyd, Jr., Ted Gioia, Scott DeVeaux, Gene Lees, Dan Morgenstern, Gunther Schuller, Mark Tucker, and many more. Thorough and detailed, and an excellent supplement to the appreciation and understanding of the artists who made the jazz.

891. Knauss, Zane. *Conversations with Jazz Musicians.* Detroit: Gale Research Company; 1977.

The book has three purposes: first, to provide a forum for musicians by preserving their comments regarding their music and careers; second, to provide readers with insight into the music profession; and, third, to portray musicians as individuals with feelings, aspirations, and as musicians who respond to the world they live in. Ten biomusical portraits covering several jazz styles. The conversations are permeated with background information, career details, role and function of individuals as agents of change, reflections on other artists, and more. The interviewed artists are Louis Bellson, Dizzy Gillespie, Eric Kloss, Jimmy McPartland, Barry Miles, Sy Oliver, Charlie Spivak, Billy Taylor, Phil Woods, and Sol Yageel. Excellent insider perspectives.

892.   Korall, Burt. *Drummin' Men, The Heartbeat of Jazz: The Swing Years.* New York: Schirmer Books; London: Collier-Macmillan; 1990.

An oral history as told by drummers, other musicians, and industry figures. Combines his experiences as a drummer and writer to provide a penetrating probe of how and why several drummers made important contributions to jazz. He discusses Sid Catlett, Jo Jones, Gene Krupa, Ray McKinley, Buddy Rich, Dave Tough, Chick Webb, Sonny Greer, Cozy Cole, and several more. Each informant's comments are woven into the text. There are chapter notes, a selected discography organized by drummer, an extensive list of interviewees, and an index.

893.   Lee, Bill. *People in Jazz: Jazz Keyboard Improvisers of the 19th and 20th Centuries.* Hialeah, Fla.: Columbia Pictures Publications/Studio P R Publications; 1984.

A compilation of the numerous biographies of pianists from the nineteenth and twentieth century, before and after the word "jazz" was coined. He describes improvisation as "the art of musical performance without aid of memorization or notation." He covers improvisers from the polyphonic period (800–1600) to the beginnings of jazz.

894.   Lees, Gene. *You Can't Steal a Gift: Dizzy, Clark, Milt, and Nat;* foreword by Nat Hentoff. New Haven, Conn.: Yale University Press; 2001.

Discusses the lives and musical careers of Dizzy Gillespie, Terry Clark, Milt Hinton, and Nat King Cole. He is concerned with how these artists were affected by racial issues in the United States. These minibiographies draw on his conversations with the artists over many years, and reveal his admiration for their immense achievements notwithstanding the racial adversity they faced.

895.   _____. *Jazz Lives; 100 Portraits in Jazz.* Toronto: Firefly (Willowdale); 1992.

Biographies and photographs of 100 jazz musicians in birth order from trombonist Spiegle Wilcox (born May 2, 1903) to bassist Christian McBride (born May 31, 1972). Lees teams with fellow Canadian and photographer John Reeves, and provides biographical essays on Ed Bikerta, Tony Bennett, Benny Carter, Dave Brubeck, Dizzy Gillespie, John Abercrombie, Gerri Allen, Carmen McRae, Max Roach, and many more. He excluded all deceased musicians as well as some living artists regardless of importance or stature, for example, Freddie Hubbard and Wayne Shorter.

896. _____. *Waiting for Dizzy.* New York: Oxford University Press; 1991.

Written by an insider and former editor of *JazzLetter,* the author has quarried this book out of a collection of previously published essays in the aforementioned publication. He profiles several musicians as cultivated and sensitive men and women, not as inarticulate persons wandering between drug fixes. Among the artists profiled are Benny Carter, Herb Elli, Al Grey, Emily Remler, Bud Shank, Spiegle Willcox, and many others.

897. Item deleted.

898. _____. *People in Jazz Keyboard Improvisers of the 19th and 20th Centuries.* Hialeah, Fla.: Columbia Pictures Publications/Studio P R Publications; 1984.

A compilation of numerous biographies of pianists from the nineteenth and twentieth century, before and after the word "jazz" was coined. He describes improvisation as "the art of musical performance without aid of memorization or notation." and presents a concise introduction to improvisation from the polyphonic period (800–1600) to the beginnings of jazz.

899. Lindgren, Carl-Erik, and Leif Anderson. *Jazzen Går Vidare.* Stockholm: Nordiska; 1958.

In Swedish. Twenty-three swing-era biomusical portraits that cover background, career significance, and style. The artists discussed are Red Allen, Charlie Barnet, Count Basie, Cab Calloway, Benny Carter, Tommy Dorsey, Duke Ellington, Benny Goodman, Lionel Hampton, Erskine Hawkins, Woody Herman, Eddie Heywood, Harry James, John Kirby, Andy Kirk, Gene Krupa, Harlan Leonard, Jimmy Lunceford, Glenn Miller, Red Norvo, Artie Shaw, Art Tatum, and Chick Webb. The essays consist mostly of rehashed materials. Still, the Charlie Barnet and Chick Webb essays are interesting and informative.

900. Locke, Graham. *Chasing the Vibration: Meetings with Creative Musicians.* London: Exter; 1994.

In addition to eight pages of photographs, the book is permeated with interviews of many modern jazz artists. They discuss the beginnings in jazz, influences, and musical philosophy. Among the interviewees are Betty

Carter, Dave Holland, Steve Lacy, Sun Ra, Horace Tapscott, Cecil Taylor, Evan Parker, Max Roach, and several more.

901.   Luzzi, Mario. *Vomini e avanguardie Jazz.* Preface by Gianni Gualberto. Milano: Gammalibri; 1980.

In Italian. Insider perspectives of 14 musicians. The interviews cover background, career, influences, and some style points. Good insights into aesthetics and into the shaping of musical styles and philosophies. The interviewees are Lester Bowie, Anthony Braxton, Willem Brevker, Ornette Coleman, Steve Lacy, Oliver Lake, Roscoe Mitchell, Enrico Rava, Sam Rivers, Roswell Rudd, George Russell, Alex Schlippenbach, Archie Shepp, and Sun Ra. The interviews are supplemented with biographical introductions and selected discographies. Excellent resource.

902.   Lyons, Len. *The Great Jazz Pianists: Speaking of Their Lives and Music;* photographs by Veryl Oakland. New York: William Morrow and Company; 1983.

Insider perspectives of their performance styles. The book is divided into two parts: "A Survey of the Jazz Pianists and Their Tradition" (pp. 19–59) and artists' responses to his questions. The book is significant because the artists provide probing insights into their styles, often with comparisons to others. The artists covered are: Teddy Wilson, Mary Lou Williams, John Lewis, Sun Ra, George Shearing, Dave Brubeck, Ahmad Jamal, Horace Silver, Oscar Peterson, William "Red" Garland, Jimmy Rowles, Paul Bley, Marian McPartland, Billy Taylor, Jaki Byard, Ran Blake, Ramsey Lewis, Randy Weston, Bill Evans, Steve Kuhn, McCoy Tyner, Toshiko Akiyoshi, Chick Corea, Herbie Hancock, and Cecil Taylor. There is a selected discography at the end of each interview. This book is useful to both the scholar and performer. Selected discography and an index.

903.   Lyttelton, Humphrey. *The Best of Jazz.* London: Taplinger; 1998.

A reprint of two volumes in one that covers New Orleans to swing-era stars. Among the numerous stars covered are Louis Armstrong, Johnny Dodds, Jelly Roll Morton, Count Basie, Duke Ellington, Benny Goodman, and many more. The artists recount their careers, and offer insight into their musical philosophies. Includes 16 pages of photographs.

904.   _____. *The Best of Jazz: Basin Street to Harlem; Jazz Masters and Master-Pieces, 1917–1930.* London: Taplinger; 1978.

Offers fresh insights into the music by analyzing several recordings. He uses biographical details to accentuate personal insight into the life and music of artists such as Louis Armstrong, Sidney Bechet, Bix Beiderbecke,

Bessie Smith, and several more. His discussion on blues and the use of rhythm and vibrato by Louis Armstrong is provocative.

905. Mandel, Howard. *Future Jazz.* New York: Oxford University Press; 1999.

Traces the cosmopolitan topographer of a future jazz, and enables one to understand that jazz continues to be an innovative art form. Uses interviews with Wynton Marsalis as a measure of the tradition, and also profiles artists such as George Benson, David Murray, John Scofield, Cassandra Wilson, and John Zorn to paint a portrait of the late 1990s jazz scene. He also discusses M-base and the Black Rock Coalition.

906. Matzner, Antonín, and Igor Wasserberger. *Jozzové profily.* Praha: Supraphon; 1969.

In Czech. Biomusical portraits of 22 artists covering styles from early jazz to the late 1960s. Included are Louis Armstrong, Count Basie, Bix Beiderbecke, Clifford Brown, Charlie Christian, Ornette Coleman, Miles Davis, Duke Ellington, Ella Fitzgerald, Dizzy Gillespie, Benny Goodman, Coleman Hawkins, John Lewis, Thelonious Monk, Jelly Roll Morton, Gerry Mulligan, Charles Parker, George Russell, Lennie Tristano, and Lester Young. The portraits cover background careers, style, and significance. There are several musical examples, bibliography, and discography.

907. McPartland, Marian. *All in Good Time.* Foreword by James T. Maher. New York: Oxford University Press; 1987.

A compilation of previously published articles written between 1960 and 1983 by an excellent jazz pianist and former host of "Piano Jazz" on National Public Radio. The portraits (Bill Evans, Eddie Gomez, Benny Goodman, Jake Hanna, International Sweethearts of Rhythm, Ron McClure, Marian McPartland, Joe Morello, and Mary Lou Williams) cover career, music, and sociocultural issues. This book won the 1988 ASCAP-Deems Taylor Award. Selected bibliography and an index.

908. Monceaux, Morgan. *Jazz; My Music, My People.* New York: Knopf; 1994.

Foreword by Wynton Marsalis, the author presents biographical sketches of blues, swing, bebop, and modern jazz artists. Forty instrumentalists and vocalists are discussed including Buddy Bolden, Nat King Cole, Ella Fitzgerald, Leadbelly, Dizzy Gillespie, Thelonious Monk, Charles Parker, Bud Powell, Bessie Smith, and many more. The author mixes his own autobiography with those he profiles, and also includes some of his multimedia paintings. Only 64 pages.

909. Moody, Bill. *Jazz Exiles: American Musicians Abroad.* Foreword by Stanley Dance. Reno, Las Vegas, London: University of Nevada Press; 1993.

Deals with musical perceptions and sociological issues that led many musicians to become expatriates. There are interviews with 29 musicians, including Don Byas, Chet Baker, Jay Cameron, Kenny Clarke, Kenny Drew, Johnny Griffin, Slide Hampton, Jon Hendricks, Mark Murphy, Bud Powell, Ben Webster, and Phil Woods. The author balances the anti-American experience of many (racism) with the convenient excuses that some use to explain this exile. He also notes that the welcome mat began to disintegrate after a while for some musicians and reveals that some (e.g., Mark Murphy) were glad to return to the United States.

910.   Oderigo, Néstor R. Ortiz. *Perfiles de Jazz.* Buenos Aires: Ricordi; 1955.

In Spanish. Biomusical portraits of Louis Armstrong, Sidney Bechet, Baby and Johnny Dodds, Pops Foster, Budd Johnson, James P. Johnson, Freddie Keppard, Tommy Ladnier, George Lewis, Jelly Roll Morton, King Oliver, Kid Ory, Bud Scott, and Omer Simeon. Coverage includes background, career, context, and style. No new insights. Footnotes.

911.   O'Neal, Hank. *The Ghosts of Harlem.* Paris: Levallois Perret; 1997.

A collection of 41 interviews about jazz and jazz musicians who were important to the development of jazz in Harlem. Included are interviews of Cab Calloway, Andy Kirk, Panama Francis, Andy Kirk, Dizzy Gillespie, Sammy Price, Buddy Tate, Benny Waters, and many more. Text in French.

912.   Panassié, Hugues. *Douze annés de Jazz (1927–1939) souvenirs.* Paris: Corréa; 1946.

In French. Biomusical portraits of several jazz musicians' activities in Paris, including Louis Armstrong, Philippe Brun, Benny Carter, Bill Coleman, Duke Ellington, Stéphane Grappelli, Coleman Hawkins, Mezz Mezzrow, Django Reinhardt, Eddie South, Muggsy Spanier, Fats Waller, Dicky Wells, and more. Provides excellent insight into the Paris musical activities of the above.

913.   Placksin, Sally. *American Women in Jazz; 1900 to the Present; Their Words, Lives, and Music.* New York: Seaview Books; 1982.

Focuses on the instrumentalists rather than vocalists by using the musical and social context of each decade and insider views from musicians. Coverage is divided into chronological chapters such as the "Twenties," with biographical essays, which include anecdotes, interviews, memories, and comments regarding each person's contribution to jazz.

914.   Polillo, Arrigo. *Jazz: La Vicenda e i Protagoniste della Musica Afro-Americana.* Milano: Mondadori, 1975; Munich, Berlin: Herbig, 1978; Mainz: Schott, München: Goldmann, 1983.

In Italian. Massive compilation that covers both history and portraits of individuals. The history focuses on evolution, styles, and significant artists. The portraits cover Louis Armstrong, Bix Beiderbecke, Charlie Christian, Ornette Coleman, John Coltrane, Miles Davis, Roy Eldridge, Duke Ellington, Ella Fitzgerald, Benny Goodman, Fletcher Henderson, Billie Holiday, Stan Kenton, John Lewis, Charles Mingus, Thelonious Monk, Jelly Roll Morton, King Oliver, Bud Powell, Django Reinhardt, Sonny Rollins, Art Tatum, and Fats Waller. The book is geared to teachers of jazz history. The German edition is entitled *Jazz: Geschichte und Peersönlichkeiten der Afroamerikanischen Musik.* Bibliography, index, and 102 photographs.

915. Ramsey, Douglas K. *Jazz Matters: Reflections on the Music and Some of Its Makers;* foreword by Gene Lees. Fayetteville: University of Arkansas Press; 1989.

A collection of essays and articles about jazz, some of which were previously published in journals such as *Texas Monthly, Radio Free Jazz, Jazz Times, Smithsonian,* and *Down Beat,* or as liner notes. The essays are concerned with sociomusical issues, and the profiles cover background, career, accomplishments, and attitudes regarding issues ranging from the state of jazz-to-jazz styles. Among the jazz artists covered are Cannonball Adderley, Don Albert, Chet Baker, George Benson, Dave Brubeck, John Coltrane, Miles Davis, Paul Desmond, Dukes of Dixieland, Art Farmer, Red Garland, Wardell Gray, John Handy, John Hardee, Budd Johnson, Charles Mingus, Modern Jazz Quartet, Thelonious Monk, Gerry Mulligan, Art Pepper, Oscar Peterson, Bud Powell, Ike Quebec, Clark Tony, Gene Ramey, and Phil Woods. Ramsey's perceptive comments about solo construction provide important insights into the references for such solos. He is equally adept at addressing both traditional and modern artists. Footnotes, selected discography, and index.

916. Renaud, Henri (editor). *Jazz moderne.* Paris: Casterman; 1979.

In French. A total of 30 biomusical portraits and essays of bebop and postbebop artists. Among the artists discussed are Clifford Brown, Don Cherry, Nat King Cole, Ornette Coleman, Tadd Dameron, Eric Dolphy, Gil Evans, Dizzy Gillespie, Milt Jackson, J. J. Johnson, Fats Navarro, Thelonious Monk, Charles Parker, and Sonny Rollins. Several essays are by Alain Gerber and André Hodier. The portraits include a selected discography and cover background, careers, acceptance and rejection of jazz, aesthetics, and style.

917. _____. (editor). *Jazz classique.* Paris: Basterman; 1979.

In French. A companion to *Jazz moderne,* this collection of 30 biomusical portraits and historical essays concentrate on prebebop musicians. Among the musicians covered are Louis Armstrong, Bix Beiderbecke, Count Basie, Duke Ellington, Jelly Roll Morton, Benny Goodman, Fletcher Henderson, and Glenn Miller. The portraits cover background, career accomplishments, influences, and issues such as acceptance and travel. Edition includes selected discography for each artist. Glossary and index.

918.   Rennert, Richard (editor). *Jazz Stars.* New York: Chelsa House; 1994.

Introduction by Coretta Scott King, and only 63 pages, the essays cover each performer's family life, early interest in music, and career development. Profiles of Louis Armstrong, Count Basie, John Coltrane, Duke Ellington, Billie Holiday, and Charles Parker. The profiles are written in encyclopedia style, are several pages long, and are objective.

919.   Rivelli, Pauline, and Robert Levin (editors). *The Black Giants.* New York: World, 1970; reprint, with new introduction by Nat Hentoff. New York: Da Capo, 1979.

A series of articles and interviews previously published in *Jazz & Pop* magazine, 1965–69. Contains articles/interviews of Bobby Bradford, Gary Bartz, Alice Coltrane, John Coltrane, Elvin Jones, Sunny Murray, Jackie Byard, Oliver Nelson, Archie Shepp, Pharoah Sanders, Horace Tapscott, Leon Thomas, and more. In addition to the editors, Nat Hentoff, David C. Hunt, Frank Kofsky, and Will Smith contributed to this volume. The essays provide important insights and the views of some of the most important exponents of 1960s avant-garde jazz.

920.   Rowland, Mark, and Tony Scherman (editors). *The Jazz Musician.* New York: St. Martin's Press; 1994.

A collection of profiles selected from *Musician Magazine* that summarize and critically assess the careers of selected jazz artists. Includes profiles of Lester Bowie, John Coltrane, Chet Baker, Ornette Coleman, Miles Davis, Dizzy Gillespie, Charlie Haden, Jaco Pastorius, Wayne Shorter, Sonny Rollins, and Tony Williams. Among the most interesting essays are Coleman's description of "harmolodic" theory, and Gillespie's discussion of the inception of bebop, and his interest in the Bahai faith. Contains new insights.

921.   Rusch. Robert D. *Jazz Talk: The Cadence Interviews.* Secaucus, New Jersey: Lyle Stuart, Inc.; 1984.

Contains a series of interviews first published in *Cadence.* His purpose is to document the views of the movers and shakers of jazz, to give their oral histories an outlet, and to make the aforementioned information available to the public. The interviews are conducted in a call and response format, and provide penetrating insights into the artists' respective lives and music. Included are interviews of Bill Dixon, Art Blakey, Von Freeman, Billy Harper, Milt Hinton, Freddie Hubbard, Milt Jackson, Paul Quinichette, Sun Ra, and Cecil Taylor,

922. Sallis, James (editor). *Jazz Guitars: An Anthology.* New York: William Morrow and Company; 1984.

Contains 17 biomusical profiles and essays some of which were previously published. Among the guitarists covered are John Abercrombie, George Barnes, Charlie Byrd, Charlie Christian, Lenny Breau, Kenny Burrell, Eddie Lang, Nick Lucas, John McLaughlin, Wes Montgomery, Oscar Moore, Joe Pass, Django Reinhardt, Howard Roberts, and James "Blood" Ulmer. Covers background, career, influences, and style. Good biographical and musical insights.

923. Schiedt, Duncan P. *Twelve Lives in Jazz.* New York: Parma; 1996.

A collection of biomusical portraits of Louis Armstrong, Count Basie, Bix Beiderbecke, Duke Ellington, Benny Goodman, Coleman Hawkins, Fletcher Henderson, Billie Holiday, Jelly Roll Morton, Charles Parker, Bessie Smith, and Fats Waller.

924. Schnabel, Tom. *Stolen Moments: Conversations with Contemporary Musicians.* Foreword by David Byrne. Los Angeles: Acrobat; 1988.

Insider perspectives from Mose Allison, Keith Jarrett, Branford Marsalis, John McLaughlin, Wayne Shorter, and Joe Zawinul. The conversations cover attitudes and philosophies concerning contemporary music, including jazz. Of particular note are the eclectic attitudes regarding contemporary American music.

925. Shapiro, Nat, and Nat Hentoff (editors). *Jazz Makers.* New York: Reinhart; 1957.

In addition to the editors, there are seven contributors to this collection of essays on the lives and music of 19 men and 2 women artists. The essays by Orrin Keepnews, Nat Hentoff, and John S. Wilson are the strongest, whereas the other essays are mostly a compilation of anecdotes and dates. The portraits are mostly romantic and often lack proper documentation.

926. Shaw, Arnold. *The Street That Never Slept: New York's Fabled 52nd Street;* foreword by Abel Green. New York: Coward, McCann, and Geohegan; 1971.

Chronicles New York nightlife in the 1930s and 1940s through the eyes of various insiders. Among the insider's interviewed were: Leonard Feather,

John Hammond, Woody Herman, Dizzy Gillespie, Erroll Garner, Red Norvo, and Mary Lou Williams. The perspectives vary among the interviewees, particularly concerning racial issues. Index.

927.   Sidran, Ben. *Talking Jazz: An Illustrated Oral History.* Petaluma, California: Pomegranate; 1992.

Contains 50 conversations from the author's National Public Radio interview program "Sidran on Record." The conversations were recorded between the summer of 1985 and the spring of 1990. The conversations cover a myriad of topics, including jazz as a business, changing taste, the impact of technology on jazz, pop jazz, and issues dealing with improvisation and style. Among the numerous musicians interviewed are Mose Allison, Art Blakey, Betty Carter, Don Cherry, Miles Davis, Herbie Hancock, Jon Hendricks Dr. John, Max Roach, Sonny Rollins, Horace Silver, McCoy Tyner, and many more. The interviews are informative, intelligent, and witty and are accompanied by two photographs.

928.   Sinclair, John, and Robert Levin. *Music and Politics.* New York: World; 1971.

An anthology of provocative "articles, reviews, interviews, polemics, and manifestos" (p. 11), originally published in *Jazz and Pop* magazine. The articles cover diverse topics dealing with sociopolitical issues, the meaning and importance of rock, and the new black music. Both authors contributed several articles/interviews; Sinclair contributes articles on Marion Brown, Chick Corea, Stanley Crouch, Charlie Haden, Maurice McIntyre, the Jazz Composer's Orchestra Association, the Rationals, and Sun Ra. In addition to his polemic on rock's declining sociopolitical outlook, Levin contributed interviews with Willis Jackson, Booker Little, Jimmy Lyons, and Sunny Murray, and reviews of Anthony Braxton and Eric Dolphy.

929.   Stokes, W. Royal. *Living the Jazz Life: Conversations with Forty Musicians about Their Careers in Jazz.* New York: Oxford University Press; 2002.

Illuminates the lives, and celebrates their creativity and musical contributions. The interviews cover brass and rhythm players, composers, pianists, saxophonists, and vocalists. He focuses on their childhood environment, role of families, and musical influences. In addition to blues and jazz musicians such as Louis Bellson and Jackie McLean, he also interviewed vaudeville stars, and includes interviews of 12 female artists, including Regina Carter, Diana Krall, and Ingrid Jensen.

930.   Sudhalter, Richard. M. *Lost Chords: White Musicians and Their Contributions to Jazz, 1915–1945.* New York: Oxford University Press; 1999.

An exposition that combines biography, commentary, narrative, reminiscences, and the specific achievements of several white musicians to jazz. He attempts to combine both a discussion of achievements and specifics of their lives to produce an accurate assessment of their contributions. He covers artists such as Bix Beiderbecke, Bunny Berigan, Bud Freeman, Jean Goldkette, Benny Goodman, Bobby Hackett, Emmett Hardy, Miff Mole, Red Nichols, Red Norvo, Artie Shaw, Frank Trumbauer, and others. He balances his discussion of their lives with astute insights into their musical styles and improvisational techniques. The transcriptions are presented in the key of the instrument, rather than concert key. Some inconsistencies in the spelling of names.

931. Taylor, Arthur. *Notes and Tones: Musician-to-Musician Interviews.* Liege: the author, 1977; New York: Perigree Books, 1982; Expanded edition. New York: Da Capo Press; 1993.

An important collection of essays conducted by an insider between 1968 and 1972. Before moving to Europe in the early 1960s, Taylor had established a reputation as an excellent jazz drummer. Taylor's objective was to determine how the musicians viewed themselves, in contrast to the opinions of critics and journalists. Among the themes that permeate the interviews are critics, drugs, the word *jazz,* music, racism, religion, and travel. Musicians interviewed are Art Blakey, Don Byas, Betty Carter, Ron Carter, Don Cherry, Kenny Clarke, Ornette Coleman, Eddie "Lockjaw" Davis, Miles Davis, Richard Davis, Kenny Dorham, Erroll Garner, Dizzy Gillespie, Johnny Griffin, Hampton Hawes, Freddie Hubbard, Elvin Jones, Sonny Rollins, Hazel Scott, Nina Simone, Leon Thomas, Charles Tolliver, Randy Weston, and Tony Williams. The expanded edition contains interviews with Dexter Gordon, Philly Jo Jones, Richard Davis, Carmen McRae, Thelonious Monk, and Max Roach. There is a new introduction.

932. Townsend, Peter. *Jazz in American Culture.* Jackson University of Mississippi Press; 2000.

The author assesses jazz as both a music and as a culture within overall American culture. He also discusses the social and institutional structures that have underpinned the music from the 1930s to around 2000. In addition to discussing Louis Armstrong, Miles Davis, Duke Ellington, Billie Holiday, and Lester Young, he covers representations of jazz in other forms, including in films, and the literary texts of Ralph Ellison, Jack Kerouac, and Toni Morrison.

933. Ullman, Michael. *Jazz Lives: Portraits in Words and Pictures.* Washington, D.C.: New Republic Books; 1980.

Contains information on the life, music, and contributions of several artists. He covers Joe Venuti, Doc Cheatham, Maxwell Cohen, Earl Hines, Dizzy

Gillespie, Neal Hefti, Marian McPartland, Sonny Rollins, Betty Carter, Horace Silver, Dexter Gordon, Maxine Gregg, Tommy Flanagan, Rahsaan Roland Kirk, Sam Rivers, John Snyder, Ken McIntyre, Karl Berger, Ran Blake, Ray Mantilla, Anthony Braxton, Steve Baxter, and Charles Mingus. The essays are permeated with information on musical careers; there are no musical examples. No new insights. Selected discography.

934. Unterbrink, Mary. *Jazz Women at the Keyboard.* New York: McFarland and Company; 1983.

Contains 55 concise biographical profiles, mostly derived from personal interviews. She devotes full chapters to some artists such as Lil Hardin Armstrong and Mary Lou Williams; however, very little attention is given to others; only two paragraphs to Toshiko Akiyoshi. In addition to uneven coverage, the information provided is often inconsistent; and birth dates are not always provided. The strength of the book is the citing of the accomplishments of many obscure female artists. There is no discography.

935. Vache, Warren W. *The Unsung Songwriters.* Lanham, Md. and Institute of Jazz Studies (Rutgers University); 2000.

Dedicated to the famous and not-so-famous songwriters. He is concerned with writers such as Irving Berlin, George Gershwin, Jerome Kern, Cole Porter, and Richard Rogers, as well as numerous freelance and unrecognized writers. Among the unsung writers discussed are Al Neiberg, composer of "It's the Talk of the Town"; Frank Perkins, who composed "Try A Little Tenderness"; and Fred Coots, who composed "You Go to My Head"; and many more.

936. Vuijsje, Bert. *Jazzportretten: Van Ben Webster to Wynton Marsalis.* Amsterdam: Van Gennep; 1983.

In Dutch. Interviews of 13 musicians covering several periods. Among the musicians interviewed are Maarten Altena, Bill Evans, Gil Evans, Rein DeGraaff, Dexter Gordon, Illinois Jacquet, George Lewis, Abbey Lincoln, Wynton Marsalis, Piet Noordijk, and Phillip Wilson. The interviews cover background, careers, influences, acceptance of jazz, racism, and more.

937. _____. *De nieuwe Jazz.* Baarn, Netherlands: Bosch and Keuning; 1978.

In Dutch. A collection of interviews previously published in *Jazzwereld, Muziekkrant Oor, Gfnddalf, Vrij Nederland,* and *Haagse Post.* The interviewees are Muhal Richard Abrams, Han Bennink, Willen Breuter, Leo Cuypers, Milford Graves, Charles Haden, Julius Hemphill, Jimmy Lyons,

Misha Mengelberg, Charles Mingus, David Murray, Sunny Murray, Piet Noordijk, Sam Rivers, Max Roach, Sonny Rollins, Pharoah Sanders, Sonny Sharrock, Archie Shepp, Sun Ra, Cecil Taylor, and McCoy Tyner. The interviews cover background, career, attitudes about jazz, influences, and racism.

938. Williams, Martin. *Jazz Changes.* New York: Oxford University Press; 1992.

Divided into four parts, the book begins with concise appreciation profiles, followed by observations of musicians rehearsing, in recording studios, in clubs, interviews about their lives and music, and artists in give-and-take conversations. He also includes some humorous parodies and opinions about the music essays. Covers numerous artists from Earl Hines to Horace Silver.

939. _____. *Jazz in Its Time.* New York: Oxford University Press; 1989.

A collection of previously published biomusical portraits, essays, and book and record reviews. Record reviews and concert dates are prominently featured and are more descriptive than they are critical assessments. Among the featured artists are Red Allen, Louis Armstrong, Count Basie, Sidney Bechet, Jaki Byard, Harry Carney, Ornette Coleman, John Coltrane, Miles Davis, Art Farmer, Bud Freeman, Dizzy Gillespie, Jimmy Giuffre, Bobby Hackett, Jim Hall, Lionel Hampton, Thelonious Monk, Sonny Stitt, Teddy Wilson, and Lester Young.

940. _____. *Jazz Heritage.* New York: Oxford University Press; 1985.

The book draws from previously published material; accounts of recording sessions, reviews, LP liner notes, material on thematic criticism, the social role and function of jazz, and jazz as a scholarly topic. Some essays describe musicians rehearsing, recording, or performing (Ornette Coleman, Jelly Roll Morton, Fats Waller, The World Saxophone Quartet, and others). In the chapter "What Does A Composer Do?," he demonstrates how improvisation uses formal musical structures. Index.

941. _____. *The Jazz Tradition.* New York: Oxford University Press; 1971.

Organized as a series of biographical sketches but focuses on analysis of performances. The 15 essays were published previously in various reviews and journals. Among the 15 artists covered are Louis Armstrong, Bix Beiderbecke, Jelly Roll Morton, Duke Ellington, and Charles Parker. His opinions are based on his perceptions of the music, however some of his conclusions are questionable, including the aesthetic connection between Louis Armstrong and Charles Parker. Annotated discography and an index.

942. _____ (editor). *Art of Jazz: Essays on the Nature and Development of Jazz.* New York: Oxford University Press; 1959.

The essays cover a myriad of jazz topics, from ragtime to bop, including Dixieland, blues, and The Modern Jazz Quartet. Among the contributors are George Avakian with two concise introductions, one on "Bix Beider-becke" and the other on "Bessie Smith"; an examination of "Boogie-Woogie" and "Jelly Roll Morton" by William Russell; a tribute to "Sidney Bechet" by Ernest Ansermet (a Swiss orchestral conductor); Marshall Stearns' assessment of "Folk Blues," and an analysis of "Art Tatum's Style" by André Hodier. The essays are unified by their focus on musical style and structure; however, some essays (George Avakian), are superficial, whereas the contributions by William Russell are provocative.

943. Wilmer, Valerie. *Jazz People.* London: Allison and Busby; Indianapolis: Bobbs-Merrill; 1971.

Details the style and approaches to performing jazz from 14 insiders. The 14 musicians interviewed include Buck Clayton, Eddie "Lockjaw" Davis, Art Farmer, Billy Higgins, Babs Gonzales, Jimmy Heath, Thelonious Monk, Howard McGhee, Archie Shepp, Cecil Taylor, Joe Turner, Randy Weston, Clark Terry, and Jackie McLean. The author combines insider perspectives with her own opinions to provide an outline of the artist's style. Index.

944. Wilson, John S. *The Collector's Jazz Modern.* Philadelphia: Lippincott, 1959; Paris: France-Empire, 1968.

A companion to the author's *Collector's Jazz: Tradition and Swing.* Contains biographical portraits and some discussion of recordings. Concentrates on artists and styles since World War II and includes portraits of Charles Parker, John Coltrane, Thelonious Monk, and several more. French edition entitled *Place au Jazz Moderne.*

945. Wilson, Peter Niklas. *Hear and Now; Gedanken zur Improvisierten Musik.* Frankfurt: Hofheim; 1999.

A collection of essays and interviews of artists such as Derek Bailey, Paul Bley, J. and M. Maneri, P. Oxley, D. Mengelberg, Bob Ostertag, Evan Parker, and many more. The artists discuss their musical beginnings, philosophies, and influences.

946. Wulff, Ingo. *Diary of Jazz: A Perpetual Calender.* Frankfurt: Kiel; 1996.

A collection of several interviews with artists such as Miles Davis, Bill Frisell, Lee Konitz, Gary Peacock, Bill Portal, and several more. The artists discuss their careers, music, and place in the jazz world.

VI

History-Surveys

947. András, Peenye. *A Jazz.* Budapest: Gondolat Kiadó; 1964.

In Hungarian. A historical survey of jazz that begins with a concise discussion of spirituals, ragtime, and Scott Joplin. Thereafter, blues and jazz, New Orleans (which includes a scholarly discussion of rhythm, "beat-off-beat"), swing, bebop, and modern jazz to the early 1961. Devotes much of the book to styles and contributions of selected artists. Selected bibliography and index.

948. Asriel, Andre. *Jazz: Analysen und Aspekte.* Berlin: Lied der Zeit; 1966. reprint, AVFL. Berlin: Lied der Zeit; 1977.

In German. A major work that is permeated with information on the musical features of jazz. Information on chronological evolution, form, harmony, rhythm, and orchestration abound. Numerous musical examples are used to illustrate concepts. The book also contains a comprehensive list of significant performers of specific jazz styles as well as indices of names and subjects.

949. Berendt, Joachim Ernst. *Der Jazz: Eine Zeit kritische Studie.* Stuttgart; Deutsche Verlag: 1950.

In German. Offers a good interpretation of jazz and jazz history but contains little new information. The author traces trends and styles from New Orleans and illuminates the styles of significant artists to 1950. Index.

950. _____. *The New Jazz Book: From New Orleans to Rock and Free Jazz;* translated by Dan Morgenstern and Helmut and Barbara Bredigkeit. New York: Hill; 1975.

Focuses on historical and analytical approaches, tracing jazz evolution from ragtime to rock and electronic jazz. He divides the evolution into decades. Included are biomusical profiles, stylistic features of jazz, evolution of the use of instruments, and a discussion of big bands and combos. Among the profiles are Buddy Bolden, Louis Armstrong, Bessie Smith, Bix Beiderbecke, Duke Ellington, Coleman Hawkins, Lester Young, Charles Parker, Dizzy Gillespie, Miles Davis, John Coltrane, and Ornette Coleman. Stylistic elements such as melody, rhythm, phrasing, improvisation, and orchestration are also covered. Additionally, significant exponents and their stylistic features, as well as the evolution of big bands and combos since swing are covered. The book was translated and expanded from the original German edition. A discography of recordings referred to in the book and name index are included.

951. _____ (editor). *Die Story des Jazz: Vom New Orleans zum Rock Jazz.* Stuttgart: Deutsche Verlag; 1975. Reprint, Reinbek: Rowohlt; 1978. In English, *The Story of Jazz: From New Orleans to Rock-Jazz.* Englewood Cliffs, N.J.; Prentice Hall: London: Bernie and Jenkins; 1978.

In German. A series of essays, organized chronologically, by several writers. The collection includes the following essays: Reimer von Essen on New Orleans, Manfred Miller on blues, Werner Burkhardt on Chicago, Dan Morgenstern on swing, Leonard Feather on bebop, Ekkehard Jost on free jazz, and Karl Lippegaus on jazz-rock. Most of the essays are compilations of ideas and conclusions by others with few fresh insights. Also, there is no coverage of jazz west of the Mississippi nor attention given to sociocultural contexts. Selected bibliography and discography; however, no index.

952. Bernhard, Edmond, and Jacques De Vergnies. *Apologie du Jazz;* prefaces de John Ouwerx et J. Stehman. Bruxelles: Les Presses de Belgium; 1945.

In French. Begins with a general assessment of jazz that focuses on origins and influences, elements (no musical examples), and the role and function of improvisation. Individual musicians such as Louis Armstrong are discussed, along with concise profiles of other selected soloists: trumpeters, trombonists, saxophonists, clarinetists, violinists, guitarists, bassists, and drummers. All discussions are concise. A selected discography by artist or group and name index is included.

953. Chilton, John. *Jazz;* foreword by George Melly. London: Hodder and Stoughton; New York: David McKay; 1979.

One of the most interesting jazz history texts of the 1970s, as it combines theoretical chapters on improvisation, harmonic and rhythmic concepts of bebop, and basic elements of modal and free jazz. The book also covers the evolution of jazz. Generally absent are derogatory or biased interpretations and conclusions. The book is geared to new students of jazz history rather than scholars. Also included are additional readings at the end of each chapter, a bibliography, selected discography, glossary, and index.

954. Clark, Andrew (editor). *Riffs and Choruses: A New Jazz Reader.* New York: Bayou Press; 2001.

A comprehensive collection of essays that deal with jazz origins, culture, history, styles, issues of race, and related areas of language, literature, and film. Essays by jazz critics and writers, and by writers like Amiri Baraka, Langston Hughes, Zora Neal Hurston, Jack Kerouac, Michael Harper, and Jean-Paul Sartre' are also included. Comprehensive, thorough, and scholarly.

955. Coeroy, André. *Le Jazz.* Paris: Aveline, 1926, 1978; Paris: Place; 1988.

In French. An analysis of the elements and structures of jazz, and an attempt to correlate jazz to West African music. The book is permeated with musical analysis and examples. One of the better attempts to compare jazz to African music. The 1988 edition contains a preface by Frank Ténot and afterwards by Lucien Malson and Jacques B. Hess.

956. _____. *Histoire générale du azz: Strette—Hot—Swing.* Paris: Les Editions Denoël; 1942.

In French. Begins with an assessment of several writers' positions on jazz, followed by a general discussion of the evolution of jazz. The book is divided into three parts: part one covers genealogy and elements; part two, structures, soloists, styles, and instruments; and part three, evolution and influences (George Gershwin, Claude Debussy, Igor Stravinsky, and Maurice Ravel). The discussion of the influence of jazz on nonjazz composers is the highlight of the book. Appendices include a chronology of jazz, selected bibliography and discography, and name index.

957. Collier, James Lincoln. *The Making of Jazz: A Comprehensive History.* Boston: Houghton Mifflin; London: Hart-Davis MacGibbon, 1978; New York: Dell, 1979; London: Macmillan, 1981.

The author states, "Because this book is intended for students and the lay public, I have not burdened it with citations of my sources" (p. x). He emphasizes that "my main sources have been the records themselves." With this methodology, the author approaches jazz chronologically, detailing the contributions of many significant jazz performers. He covers topics

ranging from "The Precursors," a superficial treatment, through Ornette
Coleman, John Coltrane, and "The Future: Some After Thoughts."
Although the book is permeated with facts about the contributions of
musicians, there are no musical examples to support the discussions. The
book is also weak on the role and function that sociocultural context
played in shaping the music of artists like Armstrong, Morton, Monk,
Parker, and Coltrane, to name a few. Selected bibliography and discography are included plus a thorough index.

958.   Cook, Richard. *Blue Note Records: The Biography.* New York: Secker and
Warburg; 2001.

A history of the recording company that was formed by Alfred Lion and
Francis Wolff in 1939. The label was sold to Liberty Records in 1966, and
is now part of the vast EMI empire. Cites the names and recordings of
numerous blues and jazz artists, and the success of its mostly African
American artists in the same communities throughout America.

959.   Dauer, Alfons. *Jazz: Die magische Musik: Ein Leitfaden durch der Jazz.*
Bremen, Federal Republic of Germany: Roth; 1961. U.P.; 1961.

In German. Surveys jazz history and style but is sometimes lacking in
documentation. The author follows the usual chronological development
from New Orleans with a focus on artists and styles. No new insights. Index
(addition to 1981).

960.   Davis, Nathan. *Writings in Jazz.* Dubuque, Iowa: Gorsuch Scarisbrick; 1978.

Written by a world-class saxophonist and professor of ethnomusicology
at the University of Pittsburgh, the book focuses on the music, musicians,
and the sociocultural context of jazz. The book is geared to introductory-
level students and contains few musical examples. The author's insight into
Kenny "Klook" Clarke's drumming is interesting. Selected bibliography
and discography.

961.   Dexter, Dave. *The Jazz Story: From the 90's to the 60's;* foreword by
Woody Herman. Englewood Cliffs, N.J.: Prentice Hall; 1964.

Contains historical and biographical information as well as personal recollections and anecdotes on the evolution of jazz. Among the specific topics
discussed are "The First Bands"; "From Goldkette to Whiteman"; "Jazz
in the West"; "The First Ladies"; "The Men: Leadbelly, Jelly, and others";
"The Cool School," and "The Bird: Internationally Speaking." The quality
of the essays is uneven: some articles are permeated with anecdotes, some
are biographical vignettes, and there are occasional egregious errors (history and facts). The "Jazz in the West" essay offers some important facts.
Selected bibliography, discography, and an index.

962. Erlich, Lillian. *What Jazz Is All About.* New York: Messner, 1962; London: Gollancz, 1963; revised edition, New York: Messner, 1975.

Chronicles the development of jazz from the antebellum period through the 1960. In addition to spirituals, some attention is given to minstrels, blues, and ragtime in the prejazz section. These genres are treated superficially with no convincing information of how they were transformed into jazz. Significant individuals are also addressed. Selected bibliography and index.

963. Feather, Leonard. *The Book of Jazz: A Guide to the Entire Field.* Foreword by Dizzy Gillespie. New York: Horizon Press, 1957; London: Barker, 1959; New York: Meridian Books, 1960; London: Jazz Book Club, 1961; revised edition, *The Book of Jazz from Then Till Now: A Guide to the Entire Field.* New York: Horizon Press; 1965.

The purpose of this book is to provide "a series of instrument-by-instrument histories enabling the reader to see each artist's role, period of impact, and relative importance" (p. 6). In addition, the author outlines the role and development of each instrument/voice, their primary proponents, and their function within combos and big bands. The guitar chapter is reprinted from James Sallis's *Jazz Guitars* (pp. 17–30). Techniques of improvisation, the future of jazz, and jazz and race issues are also discussed. The author cites recordings in the text. Musical examples, index, and illustrations. Selected bibliography, discography, and reference notes.

964. Finkelstein, Sidney. *Jazz: A People's Music.* New York: Macmillan, 1968; New York: Da Capo, 1978.

Surveys jazz to the beginning of bop from the blues. The author examines the evolution of jazz from a social viewpoint and is concerned with the development and appreciation of all musical genres. Selected bibliography and an index.

965. Fox, Charles. *Jazz in Perspective.* London: Barrier Jenkins; 1969.

Traces the roots of jazz and the personalities involved in its development. The book uses many musical examples to illustrate the growth and evolution of jazz. Originally written for a BBC radio series, this text covers jazz to the late 1960s. He spotlights Louis Armstrong, Jelly Roll Morton, Duke Ellington, and many more. He views jazz as a performer's art (addition to 1981).

966. Gammond, Peter (editor). *The Decca Book of Jazz;* foreword by Milton "Mezz" Mezzrow. London: Muller, 1958; London: Jazz Book Club, 1960.

A collection of 25 essays by mostly British critics and historians. The essays cover jazz styles of specific cities (Harlem, Kansas City, New Orleans) and current (1960) trends on both the East Coast and the West Coast; individual artists, including composers (Ellington), pianists, vocalists, instrumentalists, white jazz, African elements, and developments in Western Europe. There are three essays on jazz-related topics, two on blues, and one on ragtime. A comprehensive discography of 78s, EPs, LPs, and an index are included.

967.   Gerard, Charley. *Jazz in Black and White.* Westport, Conn.: Praeger Publishers; 1998.

A provocative study and discussion of black versus white identity in jazz. He addresses questions like "Is Jazz a Specifically African American Music?" and "Can White Musicians Play the Music with any Authenticity?" He argues that jazz has been and continues to be a music whose developments are linked to African American strategies of achieving sociopolitical goals. Provides informed and thorough discussion, rejects what he terms extreme arguments from both sides, and concludes with the middle ground as the most logical answer to the questions he researched in his study.

968.   Giddins, Gary. *Visions of Jazz: The First Century.* New York: Oxford University Press; 2001.

Jazz history told primarily through a series of profiles of prominent musicians, including some persons on the periphery such as Ethel Waters, Frank Sinatra, Chico O'Farrell, and Spike Jones. The book is accompanied by a CD of performances selected by Giddins and released by Blue Note.

969.   _____. *Riding on a Blue Note: Jazz and American Pop.* New York: Oxford University Press; 1981.

Covers topics ranging from jazz's earliest days to developments around 1981. His appreciations of Ornette Coleman, Sonny Rollins, and Cecil Taylor deftly balance listening, analysis, and aesthetics with good writing skills. In addition to established musicians, including Frank Sinatra, he also discusses the contributions of artists such as Otis Blackwell and Donald Lambert. The articles on early rock 'n' roll and rhythm and blues are not as informative as his jazz articles.

970.   Gillenson, Lewis N. (editor). *Esquire's World of Jazz;* commentary by James Poling. New York: Grosset and Dunlap, 1962; London: Barker, 1963; London: Jazz Book Club, 1964.

Covers the evolution of jazz, significant exponents, insider perspectives, women in jazz, and future directions. Excellent photographs and paintings. Selected discography.

971. Gioia, Ted. *The History of Jazz.* New York: Oxford University Press; 1997.

Covers the major trends and personalities that have shaped jazz, including those in California and other parts of the West Coast. A discussion of styles, artists, and trends. A bibliography and good references.

972. Goffin, Robert. *Jazz: From the Congo to the Metropolitan;* introduction by Arnold Gingrich. Garden City: Doubleday; reprint New York: Da Capo, 1975; *Histoire du Jazz.* Montreal: Parizeau, 1945; *Jazz: From the Congo to Swing.* London: Musicians Press; 1946.

Traces the development of jazz from New Orleans to the 1960s. The author, known for his ability to distinguish technically between hot and commercial jazz, draws informative and perceptive portraits of several musicians, particularly Louis Armstrong and Benny Goodman. He argues that each continent will eventually develop an indigenous jazz style (1981).

973. Gonda, Janos. *Jazz: Történet elmélet, gyakorlat.* Budapest: Zeneműkiadó; 1965.

In Hungarian. Focuses on the history, theory, and practice of jazz to the early1960s. The coverage is thorough. Selected bibliography, three recordings.

974. Gridley, Mark. *Jazz Styles.* Englewood Cliffs, N.J.: Prentice Hall, 1978; second edition, 1985; third edition, 1988; fourth edition, 1991; fifth edition, 1993.

Treats jazz as a chronological evolution from New Orleans to contemporary styles. He addresses individuals and groups within styles with the exception of selected artists such as Duke Ellington, Miles Davis, John Coltrane, Bill Evans, Herbie Hancock, Keith Jarrett, and several jazz-rock fusion artists who are treated separately. The text is coordinated to the Smithsonian Collection of Classic Jazz; however, these are supplemented with the cassettes that accompany later editions. The text is geared to general students and is permeated with listening guides. Included is a chapter summary for quick reference to issues covered in previous chapters. The strengths of the book are that it is written in a nontechnical music format, and that it has a glossary provided for terms and concepts. The weakness is its failure to understand issues such as transformation and reinterpretation in the "origins" of jazz. Beginning with the fourth edition, he added new listening guides, dropping the concise profiles of Buck Clayton, Don Ellis, Herschel Evans, Artie Shaw, Frank Teschemacher, and Lucky Thompson. The appendices are chronology of jazz styles chart, elements of music, guide to record buying, glossary, supplementary reading, sources for notated solos for musicians (scales and harmonic progressions), a small basic video collection, jazz styles cassette contents, and an index.

975. _____. *How to Teach Jazz History: A Teacher's Manual and Test Bank.* Manhattan, Kans.: National Association of Jazz Educators; 1984.

A companion volume to his text that provides advice on teaching jazz history. He treats the subject as a history of styles and people, and includes suggestions regarding teaching listening through graph analysis. Also includes sample test questions; many questions require students to recognize soloists from a list of performers on the same instrument. The author does not situate the teaching of jazz within its sociocultural context.

976. Griffin, Clive D. *Jazz.* London: Dryad Press; 1989.

Addresses the roots of jazz in African and European music, after which he traces the evolution of jazz through four cities; New Orleans, Chicago, New York, and Kansas City. He traces the roots of jazz to Africa, brass band marches, and the Klezmer music of nineteenth-century immigrant Jews. In addition to highlighting the contributions of numerous musicians in a historical context, the author discusses styles, including New Orleans, Chicago, New York, Kansas City, bop, cool, free, electric jazz, and more. Geared to beginners. Contains a chronology, glossary, selected discography, and an index.

977. Harris, Rex. *Jazz.* Harmondsworth: Penguin, 1952; second edition, Harmondsworth: Penguin, 1953; third edition (same publisher), 1956; retitled, *The Story of Jazz;* with an afterward and discography by Sheldon Meyer. New York: Grosset and Dunlap; 1955.

An attempt to trace the evolution of jazz from a "purist" point-of-view. He covers topics ranging from African influences to the 1950s. Strangely, he does not cover the contributions of Fletcher Henderson and Duke Ellington because he views their music as being influenced by European music. The strength of the book is the thoroughness of his discussions of African roots, early influences, and early history. No musical examples. Selected bibliography, discography, and an index.

978. Haskins, Jim. *The Cotton Club.* New York: Random House; 1977.

Recreates the show business politics and the vitality that nurtured the Cotton Club's contributions to popular culture and jazz. Includes portraits of artists like Bojangles Robinson, Duke Ellington, Lena Horne, and others. Haskins covers mobsters, celebrity slumming, the rise to prominence of dancers and musicians, and racism.

979. Hentoff, Nat, and Albert J. McCarthy (editors). *Jazz: New Perspectives on the History of Jazz by Twelve of the World's Foremost Jazz Critics and Scholars.* New York: Reinhart, 1959; London: Cassell, 1960; New York: Grove Press, 1961; London: Jazz Book Club, 1962; reprint: Da Capo, 1974.

Presents critical and scholarly essays on the history and development of jazz, on different jazz styles, and on individual jazz musicians. The essays are arranged into several categories including general, historical, and regional studies. Among the contributors are Ernest Borneman, Charles Edward Smith, John Steiner, Franklin Driggs, Gunther Schuller, Martin Williams, and Guy Waterman. Some musical examples, a comprehensive discography, and an index.

980. Hobsbawm, Eric. *The Jazz Scene.* New York: Pantheon Books; 1993.

A history that covers the music and its practitioners from New Orleans to the clubs of New York. Includes 23 essays that have never appeared in book form. Also contains some concert and record reviews from *The New Statesman,* and the *New York Review of Books* on artists such as Ray Charles, Count Basie, Duke Ellington, Thelonious Monk, and Mahalia Jackson.

981. Hobson, Wilder. *American Jazz Music.* New York: W. W. Norton, 1939; London: Dent, 1941; London: Jazz Book Club, 1956; New York: Da Capo, 1978.

Examines the roots of jazz historically (through the swing era), and analytically (by treating the technical features of jazz and swing). The author's objective is to tell the story of jazz and to make its rhythms more understandable. A selected discography of 30 records illustrates the author's view of the development of jazz. A good index is included (addition to 1981).

982. Hodier, André. *Hommes et Problèmes du Jazz; suivi de la Religion du Jazz.* Paris: Portulan, 1954; *Jazz; Its Evolution and Essence;* translated by David Noakes. New York: Grove Press; London: Secker and Warburg, 1956; London: Jazz Book Club, 1958; New York: Da Capo, 1975.

In French. Examines the elements of jazz with a focus on modern styles. He covers five periods and examines the style of selected artists: Louis Armstrong's Hot Five, Duke Ellington's "Concerto for Cootie," Dicky Wells, and Miles Davis. Among the basic issues discussed are improvisation, what is swing, rhythm, the state of jazz to around 1955, and the influence of jazz on European classical music. Numerous musical examples. Selected discography and an index.

983. _____. *Le Jazz, cet inconnu.* Preface by Charles Delaunay. Paris: Collection "Harmoniques"; 1945.

In French. Covers a myriad of jazz topics and people, including music and culture, African Americans and jazz, and swing, all with concise references to trumpeters and cornetists, clarinetists, trombonists, and pianists. Position of artists, aesthetics, and justification of jazz are also alluded to. The coverage is opinionated and lacks documentation. Appendices on jazz discs and titles of tunes. Index of musicians.

984.   Joachim, Ernst. *The Jazz Book; From Fusion and Beyond.* New York: Hill; 1982.

An introduction to jazz with chapters on styles, major individual musicians, musical elements, instruments, vocalists, big bands, combos, and more. Revised and expanded from the 1975 edition, this book, like the earlier edition, approaches the subject from four different angles. However sections like the description of jazz styles and elements are limited in their coverage. Much of the book is an instrument-by-instrument evolution of jazz; however, criteria for inclusion and exclusion are not clearly stated. Originally published in Germany in 1953 under the title *Das Grosse Jazzbuch.*

985.   Jones, R. P. *Jazz.* New York: Roy Publishers; 1963.

Geared to young nonjazz specialists. In 96 pages, the author covers "Pre-History," "New Orleans," "Early Jazz in New Orleans," "The Spread of Jazz," "The Jazz Age: White," "The Jazz Age: Negro," "The Depression and Kansas City," "Swing," "The Revival," "Bop," and "Cool, Commercial, and Collected." The essays are concise but contain no musical analysis. He focuses on major developments, styles, and exponents to the early 1960s. Selected bibliography, discography, and an index.

986.   Kernfeld, Barry. *What to Listen for in Jazz.* New Haven: Yale University Press; 1995.

In this introduction to jazz he discusses context, musical concepts, procedures, and styles. Organized around 21 historical recordings from New Orleans to Ornette Coleman illustrating arrangement, composition, form, improvisation, sound, and tuning concepts. Permeated with musical examples. Includes a compact disc. Comprehensive and scholarly.

987.   Leonard, Neil. *Jazz: Myth and Religion.* New York: Oxford University Press; 1987.

The author of *Jazz and the White Americans,* he views jazz as a religion evoking messages of joy and transcendence in a stress-ridden society. He develops his theory, referencing writers such as Mircea Eliade and Nat Hentoff, by using anecdotal and biographical accounts of jazz artists as ethnographic paradigms. He does not distinguish between ritual and routine, nor does he address issues like transformation and reinterpretation of African aesthetics into African American culture. Chapter notes, references, and an index.

988. Lyttelton, Humphrey. *The Best of Jazz.* London: Taplinger; 1998.

A reprint of two volumes in one, which covers New Orleans to swing era stars. Among the numerous stars covered are Louis Armstrong, Johnny Dodds, Jelly Roll Morton, Count Basie, Duke Ellington, Benny Goodman, and many more. The artists recount their careers, and offer insight into their musical philosophies. Includes 16 pages of photographs.

989. Malson, Lucien. *Des Musiques de Jazz.* Preface by Michel Philippot. Roquevaire, France: Parenthèses; 1983.

In French. Surveys some of the different styles of jazz including New Orleans, swing, and bop. Selected bibliography, index.

990. _____. *Histoire du jazz.* Lausanne: Editions Rencontre; 1967.

In French. Traces the development of jazz from the early New Orleans style to the 1960s. The book, although short, contains some excellent photographs, especially those depicting the roots of jazz in black culture supplementing the historical information (1981).

991. Martin, Henry. *Enjoying Jazz.* New York: Schirmer Books; 1986.

Divided into three main parts: part one details the background, evolution, African, African American, and European legacies, types of songs, and includes an introduction to improvisation; part two is organized into categories like small groups, big bands, instruments, and vocalists; part three deals with "Jazz from 1970 to the Present" (trends, influences like world music, and related arts). The artists in part two are treated in a biomusical manner, including some musical examples. Although not in-depth, this book contains a wealth of information for both aficionados and scholars. The appendices contain transcriptions, a selected discography, glossary, chronology, and bibliography. Index.

992. McCalla, James. *Jazz: A Listener's Guide.* Englewood Cliffs, N.J.: Prentice Hall; 1982.

A historical evolutionary approach to jazz from its prejazz roots through the beginnings of free jazz and jazz-fusion. The chapters include a presentation of historical and musical information and a discussion of specific performers and recordings, many of which were taken from the Smithsonian Collection of Classic Jazz. The strength of the book is that it concisely outlines a historical developmental view of jazz.

993. McCarthy, Albert. *The Trumpet in Jazz.* London: Citizen Press; 1943.

Traces the evolution of jazz through the selected recordings of trumpeters from Armstrong to swing. No criteria was given for the selection of recordings; comments are mostly laudatory and limited to style characteristics.

994.   McRae, Barry. *The Jazz Handbook.* Boston: G.K. Hall; 1989.

The entries "are organized by decade, beginning with the pre-1920's and finishing with the present day, and then alphabetically by performer's name." The book is divided into seven periods covering jazz from the teens to the late 1980s. Each entry contains a concise overview followed by brief profiles of artist's accomplishments, highlights, media appearances (films, TV), and a selected discography. Appendices include a list of record labels, a glossary, selected bibliography, jazz periodicals by country, and a list of festivals (weighted to British).

995.   Megill, David, and Paul O. Tanner. *Jazz Issues: A Critical History.* Madison, Wisc.: Brown and Benchmark Publishers; 1995.

Focuses on cultural and musical forces. Covers topics such as early influences, prejazz, bop to the present, and theoretical concerns in part one. Part two is devoted to the role and function of jazz in culture covering topics such as ensemble composition, the engine of popularity, notation, improvisation, and fusion. Epilogue, glossary, bibliography, discography, and index.

996.   Megill, Donald D., and Richard S. Demory. *Introduction to Jazz History,* third edition. Englewood Cliffs, N.J.: Prentice Hall; 1993.

Examines jazz from its beginnings to the present by outlining styles and influences within its evolution. Also attempts to illustrate how styles have evolved as a result of both individual creativity and sociocultural influences. Covers numerous artists and styles. The third edition updates modern big bands, crossover, and piano styles. The treatment is geared to a beginning approach to appreciation. Glossary, selected bibliography and discography, instructor's manual, cassettes/compact discs, and an index.

997.   Middleton, Richard. *The Rise of Jazz.* Milton Keynes: Open University Press; 1979.

A manuscript that combines history, musical analysis, and to a lesser degree, sociocultural contexts, to discuss jazz historiography. Primarily focused on early jazz; some attention given to modern jazz. Topics covered include the origins of jazz and the importance of New Orleans, Chicago combo jazz, and the evolution and development of the big band in New York. Individuals are discussed within the context of history and include Louis Armstrong, Bix Beiderbecke, James P. Johnson, Bessie Smith, Fletcher Henderson, Duke Ellington, and Luis Russell. He uses recordings such as "Dippermouth Blues" and several transcriptions (8), which are contained in a separate volume. Bibliography.

998.   Mongan, Norman. *The History of the Guitar in Jazz.* Foreword by Barney Kessel. New York, London, Sydney: Oak; 1983.

Documents the role and function of the guitar in the history and evolution of jazz. Discusses the roles and musical styles of several guitarists, including Charlie Christian, Django Reinhardt, Joe Pass, and Wes Montgomery. Musical examples and solo transcriptions, including Reinhardt's solo on "Dinah." References, index, and illustrations.

999.   Morris, Ronald L. *Wait until Dark: Jazz and the Underworld, 1880–1940.* Bowling Green, Ohio: Bowling Green State University Press; 1980.

Demonstrates that "gangsters befriended, encouraged, and marketed hundreds of jazz performers 1880–1940." The author examines the attitudes and behavior of the underworld. His conclusions on seminal artists such as Duke Ellington and Charles Parker are questionable. Morris believes "individual success and recognition had little to do with innate talent, technical skill, or, for that matter, their own free will." A debatable conclusion.

1000.   Myrus, Donald. *I Like Jazz.* New York: Macmillan and Company; 1964.

A history of jazz from its beginnings to the mid-1960s. There is a discussion of the music and contributions of selected artists including Louis Armstrong, Jelly Roll Morton, Jimmy Gunfire, Thelonious Monk, Charles Parker, and, inexplicably, Mahalia Jackson. There are no new insights. Geared to beginning jazz enthusiasts. Selected discography and an index.

1001.   Nicholson, Stuart. *Jazz Rock: A History.* New York: Schirmer Books; 1998.

Details the history and evolution of jazz-rock from the 1960s to the 1990s. He distinguishes between jazz-rock, fusion, and its modern equivalents. The author argues that jazz is an inclusive music that not only allows but also demands both individuality and new concepts. In addition, he discusses the roles and importance of artists/groups such as Blood, Sweet and Tears, Chicago, Chick Corea, Miles Davis, Maynard Ferguson, Herbie Hancock, Mike Mainieri's White Elephant Band, John McLaughlin, Buddy Rich, Weather Report, Wayne Shorter, Joe Zawinul, and many more. He also discusses rock musicians who have influenced jazz, including Jimi Hendrix, Carlos Santana, and Sly Stone. Well-researched and written.

1002.   Ostransky, Leroy. *The Anatomy of Jazz.* Tacoma: University of Washington Press; 1964.

Details problems in jazz composition and performance providing information on the history of jazz as music. He has several purposes: to present jazz to those whose interest is "serious" or classical music; to relate jazz theory to music theory; to relate jazz to the history of music in general; and to indicate to jazzmen what he believes to be their position as well as their responsibility to the future. He begins with an explanation of musical elements and follows with an analysis of jazz styles from New Orleans to the 1950s. He uses musical examples to illustrate his insightful perceptions of the styles. There are chapter notes, a bibliography, and an index.

1003. _____. *Jazz City: The Impact of Our Cities on the Development of Jazz.* Englewood Cliffs, N.J.: Prentice Hall; 1978.

Develops the theory that "jazz developed in proximity to poverty and commercial sin." Ostransky also focuses on what he feels are "The Principal Urban Places That Spawned or Nurtured Jazz: New Orleans, Chicago, Kansas City, and New York." He deals at length with business and political figures, underworld activities, prohibition, prostitution, social entertainment of African American and Anglo-American populations, and the urban development of each city. Ostransky offers insights into the development of regional jazz styles. Substantiated by references, a selected bibliography, a discography arranged by city, and a comprehensive index.

1004. Panassié, Hugues. *Histoire de vrai jazz.* Paris: R. Laffont; 1959.

In French. Extols the virtues of traditional jazz over the emerging jazz trends of the time. The discussion focuses on jazz styles from early New Orleans to the late 1950s. The author champions early jazz over jazz of the 1950s (addition to 1981). Index.

1005. _____. *The Real Jazz;* translated by Anne Sorelle Williams; adapted for American publication by Charles Edward Smith. New York: Smith and Durrell, 1942; revised, New York: Barnes, 1960; London: Jazz Book Club, 1967; *La Véritable musique de jazz.* Paris: Laffont; 1946.

Panassié focuses on the elements of styles, and he critiques artists by instrument. He believes that white musicians are inferior to African American musicians and he disdains the contemporary jazz movements evolving during the time of writing, especially bebop. Selected discography.

1006. Pedro, Rogue De. *El Jazz: Historia y presencia.* Buenos Aires, Argentina: Editorial Convergencia; 1977.

In Spanish. Begins with a discussion of the role of blues and spirituals in the development of jazz, a regional New Orleans focus, and later developments. New Orleans and Chicago are discussed in "Primer Movimiento." Gives a chronology (dates) of Louis Armstrong's career 1900 to 1971 and concise discussions of swing, ragtime, boogie-woogie, cool, hard bop, and selected musicians such as Albert Ayler, Count Basie, and John Coltrane. A map of the "Evolution of Jazz," selected discography, and name index included.

1007. Perrin, Michel. *Histoire du Jazz.* Paris: Larousse; 1967.

In French. Traces the evolution of jazz from New Orleans to the early 1960s. Covers New Orleans, Chicago, swing, bop, and postbebop styles, and includes a career overview of Miles Davis, with portraits of his band members. Selected bibliography, chronology, index, and illustrations.

1008. Piazza, Tom (editor). *Writing the Tempo.* New York: Anhor Books; 1996.

A collection of jazz liner notes representing different persons and styles from throughout jazz history. Includes two essays by the author, however the majority of the essays are from other writers, not musicians, such as Nat Hentoff, Dan Morgenstern, and Martin Williams. The essays include anecdotes, historical information, and some musical analysis.

1009. Polillo, Arrigo. *Le Voci del Jazz: Origini e sviluppo del canto vella Musica Afro-Americana.* Milano: Mondadori; 1977.

In Italian. Concerned with the origins and development of singing in African American music. Although the focus is on jazz, he draws upon blues and spirituals to illustrate vocal aesthetics and styles.

1010. Porter, Lewis (editor). *Jazz: A Century of Change.* New York: Schirmer Books; 1997.

The author approaches the topic by posing the question "What is Jazz?" After posing the question he explores the evidence from stylistic change to artistic innovation. Also, he explains the technical composition of jazz and examines the race politics of jazz in the 1950s. The book is divided into essays that deal with early and modern jazz. Good documentation and coverage of topics that are not commonly covered in jazz literature.

1011. Porter, Lewis, and Michael Ullman. *Jazz: From its Origins to the Present.* Englewood Cliffs, N.J.: Prentice Hall; 1993.

Provides an account of both the evolution of jazz and its major contributors. The authors balance information on lives with information on the styles and movements. They detail the lives and contributions of artists such as Louis Armstrong, Count Basie, John Coltrane, Ornette Coleman, Duke Ellington, Miles Davis, and Bill Evans, as well as topics like "Popular Jazz: Bossa Nova, Big Band and Soul"; "Fusion"; and "The Avant-Garde since Coltrane." There are numerous musical examples. The appendices contain suggestions on "How to Listen to Jazz," a glossary, selected bibliography and discography, a CD-Rom version, and a 60-minute Listening to Jazz video cassette featuring a survey of jazz instruments and performance demonstrations.

1012. Sales, Grover. *Jazz: America's Classical Music;* foreword by Gene Lees. New York: Da Capo Press; 1992.

An introduction to the lives and music of several significant jazz artists with historical insights and anecdotes. The book is designed as a textbook for jazz appreciation classes rather than jazz performers or scholars. Among the artists covered are Louis Armstrong, Duke Ellington, Benny Goodman, Charles Parker, and John Coltrane. Includes a selected discography of recommended listening, a bibliography, numerous photographs, and an index.

1013. Sargeant, Winthrop. *Jazz Hot and Hybrid.* New York: Arrow, 1938; new and enlarged edition, New York: Dutton, 1946; London: Jazz Book Club, 1959; third edition, New York: Da Capo, 1975.

One of the first scholarly assessments of the character and musical structure of jazz. The author's discussion of jazz rhythm and melody, scalar structures, and the derivation and evolution of blues harmony and the blues scales is noteworthy. In each case, he draws his conclusions by examining other African American genres (e.g., spirituals). Sargeant was the first scholar to suggest a "blues scale." Although this was published before much of the research on African music was done (for example, A. M. Jones, *Studies of African Music*), Sargeant suspected but did not conclude that the "blues scale" was an African retention. Musical form, the jazz orchestra, and jazz as an art form are also examined. Comprehensive bibliography in later editions, musical examples, and an index.

1014. Seymour, Gene. *Jazz: The Great American Art.* New York: Franklin Watts (Grolier Publishing); 1995.

Concise opinion and rehashing of topics such as "Roots and Blues," through "Rock and Retrenchment." The author's coverage is limited, and lacks both the in-depth discussion and references that one can find in other books on the topic.

1015. Shapiro, Nat, and Nat Hentoff (editors). *Hear Me Talkin' to Ya: The Story of Jazz by the Men Who Made It.* New York: Rinehart, 1955; reprint, New York: Dover Publications, 1966; London: Davies, 1955; London: Jazz Book Club, 1967.

Insider perspectives of their lives, fellow musicians, and styles gleaned from interviews and printed sources. Numerous musicians were involved. The material is organized chronologically from New Orleans to the West Coast style of the 1950s and the New Orleans revival. Another significant inclusion is the insider views of 12 musicians detailing what jazz means to them. Both an interview index and a regular index.

1016. Shipton, Alyn. *A New History of Jazz.* New York: Bayou Press; 2001.

One of the most comprehensive and thoroughly researched histories of jazz to date. In addition to covering styles, people, and characteristics of jazz before John Coltrane's death in 1967, the author also provides comprehensive coverage of people, styles, and trends in jazz in the last 30 years of the twentieth century. Included is a discussion of free jazz, jazz rock, world music influences, the new historicism of the repertory movement, and the continuing trend to internationalize the genre. He rejects myths such as jazz was born in New Orleans and provides solid reasons to back his assertions. Although thorough, he does not discuss artists such as Red Norvo, Pee Wee Russell, or Dave Tough.

1017. Stearns, Marshall W. *The Story of Jazz.* New York: Oxford University Press, 1956; London: Sidgwick and Jackson, 1957; an expanded bibliography and a syllabus of 15 lectures on the history of jazz. New York: New American Library; 1958.

Written by an English professor, the book is significant because the author addresses issues such as jazz and West Africa, the meshing of cultures in the United States, and the cultural transformations that evolved in both the United States and the West Indies. He covers the evolution of jazz from its roots through the 1940s. He also addresses future directions, the elements of jazz (harmony, melody, and rhythm), and Afro-Cuban influences, especially in New York during the bebop era. No musical examples. There are chapter notes, a bibliography by R. G. Reisner, an index, and an outline of jazz lectures.

1018. Stewart, Earl. *African-American Music: An Introduction.* New York: Thomson/Schrimer; 1998.

Although not devoted solely to jazz, the author provides an introduction to the richness and diversity of African American musical styles. In addition to gospels and spirituals, he also covers jazz related genres like blues and ragtime, as well as jazz. Also contains information on classical and popular musics.

1019. Stokes, W. Royal. *The Jazz Scene: An Informal History from New Orleans to 1990.* New York: Oxford University Press; 1991.

An oral history of people, places, periods, and styles as viewed by numerous insiders. He covers the evolution of jazz in cities and regions except the early West Coast (he covers California after 1950). The California coverage is superficial. There are no new revelations. Selected bibliography.

1020. Summerfield, Maurice J. *The Jazz Guitar: Its Evolution and Its Players.* Milwaukee: Ashley Mark Publications/Music Dispatch; 1991.

Details the history of the guitar's role in jazz. The primary focus is the detailed biographies of all the major jazz guitarists since 1895, including Charlie Christian, Eddie Durham, Django Reinhardt, Joe Pass, Wes Montgomery, Barney Kessel, Kenny Burrell, Tal Farlow, Jimmy Raney, and Herb Ellis. In addition, there is a chapter on the instruments used by jazz guitarists and a section on "Sources of Supply," which contains full citations of all references mentioned in the text. Excellent photographs.

1021. Tanner, Paul, David Megell, and Maurice Gerow. *Jazz*. New York: McGraw-Hill Higher Education; 2001.

A jazz appreciation text that uses listening to help students understand and appreciate the history and styles of jazz and its predecessors. Also includes a series of boxed essays entitled "Witness to Jazz." A series of photographs by William Gottlieb that depicts scenes from some of the most important periods of jazz. Does not cover transformation, and coverage of "Jazz Heritages African and European," "Music of Africa," and other prejazz topics do not reflect the anthropological and ethnomusicological literature on the respective topics.

1022. Tanner, Paul, Ora Warren, and Maurice Gerow. *A Study of Jazz*. Dubuque, Iowa: William Brown, 1964; second edition, 1973; third edition, 1977, fourth edition; 1981.

Written by two former UCLA faculty members, this book is geared to both teachers and students of jazz. The book contains an introduction to the basic elements of jazz as well as suggestions for listening. The primary focus is historical with specific attention given to styles (New Orleans, bop, swing, contemporary, etc.), augmented with musical examples. Each chapter has a list of suggested classroom activities. Includes a list of scores, an accompanying disc that chronicles styles and a glossary. The authors treat jazz as an isolated phenomena independent of socio cultural influences.

1023. Taylor, Billy. *Jazz Piano: A Jazz History*. Dubuque, Iowa: William C. Brown; 1983.

The author draws from his extensive experience as a composer, educator-scholar, and performer to detail the role and function of the piano in jazz history. He calls jazz "African American classical music" and traces its evolution via the piano by analyzing styles and concepts such as boogie-woogie, bebop, and hard bop through the contributions of significant pianists. Among the numerous pianists cited are Bud Powell, Art Tatum, and Teddy Wilson. There are several musical examples. Selected bibliography, discography, and an index.

1024. Ténot, Frank, and Phillippe Carles. *Le Jazz*. Paris: Larousse; 1977.

In French. A collection of jazz articles previously written for and published by the *Encyclopédie Larousse*. The articles are categorized into three topics: (1) "Les Phases de la Musique Noire" contains chapters on blues, spirituals and gospels, New Orleans jazz, big bands, bebop, rock and roll, free jazz, and post-free jazz; (2) 17 portraits of major musicians; and

(3) 13 short chapters on the performers and role and function of instruments in the evolution of jazz. The essays reflect a thorough understanding of the literature and are well-written, particularly the essay on Lionel Hampton. Index of names and a bibliography.

1025. Tirro, Frank. *Jazz: A History.* New York: W. W. Norton, 1977; second Edition, New York: W. W. Norton; 1993.

Written by a musicologist, former jazz performer, and dean of the School of Music at Yale University, the book is organized chronologically from "The State of Music in the U.S. in the Late Nineteenth-Century" through contemporary idioms. Although the author states: "Of all the works presently available, however, no single volume offers the reader an analysis and interpretation of jazz, both historical and musical (which incorporates recent research from allied fields—sociology, cultural anthropology, American history—as well as from music history and theory," the text does not reflect a knowledge of issues like transformation, reinterpretation, and adaptation (see chapter on African music). The author also appears to be highly influenced by the writings of Winthrop Sargeant and Gunther Schuller (*The Blues*). The first edition contains inaccurate transcriptions of "I Can't Get Started" and "Embraceable You." The second edition addresses the social forces that shaped jazz and contains an analysis of techniques and styles with more attention given to contemporary musicians and styles, for example, "A Plurality of Styles." The book contains over 200 pages of indices and appendices: listening guides, transcriptions, synoptic table, annotated bibliography, selected discography, indices to the record collections, glossary, and index.

1026. Traill, Sinclair, and Gerald Lascelles. *Just Jazz.* Vol. 1, London: Davies, 1957; Volume 2, London: Davies, 1958; Volume 3, London: Landsborough Publications, 1959, and Volume 4, London: Souvenir Press, 1960.

Contains essays by British scholars covering a myriad of jazz topics including style, history, criticism, and biographies. Each volume also contains a yearly discography complete with details. In addition to American recordings a significant number of British recordings are cited. There are different authors for each of the four volumes (addition to 1981).

1027. Ulanov, Barry. *A History of Jazz in America.* New York: Viking Press, 1952; London: Jazz Book Club, 1957; London: Hutchinson, 1958; reprint New York: Da Capo, 1975.

Traces the evolution of jazz to the cool style of the 1950s. The book contains a glossary of jazz terms and phrases and an index but no musical examples or references.

1028. Vulliamy, Graham. *Jazz and Blues.* London: Routledge and Kegan Paul; 1982.

Covers the origins and development of these two genres. Although a few pages deal with British blues and recent trends, the majority of the book is devoted to pre-1960 forms. The focus is on the sociohistorical context rather than the music.

1029. Walser, Robert (editor). *Keeping Time: Readings in Jazz History.* New York: Oxford University Press; 1998.

To date, this is the best collection of essays that illustrate how critics, musicians, and writers wrote about jazz from the early styles to the 1990s. Also includes insightful and accurate introductions to the essays.

1030. Ward, Geoffrey C., and Ken Burns. *Jazz: A History of America's Music.* New York: Alfred A. Knopf; 2000.

Based on the jazz documentary that Burns produced for public television. Includes contributions by Stanley Crouch, Gerald Early, Garry Giddins, Wynton Marsalis, Dan Morgenstern, and Albert Murray. Permeated with factual insights, lots of insider perspectives, and lots of photographs. Coverage of pre-1960s jazz is good, however not much space was devoted to post-1960 jazz.

1031. Werner, Otto. *The Origin and Development of Jazz,* second edition. Dubuque, Iowa: Kendall/Hunt Publishing; 1989.

Concise and limited discussion of the evolution of jazz from Africa to the beginning of jazz rock. Includes style characteristics, references to recordings, and some musical analysis. The author does not address issues of transformation, reinterpretation, and syncretism, and lacks the in-depth knowledge and discussion offered by others covering the topic.

1032. Wheaton, Jack. *All That Jazz.* New York: Ardsley House Publishers; 1994.

The 13 chapters cover the history and evolution of jazz from "The Development of Afro-American Music" to "The Present and Future Status of Jazz" and "Special Topics." Chapters that deal with history and origins and retentions do not use ethnomusicological literature to demonstrate transformation, synthesis, or reinterpretation. The book contains numerous biomusical portraits, listening assignments, chapter summaries and questions, topics for further research, and further reading recommendations. Geared to the jazz-appreciation market rather than a scholarly audience. Contains a glossary, bibliography, discography, jazz video listings, and an author-subject index.

1033. Williams, Martin. *Jazz Changes.* New York: Oxford University Press; 1992.

Begins with profiles of jazz artists, focusing on recording sessions, club dates, life and music, and point-counterpoint sessions. He covers "Jelly Roll at the Library of Congress," "Program Notes" (on artists), and "Reviews and Observations" (artists and other topics). The book contains anecdotes and stories and specifically details recording sessions, rehearsals, performances, liner notes, and discussions of musicians and their music. His interview of Ross Russell about the Dial Record sessions with Charles Parker and his account of the recording session with Jelly Roll Morton at the Library of Congress in 1938 are very informative. Index.

1034. Yurochko, Bob. *A Short History of Jazz;* introduction by Wynton Marsalis. Chicago: Nelson-Hall Publishers; 1992.

Begins with a note from Wynton Marsalis, and chronicles the evolution of jazz from West Africa to the 1990s. This text is unique in that Yurochko outlines developments of the 1970s, 1980s, and 1990s, and covers jazz-rock, fusion, Latin, Brazilian, young masters (Hollyday, Jordan, etc.), and other individuals. The coverage is concise. He suggests recordings for listening, outlines the form of compositions, and includes some musical notation. Contains a glossary, bibliography, discography, videography, and study guides.

Early Jazz

1035. Ballantine, Christopher. *Marabi Nights: Early South African Jazz and Vaudeville.* Athens, Ohio: Ohio University Press (North American Distributor); 1994.

Focuses on the "black jazzing subculture" era(s) of development, inventing, and perfecting of its styles, and dance. He details the music and contributions of Peter Rezant, "Zuluboy" Cele, The Jazz Revellers, The Merry Blackbirds, and The Pitch Black Follies. He also describes the social context, which gave birth to the music. The book is accompanied by a cassette tape of 25 tracks (vaudeville, jazz) recorded between 1930 and 1945.

1036. Blesh, Rudi. *Shining Trumpets: A History of Jazz.* New York: Knopf, 1946; London: Cassell, 1949; second revision, New York: Knopf, 1958; reprint, New York: Da Capo, 1975; revised and enlarged, London: Cassell, 1958.

The book is divided into two parts. In the first part, Blesh discusses prejazz issues such as African elements, the evolution of African American secular and sacred music, and the elements and importance of the blues. This part offers insights by Warren "Baby" Dodds on his maternal grandfather, who played in Congo Square and transmitted African drumming concepts to him. In part two, he traces the evolution of jazz from New Orleans to the swing era. This part is supplemented with analyses of performances and numerous musical examples. There is, however, too much reliance on New Orleans as the birthplace of jazz. In spite of this fault, this is one of the best books on the topic. Selected discography and an index.

1037. Chilton, John. *A Jazz Nursery: The Story of the Jenkins's Orphanage Bands.* London: Bloomsbury Book Shop; 1980.

A significant addition to African American scholarship because the author details both the history and influence of Reverend Daniel Jenkins's band from the late nineteenth century through its performance in DuBose Heywood's *Porgy* in both New York and London in 1927–28. Chilton's account is significant because he reveals that the Jenkins's band visited Europe before both James Reese Europe and Will Marion Cook. The band was also significant because jazz musicians such as Gus Aitken, Cat Anderson, Peanuts Holland, and Jabbo Smith came through the band. Chilton believes that because of the band's tours in the 1910s and 1920s, it may have influenced numerous aspiring African American musicians. He also believes the band played "a robust music that loosened up the formal ragtime arrangement and produced emphatic syncopation when playing marches and two-steps" (p. 30). Bibliography and references.

1038. Dupont, Jean. *Introduction a la musique de Jazz.* Vaucluse, France: the author; 1945.

In French. Concise, general introduction to jazz focusing on New Orleans and origins, with some references to swing and selected recordings, including those of Louis Armstrong and Duke Ellington. The book is significant because it contains a chapter on the evolution of French jazz before 1945. Selected discography and reference notes.

1039. Hadlock, Richard. *Jazz Masters of the Twenties.* New York: Macmillan, 1965; London: Collier-Macmillan; 1966.

Details the contributions of Louis Armstrong, Bix Beiderbecke, Mezz Mezzrow, Benny Goodman, Fletcher Henderson, James P. Johnson, Eddie Lang, Don Redman, Bessie Smith, and Jack Teagarden. In addition to assessing their styles, the author also focuses on the significance of each of the artists in jazz of the period. Selected readings and a discography for each artist. No index.

1040. Harris, Rex. *Jazz.* Harmondsworth, Middlesex, England: Penguin Books; 1952.

Traces the roots, formation, and evolution of jazz through swing. The chapters dealing with roots, slave code(s), formation of class jazz, and ragtime and early white jazz are well-researched and permeated with factual information. Several references to recordings, however no musical examples. Includes an "African melody/African rhythm chart," notes on recordings cited in the text, and a selected bibliography.

1041. Hellström, Nils (editor). *Jazz: Historia teknik, utövare*. Stockholm: Estrad; 1940.

In Swedish. Contains both analysis of styles and biographical portraits. The analysis covers styles to the late 1930s and the portraits include career highlights and some references to recordings. No new insights. Index, musical examples, illustrated.

1042. Hennessey, Thomas. *From Jazz to Swing: African American Jazz Musicians and Their Music, 1890–1935*. Detroit: Wayne State University Press; 1994.

Focuses on the historical context of jazz in light of the changes in the African American community. He traces the development of jazz from a series of regional styles to its popularity in the swing era. He divides the early history of jazz into four periods: 1890–1914, when jazz precursors such as blues and ragtime evolved throughout the nation; 1914–1923, when the great migration, dance fads, and the phonograph synthesized the music into jazz; 1923–1929, the classic jazz era of Chicago and New York, and 1929–1935 when New York became the control center of the music. His regional focus includes New Orleans, Chicago, New York, and the Territories; artists covered include Louis Armstrong, Coleman Hawkins, Duke Ellington, James Reese Europe, King Oliver, Don Redman, Fletcher Henderson, and more. He used African American newspapers such as the *Chicago Defender,* oral history interviews, and other published materials to piece together his account of the development of jazz to 1935. Index.

1043. Hobsbawn, Eric. *The Jazz Scene.* New York: Pantheon Books; 1993.

A history that covers the music and its practitioners from New Orleans to the clubs of New York. Includes 23 essays that have never appeared in book form. Also, some concert and record reviews, and essays from *The New Statesman* and the *New York Review of Books* on artists such as Ray Charles, Count Basie, Duke Ellington, Thelonious Monk, and Mahalia Jackson.

1044. Hobson, Wilder. *American Jazz Music.* New York: W. W. Norton, 1939; London: Dent, 1940; revised edition, London: Dent, 1941; London: Jazz Book Club, 1956; New York: Da Capo, 1978.

Examines the roots of jazz historically (through the swing era), and analytically (by treating the technical features of jazz and swing). Provides a discography of 30 recordings that, in his opinion, articulate the development of jazz. The major flaw of the book is his assumption that jazz evolved and spread south to north without discussing transformation and reinterpretation. The British editions contain discographical references. Index (addition to 1981).

1045. Lang, Iain. *Background of the Blues.* London: Worker's Music Association, 1943; *Jazz in Perspective: The Background of the Blues.* London, Sydney, Cape Town, New York: Hutchinson, 1947; Milano: Mondadori, 1951; London: Jazz Book Club, 1957; New York: Da Capo, 1976.

The 1947 edition chronicles the evolution of jazz from early New Orleans to Kansas City of the 1930s. He provides information on the sociocultural context from which jazz evolved. Also included is a penetrating account of blues, including thematic content, musical and textual elements, and numerous examples. Selected discography and an index. Swedish edition, *Blues Øch Jazz,* and the 1976 edition are indexed, Italian edition is entitled *Il Jazz.*

1046. McCarthy, Albert. *The Trumpet in Jazz.* London: Citizen Press; 1943.

Traces the evolution of jazz through the selected recordings of artists like Armstrong, Beiderbecke, Oliver, and Johnson to the swing era. Focuses on style and the role and function of trumpet in jazz. Recordings reflect personal tastes, and comments are mostly laudatory rather than critical assessments.

1047. Mendl, R.W.S. *The Appeal of Jazz.* London: Philip Allan; 1927.

The title is misleading because coverage is devoted to dance music, spirituals, ragtime, the Charleston, and to selected individuals such as George Gershwin and Paul Whiteman. Only the surface comments on Gershwin and Whiteman might be of interest to jazz scholars.

1048. Nogawa, Kobun. *Jazz Kara Swing é.* Tokyo: Sanyo; 1947.

In Japanese. Covers the evolution of jazz from its origins and early history in New Orleans to swing. Mentions the contributions of Louis Armstrong, Jelly Roll Morton, Duke Ellington, and more.

1049. Oderigo, Néstor R. Ortiz. *História del Jazz.* Buenos Aires: Ricordi; 1952.

In Spanish. Focuses on the origin, history, and evolution of jazz to the 1940s. The book is weighted toward early styles (New Orleans and Chicago) with some attention given to swing. Index.

1050. Orgen, Kathy J. *The Jazz Revolution: Twenties America and the Meaning of Jazz.* New York: Oxford University Press; 1989.

A historical and sociological study of America in the 1920s. The book is an outgrowth of the author's doctoral dissertation. She believes that "For

Blacks, jazz was a cultural force influential in the development of the Harlem Renaissance"; "For Whites, it was a catalyst for the loosening of residual Victorian constraints." She does not cover adequately African American responses to jazz, the meaning of jazz, or the music. However, she does cover the historical and musical context that provided the background for the development of jazz in the 1920s. Index.

1051. Osgood, Harry O. *So This Is Jazz.* Boston: Little, Brown; 1926.

Approaches jazz history from a biased viewpoint by failing to consider the contributions of musicians such as Jelly Roll Morton, King Oliver, Sidney Bechet, and many other [*sic*] African American musicians. Instead, the focus is on artists such as Paul Whiteman and Zez Confrey. Although the book should not be considered a serious or authoritative work on jazz history, it does contain some good information on Paul Whiteman, Ferde Grofé, and George Gershwin. The author also suggests an origin of the word "jazz" and discusses [*sic*] African American folk music. There are two chapters devoted to the jazz orchestra and orchestration (addition to 1981).

1052. Panassié, Hugues. *Le jazz hot;* Présenté par Louis Armstrong; preface par Eugène Marsa. Paris: Correa, 1934; *Hot Jazz: The Guide to Swing Music;* translated by Lyle and Eleanor Dowling; New York: Witmark; London: Cassell; 1936.

In French. An attempt to correct his earlier critical assessment of selected African American musicians. The author admits that his earlier criticism was incorrect and in this book he treats African American contributions on their own cultural terms. This is one of the earliest attempts to correctly delineate African American contributions.

1053. _____. *The Real Jazz;* translated by Anne Sorelle Williams; adapted for American publication by Charles Edward Smith. New York: Smith and Durrell, 1942; revised, New York: Barnes, 1960; London: Jazz Book Club, 1967; *La Véritable Musique de jazz.* Paris: Laffont; 1946.

Focuses on elements of styles and critiques artists in groups by instrument. He believes white musicians are inferior to African American, and he disdains the contemporary jazz movements evolving during that time, especially bebop. Selected discography.

1054. Porter, Lewis. *Jazz: A Century of Change.* New York: Thomson/Schrimer; 1997.

Uses primary documents to introduce the major topics in the history of jazz. Also uses interviews, articles, and other writings to explore key issues, including the struggle to define jazz and to locate its origins, race politics in the 1950s and 1960s, and the debate over traditionalism and revivalism.

1055. Schuller, Gunther. *Early Jazz: Its Roots and Musical Development.* New York: Oxford University Press; 1968.

Using the research of A. M. Jones and Winthrop Sargeant, Schuller discusses the building blocks of jazz (harmony, melody, and rhythm), and their relationship to Africa. He concludes that these elements are strongly influenced by West African practices. He also discusses the acculturation of African and European musical elements in producing the distinct American genre known as jazz. The biomusical analyses and portraits are of Louis Armstrong, Jelly Roll Morton, Bix Beiderbecke, Bessie Smith, James P. Johnson, Fats Waller, Sidney Bechet, Johnny Dodds, and Duke Ellington. He also addresses the beginnings of big bands. Numerous musical examples, a glossary, selected discography, a transcribed interview of George Morrison, and an index.

1056. Shaw, Arnold. *The Jazz Age: Popular Music in the 1920's.* New York: Oxford University Press; 1987.

Examines the acculturation of blues, jazz, Harlem piano styles, and Broadway shows into tangible music expressions. He alludes to Gershwin's "Rhapsody in Blue," the movie *The Jazz Singer,* and the music of Ziegfeld's *Follies* as examples of the fusion of American musical genres. Selected bibliography, discography, and an index.

1057. Wyndham, Tex. *Texas Shout; How Dixieland Jazz Works.* Seattle: University of Washington Press; 1997.

An illustrated collection of the author's previously published articles in jazz magazines. The articles are focused primarily on the music and artists of Dixieland jazz.

1058. Yui, Shoichi (editor). *Dixieland Jazz Nyumon.* Japan: Shippan; 1962.

In Japanese. A guide to Dixieland jazz, including artists, places of origin, and role and function in culture. Geared to the novice.

Big Band and Swing

1059. Belaire, David. *A Guide to the Big Band Era: A Comprehensive Review of All the Recorded Hits and All The Hitmakers.* Santa, Ana, Calif.: Winged Note Press; 1996.

A reference book of bands, vocalists, and hundreds of recordings performed on radio and jukeboxes. He covers the 1935 to 1946 period.

1060. Belker, Loren B. *Seems Like Old Times: A Story of Midwest's Big Bands.* Lincoln: University of Nebraska Press; 1992.

Discusses known and under represented big bands throughout the Midwest. He chronicles bands from Chicago, Kansas City, St. Louis, and other Midwestern cities. Included are the bands of Count Basie, Benny Goodman, and others.

1061. Bied, Dan. *Dan Bied's Jazz Reader.* Burlington, Iowa: William Brown; 1997.

There are 50 photographs in this reader about the musical careers of selected jazz musicians. Although artists such as Bix Beiderbecke, Art Hodes, and Stan Kenton are covered, much of the book deals with swing artists such as Count Basie, Benny Goodman, Ray McKinley, and Artie Shaw.

1062. Bindas, Kenneth J. *Swing That Modern Sound.* Jackson: University of Mississippi Press; 2001.

Concerned with the symbols that define the swing era of jazz, for example, the dress, language, and dance styles that one see when experiencing the modern revival of swing music. He advocates that the tempers and tempos of swing defined modernity in America. Also, he explores the cultural, significance, and social structures that encouraged swing's creation, acceptance, and popularity.

1063. _____. *The World of Swing.* New York: Charles Scribner's Sons, 1974; New York: Da Capo, 1985.

Contains interviews conducted in the 1960s and 1970s first published in journals/magazines such as *Down Beat, Metronome, Jazz Journal, Jazz, Just Jazz No. 4,* and *Saturday Review.* In addition to innovative musicians such as Count Basie, Benny Goodman, and Lionel Hampton, Dance also interviewed musicians who were associated with the bands of Benny Carter, Erskine Hawkins, Fletcher Henderson, Jimmie Lunceford, and Chick Webb. Helen Dance contributed essays on Mildred Bailey, Billie Holiday, and Chick Webb. Although the recollections are somewhat repetitive, the personal accounts allow the reader to recapture what it was like to be an African American musician. Selected bibliography, discography, photographs, and an index.

1064. Deffa, Chip. *Swing Legacy;* foreword by George T. Simon. Lanham, Md.: Scarecrow Press, and Institute of Jazz Studies (Rutgers University); 1989.

Based on the insider perspectives of several musicians, including Benny Carter and Lionel Hampton, and covers the artists' life and times in the swing era. The insiders provide numerous anecdotes and recollections about topics ranging from bands to travel and racism. Index.

1065. Erenberg, Lewis A. *Swingin' The Dream: Big Band Jazz and the Rebirth of American Culture.* Chicago University of Chicago Press; 1998.

A cultural and social history of the swing era, 1935 to 1948, when big band jazz dominated popular music. He traces the development of big band jazz from the 1920s through the early 1950s as a vehicle for understanding American culture and society during these years. Included is a discussion of Paul Whiteman's attempts to "civilize" African American music. Duke Ellington's use of Eurocentric techniques in black jazz, how African Americans became more centered and visible in the bands of the 1930s and 1940s, and more.

1066. Fernett, Gene. *Swing Out: Great Negro Dance Bands.* Midland, Mich.: Pendell; 1970.

Discusses 25 African American bandleaders and their careers. In addition, there is a discussion of musical style(s) and significant musicians who played in the respective bands. Among the bands are those of Ellington, Basie, Henderson, Lunceford, Marable, and Gillespie. Also included are the dates and places of birth of 54 musicians and a list of theme songs. Excellent photographs.

1067. _____. *A Thousand Golden Horns: The Exciting Age of America's Greatest Dance Bands.* Midland, Mich.: Pendell; 1966.

Treats the work of some swing as well as some pseudojazz bands from 1925 to 1945. Focuses on artists, context, and the role and functions of bands. Selected bibliography and discography (addition to 1981).

1068. Gammond, Peter, and Raymond Horricks (editors). *Big Bands.* Cambridge, England: Stephens; 1981.

Discusses the history, significance, and role and function of bands generally associated with the swing era. Includes information on numerous bands, including Count Basie, Duke Ellington, Benny Goodman, Fletcher Henderson, and Jimmy Lunceford. No new insights.

1069. Gitler, Ira. *Swing to Bop: An Oral History of the Transition in Jazz in the 1940's.* New York: Oxford University Press; 1985.

A significant addition to jazz literature because the book is permeated with the comments of African American musicians concerning there struggle to regain control of jazz from white big band leaders. The insider comments provide insights into innovators versus control, perceptions of jazz, and racism. The book is based on interviews with numerous musicians. Selected bibliography and an index.

1070. Hall, Fred. *Dialogues in Swing: Intimate Conversations With the Stars of the Big Band Era.* Ventura, Calif.: Pathfinder Publishing; 1989.

Based on interviews he conducted on his syndicated radio show "Swing Thing." Includes interviews of Maxine Andrews, Bob Crosby, Dick Haymes, Jo Stafford, Woody Herman, Wild Bill Davison, Peggy Lee, Jimmy Van Heusen, Glenn Miller, George Shearing, Mel Torme, and Paul Weston. The interviews contain few new insights into the lives and careers of the respective musicians.

1071. _____. *More Dialogues in Swing: Intimate Conversations with the Stars of the Big Band Era.* Ventura, California: Pathfinder Publishing of California; 1991.

Insider perspectives from several members of the bands of Count Basie, Les Brown, Tony Bennett, Harry James, Helen O'Connell, and Kay Starr among others. Included are conversations with Steve Allen, Count Basie, Tony Bennett, Johnny Green, Harry James, Herb Jefferies, and Teddy Wilson. The insights focus on audiences, life on the road, changing musical tastes, economics, and more. Bibliography and an index.

1072. Kennedy, Don. *Big Band Jump Personality Interviews.* Atlanta: Unknown Publisher; 1993.

A concise but informative collection of interviews with artists like Ray Anthony, Count Basie, Charlie Barnet, Stan Kenton, Erskine Hawkins, Yank Lawson, Ray McKinley, Mel Torme, and others.

1073. Korall, Burt. *Drummin Men—The Heartbeat of Jazz: The Swing Years.* New York: Oxford University Press; 2002.

Details the importance of drummers to the bands of Count Basie, Jimmy Dorsey, Benny Goodman, Artie Shaw, and others. Among the drummers discussed are Jo Jones, Gene Krupa, Ray McKinley, and Buddy Rich. Also celebrates the music, important performers, and life of the times.

1074. Mandel, Howard. *Future Jazz.* New York: Oxford University Press; 2000.

Combines jazz criticism, historiography, and ethnography with interviews and analytical statements to produce a study of the recent jazz scene. His description of musical events, musicians, and history enables one to see that jazz continues to be an innovative art form.

1075. McCarthy, Albert. *Big Band Jazz.* London: Barrie and Jenkins; 1974.

Surveys the development of big band jazz with reference to the outstanding personalities involved. This comprehensive and well-illustrated volume covers the contributions of artists such as James Reese Europe, Wilbur Sweatman, Fletcher Henderson, Count Basie, Benny Goodman, and Duke Ellington as well as many less well-known big band leaders. Numerous photographs, an extensive name index, a list of references, and bibliographical and discographical information (1981).

1076. _____. *The Dance Band Era: The Dancing Decades from Ragtime to Swing: 1910–1950*. Philadelphia: Chilton; London: Studio Vista; 1971.

Introduces and discusses British and European dance bands along with a selected number of American dance bands such as Paul Whiteman, Jean Goldkette, Ben Pollack, Casa Loma, and Benny Goodman. The approach is biomusical; however, there are no musical examples. There is no coverage of African American bands and no new insights are provided. Excellent photographs (addition to 1981).

1077. Miller, Paul Edvard. *Down Beat's Yearbook of swing:* introduction by Fletcher Henderson. Chicago: Down Beat, 1939. Reprint, Westport, Conn.: Greenwood Press. Also titled *Miller's Yearbook of Popular Music*. Chicago: PEM Publications; 1943.

A potpourri of information, including a concise history of jazz, a suggested discography, an assessment of collector's items and a selected bibliography, all of which have been replaced by more detailed and scholarly studies. The 200 concise biographies of swing musicians and the jazz argot chapters are of some use.

1078. Pener, Degen. *The Swing Book*. Boston: Back Bay Books; 1999.

Details the rebirth and new interest in swing, and new artists promoting the music. She covers the legends of swing, the most swinging new bands, issues of fashion and lifestyle, a city-by-city guide to clubs, dance classes, films, and more.

1079. Raymond, Al. *Swinging Big Bands into the 1990s*. Broomall, Pennsylvania: Harmony Press; 1992.

Based on his 50-plus years in music, the author's primary purpose is to inform readers that swinging big bands are still active, exciting, and creative. The 21 chapters are mostly concise commentaries of around 7 pages, none are more than 13 pages. He covers arrangers, music business, big bands of the 1990s, recording, and much more.

1080. Rollini, Arthur. *Thirty Years with the Big Bands*. Urbana: University of Illinois Press; 1987.

This book details the experience of a sideman who lived and performed through the big band era. The book is permeated with anecdotes and reminiscences of numerous musicians the author either performed with or encountered. Contains very little on African-American bands.

1081. Rust, Brian. *The Dance Bands*. London: Allan, 1972; New Rochelle: Arlington House; 1974.

Focuses on American and British dance bands' differences and influences. In the historical discussion he provides numerous biographical portraits on both individuals and bands covering 1910 to the early 1940s. Index.

1082. Scanlan, Tom. *The Joy of Jazz; Swing Era, 1935–194.* Golden, Colo.: Unknown Publisher; 1996.

The author recounts his many years as a jazz reporter. His recollections include personal contact with many jazz artists, personal stories, and insight into the era as he observed and experienced it.

1083. Schuller, Gunther. *The Swing Era: The Development of Jazz, 1930–1945.* New York and Oxford: Oxford University Press; 1989.

The sequel to the author's classic study, *Early Jazz: Its Roots and Musical Development.* This is the most scholarly study of 1930–45 jazz to date. The author examines how the arrangements of Fletcher Henderson and Eddie Sauter contributed to Benny Goodman's success; how Duke Ellington orchestrated, and used the trombone trio of Joe "Tricky Sam" Nanton, Juan Tizol, and Lawrence Brown to enrich his compositions; how Billie Holiday developed her horn-like vocal style; and how the compositions of John Nesbitt influenced the swing styles of Gene Gifford and the Casa Loma Orchestra. He also provides penetrating accounts of the music and contributions of Cab Calloway, Henry "Red" Allen, Horace Henderson, Pee Wee Russell, and Joe Mooney. The majority of the book is devoted to the famous swing bands, and is divided into "The Great Black Bands" (Earl Hines, Andy Kirk, Jimmy Lunceford, Count Basie, Duke Ellington, Benny Carter, Don Redman, etc.), and "The White Bands" (Casa Loma, Dorsey Brothers, Claude Thornhill, Les Brown, etc.). There are also probing accounts of soloists such as Art Tatum, Teddy Wilson, Coleman Hawkins, Lester Young, Bunny Berigan, and Jack Teagarden and vocalists Billie Holiday, Frank Sinatra, Peggy Lee, and Helen Forrest. The discussions are permeated with musical analysis by the author. The appendix contains a visual representation of the elements of swing, a glossary, and an index.

1084. Simon, George. *The Big Bands;* with a foreword by Frank Sinatra. New York: Macmillan, 1967; revised edition, New York: Macmillan; London: Collier-Macmillan, 1971.

Rich repository of information on bands of the 1930s and 1940s. Before Schuller's classic, *The Swing Era: The Development of Jazz 1930–1945,* this was one of the most frequently consulted books on the topic. The book is divided into four parts: surveys of artists, groups, businessmen, and media that constituted the big band era; portraits of 72 bands; categories of musicians not in bands into groupings like "arranger, leader, etc."; and portraits of Count Basie, Benny Goodman, Woody Herman, Harry James, Stan Kenton, Guy Lombardo, and Artie Shaw. Selected discography and an index.

1085. _____. *Simon Says: The Sights and Sounds of the Swing Era, 1935–1955.* New Rochelle, N.Y.: Arlington House; 1971.

A selected compilation of essays published by the author in *Metronome* between 1935 and 1955. The essays cover a myriad of topics; interviews of band leaders, reviews, histories of five bands, and chapters on Bix Beiderbecke and Bunny Berigan. Interviews cover arrangers, composers, and vocalists (Ella Fitzgerald, Peggy Lee, Sy Oliver, Fletcher Henderson, and many more). *Metronome* band reviews from 1935–46 are listed in the appendix. Index.

1086. Specht, Paul L. *How They Became Name Bands: The Modern Technique of a Dance Band Maestro.* New York: Fine Arts Publications; 1941.

Draws on anecdotes, personal experiences and communication with band-leaders to provide advice on how to build a good band. The author conducted the first dance band to broadcast and draws heavily upon his personal experiences between 1920 and 1940. One significant aspect of the book is the chapter on early radio bandleaders by Ken Farnsworth.

1087. Stewart, Rex. *Jazz Masters of the Thirties.* New York: Macmillan; London: Collier-Macmillan; 1972.

Written by a former cornetist with Duke Ellington and Fletcher Henderson, this book provides insightful comments by an insider. The author relies on anecdotes gleaned from his acquaintances with the musicians he discusses. He discusses artists from the 1920s and 1930s; Harry Carney and Joe Nanton (Ellington orchestra), Louis Armstrong, Sid Catlett, Benny Carter, John Kirby, Fletcher Henderson, Jimmy Harrison, Coleman Hawkins, Red Norvo, Art Tatum, and members of Jean Goldkette's band. Contributions include an essay on Count Basie by Hsio Wen Shih, and Francis Thorne an essay on Rex Stewart. The essays focus primarily on stories rather than styles. No index.

1088. Stowe, David. *Swing Changes: Big-Band Jazz in New Deal America.* Cambridge, Mass.: Harvard University Press; 1994.

Proposes the notion that the 1930s and the 1940s was a swing-shaped culture. He believes swing was a broad-based, unified but heterogeneous social practice, which encompassed a variety of ideologies and touched the lives of people representing different classes, ethnicities, and races. He discusses the life of the times, incorporation, conscription, discontents, and the modern dilemma. Also included is a discussion of "Are Colored

Bands Doomed" (pp. 121–130), and "Gender in the Gender Front" (pp. 167–180). Well-researched, referenced, and scholarly.

1089. Tracy, Sheila. *Bands, Booze and Broads.* Edinburgh: Trafalgar Square Publishing; 1995.

In addition to the 24 pages of photographs, the book contains interviews of 60 musicians who played with bandleaders like Tommy Dorsey, Benny Goodman, Harry James, Glenn Miller, and more. The sidemen discuss the roles and functions within the respective bands, careers, successes and failures.

1090. Treadwell, Bill. *Big Book of Swing.* New York: Cambridge House; 1946.

Covers swing and nonswing artists. There are chapters on Louis Armstrong, Count Basie, Les Brown, Charlie Barnet, Tex Benecke, the Dorsey brothers, Benny Goodman, Gene Krupa, Woody Herman, Stan Kenton, Harry James, and Glenn Miller. The swing-related artists detail their roles, successes, and influences in that style. Selected bibliography and an index.

1091. Vale, V., and Marian Wallace (editors). *Swing! The New Retro Renaissance.* New York: Search Publications; 1998.

The essays are concerned primarily with the rebirth of swing and the meaning of this rebirth within modern America. They discuss events and artists, and reasons why the rebirth is taking place.

1092. Walker, Leo. *The Big Band Almanac.* Pasadena, Calif.: Ward Ritchie Press; 1978.

Primarily a biographical dictionary of bandleaders of the swing era. Contains numerous listings with information on sidemen and vocalists, theme songs, radio shows, and sponsors. Includes information on stars like Basie, Goodman, and Ellington, as well as lesser-known leaders. Name index.

1093. Woods, Bernie. *When the Music Stopped: The Big Band Era Remembered.* New York: Barricade Books; 1994.

Written by a former music editor of *Variety* magazine, the author chronicles the lives and loves of the men and women who controlled the music industry at the time. The book is not documented, and is permeated with the author's assessments, insights, and conclusions regarding selected musicians, critics, press agents, disk jockeys, and others.

1094. Yanow, Scott. *Swing.* San Francisco: Freeman Books; 2000.

Reviews and rates 1,500 recordings from the classic 1930s through the retro-swing movement. He also profiles over 500 bandleaders, players, vocalist, sidemen, and composers. He begins with concise essays on swing, and thereafter divides the musicians by instrument and voice. Includes a list of recommended swing books.

World War II: Bebop and After

1095. Aboucaya, Jacques, and Jean-Pierre Peyrebelle. *Du Be-Bop au Free Jazz; Formes et Techniques d'Improvisation Chez Charles Parker, Miles Davis, and Ornette Coleman.* Paris: Toulouse; 2001.

In French. Discusses the forms and techniques of improvisation used by several artists in the bebop and free styles. The book is permeated with musical examples, and insightful discussion of the methods used in bebop and free jazz.

1096. Appel, Alfred. *Jazz Modernism; From Ellington to Matisse and Joyce.* New York: Knopf; 2002.

His purpose is to establish the place of classic jazz (1920–50), especially Louis Armstrong, Duke Ellington, Fats Waller, Billie Holiday, Jack Teagarden, and Charles Parker, in the great modernist tradition of the arts. He considers Armstrong, Ellington, and Waller to be equal to Joyce, Picasso, and Matisse. He is very insightful and idiosyncratic on issues of race.

1097. Bergerot, Frank, and Arnaud Merlin. *The Story of Jazz: Bop and Beyond.* New York: Harry N. Abrams, Inc.; 1993.

Anecdotal and historical coverage of styles and selected individuals associated with the evolution from bop to free jazz. Among the numerous contributors cited are Miles Davis, John Coltrane, Charles Mingus, and Ornette Coleman. The "Documents Section" includes quotes, remembrances, and anecdotes regarding the music and contributions of several significant artists. Concise but informative. Selected discography, further reading, index, illustrations, and photographs.

1098. Brinkmann, Reinhold (editor). *Die Neue Musik und die Tradition: Seiben Kongressbeiträge und eine analytische Studie.* Mainz: Schott; (Veröffentlichungen des Instituts für Neue Music und Musikeerziehung, Darmstadt, Band 19).

In German. Essays that deal with continuity and change in music. Topics are not limited solely to jazz and cover concepts like processes and tradition in free jazz and pop (Ekkehard Jost).

1099. Budd, Michael J. *Jazz in the Sixties: The Expansion of Musical Resources and Techniques.* Iowa City: University of Iowa Press; 1978, expanded edition, 1990.

One of the limited number of texts that focuses on jazz in the 1960s. After a concise "Survey of Jazz Styles Before 1960," the author focuses on "Color and Instrumentation," "Texture and Volume," "Melody and Harmony," "Meter and Rhythm," "Structural Design," and "Other Influences" (bossa nova and rock). Each topic is treated concisely, and is occasionally illustrated with musical examples and harmonic progressions. The new edition covers "Extra-Musical Connotations: New Purpose" and a retrospective on the significance of the developments in jazz during the 1960s. Selected discography, bibliography, organized topic areas, and an index.

1100. Carl Gregor, Herzog Zu Mecklenburg, and Waldemar Scheck. *Die Theorie des Blues im Modernen Jazz.* Strasbourg: Heitz; 1963.

In German. An analysis of the musical elements of the blues and their use in instrumental jazz. Among the elements addressed are blue notes, blues tonality, form, ornamentation, and rhythm. There are numerous musical examples and several transcriptions and analyses of selected solos in the appendix

1101. Carles, Phillippe, and Jean-Louis Comolli. *Free Jazz/Black Power.* Paris: Editions du Champ Libre, 1971; Paris: Union Générale d'Editions, 1972; aus dem Französichen von Federica und Hansjorg Pauli. Frankfurt: Fisher, 1974; and Hofheim: Raymund Dillmann, 1980.

In French. Focuses on the development of free jazz. A significant study that espouses the view that African American music is best understood as an outgrowth of social, political, and economic conditions affecting that community. The book is divided into three sections; the first section focuses on economic and cultural colonization of the music by the white power structure, including jazz critics; the second section is entitled "Contributions to a History of Black Jazz," which focuses on economic, political, and social issues that have shaped African American musics (blues, work songs, spirituals, and different jazz genres), and the final section refocuses on free jazz and demonstrates how its diverse features are a reflection of societal contradictions and political views. The 1974 edition contains biographical portraits. Bibliography and references.

1102. Coryell, Julie, and Laura Friedman. *Jazz-Rock Fusion: The People, the Music;* preface by Ramsey Lewis. London: Marion Bayars; New York: Dell; 1978.

The book contains 58 interviews of musicians who play "jazz-inspired improvisatory music." In the author's view, these musicians "had a hand in shaping the course of music from the late sixties to the late seventies" (p. i). The musicians are organized by instruments (bass, brass, etc.), groups, or as composers. In addition to concise biographical details, a photograph of each interviewee is included. The weaknesses of the book are the cursory approach, the lack of musical analysis, and the failure to connect the emergence of fusion jazz with sociocultural issues. Extensive discography contains significant albums as well as albums on which the musicians appeared as sidemen.

1103. Davis, Francis. *Bebop and Nothingness: Jazz and Pop at the End of the Century.* New York: Schirmer Books; 1996.

This is the author's third collection of essays on jazz and tangential musics. The unifying theme is the author's growing disenchantment with contemporary jazz. He believes youth is the new product in jazz, revival, and the museum like approaches to performing the music. In addition, he believes as jazz becomes more predictable, more people are finding qualities they admire in both popular and world musics. The collection includes profiles of musicians and critical essays; however, most are hybrids of people as issues. Informative and provocative.

1104. _____. *Outcats: Jazz Composers, Instrumentalists, and Singers.* New York: Oxford University Press; 1990.

Written by the jazz critic for the *Philadelphia Inquirer,* this book focuses on jazz composers and instrumentalists such as Butch Morris, Ella Fitzgerald, Bobby Short, and Edward Wilkerson. The thesis of the book is the alienation of "Outcats" from mainstream American culture. One of the strengths of the book is the introduction of emerging jazz artists such as Butch Morris and Edward Wilkerson.

1105. DeVeaux, Scott. *The Birth of Bebop: A Social and Musical History.* Berkeley: University of California Press; 1997.

Combines history, social context, and musical analysis to present an account of the origins of this revolutionary jazz style. He addresses the impact of bebop on the commercial, political, and aesthetic realms of American culture. In addition, he reveals it as an artistic and cultural movement situated within the social and cultural politics of the time. He presents first-persons accounts of Dizzy Gillespie and Billy Eckstine, and in-depth analyses of several compositions.

1106. Donati, William. *Jazz Americanco del dopoquerra.* Milano: Schwarz; 1958.

In Italian. Covers artists and their styles complete with musical examples. The portraits include Dave Brubeck, Miles Davis, Errol Garner, Dizzy Gillespie, Stan Kenton, Modern Jazz Quartet, Charles Parker, Lennie Tristano, and Sarah Vaughan. No new insights. Selected bibliography, discography, index, and illustrations.

1107. Dulker, Hans. *Jazz in China: En Andere Perikels uit de geïmproviseerde Muziek.* Amsterdam: Bakker; 1980.

In Dutch. Has nothing to do with jazz in China. Profiles the styles of Albert Ayler, Don Byas, Arnett Cobb, Booker Ervin, Paul Gonsalves, Benny Goodman, Illinois Jacquet, J. R. Monterose, Big Nick Nichols, Archie Shepp, Toon Van Uliet, and Ben Webster. The essays were previously published in *Jazzwereld, Muziekkrant Oor,* and *Het Gewicht.* Good insights into their improvisational styles.

1108. _____. *In the Moment: Jazz in the 1980's.* New York: Oxford University Press; 1986.

Essays devoted to capturing the 1980s jazz evolution and how it relates to our vision of the times. Although he cites Miles Davis, Josef Zawinul, Wayne Shorter, and jazz fusion, his overall objective is to assess music in culture and how subsequent musical change alters a person's view of a particular period or time. Named an Outstanding Academic Book of 1988–89 by *Choice.* Selected bibliography and an index.

1109. Feather, Leonard. *Inside Be-bop.* New York: Robbins, 1949; retitled, *Inside Jazz;* with a new introduction. New York: Da Capo; 1977.

Written by a legendary jazz critic, this is one of the first attempts to analyze the musical elements of bebop. Describes Afro-Cuban influences, rhythm (tempos), unison ensemble passages, offbeat bass drum punctuations, and selected personalities. The first section, "When," focuses on Gillespie and Parker within the history of bebop. In the second section, "How," Feather provides an analysis and explanation of bebop musical elements; harmony, rhythm, articulation and phrasing, and form. Finally in "Who," he profiles numerous musicians, famous and not so famous. A selected list of compositions based on the contrafact and a biographical index that cites selected recordings of 92 artists are also included. The strength of the book is the explanation of the musical elements of bebop, whereas the weakness is the failure to connect the music to sociocultural contexts. No index.

1110. Fox, Charles. *The Jazz Scene.* Photography by Valerie Wilmer. New York: Hamlyn; 1972.

Details jazz and jazz-related music in the 1960s and 1970s. Covers composers and vocalists in blues, gospels, and jazz active during these periods. Also details the influence of rock, the status of big bands, and the impact of Miles Davis. Selected bibliography.

1111. Gitler, Ira. *Jazz Masters of the Forties.* London, Toronto, New York: Macmillan, 1966; New York: Collier Books, 1974; New York: Da Capo, 1983; New York: Da Capo, 1984.

Assessments of significant artists of the bebop era and selected artists of the postbop style. Critical biomusical portraits of Kenny Clarke, Dexter Gordon, Dizzy Gillespie, J. J. Johnson, Oscar Pettiford, Max Roach, Bud Powell, Tadd Dameron, Lee Konitz, and Lennie Tristano. Selected discographies after each chapter. Index.

1112. Goldberg, Joe. *Jazz Masters of the Fifties.* New York: Macmillan; London: Collier/Macmillan; 1965.

Outlines musical careers and styles, contributions of individuals to jazz, and influences on careers and styles. The profiled artists are Art Blakey, Ray Charles, Ornette Coleman, John Coltrane, Miles Davis, Paul Desmond, Thelonious Monk, Gerry Mulligan, Charles Mingus, the Modern Jazz Quartet, Sonny Rollins, and Cecil Taylor. Selected musician discographies and an index.

1113. Goldsher, Alan. *Hard Bop Academy: The Sidemen of Art Blakey and The Jazz Messengers.* Milwaukee: Hal Leonard Publications; 2002.

Contains a biographical assessment of Blakey's sidemen divided into categories. He discusses bassists, trumpeters, saxophonists, pianists, and the musical philosophy of Blakey. Among the numerous musicians discussed are Clifford Brown, Branford and Wynton Marsalis, Lee Morgan, Freddie Hubbard, Horace Silver, Donald Williams, Wayne Shorter, and many more.

1114. Haydon, Geoff. *Quintet of The Year.* London: U.P.; 2002.

An important book that describes the story behind the famous Jazz at Massey Hall concert in Toronto in 1953. He discusses Charles Parker, Dizzy Gillespie, Bud Powell, Charles Mingus, and Max Roach.

1115. Hellhund, Herbert. *Cool Jazz.* Mainz, Germany: Schott; 1985.

In German. Discusses the music and contributions of Lennie Tristano, Miles Davis's Capitol Band, Lee Konitz, Stan Getz, Modern Jazz Quartet, West Coast Jazz, Dave Brubeck, and Gerry Mulligan. The emphasis is on a scholarly analysis of styles and contributions. Numerous transcriptions. Lennie Tristano discography, glossary, and selected references.

1116. Hentoff, Nat. *The Jazz Life.* New York: Da Capo Press; 1978.

Explores the social, economic, and psychological elements that made the context of the then-modern jazz. He discusses Count Basie, Ornette Coleman, Miles Davis, John Lewis, Thelonious Monk, Charles Mingus, and more. He espouses that the rise of black consciousness and its search for roots and meaning in the American experience was one of several reasons why jazz made a comeback in the 1960s and 1970s.

1117. Horricks, Raymond. *These Jazzmen of Our Time*. London: Gollancz, 1959, 1962; London: Jazz Book Club, 1960; Toronto: Doubleday, 1959; Paris: Buchet-Chastel, 1960.

Biomusical portraits of 16 musicians active in jazz beginning with bebop and expanding to the late 1950s. The portraits contain both biographical and critical appraisals of styles, and in addition to Horricks, are contributed by Charles Fox, Benny Green, Max Harrison, Nat Hentoff, Ed Michel, Alun Morgan, and Martin Williams. The essays cover Miles Davis, Gil Evans, Art Blakey, Dave Brubeck, Gigi Gryce, J. J. Johnson, Thelonious Monk, Milt Jackson, John Lewis, Jimmy Giuffre, Gerry Mulligan, Quincy Jones, Bud Powell, and Sonny Rollins. Index. Photographs by Herman Leonard.

1118. Jones, Leroi. *Black Music*. New York: W. W. Morrow and Company; 1967.

Primarily a collection of previously published reviews, liner notes, interviews, articles, and comments, which appeared in journals such as *Down Beat, Negro Digest, The Jazz Review,* and *Metronome*. Only the final chapter, which focuses on the new jazz and jazzmen, was not published previously. The contents include essays on the growth of the jazz avant-garde and the New York loft-and-coffeehouse jazz scene, as well as interviews with Don Cherry, Wayne Shorter, and Cecil Taylor. In addition, Jones attributes the lack of understanding of avant-garde jazz to the fact that most of the critics were Anglo-American.

1119. Jost, Ekkehard. *Free Jazz*. Graz: Universal Edition; 1974.

An attempt to codify and analyze the music of several significant exponents of jazz of the 1960s and 1970s. Analysis of styles predominates and includes artists such as AACM, Don Cherry, Ornette Coleman, John Coltrane, Albert Ayler, Charles Mingus, Archie Shepp, Sun Ra, and Cecil Taylor. The essays on Coltrane's modal style and Coleman's musical approaches in melody, rhythm, and improvisation are especially noteworthy. The book is permeated with musical examples and includes a selected bibliography and discographies.

1120. Klopotek, Felix. *How They Do It: Free Jazz, Improvisation und Niemandsmusik*. Mainz: Ventil Verlag; 2002.

Describes the uses, functions, and procedures of free jazz, and creative improvisation. Also covers some of the approaches used by many of the most successful performers of this jazz.

1121. Kofsky, Frank. *Black Nationalism and the Revolution in Music*. New York: Pathfinder Press; 1970.

An outgrowth of the author's doctoral dissertation of 1973 at the University of Pittsburgh, entitled "Black Nationalism and the Revolution in Music: Social Change and Stylistic Development in the Art of John Coltrane and Others, 1954–1967." Correctly assesses the creative and social forces affecting African American jazz musicians as well as the sociological forces shaping the nationalistic movement in jazz. The author, one of the first white critics to treat this subject accurately, presents a controversial and penetrating commentary on Leroi Jones's *Blues People* as well as an illuminating critique of critics' attitudes toward African American musicians, particularly creative and innovative musicians. The second part of the book deals with the music of several outstanding artists as a reflection of black nationalism. The author gives special attention to the music of Coltrane, Coleman, and Cecil Taylor and also acknowledges the contributions of Albert Ayler, Elvin Jones, and McCoy Tyner. There is an analysis of Tyner and Coltrane as well as an attempt to relate the nationalistic jazz movement to the career of Malcolm X (addition of 1981). Index.

1122. Korall, Burt. *Drummin Men—The Heartbeat of Jazz: The Bebop Years.* New York: Oxford University Press; 2002.

A follow-up to his first book *Drummin Men—The Heartbeat of Jazz: The Swing Years.* He offers a history of the drumming of the bebop era as portrayed through the styles of Art Blakey, Kenny Clarke, and Max Roach. The book also contains Korall's own memoir of nearly 50 years in the jazz world, a career linked by the careers of the aforementioned drummers. Unlike many books on the topic, Korall attempts to penetrate the thinking as well as the drumming of the artists within the social context, and music of the period.

1123. Levey, Joseph. *The Jazz Experience: A Guide to Appreciation.* Englewood Cliffs, N.J.: Prentice Hall; 1983.

This book differs from other jazz appreciation or history texts because it does not cover jazz chronologically. Instead, it focuses on jazz of the early 1980s as it exists within American popular genres. He covers significant improvisers, African and European origins, and devotes the same amount of attention to Coleman Hawkins and Tom Scott, devotes more space to Don Ellis than to Louis Armstrong. He also believes the younger performers are better trained and more innovative. The latter views are questionable at best; several additional assertions are made. Index, selected discography.

1124. Litweiler, John. *The Freedom Principle: Jazz After 1958.* New York: W. W. Morrow; 1984.

Demonstrates "how modern jazz pioneers such as Ornette Coleman and John Coltrane stretched the traditional harmonic, melodic, and rhythmic structures of the 1950's and inspired contemporary artists such as Anthony Braxton and Roscoe Mitchell." Some of his descriptions of performances are impressionistic, and his comments about artists graphic, for example, dismissing Woody Herman as a "mediocre eclectic," and describing Anthony Braxton's music as "distorted, nonconsecutive tones," and inclusive of "growls and squalls." Excellent discography.

1125. Locke, Graham. *Chasing The Vibration: Meetings With Creative Musicians.* London: Exter; 1994.

In addition to eight pages of photographs, the book is permeated with interviews of many modern jazz artists. They discuss the beginnings in jazz, influences, and musical philosophy. Among the interviewees are Betty Carter, Dave Holland, Steve Lacy, Sun Ra, Horace Tapscott, Cecil Taylor, Evan Parker, Max Roach, and several more.

1126. Malson, Lucien. *Histoire du Jazz et de la musique Afro-Américaine.* Paris: Union Générale, 1976; revision of *Histoire du Jazz moderne.* Paris: Table Ronde, 1961; Lausanne, Switzerland: Recontre, 1967.

In French. Portraits of Clifford Brown, Miles Davis, Dizzy Gillespie, John Lewis, Gerry Mulligan, Thelonious Monk, and Charles Parker. The selected discography includes a separate listing of recordings made in France. Also included are birth dates and places, artist's instrumentation, a filmography, and a selected discography.

1127. Mandel, Howard. *Future Jazz.* New York: Oxford University Press; 1999.

Espouses that we should not reject change or attempt to hold onto the past as the only true jazz. Instead, we should try to understand today's jazz with today's insights and within its social and cultural context. He discusses persons and topics such as Wynton Marsalis, avant-garde, and new thinkers and performers like Gerri Allen, Anthony Davis, and several more.

1128. Mathieson, Kenny. *Giant Steps: Bebop and the Creators of Modern Jazz, 1945–65.* Edinburgh: Payback Press; 1999.

Examine he development of modern jazz through the music of 11 artists from bebop to free jazz. The contributions are examined in some detail, however with no musical analysis. He examines the contributions of John Coltrane, Miles Davis, Dizzy Gillespie, Charles Mingus, Thelonious Monk, Herbie Nichols, Fats Navarro, Charles Parker, Bud Powell, Max Roach, and Sonny Rollins. No criteria for inclusion were given.

1129. _____. *Cookin'; Hard Bop and Soul Jazz, 1954–1965.* Edinburgh: Canongate; 2002.

Cover artists and philosophies of performing hard bop and soul jazz. Included is an assessment of the styles of artists such as Clifford Brown, Harold Land, Lee Morgan Sonny Rollins, The Crusaders, Stanley Turrentine, and many more. He discusses jazz 1951–1960 and 1961–1970.

1130. McRae, Barry. *The Jazz Cataclysm.* London: Dent; South Brunswick, New Jersey: A. S. Barnes; 1967.

Attempts to analyze and survey developments in jazz styles from the so-called cool era to free jazz of the late 1960s. He focuses on the musical contributions and styles of several significant exponents, especially Ornette Coleman, John Coltrane, and Sonny Rollins. While the author is a proponent of most modern jazz styles, he disdains cool jazz because, in his opinion, it lacks vitality. Selected discography and an index.

1131. Meadows, Eddie S. *Bebop to Cool: Context, Ideology, and Musical Identity.* Westport, Conn.: Praeger Publishers; 2003.

The author explains that bebop was more than a style that burst suddenly on the jazz scene. He traces the evolution of the style to 1920s Harlem until its maturation in the 1940s. The book includes the perspectives of Marcus Garvey, W.E.B. Du Bois, other leaders of the Harlem renaissance, and for the first time the role that Islam played in the formation of bebop identities. In addition, he includes analytical musical studies of bebop artists such as Dizzy Gillespie, Thelonious Monk, and Charles Parker, and cool artists like Stan Getz, Lee Konitz, and Lennie Tristano. The role of Miles Davis in both bebop and cool is also discussed.

1132. Metzger, Günther. *Darmstädter JazzForum 89.* Darmstadt: Jazz-Institut, 1989; Wolke, Verlag, Hofheim, 1990.

In German. A collection of essays that deal with topical issues such as improvisation in free jazz, bebop and free jazz, jazz pedagogy, the swing phenomenon, harmolodics, and artists such as Bix Beiderbecke, Cecil Taylor, and Ornette Coleman. The articles on swing as a phenomenon and the theory, aesthetics, and syntax of harmolodics are noteworthy. Profiles of the contributors.

1133. Morgan, Alun, and Raymond Horricks. *Modern Jazz: A Survey of Developments Since 1939;* foreword by Don Randell. London: Gollancz, 1956; reprint, Westport, Conn.: Greenwood Press, 1977.

The strength of the book is its perceptive insight into the origins of bebop and the role that Christian, Gillespie, Parker, and lesser-known contributors such as Clyde Hart and Jimmy Blanton played in its development. Also included are three essays on post-1939 big bands: Stan Kenton and Charlie Barnet, Duke Ellington, and Count Basie. Although musical analysis and social contexts are minimized, the author's discussion of the 1948–49 Miles Davis group centers on specific compositions. Selected discography and index.

1134. Nicholson, Stuart. *Jazz: The 1980s Resurgence.* New York: Da Capo Press; 1995.

Addresses new players, new recordings, reissues, and recycled players of the 1980s. Surveys major developments, including the neoclassicists, bop and postbop, free jazz, big bands, fusion, vocal jazz, and related movements. Permeated with photographs, offers penetrating insights into artists and developments.

1135. Nisenson, Eric. *Blue: The Murder of Jazz.* New York: St. Martin's Press; 1997.

Draws on his book *Ascension: John Coltrane and His Quest,* where he discussed among other things what happen to jazz after the death of Coltrane in 1967. He has misgivings about post–Coltrane jazz, and grave feelings about the present course of contemporary jazz. The author does not advocate that jazz is dead; rather, he attempts to reconcile the views of those who believe it is, and others who see the newer styles as creative and provocative.

1136. Nogawa, Kobun. *Jazz Gendaijin no Ongaku.* Tokyo: Hakubi; 1949.

In Japanese. A follow-up to *Jazz Kara Swing,* which covers the history and evolution of jazz from swing to the late 1940s. The book is written for the novice rather than the scholar. Covers contributions by selected artists.

1137. Noglik, Bert. *Klangspuren: Wege Improvisierter Musik.* Frankfurt: Kiel; 1992.

Illustrations of Jeanne Lee, Harry Miller, and others, and a discussion of the philosophy and procedures used in improvised music. Includes lots of names, techniques of improvisation, and accomplishments of performers.

1138. Oliphant, Dave (editor). *The Bebop Revolution in Words and Music.* Austin: University of Texas Press; 1994.

A collection of papers from the 1992 Bebop Symposium. The papers dealt with the social environment, music, artists, and the impact of bebop on modern jazz.

1139. O'Meally, Robert G., Brent Hayes Edwards, and Farah Jasmine Griffin. *Uptown Conversation: The New Jazz Studies.* New York: Columbia University Press; 2003.

Covers a variety of topics, including how jazz outside the United States has transformed American jazz, new insights into the jazz avant-garde, and new assessments of canonical figures such as Louis Armstrong, Miles Davis, Duke Ellington, and Thelonious Monk.

1140. Owens, Thomas. *Bebop: The Music and the Players.* New York: Oxford University Press; 1995.

Scholarly study of bebop and the musicians of bebop from its origins in the 1940s to the present. Permeated with cultural context and analysis, including the music and contributions of artists such as Dizzy Gillespie, Thelonious Monk, Charles Parker, and others. Contains numerous musical examples. The most in-depth and scholarly assessment of the context, music, and its practitioners to date.

1141. Rosenthal, David H. *Hard Bop: Jazz and Black Music 1955–1965.* New York: Oxford University Press; 1992.

The title is misleading because the book focuses on the 10-year period commonly referred to as hard bop. No other African American genre is examined in any detail. Yet, he does examine the musical developments of this period and also relates these developments to sociocultural contexts. This is the first book-length manuscript on hard bop. Selected bibliography and discography.

1142. Rusch, Robert D. *Jazz Talk: The Cadence Interviews.* Secaucus, N.J.: Lyle Stuart Inc.; 1985.

Provides insider perspectives from Freddie Hubbard, Paul Quinichette, Milt Jackson, Cecil Taylor, Sun Ra, Milt Hinton, Von Freeman, Billy Harper, Art Blakey, and Bill Dixon. They cover topics ranging from business and music to travel and racism.

1143. Such, David G. *Avant-Garde Musicians: Performing out There.* Iowa: University of Iowa; 1993.

Focuses on musicians, approaches to performance, and on selected socio-historical and personal assessments related to the music. He probes the worldviews of the "second generation" musicians like Jemool Moondoc and Billy Bang. He also presents the worldviews of William Parker, Dewey Johnson, and Daniel Carter, all of New York, the venue of his research. The book is based on the author's doctoral dissertation in Folklore at UCLA.

1144. Tomens, Robin. *Points of Departure; Essays on Modern Jazz.* London: Exeter; 2001.

Discusses the artistry and musical contributions of selected path breakers such as John Coltrane, Thelonious Monk, Charles Parker, Cecil Taylor, and more. The artists are profiled as persons who challenged the status quo in jazz.

1145. Werther, Iron. *Die Geschichte einer Musikalischen Revolution und ihrer Interpreten.* Frankfurt: Fisher Taschenbuch Verlag; 1988.

In German. Provides insights into Harlem, Minton's Playhouse, 52nd Street, Revival, and the music as evolution. In addition, he provides musical analysis of the elements, and gives his perspective on the roles and contributions of artists such as Charlie Christian, Kenny Clarke, Dizzy Gillespie, Charles Mingus, Thelonious Monk, Charles Parker, Oscar Pettiford, Bud Powell, and Max Roach. The author also quotes David Baker's bebop scale and compares/illustrates many of the scales used by beboppers.

1146. Williams, Martin. *Jazz in Its Time.* New York: Oxford University Press; 1989.

In this collection, Williams combines many of his past essays with new pieces to produce an insightful overview of trends and developments in jazz since around 1969. Arranged by topics, for example, music reviews, he examines the contributions of several giants of jazz including Sidney Bechet, Lee Konitz, Art Farmer, Ornette Coleman, Lionel Hampton, George Winston, Teddy Wilson, and many more. He also examines the current state of jazz, developments and directions, and jazz scholarship. Selected bibliography and an index.

1147. _____. *Jazz Masters in Transition, 1957–69.* New York: Macmillan; London: Collier-Macmillan; 1970.

Highlights the transformation of jazz, late 1950s to late 1960s, by focusing on the contributions of old, new, and revived artists. The 87 essays are arranged into portraits, interviews, reviews, recording dates, television appearances, details of rehearsals, and nightclub dates. The author wrote the essays; some are superficial and reflect information gathered from secondary sources.

1148. Wilmer, Valerie. *As Serious as Your Life: The Story of the New Jazz.* London: Allison and Busby; London and New York: Quartet; 1977.

An illuminating account of insider's attitudes of the role and function of jazz in American culture. The book is permeated with the sociopolitical views and music of selected contemporary musicians. An underlying objective of the musicians' views is that they can now voice concerns that previous jazz musicians either could not, or did not, voice. The book is organized as follows: part one contains biographical portraits of selected giants of the 1960s—Ayler, Coltrane, Coleman, Sun Ra, and Cecil Taylor (the portraits are compiled through the views of their contemporaries);

part two contains biographical portraits of selected giants of the 1970s—Earl Cross, Leroy Jenkins, Art Lewis, and Frank Lowe; part three focuses on the importance of selected contemporary jazz drummers—Ed Blackwell, Milford Graves, Elvin Jones, and Sunny Murray. There are also interesting sections on women's roles and obstacles in jazz. The final part details perceived obstacles and conspiracies these musicians face and their need to create their own outlets to combat this type of discrimination. Concise biographies of over 150 musicians, a selected bibliography of books, a list of journals, and a name index are included.

1149. Wilson, John S. *Jazz: The Transition Years, 1940–1960.* New York: Appleton-Century-Crofts; 1966.

Surveys and analyzes jazz styles from 1940 to 1960. The author divides the jazz styles into five separate categories: bop, that is, the contributions of Roy Eldridge, Charles Parker, and Dizzy Gillespie; cool, that is, the music of Miles Davis, Stan Getz, and Gerry Mulligan; return to the roots, that is, the music of Horace Silver and Ray Charles; intellectualization, that is, Stan Kenton, Dave Brubeck, and the Modern Jazz Quartet; and reacceptance, that is, musicians who revived traditional jazz. The essays contain good information on contrasting movements, transformations, and changing attitudes (addition to 1981).

1150. Wilson, Peter Niklas. *Hear and Now; Gedanken zur Improvisierten Musik.* Frankfurt: Hofheim; 1999.

A collection of essays and interviews of artists such as Derek Bailey, Paul Bley, J&M Maneri, P. Oxley, D. Mengelberg, Bob Ostertag, Evan Parker, and many more. The artists discuss the musical beginnings, philosophies, and influences.

1151. Yanow, Scott. *Bebop.* San Francisco: Miller Freeman Books; 2000.

The author seeks to answer several questions including what is bebop, where did it come from, how it evolved, and where is it today? Also concentrates on some of its main contributors, and suggests the best CDs to buy. Concise primarily of short biographies of numerous artists organized by instrument. Includes some questionable artists like Billy Bauer (guitar), Erroll Garner (piano), and Toots Thieleman (harmonica), to name a few. His definition of bebop (pp. 3–4) is both limited and questionable. Good biographical profiles with references and a selected discography at the end of each entry.

1152. Yui, Shoichi (editor). *Modern Jazz Nyumon.* Arechi, Japan: Shippan; 1961.

In Japanese. Discusses people and styles associated with jazz since bebop. The book is current to the late 1950s and is geared toward the novice.

Regional Studies

California

1153. Cox, Bette Yarbrough. *Central Avenue: Its Rise and Fall,* 1890–c1955. Los Angeles: Beem Publications; 1996.

The book is permeated with important historical information and oral histories. She discusses Central Avenue from the early pioneers, early jazz explosion, formation of the Musician's Union #767, the black and white union amalgamation, and its eventual demise. She provides concrete racial and social reasons for Central Avenue's fame and subsequent demise. In addition to the many nonjazz oral histories, she interviewed jazz artists such as Teddy Buckner, Buddy Collette, Ginger Smock Shipp, Marl Young, and Marshall Royal.

1154. DjeDje, Jacqueline, and Eddie S. Meadows (editors). *California Soul: Music of African Americans in the West.* Berkeley: University of California Press; 1998.

The first book to discuss collectively the rich musical heritage and creativity of African Americans in California. Focusing on blues, jazz, gospel, rhythm and blues, and soul music, this collection describes the history, people, and places involved in shaping these genres. Relying on oral histories, musical recordings and newspapers articles and advertisements of the day, the essays offer original research on the importance of Central Avenue in the history of Los Angeles jazz, the first in-depth essay on jazz in San Diego, a comprehensive essay on the evolution of gospel music in California, and important insights into the development of West Coast blues. To date, the book contains the most extensive compilation of source materials on African American music and culture in California.

1155. Gioia, Ted. *West Coast Jazz: Modern Jazz in California, 1945–1960.* New York: Oxford University Press; 1992.

Provides the only account of California jazz from World War II to 1960. He traces this evolution from Central Avenue (Los Angeles), Club Alabam, The Downbeat, and other venues. He discusses the pivotal moments in the beginnings of California jazz, provides portraits of significant artists, and champions the importance of California, especially Los Angeles, in the development of jazz.

1156. Gordon, Robert. *Jazz West Coast: The Los Angeles Jazz Scene of the 1950's.* New York, London: Quartet; 1986.

Details of jazz musicians on the West Coast (Dizzy Gillespie, Charlie Parker, The Gerry Mulligan Quartet, and a career overview of Shorty Rogers). Art Pepper is the only native Californian represented. Index.

1157. Hoskyns, Barney. *Waiting for the Sun: Strange Days, Weird Scenes and the Sound of Los Angeles.* New York: St. Martin's Press; 1996.

Although most of the book deals with rock 'n' roll, the author does include information on jazz activities on Central Avenue, and the cool jazz movement. Also, offers insights into R&B artists, artists in other genres, clubs, and other performance venues.

1158. Isoardi, Steven, Clora Bryant, Buddy Collette, William Green, Jack Kelson, Horace Tapscott, Gerald Wilson, and Marl Young. *Central Avenue Sounds: Jazz in Los Angeles.* Berkeley: University of California Press; 1998.

Reveals and recounts the flourishing jazz life on Central Avenue in Los Angeles, the integration of the black and white music unions and the Hollywood studios, important clubs, and contains the reminiscences of several important musicians of the 1940s to 1970s. The book brings to life a Los Angeles of yesteryear, a city with an increasing black population, gambling, explosive creativity, and a city separated by race. Offers important and factual insights by the people who made the music.

1159. _____. *Central Avenue Sounds.* Los Angeles: UCLA Oral History Program; 1990s.

Contains transcripts of numerous interviews done as part of the *Central Avenue Sounds* project. The artists reveal memories of Central Avenue at its peak, and provide details on the nightlife, clubs, and persons who performed on this famous street. All of the interviewees are either natives of Los Angeles or spent major portions of their careers in the city. The UCLA Oral History program does not sell the transcripts, however they are available for scholars to use in person at the Oral History Program. There are interviews of Ernie Andrews, Gil Bernal, Joseph Bihari, Rene Bloch, Hadda Brooks, Clora Bryant, David Bryant, Buddy Collette, William Douglas, John Ewing, Art Farmer, William Ernest Green, Leroy Hurte, Jackie Kelso, Ruben Leon, Melba Liston, Larance Marable, Cecil McNelly, Frank Morgan, Anthony Ortega, Minor Robinson, Marshall Royal, Fletcher Smith, Clifford Solomon, Anthony Sweeting, Horace Tapscott, Gerald Wiggins, Gerald Wilson, Britt Woodman, Coney Woodman, William Woodman, Lee Young, and Marl Young.

1160. Levin, Floyd. *Classic Jazz: A Personal View of the Music and the Musicians.* Berkeley: University of California Press; 2000.

Drawing on 50 years of devotion, friendship, and acquaintances in jazz, the author covers the life and contributions of numerous musicians. He weaves anecdotal material, primary research, personal observations, and interpretation to present a history of jazz in New Orleans and in Los Angeles. Contains important information on the migration of New Orleans musicians to Los Angeles, and new information on the musical activities of Jelly Roll Morton and Kid Ory in Los Angeles. Also contains a wealth of information on the jazz revival, and the influence of New Orleans musicians on Los Angeles jazz.

1161. Tercinet, Alain. *West Coast Jazz*. Marseille: Parenthèses; 1986.

In French. Covers the evolution, events, history, and artists concerned with West Coast jazz from the late 1940s to the early 1960s. Cites West Coast musicians such as Dave Brubeck, the impact of the cool school, and makes frequent references to recordings. Selected discography and filmography.

1162. Wilson, Burt. *A History of Sacramento Jazz, 1948–1966: A Personal Memoir.* Canoga Park, California: the author; 1986.

Permeated with personal experiences, recollections, anecdotes, and historical data. He recalls venues, artists and their music, acceptance, and the overall role and function of jazz in Sacramento during this period. The only history to date on Sacramento jazz.

Chicago

1163. Collier, James Lincoln. *The Jazz Kid.* New York: Holt and Company; 1994.

Touches on the origins of jazz, public response to 1920s jazz, relationships of black and white musicians, and the role and function of organized crime in jazz clubs. The focus is the 1920s jazz world of Chicago, and he discusses individuals/groups such as Bix Beiderbecke, King Oliver, and the New Orleans Rhythm Kings.

1164. Demlinger, Sandor, and John Steiner. *Destination: Chicago Jazz.* Stroud, Gloucestershire, U.K.: Tempus; 2003.

A collection of nearly 300 photographs covering the rich history of Chicago jazz. There are photographs of visitors to Chicago, and musicians, clubs, and other venues native to Chicago.

1165. Kenney, William Howland. *Chicago Jazz: A Cultural History, 1904–1930.* New York: Oxford University Press; 1993.

Details Chicago jazz in its early years with special focus on the 1920s. He discusses several Chicago musicians/groups including Bix Beiderbecke and The Austin High Gang and demonstrates how the music was molded by historical trends. The book is equally important as a musical and cultural history of Chicago, especially the 1920s.

1166. Ramsey, Frederic. *Chicago Documentary: Portrait of a Jazz Era.* London: Jazz Music Books; 1944.

Treats the history of jazz in Chicago in the 1920s. The book lacks detail and overlooks several key Chicago jazz musicians. Focuses on Bix Beiderbecke and Chicago musicians such as Jack Teagarden but does not cover the exploits of musicians such as Kid Punch Miller.

1167. Sengstock, Charles A. *Jazz Music in Chicago's Early Southside Theatres.* Northbrook, Illinois: Canterbury Press; 2000.

A concise collection of previously published articles that cite the names and venues that featured jazz in early Chicago. The discussion includes some African American venues as well as those that were segregated.

1168. Travis, Dempsey J. *An Autobiography of Black Jazz;* introduction by Studs Terkel. Chicago: Urban Research Institute; 1983.

A thorough discussion of African American jazz life in Chicago from 1920 to 1940. Travis provides anecdotes and recollections about numerous artists and bands and their relationship with club owners and promoters in a myriad of performance venues. He also provides information on the difficulties that African American artists encountered on the T.O.B.A. circuit. Covers many aspects that previous scholars have ignored. Selected bibliography, an index, and nearly 500 photographs.

1169. Wolf, Robert. *Story Jazz: A History of Chicago Jazz Styles.* Lansing, Iowa: Free River Press; 1995.

An illustrated history of jazz in Chicago, and performers who resided in the city. Covers artists such as The Austin High Gang, Bix Beiderbecke, Art Hodes, Muggsy Spanier, and many more.

Columbus, Ohio

1170. *Listen for the Jazz.* Columbus, Ohio: Arts Foundation of Olde Towne; 1990.

Details the history of jazz in Columbus, Ohio. There are details on artists, venues, groups, and the changes that transpired over the decades. Information on styles and personnel are also provided. Includes a contribution by Ted McDaniel, Director of Jazz Studies, Ohio State University. Selected bibliography and an index.

Detroit, Michigan

1171. Boyd, Herb, and Leni Sinclair. *Detroit Jazz Who's Who.* Preface by Ken Cox. Detroit: Jazz Research; 1984.

Biomusical portraits and several concise essays covering birth/death dates (where warranted), career highlights, occasional references to significant recordings, and more. Several photographs by Leni Sinclair. Among the inclusions are Kenny Burrell, Donald Byrd, Sheila Jordan, Eddie Locke, J. R. Monterose, and Marcus Belgrave.

Indiana

1172. Scheidt, Duncan. *The Jazz State of Indiana.* Pittsboro, Indiana: The author and Indiana Historical Society 1977.

A significant addition to jazz literature because the importance of Indiana in the evolution and development of jazz is detailed. The impetus for this book stems from the author's belief that Indiana has been overlooked, whereas geographical areas/centers such as New Orleans, Chicago, Kansas City, and New York have been thoroughly discussed. Scheidt asserts that Indiana developed its own style by interpreting music composed elsewhere. He focuses on the 1910s and 1920s with information on the role and function of various ethnic groups in shaping an Indiana style. Also included are concise biographical sketches on Indiana musicians such as Hoagy Carmichael, Red Nichols, Jim Riley, Emil Seidel, and Speed Webb, bands lead by Charlie Davis, the Royal Peacocks, and African American musicians/bands such as Leroy Carr, Slide Hampton, and The Paris Family Band. Index.

Kansas City

1173. Hester, Mary Lee. *Going to Kansas City.* Foreword by Stanley Dance. Sherman, Texas: Early Bird Press; 1980.

Based on insider recollections of the music, musicians, and life in the heyday of Kansas City. The informants extol the musical contribution of each other as well as the importance of Kansas City as an innovative oasis of jazz. Among the interviewees are Count Basie, Buck Clayton, Eddie Durham, Jo Jones, Budd Johnson, Jay McShann, Gene Ramey, Buster Smith, Stuff Smith, and Joe Turner. The interviews are not organized by themes, hence, other than self-adulation and the importance of Kansas City as a mecca of jazz activity. The interviews are wide-ranging and mostly anecdotal. No index.

1174. Person, Jr., Nathan W. *Goin' to Kansas City.* Urbana and Chicago: University of Illinois Press; 1987.

Details the story of the great bands of the Kansas City era: the Blue Devils, Benny Moten, Andy Kirk, The Kansas City Rockets, Count Basie, and Jay McShann. In addition, first-hand accounts of Buck Clayton, Buster Smith, and Mary Lou Williams are presented. The authors use an ethnomusicological approach, including interviews, to craft an intimate view of the life and lore of the times, music, and musicians. The 18 chapters are organized as follows: chapters 1 and 2 focus on the broad cultural, musical, and theatrical roots of the music (ragtime and New Orleans jazz); chapters 3–6 treat the proliferation of jazz in the mid- and southwest (territories), during the 1920s; chapter 7 begins the Kansas City accounts with the political and economic environment dominated by Tom Pendergast's administration; chapters 8 and 9 focus on the open and corrupt Kansas City night life of the 1920s and 1930s; in chapter 10 the Kansas City lifestyle is described followed by histories of orchestras led by Benny Moten, Count Basie, George E. Lee, the Kansas City Rockets, and Jay McShann; chapter 16 covers the demise of Kansas City's open entertainment era; chapter 17 treats some of the most important musicians who transferred this tradition into modern jazz (Charles Parker, Buster Smith, Lester Young); and chapter 18 details attempts to preserve the Kansas City tradition. Although the book is well-researched, there are some problems, including a failure to clearly document how ragtime and New Orleans influences were transformed and adapted into Kansas City style, inadequate coverage of blues (p. 4–5), and the author's assertion, without proof, "that New Orleans can be reliably recognized as the birthplace of jazz" (p. 25). There are no musical examples. The appendix contains a chronology of jazz-related events, concise biographies, a selected discography, and bibliography. Index.

1175. Russell, Ross. *Jazz Style in Kansas City and the Southwest.* Berkeley and Los Angeles: University of California Press; 1971.

Recognizes the importance of Kansas City in the development of jazz. In addition to sociological information (e.g., on the Pendergast's Machine and on the musical preferences of the black population), the author discusses individual artists and bands such as Buster Smith, Benny Moten, Count Basie, Andy Kirk, Harlan Leonard, Jay McShann, and Charles Parker. He also treats territorial bands (Jack Teagarden and the Texas School). The approach in this well-illustrated and well-researched study, which was one of the first to examine the Kansas City influence in jazz, is descriptive rather than analytical. A selected discography and bibliography are included (1981).

Newark, New Jersey

1176. Kukla, Barbara J. *Swing City: Newark Nightlife 1925–1950.* Philadelphia: Temple University Press; 1991.

A broad social history of nightlife in Newark, New Jersey, 1925–50. Focuses on black life of the vaudeville and swing eras, and the tool African Americans devised and used to survive economically and socially in a segregated city. Equal emphasis is given to the entertainment and vicissitudes of life in an urban city. The coverage includes Foundations 1925–35,

The Performers 1935–45, The Bands 1935–42, and The Clubs 1935–44. In addition, they cover the Coleman Hotel, and Herman Lubinsky and Savoy Records. Important and informative.

New Orleans/Louisiana

1177. Berry, Jason. *Up from the Cradle of Jazz: New Orleans Music Since World War II;* with Jonathan Foose and Tad Jones. Athens: University of Georgia Press; 1986.

Traces the development of "non-classical music in New Orleans from the late 1940s to the present (mid-eighties)." He documents New Orleans's seminal role in the development of rhythm and blues and rock and roll. In addition, he covers the jazz scene with detailed attention given to some of its most famous exponents including the Marsalis brothers and Alvin Baptiste. Among the nonjazz portraits are Fats Domino, Allen Toussaint, Mac (Dr. John) Rebennack, Henry Roeland (Professor Longhair) Byrd, and others. He also covers the Mardi Gras Indians. Unfortunately, he devotes only limited attention to the impact that the New Orleans Jazz and Heritage Festival has had on modern jazz in New Orleans.

1178. Bissonnette, William E. *The Jazz Crusade: The Inside Story of the Great New Orleans Jazz Revival of the 1960's.* Bridgeport, Conn.: Special Request Books; 1992.

Details how, in the 1960s, a record producer and a musical helped to revive early New Orleans jazz. Also included are details of the friendship the author forged with many of the musicians who were active in this revival. This is the first book to include a compact disc of the music. Discography, index, and 60 pages of photographs.

1179. Blesh, Rudi. *This Is Jazz: A Series of Lectures Given at the San Francisco Museum of Art.* San Francisco: the author, 1943; London: Jazz Music Books, 1945.

Some of these viewpoints appear in *Shining Trumpets,* and clearly articulate the author's passion for New Orleans jazz. The lectures focused on the evolution and musical characteristics of New Orleans jazz. The author's disdain of related styles (Chicago style) and white imitators of New Orleans jazz is also evident in the lectures. The lectures on the development of New Orleans jazz are important because he connects the music and musicians to the culture. Selected bibliography and discography as well as reference notes.

1180. Bokelund, Henning. *High Society: My Friends, The New Orleans Clarinetists.* London: Holte; 2002.

Discusses the role and function of several New Orleans clarinetists in jazz. Included are Johnny Dodds, George Lewis, Pete Fountain, and many more.

1181. Buerkle, Jack V., and Danny Barker. *Bourbon Street Black: The New Orleans Black Jazzman.* New York: Oxford University Press; 1973.

Provides a glimpse into the lives of several New Orleans musicians. The authors use a sociohistorical approach to discuss issues like musical apprenticeship, Union Local 496, racism, travel, and the role and function of community groups in maintaining and nurturing jazz (church and social classes). Fifty musicians were interviewed and provide important insider insights into the culture that nurtured jazz in New Orleans. Selected bibliography, reference notes, and an index.

1182. Carter, William. *Preservation Hall: Music from the Heart.* New York: W. W. Norton and Company; 1991; reprinted by New York: Bayou Press; 2000.

The book is based on several taped interviews with Preservation Hall personnel and others made by the author between 1984 and 1987. He also consulted letters, memorabilia housed at Preservation Hall, newspaper clippings, and photographs. He discusses the roots of New Orleans jazz, early pioneers, the story of Preservation Hall and the people who managed it, survival of New Orleans jazz artists during the swing and bebop eras, and the eventual renaissance of New Orleans jazz in the early 1960. Other strong points of the book are his interview of William Russell and the 200-plus photographs of artists and places. Index.

1183. Charters, Samuel B. *Jazz: New Orleans, 1885–1963: An Index to the Negro Musicians of New Orleans.* Originally published by William Allen in 1958 as *Jazz: New Orleans 1885–1957.* Belleville, N.J.: W. C. Allen, 1958; London: Jazz Journal, 1959; revised edition, New York: Oak Publications, 1963; New York: Da Capo, 1983.

A comprehensive compilation of portraits of more than 200 musicians who were active in New Orleans between 1885 and 1931. The collection is limited to artists who remained in New Orleans rather than artists who migrated to other locales. The portraits are organized into year periods, for example 1885–1899, and preceded by a concise introductory essay. The portraits include information on birth, musical life and career, information on brass bands and orchestral ensembles, instrument performed, and death date. A discography of recordings made in the 1920s and the revival recordings of the 1950s and 1960s is also included. The strength of this book is that it provides the names and important facts on lesser-known New Orleans musicians. Bands, performance halls, musicians, and tune title indexes are included.

1184. Colyer, Ken. *New Orleans and Back.* Delp, Yorks: Brooks and Pratt; 1969.

Contains anecdotal information on the author's visit to New Orleans in the 1950s. The author recounts stories about the artists he met and provides some general observations about the bands he heard.

1185. *French Quarter Interviews.* New Orleans: Vagabond Press; 1969.

Contains transcriptions of several interviews of New Orleans artists including Danny Barker.

1186. Goffin, Robert. *La Nouvelle-Orleans, Capitale Du Jazz.* New York: Francaise; 1946.

In French. Biomusical portraits of Louis Armstrong, Sidney Bechet, Buddy Bolden, Bunk Johnson, New Orleans Rhythm Kings, Leon Roppolo, Tony Sbarbara, and Muggsy Spanier (who is not indigenous to New Orleans). The portraits contain birth/death dates (where warranted), career highlights, contributions, and selected references to recordings.

1187. Graves, James. *Damals in New Orleans: Eine Bildchronik des frühen Jazz.* Zürich: Sanssouci Verlag Zürich; 1960.

In Swiss. Divided into parts; part one deals with context and history of jazz in New Orleans, and covers topics such as Congo Square, Mardi Gras, Buddy Bolden, Storyville, and the Riverboats. The coverage is concise (most of four or fewer pages). The second part profiles the history, contributions, and style of Sidney Bechet, Paul Dominquez, Jelly Roll Morton, and has contributions by Alan Lomax on Johnny St. Cyr, Bob Whitman, Bunk Johnson, and Louis Armstrong, and William Russell on Stephen W. Smith. The portraits are limited (less than three pages) and offer no new insights. Selected discography.

1188. Grossman, William Leonard, and Jack W. Farrell. *Heart of Jazz; Line Drawings by Lamartine Le Goullon.* New York: New York University Press; 1956.

There are contributions by both authors; Farrell covers selected instruments and their roles and functions in a jazz band as well as providing provocative essays that detail the New Orleans revival of the 1940s and early 1950s. Grossman develops the thesis that jazz is a "Christian" music, which, in his opinion, is the reason why it is good music. Some of his views are personal rather than documented by facts.

1189. Hazeldine, Mike (compiler and editor). *Bill Russell's American Music.* New York: Jazzology Press; 1993.

The editor combines Russell's production notes and interviews to produce a history of the American Music recordings. Russell founded this jazz record label in the 1940s, and subsequently introduced some forgotten and overlooked musicians connected to the earliest days of unrecorded jazz. The music was recorded in dance halls, homes, storerooms, backyards, and other less than desirable settings, because many professional studios would not allow African Americans inside.

1190. Kennedy, Al. *Chord Changes on the Chalkboard: How Public School Teachers Shaped Jazz and the Music of New Orleans.* Lanham, Md.: Scarecrow Press, and Institute of Jazz Studies (Rutgers University); 2002.

Uses more than 90 interviews and extensive research in New Orleans historical collections to document how public school teachers pushed to have jazz and other indigenous musical traditions to be taught in the city schools. The result was a series of successful students, and a teaching outlet for the teachers' own musical experiences, recordings, and performances. In addition to discussing high school programs, he detailed the contributions of teachers such as Clyde Kerr, Sr., and Clyde Kerr, Jr., Yvonne Busch, Dr. Bert Braud, Ellis Marsalis, and several others. Foreword by Ellis Marsalis.

1191. Knowles, Richard H. *Fallen Heroes: A History of New Orleans Brass Bands.* New Orleans: Basin Street; U.P.; 1996.

Insider perspectives about the history and function of New Orleans brass bands. Discusses the Eureka, Young Tuxedo Brass Band, E. Gibson brass Band, Olympia Brass Band, and others. Lots of previously unpublished photographs and a CD that includes 13 tracks, 5 by Bunk Johnson, and Peter Bocage, Alex Bigard, and Alfred Williams discussing brass bands.

1192. Koening, Karl. *Jazz Map of New Orleans.* New Orleans: Basin Street; 1985.

Annotated references to important venues and significant homes in the history and evolution of jazz in New Orleans. Index.

1193. Koster, Rick. *Louisiana Music: A Journey from R&B to Zydeco, Jazz to Country, Blues to Gospel, Cajun Music to Swamp Pop to Carnival Music and Beyond.* New York: Da Capo Press; 2002.

Surveys the lush musical landscape of Louisiana and produces a book that deals with the roots of its cultural and music. Discusses the past and present of several genres, and includes important information on brass bands, several modern jazz artists, voodoo music, Mardi Gras Indian tribes, and the genres cited in his title.

1194. Lichtenstein, Grace. *Musical Gumbo: The Music of New Orleans.* New York: W.W. Norton and Company; 1993.

An overview of twentieth-century musical development in New Orleans. They begin with a discussion of early jazz, and focus on Louis Armstrong,

Sidney Bechet, and Jelly Roll Morton. In addition, they discuss post–World War II rhythm and blues, cajun, contemporary jazz, survey festival and record stores, and more. Other than a discussion of the early giants, they discuss Clifton Chenier, Harry Connick, jr., Fats Domino, Michael Doucet, The Dirty Dozen Brass Band, Dr. John, the Marsalis family, the Neville brothers, Irma Thomas, Allen Toussaint, and many more.

1195. Longstreet, Stephen. *The Real Jazz Old and New.* Baton Rouge: Louisiana State University, 1956; Stockholm: Wennerberg, 1958; New York: Greenwood, 1969.

Insider perspectives (notebook material and taped interviews), with selected New Orleans musicians including Louis Armstrong, Buddy Bolden, and King Oliver. The perspectives cover their embryonic musical experiences, jazz in early New Orleans, career highlights, and sociocultural issues. Index, illustrations (author).

1196. _____. *Sportin' House: A History of the New Orleans Sinners and the Birth of Jazz;* text and pictures by Stephen Longstreet. New York: Sherbourne; 1965.

Details the relationship between prostitution and jazz, until Newton D. Baker and Josephus Daniels crafted rules, which lead to the closing of Storyville. His 1933 interview of Nell Kimball, a New Orleans madam from 1880 to 1917, provides a graphic insight into the drugs, gambling, and prostitution available in Storyville before it officially closed in 1917.

1197. Martinez, Raymond J. *Portraits of New Orleans Jazz: Its People and Places.* New Orleans: Hope Publications; 1971.

Discusses elements important to the development of jazz in New Orleans. There is information on Storyville, New Orleans funerals, and Congo Square; also on L. M. Gottschalk, Louis Armstrong, King Oliver, Jelly Roll Morton, and George McCullum. Of particular importance is the information on Mardi Gras Indians. There is a list of nearly 1,000 artists, and the book is richly illustrated. This is a brief but valuable study (addition to 1981).

1198. Martyn, Barry. *New Orleans Jazz: The End of The Beginning.* New Orleans: Jazzology Press; 1998.

A collection of interviews with several veterans of New Orleans style jazz conducted over a 37-year period. The interviews include artists such as Louis Armstrong, Baby and Johnny Dodds, Jelly Roll Morton, and many more. The book also includes a CD of interviews about Chris Kelly.

1199. Martyn, Barry, and Mike Hazeldine (compilers and editors). *New Orleans Style by Bill Russell.* New Orleans: Jazzology Press; 1994.

The editors completed the book that Bill Russell began but did not finish before his death. In compiling the chapters, the authors used material that Russell had collected for the project. Included are numerous interviews. The chapters are divided by instrument, specifically drums, guitar and banjo, string bass, piano, trumpet, trombone, and clarinet. Among the interviewed musicians are Baby Dodds, Johnny St. Cyr, Natty Dominique, Pops Foster, Kid Ory, and others. The editors eliminated Jelly Roll Morton because Russell had written a book on him, and added short chapters on Lawrence Duhe, Louis Keppard, and the recollections of Judy Garland and Roy Palmer. Although concise, Russell's description of New Orleans jazz is informative.

1200. Olivier, Adam. *New Orleans Jazz.* Amsterdam: Inter/View; 1981.

In Dutch. Concerned with history, role and function, and relationship of New Orleans jazz to New Orleans culture. Discusses the role of brass bands, Storyville, and the contributions of Louis Armstrong, Jelly Roll Morton, Buddy Bolden, King Oliver, and many more. Illustrated.

1201. Paul, Elliott. *That Crazy American Music.* Port Washington, N.Y.: Kennikat Press; 1975.

Begins with an appraisal of music in the early colonies and some comments on the vitality of antebellum African American music and moves to a discussion of jazz, boogie-woogie, and rock. The book transcends jazz because he discusses the works of Edward MacDowell, the songs of Stephen Foster, opera, church music, and more. His discussion of jazz focuses on "Dixieland Jazz" (pp. 166–186), followed by chapters on Joe Oliver, Louis Armstrong, and bop. The focus is historical. Occasionally there are some important points made, for example, his discussion of Buddy Bolden, Bunk Johnson, and Storyville (pp. 173–186). Selected bibliography and an index.

1202. Rockmore, Noel. *Preservation Hall Portraits:* paintings by the author; text by Larry Borenstein and Bill Russell. Baton Rouge: Louisiana State University Press; 1968.

Combines texts on each artist with graphic reproductions of paintings of New Orleans jazz musicians. The author attempts to capture the essence of the funeral as well as realistic scenes of people and places. The photographs focus primarily on artists that have performed at Preservation Hall; however, he also includes portraits of the Eureka Brass Band.

1203. Rose, Al. *Storyville, New Orleans.* Tuscaloosa: University of Alabama; 1974.

Discusses the beginning and importance of Storyville, from its inception in 1897 to its closing in 1917. Permeated with references. More of a bibliographic essay than a history. Index and illustrations.

1204. Rose, Al, and Edmond Souchon. *New Orleans Jazz: A Family Album.* Baton Rouge: Louisiana State University Press; 1967.

Contains numerous photographs of both New Orleans and the artists that performed there from its embryonic stages to the late 1960s. Also included are biographical portraits of nearly 1,000 musicians, which include birth, career achievements, and the date of death. There is information of jazz and brass bands, personnel, instruments, venues, and dates of performances. Name index.

1205. Russell, Bill. *Jazz Scrapbook: Bill Russell and Some Highly Musical Friends.* New Orleans: New Orleans Historical Society; 1998.

A book of photographs about the New Orleans jazz scene. The photographs depict musicians performing, and in other contexts. Includes photographs of many of the most important New Orleans artists like Louis Armstrong, Baby and Johnny Dodds, Pops Foster, Kid Ory, and many more.

1206. Schafer, William J. *Brass Bands and New Orleans Jazz;* with assistance from Richard B. Allen. Baton Rouge: Louisiana State University; 1977.

The primary focus is to detail how the American band tradition and African American musical tradition met, acculturated, and produced the brass band tradition. The book also details the history, playing styles, repertories, and musicians of New Orleans African American brass bands. The author believes the relationship between brass bands and jazz was symbiotic, "Two musics co-existing and mingling, never quite merging" (p. 50). In addition, the importance of African American culture to the history and preservation of the bands is detailed; especially funeral parades, where he details how elements of ritual, music, theater, and religion are mixed to form a unique African American cultural expression. Included are photographs of New Orleans brass bands from the 1860s through the 1970s. A roster of brass bands, microgroove discography, selected bibliography of books and articles, end the book.

1207. Spedale, Rhodes, Jr. *A Guide to Jazz in New Orleans.* New Orleans: Hope; 1984.

Contains an historical overview of jazz in New Orleans and several portraits of artists/groups. The portraits include a profile/ interview of Pud Brown, with a lead sheet of his "Tenor For Two"; a history of Dejan's Olympia Brass Band, and the Dukes of Dixieland; a career overview of Pete Fountain; biomusical portraits of Branford, Ellis, and Wynton Marsalis, Germaine Bazzle, Al Belleto, Roger Dickerson, Patrice Fisher, Pete Fountain, Banu Gibson, Allan Jaffe and the Preservation Hall Jazz, LaVergne Smith, Allen Toussaint, and several others, and an obituary of Art Pepper (who was not a native, or proponent of, New Orleans–style jazz). Illustrations.

1208. Stramacci, Fabrizio. *New Orleans: Alle Origina del Jazz.* Roma: LatoSide; 1982.

In Italian. Promotes the theory that jazz originated in New Orleans and details the importance of Storyville and the accomplishments of several artists (Louis Armstrong, Johnny and Baby Dodds, Jelly Roll Morton, and King Oliver). Includes information on the uses and functions of jazz in New Orleans.

1209. Suhor, Charles. *Jazz in New Orleans: The Postwar Years Through 1970.* Lanhan, Md., and the Institute of Jazz Studies (Rutgers University); 2001.

A credible interpretation of jazz in New Orleans from the end of World War II through 1970. The book is divided into three sections, each with an overview essay followed by other essays. Section one, "Jazz and the Establishment," focuses on cultural and institutional setting; section two, "Traditional and Dixieland Jazz highlights music and musicians"; and section three, "An Invisible Generation," dispels the myth that no one was playing bebop or other modern styles in New Orleans before the current modernists appeared in the 1980s. He also discusses the Tulane Jazz Archive, Jazz Fest 1968 and 1969, revival, The Dukes of Dixieland, Pete Fountain, Al Hirt, Raymond Burke, George Lewis, and others.

1210. Tallant, Robert. *Voodoo in New Orleans.* New York: Macmillan, 1946; New York: Collier Books, 1962.

Investigates the history of cult practices in New Orleans with a special attempt to connect them to jazz in that city. The book is important because the author investigates the role and function of jazz within religious practices. A later study by Susan Cavin, "Missing Women: On the Voodoo Trail to Jazz," references Tallant; however, she also offers insights into the role that women play in voodoo (addition to 1981). Selected bibliography.

1211. Turner, Frederick. *Remembering Song: Encounters with the New Orleans Jazz Tradition.* New York: Viking; 1982.

A sociocultural history of the origins and development of New Orleans jazz. The specific foci are the traditions, roots, meaning, and ultimate decline of the music, intertwined with the musician's lives that embodied it. He emphasizes the cultural and historical significance of Buddy Bolden, Bunk Johnson, Freddie Keppard, and Jim Robinson. Overall, the book is concerned with the role and function of jazz in culture. Some excellent material gleaned from oral history; however, the book is, unfortunately, permeated with romanticized and morbid personal impressions.

1212. Williams, Martin. *Jazz Masters of New Orleans.* New York, London, Toronto: Macmillan, 1967; New York: Da Capo, 1978.

Presents biomusical portraits of Buddy Bolden, Jelly Roll Morton, Joe "King" Oliver, Sidney Bechet, Zutty Singleton, Kid Ory, Bunk Johnson, Red Allen, The Original Dixieland Jazz Band, and the New Orleans Rhythm Kings. He focused on artists whose styles were codified in New Orleans, although they might have spent a substantial amount of their careers outside of New Orleans. The one exception is that only the early years of Louis Armstrong are covered. His musical assessments are based on selected recordings, however, the chapter on Buddy Bolden focuses more on Bolden's musical practices within New Orleans culture. Each chapter contains selected bibliographical and discographical listings. Includes part of Sidney Bechet's *Treat It Gentle,* and the author's article, "Condition Red" (on Red Allen, previously published in *Down Beat*). Index.

New York

1213. Bastin, Bruce. *Never Sell A Copyright: Joe Davis and His Role in the New York Music Scene 1916–1978.* London: Chigwell; 1990.

In addition to his life and role in music, the book contains important information on the history and evolution of jazz in New York. Discusses how some musicians sold the rights to their compositions and the affect that ownership of copyrights had on the New York music scene.

1214. Charters, Samuel B., and Leonard Kunstadt. *Jazz: A History of the New York Scene.* New York: Doubleday; 1962.

Charters details the evolution of jazz in New York from the turn of the century to the late 1950s. Using a myriad of printed sources (articles, newspaper announcements, and reviews), the authors discuss ragtime, the first visits of New Orleans bands, Freddie Keppard and the Original Dixieland Jazz Band, and African American military bands of World War I (James Reese Europe). They also extol the virtues of Perry Bradford and detail the first blues recording by Mamie Smith in 1920. Female blues artists, the roles of Paul Whiteman, Fletcher Henderson, and Don Redman, subsequent developments in ensembles, the swing era, piano greats James P. Johnson and Fats Waller, and the rise of bebop (Gillespie, Monk, and Parker), are also covered. Selected discography, bibliography, and an index.

1215. Cohen, Maxwell. *The Police Card Discard.* Lanham, Md.: Scarecrow Press, and the Institute of Jazz Studies (Rutgers University, 1993.

Presents a history of conflict ending in the 1960s between musicians and the police in New York. Covers important trials, social issues, and the ultimate victory that some entertainers and musicians won. Thorough and well-documented.

1216. Freeman, Phil. *New York is Now: The New Wave of Free Jazz.* Brooklyn: The Telegraph Company; 2001.

A passionate account of the renaissance transpiring in the world of free jazz and its players. He covers the 1990s by exploring the musical scene, venues, independent record labels, and the magazines that cover the music and musicians. He covers David S. Ware, Matthew Shipp, William Parker, Roy Campbell, Charles Gayle, Joe Morris, and Daniel Carter.

1217. Lees, Gene. *Meet Me at Jim and Andy's: Jazz Musicians and Their World.* New York: Oxford University Press; 1988.

Portraits of some of the great artists who frequented the New York bar Jim and Andy's in the 1960s. Based on his second jazz letter collection, and concentrates on bandleaders and instrumentalists. Several essays deal with artists such as Paul Desmond, Duke Ellington, Bill Evans, Art Farmer, John Heard, Woody Herman, Frank Rosolino, and Artie Shaw.

1218. O'Neal, Hank. *The Ghosts of Harlem.* Paris: Levallois-Perret; 1997.

A collection of 41 interviews about jazz and jazz musicians who were important to the development of jazz in Harlem. Included are interviews of Cab Calloway, Andy Kirk, Panama Francis, Andy Kirk, Dizzy Gillespie, Sammy Price, Buddy Tate, Benny Waters, and many more. Text in French.

1219. Stokes, W. Royal and Charles Peterson. *Swing Era—New York.* Philadelphia: Temple University; 1994.

Concerned with the history and accomplishments of many of the swing era bands in New York. Discusses the context, and accomplishments of individuals and groups, and offers insight into why swing bands flourished in New York.

Seattle, Washington

1220. De Barros, Paul. *Jackson Street After Hours: The Roots of Jazz in Seattle.* Seattle: Sasquatch; c. 1993.

A significant addition to the literature because the author chronicles the embryonic careers and achievements of several jazz artists who got their start in Seattle. He covers the 1940s and 1950s and covers Ernestine Anderson, Mildred Bailey, Ray Charles, and Quincy Jones. In addition, he covers the careers of several significant artists who remained local, including bassist Red Kelly, and pianists Jack Perciful and Junior Raglin. The musician interviews provide a rich perspective on local jazz history, including the impact of racism on their respective careers. There are several photographs by Eduardo Calderon, and 24 contemporary portraits. Ted Dzieick provided research assistance.

Texas

1221. Oliphant, Dave. *Texas Jazz.* Austin: University of Texas Press; 1996.

Examines the evolution of jazz in Texas, and discusses the contributions of artists who launched their careers in the state. Among the discussed artists are Ornette Coleman, Charlie Christian, Eddie Durham, Blind Lemon Jefferson, Scott Joplin, Jimmy Guiffre, David "Fathead" Newman, Buster Smith, and Jack Teagarden. Includes some technical analysis but is readable for the average reader. Meticulously researched and an important addition to the growing collection of literature on regional jazz.

VII

Discography

Science of Discography

1222. Allen, Walter C. (editor). *Studies in Jazz Discography, I.* Newark: Institute of Jazz Studies (Rutgers Extension Division); 1971.

A collection of the presentations made at three different discography-related conferences; the 1968 and 1969 Discographical Research, and the July 1969 conference on Preservation and Extension of the Jazz Heritage. The proceedings can be summarized as follows: the first conference papers addressed goals and methods, dating and performer identification, and jazz and social science; the second conference papers addressed archival practices, historical issues, areas of needed discographical research, and African American newspapers as primary source materials; the third conference on Preservation and Extension covered the function and purpose of Tulane University's Jazz Archive, collection and preservation of materials, jazz education, and related topics. Selected bibliography and reference notes.

1223. Black, Douglas C. *Matrix Numbers: Their Meaning and History.* Melbourne: Australia Jazz Quarterly; 1946.

Contains a brief introduction to the significance of matrix numbers and their utility for collectors. Also provides notes on different matrix number series, such as Decca, Okeh, Columbia, Brunswick, and Victor. A good manual for the beginning discographer.

1224. Langridge, Derek. *Your Jazz Collection.* London: Archon Books; 1970.

Discusses collecting, and the literature relating to it, with much of the book devoted to classifying and indexing both literature and recordings (1981).

1225. Rust, Brian. *Brian Rust's Guide to Discography.* Westport, Conn.: Greenwood Press; 1980.

According to the author, his purpose is "to define the purposes and functions of a discography and to show what is involved in the compilation of one" (p. 3). Although he provides some insights into the science of discography, the book focuses more on Rust's approach, for example, his infatuation with pre-1942 jazz recordings. Among the numerous topics he discusses are: major types of discography, significant discographies (with samples), and an introductory chapter on the purpose and function of discography. There are three appendices: a glossary of discography terms, a list of discographical organizations, and a list of journals that cover discographies.

1226. Taubman, Howard (editor). *The New York Times Guide to Listening Pleasure.* New York: Macmillan; 1968.

Concentrates on classical music, with some limited attention to jazz. Essentially this is a how-to guide for the novice record collector.

1227. Wyler, Michael. *A Glimpse at the Past: An Illustrated History of Some Early Record Companies That Made Jazz History.* West Moors, Dorset: Jazz Publications; 1957.

Provides information on 14 jazz labels, giving significant information for early 1950s collectors. Record labels such as "Black Patti," "Black Swan," "Famous," and "Herwin" are covered. Brian Rust's *The American Record Label Book* is much more comprehensive; however, some of his listings are incomplete when compared to Wyler's.

Individual Discographies

Andrews Sisters

1228. Garrod, Charles. *Andrews Sisters Discography.* Zephyrhills, Fla.: Joyce Music Publications; 1992.

Chronicles all known recordings of this pseudojazz group, including all recording sessions, titles, dates, venues, personnel, and master numbers. Where known, reissues all listed, as are broadcasts, film work, and transcriptions. Title index.

Ray Anthony

1229. Garrod, Charles, and Bill Korst. *Ray Anthony and His Orchestra.* Zephyrhills, Fla.: Joyce Music Publications; 1988.

Focuses primarily on his bandleader career after Glenn Miller. Includes all recording sessions, titles, dates, venues, labels, personnel, master numbers, and, when known, reissues. Broadcasts, film work, and transcriptions are included. Title index.

Louis Armstrong

1230. Brooks, Edward. *The Young Louis Armstrong on Records: A Critical Survey of the Early Recordings, 1923–1928.* Lanham, Md., and Institute of Jazz Studies (Rutgers University): Scarecrow Press; 2002.

A comprehensive and chronological survey and analysis of the recordings Armstrong made between 1923 and 1928. Brooks focuses on meaning with copious details on musical structure. Also contains introductory and concluding chapters, and appendices covering reference systems, American practice, instrument abbreviations, glossary, bibliography, and an alphabetical list of titles.

1231. Jepsen, Jorgen Grunnet. *A Discography of Louis Armstrong.* Copenhagen: Knudsen; 1968.

A chronological listing of all recordings covering both the performer's bands and recordings with other bands. Complete discographical details are provided including date of recording, recording venue, matrix and take numbers, original and LP reissue numbers, and titles of compositions. No index.

George Auld

1232. Garrod, Charles, and Bill Korst. *George Auld and His Orchestra.* Zephyrhills, Fla.: Joyce Music Publications; 1992.

A comprehensive listing of all recordings, including those with Bunny Berigan and Benny Goodman. Details all recording sessions, including titles, dates, venues, labels, personnel, master numbers, and reissues where known. Also includes broadcasts, film work, and transcriptions. Title index.

Mitchell Ayres

1233. Garrod, Charles. *Mitchell Ayres and Orchestra 1933–1973.* Zephyrhills, Fla.: Joyce Music Publications; 1991.

List all recording sessions, including dates, labels, personnel, titles, master numbers, and reissues when known. Broadcast and film work are also included.

Charlie Barnet

1234. Edwards, Ernest. *Charlie Barnet and His Orchestra:* New Revised Edition. Whittier, Calif.: Erngeobil Publications; 1967.

Covers all known Barnet recordings including some as a sideman. Each entry contains title, date, venue, label, master number, and personnel. This edition contains corrections and omissions related to an earlier transcript.

1235. Garrod, Charles. *Charlie Barnet and His Orchestra.* Zephyrhills, Fla.: Joyce Music Publications; 1984.

Includes contributions from Ernest Edwards, Bill Korst, and George Hall and contains all known recording sessions. Each entry contains title, date, venue, label, personnel, master numbers, and reissues. Also includes broadcasts, film work, and transcriptions. Title index.

Blue Barron

1236. _____. *Blue Barron and His Orchestra.* Zephyrhills, Fla.: Joyce Music Publications, revised; 1992.

The revised edition includes corrections and omissions from an earlier draft. Lists all recordings, including titles, dates, venues, personnel, master numbers, and reissues when known.

Count Basie

1237. _____. *Count Basie and His Orchestra.* Three volumes. Zephyrhills, Fla.: Joyce Music Publications; 1987; 1988.

The three-volume discography is organized as follows: volume 1 1936–1945, volume 2 1946–1957, and volume 3 1958–1967. Lists all known recordings and includes titles, dates, venues, personnel, label, master numbers, and reissues where known. Also includes broadcasts, film work, and transcriptions. Not as comprehensive as Chris Sheridan's *Count Basie: A Bio-Discography.* Title index.

1238. Jepsen, Jorgen Grunnet. *A Discography of Count Basie.* Two volumes. Copenhagen: Knudsen; 1969.

Volume 1, compiled by Bo Scherman and Carl A. Haellstrom, covers listings from 1929 to 1950; volume 2, compiled by Jepsen, covers listings from

1951 to 1968. A chronological listing of all recordings made with the Basie band. Complete discographical details are provided including date of recording, recording venue, matrix and take numbers, original and LP reissue numbers, and titles of compositions. No index.

1239. Sheridan, Chris. *Count Basie: A Bio-Discography.* Westport, Conn.: Greenwood Press; 1986.

Begins with a concise biographical profile of Basie liberally sprinkled with photographs, dates, personnel, and other facts. The discography entries are preceded in each of the 10 categories by a short essay, which provides information on the context. The categories and subsequent entries are divided by years and contain full discographical information. The entries cover five broad categories: commercial recordings, electrical transcriptions, films, broadcasts, and location recordings, and cover nearly 1,300 pages. The appendices contain record listings, band itinerary, and a selected bibliography. There are five indices: Basie on film and video, general index, arrangers, musicians, and index of tune titles. This is one of the most comprehensive biodiscographies on any jazz artist.

Sidney Bechet

1240. Mauerer, Hans J. *A Discography of Sidney Bechet.* Copenhagen: Karl E. Knudsen; 1969.

Covers Bechet's entire career, including recordings of Bechet's own group as well as those he made with others from 1921 to 1964. Each entry is coded to indicate who supervised the recording session. There are artist and title indices (1981).

Bix Beiderbecke

1241. Castelli, Vittorio, Evert Kaleveld, and Liborio Pusateri. *The Bix Bands: A Bix Beiderbecke Discography.* Milan: Raretone; 1972.

Includes biographical and discographical information. Entries are arranged in chronological order and include details on the band, date of recording, matrix and take numbers, place, titles, and both release and reissue numbers. Improvised solo information includes form and details on choruses taken by soloist (including the number of measures). There are four indices: titles (with composer credits); musicians and orchestras; 78 release numbers; and details of The microgroove reissues.

Tex Beneke

1242. Garrod, Charles. *Tex Beneke and His Orchestra.* Zephyrhills, Fla.: Joyce Music Publications; 1973.

Based on an earlier draft by Ernest Edwards. Each entry includes titles, labels, dates, venues, personnel, master numbers, and record numbers, including reissues where known. Also includes broadcasts, film work, and transcriptions. Title index. The discography was revised in 1997.

Ben Bernie

1243. _____. *Ben Bernie and His Orchestra.* Zephyrhills, Fla.: Joyce Music Publications; 1991.

Contains all recording sessions, including titles, dates, venues, personnel, label, master numbers, and reissues when known. Also includes all known broadcasts, film work, and transcriptions. Title index.

Will Bradley and Freddie Slack

1244. Garrod, Charles, and Bill Korst. *Will Bradley/Freddie Slack.* Zephyrhills, Fla.: Joyce Music Publications; 1986.

Covers all known recordings by two little-known artists. As in other Joyce publications, each entry includes title, date venue, personnel, label, and master numbers. Broadcasts and transcriptions are also included. Title index. Revised in 1997.

Tiny Bradshaw and Lucky Millinder

1245. Garrod, Charles. *Tiny Bradshaw and His Orchestra/Lucky Millinder and His Orchestra.* Zephyrhills, Fla.: Joyce Music Publications; 1994.

Lists all known recordings, broadcasts, and transcriptions. Includes titles, dates, venues, labels, personnel, and master numbers. Also covers Millinder's recordings as a sideman. Title index.

Anthony Braxton

1246. deCraen, Hugo, and Eddy Janssens. *Anthony Braxton Discography.* Brussels, Belgium: New Think Publications; 1982.

Chronicles his entire discographical output and includes titles, labels, dates, venues, personnel, master numbers, broadcasts, film work, and transcriptions.

1247. Wachtmeister, Hans. *A Discography and Bibliography of Anthony Braxton;* photographs by Gunnar Holmberg. Stocksund, Sweden: Blue Anchor Jazz Book Shop; 1982.

Recognizes the problem of documenting Braxton's composition titles and intervals between recordings and provides reasons why some album titles appear in more than one place. Limited to commercially issued recordings where Braxton is either a leader or sideman. The bibliography includes books, periodicals, and record reviews. Artist index, author index, abbreviations of periodicals and instruments.

Clifford Brown

1248. Weir, Bob. *Clifford Brown Discography.* Wales, U.K.: Weir, 1982, revised edition; 1983.

The revised edition contains corrections to the first edition. Lists titles, label, dates, venue, personnel, and reissues. Also includes an index of tunes, musicians, lists of records, lists of magazine articles, and unissued tapes and recordings. Illustrations on pages 16, 20, and 32.

Les Brown

1249. Garrod, Charles. *Les Brown and His Orchestra 1936–1960.* Zephyrhills, Fla.: Joyce Music Publications; 1974.

Draws on the work of Ernest Edwards, and includes all known recordings, transcriptions, film work, and broadcasts. Each entry includes title, dates, venue, label, personnel, master numbers, and record numbers, including reissues where known. Artist index. The discography was revised in 2001.

Sonny Burke/Skinnay Ennis

1250. _____. *Sonny Burke and His Orchestra/Skinnay Ennis and His Orchestra.* Zephyrhills, Fla.: Joyce Music Publications; 1994.

Follows the format of other Joyce music publications by listing all known recordings, broadcasts, film work, and transcriptions. The entries contain title, date, venue, label, personnel, and if appropriate, reissues. Title index.

Henry Busse and Clyde McCoy

1251. _____. *Henry Busse and His Orchestra/Clyde McCoy and His Orchestra.* Zephyrhills, Fla.: Joyce Music Publications; 1990.

Includes all known recordings, broadcasts, film work, and transcriptions. Each entry contains title, date, venue, personnel, label, master numbers, and reissues where known. Title index. Revised in 2000.

Bobby Byrne/Dean Hudson

1252. Garrod, Charles and Bill Korst. *Bobby Byrne and His Orchestra/Dean Hudson and His Orchestra.* Zephyrhills, Fla.: Joyce Music Publications; 1992.

Cites all known recording sessions, broadcasts, and transcriptions. Entries list titles, dates, venues, personnel, label, master numbers, and reissues. Title index. Revised in 2001.

Cab Calloway

1253. Popa, James. *Cab Calloway and His Orchestra 1925–1958.* Zephyrhills, Fla.: Joyce Music Publications; 1976.

Draws on the work of Charles Garrod, Charles Delaunay, Jorgen Grunnet Jepsen, Brian Rust, and Albert McCarthy. Lists all known Calloway recordings. Each entry contains titles, dates, venues, labels, master numbers, and reissues. There are inaccuracies and omissions. Broadcasts, film work, and transcriptions are also included. Title index. Revised in 1987.

Frankie Carle

1254. Garrod, Charles. *Frankie Carie and His Orchestra.* Zephyrhills, Fla.: Joyce Music Publications; 1989.

Comprehensive listing of all known recordings, broadcasts, film work, and transcriptions. Entries contain title, date, venue, personnel, label, master numbers, and reissues. Title index. Revised in 2000.

Carmen Cavallaro

1255. _____. *Carmen Cavallaro and His Orchestra.* Zephyrhills, Fla.: Joyce Music Publications; 1989.

Covers known recordings, broadcasts, film work, and transcriptions. The entries include title, date, venues, labels, personnel, master numbers, and reissues. Title index. Revised in 2001.

Bob Chester

1256. Garrod, Charles and Bill Korst. *Bob Chester and His Orchestra.* Zephyrhills, Fla.: Joyce Music Publications; 1974.

Expands on the work of Ernest Edwards and includes titles, dates, venues, labels, master numbers, and reissues. Title index. Revised in 1997.

Charlie Christian

1257. Callis, John. *Charlie Christian 1939–1941: A Discography.* London: Tony Middleton; 1978.

Attempts to list all recordings made by Christian, even when the same numbers have been issued in more than one country. Each entry includes title, date, venue, label, master numbers, and when necessary, reissues. Title index.

Buddy Clark

1258. Garrod, Charles, and Bob Gottlieb. *Buddy Clark.* Zephyrhills, Fla.: Joyce Music Publications; 1991.

Lists both his recordings as a leader and sideman. In addition, broadcasts, film work, and transcriptions are covered. The entries contain title, date, venue, label, personnel, master numbers, reissues. Title index.

Larry Clinton

1259. Garrod, Charles. *Larry Clinton and His Orchestra.* Zephyrhills, Fla.: Joyce Music Publications, revised; 1990.

This revision includes corrections and omissions from an earlier edition. Includes all known recordings, broadcasts, film work, and transcriptions. Standard discographical information including title, date, venue, label, personnel, master numbers, and reissues. Title index. Second revision in 2000.

Nat "King" Cole

1260. Garrod, Charles, and Bill Korst. *Nat "King" Cole: His Voice and Piano.* Zephyrhills, Fla.: Joyce Music Publications; 1987.

Focuses on his known recordings as a solo pianist, trio leader, and bandleader, and his broadcasts, film work, and transcriptions. The entries include title, date, venue, label, personnel, master numbers, and reissues. Title index.

Ornette Coleman

1261. Wild, David, and Michael Cuscuna. *Ornette Coleman 1958–1979: A Discography.* Ann Arbor: University of Michigan Press; 1980.

Combines biographical, stylistic, and discographical information. The discography contains readings as well as commercial recordings. The recordings are arranged chronologically and include details on composer credits, date of recording, name of group, matrix and release numbers, personnel, length of recording, instrument that Coleman performs, record label and number, and indication of whether a recording was commercial or private. Cuscuna discusses style, and Wild contributed a concise biography. There are indices for album titles, performers, and titles. Selected bibliography and references.

Buddy Collette

1262. Hoffman, Coen. *Man of Many Parts: A Discography of Buddy Collette.* Two volumes. Amsterdam: Micrography; 1985.

Includes an extended interview with Collette in which he details his career and relates important information on Central Avenue, visits by artists, and the activities of many Los Angeles jazz musicians. Sixty pages of lead sheets and a comprehensive discography.

John Coltrane

1263. Davis, Brian, and Ray Smith. *John Coltrane Discography.* Discography and supplement. London: the author, 1976; Hockley, Essex: Brian Davis and Ray Smith, 1977.

Complete listing of Coltrane's recordings as both a leader and a sideman. The listings began with Coltrane's first recording with Dizzy Gillespie (November 1949), and continue to his last session (March 17, 1967), in New York. Reissues and private recordings (uses research by Nils Winther Rasmussen and Jan Lohmann) are also included.

1264. Jepsen, Jorgen Grunnet. *A Discography of John Coltrane.* Copenhagen: Knudsen; 1969.

A chronological listing of all recordings covering both the performer's bands and recordings with other bands. Complete discographical details are provided, including date of recording, recording venue, matrix and take numbers, original and LP reissue numbers, and titles of compositions. No index.

1265. Wild, David. *The Recordings of John Coltrane: A Discography.* Two supplements. Ann Arbor: Wildmusic; 1977.

This discography covers the same time span as the Brian Davis *John Coltrane Discography;* however, Wild augments his discography with composer credits, durations of solos, and private tapes. Neither Davis nor Wild provides the order of soloists on the recordings. The two supplements contain additions and corrections and an index of musicians.

Del Courtney

1266. Garrod, Charles. *Del Courtney and His Orchestra/Gray Gordon and His Orchestra.* Zephyrhills, Fla.: Joyce Music Publications; 1992.

Lists all known broadcasts, dates, recordings, titles, film work, personnel, venues, master numbers, and more of these bandleaders.

Bob Crosby

1267. Garrod, Charles, and Bill Korst. *Bob Crosby and His Orchestra.* Zephyrhills, Fla.: Joyce Music Publications; 1987. Two volumes.

Volume one covers the 1935–45 years, and volume two covers the 1946 to 1985 years. Chronicles all known recordings, broadcasts, film work, and transcriptions. The entries include titles, dates, venues, labels, personnel, master numbers, and reissues. Includes several listings on the "Bobcats." Title index.

Xavier Cugat

1268. Garrod, Charles. *Xavier Cugat and His Orchestra.* Zephyrhills, Fla.: Joyce Music Publications; 2002.

A comprehensive listing of all known dates, broadcasts, film work, titles, labels, venues, personnel, master numbers, and reissues.

Vic Damone

1269. Brown, Denis, Ed Novitsky, and Fiona Webster. *Vic Damone Discography: 40 Years of Musical Magic.* Portland, Oreg.: Joyce Music Publications; c. 1991, revised 1999.

Although he was not known solely as a jazz vocalist, he did perform jazz on some occasions. The discography includes a complete listing of all dates, film work, labels, reissues titles, venues, master numbers, personnel, and more. Also contains the name of bands he performed with throughout his long and productive career.

Miles Davis

1270. Jepsen, Jorgen Grunnet. *A Discography of Miles Davis.* Copenhagen: Karl Emil Knudsen; 1969.

A chronological listing of all recordings covering both Davis's bands and recordings with other bands. Complete discographical details are provided, including date of recording, recording venue, matrix and take numbers, original and LP reissue numbers, and titles of compositions. Also incorporates details on many transcriptions taken from radio broadcasts and television shows. No index.

1271. Mortensen, Tore. *Miles Davis: den ny Jazz.* Århus: Forlaget; 1977; Kobenhavn, Den.: Hasse, 1977.

A comprehensive discography covering the 1969–75 period. Each entry includes full discographical information. The entries also include personnel, dates, and venues.

Eric Dolphy

1272. Reinhardt, Uwe. *Like a Human Voice: The Eric Dolphy Discography.* Schmitten: Ruecker; 1986.

In German. Includes all known recording sessions in which Eric Dolphy participated (leader and sideman). Private tapes are excluded. The entries include title, label, date, venue, personnel, master numbers, and reissues.

Al Donahue

1273. Garrod, Charles, and Bill Korst. *Al Donahue and His Orchestra/Van Alexander and His Orchestra.* Zephyrhills, Fla.: Joyce Music Publications; 1991.

Details known recordings, film work, broadcasts, and transcriptions. The entries follow the standard format, including titles, dates, venues, label, personnel, master numbers, and reissues. Title index.

Sam Donahue

1274. Garrod, Charles. *Sam Donahue and His Orchestra.* Zephyrhills, Fla.: Joyce Music Publications; 1992.

Covers all known film work, labels, recordings, titles, venues, reissues, dates, personnel, master numbers, and more.

Kenny Dorham

1275. Raftegard, Bo. *The Kenny Dorham Discography.* Karlstad, Sweden: the author; 1982.

Covers all known recordings, including those on Blue Note and Riverside. The entries include title, date, label, venue, matrix numbers, known reissues, personnel, and broadcasts. The author referenced several known discographical works, including Jepsen's *Jazz Records* (volumes 1–8), Michel

Ruppli and B. Porter's *The Savoy Recordings,* and David Wild's *The Recordings of John Coltrane.*

Jimmy Dorsey

1276. Garrod, Charles. *Jimmy Dorsey and His Orchestra.* Zephyrhills, Fla.: Joyce Music Publications, revision; 1988.

Concentrates on his recordings as a leader and sideman. All known broadcasts, film work, venues, and transcriptions are included. The entries include title, date, venue, label, personnel, master numbers, and reissues. Title index.

Tommy Dorsey

1277. _____. *Tommy Dorsey and His Orchestra.* Two volumes. Zephyrhills, Fla.: Joyce Music Publications, revision; 1988.

Volume 1 covers 1928–45, and volume 2 covers 1946–52. Contains all known broadcasts, film work, and transcriptions. The entries include title, date, venue, label, personnel, master numbers, and reissues. Title index.

Dorsey Brothers

1278. _____. *The Dorsey Brothers.* Zephyrhills, Fla.: Joyce Music Publications; 1992.

A compilation of the recordings, including broadcasts, film work, and transcriptions. Entries include title, date, venue, label, personnel, master numbers, and reissues. Title index.

Eddy Duchin

1279. _____. *Eddy Duchin and His Orchestra.* Zephyrhills, Fla.: Joyce Music Publications; 1989.

Detailed listing of all known recordings, including titles, dates, venues, label, personnel, and master numbers. Also cites broadcasts, film work, transcriptions, and reissues. Title index. Revised in 2000.

Sonny Dunham and Ziggy Elman

1280. _____. *Sonny Dunham and His Orchestra/Ziggy Elman and His Orchestra.* Zephyrhills, Fla.: Joyce Music Publications; 1990.

The Dunham entries include some of his recordings with Gene Gifford and Elman's include some with Benny Goodman. The entries include titles, dates, venues, label, personnel, master numbers, and reissues. Broadcasts, film work, transcriptions are included. Title index.

Billy Eckstine

1281. Brown, Denis. *Billy Eckstine: A Discography.* Zephyrhills, Fla.: Joyce
Music Publications; 2000.

A complete discography that contains his recordings as both a bandleader
and sideman. Also includes dates, labels, titles, personnel, venues, and
master numbers. In addition to his many vocal recordings, the discography
includes citations of the recordings he made as a trumpet player and as
leader of a big band that featured Dizzy Gillespie, Charles Parker, and Sarah
Vaughan.

Les and Larry Elgart

1282. Palmer, Richard F., and Charles Garrod. *Les and Larry Elgart.*
Zephyrhills, Fla.: Joyce Music Publishers; 1992.

Covers all known recordings, broadcasts, film work, and transcriptions.
Discographical details include title, date, venue, label, personnel, master
numbers, and reissues. Title index.

Duke Ellington

1283. Aasland, Benny. *The "Wax Works" of Duke Ellington: The 6th March
1940–30th July 1942 RCA Victor Period.* Jarfalla, Sweden: Dems; 1978.

A comprehensive list of Ellington's works, including some reprints, with
information on date, personnel, place, label, and titles. Includes all air shots
and transcriptions along with broadcasts, studio sessions, and personnel.
The soloists are cited in the index of titles, however, composer credits are
omitted. A comprehensive Microgroove section, illustrations of 78 and
EP labels from the Jazz Society Forgo issue, and volumes 9 to 18 of the
French RCA series are included.

1284. _____. *The "Wax Works" of Duke Ellington: 31st July, 1942–11th
November, 1944. The Recording Ban Period.* Jarfalla, Sweden: DEMS; 1979.

The book covers: (1) the 106 recording sessions, broadcasts, and stage
performances leading up to the Petrillo ban; and (2) the 222 sessions that
transpired during the ban (primarily radio broadcasts). There are two
sections; the title section provides date of recording and the initials of the
soloist, and the chronological section provides date of recording, personnel,
record numbers, titles, and the existence of an acetate. Microgroove listings
are also detailed and contain liner notes to specific volumes in the "Works
of Duke" series (RCA).

1285. Bakker, Dick. *Duke Ellington on Microgroove, 1923–1942.* Alphen aan den Rijn: Micrography; 1974.

Lists all broadcasts and recordings made during a 19-year period. Full discographical information with the exception of matrix and original release numbers. He also includes some films among his listings. Personnel are provided in a separate table in the introduction. Title index.

1286. Jepsen, Jorgen Grunnet. *Discography of Duke Ellington.* Three volumes. Copenhagen: Knudsen; 1959.

A comprehensive listing of Ellington's recordings in chronological order. Includes title, label, personnel, date, venue, issues, reissues, and some out-of-print recordings. Compliments other Ellington discographies.

1287. Massagli, Luciano, Liborio Pusateri, and Giovanni M. Volonté. *Duke Ellington's Story on Records.* Nine volumes. Milan: Musica Jazz: 1966–1975.

Covers Ellington's career from 1923 to 1955. This outstanding discography includes complete information on commercial recordings, sound tracks, concerts, and radio and television performances. In addition, the authors provide a structural analysis of each piece, for example, the number of bars comprising the theme, the successions of choruses, and the contribution of specific soloists in order of entry. Each volume has indices of titles (with composers), personnel (with dates of each musician's stay in the band and references to solos), and Microgroove releases (with contents). The volumes cover the following dates: Vol. 1: 1923–31; Vol. 2: 1932–38; Vol. 3: 1939–42; Vol. 4: 1943–44; Vol. 5: 1945; Vol. 6: 1946; Vol. 7: 1947–50; Vol. 8: 1951–52; Vol. 9: 1953–55 (1981).

1288. San Filippo, Luigi. *General Catalog of Duke Ellington's Recorded Music with Discographical Notes.* Palermo, Italy: Centro studi di Musica Contemporea; 1964; Second edition, 1966.

Lists 1,472 titles covering the years 1924 to 1965, but not as comprehensive as the Massagli discography. The entries are listed in chronological order and include title, label, personnel, date, venue, issues, and reissues, with a title index. Priority is given to American and British labels. The author provides information on V-discs, films, and radio and television transcriptions. The author used Benny Aasland's *The "Wax Works" of Duke Ellington* and Jorgen Grunnet Jepsen's *Discography of Duke Ellington* Volumes 1, 2, and 3 as references (1981).

1289. Timner, W. E. *The Recorded Music of Duke Ellington and His Sidemen: A Collector's Manual.* Montreal: the author; 1976; revised and updated edition, Montreal: the author; 1979, *Ellingtonia: The Recorded Music of*

Duke Ellington, and His Sidemen (3rd edition). Metuchen, N.J.: Scarecrow Press; 1988.

A definitive collection of Ellington's and his sidemen's recordings organized into five sections: (1) orchestras (details on band names under which Ellington recorded or under which his recordings have been issued); (2) personnel; (3) chronological list of recordings (broadcasts, concerts, movie soundtracks, radio and television appearances, studio sessions, and private recordings of both Ellington and some of his sidemen including date of recordings, label names, place of recording, personnel, and titles, however there are no issue numbers; (4) title index, with different versions of tunes such as "Mood Indigo"; and (5) an attendance list. The collection lists many out-of-print recordings and also covers Ellington's European recordings. Index.

1290. Valburn, Jerry. *The Directory of Duke Ellington's Recordings*. Hicksville, N.Y.: Marlor Productions; 1986.

Not meant to be a discography but rather a complete insight into Ellington's recorded efforts. This book is best suited as a cross-reference, index, and inventory. Does not include cassettes, reel-to-reel tapes, compact discs, laser discs, or videocassettes. Covers Ellington through 1953.

Bill Evans

1291. Larsen, Peter (compiler). *Bill Evans: The Complete Discography*. Holte, Denmark: the author; 1981.

Lists all known recordings, 1954–80, including those with Eddie Gomez, Scott LaFaro, and Miles Davis. The entries cover broadcasts, film work, transcriptions, and recording sessions. Each entry includes title, personnel, date, venue, master numbers, record numbers, and reissues where known. Index.

Maynard Ferguson

1292. Harkins, Edwin. *Maynard Ferguson: A Discography*. Holte, Denmark: Karl Emil Knudsen; 1976.

Uses standard discographical format; alphabetical listing by leader's surname, personnel by instrument, date and venue of recording, matrix numbers, titles, record numbers, and album titles. Album titles and numbers are at the end of the appropriate leader's section.

Shep Fields

1293. Garrod, Charles. *Shep Fields and His Orchestra.* Zephyrhills, Fla.: Joyce Music Publishers, revised; 1994.

Comprehensive, thorough, and includes corrections and updates to an earlier version and lists all known broadcasts, film work, recordings, and transcriptions. The entries include title, date, venue, label, personnel, master numbers, and reissues. Title index.

Ted Fio Rito and Ina Ray Hutton

1294. _____. *Ted Fio Rito and Ina Ray Hutton and Their Orchestras.* Zephyrhills, Fla.: Joyce Music Publishers; 1989.

The discography covers two important but little known artists. Fio Rito led groups that fit a myriad of situations, and Hutton (dancer, singer) led a female swing band in 1934. The entries include broadcasts, film work, recordings, and transcriptions. The entries include full discographical details: title, date, venue, label, personnel, master numbers, and reissues. Title index.

Ralph Flanagan

1295. _____. *Ralph Flanagan and His Orchestra.* Zephyrhills, Fla.: Joyce Music Publishers; 1990.

Details the broadcasts, film work, recordings, and transcriptions of this entertainment/jazz band. Entries cover the basic discographical information, including title, date, venue, label, personnel, master numbers, and reissues. Title index. Revised in 2000.

Helen Forrest

1296. _____. *Helen Forrest.* Zephyrhills, Fla.: Joyce Music Publications; 1993.

The first discography on this primarily big band vocalist. Contains a listing of all recordings and film work, and includes dates, labels, titles, venues, master numbers, reissues, and more.

Chuck Foster

1297. _____. *Chuck Foster and His Orchestra.* Zephyrhills, Fla.: Joyce Music Publishers; 1992.

Documents all known recordings, broadcasts, film work, and transcriptions. The entries include title, date, venue, label, personnel, master numbers, and reissues. Title index.

Jan Garber

1298. _____. *Jan Garber and His Orchestra.* Zephyrhills, Fla: Joyce Music Publishers; 1992.

A comprehensive listing of all broadcasts, film work, recordings, and transcriptions. Entries contain title, date, venue, label, personnel, master numbers, and reissues. Title index.

Stan Getz

1299. Astrup, Arne. *The Stan Getz Discography.* Foreword by Jerry L. Atkins. Texarkana, Tex.: Jerry L. Atkins; Hellerup, Copenhagen, Denmark: Arne Astrup; 1978.

Follows standard discographical methodology with date of recording, chronology, personnel, record number, and venues. The entries cover 1943–78 and include broadcasts, live sessions, and studio recordings. Appendix contains a list of album titles arranged by record label.

Dizzy Gillespie

1300. Jepsen, Jorgen Grunnet. *A Discography of Dizzy Gillespie.* Two volumes. Copenhagen: Knudsen; 1969.

A chronological listing of all recordings covering both the performer's band(s), and recordings with other bands. Complete discographical details are provided including date of recording, recording venue, matrix and take numbers, original and LP reissue numbers, and titles of compositions. No index.

Glen Gray

1301. Garrod, Charles, and Bill Korst. *Glen Gray and The Casa Loma Orchestra.* Zephyrhills, Fla.: Joyce Music Publications, revision; 1993.

In this revision, corrections and additions were made to the broadcasts, film work, recordings, and transcriptions previously listed. The entries include full discographical details, including title, date, venue, label, personnel, master numbers, and reissues. The Casa Loma band influenced several swing bands. Title index.

Jerry Gray

1302. Popa, Chris. *Jerry Gray and His Orchestra.* Zephyrhills, Fla.: Joyce Music Publications, revision; 1989.

Covers known broadcasts, film work, recordings, and transcriptions. Entries include title, date, venue, label, personnel, master numbers, and reissues. Although the band was popular, it never achieved the status of Basie, Ellington, Goodman, or Miller. Title index.

Wardell Gray

1303. Schlouch, Claude. *In Memory of Wardell Gray: A Discography.* Marseille, France: the author; 1983.

There is no introduction or preface. Includes full discographical citations of Gray's role as both leader and sideman. Entries include title, date, venue, label, personnel, master numbers, and reissues. Index of musicians and titles.

Coleman Hawkins

1304. Villetard, Jean Francois. *Coleman Hawkins, Volume One, 1922–1944 and Volume Two, 1945–1957.* Amsterdam: Micrography; 1984.

This discography does not include the numerous recordings that Hawkins made with the Fletcher Henderson orchestra from August 8, 1923, until March 6, 1936. Notwithstanding, this is a comprehensive chronological listing of all known preserved recordings. Unissued takes are only listed when a test pressing or tape was made. 78-rpm issues are not listed. Each entry includes title, label, date, venue, personnel, and matrix numbers. A description of each recording will be given in a future volume.

Erskine Hawkins

1305. Garrod, Charles. *Erskine Hawkins and His Orchestra.* Zephyrhills, Fla.: Joyce Music Publications; 1992.

Documents the broadcasts, recordings, and transcriptions of this important swing era band. Entries include title, label, date, venue, personnel, master numbers, and reissues.

Dick Haymes

1306. Garrod, Charles, and Denis Brown. *Dick Haymes and His Orchestra.* Zephyrhills, Fla.: Joyce Music Publications; 1990.

A comprehensive compilation of all known broadcasts, films, recordings, and transcriptions. Each entry includes title, label, date, venue, personnel, master numbers, and reissues.

Horace Heidt

1307.   Garrod, Charles. *Horace Heidt and His Orchestra*. Zephyrhills, Fla.: Joyce Music Publications; 1993.

Lists the broadcasts, films, recordings, and transcriptions of this swing band. Entries contain full discographical details including title, label, date, venue, personnel, master numbers, and reissues. Title index.

Woody Herman

1308.   _____. *Woody Herman and His Orchestra; Volume One (1936– 1947), Volume Two (1948–1957), and Volume Three (1958–1987)*. Zephyrhills, Fla.: Joyce Music Publications; 1985, 1986, 1988.

A comprehensive coverage of all known recording sessions, film work, broadcasts, and transcriptions. The entries include title, dates, venues, personnel, master numbers, and record numbers including reissues where known. Each volume contains an artist index.

1309.   Morrill, Dexter (compiler). *Woody Herman: A Guide to the Big Band Recordings, 1936–1987*. Westport, Conn.: Greenwood Press; 1990.

Begins with a preface that briefly outlines his interest in Herman, followed by an essay on "The Essential Recordings." In this section he uses recordings to provide insights into Herman's style (The Herd Bands to the Reunion years). The big band recordings are organized as: Early Bands; First Herd; Second Herd; Third Herd; Thundering Herds; and the Carnegie Hall Concert. There are also sections on "Trombone Solo Ballads," "Stan Getz Solos," "First Herd Repertoire," and "Twelve-Inch Long-Playing Records," and "Woody Herman on Compact Disc."

1310.   Treichel, James A. *Keeper of the Flame: Woody Herman and the Second Herd, 1947–1949*. Zephyrhills, Fla.: Joyce Music Publications; 1978.

Contains all recording sessions, including dates, title, venue, personnel, master numbers, record numbers, and reissues where known. Also includes film work, broadcasts, and transcriptions. Index.

Tiny Hill and Ray Herbeck

1311.   Garrod, Charles. *Tiny Hill and His Orchestra/Ray Herbeck*. Zephyrhills, Fla.: Joyce Music Publications; 1992.

Includes known broadcasts, films, recordings, and transcriptions. Each entry contains title, date, venue, label, personnel, master numbers, and where necessary, reissue(s). Title index.

Richard Himber

1312. _____. *Richard Himber and His Orchestra.* Zephyrhills, Fla.: Joyce Music Publications; 1993.

Lists all known dates, recordings, labels, titles, venue, master numbers, and reissues.

Billie Holiday and Teddy Wilson

1313. Bakker, Dick M. *Billie and Teddy on Microgroove, 1932–1944.* Alphen aan den Rijn: Micrography; 1975.

Focuses on LP collectors, contains the 181 Billie Holiday reissues and Teddy Wilson's 371 recordings for Brunswick, Okeh, and Vocalion. Holiday's 1944 Commodore recordings are also included. Full discographical details with the exception of matrix and original LP numbers; he chose to include LP reissue numbers instead. The recordings are numbered sequentially. Artist and title indexes.

1314. Jepsen, Jorgen Grunnet. *A Discography of Billie Holiday.* Copenhagen: Knudsen; 1969.

A chronological listing of all recordings covering both Holiday's band(s), and recordings with other bands. Complete discographical details are provided, including date of recording, recording venue, matrix and take numbers, original release and LP reissue numbers, and titles of compositions. No index.

1315. Miller, Jack. *Born To Sing: A Discography of Billie Holiday.* Copenhagen: Jazzmedia; 1979.

A continuation and expansion of Jorgen Grunnet Jepsen's *A Discography of Billie Holiday,* by detailing numerous radio broadcasts, television shows, and performances, and by providing a comprehensive list of LP reissues, Holiday sessions (but not titles of all the compositions recorded), an artist name index, and some comments and notes.

Eddy Howard

1316. Garrod, Charles. *Eddy Howard and His Orchestra.* Zephyrhills, Fla.: Joyce Music Publishers; 1994.

Follows the format of other Joyce publications by listing all known broadcasts, films, recordings, and transcriptions. The entries follow standard discographical format, including title, date, venue, label, personnel, mater numbers, and reissues. Title index.

Milt Jackson

1317. Wilbraham, Roy. *Milt Jackson: A Discography and Biography,* including recordings made with the M.J.Q. London: the author; 1968.

Complete listing of Jackson's recordings as a bandleader and sideman (M.J.Q.) to 1968. The listings are organized chronologically, and include dates, recording, venues, and titles. The biography covers his life and musical career. Index of compositions included.

Harry James

1318. Garrod, Charles, and Peter Johnson. *Harry James and His Orchestra, Volumes 1, 2, and 3.* Zephyrhills, Fla.: Joyce Music Publications; 1975.

Volume 1 covers 1937–1945, volume 2, 1946–1954, and volume 3, 1955–1982. Draws on the work of Ernest Edwards, and includes all recording sessions, dates, locations, titles, master numbers, and record numbers with reissues where known. Broadcasts, films, and transcriptions are also included. Title index.

Isham Jones

1319. Garrod, Charles. *Isham Jones and His Orchestra.* Zephyrhills, Fla.: Joyce Music Publications; 1993.

Chronicles the broadcasts, films, recordings, and transcriptions, including dates, venues, titles, label, personnel, master numbers, and reissues. Title index.

Spike Jones

1320. _____. *Spike Jones and His City Slickers.* Zephyrhills, Fla.: Joyce Music Publications; 1989.

Although not known solely as a leader of jazz band, the discography is important because of Jones's jazz-related recordings. The discography includes all known dates, labels, recordings, films, personnel, master numbers, and reissues.

Louis Jordan

1321. _____. *Louis Jordan and His Orchestra.* Zephyrhills, Fla.: Joyce Music Publications; 1994.

Contains the dates, recordings, titles, labels, venues, master numbers, films and more. Lists all known popular and jazz-related compositions.

Dick Jurgens

1322. _____. *Dick Jurgens and His Orchestra.* Zephyrhills, Fla.: Joyce Music Publications; 1988.

Cites all known broadcasts, films, recordings, and transcriptions. Entries include title, date, venue, label, personnel, master numbers, and reissues. Title index.

Art Kassell and Johnny Messner

1323. _____. *Art Kassell and His Orchestra/Johnny Messner and His Orchestra.* Zephyrhills, Fla.: Joyce Music Publications; 1993.

Documents known broadcasts, films, recordings, and transcriptions. Entries include title, date, venue, label, personnel, master numbers, and reissues. Title index.

Sammy Kaye

1324. _____. *Sammy Kaye and His Orchestra.* Zephyrhills, Fla.: Joyce Music Publications; 2000. Two volumes.

The first volume covers the 1937–48 years, and the second covers the 1949–75 years. The citations cover dates, titles, personnel, venues, labels, master numbers, and reissues. All known broadcasts and film work are also included.

Hal Kemp and Art Jarrett

1325. _____. *Hal Kemp/Art Jarrett.* Zephyrhills, Fla.: Joyce Music Publications; 1990.

Provides known broadcasts, films, recordings, and transcriptions. Entries cover essential discographical details, including title, date, venue, label, personnel, master numbers, and reissues. Title index.

Stan Kenton

1326. _____. *Stan Kenton and His Orchestra; Volume One (1940–1951), Volume Two (1952–1959), and Volume Three (1960–1979).* Zephyrhills, Fla.: Joyce Music Publications; 1984, 1991.

Comprehensive coverage of all known broadcasts, films, recordings, and transcriptions. Includes title, date, venue, label, personnel, master numbers, and reissues. Coverage is accurate and thorough. Title index.

1327. Pirie, Christopher A., and Siegfried Mueller. *Artistry in Kenton: The Bio-Discography of Stan Kenton and His Music.* Volume 1. Vienna: Siegfried Muller, 1969; Volume 2, Vienna: Mueller, 1972.

Lists all Kenton broadcasts, commercial releases, and transcriptions of radio programs made from 1937 to late November 1953. Full discographical details and comments on each session are included in the biographical essay. There is an index of first recordings, artists, itinerary, and a list of arrangers in each volume.

1328. Venudor, Pete, and Michael Sparke. *The Standard Kenton Directory. Volume 1, 1937–1949.* Amsterdam: Pete Venudor; 1968.

Detailed listing of broadcasts, recordings, and sound tracks. An index of titles, choreographed "Kentonia," and filmography are also provided.

Henry King

1329. Garrod, Charles. *Henry King and His Orchestra.* Zephyrhills, Fla.: Joyce Music Publications; 1994.

Covers all jazz and popular recordings, broadcasts, and transcriptions. Includes title, date, venue, personnel, master number, and reissues where warranted for each entry. Title index.

Wayne King

1330. _____. *Wayne King and His Orchestra.* Zephyrhills, Fla.: Joyce Music Publications; 1994.

Documents known broadcasts, films, recordings, and transcriptions. The entries contain title, date, venue, personnel, master number, and reissues where appropriate. Title index.

John Kirby and Andy Kirk

1331. _____. *John Kirby/Andy Kirk and Their Orchestras.* Zephyrhills, Fla.: Joyce Music Publications; 1991.

Provides details of known broadcasts, films, recordings, and transcriptions of these two giants. The discographical details include title, date, venue, personnel, master number, and some reissues. Title index.

Gene Krupa

1332. _____. *Gene Krupa and His Orchestra, Volume One (1935–1946) and Volume Two (1947–1973)*. Zephyrhills, Fla.: Joyce Music Publications; 1992.

Covers his broadcasts, films, recordings, and transcriptions as a leader and sideman. The entries include title, date, venue, personnel, master number, and reissues where appropriate. Title index.

Kay Kyser

1333. _____. *Kay Kyser and His Orchestra*. Zephyrhills, Fla.: Joyce Music Publications, revision; 1992.

Revision, correction, and expansion of an earlier edition. The entries include broadcasts, films, recordings, and transcriptions. Entries include title, date, venue, label, personnel, master numbers, and some reissues. Title index.

Elliott Lawrence

1334. _____. *Elliott Lawrence and His Orchestra*. Zephyrhills, Fla.: Joyce Music Publications; 1987.

Lists all known broadcasts, films, recordings, and transcriptions. The entries include title, date, venue, label, personnel, master numbers, and reissues where appropriate. Title index.

Ted Lewis

1335. _____. *Ted Lewis and His Orchestra*. Zephyrhills, Fla.: Joyce Music Publications; 1994.

A compilation of all dates, recordings, labels, personnel, venues, master numbers, reissues, and film work.

Guy Lombardo

1336. Kressley, Dave, and Charles Garrod. *Guy Lombardo and His Royal Canadians*. Zephyrhills, Fla.: Joyce Music Publications; 1995–1996. Four volumes.

The four volumes cover the 1924–45, 1946–50, 1952–61, and 1962–77 years, respectively. Comprehensive and thorough, the discography contains all known recordings and film work. Each entry also includes a date, title, label, list of personnel, master numbers, venues, reissues, and more.

Johnny Long

1337. Garrod, Charles. *Johnny Long and His Orchestra.* Zephyrhills, Fla.: Joyce Music Publications, revision; 1993.

The revision includes corrections and expanded entries along with broadcasts, films, recordings, and transcriptions. The entries include title, date, venue, label, personnel, master numbers, and reissues where appropriate. Title index.

Vincent Lopez

1338. _____. *Vincent Lopez and His Orchestra.* Zephyrhills, Fla.: Joyce Music Publications; 1994.

Lists all broadcasts, films, recordings, and transcriptions. The entries include title, date, venue, label, personnel, master numbers, and reissues where appropriate. Title index.

Clyde Lucas, Al Kavelin, Carl Ravazza, and Ted Straeter.

1339. _____. *Clyde Lucas, Al Kavelin, Carl Ravazza, and Ted Straeter and Their Orchestras.* Zephyrhills, Fla.: Joyce Music Publications; 1995.

Includes all discographical information including dates, labels, recordings, titles, personnel, venue, master numbers, and some reissues.

Jimmie Lunceford

1340. _____. *Jimmie Lunceford and His Orchestra.* Zephyrhills, Fla.: Joyce Music Publications; 1990.

Documents the broadcasts, films, recordings, and transcriptions of this significant band. The entries include title, date, venue, label, personnel, master numbers, and reissues where appropriate. The entries are inclusive of jazz versions of popular songs and jazz tunes. Title index.

Abe Lyman

1341. _____. *Abe Lyman.* Zephyrhills, Fla.: Joyce Music Publications; 1995.

Contains all known recordings plus dates, titles, personnel, venues, master numbers, reissues, and more.

Richard Maltby

1342. _____. *Richard Maltby and His Orchestra.* Zephyrhills, Fla.: Joyce Music Publications; 1994.

Chronicles the broadcasts, films, recordings, and transcriptions of this pseudojazz band. The entries include title, date, venue, label, personnel, master numbers, and reissues where appropriate. Title index.

Wingy Manone

1343. _____. *Wingy Manone and His Orchestra.* Zephyrhills, Fla.: Joyce Music Publications; 1994.

Concise but complete listing of all recordings with dates, titles, personnel, venues, master numbers, and reissues.

Ralph Marterie

1344. _____. *Ralph Marterie and His Orchestra.* Zephyrhills, Fla.: Joyce Music Publications; 1994.

Includes known broadcasts, films, recordings, and transcriptions. Although most of the entries are devoted to his popular recordings, some jazz citations are included. Each entry includes title, date, venue, label, personnel, master numbers, and reissues where appropriate. Title index.

Freddy Martin

1345. _____. *Freddy Martin and His Orchestra.* Zephyrhills, Fla.: Joyce Music Publications; 1990.

A comprehensive compilation of broadcasts, films, recordings, and transcriptions. The entries include title, date, venue, label, personnel, master numbers, and reissues where appropriate. Title index.

Frankie Masters

1346. _____. *Frankie Masters and His Orchestra.* Zephyrhills, Fla.: Joyce Music Publications; 1992.

Details known broadcasts, films, recordings, and personnel of this dance band. The discography is weighted heavily toward popular recordings and contains title, date, venue, label, and personnel for each entry. Title index.

Billy May

1347. _____. *Billy May and His Orchestra*. Zephyrhills, Fla.: Joyce Music Publications; 1991.

A comprehensive listing of broadcasts, films, recordings, and transcriptions. Entries cover title, date, venue, label, personnel, master numbers, and reissues where appropriate. Title index.

Hal McIntyre

1348. _____. *Hal McIntyre and His Orchestra*. Zephyrhills, Fla.: Joyce Music Publications; 1988.

Covers his broadcasts, films, recordings, and transcriptions. Included are some of his vocal recordings. Each entry includes title, date, venue, label, personnel, master numbers, and reissues where appropriate. Title index.

Ray McKinley

1349. _____. *Ray McKinley and His Orchestra*. Zephyrhills, Fla.: Joyce Music Publications; 1988.

Revision of an earlier edition, includes known broadcasts, films, recordings, and transcriptions. The entries are comprehensive and contain title, date, venue, label, personnel, master numbers, and reissues where appropriate. Title index.

McKinney's Cotton Pickers

1350. Chilton, John. *McKinney's Music: A Bio-Discography of McKinney's Cotton Pickers*. London: Bloomsbury Book Shop; 1978.

An excellent work on an unsung band that rivaled the greatness of Moten, Ellington, and Jay McShann during its heyday (1920s). The band included jazz greats like Don Redman (who later became known as an arranger), Ben Webster, and Clarence Holiday (Billie Holiday's father, a banjoist). Information was gleaned from guitarist/vocalist Dave Wilborn. Includes information on the music and musical context. Biographical portraits of musicians, discography, matrix numbers, titles, personnel, arranger of each recorded composition, and names of all soloists. Selected bibliography and references.

Jackie McLean

1351. Wilbraham, Roy. *Jackie McLean: A Discography with Biography.* London: the author; 1967.

Complete listing of McLean's recordings to 1967. The listings are organized chronologically and include detailed information including dates, recording venues, and titles. A succinct biographical sketch and an index of compositions are included.

Carmen McRae

1352. Brown, Denis. *Carmen McRae: A Discography.* Zephyrhills, Fla.: Joyce Music Publications; 2001.

Complete listing of all recordings with dates, titles, labels, master numbers, venues, and reissues.

Glenn Miller

1353. Garrod, Charles. *Glenn Miller and His Orchestra.* Zephyrhills, Fla.: Joyce Music Publications; 1995. Three volumes.

The three volumes cover the 1935–40, 1941–42, and 1943–44 years, respectively. Includes all known recordings, titles, dates, labels, personnel, master numbers, and reissues. Also includes all known film work and transcriptions of Miller.

Charles Mingus

1354. _____. *Charles Mingus: A Biography and Discography.* London: the author; 1967.

Complete listings of Mingus's recordings to 1967. The listings are organized chronologically and include detailed discographical information, including dates, recording venues, and titles. A concise biographical sketch and an index of compositions are included.

Thelonious Monk and Bud Powell

1355. Jepsen, Jorgen Grunnet. *A Discography of Thelonious Monk and Bud Powell.* Copenhagen: Knudsen; 1969.

A chronological listing of all recordings covering both the performers' bands and recordings with other bands. Complete discographical details are provided including date of recording, recording venue, matrix and take

numbers, original release and LP reissue numbers, and titles of compositions. No index.

Vaughan Monroe

1356. Garrod, Charles. *Vaughan Monroe and His Orchestra*. Zephyrhills, Fla.:
Joyce Music Publishers; 1987.

Contains known broadcasts, films, recordings, and transcriptions of this
popular dance band. Lists titles, dates, venues, labels, personnel, master
numbers, and reissues. Title index.

Russ Morgan

1357. _____. *Russ Morgan and His Orchestra*. Zephyrhills, Fla.: Joyce Music
Publishers; 1993.

Provides known broadcasts, films, recordings, and transcriptions of his
entire repertoire. Most of the entries are dance band recordings rather than
jazz compositions. Each entry contains a title, date, venue, label, personnel,
master number, and if necessary, a reissue. Title index.

Buddy Morrow

1358. _____. *Buddy Morrow and His Orchestra*. Zephyrhills, Fla.: Joyce Music
Publications; 1995.

Details all known recordings, dates, labels, titles, personnel, master numbers, venues, reissues, and film work.

Jelly Roll Morton

1359. Cusack, Thomas. *Jelly Roll Morton: An Essay in Discography*. London:
Cassell; 1952.

Discusses the musical characteristics of selected recordings focusing on
continuity and change.

1360. Davies, John R. T., and Laurie Wright. *Morton's Music*. London: Storyville
Publications; 1968.

The discography is divided into three sections: piano rolls, commercial
discs, and Library of Congress recordings. Full discographical information
including date and venue of recording, matrix and catalog numbers, personnel, and titles, is provided for the commercial discs and the Library
of Congress recordings. Mirogroove reissues and alternate takes are also
noted. Disposition instructions are provided for change of intent and title,

and the original instructions are provided for the Columbia and Victor recordings.

1361.   Hill, Michael, and Eric Bryce. *Jelly Roll Morton: A Microgroove Discography and Musical Analysis.* (Occasional Papers, No. 16). Salisbury East, South Australia: Salisbury College of Advanced Education; 1977.

A limited approach to both analysis and discography. Only three transcriptions (analyses are offered): "Seattle Hunch," "Mr. Jelly Lord," and "Kansas City Stomp." Includes a two-part listing of Morton's LP reissues. Both the analyses and discography are deficient; therefore, the book is of limited use to Morton scholars. The book does not rival James DaPogny's classic Morton study. Selected bibliography.

1362.   Wright, Laurie. *Mr. Jelly Lord;* with special contributions by John H. Cowley, John R. T. Davies, Mike Montgomery, Roger Richards, and Horace Spear. Chigwell, Essex: Storyville Publications; 1980.

Details all Morton recordings including radio broadcasts, Library of Congress sessions, Microgroove reissues, and piano rolls. Included in the text is biographical and historical information. The usual discographical information on composer credits, date of recording, recording venues, matrix and take numbers, issue numbers, instruments, personnel, title, and take numbers, is given. Davies contributes notation on alternative recordings, reference notes, and concise vignettes on session personnel. The Library of Congress listings contain original comments from John H. Cowley as well as notes originally made by Alan Lomax. In addition, there is a Microgroove reissues section and a section entitled "Miscellaneous Mortonia," which contains the text of unissued Library of Congress recordings, a list of copyright holders of Morton's compositions, and a photographic essay. There are indices of names, places, and titles.

Ozzie Nelson

1363.   Garrod, Charles, and Bill Korst. *Ozzie Nelson and His Orchestra.* Zephyrhills, Fla.: Joyce Music Publications; 1991.

Concise but complete listing of broadcasts, films, recordings, and transcriptions. The discography is permeated with dance band recordings rather than jazz compositions. Each entry contains a title, date, venue, label, personnel, and master number. Reissues are cited where appropriate. Title index.

Ray Noble

1364.   Garrod, Charles. *Ray Noble and His Orchestra.* Zephyrhills, Fla.: Joyce Music Publications; 1991.

In addition to the broadcasts, films, recordings, and transcriptions, this comprehensive discography includes several reissues. Each entry contains a title, date, venue, label, personnel, and master number. Contains several reissues of "Cherokee," a composition written by Noble. Title index.

Anita O'Day

1365. Wolfer, Jurgen. *Anita O'Day.* Zephyrhills, Fla.: Joyce Music Publications; 1990.

Among the comprehensive listings are broadcasts, films, recordings, and transcriptions, including several with Stan Kenton. The entries contain title, date, venue, label, personnel, master number, and if necessary, a reissue. Title index.

King Oliver

1366. Allen, Walter C., and Brian A. C. Rust. *King Joe Oliver.* Bellville, New Jersey: Allen, 1955; London: Jazz Book Club, 1957; London: Sidgwick and Jackson, 1958, 1960; Chigwell, England: Storyville, 1987.

A biodiscography that focuses on Oliver's influences and compositions. The discography is comprehensive and includes composer, catalogue numbers, date, personnel, venue, and soloists for each entry. The discography is organized in chronological order. The appendix contains Oliver's orchestra's itinerary, 1934–35. There are indices of recorded titles, personnel, catalog numbers, and rare recordings. The 1987 edition was revised by Laurie Wright and includes a foreword by Ann Allen. Also includes some unpublished interview material. Index.

Sy Oliver

1367. Garrod, Charles. *Sy Oliver and His Orchestra.* Zephyrhills, Fla.: Joyce Music Publications; 1993.

Gives the broadcasts, films, recordings, and transcriptions of this excellent swing band. Sy Oliver is known for both his arranging-composing and bandleader skills. The entries contain a title, date, venue, label, personnel, master number, and if necessary, a reissue. Title index.

Will Osborne

1368. _____. *Will Osborne and His Orchestra.* Zephyrhills, Fla.: Joyce Music Publications; 1991.

Presents all dates, known recordings, labels, titles, personnel, master numbers, venue, reissues, and film work.

Oran "Hot Lips" Page

1369. Demeusy, Bertrand, Otto Flückiger, Jorgen Grunnet Jepsen, and Kurt Mohr. *Hot Lips Page.* Basel: Jazz Publications; 1961.

Follows the format established by Charles Delaunay in *New Hot Discography.* Oran "Hot Lips" Page was one of the great trumpet players in Kansas City in the 1930s; his style was rooted in Louis Armstrong. This discography includes a concise biography and a complete listing of Page's recordings with both his band and other bands. The listings cover the 1935–54 period. Some listings lack complete discography details; however, personnel listings and travel itineraries are cited for some listings.

Charlie Parker

1370. Jepsen, Jorgen Grunnet. *A Discography of Charlie Parker.* Copenhagen: Knudsen; 1968.

A chronological listing of all recordings covering both Parker's band and recordings with other bands. Complete discographical details are provided including date of recording, recording venue, matrix and take numbers, original release and LP reissue numbers, and title of compositions. No index.

1371. Koster, Piet, and Dick M. Bakker. *Charlie Parker.* Volume 1, 1940–1947. Alphen aan den Rijn: Micrography; 1974; Volume 2, 1948–1950; 1975.

Two volumes of a projected four volume series containing listings on broadcasts, private recordings, and commercial releases. The published and projected volumes are organized as follows: Volumes 1 and 2 contain the Dial recordings; volume 3 is projected to cover 1951–54; and volume 4 will focus on additions, corrections, combined indices, omissions, and a list of compositions based on the contrafact. Full discographical details and a list of the Microgroove releases are included.

1372. Koster, Piet, and Harm Mobach. *Bird Lore: A Revised Charlie Parker Discography.* Amsterdam: Spectrum U.P., 2002.

The revised discography is issued in three volumes and is a complete listing of his recordings as a leader and sideman.

1373. Williams, Tony. "Charlie Parker Discography." *Discographical Forum* 2, no. 1 (Nov. 1968): 8–20.

Provides comprehensive and accurate discographical information.

Tony Pastor

1374. Garrod, Charles. *Tony Pastor and His Orchestra.* Zephyrhills, Fla.: Joyce Music Publications; 2000.

The only known discography on this artist. The discography cites recordings, date, titles, labels, master numbers, venues, reissues, and film work.

Bud Powell

1375. Schlouch, Claude. *Bud Powell: A Discography.* Marseille, France: the author; 1983.

There is no biography, introduction, or preface. Lists all known Powell recordings as a leader and sideman. Each entry contains a title, date, venue, label, personnel, matrix number, and when known, reissue. Index of titles, 1944–1966.

Louis Prima

1376. Garrod, Charles. *Louis Prima and His Orchestra.* Zephyrhills, Fla.: Joyce Music Publications; 1991.

This discography includes broadcasts, films, recordings, and transcriptions, with listings of title, date, venue, label, personnel, master numbers, and where appropriate, reissue, for each entry. Title index.

Boyd Raeburn

1377. Garrod, Charles, and Bill Korst. *Boyd Raeburn and His Orchestra.* Zephyrhills, Fla.: Joyce Music Publications; 1985.

Covers both his dance band and fusion of bebop and European concert music recordings, plus broadcasts, films and transcriptions. Each entry contains a title, date, venue, label, personnel, master numbers, and where appropriate, reissue, for each entry. Title index.

Harry Reser

1378. Triggs, W. W. *The Great Harry Reser.* London: Henry G. Alker; 1980.

A biodiscography of the 1920s band leader and banjoist. In addition to the biographical details, Triggs also provides an informative assessment of Reser's musical attributes. Discographical listings include date of recording, matrix numbers, release numbers, titles, and recording venues. No personnel are cited. A meticulous piece of research, as Reser used numerous pseudonyms, and because it provides informative material on a good, but not highly significant, musician of the 1920s.

Alvino Rey and The King Sisters

1379. Garrod, Charles, and Bill Korst. *Alvino Rey and The King Sisters, 1939–1958.* Zephyrhills, Fla.: Joyce Music Publications; 1986.

Documents the broadcasts, films, recordings, and transcriptions of these dance band musicians. The groups were known primarily for their popular music contributions rather than jazz. A title, date, venue, label, list of personnel, and master number is included for each entry. Reissues are also cited. Title index.

Buddy Rich

1380. Cooper, David J. *Buddy Rich Discography.* Blackburn, Lancaster: the author; 1975.

A biodiscography of broadcasts and recordings from 1938 to 1973. Broadcasts are arranged chronologically and are supplemented with succinct biographical comments. Each listing contains the date of recording, recording venue, release numbers, personnel, and titles.

Shorty Rogers

1381. Hofmann, Coen, and Erik M. Bakker. *Shorty Rogers: A Discography.* Two volumes. Amsterdam: Micrography; 1983.

Volume 1 (1945–51) covers his career as a sideman through Woody Herman, and volume 2 focuses on the 1952–69 years. Includes recording sessions as a sideman and leader, with dates, venues, personnel, master numbers, record numbers, transcriptions, and reissues.

1382. Hofmann, Coen, and Gerard Hoogeveen. *Shorty Rogers Discography.* Amsterdam: Spectrum U.P., 2002.

A revised edition of the 1983 discography that includes updated performances and personnel that was either omitted or needed correcting from the first edition.

Sonny Rollins

1383. Keepnews, Orrin (producer). *Sonny Rollins: The Complete Prestige Recordings.* New York: Fantasy; 1992.

Discusses the recordings and associations with several significant sidemen. The booklet is concise and includes anecdotes and some historical information. Among those that accompanied Rollins on the recordings were Walter Bishop, Jr., Art Blakey, Clifford Brown, Paul Chambers, John Coltrane, Miles Davis, Kenny Dorham, Bennie Green, Ray Haynes, J. J. Johnson, Jackie McLean, Thelonious Monk, Charlie Parker, Max Roach, and Horace Silver.

Pee Wee Russell

1384. Hilbert, Robert, with David Niven. *Pee Wee Speaks: A Discography of Pee Wee Russell.* Metuchen, N.J.: Scarecrow Press; 1992.

Documents Russell's recording career from his first recording in 1922 to his last recording on a Mississippi riverboat in 1968. This discography contains all of his known commercial recordings as well as information on film soundtracks, private recordings, broadcasts, and concerts, including recordings with Bix Beiderbecke and Thelonious Monk. The entries are listed in alphabetical order with band names and song titles. Index.

Bob Scobey

1385. Goggin, Jim. *Bob Scobey: A Bibliography and Discography.* San Leandro, Calif.: the author; 1977.

Attempts to cover all known recordings where he is either a leader or a sideman, including dates, venues, instruments, personnel, privately held tapes, and records. The bibliography includes books, newspapers, and periodicals that refer to Scobey. The discography is permeated with gaps and inaccuracies.

Artie Shaw

1386. Garrod, Charles, and Bill Korst. *Artie Shaw and His Orchestra.* Zephyrhills, Fla.: Joyce Music Publications; 1986.

Comprehensive listing of broadcasts, films, personnel, and transcriptions. Discographical information includes title, date, venue, label, personnel, master number, and reissues. Title index.

Zoot Sims

1387. Astrup, Arne. *The John Haley Sims (Zoot Sims) Discography.* Lyngby, Denmark: Danis Discographical Publishing Company; 1980.

Contains a concise biography (only two pages) that outlines his beginnings, musical associations, and successes. The discography details recordings that he made as a sideman plus those he made as a bandleader. The entries include titles, personnel, venue, labels, and matrix numbers. There is also a list of "The Most Important Album Titles" in the index.

Frank Sinatra

1388. Garrod, Charles. *Frank Sinatra; Volume One, 1935–1951, and Volume Two, 1952–1981.* Zephyrhills, Fla.: Joyce Music Publications; 1986.

Comprehensive and detailed coverage of broadcasts, films, recordings, and transcriptions to the early 1980s. Includes listings as a sideman and leader, and each entry contains a title, date, venue, label, personnel, and master number. Reissues are also cited. Title index.

1389. Lonstein, Albert, and Vito R. Marino. *The Revised Complete Sinatra: Discography, Filmography, Television Appearances, Motion Picture Appearances, Radio Appearances, Concert Appearances, and Stage Appearances.* Ellenville, N.Y.: Cameron Publications, LTD; 1970. Second edition.

Unlike the first edition, which did not contain a usable song index, and omitted some performances, this edition is complete to the date of publication. Also, in this edition the authors include dates and names with thee photographs. Whereas the first four chapters are complete, some songs of his later appearances are missing. For example, Frank Driggs made Capitol and Reprise Records files available, however the Paramount Theater files were not, hence the lack of illusion without verification. Contains an index of arranger, orchestras, songs, composers, soloist, and vocalists and vocal groups.

Charlie Spivak

1390. _____. *Charlie Spivak and His Orchestra.* Zephyrhills, Fla.: Joyce Music Publications; 1974.

Draws on the work done by Ernest Edwards, and lists all recordings sessions, broadcasts, films, and transcriptions. Each entry contains a title, date, venue, label, personnel, and master number. Reissues are also cited. Title index and other references.

Art Tatum

1391. Laubich, Arnold, and Ray Spencer. *Art Tatum: A Guide to His Recorded Music.* Metuchen, N.J., and London: Scarecrow Press and The Institute of Jazz Studies; 1982.

A comprehensive and detailed listing of Tatum's issued and unissued discs and sessions. The entries include title, date, venue, label, personnel, master number, record number, transcriptions, published music, and piano rolls. Also includes a matrix cross reference list, a list of other discographies examined, and a quick-dating guide. Very thorough.

Jack Teagarden

1392. Garrod, Charles. *Jack Teagarden and His Orchestra.* Zephyrhills, Fla.: Joyce Music Publications; 1993.

Covers his career as a sideman and bandleader by surveying broadcasts, films, recordings, and transcriptions. Entries include title, date, venue, personnel, label, master number, and reissues. Title index.

1393. Waters, Jr., Howard J. *Jack Teagarden's Music: His Career and Recordings;* foreword by Paul Whiteman and artwork by E. Richard Frerière. Stanhope, N.J.: Walter C. Allen; 1960.

Begins with a biography, and includes several photographs divided into "Jack Teagarden and his Trombone," "The 1923–1938 Period," and "1939–1959 Period." The biography is limited to his professional career beginning with his formative years in Texas and the Southwest to his tour of Asia in 1958 for the U.S. State Department. The discography covers his career to 1959 and includes titles, personnel, venues, dates, master numbers, and record numbers. Also includes transcriptions, tapes, 45s, and 78s. The appendices are entitled "Characteristics of the Teagarden Style," "A Selection of 21 Representative Teagarden Recordings," and "Itinerary of Jack Teagarden's Professional Engagements." Index of catalogue numbers, tune titles, personnel, and recording groups. Bibliography.

Clark Terry

1394. Raditzky, Carlos de. *A 1960–1967 Clark Terry Discography, with Biographical Notes.* Antwerp: United Hot Club of Europe; 1968.

Continuation of the 1947–1960 discography by Malcolm Walker (*Jazz Monthly,* December 1961 to April 1962, Five Issues). Unfortunately, Terry's excellent recordings with the Duke Ellington band are omitted. Includes a concise biographical essay (few musical details) and standard discographical information. Additions and corrections were published in the October 21, 1968, and January 22, 1969, issues of *Jazz Journal.* No indices.

Claude Thornhill

1395. Garrod, Charles. *Claude Thornhill and His Orchestra.* Zephyrhills, Fla.: Joyce Music Publications; 1985.

Documents the broadcasts, films, recordings, and transcriptions of this influential big band. The entries feature several arrangements by Gil Evans, and a title, date, venue, label, personnel list, master numbers, and reissues. Title index.

Sarah Vaughan

1396. Brown, Dennis (compiler). *Sarah Vaughan: A Discography.* Westport, Conn.: Greenwood Press; 1991.

Begins with a preface that concisely outlines Brown's first introduction to Vaughan, and includes details concerning how to use the discography. The discography is divided into: The Chronological Sessions Data; Song Titles and Composers; Record Company Issues; and Indexes of Musicians and Orchestras. Each section is subdivided; each part contains titles, orchestra type, personnel, date, and venue. Selected references (bibliography).

Joe Venuti

1397. Garrod, Charles. *Joe Venuti and His Orchestra.* Zephyrhills, Fla.: Joyce Music Publications; 1993.

Among the comprehensive entries, includes those featuring Eddie Lang and the All-Star Orchestra. Also covers broadcasts, films, recordings, and transcriptions. Each entry contains a title, date, venue, label, personnel list, master numbers, and reissues where warranted. Title index.

Thomas "Fats" Waller

1398. Davies, John R. T. *The Music of Thomas "Fats" Waller with Complete Discography.* London: Jazz Journal Publications, 1950; revised by R. T. Cooke, London: "Friends of Fats" (Thomas "Fats" Waller Appreciation Society); 1953.

Covers discs, films, soundtracks, and radio broadcasts made between 1922 and 1943 as bandleader, accompanist, sideman, and soloist. Full discographical details are provided. The revised version lists more sessions, contains insightful comments, and includes a title index. Both editions contain introductory essays and a list of piano roll titles. Subsequent revisions appeared in *Storyville* editions, beginning with number 2. There are approximately 600 recordings cited.

Ted Weems

1399. Garrod, Charles. *Ted Weems and His Orchestra.* Zephyrhills, Fla.: Joyce Music Publications; 1990.

Lists known broadcasts, films, recordings, and transcriptions. The entries are concentrated on both dance and popular recordings. Discographical information includes title, date, venue, label, personnel list, master numbers, and reissues. Title index.

Clarence Williams

1400. Bakker, Dick M. *Clarence Williams on Microgroove.* Alphen aan den Rijn: Micrography; 1976.

An attempt to improve the reliability and validity of Tom Lord's Clarence Williams discography. Contains full discographical information and a complete list of the Microgroove recordings.

1401. Lord, Tom. *Clarence Williams.* Chigwell, Essex: Storyville Publications; 1976.

Detailed biodiscography of Williams's life and music. The biographical portrait contains critical comments and was fashioned from numerous written sources. Each listing includes composer credits, copyright composer, copyright holder, date of recording, instrumentation, recording venue, matrix and take details, and personnel information. He provides session details like the number of choruses, name of performer, and key of composition. Unfortunately, some of Lord's discographical details are both incomplete and inaccurate. Also included are transcriptions of musical phrases, an inaccurate discography of sessions, titles of his compositions, a list of his compositions recorded by other artists, personnel associated with him (with dates of recordings), and live performances. The index contains record catalogue numbers (some Microgroove are incorrect).

Lester Young

1402. Jepsen, Jorgen Grunnet. *A Discography of Lester Young.* Copenhagen: Knudsen; 1968.

A chronological listing of all recordings with other bands. Complete discographical details are provided including date of recording, recording venue, matrix and take numbers, original release and LP reissue numbers, and title of compositions. No index.

Sy Zentner

1403. Wolfer, Jurgen. *Sy Zentner and His Orchestra.* Zephyrhills, Fla.: Joyce Music Publications; 1981.

Chronicles broadcasts, films, recordings, and transcriptions. Follows standard discographical information with title, date, venue, label, personnel list, master numbers, and reissues. Title index.

Collective Discographies

1404. Avakian, George. *Jazz from Columbia; A Complete Jazz Catalog.* New York: Columbia Records; 1956.

A limited listing devoted to jazz albums recorded on Columbia records. There are 150 entries arranged by categories, with each category preceded by a concise introductory essay. The essays cover basic information and are geared to nonjazz audiences. Although titles of albums are cited, the entries lack any other discographical details.

1405. Bauza, Jose. *Jazz: Grabaciones maestros.* Alicante: Instituto de Estudios Jaun Gil-Albert; 1982.

In Spanish. A discography that highlights the most significant recordings of numerous jazz and blues musicians. Bauza offers concise essays on the characteristics of various individuals' style, spirituals, minstrels and cake-walks, blues, and New Orleans. The second section includes discussions of "Livery Stable Blues" (ODJB), the New Orleans Rhythm Kings, Ma Rainey, Duke Ellington, and Louis Armstrong to 1929, focusing on personnel with some historical comments. Contains an epilogue and a chronological listing by artist or group of recordings discussed.

1406. Belaire, David. *A Guide to the Big Band Era: A Comprehensive Review of All Recorded Hits and All the Hitmakers.* Santa Ana, Calif.: Winged Note Press; 1996.

Lists facts about popular music in America prior to the middle of the twentieth century, ostensibly around 1933 to 1945. Focuses on swing, and mostly white popular artists.

1407. Bell, Malcolm F. (compiler). *Theme Songs of the Dance Band Era.* Memphis: KWD Corporation; 1981.

Does not include themes of studio bands, radio orchestras, or broadcasting themes. Among theme songs included are those of Benny Goodman, Artie Shaw, Tommy Dorsey, Wayne King, Hal Kemp, Sammy Kaye, and Guy Lombardo.

1408. Bennett, Bill. *Capitol Record Listings 101–3031.* Zephyrhills, Fla.: Joyce Music Publications; 1987.

Covers master number or record listing, artist, date venue, personnel, and title. Includes recordings by Jimmy Giuffre, Shorty Rogers, Miles Davis, Duke Ellington, Benny Carter, Art Tatum, Charlie Barnet, King Cole, and many more.

1409. Blackstone, Orin. *Index to Jazz.* Four volumes. London: Gordon Gullickson, 1945, 1947, 1948. Reprinted, Westport, Conn.: Greenwood Press; 1978.

Attempts to list all recordings "of interest to jazz collectors," 1917 through 1944. It expands the entries covered in *Hot Discography* and *Rhythm of Record,* drawing on data from catalogues, periodicals, private lists, and other sources. He does not list "purely commercial or vocal records"; however many "non-hot" items are included because they are important to complete the discographies of selected artists. Recordings are listed in the order, that they were issued; the catalogue number appears first followed by the title with master number and, where warranted, reissue numbers, personnel, title, and dates. Reissues with different masters are listed separately, even when they have identical catalogue numbers. Volume 1 (A–E), volume 2 (F–L), volume 3 (M–R), and volume 4 (S–Z).

1410. Bruyninckx, Walter, and Domi Truffandier. *Jazz Discography: 85 Years of Recorded Jazz.* Mechelen, Belgium: Copy Express; 2000.

The data is presented on CD-Rom, and can be loaded on all or parts of it on to the hard disc of your computer. The complete data was issued on CD-Rom in five steps from 2000 to 2003. With each edition, additional data of over 5,000 printed pages were added, plus the updated version of the content of the previous edition.

1411. _____. *Swing 1920–1988: Swing/Dance Bands and Combos.* Twelve volumes. Mechelen, Belgium: Copy Express; 1988.

A continuation of the discography series, divided by styles/genres and organized alphabetically by persons/groups. As in his "Traditional Jazz" series, the entries contain standard discographical information and are limited primarily to recorded works and some reissues.

Volume 1 (A–B) mostly devoted to the recordings of Louis Armstrong.
Volume 2 (B–Ca)
Volume 3 (Ca–D)
Volume 4 (Ea–Go)
Volume 5 (Go–He)
Volume 6 (He–Jo)
Volume 7 (Jo–Ma)
Volume 8 (Ma–Po)
Volume 9 (Po–Se)
Volume 10 (Se–Th)
Volume 11 (Th–W)
Volume 12 (W–Z)

Comprehensive musicians index. Entries cover many non-American artists/groups. Excellent for both collectors of individual artists and groups, and cross-referencing.

1412. _____. *Jazz: The Vocalists, 1917–1986: Singers and Crooners.* Three volumes. Mechelen, Belgium: Copy Express; 1988.

A comprehensive, three-volume discography of jazz and jazz-related vocalists. The entries are organized alphabetically: volume 1 (A–Du); volume 2 (Du–Le); and volume 3 (Le–Si). The entries include title, venue, date, and matrix numbers. This is the most comprehensive discography to date on jazz vocalists.

1413. _____. *Modern Jazz: Be-Bop/Hard Bop/West Coast.* Six volumes. Mechelen, Belgium: 60 Years of Recorded Jazz Team; 1985.

Organized identically to other discographies in the series. All major artists/ groups are included, and some non-American artists such as Roffe Soderberg (Swedish), Piero Soffici (Italy), Martial Solal (France), Infried Hoffman (Germany), among others. Volume 1 (A–C), volume 2 (D–H), volume 3 (H–M), volume 4 (M–P), volume 5 (P–S), and volume 6 (S–Z). Comprehensive musicians index.

1414. _____. *Traditional Jazz 1897–1985: Origins/New Orleans/Dixieland/ Chicago Styles.* Six volumes. Mechelen, Belgium: 60 Years of Recorded Jazz Team; 1985.

A series of "Pocket Books" (discographies), each about 400 pages, that is intended to provide information on specific styles/genres. The division of people/groups into styles/categories is sometimes problematic; for example, Louis Armstrong recordings are listed in both "Origin of Jazz" and in "Swing" (another discography series by the author). This discography lists, in most cases, the recorded works and occasionally broadcast or concert performances if the author felt they would soon be recorded. The entries contain original label, release number, name, title of composition, personnel, date of performance, and some recent reissues. Foreign artists are also covered. Comprehensive, and excellent for cross-referencing. Volume 1 (A–C), volume 2 (C–H), volume 3 (H–M), volume 4 (M–R), volume 5 (R–Y), and volume 6 (Z plus a comprehensive musicians index).

1415. _____. *Progressive Jazz: Free/Third Stream/Fusion.* Five volumes. Mechelen, Belgium: 60 Years of Recorded Jazz Team; 1984.

Covers American and foreign artists/groups. Comprehensive. Volume 1 (A–D), volume 2 (D–L), volume 3 (L–S), volume 4 (Sh–V), and volume 5 (additions Be–Ly).

1416. _____. *50 Years of Recorded Jazz: 1917–1967.* Mechelen, Belgium: the author; 1968.

Contains full discographical information arranged alphabetically by artist. The author's objective was to overcome the problem of new releases and reissues by offering a subscription service. The entries are arranged alphabetically by artist (addition to 1981).

1417. _____. *60 Years of Recorded Jazz.* Belgium: the author; 1978.

Published in twos from 1978 to 1980. Contains both blues and jazz recordings, complete with information on date, titles, venues, personnel, and more.

1418. Carey, David A., and Albert J. McCarthy. *The Directory of Recorded Jazz and Swing Music.* Fordingbridge: Delphic Press; 1949–1952 (volumes 1–4); London: Cassell; 1955–1957 (volumes 5,6). Six volumes. (A-Longshaw); second edition, (volumes 2–4). London: Cassell; 1957.

Covers gospels, spirituals, some commercial recordings of "prestigious artists or soloists of merit," and "rare records." Included in the numerous number of jazz listings are several entries on swing and bebop. Although this discography is complete through the letter "K," the publication (*Jazz Dictionary*) ceased publication with the letter "L." Its coverage is replete with discographical information, including date of performance, recording venue, titles, and catalogue numbers. The catalogue numbers are limited primarily to American and British labels. Contains broad, comprehensive listings for recorded jazz (particularly bebop and swing) through 1957, when publication ceased.

1419. Cherrington, George, and Brian Knight. *Jazz Catalogue: A Discography of All British Releases Complete with Full Personnel and Recording Dates.* Ten volumes, 1960–1971. London: Jazz Journal.

An outgrowth of a need to document recordings as they appear, an issue first addressed by Albert J. McCarthy in *Jazz Dictionary I: An International Discography of Recorded Jazz, Including Blues, Gospel, and Rhythm-and-Blues for the Year January–December 1958.* The volumes cover blues, gospel, and jazz releases in Britain for a single year, with the only exception being the combination of the 1968–69 releases (which were published in 1970). Among the American labels represented are Blue Note, Prestige, and Riverside. The entries are arranged alphabetically by performer. There are collections in the appendix of each volume and excellent bibliographies. The entries contain full discographical details. Unfortunately, no additions have been made to these significant volumes since 1971.

1420. Cook, Richard, and Brian Morton. *The Penguin Guide to Jazz on CD, LP, and Cassette.* New York: Penguin USA; 1993.

A comprehensive jazz reference book that includes a thorough list of currently available jazz recordings, full information for each recording, label details, critical assessments of recordings, and a rating system. The index includes special sections on collections labeled "Anthologies" and "Various Artists." The authors address questions such as best collection, most sought-after recording, and label where one might find the finest recording of an individual.

1421. Cooper, David E. *International Bibliography of Discographies: Classical and Jazz and Blues, 1962–1972: A Reference Book for Record Collectors, Dealers, and Libraries.* Littleton, Colo.: Libraries Unlimited; 1975.

Deals in the first section with classical music and in the second with blues and jazz. A carefully organized and categorized bibliography arranged alphabetically. Each entry contains full discographical details (addition to 1981).

1422. Crawford, Richard, and Jeffrey Magee. *Jazz Standards on Record, 1900–1942: A Core Repertory.* Chicago: Center for Black Music Research (Columbia College, Chicago); 1992.

According to the authors, "The idea of a core repertory is that, however powerful the authority of canon makers, something can also be learned about a musical genre by discovering and studying the preferences of its own heyday" (p. v). They began with a listing of tables that cite "Jazz Standards in the Core Repertory," "Jazz Standards in Order of Publication," "Jazz Standards by Genre," "Jazz Standards with 'Blues' in the Title," "Blues Standards with Six or More Recordings Per Year," "Jazz Standards with Six or More Recordings Per Year," and "'I Got Rhythm' and Its Contrafacts to 1942." There are notes and references after the tables. The main body cites the date, performer, vocalist, place, label, issue, and matrix number of each recording made of the *Jazz Standards in the Core Repertory* (table 1). Also included are an introduction that outlines their selection process and "a note on procedure." A significant addition to jazz discography.

1423. Crowther, Bruce, and Mike Pinfold. *The Jazz Singers: From Ragtime to the New Wave.* Poole, England, and New York: Blandford; 1987.

Analysis of styles, approaches, and text. Makes critical assessments regarding numerous vocalists to the mid-1980s. Well-researched and clearly presented. Index.

1424. Cullaz, Maurice. *Guide des disques de jazz.* Paris: Buchet/Chastel; 1971.

In French. Contains over 1,000 selected jazz, spiritual, gospel, and blues recordings. They are organized alphabetically and contain full discographical details (addition to 1981).

1425. Cuscuna, Michael, and Michel Ruppli. *The Blue Note Label: A Discography.* Westport, Conn.: Greenwood Press; 1988.

A discography of all known recordings made or issued on the Blue Note label. The discography is organized into several parts:

1) details all sessions made by founders Alfred Lion and Francis Wolff from the inception of the label in 1939 until mid-1967;
2) lists Blue Note sessions made between 1967 and 1969;
3) lists reissues on the Blue Note label of material coming from various EMI labels;
4) lists reissues from other labels, made of purchased or leased sessions;
5) details Blue Note sessions made or issued in a new Blue Note series that began with the Blue Note Revival in 1985;
6) lists single series used, each issue being listed with reference to pages where titles are detailed;
7) lists album series;
8) lists compact disc issues;
9) lists Blue Note cassettes; and
10) artist index contains full discographical information. Comprehensive.

1426. Delaunay, Charles. *Hot Discography.* Paris: *Hot Jazz,* 1936; 2nd ed., Paris: *Hot Jazz,* 1938; 3rd ed., New York: Commodore Music Shop, 1940; *Hot Discographie,* 1943. Paris: Collection du Hot Club de France; 1944; *New Hot Discography: The Standard Dictionary of Recorded Jazz.* Edited by Walter Schaap and George Avakian. New York: Criterion, 1948; *Hot discographie encyclopédoqie avec la collboration de Kurt Mohr.* 3 vols., Paris: Jazz disques, 1951.

Although Hilton Schleman's *Rhythm on Record: A Who's Who and Register of Recorded Dance Music* preceded this work by a few months, Delaunay set the methodology for jazz discography research. Specifically, he was the first to cite the date of recording, venue, matrix numbers, personnel, release numbers, and titles. In this monumental work, he organized his entries into categories by styles. He also uses an alphabetical sequence rather than a historical approach. He began with a modest number of entries, and by 1952 had expanded to a comprehensive three volume set.

1427. Dexter, Dave. *Playback: A Newsman/Record Producer's Hits and Misses from the Thirties to the Seventies.* New York: Billboard Publications; 1976.

Anecdotal reminiscences of both music and musicians experienced during the author's career as both a jazz writer (*Down Beat)* and record producer (Capitol). The author's affection for big band leaders is evident (Basie, Ellington, Goodman, Kenton, etc). In addition, reminiscences of musicians like Mildred Bailey, Benny Carter, Peggy Lee, and Frank Sinatra are also included. A list of big band themes is also included.

1428. No Author. Discography of *Jazz on LPs: A Collector's Guide to Jazz on Decca, Brunswick, London, Felsted, Ducretet-Thomsen, Vogue Coral, Telefunken and Durium Long Playing Records.* Westport, Conn.: Greenwood Publishers (revised edition), 1978; first edition published by Decca Record Company, 1955.

Lists all jazz LPs on these labels issued up to July 1956. The text consists of suggestions concerning rare, historical, and modern jazz records as well as complete discographical details of the recordings. The entries are arranged alphabetically by artists' surnames, with cross-references. Availability is also noted. Index of titles, list of extended play records available that was not cited in the body of the book.

1429. Edwards, Ernest, Jr. *Big Bands.* Volume 6. Whittier, Calif.: Erngeobil Publications; 1968.

Includes revisions from earlier volumes and new listings. Revisions include Danny Belloc and His Orchestra, The Commanders, Ray DeMichel and His Orchestra, Ralph Flanagan and His Orchestra, and Freddie Slack and His Orchestra. The new entries are "Peanuts" Hucko and His Orchestra, Terry Gibbs and His Big Band, Buddy Morrow and His Orchestra, Herb Pomeroy and His Orchestra, The Sauter-Finegan Orchestra, Larry Sonn and His Orchestra, and Earle Spencer and His Orchestra (soloists and composers). Entries include title, date venue, label, master numbers, and more.

1430. Evensmo, Jan (compiler). *Jazz Solography Series.* Fourteen volumes. 1975–83. Hosle, Norway: Evensmo; 1975–1983.

A complete listing, in chronological order for a specific period, of all known studio recordings and preserved live recordings, which includes information on dates, places, personnel, matrix numbers, and critical commentary. The author also cites the number of measures of improvised solos. The volumes, titles, and chronological listing is as follows:

Volume 1—The Tenor Saxophone of Leon "Chu" Berry;

Volume 2—The Tenor Saxophones of Henry Bridges, Robert Carroll Herschel Evans, and Johnny Russell;

Volume 3—The Tenor Saxophone of Coleman Hawkins, 1929–1942;

Volume 4—The Guitars of Charlie Christian, Robert Norman, Oscar Aleman (in Europe);

Volume 5—The Tenor Saxophone and Clarinet of Lester Young, 1936–1942;

Volume 6—The Tenor Saxophone of Ben Webster, 1931–1943;

Volume 7—The Tenor Saxophones of Budd Johnson, Cecil Scott, Elmer Williams, and Dick Wilson, 1920–1942;

Volume 8—The Trumpet and Vocal of Henry "Red" Allen, 1920–1942;

Volume 9—The Trumpets of Bill Coleman, 1929–1945, and Frankie Newton;

Volume 10—The Trumpet of Roy Eldridge, 1929–1944;

Volume 11—The Alto Saxophone, Trumpet, and Clarinet of Benny Carter, 1927–1946;

Volume 12—The Trumpets of Dizzy Gillespie, 1937–1943, Irving Randolph, and Joe Thomas;

Volume 13—The Tenor Saxophone and Clarinet of Lester Young, 1936–1949 (revised edition);

Volume 14—The Flute of Wayman Carver, the Trombone of Dickie Wells, 1937–1942, and the Tenor Saxophone of Illinois Jacquet.

1431. _____. *The Tenor Saxophonists of the Period 1930–1942. Volume 1.* Oslo, Norway: Evensmo; 1969.

To date, this is the sole discography devoted to tenor saxophonists. It contains comprehensive listings of selected artists: Leon "Chu" Berry, Herschel Evans, Coleman Hawkins, Ben Webster, and Lester Young. In addition to complete discographical details on recordings and broadcasts, Evensmo provides pertinent information on each improvisation, including durations and analytical comments.

1432. Eyle, Wim Van. *Jazz Pearls.* Dudkarspel, Amsterdam: Spectrum; 1975.

Surveys recordings the author believes are crucial to establishing a jazz record collection (most of the records are owned by the author). In addition to personal preferences, the criteria for inclusion involved musical quality of recording, importance of recording in relation to jazz history, musical standard of musicians, musical standard of a sideman or soloist, and creativeness, inventiveness, devotion, drive, humor, and swing. The entries include title, master number, date, title, person/group, original label, and personnel. He does not list all reissues of a recording.

1433. Fox, Charles, Peter Gammond, Alun Morgan, and Alexis Korner. *Jazz on Record: A Critical Guide.* London: Hutchinson; London: Arrow Books; 1960.

Contains blues and jazz entries arranged alphabetically by artist. The entries include artist's name, date, instrument, venue, and matrix numbers. This is a selective discography of what the authors believe are the best or most significant of selected blues and jazz recordings. Although American and British recordings dominate, there are entries from other countries. There are several female entries. Each entry contains artist's dates, instrument, role in the development of the style, and information on stylistic development. Selected discographies and complete name index.

1434. _____. *Jazz on Record.* Westport Conn.: Greenwood Press; 1978.

Focuses on record collectors and is concerned with recordings that were available at press time. Selected artists with an EP or LP are the primary focus, therefore, one will not find a complete listing of recordings by such artists as John Coltrane or Lester Young. The entries are chronologically arranged by artist and each contains an essay that discusses the recordings, some history, personnel, and points of musical interest, for example, soloists. Index.

1435. Furusho, Shinjiro. *Riverside Jazz Records.* Chiba City, Japan; 1984.

Began as an interest in the history and importance of Riverside as a jazz record label. The author details the recordings of numerous artists, including Cannonball Adderly, Bill Evans, Thelonious Monk, Wes Montgomery, and Sonny Rollins. The entries are different from standard discographies in that the album units are made with pictures. There are several errors and omissions.

1436. Gammond, Peter, and Raymond Horricks (editors). *Music on Record 2: Big Bands.* Cambridge: Patrick Stephens; 1981.

This is not a discography in the strict sense; rather, they provide concise biographical information and a selected list of recordings, absent matrix numbers. Includes lots of jazz-related information.

1437. Gammond, Peter, and Peter Clayton. *Fourteen Miles On a Clear Night: An Irreverent, Skeptical, and Affectionate Book About Jazz Records.* London: Peter Owen Limited; 1966.

Not a systematic in-depth discography. Instead this is a random selection of recordings admired by the authors. In place of a full discographical citation, each of the 47 entries is proceeded by a monologue, which can best be described as a discussion of why they liked the record. After the monologue the personnel of the specific recording are given. Several blues and one ragtime composition, "Maple Leaf Rag" (instrumental version featuring Sidney Bechet). Geared to aficionados.

1438. Garrod, Charles. *Standard Transcription Listings: Volume 1, Series A–T, and Volume 2, Series V–Z.* Zephyrhills, Fla.: Joyce Music Publications; 1993.

Follows the same format as the author's *Associated Transcription Master Numbers and Listing Series.* Lacks some dates. The entries are organized alphabetically and include artist, date, venue, personnel, label, and master numbers. Each volume contains an artists index.

1439. _____. *World Transcription Listing 100–758, and World Transcriptions Original Series, 1–11268, Working Drafts.* Zephyrhills, Fla.: Joyce Music Publications; 1993.

Includes transcriptions of the recordings leased to radio stations by Decca records. The transcriptions cover the 1930s, 1940s, and 1950s, are organized by order of broadcast, and contain artists, date, venue, title, and personnel. To date, the volumes are not complete. Title index.

1440. _____. *Associated Transcription Master Numbers, 10/2/1934–7/24/1942; Associated Transcription Listing, Original and A Series, and Associated Transcription Listing, 60000–60999.* Zephyrhills, Fla.: Joyce Music Publications; 1992.

Volume 1—master numbers, titles, dates, venues, artist, and personnel of studio sessions; volume 2—a different series, beginning with 10,000, contains artists, dates, venues, personnel, and titles; volume 3—continues volume 2, covers 60000–60999 master numbers.

1441. _____. *MacGregor Transcription Listing, 1–920.* Zephyrhills, Fla.: Joyce Music Publications; 1990.

Transcription of the C. P. MacGregor broadcasts of the 1930s and 1940s. Each transcription contains artist, date, venue, title, and personnel. Includes several major artists.

1442. Garrod, Charles, and Robert Olson. *Crown Record and Master Numbers Listing.* Zephyrhills, Fla.: Joyce Music Publications; 1990.

Contains the recordings of this major label from the 1920s and 1930s. The coverage is comprehensive. Each entry includes artist, date, venue, title, personnel, and master number. Title index.

1443. Garrod, Charles. *Elite, Hit, and Majestic Record Listings by Master Numbers.* Zephyrhills, Fla.: Joyce Music Publications; 1990.

The entries are organized by master numbers and contain artist, date, venue, personnel, and title. These are minor labels of the 1940s that featured lesser-known artists.

1444. _____. *Four Star and Gilt Edge Records: Covers 1945.* Zephyrhills, Fla.: Joyce Music Publications; 1990.

Chronicles the recordings made on these little known but significant labels. Entries include artist, title, date, venue, personnel, and master numbers.

1445. Garrod, Charles, and Bill Korst. *RCA Victor Record Listing 20–1500 to 20–7300.* Zephyrhills, Fla.: Joyce Music Publications; 1989.

Lists approximately 5,800 entries, including the recordings of Benny Goodman, Duke Ellington, Louis Armstrong, Jimmy Lunceford, Earl "Fatha" Hines, Jean Goldkette, Don Redman, Lionel Hampton, Coleman Hawkins, Red Allen, Glenn Miller, Bob Chester, and many more. Each entry contains artist, date, venue, personnel, and title. The entries are organized by record listing.

1446. Garrod, Charles. *Columbia Record 78 RPM Record Listing 37000–41963; Columbia Chicago Master Number Listing 501–4999, and Columbia LA and H'Wood Master Number Listing 8/27/1933–7/30/1945.* Zephyrhills, Fla.: Joyce Music Publications; 1989.

The first volume is almost complete and is limited to 78s, whereas the Chicago listings cover master numbers issued in those venues. In all cases, the entries include artist, title, date, venue, and personnel. The entries are organized by master numbers. Some reissues listed. Among the artists covered are Benny Goodman, Duke Ellington, Jimmy Lunceford, Earl "Fatha" Hines, Claude Hopkins (only 12 of the 20 sides that he recorded with Columbia between May 1932 and March 1933 were released), Benny Carter, George Avakian, Art Tatum, Red Norvo, Billie Holiday, Red Allen, Artie Shaw, Woody Herman, and Will Bradley.

1447. _____. *MGM 78 Master Number Listing, 1946 thru 1953; Volume Two 1953 thru 1956; Volume Three MGM Record Listing 10000 thru 13506, 1946–1966, and Volume Four MGM Record Listing 30000,20000, 50000, 55000, 60000* (Charles Garrod and Bill Korst). Zephyrhills, Fla.: Joyce Music Publications; 1989.

Two volumes are devoted to master numbers and two to record listings. The entries include artist, title, date, venue, and personnel.

1448. Garrod, Charles, Ken Crawford, and Dave Kressley. *Thesaurus Transcriptions; Volume 1, 1–1000, and Volume 2, 1001–on* (through the 1950s). Zephyrhills, Fla.: Joyce Music Publications; 1993.

Covers the RCA Victor broadcasts that were leased to radio stations in the 1930s, 1940s, and 1950s. Entries include artists, dates, venues, titles, and personnel. The entries are organized by order of the broadcast. Both volumes contain an index.

1449. Garrod, Charles. *Decca Record Listings and Master Numbers.* Zephyrhills, Fla.: Joyce Music Publications; 1991–1994.

A massive compilation of Decca listings and master numbers 1934–1960, including all 78s and 45s. There are 22 volumes in the series, each with an artist index. The entries cover artists, date, venue, titles, record or master numbers, and personnel. The series is organized as follows:

A. Decca Record Listing 100–222
B. Decca Record Listing 2226–4455
C. Decca New York Master Numbers Volume 1, 38277–62999
D. Decca LA Master Volume 1, 1–5000
E. Decca Chicago Masters, 1934–1941
F. Decca New York Master Numbers Volume 2, 63000–67999
G. Decca New York Master Numbers Volume 3, 68000–71999
H. Decca New York Master Numbers Volume 4, 72000–75999
I. Decca Records 5000 and 7000 Series
J. Decca Records 18000 Series
K. Decca LA Masters Volume 2, 5001–8999
L. Decca New York Master Numbers Volume 5, 76000–82999
M. Decca 10000 Record Listing, 10000–10530
N. Decca New York Master Numbers Volume 6, 83000–86999
O. Decca New York Master Numbers Volume 7, 87000–89999
P. Decca 8500, 11000, 12000, 14000, 15000, 16000 Record Listings
Q. Decca 23000 and 24000 Record Listings
R. Decca 25000 and 27000 Record Listings
S. Decca 28000 and 29000 Record Listings
T. Decca LA Masters Volume 3, 9000–11999
U. Decca Record Series 30000–31999
V. Decca New York Master Numbers Volume 8, 100000–103999

The Decca recordings include those with Lil Hardin (house pianist at Decca [Chicago] in the 1930s), Fletcher Henderson, Louis Armstrong, Luis Russell, Jimmy Dorsey, Bing Crosby, the Mills brothers (including recordings with Louis Armstrong), Jimmy Lunceford, Earl "Fatha" Hines (including some broadcasts from the Grand Terrace), Chick Webb (including some vocals by Ella Fitzgerald), Fred Norman, Benny Carter, Tiny Bradshaw, Billie Holiday (after the recording ban), Pat Davis, Bob Crosby, Glenn Miller, Carl Barriteau (Trinidadian clarinetist), The King Cole Trio, and many more.

1450. Giddins, Gary. *Riding on a Blue Note: Jazz and American Pop.* New York: Oxford University Press; 1981.

The book addresses issues related to jazz and popular music including influences, contributions, and styles. There are four sections: singers;

instrumentalists; composers and movements, and adventures in the jazz trade. He outlines the influence of Otis Blackwell on Elvis Presley and provides insightful comments on Arthur Blythe, Charles Mingus, Sonny Rollins, George Benson, and Wes Montgomery. The essays on Benson and Montgomery provide insider's views on control of their music careers. Selected discography, bibliography, and an index.

1451. Hallstrom, Carl A., and Bo Scherman. *AFRS Jubilee Transcriptions.* Portland, Oreg.: Joyce Music Publications; 2003.

A revised and augmented listing of the original series, numbers 1 to 365, from Christmas 1945, 1947, and 1948. The comprehensive discography will be issued in three volumes.

1452. Harris, Rex, and Brian Rust. *Recorded Jazz: A Critical Guide.* Harmondsworth: Penguin Books; 1958.

Covers biographical information and stylistic comments on both artists and groups. The recordings cover both American and British LPs and EPs of the 1950s, and artists like Louis Armstrong and Jelly Roll Morton. Index.

1453. Harrison, Max, Stuart Nicholson, and Eric Thacker. *The Essential Jazz Records: Volume II: Ragtime to Swing.* New York: Bayou Press; 2001.

A selection of the best 250 modern jazz records and CDs. Also places the recordings in musical context, and provides an in-depth review of each recording. Includes an index of album/CD titles, track titles, and musicians.

1454. Harrison, Max, Alun Morgan, Ronald Atkins, Michael James, and Jack Cooke. *Modern Jazz: The Essential Records.* London: Aquarius Books; 1975.

Assesses what these British critics selected as the 200 best postwar jazz recordings. Critical essays on each of the recordings are arranged according to eight chronological styles/categories. Although 1,000 artists are covered, Parker, Coleman, Coltrane, Monk, and Rollins dominate the book. Each entry has complete discographical information as well as the later available British and American record numbers (1981).

1455. Harrison, Max, Charles Fox, and Eric Thacker. *The Essential Jazz Records: Volume I, Ragtime to Swing.* New York: Da Capo; 1974.

Reviews recordings on ragtime, jazz, the influence of jazz on European composers, blues singers and jazz, and the transition to modern jazz. The book is topical and includes indices of LP titles, tune titles, and musicians. Reference notes and a bibliography.

1456. Hibbs, Leonard. *21 Years of Swing Music on Brunswick Records.* London: White; 1937.

Surveys recordings pressed between 1961 and 1937, including those of Duke Ellington, Earl "Fatha" Hines, Chick Webb, Glenn Miller, and Mary Lou Williams. The entries contain title, date, venue, personnel, and master number. Illustrated.

1456a. Holtje, Steve, and Nancy Ann Lee. *MusicHound Jazz: The Essential Album Guide.* Unknown City: Visible Ink Press; 1998.

A compilation of around 1,300 jazz artists is profiled in this guide to jazz recordings on compact disc. The focus is on recordings rather than jazz history, however notes on solos, musical influences, band members, producers, radio stations, books, periodicals, and Web sites are provided. Albums are described under the headings of "What to Buy," "What to Buy Next," and "What to Avoid."

1457. *Jazz on 78's: A Guide to the Many Examples of Classic Jazz on Decca, Brunswick and London 78 R.P.M. Records.* London: Decca Records; 1954.

Contains general stylistic critiques rather than assessments of individual recordings. The booklet lists 78s only, including personnel and dates. Each artist entry contains a selected discography, date of recording, and personnel. Concise and informative (addition to 1981).

1458. *Jazz on LP's: A Collector's Guide to Jazz on Decca, Brunswick, Capitol, London and Felsted Long Playing Records.* Revised edition London: Decca Records; 1956.

Recordings are listed first, followed by stylistic assessments. Entries include date of the recording, names of the personnel involved, venue, and matrix numbers. The entries are arranged alphabetically (addition to 1981).

1459. *Jazz Records, 1897–1942.* Revised edition London: Storyville Publications; 1970.

Lists all known American and British recordings in the ragtime, jazz, and swing styles, made up to the Petrillo ban. Arrangement is alphabetical by artist or band, with composers names given. There is a 90-page artist index in this revised edition. Discographical details include title, date, venue, personnel, and matrix numbers (addition to 1981).

1460. Jepsen, Jorgen Grunnet. *Jazz Records: A Discography.* Eight volumes. Copenhagen: Knudsen; 1963–1970.

Rivals Brian Rust's *Jazz Records A–Z, 1987–1942,* as one of the most scholarly achievements in jazz discography. The author lists recordings made, 1942–1962 (volumes 5–8); 1965 (volumes 1–3); and 1967 (volume 4). The volumes were published out of order; volumes 5–8 were the first to be published because the author wanted to continue the unfinished listings of David A. Carey and Albert J. McCarthy, *The Directory of Recorded Jazz and Swing Music,* which ceased publication with the letter "L." Coverage includes blues, gospel, rhythm and blues, and jazz. Entries are arranged alphabetically by band or performer and chronologically within the performer category. Full discographical information is given, including date and venue of recording, matrix numbers for original recordings, instrumentation and personnel, release numbers of 78s, EPs, LPs, and whether mono or stereo. The entries are cross-referenced. There are no listings of tapes. Due to the massive number of entries, an additional index might help the search for information.

1461. Jones, Morley. *Jazz.* New York: Simon and Schuster; Poole, Dorset: Blandford Press; 1980.

Geared to the nonspecialist, this listening guide is arranged chronologically. It includes chapters on blues, bebop, swing, and fusion and beyond. There is biographical information and a selected discography after each chapter. The discographies are incomplete because only label names are listed.

1462. Karlin, Fred. *Edison Diamond Discs 50001–52651. Volume One.* Santa Monica, Calif.: Bona Fide Publishing Company; 1972.

Designed to provide information on both artists and discs released as Edison Diamond Discs. This discography contains all entries listed in the Edison catalogs 1914–1928, the 1927–1929 supplements, and the 132 "Weekly Bulletins" (lists all the recordings made from the beginning of 1927 until November 1, 1929). Of particular note to scholars is a list of "Edison Diamond Disc Artists." Although some titles are missing, each entry contains record numbers, matrix numbers (in 1927, the missing matrix numbers from 12001–17999 were reserved for Edison's new long playing discs), composer/lyricist, title, and artist. There are lists of medleys, songs from films, songs from musicals, and several photographs.

1463. Kernfeld, Barry (editor). *The Blackwell Guide to Recorded Jazz.* Oxford, England and Cambridge, Mass.: Basil Blackwell Publishers; 1991.

Attempts to identify "a rare collection of recordings representing the best works from the field of jazz music." He covers genres dating from the turn-of-the century to the fusion styles of the 1970s and 1980s. The 11 chapters are arranged chronologically with major artists of each genre highlighted. The bop chapter includes the contributions of Dizzy Gillespie,

Thelonious Monk, Charlie Parker, Bud Powell, and others. John Coltrane, Louis Armstrong, Miles Davis, and several additional artists are also highlighted. Each chapter contains an overview as well as critical assessments of significant recordings of a particular genre. Bibliography and index.

1464. Laird, Ross, and Brian Rust. *Discography of Okeh Records, 1918–1934.* Westport, Conn.: Praeger Press; 2004.

Documents all recordings made by this pioneering and influential record label of popular, blues, jazz, country, and ethnic music before, during, and after the 1920s into the 1930s. It contains all known 78-rpm record releases in the United States, Britain, Canada, Australia, and Japan.

1465. Laird, Ross. *Tantalizing Tingles: A Discography of Early Ragtime, Jazz, and Novelty Syncopated Piano Recordings, 1889–1934.* Westport, Conn.: Greenwood Press; 1995.

A compilation of recordings of nonclassical piano music made for issue on disc and cylinder records prior to 1935. Included are piano solos, duets, trios, quartets, as well as soloists featured with a dance band or orchestra. He covers jazz, boogie-woogie, blues, novelty, syncopated, ragtime, and stride. Most of the entries have not been cited in other discographies.

1466. Lange, Horst H. *Die Deutsche Jazz-Discographie: Eine Geschicte des Jazz auf Schallplatten von 1902 bis 1955.* Berlin: Bore and Bock; 1955.

In German. Offers a good cross section of listings on jazz to 1955, covering many of the most significant artists. Each entry contains date, title, venue, personnel, and matrix numbers.

1467. _____. *The Fabulous Fives.* Lübbecke: Uhle and Kleimann, 1959; revised by Ron Kewson, Derek Hamilton-Smith, and Ray Webb. Chigwell: Storyville Publications; 1978.

Lists the recordings of eight Anglo-American jazz bands: The Original Dixieland Jazz Band; Earl Fuller's Famous Jazz Band; Louisiana Five; Original Memphis Five (also known as Ladd's Black Aces and Lanin's Southern Serenaders); Southern Five; New Orleans's Jazz Band; and the Original Georgia Five and Original Indiana Five. The discographies are arranged chronologically and are replete with information on date of recording, composer credits, personnel, titles, recording labels, and numbers (including reissues). In addition, ODJB entries include a filmography, a list of broadcasts, and a listing of Joe LaRocca's private recordings. A questionable aspect of the collection is the assertion that white musicians were most responsible for the creation of jazz. There are several indices for artist credits, catalogue numbers, label illustrations, personnel, and titles.

1468. Langridge, Derek. *Your Jazz Collection.* London: Bingley; Hamden: Archon Books; 1970.

Discusses the attributes of collecting and contains bibliographies of biographies, discographies, histories, social and musical analysis, introductions, and reference works. Index.

1469. Larkin, Philip. *All What Jazz: A Record Diary, 1961–68.* New York: St. Martin, London: Faber and Faber, 1970; New York: Farrar, Straus and Giroux, 1985; London, Boston: Faber, 1985.

A collection of articles and record reviews originally published in the *Daily Telegraph* by the British poet covering 1961–71. The 1969–71 reviews were omitted from the first publication, hence their addition to the 1985 edition. The reviews cover mostly jazz and to a lesser degree blues. Although his writing displays a keen sense of musical detail, he displays a strong bias against jazz from bebop on, especially the 1960s. He laments that his obvious dislike for later jazz styles "seemed to type me as a disliker rather than a liker" (p. 30). The index contains a list of the records reviewed. Larkin also wrote *Required Writing: Miscellaneous Pieces 1955–1982* (London: Faber and Faber, 1983), a collection of articles.

1470. Leder, Jan. *Women in Jazz: A Discography of Instrumentalists, 1913–1968.* Westport, Conn.: Greenwood Press; 1985.

Draws from Charles Delaunay's *New Hot Discography;* Brian Rust's *Jazz Records 1897–1942;* Jorgen Jepsen's *Jazz Records 1942–1968;* and Walter Bruyninckx's *60 Years of Recorded Jazz, 1917–1977.* The discography is divided into two sections, alphabetical by artist and chronological within each player's section, and a chronologically listed collective section containing recordings with two or more women players. The entries cover some blues artists as well as an occasional gospel artist (Sister Rosetta Tharpe), and include date, venue, personnel, titles, labels, and matrix numbers. Name index.

1471. Litchfield, Jack. *This Is Jazz.* Montreal: the author; 1985.

Lists all recordings of "This Is Jazz," a half-hour program of live jazz, broadcast weekly during 1947 over the Mutual Broadcasting System. The personnel on the broadcasts included Muggsy Spanier, Georg Brunis, Albert Nichols, Danny Barker, Pops Foster, Baby Dodds, James P. Johnson, Luckey Roberts, and others. One page is devoted to each broadcast and includes the date, personnel, titles, solo sequence, and the issued records.

1472. Lord, Tom. *The Jazz Discography.* Redwood, N.Y.: North Country Distributors; 1992.

The first three volumes of a projected 24-volume series have been published. The complete discography is projected to list over 100,000 recording sessions with the appropriate information. The discography utilizes computer technology; the author designed the database. Lord will document jazz and its styles, including ragtime, swing, bebop, modern, avant-garde, fusion, and third stream. Each entry contains album titles, group leader name, tunes, instruments, personnel, date, and venue of recorded performances. The entries are cross-referenced in each of the first three volumes. Contains entries on around 6,000 recording sessions.

1473. Lotz, Rainer E., and Ulrich Nevert. *The AFRS "Jubilee" Transcriptions Programs, an Exploratory Discography;* foreword by Richard S. Sears. Two volumes. Frankfurt: Norbert Ruecker; 1985.

A comprehensive discography of mostly African American performances during World War II and the immediate postwar years. Major Mann Holiner, Special Services Division, United States Army, conceived the "Jubilee" shows in 1942. The Army "Jubilee" shows were designed to showcase both African American talent and white variety programs such as "Command Performance" and "Mail Call." The transcriptions cover the 1942–1945 years and are organized by sessions beginning with the first session in October 9, 1942, which featured Eddie "Rochester" Anderson, Duke Ellington and His Orchestra, The Hall Johnson Choir, Rex Ingram, and Ethel Waters. Volume II contains featured vocalists (nonband members), arranged alphabetically and grouped by dates. Tune and artist index in Volume II. Contains numerous entries not cited in other discographies and is not limited to jazz.

1474. Lucas, John. *Basic Jazz on Long Play.* Northfield, Minn.: Carleton Jazz Club (Carleton College); 1954.

An outgrowth of several jazz lectures given at Carleton College in the early 1950s. He recommends 30 jazz recordings for listening. The book is divided into two parts: part one, the great soloists (Jelly Roll Morton, Lead Belly, Bessie Smith, Sidney Bechet, and Louis Armstrong), and part two, the great bands (King Oliver New Orleans Rhythm Kings, Bob Crosby, Muggsy Spanier, and Kid Ory). Numerous references to the 30 recordings are made in essays on the artists. The recordings were chosen based on availability, no duplication of tunes, and if at least two tunes could be drawn from each recording.

1475. Lyons, Len. *The 101 Best Jazz Albums: A History of Jazz on Records.* New York: Morrow; 1980.

One of the best guides to date. In short, the author approaches the topic through the history of jazz, although he limits himself to 101 albums. Equal weight is given to the biographical data and to informative comments regarding style; references to other recordings are also frequently made. There are seven historical chapters. There are indices of names, subjects, and titles.

1476. Mackenzie, Harry, and Lothar Polomski. *One Night Stand Series, 1–1001.* New York, London, Westport, Conn.: Greenwood Press; 1991.

A discography of selected United States Armed Forces Service broadcasts, 1943–46. The discography contains transcriptions of a wide variety of bands: dance, Hawaiian, Latin, novelty, large and small, African American, and white. Cab Calloway, Count Basie, Lionel Hampton, Louis Armstrong, John Kirby, Jimmie Lunceford, Tiny Bradshaw, Erskine Hawkins, Buddy Johnson, and several more represent the African American bands. The entries are organized by One Night Stand (ONS), beginning September 29, 1943. Each entry contains title of group, vocalist (where warranted), venue, date, program, and occasional notes. An introduction to "the Armed Forces Radio Service" and several appendices (location addresses, directory of bandleaders, themes, commercial issues, bibliography, and label illustrations), and indices (band index 1, band index 2, and addenda).

1477. Mackenzie, Harry. *AFRS Downbeat Series, Working Draft.* Zephyrhills, Fla.: Joyce Music Publications; 1986.

This compilation is derived from *Downbeat* recordings, live sessions, and transcriptions. Each entry includes an artist, date, venue, title, and personnel. The entries are organized by dates.

1478. Malson, Lucien. *Les Maitres du Jazz.* Paris: Universitaires, 1952, 1955, 1958, 1962, 1966; Milano: Garzanti, 1954; Stockholm: Bonnier, 1956; Milano: Garzanti, 1957; Hamburg: Hoeppner, 1960; Paris: PUF, 1972.

In French. Biomusical portraits that focus on discographies. Among the artists covered are Louis Armstrong, Sidney Bechet, John Coltrane, Duke Ellington, Coleman Hawkins, King Oliver, Charles Parker, Fats Waller, and Lester Young. The discographies are limited to several significant recordings rather than a discussion of the entire repertoire. There are Italian and Swedish editions: *I. Maestri del Jazz* and *Jazzens Mästaare,* respectively. Footnotes, index, and some musical examples.

1479. Mauro, Walter. *Jazz e universo Negro.* Milano: Rizzoli; 1972.

In Italian. Champions the African American role in the origin and development of jazz. Cites the recordings of several artists, and includes an assessment of the contributions of Duke Ellington and Miles Davis. Selected bibliography and discography.

1480. McCarthy, Albert J. *Jazz Discography I: An International Discography of Recorded Jazz, Including Blues, Gospel, and Rhythm-and-Blues for the Year January–December, 1958.* London: Cassell; 1960.

An attempt to provide a comprehensive coverage of both new and reissue releases for a year. This daunting task proved to be overwhelming, and it was not until publication of *Jazz Catalogue* by George Cherrington and Brian Knight that it was accomplished. Although ambitious, this one-year discography contains numerous jazz and jazz-related recordings complete with discography details.

1481. McCarthy, Albert, Alun Morgan, Paul Oliver, and Max Harrison. *Jazz on Record: A Critical Guide to the First 50 Years, 1917–1967.* New York: Oak; London: Hanover Books; 1968.

Extends the discography by Fox, Gammond, Morgan, and Korner. It includes entries of blues and jazz representing both American and British labels as well as a second section in which artists that do not appear in the first work. These artists are treated in categories as follows: geographical blues, piano blues, ragtime, New Orleans jazz, big bands, postwar pianists, progressives, spirituals, and songs. A name index is included. Each entry contains date, title, venue, personnel, and matrix numbers (addition to 1981).

1482. McCarthy, Albert (editor). *Jazz on Records, 1917–1967.* Second edition. New York: Oak; 1969.

Contains alphabetically arranged biographical articles with selective discographies for each artist. Also included are general articles, surveys of musical appeals (e.g., "Post-War Reeds"), and geographical surveys of blues. There is full discography information for each entry (1981).

1483. McCoy, Meredith, and Barbara Parker (editors). *Catalog of the John D. Reid Collection of Early American Jazz.* Little Rock: Arkansas Arts Center; 1975.

A comprehensive listing of recordings organized into five categories: (1) "original" recordings of several different musicians recorded between 1939 and 1949, containing several recordings by Sidney Bechet; (2) blues; (3) bands; (4) piano and organ solos; and (5) gospel and spirituals. There are 4,000 recordings, dating from 1935 to 1945, including commercial recordings and recordings made by Reid. In addition, the collection contains correspondence, memorabilia, and photographs. The original recordings are especially noteworthy, and most of the other recordings (78s) are collector's items.

1484. Panassié, Hugues. *Discographie critique des meilleurs disques de jazz.* Paris: Laffont; 1958.

In French. Contains valuable comments on a wide range of jazz recordings up to 1957. The recordings represent several styles and numerous artists. Comments include information on styles as well as significance (addition to 1981).

1485. Panassié, Hugues, and Madeleine Gautier. *Guide to Jazz;* translated by Desmond Flower; edited by A. A. Gurwitch; introduction by Louis Armstrong. Boston: Houghton; 1956.

The guide is designed "to provide, in alphabetical order, a ready reference source to all aspects of authentic jazz: History and Background, Musicians and Bands, Styles, Instruments, the great Standard Tunes, and Definitions of Technical Terms." The book consists primarily of biographies, which are supplemented with comments on individual styles and a selected discography. He disdains jazz of the late 1950s, and favors African American artists in his biographical entries. Selected discography.

1486. Piazza, Tom. *The Guide to Classic Recorded Jazz.* Iowa City: University of Iowa Press; 1995.

The guide is organized into two main sections; one highlighting ensembles and the other soloists. Among the bands/individuals included are Art Blakey Duke Ellington, Benny Goodman, King Oliver, Charles Mingus, and Jelly Roll Morton. Soloists are arranged by instrument, and each category contains a chronological listing of one to two dozen soloists. The author defines "classic" recordings that have formed or that exemplify the definitive elements of the jazz style in as undiluted form as possible. He covers more than 800 recordings, with most dating from the 1920s to the 1970s. The breadth and depth is limited because he does not include bassists, drummers, guitarists, trombonists, and vocalists.

1487. Pickney, Warren R. *Jazz: A Guide to Perceptive Listening.* Dubuque, Iowa: Kendall/Hunt Publishing Company; 1986.

The book is divided into two broad parts: development of Jazz, 1890s–1940s, and development of jazz, 1940s-1980s. The author provides listening guides for each style or individual covered under the broad parts, for example, Chicago jazz, Afro-Cuban jazz, Duke Ellington, and Benny Goodman. Only styles are covered in part two. The weakness of the guide is that very little is provided on the history and context of the styles or individuals. The guides are an outgrowth of the jazz history classes that Dr. Pickney previously taught at UCLA. Appendices include sample listening exams for the development of Jazz 132 A & B (UCLA); record list for the development of jazz; chronology of listening guide topics; selected

Los Angeles-area jazz entertainment centers; course outlines for development of Jazz A & B; glossary; and a recommended reading list.

1488. Porter, Bob. *Signature Record Listing by Master Numbers.* Zephyrhills, Fla.: Joyce Music Publications; 1989.

Documents the recordings of some of the most important artists of the 1940s and 1950s. The entries are organized by master numbers and contain artist, date, venue, title, and personnel. Bob Thiele owned the label.

1489. Raben, Erik (editor). *Jazz Records 1942–80: A Discography.* Eight volumes. Copenhagen: Jazz Media Aps; 1984.

Lists issues, and reissues where possible, organized alphabetically. Nonjazz recordings are sometimes included to complete the discography of an artist or group. Live recordings, broadcasts, and transcriptions are only included when one or more titles have been or were scheduled to be issued. Broadcasts are occasionally included. The entries include recording sessions, dates, venues, personnel, master numbers, record numbers, and transcriptions. Some entries begin with an article. Each volume includes an index with a reference to each page on which an artist is cited.

1490. _____. *A Discography of Free Jazz: Albert Ayler, Don Cherry, Ornette Coleman, Pharoah Sanders, Archie Shepp, Cecil Taylor.* Copenhagen: Karl Emil Knudsen; 1969.

Organized alphabetically by artist. the recordings are arranged alphabetically by groups under which the recording was made. Most of the entries include personnel, title of album, date and place of recording, and titles of individual sides.

1491. Ramsey, Jr. Frederic. *A Guide to Long Play Records.* New York: Long Player Publications, 1954; reprint, New York: Da Capo, 1977.

An annotated guide to about 400 entries of individual artists and bands. The book contains short discussions of select available recordings as well as artist and title indices. He discusses styles, cites personnel, and gives reasons why the recording is important. The 1977 edition includes a new introduction and supplementary record listings (addition to 1981).

1492. Ruppli, Michel. *The Aladdin/Imperial Labels: A Discography.* New York, Westport, Conn., London: Greenwood Press; 1991.

Lists all recordings made or issued by the Aladdin and Imperial labels, and their subsidiaries (Intro, Jazz West, Lamp, Score, Ultra, and 7–11 for Aladdin, and Bayou, Bonnie, Colony, Knight, Moppett, and Post for Imperial). The discography is divided into six parts: (1) details all recordings coming from Alladin labels made between 1945 and 1961 (includes separate sections for leased materials and sessions not precisely dated); (2) lists all Imperial folk and dance recordings, using various master series according to the field covered; (3) lists the Imperial popular IM Master Series (popular, blues, rhythm and blues, and jazz artists); (4) lists reissues from other labels along with those with assigned master numbers; (5) contains the single series used on various labels; and (6) includes the album series (45 rpm EPs, 33 rpm 7, 10, and 12 inch LPs, and compact discs). Artists and album numbers are provided for each album. Parts 5 and 6 include comprehensive lists of foreign issues (European and Japanese) along with tables of equivalent foreign/U.S. issues. Very thorough.

1493. _____. *The Clef/Verve Labels: A Discography; Volume I, The Norman Granz Era, and Volume II, the MGM Era;* with assistance from Bob Porter. Westport, Conn.: Greenwood Press; 1986.

Lists all recordings made or issued by the Clef and Verve labels and their subsidiaries (Norgran, Verve-Folkways, Verve-Forecast, and VSP). Volume 1 is subdivided into four parts and is devoted to all recordings made or issued between 1944 and 1961 under the ownership of Norman Granz: part one includes many of the Jazz at the Philharmonic Concerts; part two lists the Clef/Norgran sessions made between 1950 and 1956; part three covers the Verve sessions made by Granz using the Verve Master numerical sequence; and part four lists reissues from other labels. Volume 2 includes all recordings made or reissued after the Verve catalogue was sold to MGM to the last sessions in 1973. Inclusive in volume 2 are parts five and six, the Verve sessions made between 1966 and 1973, when MGM master numerical sequences were used for all recordings.

1494. _____. *The King Labels: A Discography.* Two volumes. Westport, Conn.: Greenwood Press; 1985.

A discographical listing of all recordings made or reissued by King and subsidiary labels: DeLuxe, Federal, and Bethlehem. Although most entries are devoted to rhythm and blues and country music, he includes some King jazz sessions previously cited by J. G. Jepsen, Albert McCarthy, and Walter Bruyninckx. The jazz entries include Benny Carter, Erroll Garner, early Roland Kirk, whereas the Bethlehem label recorded several West Coast jazz groups, Carmen McRae, Nina Simone, Duke Ellington, and Johnny Richards. Volume one is devoted to the King Masters, and volume two to the associated labels. Index of artists (volume two).

1495. _____. *The Chess Labels: A Discography.* Westport, Conn.: Greenwood Press; 1983.

Covers Chess recordings of blues and jazz from its beginnings in 1947 to its demise in 1975. The discography is divided into six parts and includes information on date, venue of session, personnel, titles, matrix and issue numbers for each title, and LP numbers, including foreign releases. In addition to jazz entries, there are blues/rhythm and blues entries on Chuck Berry, Muddy Waters, and Howlin' Wolf.

1496. _____. *The Savoy Label: A Discography.* Westport, Conn.: Greenwood Press; 1980.

Contains listings on gospel, rhythm and blues, and jazz. Among the listings contained are vintage recordings of Alex Bradford and James Cleveland, Big Maybelle and Big Jay McNelly, and Charles Parker. Savoy championed the 1940s bebop recordings of Charles Parker. Included are recordings with a young Miles Davis. The listings cover the 1939–65 era and are arranged chronologically. Whenever matrix numbers differed and were used concurrently, the listings are given separately.

1497. _____. *Atlantic Records: A Discography.* Four volumes. Westport, Conn.: Greenwood Press; 1979.

Documents all African American recordings made on Atlantic records, 1947 to October 1978. There are 36,000 listings covering blues, jazz, rhythm and blues, and soul. The four volumes are arranged chronologically by number sequences; the jazz section includes personnel listings, date of session, place, titles, and release numbers. Organized as follows: volume 1, covers 1947–66; volume 2, covers 1966–70; volume 3, covers 1970–74; and volume 4, covers 1974–78. An index of session leaders is included in volumes 1 through 3, and volume 4 has a cumulative index of the session leaders listed in the four volumes.

1498. _____. *Prestige Jazz Records 1949–1969: A Discography.* Copenhagen: Karl E. Knudsen; 1972.

Includes original blues, gospel, and jazz recordings as well as all reissues made by Prestige during this period. The original recordings are arranged in chronological order of recording session. Reissues from other labels are also included and listed chronologically by original recording date covering 1944 to 1962. A supplementary section of 1933 to 1968 reissues are also included. There are several additional supplements: 12″ LP numbers with performers; 12″ English and French issues; 45 RPM singles, 78 RPM, 10″ LP, and 45 RPM EP issues. The listings contain full discographical details. Index of bandleaders.

1499. Ruppli, Michel, and Ed Novitsky. *The Mercury Labels: A Discography.* Five volumes. Westport, Conn.: Greenwood Press; 1993.

Mercury Records was founded in 1945 and soon became a major recorder of blues and jazz. This discography provides a listing of all recordings made or issued by Mercury and its subsidiaries (Blue Rock, Cumberland, Emarcy, Fontant, Limelight, Philips, Smash, and Wing). Also included are leased and purchased materials and recordings (independent labels) distributed by Mercury. The five volumes contain 4,240 pages.

1500. Rust, Brian. *The American Dance Band Discography, 1917–1942.* Two volumes. New Rochelle, N.Y.: Arlington House; 1975.

Covers the recordings of nearly 2,000 bands with detailed discographical information and succinct biographical essays. The primary weakness of this work is that it omits African American bands, which were thoroughly covered in his monumental work, *Jazz Records.* He also omits the recordings of Benny Goodman and Glenn Miller, perhaps because D. Russell Connor and W. Warren Hicks published *B. G.—Off the Record: A Bio-discography* and John Flower published *Moonlight Serenade: A Bio-discography of the Glenn Miller Civilian Band* in 1975 and 1972, respectively. The listings are highly accurate.

1501. _____. *Jazz Records, A–Z, 1897–1931.* Middlesex: the author. 1961; Second edition, Hatch End, Middlesex, 1962; *Jazz Records, A–Z, 1932–1942.* Hatch End, 1965. *Jazz Records 1897–1942* (revised edition). London: Storyville Publications. Two volumes; 1970.

A monumental compilation of jazz and ragtime. The author lists cell recordings made primarily in America and England to the Petrillo ban. The books/volumes are organized systematically as follows: alphabetically by performer or band; sessions are organized chronologically with details on date of recording, instrumentation and personnel, matrix numbers, take and issue numbers, and venue of recording; abbreviations are used for instruments, labels, soloists, and vocalists in selected compositions; and cross-references for fictitious names where warranted. Incorrect citations were corrected in *Storyville* No. 36. Richard Grandorges's *Index* was also an integral part of this series.

1502. _____. *Jazz Records A–Z, 1897–1942.* Two volumes/Fourth edition. New Rochelle, N.Y.: Arlington House; 1972.

Contains listings of all jazz recordings to 1942. The arrangement is alphabetical by artist or orchestra with the orchestra's personnel, place and date of recording, song titles, matrix numbers, and label and issue numbers, with notes relating to each recording given in each entry. Updated in a variety of sources, including *Jazz Journal* and *Storyville;* similar to Jepsen's discography (1981).

1503. Salemann, Dieter, Dieter Hartmann, and Michel Vogler. *Solography Series.* Basle: Salemann, 1986–1988; Ithaca, N.Y.: Jazz Circle, 1986–1988.

This solography includes a chronological listing of solos, recordings, band routes, and engagements. The solos include information about duration, and the discography includes titles, dates, venues, labels, and personnel. The series is as follows:

A. Edmund Gregory (Sahib Shibab): Solography, Discography, Band Routes, Engagements in Chronological Order.

B. Sonny Stitt: Solography, Discography, Band Routes, Engagements in Chronological Order.

C. Jimmy Heath: Solography, Discography, Band Routes, Engagements in Chronological Order.

D. Wardell Gray: Solography, Discography, Band Routes, Engagements in Chronological Order.

E. Sonny Criss: Solography, Discography, Band Routes, Engagements in Chronological Order.

F. Rudy Williams: Solography, Discography, Band Routes, Engagements in Chronological Order.

G. Åke "Stan" Hasselgård: Solography, Discography, Band Routes, Engagements in Chronological Order.

H. Ernie Henry: Solography, Discography, Band Routes, Engagements in Chronological Order.

I. John Brown: Solography, Discography, Band Routes, Engagements in Chronological Order.

1504. Schleman, Hilton. *Rhythm on Record: A Who's Who and Register of Recorded Dance Music.* London: Melody Maker; 1936.

One of the earliest attempts to systematically list jazz recordings in book form. This book is significant for at least two reasons: (1) he includes dance bands, and (2) this discography preceded Charles DeLaunay's *Hot Discography* by several months. By today's standards, the discographies lack detailed information; however, each artist or band is given a concise biography. This book has been cited by David Horn in *Literature of American Music,* and Paul Sheatsley, "A Quarter Century of Jazz Discography," *Record Research,* February, 1964.

1505. Sears, Richard S. *V-Discs: A Historical Discography.* Westport, Conn.: Greenwood Press; 1980.

This discography also includes a V-Discs First Supplement and phonograph records produced during and after World War II by a military group in New York. Divided into three sections: historical, synthesis, discography, and an appendix. Details the events that led to the formation of the V-Disc group and surveys organization and operation of the program; how, where, and by whom the records were made, processed, produced, and distributed. Also includes an annotated discography of all issued army and navy V-Discs, including unissued sessions. The supplement includes corrections and additions to the book. The V-Discs were issued from October 1943 to May 1949. This discography includes special recording sessions, radio broadcasts, broadcast rehearsals, film soundtracks, radio transcriptions, and issued and unissued commercial recordings. The entries are organized alphabetically. Comprehensive and scholarly.

1506. Smith, Charles Edward, Frederic Ramsey Jr., Charles Payne Rogers, and William Russell. *The Jazz Record Book.* New York: Smith and Durrell; 1942.

Divided into two broad sections: a section on jazz history precedes the record entries, and the second section is devoted to recorded jazz. The jazz history also includes a chapter on blues and boogie-woogie and is not chronologically arranged. The authors cover phases of jazz growth, technical changes, instrumentation, and jazz intonation in the New Orleans period. The recordings are organized into sections on "Chicago Breakdown," "New York and Harlem," "Blues and Boogie-Woogie," "Seven Brass," "Four Reed," and "They Still Play Jazz." Each section contains titles, labels, personnel, date, venue, and concise background comments. Geared to an audience interested in selected recordings of big bands and ensembles. Selected bibliography of books and periodicals and an index of bands and other recording units.

1507. Stagg, Tom, and Charlie Crump. *New Orleans, the Revival: A Tape and Discography of Negro Traditional Jazz Recorded in New Orleans or by New Orleans Bands, 1937–1972.* Dublin: Bashall Eaves; 1973.

Primarily lists New Orleans black musicians, including brass bands. First releases, reissues, and unissued (much of the book) recordings are included as well as private tapes and taped interviews. The entries are arranged alphabetically by bandleader or group name. Among the recordings cited are Bunk Johnson, Papa Celestin, Papa French, George Lewis, the Onward Brass Band, Kid Ory, and the Eureka Brass Band. There is also a section on "The Religious Recordings of New Orleans," which feature artists or groups like Sister Elizabeth Eustis, the Holy Family Spiritual Church of Christ, the New Orleans Street Gospel Singers, and the New Orleans Humming Four. There are four indices: black New Orleans musicians;

white New Orleans musicians; non-New Orleans musicians; and miscellaneous persons.

1508. Swenson, John. *The Rolling Stone Jazz Record Guide.* New York: Random House; 1985.

An alphabetical listing of currently available LPs on artists and groups, including concise biographical portraits, comments on the albums, and a zero- to five-star rating for each album. There are 4,000 jazz albums; however, there are some omissions, including Milt Jackson, Joe Williams, and Teddy Wilson. The albums are identified by manufacturer only.

1509. Testoni, Gian Carlo. *Enciclopedia del Jazz. Second edition* Milan: Messaggerie musicale; 1954.

In Italian. Contains brief biographies and detailed discographies of recordings issued in Italy from 1920 to 1950. The recordings cover both American and non-American artists and contain information on their life and musical careers, as well as date, place, title, label, personnel, and matrix numbers of releases (addition to 1981).

1510. Tudor, Dean, and Nancy Tudor. *Jazz: American Music on Elpee.* Littleton, Colo.: Libraries Unlimited Inc.; 1979.

A survey and buying guide to around 1,300 jazz recordings. The recordings are organized as follows: anthologies, ragtime, geographic, origins and stylings, mainstream swing and big bands, bop, cool, modern, and dance themes. Each entry includes name of artist, country of origin, title, and serial number. Each entry is annotated and is preceded by an essay that focuses on definitions, criteria for selection, history and development, hybrid forms, and more. There are some factual errors in the essays. Includes an annotated bibliography of 136 books and 18 periodicals, a label directory, and an artists index.

1511. Tuft, Harry M. *The Denver Folklore Center Catalogue and 1966 Almanac of Music.* Denver: Denver Folklore Center; 1965.

Contains a listing of some early jazz recordings.

1512. Van Eyle, William. *Jazz Pearls.* Oudkarged, Holland: Van Eyle; 1975.

Surveys 3,102 jazz recordings listed chronologically, covering many styles and periods. The entries contain full discographical information (addition to 1981).

1513. White, Bozy. *AFRS Basic Music Library Volume One 1–1200, Volume Two 1201–2400, Volume Three 2401–3603.* Zephyrhills, Fla.: Joyce Music Publications; 1988, 1989.

A comprehensive coverage of Armed Forces Radio Service's broadcasts. Each volume contains 1,200 entries with artist, date, venue, title, personnel, and index.

1514. Wilson, John S. *The Collector's Jazz Modern.* New York: Audiocom, Inc., 1955, 1956, 1957, 1958, 1959; Philadelphia, New York: J.B. Lippincott, 1959.

Deals with jazz styles of post-World War II, proceeding from the end of *Collector's Jazz: Traditional and Swing.* Artists who might have been assigned to either volume are arbitrarily assigned. Discusses numerous recordings in part two where the individual artist is either the leader or plays a significant role. References to sidemen can be checked in the index.

1515. _____. *Collector's Jazz: Tradition and Swing.* Philadelphia: J.B. Lippincott; 1958.

A guide covering jazz styles developed before World War II. The coverage is limited to "Traditional" and "Swing," and contains discographies and biographical notes on several artists. In addition, there is a brief essay on the histories of traditional and swing jazz. The guide is limited to selected artists and their recordings of the previously mentioned genres.

1516. Wynn, Ron, with Michael Erlewine, et al. (editors). *All Music Guide to Jazz.* San Francisco: Miller Freeman; 1994.

Focuses on 26 styles of African American music, including boogie woogie, and all jazz styles from early to soul. Includes biographical sketches of about 1,150 artists, and groups with reviews and ratings of their best recordings. More than 9,000 records, tapes, and CDs are listed. Concise introductory summaries of the styles, jazz terms, and entries of numerous musicians are also included. Each entry contains birth and death dates, where applicable, types of jazz played, biocritical statements, and a chronological list of recordings with record label, number, date, and a signed review. The appendices include a directory of record labels, list of producers, clubs, annotated list of periodicals, mail order sources for jazz recordings, and a bibliography.

1517. Yanow, Scott. *Classic Jazz: The Musicians and Recordings that Shaped Jazz, 1895–1933.* San Francisco: Backbeat Books; 2001.

Begins with an exploration of ragtime, early blues, and blues-infused New Orleans jazz from 1895 to 1916. However, the author focuses on the 1917–33 years, and profiles artists such as Louis Armstrong, Sidney Bechet, Bix Beiderbecke, Duke Ellington, Coleman Hawkins, Earl Hines, James P. Johnson, Freddie Keppard, Jelly Roll Morton, King Oliver,

Bessie Smith, and Paul Whiteman. Provides reviews, rating of recordings, and historical insight often absent from other listening guides.

Educators, performers, and scholars are also urged to access the discographies of Hans Westerberg, which were unavailable to the author at the time of publication.

VIII

Theses and Dissertations

This section is limited to selected studies cited primarily in both the master's and dissertation abstracts. The jazz education citations were limited primarily to studies on jazz improvisation. Each entry includes the author, title, degree, university, year of completion, and a concise annotation.

Theses and Dissertations on Individuals/Groups

Julian "Cannonball" Adderley

1518. Crawley, Ricky Alonzo, Ph.D. *Julian "Cannonball" Adderley: Selected Highlights of His Life and Music.* Tallahassee: The Florida State University; 2001.

> The first six sections describe the early years, provides an overview of Adderley's family, high school, college, teaching, and military years. In the second section, his debut as a professional, events surrounding his performance at the Café Bohemia in New York, his recruitment by Miles Davis, and his return to teaching before organizing his own quintet. In section three, his 16-year stint as a leader, selected recordings, festival appearances, concerts, and tours are discussed. Section four describes the circumstances surrounding his death. In section five, there are transcriptions of 50 selected improvisations by Adderley replete with articulation and phrase markings. The transcriptions are dated and referenced to the original recordings. Section six details activities after his death, including

memorials, tributes, festivals, scholarships, and posthumous recordings. After Adderley's death, Florida A&M, his alma mater, established a jazz program in his honor.

1519. Kernfeld, Barry Dean, Ph.D. *Adderley, Coltrane, and Davis at the Twilight of Bebop: The Search for Melodic Coherence (1958–59).* Ithaca: Cornell University; 1981.

An analysis of the 1958–59 solos of Julian "Cannonball" Adderley, Miles Davis, and John Coltrane while performing in the Miles Davis sextet. The author argues that "two" Coltranes competed artistically throughout the 1950s; that Adderley displayed several improvisational techniques, and that Miles Davis used "paraphrasing" (André Hodier's definition), on the four analyzed compositions. He focuses on four blues in "F," "Dr. Jekyll," "Straight, No Chaser," "Jazz at the Plaza" (a retitled version of "Straight, No Chaser") and specifically motivic improvisation on "So What," "Flamenco Sketches," "All Blues," and "Milestones" (Also cited under John Coltrane, Miles Davis, and Collective Biographies).

Louis Armstrong

1520. Harker, Brian Cameron, Ph.D. *The Early Years of Louis Armstrong.* New York: Columbia University; 1998.

The author attempts to identify and trace the origins of important traits of Armstrong's early style through recordings he made as a sideman and leader in Chicago and New York. He traces traits such as the clarinet-type musical figures and high notes, arpeggiated solo construction, rubato rhythms, triadic extensions, rhythmic concepts like his accented upbeats, downbeat slurring, and complimentary relations among rhythmic patterns. The author surveyed Armstrong's first recordings with blues vocalists, recordings made with Erskine Tate's Vendome Theater Orchestra, the Hot Five, and Hot Seven. He argues that Armstrong's style was codified in these recordings, thereby transforming the New Orleans idiom, and for many conceptualizing the art of jazz itself.

1521. Harrington, Richard Charles, Ph.D. *The Young Artist As Old Bad Air: Louis Armstrong as Model "Invisible Man."* Charlottesville: University of Virginia; 1981.

In addition to gathering information from Ralph Ellison's *Invisible Man* and elsewhere, the author uses two recordings of Armstrong's *Black and Blue*, the original from 1929, and the 1947 recording, to reveal a link between Armstrong and the novel. He discusses masking, and how Armstrong inspires young artists to grasp and arrange conflicting sounds of their own culture and being. He uses Armstrong as an artistic model, summarizes the highlights of his career and improvises his autobiography as a performing artist.

1521a. Association for the Advancement of Creative Musicians (AACM).

De Jong, Nanette T. *Chosen Identities and Musical Symbols: The Curacaoan Jazz Community and the Association for the Advancement of Creative Musicians.* Ann Arbor: University of Michigan; 1997.

She examines the similarities between identity formation of the Curacaoan jazz community and the Chicago-based Association for the Advancement of Creative Musicians (AACM). Because both groups have revised and reinvented musical traditions, she investigated the complexities of identity formation via the music produced by the groups. In addition to Africa, her findings indicate that the Curacaoan jazz musicians embraced a variety of identity choices, ranging from Indian to Cuban, Dutch to Venezuelan, and Colombian to Brazilian. Regarding AACM, she discovered that they used their performances and compositions to reinvent Africa via the use of compositional structures, text, instrumentation, rhythm, and visual effects.

Bix Beiderbecke

1522. Perhonis, John Paul, Ph.D. *The Bix Beiderbecke Story: The Jazz Musician in Legend, Fiction, and Fact: A Study of the Images of Jazz in the National Culture: 1930–The Present.* Minneapolis: University of Minnesota; 1978.

Began as a study of Leon "Bix" Beiderbecke and evolved into a case study in jazz historiography focusing on the writings of cultural and historical scholars. An assessment of Beiderbecke's life and music within its cultural context. Divided into Bix Beiderbecke: The Jazz Musician as Romantic Artist, From Romantic Artist to Artist-Craftsman and Tough Artist-Hero: The Jazz Musician in Popular Writings during the Thirties, and From Romantic Legend and Literary Art to Critical Evaluation: The Jazz Musician in the Critical Establishment. Perhonis argues that acculturation processes are central in the evolution of jazz within American culture. Excellent study of Beiderbecke within his cultural context.

Edward Joseph Blackwell

1523. Schmalenberger, David J., D.M.A. *Stylistic Evolution of Jazz Drummer Ed Blackwell: The Cultural Intersection of New Orleans and West Africa (Louisiana).* Morgantown: West Virginia University; 1991.

Traces his drumming influences to bebop, and the conceptual ideas of Max Roach. Also discusses the role and function that his New Orleans roots had on the evolution of his drumming style. Blackwell's roots in New Orleans parade drumming, blues, big band swing, music of the Mardi Gras Indians, Caribbean music, and rhythm and blues all shaped his approach to drumming. In addition to his formative years in New Orleans, the author discusses his association with Ornette Coleman, the influence of traditional West African rhythmic concepts upon his musical development, and uses several transcriptions to illustrate these influences.

Jimmy Blanton

1524. Nash, Robert, D.M.A. *The Solo Vocabulary of Jazz Bassist Jimmy Blanton.* Baton Rouge: The Louisiana State University and Agricultural and Mechanical College; 1998.

The purpose of this study was to examine various aspects of Jimmy Blanton's solo vocabulary by transcribing and comparing 18 of his solos. The author traces and compares specific melodic, harmonic, and rhythmic phenomenon in different musical contexts and settings. A review of Blanton's life and musical career, jazz bass solos to 1939, and detailed analysis of 18 transcriptions are also included.

Charles Bowen

1525. Closson, David Lee, Ph.D. *One Life In Black Music: An Ethnography of a Black Jazz Musician.* Philadelphia: University of Pennsylvania; 1980.

The dissertation has two objectives: first, to place black music within the total culture, from a folklore perspective; and, second, to spell out explicitly assumptions concerning the relation between the music, the people who created it, and the larger American culture. With Charles Bowen as a case study, Closson focuses on the sociocultural context using ethnographic methodology, humanism, and symbolism. Excellent study of the role and status of an African American musician in American culture.

Anthony Braxton

1526. Radano, Ronald Michael, Ph.D. *Anthony Braxton and His Two Musical Traditions: The Meeting of Concert Music and Jazz. (Volumes I and II).* Ann Arbor: The University of Michigan; 1985.

Concerned with mediating Braxton's theories on avant-garde concert music and jazz aesthetics. Addresses the changes in Braxton's musical perception after encountering Schoenberg's music and the journalistic formulae of his critics. Presents an analysis of Braxton's music for improvising ensembles and examines his approach to improvisation. Radano critiques Braxton's treatise on harmony and aesthetics, "Tri-Axiom Position," demonstrating the connection between his African American nationalist views and his preference for avant-garde art forms. Radano's research led to the publication of *New Musical Figurations: Anthony Braxton's Cultural Critique* in 1993.

Randy Brecker

1527. Davison, Michael Allyn, D.M.A. *A Motivic Study of Twenty Improvised Solos of Randy Brecker Between the Years of 1970–1980.* Madison: The University of Wisconsin, Madison; 1987.

Davison identifies and examines six motives used by trumpeter Randy Brecker in 20 improvised solos recorded between 1970–1980. The study includes an interview with Brecker and verification of the transcriptions, chord symbols, and jazz nomenclature. Davison postulates that Brecker's use of six motivic cells throughout the 20 solos reveals a deep structural language that informs his style.

Clifford Brown

1528. Stewart, Milton Lee, Ph.D. *Structural Development in the Jazz Improvisational Technique of Clifford Brown.* Ann Arbor: The University of Michigan; 1973.

Stewart focuses on the structural development in Brown's improvisation in four choruses of "I Can Dream, Can't I?" (Prestige 7761). Stewart's specific purpose was to test Brown's awareness of the mental constructs (composition and patterns) of the original composition. Stewart concludes that: (1) rhythmic patterns operate on different levels, (2) the phenomenon of "swing" is a by-product of rhythmic displacement, and (3) a "blue-note-effect" (pitch interval patterns) exists in different forms in the improvisation. This is one of the first jazz studies to test mental constructs.

Dave Brubeck

1529. Zirpoli, Danny Ronald, Ph.D. *An Evaluation of the Work of Jazz Pianist/ Composer Dave Brubeck.* Gainesville: University of Florida; 1990.

Zirpoli assesses the contributions, influence, quality of work, and educational significance of Brubeck through analysis examining meter and rhythm, classical music influences, compositional, pedagogical, and educational contributions, and sociological issues. Excellent presentation of the man, his music, and his contributions to jazz.

Betty Carter

1530. Bauer, William R., Ph.D. *Betty Carter: Biography and Style Analysis.* New York: City University of New York; 1999.

Focuses on Carter's contributions as a jazz vocalist, composer, and arranger. Uses interviews of Carter to illuminate the events of her life, and views her musical development and evolution within the context of history. He explores how the changes that occurred in the music industry from 1946 to 1996 have affected her musical career. Also includes details on the formation of her record company, and uses Jan LaRue's guideline for style analysis to analyze several transcriptions of her vocalizing. Uses sound, harmony, melody, rhythm, and growth in conjunction to the lyrics of popular songs to raise questions about the creative process of jazz and jazz vocals.

1531. Buckley, Diedre Lorea, D.M.A. *Betty Carter: The Voice.* Madison: The University of Wisconsin, Madison; 2002.

The primary objective of this dissertation is to ascertain what contributions Betty Carter has made to the ongoing redefinition and evolution of jazz. A secondary objective is to consider the appropriateness of various methods, which are, or could be, used in jazz criticism. Her contributions as an arranger, composer, mentor, performer, and owner of her own record label are discussed. In addition, the author contextualizes Carter's music by using her perspectives, by placing Carter's performance concepts within the broader context of American performance tradition, and uses Henry Louis Gates's notions of signifyin(g), and George Steiner's and Hans Keller's ideas of criticism to draw conclusions.

Ron Carter

1532. Butterfield, Matthew W., Ph.D. *Jazz Analysis and the Production of Musical Community: A Situational Structure.* Philadelphia: University of Pennsylvania; 2001.

Develops a rationale and method of analysis that seeks to transcend the solitary listening practices implied by conventional musical analysis and the socially integrative nature of jazz performance events. He develops an interdisciplinary approach that he labels "Situational Structure," a function of the social, economic, temporal, spatial, and acoustic organization of musical events. He uses case study analyses of two Ron Carter performances, one recorded and one live, to draw his conclusions. In addition, he examines recent trends in jazz history regarding the typical situation in which we listen to the music today.

Sidney "Big Sid" Catlett

1533. Hutton, James Michael, D.A. *Sidney "Big Sid" Catlett: The Development of Modern Jazz Drumming Style.* Greely: University of Northern Colorado; 1991.

Details his contributions as a drummer and a catalyst in the transformation in jazz drumming. Focuses on Catlett's rhythm section and solo performances in New Orleans, Chicago, swing, and bebop styles. According to Hutton, Catlett's ability to accompany, solo, and use dynamics (and silence) enabled him to function in both early and more modern contexts. Good study of role and function, context, and musical contributions.

Charlie Christian

1534. Antonich, Mark E., M.M. *The Jazz Style and Analysis of the Music of Charlie Christian, Based upon an Examination of His Improvised Solos, and the Various Components of His Playing.* Pittsburgh: Duquesne University; 1982.

Antonich discusses Christian's influence by examining his musical contributions, influences, style, most significant melodic, harmonic, and rhythmic patterns and improvisations. Includes a biographical sketch, musical portrait, explanation of symbols and notation used in the musical examples, a selected list of available transcriptions, a bibliography, and a cassette tape of compositions.

Zez Confrey

1535. Dossa, James Richard, Ph.D. *The Novelty Piano Style of Zez Confrey: A Theoretical Analysis of His Piano Solos and Their Relation to Ragtime and Jazz.* Evanston: Northwestern University; 1986.

A study of Zez Confrey, a composer of ragtime and early jazz. Dossa traces Confrey's musical influences to classical music, percussion, ragtime, early jazz, and piano roll arrangements. Between 1918 and 1959, Confrey composed more than 150 novelty pieces, making significant contributions to novelty piano methods and piano literature for children. Confrey's early compositions feature complex rhythmic formulas in large structural schemes. His middle period pieces, lyrical with rich harmonic textures, use French impressionist concepts. Annotated bibliography of novelty piano literature, piano ragtime, and jazz piano styles.

Ornette Coleman

1536. Cogswell, Michael Bruce, M.M. *Melodic Organization in Four Solos by Ornette Coleman.* Denton: University of North Texas; 1989.

Presents an assessment of Coleman's career and a discussion of "harmolodics" through analysis of four improvised solos recorded in 1959—"Ramblin,'" "Lonely Woman," "Congenial," and "Free"—with conclusions regarding melodic continuity and development. Insightful and informative study on melodic organization. Selected bibliography and discography.

1537. Westendorf, Lynette, D.M.A. *Analyzing Free Jazz (Coleman, Ornette, Coltrane, John, and Taylor, Cecil).* Seattle: University of Washington; 1994.

An examination of several stylistically diverse works within their respective cultural contexts. The first two chapters address the origins and influence of free jazz, and it relationship to blues and earlier jazz styles. In addition, she discusses the methodological approaches of selected artists, the Black Nationalist Movement, treatment of free jazz in the scholarly literature, and analytical techniques appropriate to jazz. In chapters 3 through 5, she analyzes Ornette Coleman's *Lonely Woman* (1959), John Coltrane's *India* (1961), and Cecil Taylor's *Indent: Second Layer* (1973). She transcribed each composition, and uses diagrams, and some graphic representations to make her points about rhythm, method of development, form, and the use of contrast. Additionally, she discusses Coleman's *Harmolodic* theory, Coltrane's adaptation of Indian aesthetics and techniques, and the poem, if warranted, that a specific composition is based on. (Also cited under John Coltrane, Cecil Taylor, and Collective Biographies.)

John Coltrane

1538. Cole, William Shadrack, Ph.D. *The Style of John Coltrane, 1955–1967.* Middletown, Conn.: Wesleyan University; 1975.

Traces the evolution of Coltrane's style from 1955 to his death in 1967. Cole uses ideas of Fela Sowande to understand Coltrane as a musician in an African to African American continuum. He focuses on Coltrane's saxophone innovations, his interest in world music and his worldview, and the influence of African cultural phenomena upon his music Provocative insights and theories. Excellent work on Coltrane's musical contributions, aesthetics, and worldview.

1539. Grey, De Sayles R, Ph.D. *John Coltrane and the "Avant-Garde" Movement in Jazz History.* Pittsburgh: University of Pittsburgh; 1986.

Concerned with refuting the negative assessments of Coltrane's avant-grade jazz period in the early 1960s Musical ignorance, misinterpretations, the social bias of critics, and the need for appropriate critical standards are cited. With educated standards Grey evaluates Coltrane's modal playing, ethical imperatives, and spiritualism.

1540. Hester, Karlton Edward, Ph.D. *The Melodic and Polyrhythmic Development of John Coltrane's Spontaneous Composition in a Racist Society.* New York: City University of New York; 1990.

Argues that Coltrane's musical evolution involved an absorption of African and Asiatic music and culture along with his mastery of at least five definitive American musical styles: blues, bebop, hard bop, modal jazz, and free jazz. He also examines Coltrane's adroit saxophone technique, and refutes the assertion that free jazz was an attempt to destroy conventional musical systems. Hester uses *Interstellar Space* as an example of Coltrane's incorporation of earlier musical devices in his free jazz style. Also covers the relationship between Coltrane's spirituality and his evolution as an improviser.

1541. Kernfeld, Barry Dean, Ph.D. *Adderley, Coltrane, and Davis at the Twilight of Bebop: The Search for Melodic Coherence (1958–59)*. Ithaca: Cornell University; 1981.

An analysis of the 1958–59 solos of Julian "Cannonball" Adderley, Miles Davis, and John Coltrane when performing in the Miles Davis sextet. The author argues that the "two" Coltranes competed artistically throughout the 1950s; that Adderley displayed several improvisational techniques, and that Miles Davis used "paraphrasing" (André Hodier's definition), on the four analyzed compositions. He focuses on four blues in "F," "Dr. Jekyll," "Straight, No Chaser," "Jazz at the Plaza" (a retitled version of "Straight, No Chaser") and specifically motivic improvisation on "So What," "Flamenco Sketches," "All Blues," and "Milestones." (Also cited under Cannonball Adderley, Miles Davis, and Collective Biographies.)

1542. Kofsky, Frank Joseph, Ph.D. *Black Nationalism and the Revolution in Music: Social Change and Stylistic Development in the Art of John Coltrane and Others, 1954–1967*. Pittsburgh: University of Pittsburgh; 1973.

Researches the relationship between social change in the African American community and concurrent developments in jazz, 1954–1967. Kofsky introduced and researched three hypotheses: (1) although jazz innovators and significant practitioners are African Americans, the business and related activities are controlled primarily by whites; (2) African American jazz artists are often the first to promote antiracist protest ideologies; and (3) the promulgation of such ideologies by the African American jazz community has impacted the course of jazz evolution. Kofsky reviewed jazz literature, interviewed John and Alice Coltrane, Ornette Coleman, Albert Ayler, Elvin Jones, Cecil Taylor, McCoy Tyner, Archie Shepp, Pharoah Sanders, Sun Ra, and others, and collected business data to supplement his participant observer views. His conclusions point to business control by whites, the exploitation of jazz as a propaganda tool by federal agencies, the view among young African Americans that this control is not commensurate with their creativity, and Coltrane's role in fermenting a jazz revolution.

1543. Porter, Lewis R., Ph.D. *John Coltrane's Music of 1960 Through 1967: Jazz Improvisation as Composition.* Waltham, Mass.: Brandeis University; 1983.

Concerned with explaining Coltrane's contributions to the control of long-range structure in "Equinox," "A Love Supreme," and "Venus." Porter begins with an overview of terminology, procedures, and history and then discusses saxophone styles and Coltrane's recordings of the 1950s and 1960s. He concludes with Coltrane's influence on younger artists. Porter demonstrates Coltrane's use of motives to build improvisation and the continuity of mood over time in Coltrane's solos. Includes transcriptions by Andrew White.

1544. Saul., Scott Andrew, Ph. D. *Freedom is, Freedom Ain't: Jazz and the Making of the Sixties.* New Haven: Yale University; 2001.

Examines the jazz culture of the 1950s and 1960s from three perspectives; musicians who elaborated its aesthetic of extreme spontaneity and extreme discipline, artists and intellectuals who associated themselves with freedom cultural values, and youth who attended jazz festivals in the 1950s and 1960s but later transferred their allegiance to rock music. Part one covers black and white intellectuals who grappled with issues of community and marginality; part two examines the rise of the jazz festival as a site of postwar youth culture; parts three and four examines the music, approaches, significance, and contributions of John Coltrane and Charles Mingus. In part five, the author traces the emergence of counterculture among white youth, and the rise of soul power in the African American community. (Also cited under Charles Mingus and Collective Biographies.)

1545. Washington, Michael Spence, Ph.D. *Beautiful Nightmare: Coltrane, Jazz, and American Culture.* Cambridge: Harvard University; 1996.

Examines the music of John Coltrane both as music and in relation to African American cultural traditions. Although he considers the full range of Coltrane's musical career, the primary focuses are his quartet performances from November 1961 to December 1965. The main goal is to examine how the quartet's musical conceptions and techniques grew out of African American musical traditions. In addition, he shows how Coltrane's oeuvre represents an authoritative, artistic response to both the environments and the sociopolitical upheavals of the late 1950s and 1960s. The two chapters of part one focus on the socioliterary uses of the blues/jazz aesthetic, and theorizes the aesthetic by correlating specific musical practices and stylistic tendencies with the cultural preferences of African Americans. The biographical sketch of Coltrane's life and musical career is combined with the blues/jazz aesthetic, musicological tools, musical analysis, cultural theory, and African American studies to arrive at his conclusions.

1546. Westendorf, Lynette, D.M.A. *Analyzing Free Jazz (Coleman, Ornette, Coltrane, John, and Taylor, Cecil).* Seattle: University of Washington; 1994.

An examination of several stylistically diverse works within their respective cultural contexts. The first two chapters address the origins and influence of free jazz, and it relationship to blues and earlier jazz styles. In addition, she discusses the methodological approaches of selected artists, the Black Nationalist Movement, treatment of free jazz in the scholarly literature, and analytical techniques appropriate to jazz. In chapters 3 through 5, she analyzes Ornette Coleman's *Lonely Woman* (1959), John Coltrane's *India* (1961), and Cecil Taylor's *Indent: Second Layer* (1973). She transcribed each composition, and uses diagrams, and some graphic representations to make her points about rhythm, method of development, form, and the use of contrast. Additionally, she discusses Coleman's *Harmolodic* theory, Coltrane's adaptation of Indian aesthetics and techniques, and the poem, if warranted, that the composition is based on. (Also cited under Ornette Coleman, Cecil Taylor, and Collective Biographies.)

Chick Corea

1547. Duke, Daniel Alan, D.M.A. *The Piano Improvisations of Chick Corea: An Analytical Study.* Baton Rouge: The Louisiana State University and Agricultural and Mechanical College; 2000.

The dissertation grew out of a need to provide a scholarly analysis of Chick Corea's piano improvisations because there was no contemporary study of them, and because they embodied a mixture of classical and jazz styles. Duke combines traditional form, harmonic, and motivic analysis with reductive techniques related to Schenkerian analysis to "Noon Song," "Ballad for Anna," "Song of the Wind," and "Sometime Ago." He discovers harmonic language that combines elements of jazz and classical music, forms generated largely by variation, and a myriad of melodic inventions. He concludes there are shared jazz and classical elements in the compositions and improvisations of Chick Corea.

Miles Davis

1548. Coolman, Todd F. *The Miles Davis Quintet of the Mid-1960s: Synthesis of Improvisational and Compositional Elements.* New York: New York University; 1997.

Focuses on reasons why the Miles Davis Quintet of the mid-1960s is considered one of the greatest combos in jazz history. He assesses the questions from two different viewpoints. First, he interviewed the four surviving members of the group to gain their perspectives and to develop the historical context of the group. Second, he analyzed selected recordings of "Agitation," "Masqualero," and "Stella By Starlight" to determine how compositional and improvisational elements were synthesized in both studio and live performances. His analysis explored uses and functions of form, modality, rhythm, tonality, and ensemble interaction.

1549. Kernfeld, Barry Dean, Ph.D. *Adderley, Coltrane, and Davis at the Twilight of Bebop: The Search for Melodic Coherence (1958–59).* Ithaca: Cornell University; 1981.

An analysis of the 1958–59 solos of Julian "Cannonball" Adderley, Miles Davis, and John Coltrane when performing in the Miles Davis sextet. The author argues that "two" Coltranes competed artistically throughout the 1950s; that Adderley displayed several improvisational techniques, and that Miles Davis used "paraphrasing" (André Hodier's definition), on the four analyzed compositions. He focuses on four blues in "F," "Dr. Jekyll," "Straight, No Chaser," "Jazz at the Plaza" (a retitled version of "Straight, No Chaser") and specifically motivic improvisation on "So What," "Flamenco Sketches," "All Blues," and "Milestones." (Also cited under Cannonball Adderley, John Coltrane, and Collective Biographies.)

1550. Stanford, David William, Ph.D. *Prelude (Part I) from "Agharta": Modernism and Primitivism in the Fusion Works of Miles Davis.* Princeton: Princeton University; 2001.

The dissertation emerged from a study of "Prelude (Part I) from *Agharta*" and responds to the positive and negative criticism of Davis's music from this period. He recognizes Davis's music of this period as a fertile, alternative trope, as well as a complex and innovative artifact that signals trends of twentieth-century musical discourse. He also discusses orchestral components of electronic timbres, rhythmic section grooves, transcriptions and analysis, and a discussion of "oppositions" (as defined by Robert Cogan). In his final chapter, he discusses the primitivism and black nationalism found in Davis fusion works, and compares it with the Russian nationalism found in the music of Igor Stravinsky.

Buddy DeFranco

1551. Barrett, Robert Hawkes, D.M.A. *The Jazz Improvisational Style of Clarinetist Buddy DeFranco.* Norman: The University of Oklahoma; 2002.

Focuses on three periods of DeFranco's improvisational style. The swing era of the 1940s, bebop era of the 1950s and 1960s, and the modern jazz era, 1970s and onward. In the swing era, he discusses how DeFranco was influenced by clarinetists such as Benny Goodman and Artie Shaw. He acknowledges that DeFranco's bebop era style was influenced by Charles

Parker and Art Tatum, and featured motivically driven melodic lines. In the modern jazz era, DeFranco maintained his smooth technique and communicated improvisational ideas through melodic fragments and rested space. He transcribes solos from each era and together with DeFranco discussed how they evolved into a style.

Duke Ellington

1552. Dietrich, Kurt Robert, Ph.D. *Joe "Trick Sam" Nanton, Juan Tizol and Lawrence Brown: Ellington Great Trombonists, 1926–1951.* Madison: The University of Wisconsin, Madison; 1989.

In addition to the biographical information on each artist, the primary focus is on the analysis of recorded improvisations by each performer. Dietrich transcribed and analyzed 8 Nanton solos, including those that featured "wa-wa," or plunger concepts, 3 of Juan Tizol's solos, and 11 of Lawrence Brown's solos. Also provides information on the role and function of each artist within the band, and the influence of the three on trombonists of the past, present, and possibly the future. (Also cited under Collective Biographies.)

1553. Hill, Wilbert Weldon, Ph.D. *The Sacred Concerts of Edward Kennedy "Duke" Ellington.* Washington D.C.: The Catholic University of America; 1998.

Discusses stylistic codifications, harmonic analysis, his use of blues, harmonic dissonance, atypical harmonic progressions, forms, melodic concepts, orchestration techniques, and instrumentation. Also discusses how Ellington interchanged vocal and instrumental voicing techniques, the influence of modern arrangers-composers such as Thad Jones, popular music of the 1960s and 1970s, free and modal jazz, gospel and rock, and complex formal schemes for each of the Sacred Concerts.

1554. Reed, Thomas Terry, D.M.A. *Jimmy Hamilton and Russell Procope: The Clarinet Soloists in the Duke Ellington Orchestra, 1943–1974.* Columbus: The Ohio State University; 1995.

Discusses their respective styles, approaches, and roles and functions within the Duke Ellington orchestras, 1943 to 1974. Also provides a biographical sketch of each artist, and discusses Ellington's relationship with each artist. Uses 17 musical excerpts to compare and contrast the roles and functions that both Ellington and Billy Strayhorn assigned to each performer. (Also cited under Collective Biographies.)

1555. Tucker, Mark Thomas, Ph.D. (musicology). *The Early Years of Edward "Duke" Ellington, 1899–1927.* Volumes I and II. Ann Arbor: University of Michigan; 1990.

According to the author, "This study focuses on Ellington's early years following him from his youth in Washington, D.C., during the first two decades of the 1900s, to his experiences as a young man in New York during the 1920s. It leaves him at the age of 28, in early December of 1927, on the eve of his debut at the Cotton Club where a new phase of his creative and professional life was about to begin" (p. 10). Dr. Tucker interviewed friends, colleagues, and relatives of Ellington from both the Washington and early New York years. He consulted the Jazz Oral History Project at the Institute of Jazz Studies in Newark, New Jersey, the Duke Ellington Oral History Project at Yale University, and tapes of meetings of the New York Chapter of the Duke Ellington Society at the Schomburg Center for Research in Black Culture, New York. To date, this is the most thorough study published on Ellington's early years. Important for the fieldwork and his discussion of culture context and music. Permeated with musical examples. Afterward, appendix of compositions, recordings of Duke Ellington 1914–November 1927, and bibliography.

Bill Evans

1556. Berardinelli, Paula, Ph.D. *Bill Evans: His Contributions As a Jazz Pianist and an Analysis of his Musical Style.* New York: New York University; 2001.

Identifies the contributions that Bill Evans has made to jazz. She analyzes several improvisations, and investigates his life, career, and recording output. Uses the methods of Jan LaRue, Jerry Cocker, and Heinrich Schenker to analyze four representative improvisations. She concludes that Evans's contributions include both open and close chord voicing, harmonic substitutions and quartal harmonies, extensive use of motivic development, and the application of both rhythmic displacement and polyrhythmic concepts.

1557. Smith, Gregory Eugene, Ph.D. *Homer, Gregory, and Bill Evans? The Theory of Formulaic Composition in the Context of Jazz Piano Improvisation.* Cambridge: Harvard University; 1983.

Smith references the oral verse-making research of Milman Parry and Albert Lord, and Leo Treitler's application of their ideas to research in Gregorian chants to formulate a theoretical paradigm to assess the jazz improvisations of Bill Evans. By applying deconstruction techniques to Evans's improvisation, Smith elucidates phenomena operative in jazz improvisation.

1558. Widerhofer, Stephen Barth, D.A. *Bill Evans: An Analytical Study of His Improvisational Style Through Selected Transcriptions.* Greely: University of Northern Colorado; 1988.

Uses improvisations from the 1929–80 period—"All of You" (*Sunday at the Village Vanguard*), "Israel" (*Trio '65*), "T.T.T." (*The Bill Evans Album*), "Since We Met" (*Since We Met*), and "Up With the Lark" (*The Paris*

Concert: Edition I)—to analyze Evans's style. Analysis focuses on scales, melodic patterns, motivic development, chord voicing, harmonic substitution, and rhythmic patterns and variation. Widerhofer concludes Evans's style changed little over his career, although his later improvisations were more "adventurous and energetic." Informative. Contains analytical material appropriate to jazz pedagogues.

Ella Fitzgerald

1559. Cartwright, Katharine, Ph.D. *Quotation and References in Jazz Performance: Ella Fitzgerald's St. Louis 1957–1979.* New York: City University of New York; 2002.

The dissertation is concerned with Fitzgerald's borrowings and references, specifically what the interpolations reveal about her musical abilities, who she listened to, how she chooses her sources, and how she weaves bits and pieces of material into improvisations. The study focuses on seven of her versions of *St. Louis Blues,* and includes 72 transcriptions from her recordings and other sources. She examines the sources of 13 quotations Fitzgerald used in a 15-chorus scat solo in her 1958 birthday concert. Also, she summarizes Fitzgerald's techniques of paraphrase and restatement, and how interpolation is used as an improvisational/compositional strategy.

John Jacob Graas, Jr.

1560. Ormsby, Verle Alvin, Jr., D.A. *John Jacob Graas, Jr.: Jazz Horn Performer, Jazz Composer, and Arranger.* Muncie, Ind.: Ball State University; 1988.

Ormsby illuminates Graas's life and career through photo albums, newspaper articles, compositions, records, tapes, and consultation with peers. Includes a melodic analysis of original compositions. Among his conclusions: Graas was the first horn player to achieve prominence in jazz (from 1955 to 1961 he was recognized by *Down Beat, Metronome,* and *Playboy*); he honed his jazz skills performing with Claude Thornhill, Tex Beneke, and Stan Kenton, and studying composition with Lennie Tristano, Shorty Rogers, and Dr. Wesley LaViolette. Graas composed works for a wide variety of groups and mediums (jazz, classical, and a television score). Ormsby relates that Graas's improvisations helped pave the way for later jazz French hornists such as Julius Watkins and Willie Ruff. Important study on a little-known player.

Urbie Green

1561. Rickard, Marlyn Kent, M.A. *Urbie Green: A Study of His Musical Career.* Eugene: University of Oregon; 1998.

Provides an overview of his life and musical career and reviews physical characteristics of the trombone and modern performance techniques. Also examines Green's playing, surveys his recorded repertoire, and analyzes transcriptions of a variety of styles.

Lionel Hampton

1562. Tangen-Foster, Laurel Jean, Ph.D. *The Lionel Hampton Jazz Festival and the Continuance of the Jazz Legacy: A Qualitative Study.* Moscow: University of Idaho; 1996.

The four-day festival consists of concerts, clinics, and competitions for more than 14,000 elementary through college students. This study focused on the festival and its activities as a social phenomenon. She used qualitative methods and fieldwork to develop a theory relating events and activities to key participants. She espouses that key participants share a perspective she labels as classic jazz ideology, an ideology that is reflective of the traditionalist movement in the jazz world. The study was conducted over eight consecutive festivals from 1989 to 1996.

Fletcher Henderson

1563. Garner, Charles, Ed.D. *Fletcher Henderson, King of Swing: A Summary of His Music and His Influences.* New York: Columbia University Teachers College; 1991.

Recognizes Fletcher Henderson as a prime designer, architect, and leader of swing and big band jazz. He organizes and reviews current scholarship on Henderson, investigates his big band technique and style, orchestration concepts, his use of harmony, melody, and rhythm, and how he built his ensembles. In addition, his role as a bandleader, entrepreneur, influence, and social legacy are studied. Includes a list of all known compositions, discography of available recordings, and an overview of his life.

Earl Hines

1564. Taylor, Jeffrey James, Ph.D. *Earl Hines and Black Jazz Piano in Chicago, 1923–1928.* Ann Arbor: The University of Michigan; 1993.

Uses musicological research and documentation, analysis of transcriptions, personal insights gained from interviews, and critical listening to research Hines's early career. The author addresses Hines from two contrasting but related viewpoints: as an innovative and influential musician who was an important contributor to early jazz piano, and an important member of 1920s black Chicago. He focuses on the recordings made between 1923 (the year the first recordings of black Chicago jazz were made), and 1928, the end of the first stage of his career in Chicago, and the year he began his long residency at the Grand Terrance Ballroom. He covers his Pittsburgh years, analyzes the music of Hines and his Chicago contemporaries, and generic approaches to harmony, phrasing, and rhythm. Also focuses on Hines's influence, his musical association with Louis Armstrong, and an investigation of his solo piano recordings.

Billie Holiday

1565. Bates, Dawn-Wisteria, M.A. *Race Women: The Political Consciousness of Billie Holiday.* Bronxville, N.Y.: Sarah Lawrence College; 2001.

Using Holiday's 1939 recording of "Strange Fruit" as a backdrop, the author examines Holiday's ties to what she terms the radical left. The aforementioned is achieved by tracing her performances at political rallies and concerts during the 1940s. She discusses Holiday's description of herself as a *Race Women* by using her autobiography, *Lady Sings the Blues,* to establish Holiday's social consciousness. She theorizes that the political activism of Holiday must be defined by nontraditional definitions of political and social action and protest.

1566. Johnson, Jacqueline Yvonne, M.A. *The Integration of Melody, Speech, and Dramatic Art in the Vocal Style of Billie Holiday.* San Diego: San Diego State University; 1998.

Discusses how Holiday integrates the use and function of melody, speech, and dramatics into her vocal style. The author believes Holiday's unique and successful vocalizing is the result of her ability to combine melody, speech, and dramatics into a holistic approach.

1567. Whalen, Doretta Lonnett, Ph.D. *A Sociological and Ethnomusicological Study of Billie Holiday and Her Music.* Pittsburgh: University of Pittsburgh; 1999.

Investigates the life and musical style of Holiday, and the sociocultural environment that shaped her singing. The author believes the key to understanding Holiday's singing is connected to an understanding of her environment and personality. She includes an investigation of Holiday's family history, early life in Baltimore, and her musical approach, including an analysis of interviews, performances, and recordings.

Freddie Hubbard

1568. Lark, Robert James, Jr., D.M.A. *Selected Contemporary Jazz Trumpet Improvisations by Frederick Dewayne Hubbard: Structure and Form in Improvisation.* Denton: University of North Texas; 1994.

Uses selected blues improvisations to examine the contemporary jazz trumpet style of Freddie Hubbard. In addition to a history of the trumpet's use in bebop and subsequent jazz styles, an account of improvisation sources, blues structure and variations, and a chronology of Hubbard's performing career is presented. He presents a detailed analysis of Hubbard's musical tendencies and structural devices in relation to the blues form in selected recorded performances.

J. J. Johnson

1569. Burgois, Louis George, III, D.M.A. *Jazz Trombonist J. J. Johnson: A Comprehensive Discography and Study of the Early Evolution of His Style.* Columbus: The Ohio State University; 1986.

Traces Johnson's musical career and analyses his improvisational style from 1941 to 1950. The biography includes information on his embryonic musical experiences, early professional forays, the J. J. Johnson-Kai Winding Quintet and his career as an arranger-composer. The improvisational analysis centers on 12 transcriptions focusing on harmonic, melodic, and rhythmic concepts. Comprehensive discography. The most accurate and comprehensive coverage of Johnson's career and style to date.

Shella Jordan

1570. Burns, Vicki-Lyn, M.A. *The Sheer Need to Sing: The Healing Effect of Jazz in Shella Jordan's Life.* San Jose: San Jose State University; 2000.

Addresses the life and career, and the relationship of the singer to the music she sings in regards to the cultural contributions of the African diaspora in America. Discusses her relationship to jazz and jazz musicians, and relates how the depth and complexity of her performances are spiritual. The author interviewed Jordan for her thesis.

Rahsaan Roland Kirk

1571. Cole, Montgomery Charles, D.M.A. *The Life and Music of Rahsaan Roland Kirk.* Cincinnati: University of Cincinnati; 1998.

Begins with a biography of Kirk's life supported by interviews with friends and musical associates who knew him well. He also addresses Kirk's musical instruments and techniques, performing with several instruments simultaneously, influence on modern musicians, and aspects of his improvisational style. He transcribed several solos to support his analysis, and includes a discography, chronology of Kirk's life, and a bibliography.

Hubert Laws

1572. Walker, Vanessa G., M.M. *Hubert Laws—Observations of His Life, Philosophy, and Jazz Improvisational Techniques.* Bowling Green, Oh.: Bowling Green State University; 1980.

Uses insider comments from Laws to assess his style, influences, approach to teaching improvisation, and philosophy. Walker reveals that Laws's performance technique is shaped by his affinity to classical music, jazz, and other genres. She also discusses his use of melodic motives as generating devices in composition. Discography and list of transcriptions.

Richmond Matteson

1573. Dickman, Marcus, Jr., D.M.A. *Richmond Matteson: Euphonium Innovator, Teacher and Performer.* Denton: University of North Texas; 1997.

Discusses his life, career, and musical styles, including a concise description of the euphonium's role in the concert band. Permeated with information on his activities as a clinician, career changes, influences, and importance as a jazz educator. Analyzes his improvisational style, and includes a transcriptions of *Dan's Blues* as well as an analysis of Claude T. Smith's *Variations for Baritone.* A list of Matteson's compositions and arrangements, selected discography, and his 1982–92 clinics and performances is included.

Charles Mingus

1574. Rustin, Nichole T., Ph.D. *Mingus Fingers: Charles Mingus, Black Masculinity, and Postwar Jazz Culture.* New York: New York University; 1999.

She addresses the problem of historicizing and theorizing black masculinity in the post–World War II period. The changing dynamics of postwar jazz culture and the career of Charles Mingus serve as the historical and cultural context of her study. Her research methodology included using business records, album notes, interviews, memoirs, Mingus's correspondence, and record reviews. She postulates that Mingus's experiences reveal how postwar jazz's counterculture enabled black men to challenge prevailing racial stereotypes by representing themselves as subjects with multiple and contradictory experiences. She focuses on his 1971 memoir *Beneath the Underdog* and situates Mingus in relationship with his contemporaries, discuss how he articulated his role as musician with a racial and sexual identity, covers his career as composer, performer, and record producer, and map the intersections between black business, migration and urban life, networking, and other concerns and relationships.

1575. Saul, Scott Andrew, Ph. D. *Freedom is, Freedom Ain't: Jazz and the Making of the Sixties.* New Haven: Yale University; 2001.

Examines the jazz culture of the 1950s and 1960s from three perspectives: musicians who elaborated its aesthetic of extreme spontaneity and extreme discipline, artists and intellectuals who associated themselves with freedom cultural values, and youth who attended jazz festivals in the 1950s and 1960s but later transferred their allegiance to rock music. Part one covers black and white intellectuals who grappled with issues of community and marginality; part two examines the rise of the jazz festival as a site of postwar youth culture; parts three and four examines the music, approaches, significance, and contributions of John Coltrane and Charles Mingus. In part five, the author traces the emergence of counterculture among white youth, and the rise of soul power in the African American community. (Also cited under John Coltrane and Collective Biographies.)

Modern Jazz Quartet

1576. Owens, Thomas, M.A. *Improvisation Techniques of the Modern Jazz Quartet.* Los Angeles: University of California, Los Angeles; 1965.

Concerned with both the improvisational techniques and the ensemble performance concepts of pre-1965 recordings. Of the 22 LPs of MJQ's music issued by 1965, the author chose seven compositions for analysis. Owens addresses instrumentation and style, the musicians (including Kenny Clarke and Ray Brown), synthesis, and the combination of fugal and jazz elements. Analysis of "Bluesology" (blues), "Between the Devil and the Deep Blue Sea" (popular standard), "Angel Eyes" (ballad), "Django" (jazz), and third-stream-fugal compositions "Versailles" and "Three Windows." Extols the superb musicianship and ability with the synthesis of jazz and classical elements. Bibliography, discography, glossary of terms. Thorough and scholarly. Two volumes.

Thelonious Monk

1577. Simon, Tom, M.A. *An Analytical Inquiry into Thelonious Monk's "Ruby, My Dear."* Ann Arbor: University of Michigan; 1978.

Uses the reductive method of Schenkerian analysis to analyze a single composition, "Ruby, My Dear," recorded solo in 1959. This model enables Simon to analyze the composition as "a spontaneous and creative phenomena involving composition, development, and memory," and concerned more with diatonic and triadic structural elements than with linear concepts. Thorough analysis.

Wes Montgomery

1578. De Stefano, Reno, Ph.D. *Wes Montgomery's Improvisational Style (1959–1963): The Riverside Years.* Montreal: Universite De Montreal; 1996.

The primary purpose is to discern Wes Montgomery's improvisational style by analyzing the recordings he made for the Riverside label from 1959 to 1963. He focuses on constructive elements, distinctive techniques, and idiosyncratic traits that characterize Montgomery's improvisational style. He also discussed the impact of Montgomery's style and approach in jazz history. He examines the musical, political and social contexts in which Montgomery learned his craft, and uses Jan LaRue's guidelines for analysis, which, in turn, the author supplemented with specific features to accommodate Montgomery's unique characteristics of performance.

Jelly Roll Morton

1579. Beecher, Randy L., M.A. *Ferdinand "Jelly Roll" Morton and Earl "Fatha" Hines Piano Styles in the 1920s: A Selected Comparison.* San Diego: San Diego State University; 2001.

In addition to a selected discussion of their early lives and musical careers, the author compares respective styles of the 1920s. Included is a discussion of musical elements such as the stride technique and chord voicing. The comparison is limited to comparing a few musical phrases that the author believed was representative of their 1920s piano styles.

1580. Osborn, Philip Arnold, M.M. *The Piano Music of Ferdinand "Jelly Roll" Morton.* Alberta, Edmonton: The University of Alberta, Edmonton; 1981.

Limited to Morton's solo piano interpretations from acoustical recordings and the Library of Congress recordings. Includes transcriptions by Osborn of "Frog-i-more Rag" (Sweetheart O' Mine), "Kansas City Stomp," "The Pearls," and "Mama 'Nita" (Mamanita). Permeated with contextual information and analysis, Osborn's work uses Morton's assessments (Library of Congress recordings) to enrich his analysis.

Bennie Moten

1581. Rice, Marc Joseph, Ph.D. *The Bennie Moten Orchestra, 1918–1935: A Kansas City Jazz Ensemble and African-American Audience.* Lexington: University of Kentucky; 1998.

Investigates the orchestra's style, role as a transitional ensemble during the 1920s and 1930s, and the symbiotic relationship between the orchestra and the Kansas City African American community. He examines the Moten orchestra from three perspectives: musical contribution, biographical events, and cultural context. He analyzes over 100 recordings to illuminate the orchestra's style, and uses history and newspaper articles to trace crucial events in the history of the orchestra. In addition, he examines the orchestra's longevity as a unit, discovery of the orchestra by record executives, tours, and the orchestra's ability to attract white audiences.

King Oliver

1582. Bowman, Robert, M.F.A. *The Question of Improvisation and Head Arrangement in King Oliver's Creole Jazz Band.* Toronto: York University (Canada); 1982.

The author focused on the 37 sides on four different record companies that King Oliver's Creole Jazz Band recorded between April and December 1923. Of the 37 recordings, five were twice recorded, and one was recorded three times. He transcribed the frontline parts (clarinet, cornet, trombone), and the ensemble strains of the six rerecorded compositions. He used the six transcriptions to compare different versions of a strain on a given recording, and the same strain on different recordings.

Charlie Parker

1583. Engelhardt, Kent John, Ph.D. *Musical and Cultural Factors in the Musical Development of Young Charlie Parker as Demonstrated Through Transcription and Analysis of the Improvised Solos of Young Charlie Parker with the Jay McShann Orchestra.* Pittsburgh: University of Pittsburgh; 2001.

Traces the musical development of Parker from the cultural environment that influenced him by investigating the musical and cultural history of Kansas City, and by reconstructing the life of young Charles Parker. He transcribed and analyzed 16 solos, and extracted musical phrases from the solos to trace Parker's musical influences. He covered the 1940–42 years, and determined that Parker used lots of emulations and quotations from a variety of sources. In the studio recordings, some quotations were traced to Lester Young, Buster Smith, Roy Eldridge, Coleman Hawkins, and popular tunes of the day. However, in the live recordings, none of the quotes are from other musicians, however one quote is traced to a popular tune of the day.

1584. Fants, Karen Lee, M.A. *The Blues of Charlie Parker.* Columbus: The Ohio State University; 1964.

The thesis is divided into seven chapters: bebop; Charlie Parker; the blues; harmony; melody; rhythm; and conclusions. The study is limited to 11 blues derived from a fake book: "Air Conditioning" (Dial-207), 1947;

"Barbados" (Savoy M69001), 1948; "Billie's Bounce" (Savoy M69001), 1945; "Bird Feathers" (Dial-207), 1947; "Bloomdido" (Clef-M6 (512), 1944; "Bongo Bop" (Dial-1024), 1947; "Buzzy" (Savoy M69001), 1947; "Cheryl" (Savoy M69001), 1947; "Mohawk" (Savoy M69000), 1945; "Now's The Time" (Savoy M69000), 1945; and "Visa" (Clef M6 (612), 1949. The author made the following conclusions: "Parker's blues had more complex harmonies and a faster harmonic rhythm than the traditional blues. He embellished the traditional harmonic pattern with many substitute chords"; "Parker used minor 2nds, 3rds, 6ths, and 7ths, and diminished 5ths. He used chromatic tones that contributed to a 'bluesy' effect. A striking characteristic of his style was his frequent use of higher chord tones; 9ths, 11ths, and 13ths appeared in great numbers"; "Parker's melodic line was predominantly in conjunct motion. Skips of more than a perfect 5th were unusual. His accents occurred in unexpected places, and Parker's originality shows most clearly in the variety of his phrase lengths. Although Parker did use some two and four bar phrases, irregular phrase lengths, as of one, three and one half, or five bars, are found even more frequently in these blues." Music examples, appendix, bibliography, and footnotes.

1585. Gray, James, M.F.A. *An Analysis of Melodic Devices in Selected Improvisations of Charlie Parker.* Athens: Ohio University; 1966.

Divided into three parts: (1) a statement and review of Charlie Parker's life and musical accomplishments, (2) a four-way melodic analysis of his improvisations, and (3) notation of the selected improvisations with the basic melodies over which they were conceived. The study is limited to notating and analyzing "Now's the Time," "Barbados," "Ornithology," and "Just Friends." Draws conclusions regarding phrase lengths, cadences, intervals, and scale range in improvisations.

1586. Henriksson, Juha. *Chasing the Bird: Functional Harmony in Charlie Parker's Bebop Themes.* Helsinki: Helsingin: Yliopisto (Finland); 1998.

The goal of the study is to develop a new method for analyzing melody and harmony in jazz, and to analyze the compositional style of Charles Parker. He analyzed 37 themes composed by Parker, and used Diether de la Motte's notation. He used functional harmonic concepts, and concluded that Parker gave preference to principal functions and secondary dominants. In addition, he concluded that Parker rarely used dominant substitutions other than a bII7 and bVii7 chords, used the major scale against the tonic chord in blues, and melodically he favors chord tones of underlying harmonies, treats the ninth as a chord tone, and that he frequently used altered and extended notes beyond the ninth in substitute sequences.

1587. Komara, Edward, M.A. *The Dial Recordings of Charlie Parker.* Buffalo: State University of New York at Buffalo; 1991.

Contains an historical introduction, a thematic catalogue, and commentary on the Dial recordings. From 1946 to 1948 Parker participated in 8 of the 16 recording sessions instituted by Ross Russell (owner and CEO of Dial Records, 1946 to 1954). Includes a list of when Parker played his Dial repertory, record titles, Dial issues of performances, and more. Excellent details on the sessions and Parker's business dealings with Dial.

1588. Owens, Thomas. Ph.D. *Charles Parker: Techniques of Improvisation.* Los Angeles: University of California, Los Angeles; 1974.

A comprehensive and scholarly assessment of Parker's method of improvisation. The author collated 250 transcriptions of improvisations recorded between 1940 and 1943 and 1944 and 1954 and organized them by key, contrafacts, and blues. The "I've Got Rhythm" and "Cherokee" contrafacts featured prominently. In his analysis, Owens identifies numerous improvisational motives and chronicles their use in improvisations. The motivic analysis is supplemented by a Schenkerian analysis of longer improvisational phrases. Owens's work offers deep structural insight into Parker's method of improvisation.

Evan Parker

1589. Borgo, David. *Reverence for Uncertainty: Chaos, Order, and the Dynamics of Musical Free Improvisation.* Los Angeles: UCLA; 1999.

Focuses on the transcultural practice and musical free improvisation, the emerging science of chaos theory, and the paradigm shift that created a moment in which uncertainty is revered instead of feared. He argues that there is similarity between the way that the modeling of the natural world by chaos theorists and the process of formation inherent in musical free improvisation. Furthermore, he argues that the dynamic understanding of order and disorder emerging in chaos theory may help to understand the dynamics and aesthetics of free improvisation. He reviews inherent biases, free jazz development, sketches an outline of the growing interest in non-linear dynamical systems with special focus on chaos theory, nonequilibrium thermodynamics, information theory, and cognitive science. He uses the solo improvisational practices and kinesthetic metaphors of Evan Parker as a model for his research.

Art Pepper

1590. Rask, Perry Joel, D.A. *Arthur Edward Pepper (1925–1982): An Analysis of his Improvisational Style Through Solos Transcriptions from 1943–1960.* Greely: University of Northern Colorado; 2001.

Researches Pepper as one of the most important contributors to West Coast jazz. The primary focus of the study is to identify and codify the musical elements that can be associated directly to Art Pepper. The dissertation is limited to an analysis of saxophone solos, and represents three of the four periods of Pepper's career: 1940–1946, his apprenticeship with Stan Kenton and Benny Carter; 1946 to 1954, when he honed his skills with Kenton and five successful years of recording; July 1956 to October 1960, highlighted by his Pacific recordings; and 1975–1982, his fourth period, when his emotional content soared to new heights, and he made numerous recordings. He charted and catalogued motivic recurrence, melodic and harmonic applications, favored forms, and number of original compositions.

Oscar Peterson

1591. Madura, Patrice Dawn, M.A. *Oscar Peterson: A Musical Biography.* San Diego: San Diego State University; 1981.

A biomusical assessment of his Canadian and non-Canadian career, study, and achievements from 1950 to 1980. The biography covers his influences, musical associations, experiences, and his thoughts on teaching. Limited to a thorough analysis of "Night Train" and portions of "That Old Black Magic" and "The Nearness of You." Includes a selected discography and bibliography.

Bud Powell

1592. Ramsey, Guthrie P., Jr., Ph.D. *The Art of Bebop: Earl "Bud" Powell and the Emergence of Modern Jazz.* Ann Arbor: The University of Michigan; 1994.

The first scholarly study of Powell, Ramsey examines his early career, and his distinctive contributions to jazz as both a soloist and composer during bebop's formative years. In his presentation, cultural and musical analysis of Powell's early recordings and other sources reveals why bebop can be interpreted as both an African American musical expression and as a modernist one.

Max Roach

1593. Brownell, John E.B., M.A. *Drum Set Improvisation: Towards a Conceptual Model.* Toronto: York University (Canada); 1994.

Investigates the conceptual schemata by which drum set players organize their improvised solos and accompaniments from a processual perspective. He reviews selected jazz improvisation literature and the theory of meter to determine their relevance to the modeling of drum set improvisations.

He develops a matrix whose central construct is the *seed pattern,* a formulaic unit defined as a gesture that is capable, through timbral and amplitude modification, of generating a large variety of outputs. He applies the model to a Max Roach improvisation to determine its utility.

1594. Sanderbeck, Rande Paul, D.M.A. *'Homage to Max': A New Work for Solo Drum Set Based on the Style of Max Roach.* Lexington: University of Kentucky; 1997.

A musical composition that is based on the transcription and analysis of selected Max Roach solos. The analysis chapters contain musical examples within the text, and the stylistic conclusions are used in the newly composed composition, *Homage to Max.* The composition has five movements and is scored for unaccompanied drum set. He includes a musical score of the composition and the transcriptions of the five Max Roach solos.

Sonny Rollins

1595. Blancq, Charles Clement, III, Ph.D. *Melodic Improvisation in American Jazz: The Style of Theodore "Sonny" Rollins, 1951–1962.* New Orleans: Tulane University; 1977.

Assesses Rollins's use of thematic and harmonic concepts. Blancq analyzed more than 200 improvisations by limiting this work to 20 Rollins transcriptions and four of other artists—"The Man I Love," "Body and Soul," and "Honeysuckle Rose" by Coleman Hawkins, and "Summertime" by Miles Davis. Contains a good overview of improvisation before Rollins and a thorough assessment of Rollins's use of melody, rhythm, harmony, and form and structure. Detailed and scholarly.

Sonny Stitt

1596. Witt, Woodrow William, D.M.A. *Sonny Stitt: His Life and Music.* Houston: University of Houston; 2000.

Based on interviews with his widow, Pamela Stitt, and musicians who performed with him, the author chronicles the life and music of this giant. He analyzed five transcribed tenor solos, recorded between 1949 and 1972, for this dissertation. Stitt bases the improvisations on the "I Got Rhythm" contrafact, and four original tunes. He examined Stitt's use of scales, development of melodic material, and the influence of Lester Young.

Billy Strayhorn

1597. Stock, Matthew Chris, M.M. *Billy Strayhorn: His Life, Familiar and Forgotten Works.* Denton: University of North Texas; 1996.

Demonstrates that Strayhorn possessed his own distinctive voice as a composer before his association with Duke Ellington. A comprehensive biography is presented in chapter 1; Strayhorn and Ellington musical training and compositional methods are compared in chapter 2; and in the remaining three chapters, the author analyzes selected compositions covering different periods of his life.

Sun Ra

1598. Martinelle, David A., M.A. (ethnomusicology). *The Cosmic-Myth Equations of Sun Ra: An Examination of the Unity of Music and Philosophy of an American Creative Improvising Musician.* Los Angeles: University of California, Los Angeles; 1991.

An ethnomusicological study of the relationship between Sun Ra's music and philosophy. Focuses on a deconstruction of his philosophy, including his Egyptian beliefs, promulgates possible influences between his philosophy and music and reveals the realization of Sun Ra's philosophy in aspects of his life and his music. An excellent integration of cultural, musical, and philosophical issues.

Ward Swingle

1599. Shannon, Kathleen, M. D. M.A. *Ward Swingle: A Study of His Choral Music and Its Jazz Influences.* Miami: University of Miami; 1990.

Assesses his choral music and his role and function as a composer/arranger, musician, and organizer/founder of the Swingle Singers. Shannon discusses his life and the influence of jazz on his compositions, rehearsal techniques, and his sound and style. She divides Swingle's output into three distinct stages, provides a concise biography and uses analysis to draw conclusions regarding his arrangements, performance practices, and approaches to rehearsal. A discography and bibliography is included.

Art Tatum

1600. Genova, Vincent, M.A. *Melodic and Harmonic Irregularities Found in the Improvisations of Art Tatum.* Pittsburgh: University of Pittsburgh; 1978.

Analyzes what the author calls the inner workings of melodic and harmonic irregularities and the substitution possibilities in "I'm in the Mood for Love," "Good Night Sweetheart," "Blues in Bb," and "Blues for the Oldest Profession." His conclusions regarding Tatum's melodic and harmonic irregularities focus on structure, variance by using the circle of fourths and fifths, reliance on classical concepts, use of diverse styles, and voice leading.

The study is supplemented with information on background, influences, style, and Tatum's influence on others. Significant addition to the literature.

1601. Howard, Joseph A., Ph.D. *The Improvisational Techniques of Art Tatum (Volumes I–III).* Cleveland, Ohio: Case Western Reserve University; 1978.

Of the 657 known Tatum recordings and transcriptions, the 372 solo performances form the basis of this comprehensive and scholarly three-volume study. Howard devised a system to chart the frequency of improvisational ideas. He includes information on song title, composer, album title, record label, recording date and place, melodic-harmonic-rhythmic tendencies, and more. Discography of all known recorded performances (solo and ensemble). One of the most in-depth and significant studies of a jazz artist to date.

1602. Item deleted.

1603. Howlett, Felicity Ann, Ph.D. *An Introduction to Art Tatum's Performance Approaches: Composition, Improvisation, and Melodic Variation.* Ithaca: Cornell University; 1983.

Examines Tatum's life and music focusing on salient features of his improvisational style. Transcriptions by the author, J. Lawrence Cook, Jed Distler, and John Mehegan. Howlett's analysis focuses on internal structure, technique, improvisational approach, and moods. Examines bass line concepts through five transcriptions (1938 to 1954) of "Sweet Lorraine." Tatum emerges as a composer of internal structures, a composer who worked with the externally provided material of a given harmony and melody to produce spontaneous and creative musical compositions.

1604. Hunt, Imelda, Ph.D. *An Oral History of Art Tatum During His Years in Toledo,1909–1932.* Bowling Green, Ohio: Bowling Green State University; 1995.

Uses oral history sources to document the life of Art Tatum from 1909 until 1932. The interviews include information about his school life, family, church life, girlfriend, friends, and musical associates in Toledo. She researched questions such as who were his parents, where did they come from, and when and how did they influence his life and music.

Cecil Taylor

1605. Bobak, Mark J., D.M.A. *The Music of Cecil Taylor: An Analysis of Selected Piano Solos, 1973–1989.* Urbana-Champaign: University of Illinois at Urbana-Champaign; 1994.

Examines both his reputation as a virtuosic performer and analyzes his improvisational concepts. He uses representative excerpts from Taylor's solo recordings, and illuminates their salient features and stylistic traits. Because Taylor does not express his music via musical scores, numerous transcriptions from several live recordings were made. After a concise biographical sketch, the author describes Taylor's interdisciplinary interests in choreography and poetry, and than discusses how he conceptualizes improvisation, composition, and musical creativity. In part two, he analyzes the tonal and rhythmic passages from several recordings, and his use of motivic material, figurations, rapid "flurries" of notes, cluster, form, and interval use and function. She also uses the views of Taylor and others to provide deeper insights into his music.

1606. Westendorf, Lynette, D.M.A. *Analyzing Free Jazz (Coleman, Ornette, Coltrane, John, and Taylor, Cecil).* Seattle: University of Washington; 1994.

An examination of several stylistically diverse works within their respective cultural contexts. The first two chapters address the origins and influence of free jazz, and it relationship to blues and earlier jazz styles. In addition, she discusses the methodological approaches of selected artists, the Black Nationalist movement, treatment of free jazz in the scholarly literature, and analytical techniques appropriate to jazz. In chapters three through five, she analyzes Ornette Coleman's *Lonely Woman* (1959), John Coltrane's *India* (1961), and Cecil Taylor's *Indent: Second Layer* (1973). She transcribed each composition, and uses diagrams, and some graphic representations to make her points about rhythm, method of development, form, and the use of contrast. Additionally, she discusses Coleman's *Harmolodic* theory, Coltrane's adaptation of Indian aesthetics and techniques, and, if warranted, the poem that Taylor's composition is based on. (Also cited under Ornette Coleman, John Coltrane, and Collective Biographies.)

Tio Family

1607. Kinzer, Charles E., Ph.D. *The Tio Family: Four Generations of New Orleans Musicians, 1814–1933.* Volumes I and II. Baton Rouge: The Louisiana State University and Agricultural and Mechanical College (LSU); 1993.

Examines the life and musical careers and contributions of Thomas Louis Marcos Tio (1828–c. 1881) and his uncle Louis Hazeur (c. 1792–1860) who were active musicians in the antebellum "free-colored society of New Orleans." Also covers the life and musical contributions of Tio's sons, Louis (1862–1922) and Lorenzo (1867–1908), who became known as excellent clarinetists and arrangers in the New Orleans marching bands, minstrel shows, and pit orchestras of the late nineteenth century. Lorenzo became the teacher of Sidney Bechet and Barney Bigard, and performed with many New Orleans, Chicago, and New York bands. The author covers the family life, contributions, and influences from 1814 to 1933. The appendices contain maps and musical transcriptions.

Lennie Tristano

1608. Shim, Eunmi, Ph.D. *Lennie Tristano (1919–1978): His Life, Music, and Teaching.* Urbana-Champaign: University of Illinois at Urbana-Champaign; 1999.

The author interviewed over 80 individuals, including family members, associates, and students to chronicle the succession of innovations made by the composer, pianist, and teacher. The individuality of his 1949 recording of a free jazz composition, his use of multitracking techniques, and contributions to advanced harmony, rhythmic complexity, and linear construction of melody are discussed. Also discusses his contributions as a teacher of artists such as Billy Bauer, Lee Konitz, Warne Marsh, and many others.

Sarah Vaughan

1609. King, Ruth Elaine, M.A. *The Stylistic Interpretations of Sarah Vaughan.* San Diego: San Diego State University; 1984.

Uses a revised method of Alan Lomax's cantometrics directed toward melodic contour, enunciations, harmonic suggestions, vocal range, registers, timbre, embellishments, vibrato, and improvisation to analyze Vaughan's interpretations. This is the first jazz study to use Lomax's paradigm. More detailed than pre-1984 vocal jazz studies.

Julius Watkins

1610. Schaughency, Steven Michael, D.A. *The Original Jazz Compositions of Julius Watkins.* Greely: University of Northern Colorado; 1994.

Deals with his contributions as a composer, and focuses primarily on his compositional style and characteristics. Half of his compositional output was transcribed and analyzed for this study, and revealed idiosyncratic writing for both jazz groups and the horn. He also chronicles Watkins use of classical elements in his compositions, and explores his development of motivic material, contrapuntal writing, harmonic movement, use of tone colors, forms, variation of musical moods, and use of rhythmic concepts. The discography contains references to compositions and recordings on which he performed improvised horn solos.

Anthony Williams

1611. Woodson, Craig DeVere, M.M. *Solo Jazz Drumming: An Analytic Study of the Improvisation Technique of Anthony Williams.* Los Angeles: University of California, Los Angeles; 1973.

Assesses the measured and free rhythm techniques of Williams by using the Melograph Model C. Woodson uses a real-time graphic printout to devise a system to study duration, loudness, rhythm, and special techniques. He discusses improvisation in rhythm instrumental combinations, including form, loudness, manual techniques, and melodic concepts. Woodson's conclusion that Williams uses free, measured, and implied rhythm is the most accurate analysis of his improvisational technique to date.

Mary Lou Williams

1612. Fledderus, Francine May, M.M. *The Function of Oral Tradition in "Mary Lou's Mass" By Mary Lou Williams.* Denton: University of North Texas; 1996.

Begins with a biography of Williams, and includes a discussion of aesthetics, elements of conventional mass settings, and oral tradition found in *Mary's Lou's Mass*. She argues because of Williams's personal faith, Catholicism, and career as a composer and pianist it was inevitable that Williams would be the first jazz composer to write a jazz setting of the mass.

1613. Kernodle, Tammy Lynn, Ph.D. *Anything You Are Shows Up in Your Music-liminate close quote': Mary Lou Williams and the Sanctification of Jazz.* Columbus: The Ohio State University; 1997.

Acknowledges Williams as one of the premiere jazz pianists, her recordings with Andy Kirk and the Mighty Clouds of Joy, her arrangements for Benny Goodman and Duke Ellington, and her extensive body of solo compositions. Focuses on her religious compositions composed after her 1954 to 1957 hiatus from jazz. The dissertation is limited to six of the over 100 religious theme compositions she composed after her return to the jazz world in 1957. She examines the separation of sacred and secular music in the African American community, and how the church and the Harlem renaissance influenced public opinion. She uses original manuscripts, personal commentaries, and her use of jazz-related forms in a sacred context.

1614. Pickeral, Charles Wilkins, Ph.D. *The Masses of Mary Lou Williams: The Evolution of a Liturgical Style.* Lubbock: Texas Tech University; 1998.

Focuses attention on the structure, circumstances of their composition, performance, and alterations of her masses. Presents a chronology of the development of each mass, an analysis of their musical components, origins, and more. The author illuminates the evolution of her late 1960s and early 1970s liturgical style, and her quest to evolve spiritual jazz into an original vision of the mass as a musical, historical, social, and didactic statement.

Theses and Dissertations on Several Individuals

1615. Aloisio, Gerard Salvatore, D.M.A. *A Historical Summary of Major Musical Developments in American Jazz from the End of World War I to the Beginning of World War II (Interwar Period).* Cincinnati: University of Cincinnati; 1995.

Traces the major changes in jazz styles, and describes how selected vocalists, instrumentalists, and composers from blues, boogie-woogie, and jazz made significant contributions to their respective genres. He discusses the contributions of Blind Lemon Jefferson, Robert Johnson, Ma Rainey, Bessie Smith, Mamie Smith, Louis Armstrong, Count Basie, Duke Ellington, Bix Beiderbecke, Benny Goodman, Fletcher Henderson, James P. Johnson, Meade Lux Lewis, Jelly Roll Morton, Kid Ory, Fats Waller, Paul Whiteman, and Jimmy Yancey. The appendix contains 27 transcriptions from Folkways Records, The Smithsonian Collection of Classic Jazz, and the Smithsonian Collection of Big Band Jazz. (Also cited under Evolution and History.)

1616. Balfany, Gregory Jay, D.M.A. *A Motivic Study of Twenty Selected Solos of David Sanborn and Stanley Turrentine.* Madison: The University of Wisconsin, Madison; 1988.

Identifies and examines seven motives used by Stanley Turrentine, and five used by David Sanborn in their improvisations. The dissertation contains 20 transcribed solos, 10 by each artist. He hypothesized that the improvisations of Sanborn and Turrentine would demonstrate similarity of motivic usage. However, he concluded the artists used the same basic material in different ways.

1617. Bauer, Scott Matthew, Ph.D. *Structural Targets in Modern Jazz Improvisation: An Analytical Perspective (Melodic Line, Fats Navarro, Clifford Brown, Kenny Dorham, Freddie Hubbard);* Ann Arbor: The University of Michigan; 1994.

Uses structural targets to analyze melodic lines, cadence points in modern blues progressions, and the preparation and resolution of targets. He transcribes and analyzes Clifford Brown's *Sandu,* Kenny Dorham's solo on *The Stanley Stomper,* Freddie Hubbard's *Birdlike,* and Fats Navarro's *The Squirrel.* He reveals that the four improvisers created direct resolutions of structural targets through the placement of chord tones at the cadence point. The use and function of chromatic dissonance in preparation of structural points is also discussed. He concludes that modern jazz improvisers, unlike most of their predecessors, tend to anticipate harmonic rhythm and create melodies during the course of their improvisations.

1618. Brown, Anthony L., Ph.D. *The Development of Modern Jazz Drumset Performance, 1940–1950.* Berkeley: University of California, Berkeley; 1997.

An ethnomusicological study of the development of modern jazz drumming in the 1940s. He uses transcriptions and critical analyses of recorded performances of Kenny Clarke, Max Roach, and others to document the stylistic achievements and changes that characterizes 1940s drumming. He argues that drummers transformed their primary role of providing dance and show accompaniment in 1930s big bands into an interactive role with frontline soloists in the modern jazz ensembles of the 1940s. He includes a survey of literature, lexical examinations of definitions of jazz and swing, a historical survey of African American drumming traditions, a discussion of identity formation and intercontextual relationships, and more.

1619. Brown, Leonard Lewis, Ph.D. *Some New England African American Musician's Views on Jazz.* Middletown, Conn.: Wesleyan University; 1990.

Presenting the views of African American artists using an ethnomusicological approach to focus on definitive performance and philosophical concerns. Brown discusses history, music in culture, analysis, performance, and Afrocentric concepts. Interview questions, selection criteria, and complete transcriptions of the interviews are included. Insights into the role and function of jazz in African American culture.

1620. Brown, Theodore D., Ph.D. *A History of Jazz Drumming to 1942.* Two volumes. Ann Arbor: The University of Michigan; 1976.

Covers "African Influence on Jazz Drumming"; "Jazz Drumming: The Beginnings"; "The Ragtime Drummer"; "Jazz Drumming in the 1920's: The New Orleans Musicians"; "Jazz Drumming in the 1920's: Chicago"; "Gene Krupa"; "Jazz Drumming in the 1930s"; and "Bop Drumming: The Beginning." Among the musicians who provided information for this study are Benny Goodman, Zutty Singleton, J. C. Heard, Nick Fatool, Butch Miles, and Ralph Berton. The study is permeated with musical analysis, references to individual styles, and reference citations. Glossary, discography, bibliography, and index. Thorough discussion of the topic.

1621. Colby, Sherri Lynn, M.A. *Divas: The Negotiation of Identity and Power: Four Contemporary Female Jazz Singers (Yve Evans, Wende Hartson, Sue Kroninger, Brady McKay).* Fresno: Fresno State University; 2001.

Uses participant observation to produce an ethnography of the traditional jazz circuit as experienced by four female jazz singers. The four life experiences are presented as first-person narratives and analyzed in regard to the subject's negotiation of power and identity within a social context. She uses the form of a jazz song as a metaphor for the structure of the thesis.

1622. Davis, Ursula Broschke, Ph.D. *The Afro-American Musician and Writer in Paris During the 1950s and 1960s: A Study of Kenny Clarke, Donald Byrd, Chester Himes and James Balwin.* Pittsburgh: University of Pittsburgh; 1983.

Discusses the four artists' lives in Paris. Specifically, she investigates why they left the United States, what influence(s) Europe had on them, and the reasons they either remained in Europe or returned to the United States. The study is based on both literary sources and oral interviews conducted between February and December of 1982. Among her findings were the artists left the United States because they felt alienated and exploited, and because they were drawn to the cultural and educational attraction of Europe.

1623. DeVeaux, Scott Knowles, Ph.D. *Jazz in Transition: Coleman Hawkins and Howard McGhee.* Berkeley: University of California, Berkeley; 1985.

Discusses the lives and music of Hawkins and McGhee within their socio-economic and musical contexts. DeVeaux begins with an assessment of the issues involved the transformation of jazz from swing to bebop. A discussion of the trials, tribulations, and musical successes, including "Body and Soul," within the sociocultural context of the time is also presented. He traces the evolution of McGhee from the territory bands to his eventual success in the 1940s. His portrayal of McGehee is within the context of the events affecting Hawkins, but as a benefactor of change. Contains numerous transcriptions.

1624. Dietrich, Kurt Robert, D.M.A. *Joe "Tricky Sam" Nanton, Juan Tizol and Lawrence Brown: Ellington's Great Trombonists, 1926–1951.* Madison: The University of Wisconsin, Madison; 1989.

In addition to the biographical information on each artist, the primary focus is the analysis of recorded improvisations by each performer. He transcribed and analyzed eight Nanton solos, including those that feature "wa-wa," or plunger concepts, three of Juan Tizol's solos, and eleven of Lawrence Brown's solos. Also provides information on the role and function of each artist within the band, and the influence of the three trombonists on the past, present, and possibly the future. (Also cited under Duke Ellington.)

1625. Emge, Jeffrey David. D.M.A. *Third-Stream Music for Band: An Examination of Jazz Influences in Five Compositions for Winds and Percussion (Gunther Schuller, Timothy Broege, Dana Wilson, John Harbison, Donald Grantham).* Cincinnati: University of Cincinnati; 2000.

Uses six indicators of jazz style and found that instrumentation played a large role in the portrayal of jazz style in the five compositions examined. He concluded that the prominent roles and functions assigned to the saxophone, trombone, use of a trap set, whether actually specified or simulated, and the use of improvisation were important indicators of jazz style. He also found that swing notation was used in three compositions, and that both Harbison and Schuller made conscious efforts to imitate bebop rhythmic concepts in their compositions. Five compositions used the major-minor seventh extensively, and blues harmonic concepts were also prominent.

1626. Gunter, John Obson, Ph.D. *Good Players.* Minneapolis: University of Minnesota; 1979.

Discusses the attitudes, experience, and musical training of six professional jazz musicians (three white, three African American, five male, and one female) from the southwestern United States. Concerned with their creative profiles, he discovers that they arrange, write, and teach exhibiting strong positive attitudes, pressures associated with living their lives as jazz musicians not withstanding.

1627. Hardin, Christopher L., Ed.D. *Black Professional Musicians in Higher Education: A Study Based on In-Depth Interviews.* Amherst: University of Massachusetts; 1987.

Interviewing Bill Barron, Marion Brown, Jaki Byard, Stanley Cowell, Clyde Criner, Bill Dixon, Natalie Hinderas, Bill Pierce, Hildred Roach, Max Roach, Archie Shepp, Hale Smith, Frederick Tillis, and Pearl Williams-Jones Hardin uses a phenomenological paradigm to assess their careers as professors and professional musicians. Many were recruited in the 1960s and feel recording/performing should not be curtailed and that their abilities are under used. Significant in the insider perspectives of renowned African American performers.

1628. Hauff, Timothy Andrew, M.A. *A Comparative Analysis of Styles and Performance Practices for Three Jazz Bassists in the Composition "Stella by Starlight."* San Jose: San Jose State University; 1990.

A comparison of the style and performance practices of Eddie Gomez, Sam Jones, and Chuck Israels through analysis of "Stella by Starlight." Assesses each artist's recording techniques, scales, rhythmic concepts, and dramatic devices. Hauff includes a concise history of acoustic bassists with a discussion of the role of these bassists in history.

1629. Kernfeld, Barry Dean, Ph.D. *Adderley, Coltrane, and Davis at the Twilight of Bebop: The Search for Melodic Coherence (1958–59).* Ithaca: Cornell University; 1981.

An analysis of the 1958–59 solos of Julian "Cannonball" Adderley, Miles Davis, and John Coltrane while performing in the Miles Davis sextet. The author argues that "two" Coltranes competed artistically throughout the 1950s; that Adderley displayed several improvisational techniques; and that Miles Davis used "paraphrasing" (André Hodier's definition) on the four analyzed compositions. He focuses on four blues in "F," "Dr. Jekyll," "Straight, No Chaser," "Jazz at the Plaza" (a retitled version of "Straight, No Chaser") and specifically motivic improvisation on "So What," "Flamenco Sketches," "All Blues," and "Milestones."

1630. Larson, Seven Leroy, Ph.D. *Schenkerian Analysis of Modern Jazz.* Ann Arbor: The University of Michigan; 1987.

Five different versions of Thelonious Monk's "Round About Midnight." Larson includes two by Monk, two by Bill Evans, and one by Oscar Peterson, and focuses on the relationship between voice leading and harmony, motives and rhythm, organization and use of structures, repetitions, the treatment of jazz dissonance, harmonic language, and more. Illuminates the musical choices and technical and stylistic concepts used by each artist.

1631. Reed, Thomas Terry, D.M.A. *Jimmy Hamilton and Russell Procope: The Clarinet Soloists of the Duke Ellington Orchestra, 1943–1974.* Columbus: The Ohio State University; 1995.

Discusses their respective styles, approaches, and roles and functions within the Duke Ellington orchestras, 1943 to 1974. Also provides a biographical sketch of each artist, and discusses Ellington's relationship with each artist. Uses 17 musical excerpts to compare and contrast the role and functions that both Ellington and Billy Strayhorn assigned to each performer. (Also cited under Duke Ellington.)

1632. Saul, Scott Andrew, Ph. D. *Freedom is, Freedom Ain't: Jazz and the Making of the Sixties.* New Haven: Yale University; 2001.

Examines the jazz culture of the 1950s and 1960s from three perspectives: musicians who elaborated its aesthetic of extreme spontaneity and extreme discipline, artists and intellectuals who associated themselves with freedom cultural values, and youth who attended jazz festivals in the 1950s and 1960s but later transferred their allegiance to rock music. Part one covers black and white intellectuals who grappled with issues of community and marginality; part two examines the rise of the jazz festival as a site of postwar youth culture; parts three and four examine the music, approaches, significance, and contributions of John Coltrane and Charles Mingus. In part five, the author traces the emergence of counterculture among white youth, and the rise of soul power in the African American community. (Also cited under John Coltrane and Charles Mingus.)

1633. Such, David Glen, Ph.D. *Music, Metaphor and Values among Avant-Garde Jazz Musicians Living in New York City.* Los Angeles: University of California, Los Angeles; 1985.

Studies the music and value system of a select group of African American musicians. Demonstrates the link between music and worldviews notably in relation to African American history, social and musical concepts and strategies of urbanization and industrialization. Uses symbolism to focus on social metaphor and discuss the transcendence of conventional Western music-making. Good insider perspectives. The first serious study of this significant group of modernists.

1634. Tallman, Thomas Jon, D.M.A. *Jazz Trumpet: A Survey of the First Fifty Years.* Austin: University of Texas, Austin; 1998.

The purpose of this treatise is to demonstrate how selected aspects of jazz improvisation evolved from one generation of trumpeters to the next. He begins with King Oliver and Louis Armstrong, and analyzes selected works of Roy Eldridge, Dizzy Gillespie, Kenny Dorham, Clifford Brown, Miles Davis, Woody Shaw, and Booker Little. He uses historical data and transcriptions to show how performers learned from each other. (Also cited under Evolution and History.)

1635. Weremchuk, George, D.M.A. *A Comparative Analysis of Improvised Solos Based on the Popular Songs "Body and Soul," "Night and Day," and "Out of Nowhere" as Performed by Selected Jazz Tenor Saxophonists Representing Different Styles.* Miami: University of Miami; 1998.

The purpose was to transcribe and analyze three popular jazz classics by three different tenor saxophonists representing different styles. Michael Brecker, John Coltrane, and Coleman Hawkins performed the "Body and Soul" solos; "The Night and Day" solos were by Jerry Bergonzi, Joe Henderson, and Zoot Sims; and Stan Getz, David Liebman, and Sonny Stitt performed the "Out of Nowhere" solos. The analysis focused on their respective uses of harmonic, melodic, and rhythmic concepts.

1636. Westendorf, Lynette, D.M.A. *Analyzing Free Jazz (Ornette Coleman, John Coltrane, and Cecil Taylor)*. Seattle: University of Washington; 1994.

An examination of several stylistically diverse works within their respective cultural contexts. The first two chapters address the origins and influence of free jazz, and its relationship to blues and earlier jazz styles. In addition, she discusses the methodological approaches of selected artists, the Black Nationalist Movement, treatment of free jazz in the scholarly literature, and analytical techniques appropriate to jazz. In chapters 3 through 5, she analyzes Ornette Coleman's *Lonely Woman* (1959), John Coltrane's *India* (1961), and Cecil Taylor's *Indent: Second Layer* (1973). She transcribed each composition, and uses diagrams, and some graphic representations to make her points about rhythm, method of development, form, and the use of contrast. Additionally, she discusses Coleman's *Harmolodic* theory, Coltrane's adaptation of Indian aesthetics and techniques, and the poem that the composition is based on. (Also cited under Ornette Coleman, John Coltrane, and Cecil Taylor.)

1637. Yampolsky, Carol Jane, D.M.A. *The Solo Piano Music of Three American Composers: Armando "Chick" Corea, William "Billy" Taylor, Mary Lou Williams: A Performance-Tape Project*. College Park: University of Maryland; 1986.

A performance-tape of the nontranscribed solo jazz piano music of Armando "Chick" Corea, William "Billy" Taylor, and Mary Lou Williams. Yampolsky focuses on these musicians because they have notated many of their compositions. Featured are: "Twenty Children's Songs," Piano Music series 1–5 (manuscript, unpublished) by Armando "Chick" Corea; "B.T.'s— D.T.'s," "Beer Barrel Boogie," "Big Horn Breakdown," "Big Shoe Shuffle," "Birdwatcher," "Bit of Bedlam," "Black Swan Rag," "Cool and Caressing," "Crazy Oak Cakewalk," "Declivity," "Different Bells," "Early Morning Mambo," "Hoghead Shout," "Hotfoot Hamfat," "Jelly-Bean Boogie," "Latin Soul," "Lucky Buck Boogie," "Midnight Piano," "Society Strut," "Sounds in the Night," and "Titoro" by William "Billy" Taylor, and "Chili Sauce" and "Deuces Wild" by Mary Lou Williams. Yampolsky, writer/performer, contributed musical elements when necessary, biomusical data and annotations-classifications. Excellent addition to the literature.

Aesthetics, Criticism, Education, and Philosophy

1638. Ake, David Andrew, Ph.D. *Being Jazz: Identities and Images*. Los Angeles: University of California, Los Angeles; 1998.

Explores some of the diverse music and related identities that jazz communities have configured over the past century. He offers a case study in each chapter, and presents ways and means that differentiate each person/ community from another. He focuses on moments of instability, dealing with the historical, and musical phenomena that gave rise to contesting ways of being in jazz. He covers the relationship between the uptown and downtown communities of New Orleans and the Creoles of Color, Ornette Coleman and codes of masculinity in jazz in the 1950s, how the performance postures and demeanors of Keith Jarrett and Bill Evans shape understandings of their work, musical values espoused by college jazz-education programs, and more.

1639. Anderson, Iain D. *This is Our Music, Free Jazz, Cultural Hierachy, and the Sixties.* Bloomington: Indiana University; 2000.

Explores the question of who makes the decisions about the value of a cultural form and on what basis, and uses the impact of 1960s free improvisation on the changing status of jazz. He used interviews with surviving participants, mainstream and trade press, archival evidence, and recorded music sources to propose that the acrimonious debate over free jazz interacted with changes in its production, presentation, and reception. He used the freedom concept as a key aesthetical and ideological trait, and advocates that John Coltrane, Ornette Coleman, and Cecil Taylor undermined the concept of a popular national style by linking avant-garde techniques to the music industry's racial and economic structures. He argues that radical claims of black ownership by cultural nationalist like Amiri Baraka, Larry Neal, and A. B. Spellman enhanced the appeal of free jazz to universities and foundations. In addition, he argues that academia and philanthropic organizations offered prestige and patronage because they were under pressure to recognize African American culture.

1640. Anderson, Paul Allen, Ph.D. *From Spirituals to Swing: Harlem.* Ithaca: Cornell University; 1997.

Reconstructs a debate among the African American intellectuals associated with the Harlem renaissance, especially Sterling Brown, W.E.B. Du Bois, Langston Hughes, Zora Neale Hurston, Alain Locke, and Jean Toomer. He discusses their views regarding the formalization of the spiritual for the concert stage. Thereafter, the views of Du Bois and Locke are contrasted with those of Brown, Hughes, and Hurston. In his final chapter, he discussed how the Harlem Renaissance spirituals debate provided a context for the cultural politics of white jazz criticism in the "swing era" of the late 1930s and early 1940s.

1641. Baskerville, John Douglas, Ph.D. *The Impact of Modern Black Nationalist Ideology and Cultural Revitalization on American Jazz Music of the 1960s and 1970s.* Iowa City: University of Iowa; 1997.

The study has three purposes: (1) to explore the development of modern black nationalist though of the 1960s and 1970s, and locate it within the tradition of modern black nationalism and cultural revitalization; (2) to explore how selected jazz musicians embraced the label "new black music," and black nationalism and fused them into the production of their music; and (3) to explore how the study of music can enhance our knowledge of both culture and American society.

1642. Carter, Mia Elizabeth, Ph.D. *Shades of Jazz: Desire, Difference, and the Politics of Culture.* Milwaukee: University of Wisconsin, Milwaukee; 1992.

This study combines criticism and historiography to assess how differences have worked their way into jazz's discursive interstices. She focuses on post–World War II culture, and the impact that event had on Europe's Jewish communities and the African American community in the United States. She analyzes critics' perspectives and feelings on jazz, and national disappointment and disaffection. The study concludes with an analysis of contemporary documents and representations.

1643. Cartwright, Joan R, M.A. *The Cultural Politics of Commercial Jazz.* Boca Raton: Florida Atlantic University; 1994.

Examines jazz as a music developed by African Americans to communicate their desire for personal freedom and community, then as a commodity exploited by the commercial industry, which European-Americans dominate. In addition, she theorizes that because real jazz is the creation of African American musicians struggling to have their voices heard, it is often critically denounced and rewarded far less than commercial jazz.

1644. Harlos, Christopher, Ph.D. *The Jazz Life-Text: Autobiography and Biography in Jazz Art.* Durham: Duke University; 1998.

Explores why scholars seek to confer cultural recognition on subjects by means of traditional life writing while simultaneously celebrating those same subjects as figures of a marginalized counterculture. He argues that although jazz is America's premier musical expression, it has been marginalized in America. However, with the significant output of "Life-Texts," an effort is being made to bring the jazz artist into the historical mainstream, while maintaining the carnival essence of their existence.

1645. Herron, Joe Craig, M.A. *The Reach of the African Art Sound (Jazz).* Dominguez Hills: California State University, Dominguez Hills; 1996.

This thesis is meant to be a multidimensional study of cultural expression that includes movement and visual elements such as dress and body painting. He argues that the African sound has been transformed to the American hemisphere, and, more important, it permeates the global art scene.

1646. Lopes, Paul Douglas, Ph.D. *The Creation of a Jazz Art World and the Modern Jazz Renaissance.* Berkeley: University of California, Berkeley; 1994.

He examines the creation of a jazz art world over a 40-year period beginning in the late 1930s and up to the early 1950s. He shows how the organization of music production in the United States engendered the creation of a jazz art world, thereby transforming jazz as a musical genre. He divides the dissertation into two periods, the first deals with the 1930s to the early 1950s when a music oligopoly had effective control over the production of music. The second period begins in the mid-1950s with the collapse of the oligopoly and rise of independent music production.

1647. McMichael, Robert Kenneth, Ph.D. *Consuming Jazz: Black Music and Whiteness.* Providence, R.I.: Brown University; 1996.

Views jazz as both an art form and as a form of social and cultural interaction, and examines relationships between white audiences and African American musicians. He uses the concept of "integrationist subcultures," in which black and white audiences and musicians worked and listened in the same space. The interracial jazz scenes of the 1920s, 1950s, and 1960s were researched. He conducted ethnographic interviews with white listeners in the San Francisco Bay area that, in turn, explored the white racial conscious of the 1990s jazz scene.

1648. Morse, Michael William, Ph.D. *The Tune in Jazz as a Social Process: Prolegomena to a Sociology of Music.* Toronto: York University (Canada); 1996.

Concerned with the relationship between music and society, and the temporal procedures of music as particular instances of broader social processes. The dissertation focuses on the Kantian question, "How is consistent musical particularity possible?" He uses the ideas of Wilhelm Furtwangler, Immanuel Kant, Talcott Parsons, Max Weber, and others to discuss the musicality of the universal fact of rhythm.

1649. Oliver, Stephen Blake, M.A. *Backwards Saints: The Jazz Musician as Hero-Figure in James Baldwin's "Sonny's Blues" and John Clellon Holmes "The Horn."* Wolfville, N.S.: Arcadia University (Canada); 2000.

Examines the iconic jazz player as hero-figure in modern American fiction. He uses the theories of Ralph Ellison and Albert Murray as a way and means of understanding jazz's status within American culture. He asserts that the jazz musician speaks to a marginalized audience and offers hope of transcending this marginalization.

1650. Ongiri, Amy Abugo, Ph.D. *Blak Arts for Black People!: The Cultural Politics of the Black Power Movement and the Search for a Black Aesthetic.* Ithaca: Cornell University; 2000.

Addresses the cultural productions of the Black Power Movement, and the critical concern of defining a black aesthetic. She examines both cultural and political factors that led to the emergence of the aforementioned movements, and the conditions that account for their continued popular appeal. She addresses topics such as the Black Panther Party, the work of Larry Neal and LeRoi Jones, the black arts movement, black films, the black arts movement engagement with blues and jazz, and nonengagement with funk, soul, rhythm and blues, and more.

1651. Panish, Jon Seebart, Ph.D. *The Color of Jazz: Race and Representation in American Culture, 1945–1966.* Irvine: University of California, Irvine; 1995.

Excavates the differences in Euro-American and African American constructions of racial meaning. He analyzes the social and cultural interaction between Euro-Americans and African Americans in New York's Greenwich Village, and espouses that even among a group of Americans with a strong attraction and commitment to an alternative cultural resource deep divisions, power differences, and misunderstandings were widespread. He compared the representations of Charles Parker and jazz performance in the fiction of authors such as James Baldwin, William Melvin Kelley, Jack Kerouac, John Clellon Holmes, Ross Russell, and John A. Williams with the goal of uncovering specific differences between Euro-American and African American use of jazz as a cultural resource.

1652. Price, Emmett George, III. *Free Jazz and the Black Arts Movement, 1958–1967.* Pittsburgh: University of Pittsburgh; 2000.

Links the free jazz of the 1960s to the blacks arts movement of the same period. His overall goal is to introduce a new method of analyzing free jazz by drawing close attention to parallel cultural, political, and social movements of the time. His new method is established by demonstrating a relationship between the black arts movement and free jazz. In addition, he chronicles the literary and musical achievements of artists such as Albert Ayler, Marion Brown, Sun Ra, and Archie Shepp, concentrates on race, black consciousness, the question of a black aesthetic, cultural nationalism, and more to both make his connection and to forge a new method of analyzing free jazz.

1653. Thorp, John Marsh, Jr., Ed.D. *Beyond Systems Theory: A Paragon of Autopoietic Organization, Mimesis and Praxis.* San Francisco: University of San Francisco; 2002.

Develops a paragon: jazz as organization. He links the work of Paul Ricoeur, specifically mimesis and narrative identity, with the autopoietic views of Maturana and Varela to refigure organization. He explains the genesis of the project, surveys the literature, traces reductionist and interpretive treatments of the anthropological literature, elucidates on jazz as a paragon for organizational action and learning, the use of jazz as a metaphor, and more.

1654. Titlestad, Michael Frank, M.A. *Representations of Jazz Music and Performance Occasions in Selected Literature.* Durban: University of South Africa; 1999.

Hypothesizes that creative writers translate jazz and performance into discourse by recourse to a number of figurative patterns. In turn, these patterns map existential, anthropological, and political spaces and situate jazz within them. He discusses the construction of alterity, the strategic deployment of blackness, the notion of existential integration, and the body of the instrument and body of the performer in representations. Overall, the three chapters are concerned with the emergence and propagation of oppositional identities in jazz writing.

1655. Toivanen, Mokko, Ph.D. *Jazz as a Natural System: Phenomenological and Semiotic Research into the Use of Modern Jazz and Its Meanings.* Helsinki: Jyvaskylan Yliopisto (Finland); 2000.

Focuses on the meaning of jazz, and attempts to reduce jazz to the level of human experience. Jazz is linked to existence and perception through fundamental assumptions of different traditions of phenomenology and semiotics. The arguments are centered on Heideggenan existentialistic concepts and jazz as a collective culture with its individualistic aspects. The semiotic issues are concerned with the research of jazz myths, narrative level of meaning of jazz, jazz's close relationship to natural languages, and more.

1656. Whaley, Preston Agee, Jr, Ph.D. *Jammin the Blues: Beat Writers, Jazz, Style and Markets in the Transformation of United States Culture.* Tallahassee: Florida State University; 2000.

Uses archival research and the theoretical eclecticism of cultural studies to investigate how jazz influenced the structure and content of Beat Generation writing and social life. In addition, he looks at the relationships between jazz and the Beats and audiences on the ground and in the popular media. He also observes how the dynamics of the vernacular and the spectacle set in motion important transformations in culture.

Analysis, Arranging, Composition, Harmony

1657. Arcaro, Peter Arnold, D.M.A. *Four Jazz Essays for Alto, Tenor, and Baritone Saxophones, Two Trumpets, Two Trombones, Piano, Bass, and Drums.* (Original Composition). Norman: The University of Oklahoma; 1991.

Uses blues, a ballad, a jazz waltz, and free bop to compose an original suite in four movements. Arcaro varies his compositional approach; the blues features a 12-tone unison line, the ballad is in free from, the jazz waltz features both Lydian and polymodal concepts, and the free bop movement proceeds from free atonal concepts to tonal concepts.

1658. Byrd, Donaldson Touissant L'Ouverture, II, Ed.D. *The Performance and Analysis of an Original Afro-American Musical Composition for Trumpet and Orchestra.* New York: Columbia University Teacher's College; 1983.

A composition for trumpet and orchestra that includes a section for improvisation accompanied by rhythm section and electronic instruments. Includes an overview of the author's life, stylistic concepts, compositional techniques, and stylistic interpretation. Purposes include filling the void of trumpet music rooted in African American tradition, helping educators to understand the musical complexities of African American music and the integration of improvisation rooted in African American music and the symphonic tradition.

1659. Chicural, Steven Robert, D.M.A. *"George Gershwin's Songbook": Influences of Jewish Music, Ragtime, and Jazz.* Lexington: University of Kentucky; 1989.

Discusses the Jewish, jazz, and ragtime influences contained in *George Gershwin's Songbook.* In addition to generic features, Chicural's analysis is concerned with melodic, rhythmic, and modulation aspects. One of the most significant findings is the importance of the minor third in his melodies. Provides deep insights into Gershwin's use of musical concepts from different cultures.

1660. Contorno, Nicholas Joseph, D.M.A. *Symphony for Concert Band and Jazz Ensemble.* Madison: The University of Wisconsin, Madison; 1985.

Focused primarily on middle and high school performers, this work provides a jazz-influenced performance for all band instruments. Contorno delineates the percentage of time that each group performs in the three-movement work. The first movement loosely follows the sonata allegro form. The second movement, a theme and variations, is an alto saxophone solo with the variations occurring in the accompaniment. The third movement begins with a fanfare by the concert band and evolves into a bossa nova. The finale allows for improvisation and themes that appeared in the first three movements reappear.

1661. Davis, Glen Roger, D.M.A. *Levels Analysis of Jazz Tunes.* Columbus: The Ohio State University; 1990.

Extends Schenkerian analysis to include new approaches to jazz analysis. Davis proposes new concepts, terminology, and notation he considers logical extensions of Schenkerian analysis. His new ideas are defined and applied to levels analysis of jazz tunes. Logical and thorough.

1662. Dimoff, Trevor Anthony, M.M. *The Third Impossible Thing Before Breakfast: An Octet for Saxophone and String Quartets.* Calgary, Alta.: University of Calgary (Canada); 1998.

The work is in three movements and is approximately 19 minutes long. He merges jazz and classical musical elements; the jazz elements include rhythm and harmony and the classical musical elements include formal structure, bitonality, and motivic generation of musical ideas The first movement is permeated with quartal chords, and the second movement features blues and contains tertian harmonies. The third movement combines elements of the first two movements while maintaining swing inflections over asymmetrical meters and changing beat lengths.

1663. Dodson, Leon, Ed. D. *Adapting Selected Compositions and Arrangements of Duke Ellington for the High School Jazz Orchestra.* New York: New York University; 1979.

Adapts "Satin Doll," "Take The 'A' Train," "Mood Indigo," "Sophisticated Lady," "Caravan," "Perdido," and "Don't Get Around Much Anymore" for high school jazz band. Dodson's identification and application of Ellington devices (harmonic concepts, sound, style, and structure) is commendable.

1664. Elliott, Scott Nelson, M.M. *A Study of Tonal Coherence in Jazz Music as Derived from Linear Compositional Techniques of the Baroque Era.* Pittsburgh: Duquesne University; 1987.

Uses Schenkerian analysis to prove the structural similarity between jazz and baroque music and to demonstrate that Schenkerian analysis is an effective method of jazz analysis. Elliott concluded that as linearity is a significant factor in the structure of jazz and as linearity coincides with Schenkerian theories of tonal music beginning in the baroque, there is a European influence in jazz.

1665. Emche, John Theodore, Jr., D.M.A. *Dialogue for Jazz Piano and Orchestra, with Preliminary Research and Analysis* (original composition). Columbus: The Ohio State University; 1980.

A third-stream composition that evolved after preliminary research to determine why some compositions were judged musically unsuccessful. Emche reviewed the qualifications/sources of selected third stream composers and through analysis concluded that the employment of form and rhythm, harmonic language, and improvisation were important when creating a successful third-stream composition.

1666. Ford, Christopher John, D.M.A. *Eleven Jazz-Influenced Works for Concert Saxophone.* College Park: University of Maryland, College Park; 1991.

Consists of an audiotape recording and a written document analyzes 11 jazz-influenced compositions composed between 1921 and 1981. He focuses on the identification of jazz influences and offers performance suggestions. Information on the composer, compositional techniques, musical form, and special instrumental techniques is also included. The compositions are by William Albright, David Amram, Edison Denisov, Werner Heider, Paul Hindemith, Jacque Ibert, Andre Jolivet, William Karlins, Darius Milhaud, Edwin Schuloff, and Phil Woods He details how the composers integrate classical and jazz techniques in their respective styles.

1667. Griswold, Erik Michael, Ph.D. *In Between States.* La Jolla: University of California, San Diego; 1997.

The culmination of his graduate works in composition, free improvisation, and jazz performance. He is focused on the abstract development of materials and the technique of information layering. Performers are asked to spontaneously extrapolate from notated scores and to incorporate their own original ideas. They also are asked to engage in group dialogue. The jazz influences draw on historical styles and practices, and are used to establish historical and emotional links to the collective body of jazz music.

1668. Heen, Carol Louise, Ph.D. *Procedures for Style Analysis of Jazz: A Beginning Approach.* Minneapolis: University of Minnesota; 1981.

Predicated on the assumption that there is a need to develop an approach for style analysis of jazz. Heen is concerned with analyzing musical elements and ascertaining their effect on style classifications and philosophy. She examines fundamental issues and practices in style analysis of jazz with the goal of developing a set of concepts and practices for analysis of jazz using musicological paradigms. Includes a review of the literature, a discussion of notation and transcription, characteristics of periods, application of procedures of analysis, and a comparison of several versions of "Dippermouth Blues/Sugarfoot Stomp" recorded between 1923 and 1957.

1669. Holmquist, Mats Goran, M.M. *Concertino for Jazz Clarinet, Electric Viola and Symphonic Orchestra.* Denton: University of North Texas; 1991.

This composition of approximately 15 minutes is scored for two flutes (second doubling on piccolo), two oboes, two B-flat clarinets, two bassoons, four F horns, two B-flat trumpets, three trombones, solo B-flat clarinet, solo electric viola, and strings. The composition is in two movements, Andante and Canon. He uses jazz-influenced harmonies and improvisation, and jazz-classical influences from composers such as Chick Corea, Wolfgang Mozart, Igor Stravinsky, and Dmitri Shostakovich.

1670. Holtz, Robert E., M.A. (theory). *Fundamental Harmonic Materials for Tonal Jazz Improvisation.* San Diego: San Diego State University; 1978.

An exploration of the relationship of modes and scale tone chords, common scale-tone harmonic progressions, 13th chords, chromatic alterations, symmetrical scales, diatonic and chromatic progressions, quartal harmonies, and more. He uses examples to demonstrate his theories and provides clear explanations.

1671. Husak, Thomas John, Ph.D. *The Development and Evaluation of Programmed Instruction in the Techniques of Jazz Ensemble Arranging.* Columbus: The Ohio State University; 1978.

Concerned with developing a programmed format for teaching the concepts of arranging for jazz ensemble. Determines what concepts, methods, and principles arrangers use to produce a programmed textbook with taped musical examples. Uses the RULEG approach to construction and sequencing and a pretest-posttest-retest procedure. Reports reliability and validity.

1672. Lillo, Kenneth John, M.M. (composition) *Jazz Mass.* Reno: University of Nevada, Reno; 1982.

The ordinary of the mass (Kyrie, Gloria, Credo, Sanctus, and Agnus Dei) in a jazz style for chorus, orchestra, and jazz band (with a revised version of the Lutheran liturgy as text). Features vocal solos and thematic unity between movements (a cantus firmus mass).

1673. Mahoney, J. Jeffrey, M.M. *The Elements of Jazz Harmony and Analysis.* Denton: North Texas State University; 1986.

A method of analyzing jazz piano music of the 1935–1950 period by focusing on root positions, circle of fifths, tritone substitutions, and more. Mahoney analyzes several compositions and arrives at a troipart categorization of harmonic motion.

1674. Martin, Henry John, Ph.D. *Jazz Harmony (with) String Quartet No. 2* (original composition). Princeton: Princeton University; 1980.

An essay on jazz harmony and a string quartet constitute this dissertation. Martin's discussion of harmony follows a chromatic model focusing on the circle of fifths, dominant seventh chords, chord functionality, and the organization of 12-bar blues and 16- and 32-bar song forms. Includes a discussion of voice leading, harmonic functional norms, harmonic-modal prolongation and formation, pedagogical jazz literature and a discussion of selected theoretical studies. The two appendices include a description of jazz pedagogical literature, and the literature the author found useful in studying jazz.

1675. Miley, James Scott, D.M.A. *In the Shadow of Angels.* Eugene: Univesity of Oregon; 1999.

The composition has three movements and is written for full ensemble and two optional interludes for guitar soloist and jazz trio. The harmonic and rhythmic language various throughout, ranging from the use of extended triads and quartal harmonies often heard in blues and jazz, and driving rhythms. The composition has a contrasting section that was inspired by the composer's childhood experiences growing up in Los Angeles. Each of the interludes is performed twice, with the soloist embellishing the written material during the repeat. Although these interludes provide insight into the improvisational nature of his jazz background, the three ensemble movements are fully notated in strict concert style. Overall, one can hear minimalist hockets, polyrhythms, metric layering, and blues-jazz influences throughout the composition.

1676. Morgan, Robert Badgett, D.M.A. *The Music and Life of Robert Graettinger (with) Cantata for Chorus and Jazz Band* (original composition). Urbana-Champaign: University of Illinois at Urbana-Champaign; 1974.

Examines the life and music of a former (1947–1954) Stan Kenton arranger. Extensive analysis is supplemented with insider perspectives from friends and colleagues of Robert Graettinger. Covers Graettinger's early development, association with Stan Kenton, and tenure at Westlake College of Music with analysis of compositions and arrangements such as "Thermopolae," "You Got to My Head," "City of Glass," and "Suite for String Trio and Wind Quartet." The appendices include a list of scores, parts held by Stan Kenton, a discography, and the extant score of "A Trumpet."

1677. Ottervik, Jennifer Robin, M.A. *The Use of Jazz in Opera.* Denton: University of North Texas; 1995.

Attempts to collectively discuss the methods of incorporating jazz into opera. Focuses on jazz rhythms, harmonies, and improvisation of selected composers. Recognizes the importance of jazz in the works of Gershwin and Krenek, and in the works of jazz artists such as Dave Burrell, Anthony Davis, George Gruntz, and others.

1678. Pinckney, Warren Richard, Ph.D. *Some Properties of Nonfunctional Chord Progressions in the Modern Jazz Opera Scenes from the Duplex.* Princeton: Princeton University; 1983.

A composition and an essay in which Pickney details the process that led him to compose an opera incorporating jazz. The analysis focuses on relationships, symmetries, and properties of the harmonic progressions that make up the composition.

1679. Rizzo, Jacques C., Ed.D. *Written Jazz Rhythm Patterns: A Series of Original, Accompanied Wind Instrument Duets of an Intermediate Degree of Difficulty with Suggestions for Their Performance.* New York: New York University; 1979.

This study evolved from the premise that traditionally trained musicians experience difficulty performing jazz (which Rizzo attributes to a 4/4 rather than a 12/8 interpretation of selected rhythms). Rhythmic patterns are categorized and arranged systematically for study. The 28 duets for wind instruments and rhythm section (bass, drums, piano) use jazz-idiomatic articulation.

1680. Rohm, Joseph William, Ph.D. *Jazz Harmony: Structure, Voicing, and Progression.* Tallahassee: The Florida State University; 1974.

Studies chord structures, voicings, and harmonic progressions. The study is limited to selected piano and instrumental scores of the 1950–70 period. Included is a discussion of harmonic structures. Formulates a theory of harmonic progressions.

1681. Rose, Richard Franklin, D.M.A. *An Analysis of Timing in Jazz Rhythm Section Performance.* Austin: The University of Texas at Austin; 1989.

Concerned with the time relationships that exist among the attack of musical tones on selected rhythm section performances. His analysis is predicated on beats and mean durations. Rose used one example each of swing style, jazz ballad, and Latin jazz. Shows that many differences occur below human perception.

1682. Ross, George Joseph, D.M.A. *An Annotated Historical Anthology of Thirty-Five Graded Duets for Two Bassoons Including Eight Original Duets in Historical Jazz Idioms.* Rochester: The University of Rochester, Eastman School of Music; 1975.

A compilation of 35 selected duets including originals and some taken from scholarly sources. He includes transcriptions from the St. Martial School, the Trecento period, the Renaissance, Baroque, Classical, Romantic, and twentieth century. The duets are designed to improve both a student's knowledge of history as well as their performance skill. Covers technical and expressive problems.

1683. Sanborn, Larry Martin, Ph.D. *Musicianship for the Jazz Performer.* Cincinnati: The Union Institute; 1992.

Advocates combining modern jazz harmonic concepts, theory, composition, and orchestration in teaching jazz improvisation. Sanborn's philosophy, derived from his experience, lies in the spontaneity of music.

1684. Santander, Andrew Michael, D.M.A. *David Baker's Sonata I for Piano: Background, Compositional Style, and Performance Considerations.* Athens: University of Georgia; 1998.

Recognizes that the scholarly studies of Baker's works are rare in spite of his recognition as an internationally renowned composer, music educator, and performer. He is concerned with Baker's use of classical and jazz elements, and wishes to introduce pianist, piano teachers, and other musicians to his important work. In the first two chapters, he presents a concise biography of Baker, and gives the compositional background of the sonata. In the following three chapters, he addresses a movement of the sonata, and in the final chapter draws conclusions from his study of the sonata.

1685. Trimmer, Dale, Ed.D. *Concerto for Percussion and Jazz Band.* New York: Columbia University Teachers College; 1994.

Recognizing the importance of the jazz band in contemporary instrumental programs, he espouses the need for an original composition that has a variety of musical influences. His overall purpose was to compose a composition that that included contemporary music, jazz, and improvisation, thereby fulfilling the void that music educators have expressed. A related paper includes a stylistic interpretive analysis as well as suggestions for teaching, rehearsing, and performance.

1686. Washut, Robert Paul, Jr., D.A. *Excursions for Jazz Quartet and Orchestra: A Preliminary Research and Analysis.* (original composition). Greely: University of Northern Colorado; 1986.

Combines jazz and classical music elements to produce an original composition in three movements. Analyzes "symbiosis" by Claus Oberman and surveys other third-stream works. Selected discography of post-1950 third-stream works.

1687. Williams, James Kent, Ph.D. *Themes Composed by Jazz Musicians of the Bebop Era: A Study of Harmony, Rhythm, and Melody (Volumes I and II).* Bloomington: Indiana University; 1982.

A comprehensive categorization of bebop harmonic, melodic, and rhythmic themes. He uses 200 themes by bebop musicians, and categorized them by using Salzerian reductive harmonic analysis and other methods. He used an analytical method developed by Leonard Meyer and Eugene Narmour to assess melodic structures. The harmonic categorization also included themes based on both blues and contrafacts. Williams used a computer program to elicit melodic motives and associate themes with rhythmic patterns. Comprehensive and scholarly.

Argot

1688. Gold, Robert S., Ph.D. *A Jazz Lexicon.* New York: New York University; 1962.

Contains over 1,000 words and phrases that have been used by jazz musicians since 1900. Includes words and phrases from jazz glossaries, slang dictionaries, jazz periodicals, African American literature, periodicals and newspapers. Good examination of the social history of African American jazz artists and their jazz vocabulary. Reveals consciousness, group dynamics, and identity concepts.

Criticism and Poetry

1689. Anderson, Thomas J., III, Ph.D. *Notes to Make the Sound Come Right: Towards a Definition of Jazz Poetry (Bob Kaufman, Stephen Jonas, Jayne Cortez, Nathaniel Mackey).* Binghamton: State University of New York at Binghamton; 1998.

A chronological and textual analysis of the use of jazz in modern and contemporary African American poetry. His primary focus is jazz poetry that has been used to transmit the historical and cultural legacies of the black community. The work of these four African American poets spans a time period of 1960 to 1990, and he focuses on how they used jazz as a technique in writing poetry.

1690. Bernotas, Robert W., Ph.D. *Critical Theory, Jazz, and Politics: A Critique of the Frankfurt School.* Baltimore: The Johns Hopkins University; 1987.

Investigates and refutes the Frankfurt School's theory of "affirmative" culture as applied to jazz. The Frankfurt School argues that once art has come under the influence of affirmative culture it loses its element of protest and becomes a means for affirmation of the status quo. Bernotas argues for an alternative aesthetic analysis of jazz.

1691. Brown, Patrick James, Ph.D. *Jazz Poetry: Definition, Analysis, and Performance.* Los Angeles: University of Southern California; 1978.

What is jazz? What is poetry? What are the principles for performance of jazz poetry? Discusses jazz within a racial, historical, geographic, and stylistic context. Jazz poetry is discussed by titles and topics related to generic jazz applications. Brown focuses on African American poetry since 1900, choosing one example each from Langston Hughes, Sterling Brown, Bob Kaufman, David Henderson, Don Lee, and Stanley Crouch. In-depth analysis and performance principles covering expression, attitudes, and moods.

1692. Jarrett, James Michael, Ph.D. *Drifting on a Read: Jazz as a Model for Literacy and Theoretical Writing.* Gainesville: University of Florida; 1988.

Examines the impact of jazz used in literary and theoretical writing. Uses Gunther Schuller's *Early Jazz* to analyze both musicological applications and images dealing with "Rhapsody," "Satura," "Obbligato," and "Charivari." Demonstrates the shaping of cultural perceptions by jazz literary representation providing a theoretical basis for the use of jazz as a model for scholarly writing.

1693. Jones, Meta DuEwa, Ph.D. *African-American Jazz Poetry: Orality, Prosody and Performance (Jayne Cortez, Michael Harper, Yusef Komunyakaa, Nathaniel Mackey, Harryette Mullen).* Palo Alto: Stanford University; 2001.

She begins with the premise that jazz has a crucial relationship to American literature. She traces the influence of jazz on contemporary African American poetry, examines what characterizes poetry within an African American literary tradition. In addition, she approaches the translatability of jazz into poetry by using by using concrete prosodic analysis, examining the relationship between rhythm, accent, and meter in poetry structurally influenced by jazz, use of typography and orthography, and the use of critical and instrumental bias in jazz on the tradition of jazz poetry.

1694. Smith, Hugh L., Jr., Ph.D. *The Literary Manifestation of a Liberal Romanticism in American Jazz.* Albuquerque: The University of New Mexico; 1955.

Reviews jazz literature to demonstrate the outgrowth of liberal romanticism in twentieth-century writing. Advocates the allegiance of jazz to American literature focusing on George Washington Cable, Lafcadio Hearn, and Mark Twain. Discusses the creation of reverence for artists like Louis Armstrong, Bix Beiderbecke, King Oliver, and Bessie Smith through jazz literature.

1695. Towler, Carmen Buford, M.A. *African Oral Tradition and Black American Jazz Structures in Langston Hughes' Montage of a Dream Deferred.* Dominguez Hills: California State University, Dominguez Hills; 1978.

Analyzes *Montage of a Dream Deferred* by recognizing Hughes's reliance on African American blues and jazz. Demonstrates Hughes's transliteration of African melodic and rhythmic structure into 86 poems based on a single theme. Good demonstration of the relationship of the poems to jazz improvisation.

1696. Welburn, Ronald Garfield, Ph.D. *American Jazz Criticism, 1914–1940.* New York: New York University; 1983.

Chronicles the contributions of R.D. Darrell and the importance of *Phonograph Monthly Review, Down Beat,* and *Metronome.* The contributions of Charles DeLaunay, Paul Edvard Miller, Winthrop Sargeant, Wilber Hobson, Marshall Stearns, Frank Marshall Davis, George Simon, and George Frazier are discussed, as is the importance of John Hammond, Hugues Panassie, and Roger Pryor Dodge. Excellent discussion.

Discography

1697. Foreman, Ronald Clifford, Ph.D. *Jazz and Race Records, 1920–32; Their Origins and Their Significance for the Record Industry and Society.* Urbana-Champaign: University of Illinois; 1968.

Historical discussion of the production and merchandising of recordings geared to African Americans between 1920 and 1932. Draws heavily on both pre- and post-1920 sociocultural contexts to illustrate the commercial inauguration, expansion, and decline of *Race Records.* Discusses marketing, merchandising, advertising, competition with radio and the importance of *Race Records* in disseminating blues and jazz.

1698. Gray, Herman S., Ph.D. *Independent Cultural Production: Theresa Records, Case Study of a Jazz Independent.* Santa Cruz: University of California, Santa Cruz; 1983.

Investigates the ideological, organizational, and structural concepts that shaped the identity, operation, and products of an independent jazz record company. Interested in reformulating cultural production to determine ideology and structure. Suggests that identity and meanings are directly related to independent status.

1699. Shockett, Bernard I., Ph.D. *A Stylistic Study of the Blues as Recorded by Jazz Instrumentalists, 1917–1931.* New York: New York University; 1964.

Traces stylistic trends in the historical evolution of the blues as demonstrated by jazz artists. Uses Brian Rust's discography to compile a list of titles recorded between 1917 and 1931. Compositions were categorized and analyzed according to form, introductions, keys, modulations, and tempos. Lists some characteristics of pre-1932 blues offering insights into structure and concepts.

1700. Tracy, Michael Alfred, M.A. *Blue Note Classics: An Analytical, Comparative and Historical Study of Eleven Jazz Recordings.* Louisville: University of Louisville; 1989.

Concerned with understanding jazz improvisation as a creative process. Analyzes 11 recordings and interviews the artists concerning personal approaches to improvisation. Insightful insider perspectives on the origin and application of phenomena to produce a creative result.

Evolution and History

1701. Aloisio, Gerard Salvatore, D.M.A. *A Historical Summary of Major Musical Developments in American Jazz from the End of World War I to the Beginning of World War II.* Cincinnati: University of Cincinnati; 1995.

Traces the major changes in jazz styles, and describes how selected vocalists, instrumentalists, and composers from blues, boogie-woogie, and jazz made significant contributions to their respective genres. He discusses the contributions of Blind Lemon Jefferson, Robert Johnson, Ma Rainey, Bessie Smith, Mamie Smith, Louis Armstrong, Count Basie, Duke Ellington, Bix Beiderbecke, Benny Goodman, Fletcher Henderson, James P. Johnson, Meade Lux Lewis, Jelly Roll Morton, Kid Ory, Fats Waller, Paul Whiteman, and Jimmy Yancey The appendix contains 27 transcriptions from Folkways Records, the Smithsonian Collection of Classic Jazz, and the Smithsonian Collection of Big Band Jazz. (Also cited under Collective Biographies.)

1702. Bough, Thomas Wayne, D.M.A. *The Role of the Tuba in Early Jazz Music from 1917 to the Present: A Historical, Pedagogical, and Aural Perspective.* Tempe: Arizona State University; 1998.

The purpose is to produce introductory pedagogical materials that will guide tuba players in a stylistically correct performance of early jazz. He transcribed the tuba parts of selected recordings of early jazz, annotated the transcriptions, and then supplemented the transcriptions with appropriate improvised solos. The dissertation included a compact disc recording of the transcriptions by the author, which in turn, are supplemented with a trumpet, trombone, banjo, and drums. An extensive discography is included in the appendix.

1703. Bird, Robert Atkinson, M.A. *Methods and Categories of Jazz Analysis: A Critical Review of Five Approaches to Jazz History and Musical Analysis.* Madison: University of Wisconsin, Madison; 1976.

The five works assessed are *Jazz: Its Evolution and Essence* by Andre Hodeir, *Early Jazz: Its Roots and Musical Development* by Gunther Schuller, *Improvisation: Zur Technik der spontanen Gestaltung im Jazz* by Alfons M. Dauer, "Constructive Elements in Jazz Improvisation," in *Journal of the American Musicological Society* 27 (1974) by Frank Tirro, and "Charlie Parker: Techniques of Improvisation" by Thomas Owens. Bird uses some definitions from Earl Spielman's dissertation *North American Fiddling: A Methodology for the Historical and Comparative Analytical Style Study of Instrumental Musical Traditions* (University of Wisconsin, Madison, 1975). Provides a detailed and scholarly account of strengths and weaknesses for each approach. Includes analysis supplemented with numerous musical examples.

1704. Coin, Gregory McAfee, M.A. *Developmental Parallels in the Evolution of Musical Styles: Romanticism, Jazz, Rock 'n' Roll, and American Musical Theatre.* Louisville: University of Louisville; 1974.

Promotes a generic theory of evolution focusing on primary, melding, dynamic, and transition developmental stages. Provocative. Somewhat parallels the cyclic theory of the evolution of musical styles.

1705. Hansen, Chadwick Clarke, Ph.D. *The Ages of Jazz: A Study of Jazz in Its Cultural Context.* Minneapolis: University of Minnesota; 1956.

Hanson believes African American folk music is superior to anglo-American folk music. Discusses origins of the jazz band, the importance of New Orleans, African American migration to the north, Chicago in the 1920s, swing, and bebop. Focuses on jazz styles and evolution as cultural phenomena and connects change with racial progress. Hanson believes jazz is becoming high art. One of the earliest dissertations connecting jazz evolution and cultural context.

1706. Harding, John Ralph, D.M.A. *A Survey of the Evolution of Jazz for the General Reader.* Miami: University of Miami; 1981.

Believes jazz evolved as a mixture of musical elements from the African and European cultures in the West Indies and the southeastern United States in the late 1700s and 1800s. Traces the evolution from antebellum genres to the 1960s, including New Orleans, swing, cool, and bebop. Also addresses Afro-Cuban jazz. The survey is intended for general readers, and provides a commercialized view of jazz history with no discussion of transformation or reinterpretation.

1707. Hennessey, Thomas Joseph, Ph.D. *From Jazz to Swing: Black Jazz Musicians and Their Music, 1917–1935.* Evanston: Northwestern University; 1973.

Addresses the 1917–1935 changes in jazz and the role and function of African American musicians. Hennessey traces jazz from a local phenomenon to the influence of media in dissemination and popularization. He addresses the 1923–29 development of African American regional styles in Chicago, New York, and six territories.

1708. Herfort, David A., Ed.D. *A History of the National Association of Jazz Educators and a Description of Its Role in American Music Education.* Houston: University of Houston; 1979.

Traces the history of NAJE from the early planning sessions in the 1960s focusing primarily on the 1968 to 1978 years. Provides a description of the organization's role in music education and a summary of progress made toward achieving its goals and objectives. Includes data on curricula and ensemble growth.

1709. High, Louchrisa E. Ford, Ed.D. *A Historical Study of the Development of Black Music and Biographies of Selected Black Composers (Gospel, Spiritual, Jazz).* Nashville: Tennessee State University; 1988.

Investigates the historical development of the spiritual, gospel music, jazz, and black concert music. She focuses on the lives and musical contributions of selected composers in each genre. She provides lists of compositions, including concert music, spirituals, and gospel songs as well as audiovisual materials, video cassettes, film and filmstrips, and discographies of concert music, gospel, jazz, and spirituals.

1710. Hischke, Jon J., M.M. *The Origin and Development of Kansas City Jazz.* Lincoln: University of Nebraska; 1977.

Although he recognizes the contributions of Frank Driggs, Ross Russell, and Gunther Schuller, Hischke believes scholars have largely ignored Kansas City jazz. Limited to origins, style, development of Kansas City jazz to World War II, and the emergence of bebop. Good discussion of origins and style with an informative interview of Jay McShann.

1711. Levin, Michael David, Ph.D. *Louise de Koven Bowen: A Case History of the American Response to Jazz.* Urbana-Champaign: University of Illinois at Urbana-Champaign; 1985.

Examines the feelings, thoughts, and perceptions of Louise deKoven Bowen regarding Chicago jazz in the 1920s. Levin discusses her rejection of jazz within the context of her concerns about Chicago and its youth focusing on her work with the Juvenile Protective Association and Hull-House and using the writings of Morroe Berger and Neil Leonard in measuring early perceptions of jazz. Offers penetrating insights into sociocultural issues of the time.

1712. Merriam, Alan Parkhurst, M.M. *Instruments and Instrumental Usages in the History of Jazz.* Evanston: Northwestern University; 1948.

The author espouses that jazz is a complex art form that should be accorded more study by institutions of higher education. His primary objective is to acquaint the reader with the role and function of specific musical instruments and their place in jazz history. Discusses history, the evolution of the jazz band, and the techniques of jazz. His discussions on organology, origins, influences, and archaic jazz are noteworthy. Excellent references to recordings and record labels.

1713. Ogren, Kathy Jo, Ph.D. *Performance Crossroads: The Significance of the Jazz Controversy for Twenties America.* Baltimore: The Johns Hopkins University; 1986.

Uses jazz to discuss context in New Orleans, Chicago, New York, and Kansas City. Ogren also addresses dissemination, participatory qualities, African American and white aesthetics and African American perceptions of jazz as viewed within the prism of sacred/secular cultural phenomena. Rooted in meaning, symbolism, and a perceptive understanding of African American culture and its ability to adapt. A scholarly treatment that demonstrates how jazz mediated controversy while adopting change.

1714. Pyke, Launcelot Allen, II, Ph.D. *Jazz, 1920 to 1927: An Analytical Study. (Volumes I and II).* Iowa City: State University of Iowa; 1962.

Analysis of 10 transcriptions of solos by Louis Armstrong, Bunk Johnson, and King Oliver recorded between 1922 and 1927. After a concise history of prejazz, Pyke discusses form, harmonic and contrapuntal practices, and meter and rhythm. Good analysis (performance techniques, harmony, melody, scales, etc.) and discussion of jazz.

1715. Quinn, James Joseph, Ph.D. *An Examination of the Evolution of Jazz as it Relates to the Pre-Literate, Literate, and Post-Literate Precepts of Marshall McLuhan.* Evanston: Northwestern University; 1971.

Discusses the performing practices, musical textures, and structures of selected jazz styles and relates these concepts to the theories of Marshall McLuhan. Discusses McLuhan's theory of preliterate, literate, and postliterate modes of communication. Scholarly discussion and revelations regarding communication, perception, and organization.

1716. Raeburn, Bruce Boyd, Ph.D. *New Orleans Style: The Awakening of American Jazz Scholarship and Its Cultural Implications.* New Orleans: Tulane University; 1991.

Focuses on jazz historiography before the publication of Marshall Stearns's *The Story of Jazz (1956).* Advocates that the preacademic era evolved from international "hot" record collectors from the 1920s to 1934. The dissemination of historical information led to the initiation of jazz journals such as *Down Beat, Esquire, The New Republic,* and *Jazz Information.* Raeburn believes that *Jazzman (1930)* and *The Jazz Record Book (1942)* began the perception that jazz originated in New Orleans, a slogan adopted in the 1940s to boost tourism.

1717. Stebbins, Robert Alan, M.A. *The Minneapolis Jazz Community: The Conflict Between Musical and Commercial Values.* Minneapolis: University of Minnesota; 1962.

Postulates that tensions exist between the practical and aesthetic requirements of jazz. Stebbins believes that jazz offers its exponents both emotional and musical values leading to the formation of quasi communities. He investigates the assumption that commercial musicians are different than jazz musicians. Interesting conclusions derived from studies of leisure time activities.

1718. Stevens, Clifford, M.A. *New Orleans to Bop and Beyond: A Comprehensive Jazz Instructional Curriculum for Secondary Level Students.* Edmonton, Alta.: Concordia University (Canada); 1997.

Offers a proposal for the development of an introductory jazz-related curriculum for secondary level students. He proposes two goals, to development knowledge of jazz history and performance. He developed and taught modules from early jazz and bebop, and concluded that students increased their knowledge of the jazz periods. He measured student's pre- and posttest results, and also compared gender differences.

1719. Tallman, Thomas Jon, D.M.A. *Jazz Trumpet: A Survey of the First Fifty Years.* Austin: University of Texas, Austin; 1998.

The purpose of this treatise is to demonstrate how selected aspects of jazz improvisation evolved from one generation of trumpeters to the next. He begins with King Oliver and Louis Armstrong, and analyzes selected works of Roy Eldridge, Dizzy Gillespie, Kenny Dorham, Clifford Brown, Miles Davis, Woody Shaw, and Booker Little. He uses historical data and transcriptions to show how performers learned from each other. (Also cited under Collective Biographies.)

1720. Tanner, Paul Ora Warren, M. A. *A Technical Analysis of the Development of Jazz.* Los Angeles: University of California, Los Angeles; 1962.

Espouses studying the development of jazz through analysis. Good insights and interesting comments regarding current and future directions.

1721. Taylor, William Edward, Ed.D. *The History and Development of Jazz Piano: A New Perspective for Educators.* Amherst: University of Massachusetts; 1975.

Predicated on the belief that jazz, having evolved from its African American roots into an internationally recognized genre, is America's classical music. Covers jazz piano styles from preragtime to the early 1970s, and includes historical, philosophical, and sociological observations. Supplemental materials for studying piano styles are found in the index (improvisation, patterns, cycles, harmonic concepts, tonal and rhythmic practices, etudes, and more). Permeated with analysis, musical examples, and socio-historical and philosophical insights. Offers the insights of a world-class pianist and educator.

Festivals

1722. Feldman, Mitchell Evan, M.A. *Impressions of Newport: A Content Analysis of the Coverage of an American Jazz Festival in Six Publications Between 1954 and 1978.* Athens: University of Georgia; 1980.

Examines the scope, form and content of the literature by focusing on the Newport Jazz Festival. The 1954–78 years are divided into five periods and limited to articles from *Time, the New York Times, Billboard, the Village Voice, Down Beat, and the New Yorker.* Provides insights into history, events, and criticism.

1723. Worsley, John Ashton, Ph.D. *The Newport Jazz Festival: A Clash of Cultures.* Worcester, Mass.: Clark University; 1981.

Although the primary focus is the clash of cultures, the dissertation includes information of the role of George Wein, class structure, the impact of Chuck Berry, the 1960 riot, protests of African American musicians, and the clash in the African American community (integrationists vs. nationalists). Thorough and scholarly, Worsley's work relates the impact of values and business practices on the music and the festival audiences.

Improvisation

1724. Allen, Jill, D.A. *A Methodical Approach to the Introduction of Jazz Improvisation for the Flutist.* Greely: University of Northern Colorado; 1999.

Primarily a teaching method for flutists interested in exploring jazz improvisation in a sequential manner. Contains two compact discs of listening examples, imitation exercises, and exercises that allow the student to create their own improvisations. Topics include the use of vibrato, blues, and AABA form. Most of the tracks feature a play-along rhythm section.

1725. Aitken, Allen Eugene, Ph.D. *A Self-Instructional Audio-Imitation Method Designed to Teach Trumpet Students Jazz Improvisation in the Major Mode.* Eugene: University of Oregon; 1975.

Concerned with designing a pedagogical approach for teaching jazz improvisation. Originally designed to fill a void in the literature by creating a method for teaching clichés, phrasing, patterns, and scales to beginning trumpet players. Aitken includes a self-instruction audio-imitation self-paced book. Logical and systematic, allowing individual pace.

1726. Anderson, Iain D. *This is Our Music, Free Jazz, Cultural Hierachy, and the Sixties.* Bloomington: Indiana University; 2000.

Explores the question of who makes the decisions about the value of a cultural form and on what basis and uses the impact of 1960s free improvisation on the changing status of jazz. He used interviews with surviving participants, mainstream and trade press, archival evidence, and recorded music sources to propose that the acrimonious debate over free jazz interacted with changes in its production, presentation, and reception. He used the freedom concept as a key aesthetical and ideological trait, and advocates that John Coltrane, Ornette Coleman, and Cecil Taylor undermined the concept of a popular national style by linking avant-garde techniques to the music industry's racial and economic structures. He argues that radical claims of black ownership by cultural nationalists such as Amiri Baraka, Larry Neal, and A. B. Spellman enhanced the appeal of free jazz to universities and foundations. In addition, he argues that academia and philanthropic organizations offered prestige and patronage because they were under pressure to recognize African American culture.

1727. Balistreri, Don L., M.A. *Intuition and Fretboard Intimacy: Approaching Improvisation on the Guitar.* San Jose: San Jose State University; 1995.

Covers concepts for developing the intuitive aspects of musical improvisation in relationship with a plan for fret board comprehension. He outlines specific techniques, activities, and guidelines designed to improve improvisational skills, and focuses on blues, jazz, and rock idioms. Overall, he is concerned with achieving a balance between the technical and intuitive aspects of guitar improvisation.

1728. Bash, Lee, Ph.D. *The Effectiveness of Three Instructional Methods on the Acquisition of Jazz Improvisation Skills.* Buffalo: State University of New York at Buffalo; 1983.

Using a multivariate analysis of covariance, Bash examines three different pedagogical methods to determine effectiveness in producing improvisation skills. Method one emphasizes scales and chords, method two presents vocal/instrumental examples of concepts, and method three analyzes examples from the Smithsonian Collection of Classic Jazz. Bash's examination points to a combination of the above.

1729. Borgo, David, Ph.D. *Reverence For Uncertainty: Chaos, Order, and the Dynamics of Musical Free Improvisation.* Los Angeles: UCLA; 1999.

Focuses on the transcultural practice and musical free improvisation, the emerging science of chaos theory, and the paradigm shift that created a moment in which uncertainty is revered instead of feared. He argues that there is similarity between the way that the modeling of the natural world by chaos theorists and the process of formation inherent in musical free improvisation. Furthermore, he argues that the dynamic understanding of order and disorder emerging in chaos theory may help to understand the dynamics and aesthetics of free improvisation. He reviews inherent biases, free jazz development, sketches an outline of the growing interest in non-linear dynamical systems with special focus on chaos theory, nonequilibrium thermodynamics, information theory, and cognitive science. He uses the solo improvisational practices and kinesthetic metaphors of Evan Parker as a model for his research.

1730. _____, M.A. *Dialogics of Free Jazz: Musical Interaction in Collectively Improvised Performance.* Los Angeles: UCLA; 1996.

He draws on interviews of Kevin Eubanks, Vinnie Golia, Ralph Jones, and Adam Rudolph to discuss musical process and interaction in collectively improvised music. He also discusses the internal tensions between structured and innovative performance for the individual, the use of collective improvisation as a mediating activity between individual assertations and egalitarian ideals, the configuring of free jazz performances in terms of time, narrative, and identity for the listener and performer, and more.

1731. Briscuso, Joseph James, Ph.D. *A Study of Ability in Spontaneous and Prepared Jazz Improvisation Among Students Who Possess Different Levels of Musical Aptitude.* Iowa City: The University of Iowa; 1972.

Researches whether "a significant interaction exists between spontaneous and prepared jazz improvisation mean scores of high, average and low scoring students on the Musical Aptitude Profile Tonal Imagery Test." The study extends to the Musical Aptitude Profile Rhythm Imagery, Music Sensitivity, and the MAP Composite tests. Concludes that there is not way to determine whether high scoring instrumental students are more apt to learn jazz improvisation than are students with low musical aptitudes.

Encourages students above the 80th percentile on the MAP test to study jazz improvisation. Excellent study.

1732. Burnsed, Charles Vernon, Ph.D. *The Development and Evaluation of an Introductory Jazz Improvisation Sequence for Intermediate Band Students.* Miami: University of Miami; 1978.

Concerned with developing and evaluating a beginning approach to jazz improvisation for an intermediate band class. The study is limited to seventh through ninth grade students, the Gordon's Music Aptitude Profile, and the Watkins-Franum Performance Scale. Draws conclusions regarding psycho-motor, cognitive, and sight-reading skills and grade ability differences. Important for the teaching of improvisation at the junior high school level.

1733. Carlson, William Ralph, D.Mus. Ed. *A Procedure for Teaching Jazz Improvisation Based on an Analysis of the Performance Practice of Three Major Jazz Trumpet Players: Louis Armstrong, Dizzy Gillespie, and Miles Davis.* Bloomington: Indiana University; 1980.

Uses 27 transcriptions of solos of Louis Armstrong, Dizzy Gillespie, and Miles Davis to sequentially organize melodic concepts. Includes objectives, explanations, and material for ear training, development of technique, style, and articulation. Geared to secondary or college students, this approach differs from other music education approaches in his use of transcriptions of great jazz musicians. Thorough and scholarly, Carlson's approach allows students to learn by analysis and application of particular concepts.

1734. Cooper, Gloria Ann, Ed.D. *A Multidimensional Instructional Approach for the Solo Singer.* New York: Columbia University Teachers College; 1992.

The purpose is to present a beginning instructional method for the jazz singer/music educator, and to present an overview of jazz, beginning music theory, vocal production, and material on blues, ballads, bebop, Latin (bossa-nova), jazz waltz, and fusion. She provides a glossary, discography, and additional resources for further study.

1735. Damron, Bert Lee, Jr., Ph.D. *The Development and Evaluation of a Self-Instructional Sequence in Jazz Improvisation.* Tallahassee: The Florida State University; 1973.

Develops and tests a programmed sequence of jazz improvisation lessons for junior and senior high wind instrument players and compares the programmed sequence students with students not exposed to the study. Uses the Kendall Coefficient of Concordance to determine reliability and a two-way analysis of variance to analyze data. His conclusions suggest that jazz improvisation can be taught by a reliable programmed approach.

1736. Esposito, Arthur. *A Methodology For Classifying Music Based on the Resident Elements of Jazz Improvisational Language.* San Diego: San Diego State University; 2002.

He believes that the absence of musical analysis in the majority of works espousing either jazz neoclassicism or jazz modernism have flawed the conclusions and philosophies promoted by the respective exponents. He offers a methodology to classify music as jazz based on empirical evidence inherent in given performances. He analyzed Miles Davis's "Bitches Brew" solo, and Wynton Marsalis's solo on "Loose Duck" from the *The Marciac Suite* album. Overall, he used a phenomenological exclusion of all but the pertinent musical elements to discover and classify a given solo.

1737. Flora, Sim A., Ph.D. *An Analytical Anthology of Improvised Solos Designed to Supplement the Formal Teaching of Jazz Improvisation and Jazz Theory at the University Level.* Norman: University of Oklahoma; 1990.

An analysis of selected early jazz, swing, bebop, cool, hardbop, free, and fusion improvisations concerned with determining salient features. Uses analysis to frame a series of questions about each transcription. Designed to present a series of concepts/models to aid the performance of university students. A catalogue of concepts from several giants of jazz. Unique and comprehensive.

1738. Fraser, Wilmot Alfred, Ph.D. *Jazzology: A Study of the Tradition in Which Jazz Musicians Learn to Improvise.* Philadelphia: University of Pennsylvania; 1983.

Concerned with drawing a paradigm of common processes generic to jazz improvisation. Uses a worldwide community to study training, values, and the development of tradition within different national and cultural settings. Fraser reviews the literature and interviews artists in determining his theory of five developmental stages for jazz improvisers. His interdisciplinary approach concludes that to understand or perform jazz improvisation one must understand and appreciate African American culture and study the great African American artists of the jazz tradition. Precedes and compliments Paul Berliner's *Thinking In Jazz: The Infinite Art of Improvisation.* Important contribution to the literature.

1739. Greennagel David Joseph, Ph.D. *A Study of Selected Predictors of Jazz Vocal Improvisational Skills.* Miami: University of Miami; 1994.

The purpose is to identify and examine the extent to which selected variables function as predictors of jazz improvisation skill. Thirty jazz vocal majors were tested, and the data were analyzed using a forward stepping multiple regression procedure. Among the variables examined were scores on the Gordon Advanced Measure of Music Audiation, creativity on an assessment designed by the researcher, grade point average at the university, prior experience in private study of an instrument, and more.

1740. Hores, Robert George, Ed.D. *A Comparative Study of Visual- and Aural-Oriented Approaches to Jazz Improvisation with Implications for Instruction.* Bloomington: Indiana University; 1977.

An experimental study of an aural and visual approach to teaching jazz improvisation. Hores also researched inter-rater reliability, Gordon's Musical Aptitude Profile tests of musical sensitivity, and the effects of selected variables upon the experiment. Limited to 42 secondary school instrumental students. Uses a pretest-posttest methodology and draws conclusions regarding improvisational improvement, inter-rater reliability, the Gordon experimental measurement effect of selected variables on experimental outcome, and more. Excellent control and valid conclusions.

1741. Jost, David Nelson, M.M. *The Sequential Learning Theory and Its Relationship to the Instruction of Jazz Improvisation at the Junior High School Level.* Lowell, Mass.: University of Lowell; 1984.

Uses a statistically reliable approach to sequential learning theory (Edwin Gordon) to demonstrate how jazz improvisation can be taught to junior high school students. He develops and adapts material to Gordon's theory of learning. Important because he uses a standardized approach to learning theory thereby eliminating the need to both develop materials and devise a reliable and valid approach to teaching them.

1742. Konowitz, Bertram Lawrence, Ed.D. *Jazz Improvisation at the Piano—A Textbook for Teachers.* New York: Columbia University; 1969.

One of the first attempts to develop a systematic approach to teaching jazz improvisation. There are two additional purposes: the introduction of the art of improvisation before teaching particular concepts, and the use of original composition to illustrate important improvisational concepts. He approaches teaching improvisation by focusing on modes, scales, form, harmonic concepts, and chord substitution. Important because it was one of the first doctoral studies to logically and systematically approach the teaching of jazz.

1743. Madura, Patrice Dawn, D.Mus. Ed. *Relationships Among Vocal Jazz Improvisation Achievement, Jazz Theory Knowledge, Imitative Ability, Previous Musical Experience, General Creativity, and Gender.* Bloomington: Indiana University; 1992.

Focuses on vocal jazz improvisation achievement (concepts of expression, tonality, and rhythm), and several variables (jazz theory, experience, gender, instrumental and voice lessons, and creativity). Madura uses three judges and limits the experiment to the measurement of variables in a blues and a ii–V–I harmonic progression. Good design and demonstration of the significance of the relationship between vocal jazz improvisation achievement and selected variables.

1744. McCauley, John Willys, Ph.D. *Jazz Improvisation for the B-Flat Soprano Trumpet: An Introductory Text for Teaching Basic Theoretical and Performance Principles.* Baton Rouge: The Louisiana State University and Agricultural and Mechanical College; 1973.

Based on the premise that jazz improvisation is an excellent vehicle for developing creativity. Specific purpose is to design a beginning approach (text) to teaching jazz improvisational concepts for Bb soprano trumpet. His study is limited to the use of intervals, chords, scales, and beginning blues concepts. He also addresses the development of improvisational skills of serious students and uses original exercises to develop technique. Good introductory approach.

1745. McDaniel, William Theodore, Jr., Ph.D. *Differences in Music Achievement, Musical Experience, and Background Between Jazz-Improvising Musicians and Non-Improvising Musicians at the Freshman and Sophomore College Levels.* Iowa City: The University of Iowa; 1974.

Concerned with determining whether a significant difference exists between a population of jazz improvisers and nonimprovisers concerning musical achievement, experience, and background. The McDaniel Background Inventory ascertained musical achievement with the Aliferis Music Achievement Test and background and experience. He found there was a significant difference between improvisers and nonimprovisers favoring the improvisers. Well-controlled, valid study.

1746. Monson, Ingrid Tolia, Ph.D. *Musical Interaction in Modern Jazz: An Ethnomusicological Perspective.* New York: New York University; 1991.

Focuses on interaction as a phenomena that transpires between selected improvisers and the process of achieving overall musical intensification. Monson advocates that musical and social variables are prerequisites to understanding jazz improvisation and views interaction on cultural, musical, and social levels. She also uses African American metaphors to examine musical interaction and to interpret the performance within a sociocultural matrix. The theoretical paradigms are used to analyze a jazz performance. The first dissertation to address this topic, Monson draws conclusions from an African American perspective. Excellent use of ethnomusicological procedures.

1747. Montgomery, Michael R., D.M.A. *Studies in Jazz Style for the Double Bassist: Twelve Original Etudes Derived from Twenty-Two Transcribed Solos.* Miami: University of Miami; 1984.

Expands the double bass literature by composing 12 original studies from 22 solo transcriptions. He focuses on pedagogical concepts such as interpretation and technique. Each of the 12 etudes is accompanied by comments and is cross-referenced. Covers the solos of several giants of bass. Also includes discographical details of the 22 transcriptions. Expands the repertoire of traditional bassists.

1748. Moorman, Dennis Lee, Ph.D. *An Analytic Study of Jazz Improvisation with Suggestions for Performance.* New York: New York University; 1984.

Draws specific recommendations regarding improvisation performance by analyzing selected improvisations of several artists. The study is limited to an analysis of 25 improvisations covering different artists and styles and focuses on melodic concepts, rhythm, tempo, and harmony (ii–V). Among the artists represented are Louis Armstrong, Bix Beiderbecke, Clifford Brown, Donald Byrd, John Coltrane, Miles Davis, Kenny Dorham, Dizzy Gillespie, Dexter Gordon, Coleman Hawkins, Thelonious Monk, Fats Navarro, Charlie Parker, Oscar Peterson, Bud Powell, Woody Shaw, Teddy Wilson, and Lester Young.

1749. Paulson, John Charles, D.M.A. *The Development of an Imitative Instructional Approach to Improvising Effective Melodic Statements in Jazz Solos.* Seattle: University of Washington; 1985.

Based on observations of music majors and nonmajors in a beginning jazz improvisation class and concerned with developing a process that utilizes systematic imitation to produce "effective melodic statements" in jazz. Paulson demonstrates the importance of imitation as a pedagogical approach to teaching jazz improvisation.

1750. Pfenninger, Richard Charles, D.M.A. *The Development and Validation of Three Rating Scales for the Objective Measurement of Jazz Improvisation Achievement.* Philadelphia: Temple University; 1990.

Develops three rating scales to measure expression, rhythm, and tonal jazz improvisation achievement. He uses standard reliability and validity procedures, the ideas of 10 jazz educators/performers, and limits his study to 20 jazz majors' improvisations on "All the Things You Are." He concludes that rating scales are reliable and valid measures of jazz improvisation achievement though expression was more subjective. Although the pretest-posttest reliability was low (.71), the author's findings are significant because he is aware that his rating scales must be proven to be reliable and valid before significant conclusions can be made.

1751. Price, Emmett George, III. *Free Jazz and the Black Arts Movement, 1958–1967.* Pittsburgh: University of Pittsburgh; 2000.

Links the free jazz of the 1960s to the black arts movement of the same period. His overall goal is to introduce a new method of analyzing free jazz by drawing close attention to parallel cultural, political, and social movements of the time. His new method is established by demonstrating a relationship between the black arts movement and free jazz. In addition, he chronicles the literary and musical achievements of artists such as Albert Ayler, Marion Brown, Sun Ra, and Archie Shepp, concentrates on race, black consciousness, the question of a black aesthetic, cultural nationalism, and more to both make his connection and to forge a new method of analyzing free jazz.

1752. Ricker, Ramon Lee, D.M.A. *A Survey of Published Jazz-Oriented Clarinet Study Materials: 1920–1970.* Rochester: The University of Rochester, Eastman School of Music; 1973.

Reviews selected publications concerned with jazz clarinet technique. Ricker includes a history of the uses and function of the clarinet in jazz to 1973, a comprehensive annotated survey of jazz-oriented clarinet study materials, an interview of Buddy DeFranco, a list of artist's solos on recordings, and life spans of significant jazz clarinetists. Excellent and thorough. Recommended for jazz clarinetists, other instrumentalists, and educators.

1753. Rinne, Henry Q., Ph.D. *Concepts of Time and Space in Selected Works of Jazz Improvisation and Painting.* Miami, Oh.: Ohio University; 1991.

A scholarly treatment of narrative, simultaneity, and timelessness as paradigms for analysis of selected jazz improvisations. The concepts are applied individually; narrative time to improvisations of J. J. Johnson and Charles Parker; simultaneity to John Coltrane's "Giant Steps" and "Countdown"; and timelessness, via Jackson Pollack, to compositions from John Coltrane's *Sun Ship* album. An interdisciplinary application of self-creation to jazz improvisation that offers insight into linearity, nonlinearity, determinacy, and indeterminacy as modes of discourse.

1754. Rose, Richard Franklin, D.M.A. *An Analysis of Timing in Jazz Rhythm Section Performance.* Austin: University of Texas, Austin; 1989.

Describes the temporal relationships among the onsets of musical tones in rhythm section performances of recorded jazz. He analyzed three rhythmic excerpts, each representing a different jazz style, compared for duration of beats and beat subdivisions. In addition, variations in the onset of tones performed by two or more instruments during each musical beat and beat subdivision. Among his findings are beats in "Swing Style" and

"Jazz Ballads" were performed with decreased means durations on beats 1 and 3, and increased mean durations on beats 2 and 4.

1755. Rubinyi, Benno, M.A. *A Systematic Course of Study in Jazz Piano Improvisation.* Los Angeles: University of California, Los Angeles; 1972.

Evolved from the premise that there is a need to develop a systematic approach to teaching jazz piano improvisation. Combines exercises and models with analysis, listening, and playing. The materials are designed to produce the capacity to improvise effectively in selected jazz forms. The author does not test his approach for reliability and validity.

1756. Salvatore, Joseph A., Ph.D. *Jazz Improvisation: Principles and Practices Relating to Harmonic and Scalic Resources.* Tallahassee: The Florida State University; 1970.

Focuses on chord/scales and connecting chords into scales and uses principles and concepts of selected artists as study materials. Salvatore analyzes solos and arrangements/compositions and reviews pertinent literature that deals with jazz harmony/scales, and compares methods of teaching improvisation. He devises a graded method of exercises.

1757. Schenkel, Steven Michael, Ph.D. *A Guide to the Development of Improvisational Skills in the Jazz Idiom.* Saint Louis: Washington University; 1980.

An approach to teaching jazz improvisation skills to students with either minimum or no music theory background. Schenkel focuses on major, minor, dominant seventh, diminished, half-diminished, and augmented chord/scale types. Divided into "Theory," "Ear Calisthenics" and "Performance" sections. He also discusses advanced improvisational concepts, the phenomena of performing "outside," and solo construction. Includes an annotated discography.

1758. Segress, Terry Dickerson, Ph.D. *The Development and Evaluation of a Comprehensive First Semester College Jazz Improvisation Curriculum.* Denton: North Texas State University; 1979.

Uses instructional objectives, equipment, materials, and strategies to devise a one-semester jazz improvisation course. Segress measures music fundamentals, jazz listening, improvement in jazz improvisation performance, and student attitudes regarding improvisation and the jazz curriculum. He elicited reliability and validity in a pretest-posttest format. He concluded that students benefited from the study of jazz improvisation. Systematic and thorough.

1759. Sessions, Charles Martin, D.M.A. *The Effectiveness of Jazz Musical Examples and Jazz Improvisation upon College Students' Acquisition of Music*

Fundamentals Concepts. Los Angeles: University of Southern California; 1980.

Concerned with the effectiveness of jazz and jazz improvisation in ascertaining music fundamentals at the university level. Uses an experimental and control group format and jazz exercises to measure cognitive and attitudinal achievement. A Likert-type questionnaire was used to measure the jazz attitudes of the experimental groups. Because no significant difference was discovered between achievement and cognitive skills and attitudes the hypothesis concerning learning musical fundamentals by using jazz compared to those who used nursery rhymes and folk songs was supported. The hypothesis concerning developing positive attitudes about using jazz was also supported. Excellent controls and significant conclusions.

1760. Shaw, George Washington, Jr., Ph.D. *Relationships Between Experimental Factors and Precepts of Selected Professional Musicians in the United States Who Are Adept at Jazz Improvisation.* Norman: The University of Oklahoma; 1979.

Researches whether relationships exist between selected experimental concepts and the views of selected professional jazz improvisers. Based on interviews of jazz educators and professional musicians such as Jamey Aebersold, David Baker, Oscar Brashear, Randy Brecker, Bobby Bryant, Al Cohn, Jerry Coker, Bill Evans, Gil Evans, Jon Faddis, William Fielder, Carl Fontana, Dan Haerle, Eddie Harris, Joe Henderson, Milt Hinton, Dave Holland, Hank Jones, Thad Jones, Dave Leibman, Marian McPartland, Blue Mitchell, Rufus Reid, Sam Rivers, Zoot Sims, Marvin Stamm, Clark Terry, Ernie Watts, and Snooky Young. Interviews focus on early improvisational experiences, improvisational concepts, current improvisational practices and more. Shaw found similarities in early and college educational experiences, music improvisation environment, techniques of learning improvisation, and much more. Important because the research is based on insider perspectives from educators and composer/performers.

1761. Tumlinson, Charles David, Ph.D. *Theoretical Constructs of Jazz Improvisation Performance.* Denton: University of North Texas; 1991.

Concerned with determining what variables are related to a single line jazz solo and how variables group into constructs for both students and professional performers. Tumlinson develops seven constructs: harmonic appropriateness, rhythmic usage, melodic usage, jazz style, individuality, expressiveness, and form. His conclusions include a finding that the work of 60 students and professional improvisers contained variables representing several different hypothesized constructs. Systematic and scholarly.

1762. Vernick, Gordon Jay, D.A. *The Development of a Jazz Improvisation Method Utilizing Sequenced Play-Along Tracks with Variable Pitch and Tempo Control.* Greely: University of Northern Colorado; 1990.

Develops a method of teaching jazz improvisation to beginners by using a play-a-long sequencer. The method includes text and exercises in major keys and Dorian and Mixolydian modes reflecting common root movements. The strength of the method is that it allows learning at an individual pace by allowing variability of tempo and transposition.

1763. Zwick, Robert A., Ph.D. *Jazz Improvisation: A Recommended Sequential Format of Instruction.* Denton: North Texas State University; 1987.

Zwick reviews selected literature and compares teaching strategies to devise a sequential format for teaching jazz improvisation. He offers percentages on emphasis of subject matter categories. Logical and systematic.

Jazz Dance

1764. Begho, Felix O., Ph.D. *Black Dance Continuum: Reflections on the Heritage Connection Between African Dance and Afro-American Jazz Dance.* New York: New York University; 1985.

Explores the relationship between African dance and African American jazz dance tracing influences from African roots to the early 1980s. Begho's study is limited to Nigeria and uses published works, interviews, participant observations, and empirical impressions drawn from performances. His conclusions focus on the importance of jazz rhythm, similarities between African and African American aesthetics, the importance of heritage, and sociopolitical relationships.

1765. Brandman, Russella, Ph.D. *The Evolution of Jazz Dance from Folk Origins to Concert Stage (Volumes I and II).* Tallahassee: The Florida State University; 1977.

Uses literary sources, interviews, correspondence, and observations to trace the origins and evolution of jazz dance. Covers African dance, early slave trade, secular and sacred dances, African American festivals in the West Indies and United States, postantebellum entertainment, and social dances to the turn of the century. Brandman examines relationships between traditional and contemporary forms. Interesting conclusions.

1766. Crosby, Jill Flanders, Ed.D. *Will the Real Jazz Dance Please Stand Up? A Critical Examination of the Roots and Essence of Jazz Dance with Implications for Education (Rhythm).* New York: Columbia University Teachers College; 1995.

Proposes and answers questions such as what makes a rhythm a jazz rhythm, are there defining qualities that shape jazz expression, is there a jazz aesthetic that embraces both music and dance, and more. She conducted fieldwork in Ghana to investigate the African roots of jazz dance, and gained from her involvement in dance activities. Her conclusions embrace jazz expression as a process of creation in the moment as expressed through structured improvisation, personal expression, and community.

1767. Dale, Vickie Lynn, M.E. *Billie's Message: An Original Dance-Drama in the Modern Dance Idiom.* Reno: University of Nevada; 1989.

Includes a selected review of the literature, an overview of Holiday's life, rehearsal photographs and more. Dale designed the choreography, wrote the script, portrays Billie's voice, and dances. Videotape available.

1768. Goler, Veta Diane, Ph.D. *Dancong Herself: Choreography, Autobiography, and the Expression of the Black Woman Self in the Work of Dianne McIntyre, Blondell Cummings, and Jawole Willa Jo Zollar.* Atlanta: Emory University; 1994.

Examines the work of three contemporary African American women modern dance choreographers. She explores each of the women as artists, delineates the importance elements and processes they use in their creative work, and describes the individual aesthetics that distinguish their artistry. She begins with a concise outline of negative stereotypes of African American women as a means of demonstrating the importance of autobiography in their self-liberation.

1769. Hill, Constance Valis, Ph.D. *Brotherhood in Rhythm: The Jazz Tap Dancing of the Nicholas Brothers.* New York: New York University; 1998.

Her thesis is that the jazz tap dancing of the Nicholas brothers extended a three-century-long percussive tradition that reached its apotheosis in the swing era of the 1930s and 1940s. She advocates that tap dancing is indigenous to America, and its roots are based on a fusion of British and West African musical and step-dancing traditions. She concludes that the Nicholas brothers evolved a style of jazz dance that was rhythmically in the feet.

Jazz and Euro-American Art Music

1770. Baskerville, David Ross, Ph.D. *Jazz Influence on Art Music to Mid-Century.* Los Angeles: University of California, Los Angeles; 1965.

Begins with an overview of jazz elements then distinguishes between art music, commercial styles, jazz, and popular music. Composers (1900–1950) discussed include Aaron Copland, George Gershwin, Morton Gould, Paul Hindemith, Darius Milhaud, and Maurice Ravel. One of the earliest and most successful forays into the influence of jazz on art music composers.

1771. Brickens, Nathaniel Owen, D.M.A. *Jazz Elements in Five Selected Trombone Solos by Twentieth-Century French Composers.* Austin: The University of Texas at Austin; 1989.

The five works analyzed include *Concerto* (1958) by Henri Tomasi; *Deux Dances* (1954) by Jean Michel Defaye; *Ballade* (1944) by Eugene Bozza; *Sonatina* (1958) by Jacques Castérère; and *Concertino d'Hiver* (1955) by Darius Milhaud. Brickens's analysis is supplemented with an historical overview of the trombone as a solo instrument, a discussion of the impact of jazz on technical developments, and an assessment of jazz influence on twentieth-century French composers. Offers important insights.

1772. Brown, Robert Loran, Jr., Ed.D. *A Study of Influences from Euro-American Art Music on Certain Types of Jazz with Analyses and Recital of Selected Demonstrative Compositions.* New York: Columbia University Teachers College; 1974.

Researches art music concepts such as form, harmony, and melody that have been adopted by the jazz idiom and discusses the confluence of jazz and classical ideas and jazz and performance media. Also a discussion on the question of jazz as art music and art music's role in its definition. Interesting and provocative.

1773. Ford, Christopher John, D.M.A. *Eleven Jazz-Influenced Works for Concert Saxophone.* College Park: University of Maryland College Park; 1991.

Includes a written document and audiotape recording based on compositions written between 1921 and 1981. Ford provides practice suggestions, concise biographies and information on compositional techniques, forms and selected orchestration techniques. The composers and compositions included are "Caramel Mou" (1921) by Darius Milhaud, "Hot-Sonate" (1930) by Erwin Schuyloff, "Konzertstück" (1933) by Paul Hindemith, "Concertino da Camera" (1935) by Jacques Ibert, "Fantasie-Impromptu" (1953) by André Jolivet, "Trio" (1958) by David Amram, "Essay in Jazz" (1959 by Werner Heider, "Sonate" (1970) by Edison Denisov, "Music" (1972) by M. William Karlins, "Doo-Dah" (1977) by William Albright, and "Three Improvisations" (1981) by Phil Woods. Performance suggestions for both jazz and classical elements. By combining history and influence with taped musical interpretations, Ford's study becomes a model for pedagogues.

1774. Hanlon, Sister Gloria, M.M. *A Comparison of Jazz Influences on Selected American and French Composers from 1917 to 1930.* Carbondale: Southern Illinois University, Carbondale; 1971.

Focuses on the influence of jazz rhythm and timbre on selected works of Aaron Copland, Arthur Honegger, Darius Milhaud, Maurice Ravel, and

Erik Satie. The study is based on "Music For The Theatre," "Piano Concerto" and two of the "Four Piano Blues" by Copland; "Petite Fille Americaine" and "Ragtime du Paguebot" from "Parade" by Satie, "Le Boeuf Sur Le Toit" and "La Création du Monde" by Milhaud; "Concertino for Piano and Orchestra" by Honegger; "Concerto in D for the Left Hand for Piano and Orchestra," the "Presto" movement of the "Concerto in G for Piano and Orchestra" and "Blues" from the "Violin and Piano Sonata" by Ravel. Hanlon identifies blue notes, instrumentation practices, and rhythmic elements. Insightful.

1775. Haydon, Geoffrey Jennings, D.M.A. *A Study of the Exchange of Influences Between the Music of Early Twentieth-Century Parisian Composers and Ragtime, Blues, and Early Jazz.* Austin: The University of Texas at Austin; 1992.

Concerned with the exchange of musical ideas between the jazz-influenced composers Claude Debussy, Darius Milhaud, Maurice Ravel, Erik Satie, and Igor Stravinsky, and the impressionist-influenced composers Bix Beiderbecke and George Gershwin. The influence of blues, cakewalks, minstrels, and ragtime on the Parisian composers and the incorporation of altered harmonies, parallel motion, whole tone scales, and extended chords on Bix Beiderbecke and George Gershwin. Excellent discussion.

1776. Pepin, Sister M. Natalie, S.N.J.M., Mus. A.D. *Dance and Jazz Elements in the Piano Music of Maurice Ravel.* Boston: Boston University, School of Fine Arts and Applied Arts; 1972.

An exploration of the role of dance and jazz elements in Ravel's music. Covers his early life and influences (Chabrier, Satie, Fauré, and the Russian Five), use of dance forms, attraction to the Spanish idiom, harmonic style, and American and jazz influences in rhythm and melody.

1777. Samball, Michael Loran, D.M.A. *The Influence of Jazz on French Solo Trombone Repertory.* Denton: North Texas State University; 1987.

A discussion of jazz-influenced compositions with special reference to the solo trombone. Samball demonstrates the incorporation of jazz trombone skills in works by Milhaud, Ravel, Satie, and the solo trombone compositions of the Paris Conservatory. Comprehensive to around 1950.

1778. Schmid, William Albert, D.M.A. *An Analysis of Elements of Jazz Style in Contemporary French Trumpet Literature.* Denton: University of North Texas; 1991.

Explores the influence of African art and American jazz on French composers and discusses jazz elements in chamberand symphonic works by Henri Tomasi, Andrè Jolivet, Eugene Bozza, Jacques Ibert, Darius

Milhaud, Igor Stravinsky, and Maurice Ravel. Elements of jazz style are discussed in terms of performance practice.

Sociology

1779. Levy, Louis Herman, Ph.D. *The Formalization of New Orleans Musicians: A Case Study of Organizational Change.* Blacksburg, Va.: Virginia Polytechnic Institute and State University; 1976.

Uses concepts of socialization, band cohesion, band-audience relations, commercialism, organization, and formalization to research the organization of New Orleans musicians. In addition to written and institutional sources, the author interviews 17 jazz musicians. Explores the dialectical relationship between orientation and organization.

1780. Nanry, Charles Anthony, Ph.D. *The Occupational Subculture of the Jazz Musician: Myth and Reality.* New Brunswick: Rutgers University, The State University of New Jersey; 1970.

Uses a participant observation model to study a presumed subculture among selected jazz musicians. Nanry interviews 108 New York area musicians using selected informants to reject the myth of jazz as a deviant subculture and occupation. Includes data on the attitudes of African American and white musicians, stages in development, and a synthesis of social science related to jazz literature. Uses a group history methodology to draw conclusions.

1781. Peretti, Burton William, Ph.D. *Music, Race, and Culture in Urban America.* Berkeley: University of California, Berkeley; 1989.

Researches the impact of music education, race relations, technique, and commercialism of jazz musicians before 1940. Investigates the socio-intellectual development of New Orleans musicians from 1890 to 1917 and from 1915 to 1930 in Chicago, New York, and other Northern venues. Advocates that by 1940 jazz had evolved into a biracial music and subculture. Investigates gender roles, big bands, and the impact of 1940s jazz. Excellent discussion of the role and function of cultural context in shaping jazz evolution.

1782. Piazzale, Steven Peter, Ph.D. *"Deviant" Subcultural Formation and Art World Change: The Case of Jazz in the 1940's.* Palo Alto: Stanford University; 1979.

Investigates hypotheses rooted in sociomusical change, deviance, and the dropping of deviance labeling. Focuses on the swing to bebop change of the 1940s. More concerned with interactional conventions than stylistic difference. Excellent methodology used assessing the move of subcultures distancing and emerging during musical evolution.

1783. Stebbins, Robert Alan, Ph.D. *The Jazz Community: The Sociology of a Musical Sub-Culture.* Minneapolis: University of Minnesota; 1964.

Takes as its premise that jazz musicians are more than a marginal subculture. Investigates the social position of jazz musicians versus commercial musicians and jazz musicians as an organized subculture. Uses historical, demographic, and ecological data to elucidate the Minnesota jazz community.

1784. Wheaton, Jack William, Ed.D. *The Technological and Sociological Influences on Jazz as an Art Form in America.* Greely: University of Northern Colorado; 1976.

Studies the impact and interrelationship of environmental, psychological, social and technological phenomena on jazz evolution. Discusses as well the confluence of African and European musical elements, West African contributions, history, and the impact of communication, media, technology, and transportation on jazz evolution.

1785. Item deleted.

Women and Jazz

1786. Richards-Slaughter, Shannon, Ph.D. *The Blossoms of Jazz: A Novel of Black Female Jazz Musicians in the 1930's.* (Original Novel). Ann Arbor: The University of Michigan; 1990.

Discusses three African American women who traveled as a trio in the 1930s. Uses social history, feminist theory, oral history, musical historiography, and creative writing to craft the story based on remembrances of the daughters of two of the musicians. Provides insight into acceptance, conditions, and events within the context of American culture of the 1930s.

1787. Sunderland, Patricia Lynn, Ph.D. *Cultural Meanings and Identity: Women of the African American Art World of Jazz.* Burlington, Vt.: University of Vermont State Agricultural College; 1992.

Uses paradigms from cultural psychology, cultural construction, and feminism to ascertain cultural meanings and identity among a select group of New York women. Limited to 30 interviews with non-musician women of New York City's jazz community and participant observations at jazz related activities and venues. Good study of meanings and symbolism.

Regional Studies

Kansas City

1788. Hischke, Jon, M.M. *The Origin and Development of Kansas City Jazz.* Lincoln: University of Nebraska; 1977.

Although he recognizes the contributions of Frank Driggs, Ross Russell, and Gunther Schuller, Hischke believes scholars have largely ignored Kansas City jazz. Limited to origins, style, development of Kansas City jazz to World War II, and the emergence of bebop. Good discussion of origins and style with an informative interview of Jay McShann.

Los Angeles

1789. Dickerson, Lowell Dwight, Ph.D. *Central Avenue Meets Hollywood: The Amalgamation of the Black and White Musicians' Unions in Los Angeles.* Los Angeles: UCLA; 1998.

A comprehensive study of the social context and musical issues that lead to the merging of the black and white Musicians' unions in Los Angeles. He discusses the American Federation of Musicians, labor unions, the importance of Central Avenue, and the roles of musicians such as Buddy Collette and Marl Young in uniting the two unions.

1790. Macias, Anthony Foster, Ph.D. *From Pachuco Boogie to Latin Jazz: Mexican Americans, Popular Music, and Urban Culture in Los Angeles, 1940–1965.* Ann Arbor: University of Michigan; 2001.

Examines the diverse communities, contradictory identities, cross-cultural productions, and interracial improvisations of Mexicans in Los Angeles by using music as a barometer of assimilation. He compares the Chicano Pachuco and African American Zoot Suiter subcultures of the war years, and delineates Mexican American styles that influenced anglo conceptions of cool. He argues that during the big band era, jitterbug dancers and swing musicians adapted African American styles to their own sensibilities. He uses race, class, and space to argue that Mexican Americans consumed and performed rhythm and blues, rock 'n' roll, rumba, bolero, Latin jazz, and cha cha cha. In addition, he documents how Mexican Americans became possessively emersed in whiteness by embracing various genres of black music while distancing themselves from black people.

Memphis, Tennessee

1791. Briggs, Ray Anthony, Ph.D. *Memphis Jazz: African American Musicians, Jazz Community and the Politics of Race.* Los Angeles: University of California, Los Angeles; 2003.

A chronological ethnography of the Memphis jazz tradition from approximately 1910 through the 1990s. This is the first scholarly study of the jazz tradition and musicians that have emanated from this important musical city. He conducted numerous interviews with musicians, educators, and jazz enthusiasts including Dee Dee Bridgewater, Garnette Brown, George Coleman, Matthew Garrett, Charles Lloyd, Mulgrew Miller, and James Williams. He also discussed the "Memphis sound," and includes information on artists like Booker Little, Harold Mabern, Louis Smith, and Frank Strozier. He concludes that individually and collectively the Memphis jazz tradition was shaped by the same social, political, and economic forces that shaped the African American community at large.

Minneapolis

1792. Stebbins, Robert Alan, M.A. *The Minneapolis Jazz Community: The Conflict Between Musical and Commercial Values.* Minneapolis: University of Minnesota; 1962.

Postulates that tensions exist between the practical and aesthetic requirements of jazz. Stebbins believes that jazz offers its exponents both emotional and musical values leading to the formation quasicommunities. He investigates the assumption that commercial musicians are different than jazz musicians. Interesting conclusions derived from studies of leisure time.

New England

1793. Brown, Leonard Lewis, Ph.D. *Some New England African American Musician's Views on Jazz.* Middletown, Conn.: Wesleyan University; 1990.

Presenting the views of African American artists using an ethnomusicological approach to focus on definitive performance and philosophical concerns. Brown discusses history, music in culture, analysis, performance, and Afrocentric concepts. Interview questions, selection criteria, and complete transcriptions of the interviews are included. Insights into the role and function of jazz in African American culture.

New Orleans

1794. Raeburn, Bruce Boyd, Ph.D. *New Orleans Style: The Awakening of American Jazz Scholarship and Its Cultural Implications.* New Orleans: Tulane University; 1991.

Focuses on jazz historiography before the publication of Marshall Stearns's *The Story of Jazz (1956).* Advocates that the preacademic era evolved from international "hot" record collectors from the 1920s to 1934.

The dissemination of historical information led to the initiation of jazz journals such as *Down Beat, Esquire, The New Republic,* and *Jazz Information.* Raeburn believes that *Jazzman (1930)* and *The Jazz Record Book (1942)* began the perception that jazz originated in New Orleans, a slogan adopted in the 1940s to boost tourism.

New York City

1795. Hunter, Delridge Laveon, Ph.D. *The Jazz Worker: Creative Musicians in Times of Crisis.* Cincinnati: The Union Institute; 1995.

An interdisciplinary study of creative musicians performing jazz from 1980 to 1994 in New York City. He uses site visits and interviews to collect data regarding the political economy of jazz as social history. Also, his research proves how the political economy of jazz created odds for creative artists during a period of decline of jazz in New York City.

1796. Jackson, Travis Arnell, Ph.D. *Performance an Musical Meaning: Analyzing "Jazz" on the New York Scene.* New York: Columbia University; 1998.

Concerned with the way participants in a musical event construct meaning. Although his primary focus is New York City, he explores negotiations and interpretations made by participants in different sittings, and the terms on which they are made. He uses paradigms from Western concert music, psychology, philosophy, and semiotics to assess performance and meaning in live performances, recording sessions, and interviews with musicians and scene participants. In addition, he coins a concept he describes as "blues aesthetic," and argues that the scene and blues aesthetic frames jazz performance as ritualized activity.

1797. Monson, Ingrid Tolia, Ph.D. *Musical Interaction in Modern Jazz: An Ethnomusicological Perspective.* New York: New York University; 1991.

Focuses on interaction as a phenomena that transpires between selected improvisers and the process of achieving overall musical intensification. Monson advocates that musical and social variables are prerequisites to understanding jazz improvisation and views interaction on cultural, musical, and social levels. She also uses African American metaphors to examine musical interaction and to interpret the performance within a sociocultural matrix. The theoretical paradigms are used to analyze a jazz performance. The first dissertation to address this topic, Monson draws conclusions from an African American perspective. The fieldwork was conducted in New York City. Excellent use of ethnomusicological procedures.

1798. Stewart, Alexander, Ph.D. *Composition and Performance in Contemporary New York City Big Bands.* New York: City University of New York; 2000.

Explores the significance of the big bands with regard to the increased study of jazz in cultural and educational institutions, emergence of the repertory movement, increased interest in jazz composition, and the increased participation of women in jazz. He argues that big bands are central networks where New York City musicians make contacts, share knowledge, and compete for recognition.

1799. Such, David Glen, Ph.D. *Music, Metaphor and Values among Avant-Garde Jazz Musicians Living in New York City.* Los Angeles: University of California, Los Angeles; 1985.

Studies the music and value system of a select group of African American musicians. Demonstrates the link between music and worldviews notably in relation to African American history, social and musical concepts, and strategies of urbanization and industrialization. Uses symbolism to focus on social metaphor and discuss the transcendence of conventional Western music making. Good insider perspectives. The first serious study of this significant group of modernists.

North Carolina

1800. Wiggins, Ira Tyrone, Ph.D. *An Assessment of the Status of Jazz Music Education in the Public High Schools of North Carolina: A Foundation for Curriculum Revision in Higher Education.* Greensboro: University of North Carolina, Greensboro; 1997.

The purpose is to assess the status of jazz education in selected high schools throughout the eight educational regions of North Carolina. He focuses on professional characteristics of band directors, high school music programs, and band director's undergraduate degree programs. He concludes that jazz education is a major component of high school music programs in North Carolina.

Northeast Ohio

1801. Berger, Harris Merle, Ph.D. *Perception in the Moral Continuum of History: An Ethnography of Metal, Rock and Jazz in Northeast Ohio.* Bloomington: Indiana University; 1995.

Explores the experiences of musicians of four musical communities in northeast Ohio. He researched commercial hard rock musicians of Cleveland, the death metal musicians of Akron, African American jazz musicians of Cleveland's east side, and older European American jazz musicians of Akron. He examines key moments in the fields of ethnomusicology, anthropology, folklore, and cultural studies and argues that ethnomusicology must not be limited to assessing musical structure, it should also assess the active constitution of musical perception by experiencing subjects. He concludes that the smallest acts of musical perception are influenced by large-scale social phenomenon and suggests that action constitutes society and history in the broadest sense.

Philadelphia

1802. Allen, George Edward, D.M.A. *Contributions of Philadelphia African American Musicians to American Jazz Music from 1945 to 1960.* Philadelphia: Temple University; 1998.

The purpose is to provide insight into Philadelphia's role in the development of jazz from 1945 to 1960. He interviewed musicians who lived in Philadelphia during the time period of his study, and covers topics such as the Philadelphia jazz families, music education of jazz musicians, marching bands in Philadelphia, gospel music influence of jazz, and analyzed selected compositions by Benny Golson, Jimmy Heath, and Lee Morgan. He also includes information on John Coltrane's years in Philadelphia.

World Cultures

China

1803. Field, Andrew David, Ph.D. *A Night in Shanghai: Nightlife and Modernity in Semicolonical China, 1919–1932.* New York: Columbia University; 2001.

Examines the influence of nightlife and related mass culture phenomena such as jazz and social dancing on Chinese politics and social life in Shanghai between the two world wars. He discusses the role and function of cafés, clubs, and dance halls that catered to Westerners in the city's settlements in the late 1920s. In addition, he discusses the role of the dance hostess, Chinese artists, intellectuals, and writers in shaping the modern city in both reality and image.

France

1804. Cashman, Scott, Ph.D. *Nightclubs Capitalism and Expatriate Jazz Musicians in Paris.* Amherst: University of Massachusetts, Amherst; 2001.

He argues that the American music business has created a power elite that shapes and controls the popular music industry. As a result, several blues and jazz musicians became expatriates as an alternative to that subjugation. He discusses the community of expatriate jazz musicians then living in Paris, and concludes that building a career in America prior to relocating to Europe is a more practical plan.

1805. Davis, Ursula Broschke, Ph.D. *The Afro-American Musician and Writer in Paris During the 1950s and 1960s: A Study of Kenny Clarke, Donald Byrd, Chester Himes and James Baldwin.* Pittsburgh: University of Pittsburgh; 1983.

Discusses the four artists' lives in Paris. Specifically, she investigates why they left the United States, what influence(s) Europe had on them, and the reasons they either remained in Europe or returned to the United States. The study is based on both literary sources and oral interviews conducted between February and December 1982. Among the reasons she found why the artists left the United States included because they felt alienated and exploited, and because they were drawn to the cultural and educational attraction of Europe

1806. Jordan, Matthew Frank, Ph.D. *Jazz Changes: A History of French Discourse on Jazz From Ragtime to Be-bop.* Claremont, Ca.: The Claremont Graduate University; 1998.

A genealogy of the acceptance and assimilation of jazz into French culture. The acceptance and assimilation is discussed by charting the changes in French discourse on jazz. He examines prejazz phenomena to demonstrate the existence of tropes, descriptive habits, and cultural riffs, as well as the eruption of jazz into French culture, species of jazz along racial lines, jazz expression in the *La Revue Negre,* cultural battles over jazz and swing, the Vichy regime, Zazou movement, and more.

1807. Schulman, Seth Matthew, Ph.D. *The Celebrity Culture of Modern Nightlife: Music Hall, Dance, and Jazz in Paris, 198–1930.* Providence: Brown University; 2000.

Explores the nature of interwar nightlife experience and its emerging role in French public life. He focuses on the music hall, dance hall, and jazz band and argues that the appeal of nightlife resided primarily in its ability to provide consumers with an intense experience of virtual celebrity. In the first three chapters, he analyzes contemporary discourse and interprets the nightlife debates as an attempt to contain celebrity culture and to return France to an imaginary prewar state of authenticity and transparency in social relations. In the last three chapters, he discusses how such containment was pursued within nightlife.

1808. Taylor, Denise Palmer, Ph.D. *La Musique Pour Tout le Monde: Jean Wiener and the Dawn of French Jazz.* Ann Arbor: University of Michigan; 1998.

Illuminates the career of Jean Wiener, and discusses many of the musical, cultural, and racial issues that arose when Paris embraced American jazz. She uses periodical literature, French music criticism, published and unpublished scores, recordings of the time, dance manuals, memoirs, concert programs, and more to both assess the complicated Parisian jazz scene of the 1920s and Jean Wiener's contribution to it.

Japan

1809. Atkins, Everett Taylor, Ph.D. *This is Our Music: Authenticating Japanese Jazz, 1920–1980.* Urbana-Champaign: University of Illinois, Urbana-Champaign; 1997.

Uses oral, documentary, and musical evidence to describe the reception of jazz in Japan and the social history and artistic development of Japan's subculture. He outlines a variety of musical and discursive methods of authentication that are designed to legitimate jazz performed by Japanese. Among these are attempts o replicate the exact sounds of American jazz, social and cultural contexts of American jazz, the phenomenon of the "Yellow Negro," the interwar period of Shanghai jazz, the concept of a national style, marginality, the search for cultural identity, and more. He also argues that in the authenticating strategies we can see both the adoption of jazz and the history of modern Japan.

Spain

1810. Hadrick, Joseph Knetch, Ph.D. *Building Bridges With the Sound of Music: Jazz and Moroccan Music (Spain).* New York: The Union Institute; 2002.

Explores the link between African American music and North African core musical traditions. He discusses the transmutation of Moroccan musical traditions to Spain during the Middle Ages, and the development of jazz in the nineteenth and twentieth centuries in North America. He composed music for an *Andalusian Suite,* which fused blues, jazz, and North African musical concepts. Also, he compares the uniqueness of American jazz as a symbol of democracy with the development of new music by the African Moors in Spain in the Middle Ages.

West Africa/Dahomey

1811. Marvin, Thomas Fletcher, Ph.D. *Children of Legba: African-American Musicians of Jazz in Literature and Popular Culture.* Amherst: University of Massachusetts, Amherst; 1993.

Considers African American blues and jazz musicians to be the children of Legba, a country (presently called Benin) Dahomey, West African deity. He provides a cross-cultural perspective on the role of musicians in Western Europe and West Africa, the derogatory stereotypes of black musicians in the nineteenth-century minstrel show, the social role of the black musician in the jazz age, considers how writers such as Sterling Brown and Langston Hughes are represented in their writings, examines the representations of blues and jazz in the novels of Ralph Ellison, Alice Walker, and Ishmael Reed, focusing on how they assume the role of improvising historian by adapting the narrative techniques of the West African Griot.

Zimbabwe

1812. Williams, Linda Faye, Ph.D. *The Impact of African-American Music on Jazz in Zimbabwe: Exploration in Radical Empiricism.* Bloomington: Indiana University; 1995.

Investigates how Zimbabwean jazz artists combine indigenous musical influences with African American paradigms to articulate the interplay of African and African American music. She interfaces analysis with a radical empirical approach with allowed her to adopt new ideas within the context of shared awareness. She used a double-voiced discourse by employing both the language of academia, and the words of the artists with whom she interacted during the course of her research.

IX

Pedagogy Materials

Arranging and Composing

1813. Alexander, Van. *First Chart.* New York: Criterion; 1971.

Acquaints the arranger with the fundamentals of scoring. In addition to information on instrumentation and voicing, the book contains charts for analysis and information on the contemporary rhythm section (1981).

1814. _____. *First Chart.* Edited and contributions by Jimmy Haskell. Hollywood, Calif.: Criterion Books; 1987.

Details the pedagogy of how to compose your first piece of music. The book is designed for beginners and covers several modern styles, including blues-rock, jazz-rock, and Latin. There is a recording of two compositions.

1815. Baker, David. *Arranging and Composing for the Small Ensemble: Jazz/ R&B/Jazz-Rock.* Chicago: Maher; 1970.

A thorough guide that covers the elements of instrumentation and nomenclature, rules for orchestration, melodic construction, arranging-composing for a rhythm section, writing for two to six voices, and incorporating the blues into arranging/composing. The book is also significant because the author provides numerous musical examples, listening assignments, blues and standard jazz tunes, and suggested bebop tunes for listening and consultation. Selected bibliography and discography.

1816. _____. *Arranging and Composition*. Bloomington, Ind.: Frangipani Press; 1983.

Focuses on small ensembles, and covers arranging and composing for jazz, rhythm and blues, and jazz-rock styles. Specific topics covered are two-through six-voice compositional/arranging techniques, orchestration techniques, rhythm section, and organizing an arrangement. There are numerous examples, a list of assignments, and listening and reading suggestions. The book was originally published in 1970.

1817. Coker, Jerry. *A Guide to Composition and Arranging*. New Albany, Ind.: Jamey Aebersold; 1998?

A thorough study that begins with preparatory activities, philosophical issues, listening lists, a list of tunes, and all elements of composing melodies and chord progressions. In addition, he covers arranging and composing for small and large ensembles, enhanced use of rhythm sections, instrumental ranges, form, texture options, and the producing of lead sheets, scores, conductor's guides, and part-coping.

1818. Dellaera, Angelo. *Creative Arranging: Complete Guide to Professional Arranging*. New York: Charles Colin; 1966.

Covers concepts pertinent to small and large group arranging. The first part of this book deals with the visual representation of sound. In addition, the author includes a series of interesting transposition exercises for each instrument.

1819. Dobbins, Bill. *Jazz Arranging and Composing: A Linear Approach*. New Albany, Ind.: Jamey Aebersold (Distributor); 1983.

Summarizes some of the linear methods used by Duke Ellington and others. He covers voice leading, form and development, and melodic line construction. There are numerous musical examples, plus a discography for each chapter. There is a cassette of the musical examples and arrangements cited in the text.

1820. Ellis, Norman. *Instrumentation and Arranging for the Radio and Dance Orchestra*. New York: Roell; 1936.

Treats such topics as harmony, transpositions, form, voicing, and instrumental combinations. Newer books have updated and expanded many of his ideas, including instrumental combinations and voicing (addition to 1981).

1821. Garcia, Russell. *The Professional Arranger-Composer*. New York: Criterion; 1968.

Lists the ranges of instruments and then discusses topics such as dance band harmony, voicing, form, dance band styles, and harmonic progression. This thorough book is one of the most popular on this topic (1981).

1822. _____. *The Professional Arranger Composer (Book Two)*. New York: Criterion; 1978.

Discusses contemporary trends in jazz, pop, and modern classical techniques, new scales, chords, and more. There are 169 musical examples and a recording of a composition by Russ Garcia.

1823. Goldstein, Gil. *Jazz Composer's Composition*. New York: Consolidated Music Publishers; 1981.

There are four sections: melody, rhythm, harmony, and the composition process. He also addresses tonal color. The book is designed to produce the knowledge necessary to compose or to improvise. One of the most significant aspects of the book is how he uses composers like Chick Corea, Randy Brecker, Bill Evans, Pat Methany, and George Russell as compositional models. There are numerous musical examples.

1824. Lapnam, Claude. *Scoring for the Modern Dance Band*. New York: Pitman; 1937.

Presents information on dance band concepts—arranging, harmony, voicing, and instrumentation. Although not an in-depth discussion and now outdated, the book is informative about the then-acceptable dance band techniques. Some examples are included. Many of his ideas have been modernized, specifically as to the use of altered harmonies, voicing, arranging concepts, and orchestration techniques (addition to 1981).

1825. Lees, Gene. *Arranging the Score*. New York: Bayou Press; 2000.

Concerned with the craft of arranging, and profiles the approaches of 13 arrangers. The essays cover arrangers such as Les Brown, Bill Challis, Miles Davis, Gil Evans, Robert Farnon, Henry Mancini, Mel Powell, and Kenny Wheeler.

1826. Mancini, Henry. *Sounds and Scores: A Practical Guide to Professional Orchestration*. Northridge, Calif.: Northridge Music; 1962.

Covers the gamut on arranging and orchestration for jazz and nonjazz groups. The chapters on harmony, voicing, and instrument combinations are particularly good. The book, well-written and concise, includes musical examples, many of which reflect Mancini's unique style (1981).

1827. Miller, Ron. *Modal Jazz Composition and Harmony*. New Albany, Ind.: Jamey Aebersold; 2000.

Volume 1 of a two-volume series. He demonstrates the uses and functions of the chromatic-modal harmonic system and free-asymmetric form. Permeated with suggestions and musical examples.

1828. _____. *Modal Jazz Composition and Harmony.* New Albany, Ind.: Jamey Aebersold: 2001.

Continues and expand the concepts he covered in volume 1. In volume 2, he introduces the concept of melody writing and analyzes the compositional styles that are generic to much of today's jazz composition. He also covers concepts of harmonization and reharmonization.

1829. Murphy, Lyle. *Swing Arranging Method.* New York: Robbins Music; 1937.

Discusses the basics of harmony and scoring, and the concepts used by swing bands. Much more attention is given to swing techniques for big bands than for small groups (1981).

1830. Nestico, Sammy. *The Complete Arranger.* New Albany, Ind.: Jamey Aebersold; 1997?

A book and CD set that covers his philosophy and techniques of arranging. Includes tips on voicing, harmonizing, and orchestrating for different groups. Demonstrates how and why he was one of the most successful arrangers for artists like Count Basie, and many more.

1831. Pease, Ted, and Ken Pullig. *Modern Jazz Voicings.* Boston: Berklee Press; 1998.

Designed to clear up clusters, and to add color and sophistication to chord voicings. The book is geared to arrangers of small ensembles, but is equally useful to other jazz musicians who are interested in advanced harmony. The book is organized into two parts (background and basics, and modern jazz voicings) and contains numerous musical examples. In addition to the informative CD, the user is asked to write dominant seventh chord scales, harmonize given notes, and to supply the correct answer to specific questions.

1832. Rinzler, Paul E. *Jazz Arranging and Performance Practices: A Guide for Small Ensembles.* Metuchen, N.J.: Scarecrow Press; 1989.

Equates arranging technique with structural elements. The elements are organized as intros; endings; accents; breaks and dynamics; style changes; time and tempo changes; form changes; and rhythm section practices. He supports his theories with references to recordings, musical examples, and recommendations for arranging. There are several appendices: notation, instrumentation with ranges and transpositions, role of each member in the rhythm section, arranging techniques, glossary, index of tunes cited, selected bibliography and discography, and an index.

1833. Russo, William. *Composing for the Jazz Orchestra.* Chicago: University of Chicago Press; 1961.

A practical guide to composing and orchestrating for jazz bands, large and small. He addresses chord symbols, chord quality, voicing, and writing for ensembles and specific instruments. Russo uses his experience as a jazz arranger-composer to inform his approach. Musical examples were written specifically for the book, rather than using examples from his compositions; he arranged-composed for Stan Kenton, the London Jazz Orchestra, the Chicago Jazz Ensemble, and for films.

1834. _____. *Jazz Composition and Orchestration.* Chicago: University of Chicago Press; 1968.

Expands on the author's earlier work. Musical examples in this volume, however, are drawn from Russo's work with several jazz groups. He discusses topics such as scoring, voicing, harmonic progressions, and instrumental combinations (addition to 1981).

1835. Sebesky, Don. *The Contemporary Arranger.* Sherman Oaks, Calif.: Alfred Publishing; 1974; *Contemporary Arranger's Workshop.* Sherman Oaks, Calif.: Alfred Publishing; 1982.

The first book is designed to eliminate many of the problems confronting the arranger who wants to write for the record industry. It shows, through scored and recorded examples, those procedures that have proven the most (and the least) successful. The second book presents a series of 30 taped lectures, combined with over 200 recorded excerpts, representing artists such as George Benson, the Brecker Brothers, Freddie Hubbard, Hubert Laws, the Mel Lewis Orchestra, Henry Mancini, Gino Vanelli, Dionne Warwick, and the Royal Philharmonic of London.

1836. White, Andrew. *Jazz Arranging.* Washington, D.C.: Andrew's Music; 1978.

Covers topics such as the brass section, saxophone voicing techniques, rhythm section, counterpoint, back-up writing, and combo writing. There are 66 musical examples, and a cassette tape.

1837. _____. *Jazz Composition.* Washington, D.C.: Andrew's Music; 1977.

The author addresses two different classifications of jazz composition: melodies and vehicles. There are numerous musical examples, which are included on a cassette tape.

1838. Wright, Rayburn. *Inside the Score.* Delevan, York: Kendor Music; 1982.

An arranging-composing text designed for advanced students. The book uses eight compositions by three artists (Bob Brookmeyer, Thad Jones, and Sammy Nestico). The Brookmeyer compositions are "Hello and Goodbye,"

"First Love Song," and "ABC Blues"; Thad Jones's contributions are "Three and One," "Kids Are Pretty People," and "Us"; and the two Nestico compositions are "Basie-Straight Ahead" and "Hay Burner." Wright discusses melodies, form, voicing (saxophone, brass, ensembles), voice leading, doubling, passing chords, substitute chords, and tonicization. An informative interview that focuses on techniques used by each artist is also included. In this book, theoretical ideas and concepts are drawn from actual musical scores.

Ear Training

1839. Baker, David N. *Advanced Ear Training for Jazz Musicians.* Lebanon, Ind.: Studio 224; 1977.

Covers the scales used in jazz including pentatonic, blues, diminished, Lydian dominant, and many more. Comes with a cassette tape (addition to 1981).

1840. _____. *Ear Training Tapes for the Jazz Musician.* New Albany, Ind.: Studio P/R; 1981.

The format is to imitate the diction material on the tape on one's instrument. Book 1 covers intervals; book 2 covers triads, and three-, four-, and five-note sets; books 3 and 4 cover seventh chord/scales; book 5 presents ii–V patterns; and book 6 works with major melodies, turnarounds, and ii–V formula. There is an outline for ear training in each book, and guide sheets accompany each exercise.

1841. _____. *A New Approach to Ear Training for Jazz Musicians.* Lebanon, Ind.: Studio P/R; 1975.

The text and cassette tape contain a comprehensive, sequentially arranged list of chords and scales for use by all instruments. In addition, there are several ear training exercises and a discography, which lists scales that the soloists use in their improvisations. The method is excellent for the intermediate or advanced performer who is serious about ear training in jazz.

1842. Diorio, Joe. *Intervallic Designs.* Milwaukee: REH/Music Dispatch (Distributor); 1991.

Designed to expand one's ears and techniques beyond the constraints of key centers. Uses exercises and techniques to transcend the parameters of diatonic harmony and chord symbols. Demonstration tape included.

1843. Donelian, Armen. *Training the Ear for the Improvising Musician.* New Albany, Ind.: Advance Music (Jamey Aebersold, Distributor); 1992.

The 12 lessons cover analyzing, naming, singing, tapping, transcribing, and performing, and include musical exercises. The lessons are organized into a three-lesson format; the first two lessons cover concepts and the third contains exercises that integrate material previously covered. Work sheets are also included.

1844. Little, Powell. *Know Your Saxophone.* Westbury, N.Y.: Pro Art; 1975.

Designed to provide the fundamentals and ear training necessary before one begins improvisation. This first volume was followed in 1976 and 1977 by *Know Your Clarinet, Know Your Trumpet,* and *Know Your Trombone* (1981).

1845. Mason, Thom David. *Ear Training for Improvisers: A Total Approach—Part 1.* Studio City, Calif.: Dick Grove; 1983.

Contains exercises designed to facilitate the hearing of intervals, chord qualities, chord progressions, and the scales that are used by many soloists.

1846. Rizzo, Phil. *Ear Training Based on 12 Tones.* Palisades, Calif.: Palisades Publishing; 1978.

Based on the use of the chromatic scale using a stationary "Do" system, this programmed text contains material designed to be studied over a four-year period. The materials are to be sung and are aimed at the beginning jazz student; however, they provide good ear training for all music students.

Chord Studies and Voicings

All Instruments

1847. Aebersold, Jamey. *Piano Voicings for All Instruments.* New Albany, Ind.: Jamey Aebersold; 1971–1988.

Geared to his Play-Along Series, the eight books/CDs contain note for note transcriptions of the transcriptions used by the pianist on the specific recording. The transcriptions focus on voicing and comping techniques from volume 1, *How To Play Jazz and Improvise* by Jamey Aebersold; volume 41, *Body and Soul* by Dan Haerle; volume 50, *Magic of Miles* by Mark Levine; volume 54, *Maiden Voyage* by Jamey Aebersold; volume 55, *Jerome Kern* by Hal Galper; volume 60, *Freddie Hubbard* by Dan Haerle and Mark Levine; volume 64, *Salsa/Latin Jazz* by Mark Levine; and volume 70, *Killer Joe* by Jamey Aebersold. Arrangers, composers, horn players, and vocalists can use these books and CDs.

1848. Arkin, Ed. *Creative Chord Substitution*. New York: Belwin Mills; 1982.

Discusses techniques of chord substitution as a means of enriching harmonic progressions. The book evolves from basic theory to chromatic alteration, tritone substitutions, blues, quartal harmony, and chord scale relationships. There are numerous musical examples, and suggestions for composing and performance.

1849. Berger, David. *Contemporary Jazz Chord Progressions. Volume 1*. New York: Charles Colin; 1981.

Demonstrates how chord progressions can be enhanced and altered. There are 21 tunes treated in three different ways; first, the tunes are cited with chord symbols; second, he demonstrates how most performers might perform chord progressions; and third, he provides chord substitutions.

1850. _____. *Contemporary Jazz Studies. Volume 2*. New York: Charles Colin; 1981.

Volume 2 covers basic theory, chords, progressions, substitutions, voicing, and more. It contains a collection of 11 standards, including "All The Things You Are," "Satin Doll," and "I May Be Wrong." There are comments regarding the form, harmonic progressions, and the availability of a recording. The solos are notated.

1851. Bower, Bugs. *Complete Chords and Progressions for All Instruments*. New York: Charles Colin; 1952.

Covers in part one such three- and four-part chords as major, minor, harmonic minor, augmented, whole-tone, and chord variations. Part two covers five- to seven-part chords such as dominant ninth, major seventh with added ninth, dominant eleventh, and thirteenth chords. This text includes arpeggio exercises (1981).

1852. Boyd, Bill. *An Introduction to Jazz Chord Voicings for Keyboard*. New Albany, Ind.: Jamey Aebersold; 2000.

Contains over 100 examples of chords and progressions in all keys with the appropriate fingering for each. He explores different voicing for seventh and other chords, discusses comping, and soloing.

1853. Cassarino, Ray. *Chord Construction and Analysis: Elements of Jazz and Pop I—Music Theory for the Contemporary Musician*. New York: Consolidated Publishers; 1978.

Explains how the combination of specific material derived from major scales is combined to form new possibilities. Covers chord quality, scales, and chord progressions (addition to 1981).

1854. Champagne, Champ. *The Real Chord Changes and Substitutions.* Four volumes. 1989–1992. Milwaukee: Hal Leonard; 1992.

The volumes are divided alphabetically: volume 1 (A–F), volume 2 (G–K), volume 3 (L–Q), and volume 4 (R–Z). The books feature suggestions, introductions, and endings for several songs. The music includes melody, lyrics, chords, and chord substitutions printed in red above the original chords. Volume 1 includes "Alice in Wonderland," "But Not For Me," "Can't Smile Without You," "Desafinado," and "For Sentimental Reasons"; Volume 2 includes "Getting to Know You," "The Girl From Ipanema," "I Love Paris," "If Ever I Would Leave You," and "It's Been a Long, Long Time"; Volume 3 contains "Love or Leave Me," "Makin' Whoopee," "Memory," "Night and Day," and "People Will Say We're In Love"; and Volume 4 includes "September Song," "Someone to Watch Over Me," "Till There Was You," "The Very Thought of You," and "Willow Weep for Me."

1855. Dunbar, Ted. *A System for Tonal Convergence for Improvisers, Composers, and Arrangers.* Kendall Park, N.J.: Dante; 1977.

Presents an inventory of 24 scales, including pentatonic, major, augmented, diminished, blues, and angular. All have from one to three tritones that cause them to gravitate toward one tonality—F major. However, they may be used to gravitate to any chord or tonality. In addition, each scale produces chords, which may be used as collated motion to produce a desired chord or tonality. This method is good for teaching modulation, cross-scale chord substitution, a chromatic approach to any tonality or chord, and new scale-chord sources for improvisation (1981).

1856. Elliott, Mike. *Contemporary Chord Solos: A Simplified Approach to Substitute Harmonies.* Milwaukee: Hal Leonard; 1992.

Provides performers with the tools necessary to substitute harmonic alterations for standard harmonies. Book 1 contains seven arrangements of popular songs, including "Moonlight in Vermont," "My Funny Valentine," "Yesterday," and "Like Someone In Love," written in the chord-melody style. In each case, he explains how the composition was reworked and he discusses reharmonization. In book 2, original lead sheet changes and melodies are presented below the reharmonized arrangements, complete with explanations provided for all substitution harmonies. The seven chord melody arrangements include "Here's That Rainy Day," "Angel Eyes," "Lover Man," and "I Remember April."

1857. Ellis, Don. *Quarter Tones.* Plainview, N.Y.: Harold Branch; 1975.

A comprehensive method covering the theory and application of quarter-tones geared to the advanced student of harmony or improvisation (1981).

1858. Eschete, Ron. *Chord Phrases*. Milwaukee: REH/Musical Dispatch (Distributor); 1991.

Reveals his approach to reharmonizations, substitution, voice leading, chord-scale relationships, and more. Concepts are demonstrated on a cassette tape.

1859. Harris, Matt, and Jeff Jarvis. *The Chord Voicing Handbook*. New Albany, Ind.: Jamey Aebersold; 2000.

A reference book for all musicians that is geared to the beginning as well as advanced musician. The book allows pianist and others to look up voicings including triads, seventh chords, and others.

1860. Mantooth, Frank. *The Best Chord Changes for the World's Greatest Standards. Volumes I and II*. Milwaukee: Hal Leonard; 1989.

Provides musicians with altered chord changes for a more interesting sound. Melody line, chord symbols, and lyrics are included, as well as a second line of altered chords in red. Also included are historic annotations of each song by David Baker. Among the 100 songs in Volume 1 are "Ain't Misbehavin," "Easy Street," "Gone With the Wind," "Here's That Rainy Day," "I Left My Heart in San Francisco," "The Lady is a Tramp," "My Favorite Things," "My Funny Valentine," "Opus One," "People," "Skylark," "Somewhere Out There," "Stompin' at the Savoy," and "Summertime."

1861. Markewich, Reese. *Inside Outside*. New York: Markewich; 1967.

Presents harmonic substitutions used in jazz and pop music, with examples drawn from transcribed solos by selected jazz artists. The author also suggests new chord possibilities as a means of harmonizing some standard jazz tunes. This well-illustrated book is recommended for advanced improvisers familiar with chord structure and voicings.

1862. Marohnic, Chuck. *How to Create Jazz Chord Progressions*. Lebanon, Ind.: Studio 224; 1979.

Covers the theory and methods of devising chord progressions by addressing specific harmonic concepts. Topics include "The Cycle of Fifths," "The ii–V–I progression," "Chord Notation," "Cycle Extension," "Further Extension," "Turn-Arounds," "Relative Majors and Minors," "Alternate Cycle," "Use of the Dominant and Alternate Cycle," "Half-Diminished," and "Diminished." There are numerous exercises as well as harmonic analyses of well-known tunes.

1863. Nairn, Ron. *Improvisation: Bridging the Gap (Bass Clef edition)*. Pacific, Mo.: Mel Bay; 2000.

Geared to those who possess little or no experience playing jazz, but want to learn to improvise on their instrument. Permeated with chords and scales to practice, however he stresses learning notes before you play them. In addition, the author suggests singing notes to train one to effectively improvise.

1864. Shumate, Ted. *Chord Concepts.* Milwaukee: REH/Music Dispatch (Distributor); 1991.

Discusses chord theory, construction, triadic and diatonic harmony, voicings, inversions, split inversions, string transfers, substitutions, and pluralities.

1865. Stuart, Walter. *Encyclopedia of Chords.* New York: Charles Colin; 1966.

Deals comprehensively with chords in chromatic order beginning on C.

1866. Ulrich, John J. *Chords and Scales.* New York: Jazz City Workshop; 1975.

Discusses the fundamentals of harmony needed for piano comping and improvisations. The text covers chord types, spellings, voice leading, chord progressions, and much more. Recommended for pianists as well as other musician.

1867. Tracy, Mike. *Jazz Chord Voicings for the Non-Pianist.* New Albany, Ind.: Jamey Aebersold; 2000.

He addresses and explains the basics of chord voicing in non-piano language. Contains written voicing over many of the Jamey Aebersold Play-A-Long tracks. He explores different voicings, and demonstrates how the chords can be used when comping.

Bass

1868. Appleman, Rich, and John Repucci. *Berklee Practice Method: Bass.* Boston: Berklee Press; 1996.

Like the other rhythm books in the series, this book begins with the basics and proceeds to other issues. Covers general musicianship on stage, playing in different keys, how to walk, following a chart, and more. He also discusses how to play in a wide range of styles. The CDs help to trade fours, contains numerous exercises, and suggestions for "thumb slapping."

1869. Carter, Ron. *Building Jazz Bass Lines.* New Albany, Ind.: Jamey Aebersold; 1999.

A book and CD that is permeated with techniques for building jazz bass lines. He discusses how to build lines with nonharmonic tones, diverse rhythms, different tempos, pitch/tone development, and more. He demon-strates with a rhythm section on the CD.

1870.   _____. *Ron Carter.* New Albany, Ind.: Jamey Aebersold; 1999.

The bass lines are transcribed from volumes 6 *Charlie Parker Bass Lines,* 15 *Payin Dues Bass Lines,* and 35 *Cedar Walton Bass Lines* of the Jamey Aebersold Play-A-Long series. The bass lines from volume 6 are "Billie's Bounce," "Confirmation," "Dewey Square," "Donna Lee," "My Little Suede Shoes," "Now's the Time," "Ornithology," "Scrapple from the Apple," "Thriving from a Riff," and "Yardbird Suite." Volume 15 transcriptions are "Body and Soul," "Cherokee," "I'll Remember April," "It's You or No One Else," "Stella By Starlight," "There Will Never be Another You," "The Song is You," and "What is This Thing Called Love." The transcrip-tions from volume 35 are "Bolivia," "Cedar's Blues," "Clockwise," "Fantasy in D," "Firm Roots," "Hand in Glove," "Maestro," "Midnight Waltz," and "Ojos De Rojo."

1871. Coolman, Todd. *The Bottom Line.* New Albany, Ind.: Jamey Aebersold; 1999.

Covers the gamut of bass playing, sound production, special effects, and practicing in the 23 chapters. In addition, he covers slow/fast tempos, time/feel, blues, and more.

1872. Cranshaw, Bob. *Bob Cranshaw Plays the Blue: Blues in All Keys Bass Lines.* New Albany, Ind.: Jamey Aebersold; 1988.

Includes the transcribed bass lines from volume 42 of the Jamey Aebersold Play-A-Long series. There are several choruses of two different blues pro-gressions in all 12 keys. See volume 42 of the Aebersold series for list of tune.

1873. Davis, Arthur. *System for Double Bass.* New Albany, Ind.: Jamey Aebersold; 2001.

The original book was published in 1976; however, in this new and revised edition he includes information on strength exercises, position exercises, bowing techniques, and his revolutionary four-finger system. He includes lots of photographs and illustrations.

1874. Davis, Richard. *Walking on Chords for String Bass and Tuba.* New York: Sympatico Musico; 1997.

Contains a series of 20 etudes designed to teach the student to play walking bass lines and chord changes. Tuba players will have to perform the etudes an octave lower (1981).

1875. Friedland, Ed. *Building Walking Bass Lines.* New Albany, Ind.: Jamey Aebersold; 2001.

A book and CD that focuses on the art of creating walking bass lines. It is a step-by-step approach loaded with good suggestions that are reemphasized on the CD.

1876. _____. *Expanding Walking Bass Lines*. New Albany, Ind.: Jamey Aebersold; 2002.

A follow up to the above book and CD, and gives concrete suggestions regarding creating swinging bass lines, and suggestions regarding how to think and solve musical problems like a bass player.

1877. Gertz, Bruce. *Walkin.* New Albany, Ind.: Jamey Aebersold; 2001.

A book and two CDs that focus on intermediate to advanced bass lines to standard chord progressions. Contains numerous examples and good demonstrations on the CDs, included are suggestions for approaching, delayed resolutions, using harmonic and nonharmonic tones, and more. Andy Laverne on piano and Joe Hunt on drums accompany the author on the play-along tracks.

1878. Gilmore, Steve. *All Time Standards Bass Lines*. New Albany, Ind.: Jamey Aebersold; 1982?

The transcribed lines are from volume 25 of the Jamey Aebersold Play-A-Long series. He transcribed "A Foggy Day," "Come Rain or Come Shine," "Have You Met Miss Jones," "I Can't Get Started," "I Could Write a Book," "I Love You," "It Might as Well Be Spring," "I've Grown Accustomed to Her Face," "My Favorite Things," "My Foolish Heart," "My Funny Valentine," "Old Devil Moon," "Our Love Is Hear to Stay," "September Song," "Speak Low," "Summertime," and "The Party's Over."

1879. _____. *Jam Session Bass Lines*. New Albany, Ind.: Jamey Aebersold; 1983?

The transcribed bass lines are from the chord changes on Volume 34 of the Jamey Aebersold Play-A-Long series. He transcribed "Blue Moon," "Don't Blame Me," "I Left My Heart in San Francisco," "Invitation," "Just Friend," "Laura," "My Secret Love," "No Greater Love," "On the Trail," "On Green Dolphin Street," "Once in Awhile," "Over the Rainbow," "Spring Is Here," "Star Eyes," "Stompin at the Savoy," "The Shadow of Your Smile," "You Stepped out of a Dream," and "Without a Song."

1880. Goldsby, John. *Bass Notes.* New Albany, Ind.: Jamey Aebersold; 1998.

A book and CD that contains transcriptions of the bass lines played by the author in volumes 41, 48, and 55 of the Jamey Aebersold Play-A-Long series. He discusses the rules of bass line construction, provides instruction and analysis of the 10 tunes, and addresses the overall role of the bass in the combo. Includes bass lines from *Alone Together, What's New, Do Nothin Till You Hear from Me, All The Things You Are,* and six more.

1881. Liebman, Jon. *Funk/Fusion Bass.* New Albany, Ind.: Jamey Aebersold; 2001.

A book and CD set that discusses the techniques and grooves of funk and fusion. He discusses the two-finger technique, string crossings, style elements, and how to build a vocabulary for funk/fusion soloing. The play-along CDs have over 90 tracks for the student to jam with. The method contains a foreword by Verdine White, bassist for Earth, Wind and Fire, and is endorsed by professional bassists such as Nathan East, Victor Wooten, and others.

1882. Del Puerto, Carlos, and Silvio Vergara. *The True Cuban Bass.* New Albany, Ind.: Jamey Aebersold; 2002.

A book that contains an introduction to the basic elements of interpreting and performing different styles of Cuban popular music. Included is information on performing salsa, rhumba, son, mambo, and other genres. The book includes transcribed lines for practicing.

1883. Raney, Chuck. *The Complete Electric Bass Player.* New Albany, Ind.: Jamey Aebersold; 2001.

A series of five books that are designed to teach an electric bass player from the basic fundamentals to professional status. He covers hand strength, finger independence, hand positions, playing concepts and dexterity, improvisation, and chording techniques. The books contain lots of original exercises, technical information, illustration, and photographs.

1884. Reid, Rufus. *How to Play Jazz, and the II-V-I Progression.* New Albany, Ind.: Jamey Aebersold; 1975?

Transcribed bass lines from volumes 1 and 3 of the Jamey Aebersold Play-A-Long series. One of the highlights of this two-in-one method book is the focus placed on walking bass lines. Also, the importance of the ii–V–I progression as generic to Bebop and later jazz styles is also inherent.

1885. Roberts, Jim. *How the Fender Bass Changes the World.* New York: Back Beat Books; 2001.

Written to celebrate the 50th anniversary of the fender bass, he traces the uses and functions of the instrument through the music of Jack Bruce, Stanley Clarke, James Jamerson, and Paul McCartney. Factual information and opinionated commentary.

1886. Stagnaro, Oscar, and Chuck Sher. *The Latin Jazz Book.* Cupertino, Calif.: Sher Music Company; 2000.

A comprehensive study of Afro-Cuban, Brazilian, Caribbean, and other Latin jazz styles. Included are baiano grooves, cha cha chas, songos, and jumbao variations and include compositions designed to help learn the styles. Includes notes on tuning tour bass to receive the desired effect. The three CDs allow one to hear, tune out, and insert your bass playing into the rhythm section.

1887. Wheeler, Tyrone. *Maiden Voyage Bass Lines.* New Albany, Ind.: Jamey Aebersold; 1989?

Contains the transcribed bass lines from volume 54 of the Jamey Aebersold series. He transcribed *Autumn Leaves, B♭, Shuffle Blue, Cantaloupe Island, Doxy, F Blues Footprints, Impressions, Maiden Voyage, Satin Doll, Song for My Father, Summertime, Watermelon Man,* and the III–VI–ii–V–I progression.

1888. _____. *Killer Joe Bass Lines.* New Albany, Ind.: Jamey Aebersold; 1992?

Transcriptions of the bass lines from volume 70 of the Jamey Aebersold Series. The transcriptions are "Sugar," "Mr. P.C.," "Blue Moon," "Birthplace Blues," "Sweet Georgia Brown," "You Stepped out of a Dream," "Girl from Ipanema," "Afternoon in Paris," "Stop-Time Blues," "Killer Joe," "Lady Bird," "Elvinish," and "Misty."

Drums/Rhythmic Instruments

1889. Chapin, Jim. *Advanced Techniques for the Modern Drummer.* New Albany, Ind.; 1998.

A book and two CDs that contains numerous exercises and polyrhythms that are designed to assist both small group and big band drummers. The method includes two demonstration CDs and has been endorsed by drummers like Billy Cobham, Elvin Jones, and Gene Krupa.

1890. DeJohnette, Jack, and Charlie Perry. *The Art of Modern Jazz Drumming.* North Merrick, N.Y.: Drum Center Publications; 1999.

Deals with the tonal concept of playing the drum set as a musical instrument. Covers the elements, principles, and techniques of contemporary jazz and related forms of drumming are presented. There are three books in one: book 1 deals with the concepts, principles, and techniques of jazz drumming; book 2 covers triplet performance patterns; and book 3 covers independent coordination. Also includes concepts for developing a feel for playing drums.

1891. Erskine, Peter. *Drum Set Essentials.* Three volumes. New Albany, Ind.: Jamey Aebersold; 2000.

A comprehensive approach and CD that transforms the student from beginning to professional status. Volume 1 covers hand and feet techniques, and elementary beats with variations. In volume 2, the author covers advanced coordination of the hands and feet, advanced beats and rhythmic comping, and the complexities of performing slow and fast tempos. In addition, brush techniques, large and small ensemble playing fills, and solos are examined in detail. Volume 3 contains information on additional brush-playing techniques, tips and studies, Brazilian and Afro-Caribbean music, metric meters, philosophy, and tips for practice.

1892. Goldenburg, Morris. *Modern School for Xylophone, Marimba, and Vibra-phone.* New Albany, Ind.: Jamey Aeberold; 1996?

This excellent method is not limited to jazz performers, but offers many tips germane to performing jazz. It includes information on this edition that was edited by Tony Cirone, and includes phrasing inherent in the music, orchestral excerpts, etudes, and information on sticking. Good for developing technique and knowledge of orchestral music.

1893. Hunt, Joe. *52nd, Street Beat.* New Albany, Ind.: Jamey Aebersold; 2002.

Written by a member of the Berklee School of Music faculty, and a drummer who has performed with artists such as Bill Evans, Stan Getz, and others, he presents a look at many of the famous drummers active from 1945 through 1965. He presents biographical information and a discography for each artist.

1894. Lipner, Arthur. *The Vibes Real Book.* New Albany, Ind.: Jamey Aebersold; 2001?

The book contains eight standards arranged eight times each. The arrangements progress from simple to four mallet arrangements. The arrangements are *Bag's Groove, Don't Get Around Much Anymore, St. Thomas, Waltz for Debbie, My Little Suede Shoes, Moonlight in Vermont,* and *Solar.* Good preparation for performing either two or four mallet compositions.

1895. Martinez, Fernando. *Funk Grooves for Drums.* New Albany, Ind.; Jamey Aebersold; 2002.

Combines advice with numerous transcriptions, concepts for practicing, and musical exercises to lead the student from the beginning to becoming a good groove drummer.

1896. Prins Jan. *Hi-Hat Integration.* New Albany, Ind.: Jamey Aebersold; 2002.

A comprehensive approach to the topic that integrates the role and function of the hi-hat with the snare and bass drum. The author uses nearly 600 exercises to illustrate his philosophy and techniques.

1897. Puente, Tito. *Tito Puente's Drumming with the Mambo King.* New York: Hudson Music; 2001.

In his own words, Puente chronicles the history of the Latin jazz movement with photographs, handwritten drum charts, and lot of drum exercises to teach the theory and method of his Afro-Cuban rhythms. The 75-minute CD features Puente in dialogue, performing examples from the text, six timbale solos, and twelve recordings from his long and distinguished career.

1898. Riley, John. *The Art of Bop Drumming.* New Albany, Ind.: Jamey Aebersold; 2002.

A book and CD set that focuses on the techniques of bebop drumming. He also situates the tried and tested techniques to the evolution and reason why drumming techniques evolved and changed over time. The play-along CD features Bob Mintzer on tenor saxophone.

1899. _____. *Beyond Bop Drumming.* New Albany, Ind.: Jamey Aebersold; 2002.

Designed to explore and introduce the student to drumming styles and concepts that have evolved since bebop. Discusses the techniques and reasoning behind the new drumming, which has evolved since bebop.

1900. Sanchez, Poncho, and A. Silverman. *Poncho Sanchez Congo Cookbook.* New Albany, Ind.: Jamey Aebersold; 2001?

A book of riffs for beginning conga players or percussionists who want to incorporate Latin or conga techniques into their performing styles. The book and CD covers riffs, grooves, and accompaniment for one of Sanchez's *Congueros.* The tracks are performed on CD by Sanchez's rhythm section.

1901. Smith, Paul. *Jazz Ballads.* New York: Creative Keyboard Publications; 2000.

Presents several hand-coordinated exercises and ballads with very little commentary. Discusses musical and nonmusical ways and means of performing jazz ballads.

Guitar

1902. Bay, Mel. *Rhythm Guitar Chord System.* Pacific, Mo.: Mel Bay; 1976.

Covers the spectrum of chords the guitarist might encounter when performing jazz. Included are exercises on chord structures, patterns, and progressions. The system proceeds from the simple to the complex and is recommended for all guitarists (1981).

1903. Ben-Hur, Roni. *Talk Jazz Guitar.* New Albany, Ind.: Jamey Aebersold; 2001?

A comprehensive collection of bebop studies in all keys, analyzed with fingerboard diagrams, and fingerings. The 10 chapters cover topics like augmented chords, arpeggios, diminished scales, chord inversions, turn-arounds, and much more.

1904. Buckingham, Bruce. *Latin Guitar: The Essential Brazilian and Afro-Cuban Rhythm Guide.* New Albany, Ind.: Jamey Aebersold; 1992.

A book and CD that covers the basics of the topic. He discusses bossa nova, samba, baiao, bolero, cha cha, mambo, nanigo, and more. Includes lots of musical exercises that are demonstrated on the CD.

1905. Christiansen, Mike. *Mel Bay's Complete Jazz Guitar Method.* Pacific, Mo.: Mel Bay; 2000.

Focuses on the basics ranging from finger positions to chord voicing. Concerned with developing a proficient guitarist regardless of the style of music performed.

1906. Damian, Jon. *The Guitarist's Guide to Composing and Improvising.* Boston: Berklee Press (Distributed by Hal Leonard); 2000.

Covers the gamut regarding composing and improvising in several styles, including jazz, rock, funk, and more. In addition to ways and means of composing and improvising, he also discusses the role of creativity in becoming successful in both areas.

1907. DiMeola, Al. *Al DiMeola: A Guide to Chords, Scales, and Arpeggios.* Milwaukee: 21st Century Publications/Music Dispatch (Distributor); 1990.

Geared to learning the basic tools necessary to become a good musician and performer. He discusses composition, blues patterns, and jazz chord exercises, provides a guide to chords, scales, and arpeggios, and suggests playing and practicing tips.

1908. Dunbar, Ted. *The ii–V Cadence as a Creative Guitar Learning Device.* Kendall Park, N.J.: Dante Publishing Company; 1982.

The book contains 42 exercises with the ii–V device in all keys using scales, different intervals, arpeggios, melodic patterns, color tones, and various articulations.

1909. _____. *New Approaches to Jazz Guitar.* Kendall Park, N.J.: Dante Publishing Company; 1977.

Contains excellent theory and techniques of guitar improvisation. A sequential guide to learning chords is provided as well as pertinent information on voicing and altered scales. One tune is used to illustrate the 13 exercises (1981).

1910. Edison, Roger. *Jazz Guitar: A Systematic Approach to Chord Progressions.* Sherman Oaks, Calif.: Alfred Publishing; 1978.

Discusses holding a pick, reading chord diagrams, the cycle of fifths, chord substitution, and jazz progressions (1981).

1911. *Incredible Chord Finder.* Milwaukee: Hal Leonard; 1991.

Diagrams over 1,000 guitar chords in numerous voicings. Topics covered include tuning, intonation, strings, 12-string tunings, picks, and tablature.

1912. *Jazz Guitar School.* Milwaukee: Hal Leonard; 1991.

Includes 150 exercises on different aspects of jazz guitar technique. The method covers several facets of chord playing and single-line phrasing with the objective of minimizing technical difficulties while simultaneously expanding musical possibilities.

1913. Johnson, Randy. *Soul Jazz Guitar.* New Albany, Ind.: Jamey Aebersold; 2001.

A collection of tunes and improvisations that are based on the author's commercial albums, with new interpretations. The transcribed tunes include "Downtime," "The Philadelphians," and "Rolling at the Summit" from his commercial CDs. The collection also includes some improvisations on standard chord progressions

1914. Marshall, Wolf. *Best of Jazz Guitar.* Milwaukee: Hal Leonard; 2001.

Contains compositions by Miles Davis, Duke Ellington, Sonny Rollins, and others. The emphasis is on understanding the varying stylistic approaches used by some of the top guitarists. He uses "All Blues," "So What," "Yesterdays," and other compositions to illustrate the "Martino Approach," "Metheny Sound," the "Montgomery Stamp," and more. He used A C D to demonstrate the different approaches.

1915. Martino, Pat. *Linear Expressions.* Milwaukee: REH/Music Dispatch (Distributor); 1992.

Discusses his formula for chord conversions with the focus on melody, not theory.

1916. Mause, Alan de. *Mel Bay's Complete Finger Style Jazz Guitar Book.* Pacific, Mo.: Mel Bay; 2001.

Concerned with developing a technically sound, and proficient method for guitarists, rather than focusing on a single style. Permeated with exercises that range from chromatic harmonic movement, the E blues scale, secondary arpeggios, and much more. The exercises contain short introductions and helpful diagrams. A background in music theory is suggested.

1917. McGuire, Edward F. *Guitar Fingerboard Harmony.* Pacific, Mo.: Mel Bay; 1978.

Emphasizes chord formations, voicing, progressions, and tonal functions.

1918. Mock, Don. *Fusion.* Milwaukee: REH Hotline Series, Musical Dispatch (Distributor); 1991.

Combines influences from rock and jazz sources (George Benson, Jimi Hendrix, George McLaughlin), with his personal fingerboard concepts to provide chromatic and intervallic fusion ideas. Concepts are demonstrated on a cassette tape.

1919. O'Mara, Peter. *Rhythmic Concept for Funk/Fusion Guitar.* New Albany, Ind.: Jamey Aebersold; 2001.

A book and two CDs that include 16 compositions permeated with funk/fusion licks, tempos, and grooves. A play-along rhythm section accompanies the aforementioned on two CDs. The rhythm-guitar riffs are incorporated into the overall groove of the composition.

1920. Pass, Joe. *Joe Pass Guitar Chords.* New York: Warner, 1975; New York: Warner, 1976.

A good text for intermediate and advanced guitarists. Shows how chords are voiced and how they function in progressions in relation to other chords. The author classifies chords into six major categories. All chord voicings are written in fingerboard as well as musical notation.

1921. Pudturo, Al. *Graded Position Studies for Jazz Guitar.* Milwaukee: Centerstream Publications/Music Dispatch (Distributor); 1990.

Focuses on how to transcend first-position guitar playing. His exercises use diverse rhythmic patterns and are melodic rather than exercise oriented. The exercises are fingered, graded, and contain chords.

1922. Rector, Johnny. *Guitar Chord Progressions.* Pacific, Mo.: Mel Bay; 1978.

Serves as more than an encyclopedia for guitar voicing, with information on chord progressions, extensions, alterations, and substitutions. Good musical examples are provided for each chord discussed.

1923. Roberts, Howard, and Gerry Hagberg. *Guitar Compendium.* Three volumes. New Albany, Ind.: Jamey Aebersold; 1989.

Volume 1 covers craft, fingerboard map, style, and chords; volume 2 covers fingerboard map, scales, trouble shooting, and intervals; and volume 3 covers arpeggios, trouble shooting, and theoretical ideas. Objectives are outlined and instructions are given to best address blues, classical music, improvisation, jazz, chord progressions, the development of musical lines, and more.

1924. Stern, Mike. *Mike Stern Guitar Instructional Video.* New York: Rittor Music; 2000.

Reveals some of the secrets of his "chops of doom," in one-on-one with guitarist-interviewer Satoshi Inove. The live performances were shot at the 55 Bar, and contains a blues, ballad, prayer, and Cole Porter's "I Love You," and Stern's "Tipitina's." Demonstrates how Stern incorporates blues on bebop. Funk and rock into his performances. He provides tips on playing octaves, single-note variations on B-flat blues, false harmonics, and how to phrase around a melody. Also, he demonstrates how chord tones trace the contour of chord changes, and incorporates patterns over ii–V–I changes by focusing on a target tone. He references guitarists and other jazz artists as major influences on his vocabulary.

1925. Voelpel, Mark. *Charlie Parker for Guitar.* Milwaukee: Hal Leonard; 2000.

This is less a tutorial than a jam session. There are 18 transcriptions from Parker's recordings, including "Ornithology," "Ko Ko," "Parker's Mood," "Blues for Alice," and 14 more. Each transcription includes performance notes, editor's notes, and advice on how to play "scoops," "falls," "ghost note," yes "slurs," and other technique's that define Parker's performance style.

1926. Zaradin, John. *Getting Into Latin Guitar.* New Albany, Ind.: Jamey Aebersold; 2000?

The book contains five parts: references and definitions of terms, exercises and pieces that demonstrate various guitar techniques, examples of Rasgueado patterns, studies for developing rhythmic ability and appreciation, and compositions in a variety of Latin styles. The exercises and compositions are demonstrated on a CD.

Keyboard

1927. Aebersold Jamey. *Killer Joe: Transcribed Piano Comping.* New Albany, Ind.: Jamey Aebersold; 1997.

A companion to volume 70 of his Play-A-Long series, and demonstrates economical piano comping techniques over standard chord changes. Like all books in his Play-A-Long series, this book can be used as a companion to the aforementioned volume in that series.

1928. Amadre, Jimmy. *Harmonic Foundation for Jazz and Popular Music.* Bala Cynwyd, Pa.: Thornton Publishers; 1982.

A keyboard method that establishes a foundation in modern harmony enabling players to create chord voicing and to harmonize a melody in a modern context.

1929. Boyd, Bill. *An Introduction to Jazz Chord Voicings for Keyboard.* New Albany, Ind.: Jamey Aebersold; 2000.

Contains over 100 examples of chords and progressions in all keys with the appropriate fingering for each. He explores different voicing for seventh and other chords, discusses comping, and soloing.

1930. _____. *Exploring Jazz Scales for Keyboard.* Milwaukee: Hal Leonard Publishing; 1992.

A comprehensive discussion of scales and their relationship to chords and progressions. A chart of scales written in all keys along with complimentary chords is included in each chapter. He also covers the blues, blues and pentatonic scales, and ii–V–I progressions in major and minor keys.

1931. _____. *Intermediate Jazz Chord Voicing for Keyboard.* Milwaukee: Hal Leonard; 1988.

A follow-up to *An Introduction to Jazz Chord Voicing for Keyboard,* in which he continues exploring contemporary chord voicings and their application to melody and accompaniment. Chord voicings and ii–V–I chord progressions are notated in all keys. He also covers comping and solo playing. Included are chapter assignments and a comprehensive list of chord voicings in the appendix.

1932. _____. *Jazz Chord Voicing for Keyboard.* Milwaukee: Hal Leonard; 1986.

Written for beginning students, he covers basic chord spellings and voicings as well as chord progressions. The chord progressions are written in all keys, and there is coverage of piano comping and solo performing techniques.

1933. DeGreg, Phil. *Jazz Keyboard Harmony: Voicing Method for All Musicians.* New Albany, Ind.: Jamey Aebersold; 2000.

A step-by-step method that proceeds from two voice to seven voice chord structures with fourths and extended harmonies. He also provides notated harmonic progressions, notated songs for both hands, comping rhythms, bass line techniques, and strategies for practicing. Includes a play-along CD, which allows you to practice bass and drums.

1934. _____. *Midi Disc Companion for Jazz Keyboard Harmony.* New Albany, Ind.: Jamey Aebersold; 2000?

A floppy disc that provides a simulated band to accompany the songs in the above book.

1935. Deneff, Peter. *Jazz Hanon.* Milwaukee: Hal Leonard; 2000.

Presents 50 exercises for jazz pianists of all levels and experience. The exercises cover pentatonic patterns, double-note patterns, blues scales, and irregular chromatic melodies. Number rather than topic labels the exercises. No table of contents

1936. _____. *Jazz Keyboard Harmony.* New York: Piano Plus; 1983.

Covers chord symbols, chord substitution, and voice leading.

1937. Evans, Lee. *Jazz Keyboard Harmony.* New York: Piano Plus, Inc.; 1986.

Covers chord substitutions, interpretation of chord symbols, and voice leading concepts. There are suggestions for realizations, exercises, and numerous assignments for which answers are provided in the appendix.

1938. Evans, Lee, and Martha Baker. *How to Play Chord Symbols in Jazz and Popular Music.* Milwaukee: Hal Leonard; 1991.

The purpose is to teach students to read chord symbols at the keyboard, which, in turn, should prepare them to read lead sheets. First, the authors discuss basic chords through seventh and altered chords. Second, they focus on ninth, eleventh, and thirteenth chords. Melodic motifs from standards are used to demonstrate how a particular chord-type functions. There are numerous lessons devoted to chord-types and other concepts.

1939. Fowler, William. *Take Another Look at the Keyboard.* Lakewood, Colo.: Fowler Music Enterprises; 1982.

Designed to assist students to see, hear, and understand tonal concepts at the keyboard without notation. There are numerous examples of intervals, various scales, and chords with their inversions.

1940. Gillespie, Luke. *Stylistic ii/V7/I Voicings for Keyboardists.* Lebanon, Ind.: Jamey Aebersold; 2001.

Written for jazz pianists, he focuses on minor harmonies, rootless chords, chords in fourths, contrapuntal, and bitonal chord voicings. He includes chord charts, tips for practicing, and numerous exercises that help to understand the chord choices of artists like Bill Evans, Red Garland, Bud Powell, and McCoy Tyner.

1941. Grove, Dick. *Jazz Open Voicings for Keyboards.* Los Angeles: Dick Grove Publications; 1984.

Focuses on alternative voicing of chord progressions, left-right hand coordination, and comping. The role and function of the piano in combos and large ensembles and solo playing are also explored. There are numerous musical examples.

1942. Haerle, Dan. *Jazz Piano Voicing Skills.* New Albany, Ind.: Jamey Aebersold; 1999.

A graded approach to voicing skills that begins with block chords over major and minor chords and proceeds to advanced polychords and substitutions. The chapters begin with a one-page set of instructions for both teachers and students, and the 123 musical examples cover all keys.

1943. _____. *Jazz/Rock Voicings for the Contemporary Keyboard Player.* New Albany, Ind.: Studio P/R; 1983.

Focuses on chord voicing, blues progressions, ii–V–I patterns, and turn-arounds.

1944. Harris, Matt, and Jeff Jarvis. *The Chord Voicing Handbook.* New Albany, Ind.: Jamey Aebersold; 2000.

A primer for beginning jazz pianists who wish to learn chord voicing in all keys for different types of chords. Includes information on seventh chords, triads, and extended chords.

1945. Hoffmann, Russell, and Paul Schmeling. *Berklee Practice Method: Keyboard.* Boston: Berklee Press; 2000.

Concentrates primarily on sharpening one's practical skills like comping, soloing, and overall musicianship on stage. Lots of exercises and suggestions regarding soloing in different keys, following a chart, how to recover if you get lost in a solo, and how to play in other styles, including rock and funk.

1946. Laverne, Andy. *Handbook of Chord Substitutions.* New York: Ekay Music; 1991.

Provides suggestions for creating chord substitutions. The suggestions are clear and are supported by numerous musical examples. He also provides arrangements of 12 compositions, including "Moonglow" and "A Nightingale Sang in Berkeley Square," in each case providing substitute chords to accentuate colors and effects.

1947. Levine, Mark. *The Jazz Piano Book.* Petaluma, Calif.: Sher Music Company; 1989.

Covers the gamut of harmony, melody, and scale concepts necessary to improvise. Among the numerous topics covered in the 23 chapters are practicing scales, fourth chords, tritone substitutions, voicing, comping, salsa, and Latin jazz. The book is permeated with musical examples.

1948. _____. *Volume 50 "Magic of Miles."* New Albany, Ind.: Jamey Aebersold; 1999.

A transcription of the chord voicing that was used on this volume in the Aebersold series. The compings are transcribed fully, and enables a student to understand how a star pianist approaches various harmonic sequences in the performing of jazz tunes in real time.

1949. _____. *Salsa/Latin Jazz: Transcribed Piano Comping.* New Albany, Ind.: Jamey Aebersold; 1998.

The author transcribed the piano comping from volume 64 of the Aebersold series. Interesting study of chord voicing situated within energetic rhythmic structures.

1950. Levine, Mark, and Dan Haerle. *Freddie Hubbard: Transcribed Piano Comping.* New Albany, Ind.: Jamey Aebersold; 1998?

The authors transcribed the voicings/comping that each used on volume 60 of the Jamey Aebersold Play-A-Long series. Several choruses of each recorded track are presented to allow the user to compare and contrast the comping/ voicing styles used by the each pianist on the different tracks.

1951. Mantooth, Frank. *Voicings for Jazz Keyboard.* Milwaukee: Hal Leonard Publishing Corporation; 1987.

Transcends tertian harmony to address voicings that are derived from non-tertian concepts. He begins by discussing basic harmonic concepts and voicing and proceeds to altered chords, polytonal applications, chord substitutions, and linear concepts. There are numerous examples and a one-semester syllabus for jazz keyboardists.

1952. Manus, Morton. *Piano Chord Dictionary.* Van Nuys, Calif.: Alfred Publications; 1978.

Discusses chord spellings and voicing including major, minor, augmented, and diminished.

1953. Richards, Tim. *Improvising Blues Piano.* New Albany, Ind.: Jamey Aebersold; 1999.

Includes over 30 compositions covering blues piano styles from the 1920s to the present. Among the arrangements are "Blueberry Hill," "St. Louis Blues," "Just A Closer Walk With Thee," and "Blue Monk." He also includes stylistic bass lines and chord voicing, and numerous exercises and suggested listening.

1954. Rinzler, Paul. *Quartal Jazz Piano Voicings.* New Albany, Ind.: Jamey Aebersold; 2000.

A guide to complex chord voicing that is prevalent in much of today's modern jazz. He includes information on quartal voicing, good voicing in all keys, every quartal voicing allowed by traditional theory, quartal voicing, applied to standard chord progressions, and the theoretical concepts behind deriving quartal voicing.

1955. Rizzo, Phil. *Spread Chord Voicing.* Palisades, Calif.: Palisades Publishing; 1978.

Presents a wealth of information for beginning arrangers, composers, and pianists. Topics covered are jazz piano fundamentals, basic chord symbols, enrichment and enlargement of given chord symbols, principles of voice leading, comping rhythms, and common substitutions. Although short, the book is well-organized and informative (1981).

1956. Robour, Jean. *Jazz Piano Method.* Milwaukee: Hal Leonard; 1990.

Geared to beginners, this text teaches theory through music by analyzing selected jazz, Latin, pop, rock, and other genres.

1957. Shumate, Ted. *Chord Concepts.* Milwaukee: REH/Music Dispatch (Distributor); 1991.

Discusses chord theory, construction, triadic and diatonic harmony, voicing, inversions, split inversions, string transfers, substitutions, and pluralities.

1958. Ulrich, John J. *Chords and Scales.* New York: Jazz City Workshop; 1975.

Discusses the fundamentals of harmony needed for piano comping and improvisations. The text covers chord types, spellings, voice leading, chord progressions, and much more. Recommended for pianists as well as other musicians.

Saxophone

1959. Ruwe, Jordan. *Jazz Exercises and Etudes for the Alto Saxophone.* New York: Houston Publishing; 2000.

Permeated with numerous exercises and etudes for the serious saxophonist. Develops harmonic sophistication with the numerous diminished whole tone scales, augmented triad exercises, and bebop mixolydian scales. Comprehensive and thorough.

Trombone

1960. Wilson, Phil, and Joseph Viola. *Chord Studies for Trombone.* Boston: Berklee; 1978.

Transcribed from *The Technique of the Saxophone.* Like *Chord Studies for Trumpet,* he studies chordal structures and chordal sequences with rhythm problems over chord changes. This text fully covers chord structures and functions (1981).

Trumpet

1961. Hagans, Tim, Greg Gisbert, and Scott Wendholt. *Maxium Mastery.* New York: Hip-Bone Music; 2000.

There are 12 jazz etudes by three trumpet players organized into four lessons on grooves and down-home blues playing for intermediate players. Contains a strong focus on nuance, articulations, and phrasing. Includes several exercises and a CD.

1962. Kotwica, Raymond S., and Joseph Viola. *Chord Studies for Trumpet.* Boston: Berklee; 1978.

Presents studies on chordal structures in all 12 diatonic keys and studies on chord sequences containing rhythm problems over various chord changes. Transcribed from *The Technique of the Saxophone,* this book includes major and minor, seventh, and diminished seventh chords. The book is thorough and good for students who want to learn the whole range of chord structures and functions (1981).

Methods, Pedagogy, and General Approaches to Improvisation

All Instruments

1963. Aebersold, Jamey. *Scale Syllabus.* New Albany, Ind.: Jamey Aebersold; 1982.

A play-along system of scales. He includes augmented chords, and modal, pentatonic, whole-tone, Hindu, and other "world" scales.

1964. Baker, David N. *How to Play Bebop, Volume I: The Bebop Scales and Other Scales in Common Use; Volume 2: Learning the Bebop Language: Patterns, Formulae, and Other Linking Materials; Volume 3: Some Techniques for Learning and Utilizing Bebop Tunes.* Bloomington, Ind.: Frangipani Press; 1986.

Volume 1 covers bebop scales, bebop scale exercises in all permutations and a scale-chord syllabus; volume 2 covers ii–V7 and iii–VI–ii–V progressions, major chord, cycles-turnback-formulae, an approach to building bass lines on bebop scales, and a list of essential bebop tunes for memorization; volume 3 focuses on the contrafact, techniques for learning tunes, use of quotations, thematic fluency, blues, rhythm tunes, and a list of essential bebop tunes for memorization. Baker also includes original compositions, exercises, lists of tunes based on the contrafact, and lists of frequently performed tunes. An excellent collection.

1965. _____. *Improvisation Patterns: The Bebop Era, Vol. I.* New York: Charles Colin; 1978.

Covers daily jazz calisthenics for all treble clef instruments (e.g., 8-, 9-, and 10-note scales, and major scales with added notes); also ii–V7 patterns covering two measures (beginning on different notes of the ii and V7 chords). A scale syllabus is included (1981).

1966. _____. *Improvisational Patterns: The Bebop Era, Vol. 2.* New York: Charles Colin; 1979.

Presents exercises for all treble clef instruments designed to develop facility with the 8-, 9-, and 10-note scales that gained ascendancy during the bebop era in the music of Parker, Gillespie, and Powell (1981).

1967. _____. *Improvisational Patterns: The Bebop Era, Vol. 3.* New York: Charles Colin; 1979.

Deals with more daily jazz calisthenics as well as tonic function patterns, special cycle patterns, turn-back patterns, a seventh scale sequence, and some modal lines based on blues for treble clef instruments (1981).

1968. _____. *Improvisational Patterns: The Contemporary Era, Vol. 4.* New York: Charles Colin; 1979.

Based on the belief, as are other volumes in this series, of pattern books that cover "the great body of improvisational materials is of high specificity with regard to its time and place within the jazz continuum." Covers such topics as pentatonic, fourths, fourths in various combinations, modal patterns, Coltrane changes, and ii–V7 progressions (1981).

1969. _____. *Improvisational Patterns: The Blues.* New York: Charles Colin; 1980.

Covers the gamut of blues, beginning with an essay and selected discussion of performers and boogie-woogie, and proceeding to original compositions for study and performance. Baker discusses blues patterns, signals, scales (whole tone, diminished, diminished whole tone, Lydian dominant, seventh scales, pentatonics, fourths, and blues), 16-bar blues, blues with bridges, piano voicing, and more. A scale-chord syllabus is included at the beginning of the book.

1970. _____. *Jazz Improvisation: A Comprehensive Method of Study for All Players.* Chicago: Maher, 1969; Maher (revised), 1983.

A pedagogical approach covering topics ranging from scales, chord progressions (ii–V–I), to the psychological approach to improvising, with examples, study questions, and selected discographies. The book contains numerous exercises, suggestions for listening, and selected bibliographies. He also covers blues and advanced chord-scale relationships used in improvisation.

1971. _____. *Techniques of Improvisation.* Three volumes. Chicago: Maher; 1971.

The three volumes, based on George Russell's *Lydian Chromatic Concept,* cover numerous aspects of jazz improvisation and include detailed studies of progressions and turnbacks. The three volumes are organized as follows: volume 1 provides a method for developing improvisational technique; volume 2 covers ii–V7 progressions; and volume 3 focuses on turnbacks and cycles.

1972. Berg, Shelton. *Jazz Improvisation: The Goal Note Method.* Evergreen, Colo.: Lou Fisher Music Publishing; 1991.

Designed as a two- to four-semester course, the approach is consonant based, emphasizing structural pitches and harmonic considerations as opposed to scale-derived ideas. The theory is that when consonant tones are surrounded with jazz formula, successful improvisation results.

1973. Berger, David. *Contemporary Jazz Duets.* Two volumes. New York: Charles Colin; 1981.

The two volumes are replete with jazz duets for different instrumental combinations. Each duet contains chord progressions and comments describing how it may be used. The duets are based on jazz standards, including "Satin Doll," "I'll Remember April," "Night and Day," and "How High the Moon." There are 21 duets in volume 1 and 11 in volume 2.

1974. Berle, Arnie. *Complete Handbook for Jazz Improvisation.* New York: Amsco; 1972.

Treats the basics of jazz theory in a clear and concise manner. Covers chord quality, harmonic progressions, scales, and more (addition to 1981).

1975. _____. *How to Create and Develop a Jazz Solo.* Pacific, Mo.: Mel Bay Publications; 1983.

Contains a myriad of approaches on learning to improvise, including playing through chord progressions, approaches to blues, extended chords, tension and release, how to use motifs, and special effects. There are numerous musical examples.

1976. Berliner, Paul F. *Thinking in Jazz: The Infinite Art of Improvisation.* Chicago: University of Chicago Press; 1994.

Discusses how musicians learn to improvise. Documents the creativity and preparation that artists such as Betty Carter, Miles Davis, Dizzy Gillespie, Coleman Hawkins, and Charlie Parker use in their improvisations. Uses extensive interview material and musical analysis and integrate data on musical development and the practice and thought that is devoted to jazz outside of performance. Presents spontaneous composition (improvisation) as an aesthetic, a language, and a tradition.

1977. Boling, Mark E. *The Jazz Theory Workbook.* New Albany, Ind.: Jamey Aebersold (Distributor); 1990.

A discussion of the harmonic language of bebop and postbebop periods through several tunes from these periods. Among the topics covered are fundamentals, chord structures, chord/scale relationships, chord progressions, and sources of chromaticism in improvisation, with suggestions for further study. There are numerous exercises associated with each chapter as well as six tunes using specific chord progressions.

1978. Bouchard, George. *Intermediate Jazz Improvisation* Lebanon, Ind.: Jamey Aebersold; 2000.

A guide for developing soloists who possess knowledge of jazz theory and desire technical knowledge of some songs. There are concise essays on chord structure, harmonic organization, melody, tempo, and other components of standard jazz tunes. He analyzes "Autumn Leaves," "The Girl from Ipanema," "Summertime," "Sweet Georgia Brown," and many more. Includes lots of exercises, commentary on the analysis, and two CDs.

1979. Bower, Bugs. *Ad Lib.* New York: Charles Colin; 1953.

Approaches improvisation in an interesting and useful manner. The author first presents a tune, then writes out the chord and scale formation of each passage of the melody. He combines chord and scale forms before proceeding to the next tune.

1980. Brinkmann, Reinhold (editor). *Improvisation und neue Musik: acht Kongressreferate.* Mainz: Schott; 1979.

Contains a series of papers on jazz improvisation. The papers were presented at a 1979 German conference and range from topics like "What is Improvisation" (Carl Dahlhaus), to papers dealing with the technical aspects of improvisation (Ekkehard Jost). Although provocative, the papers do not break new ground.

1981. Burbat, Wolf. *Die Harmonik des Jazz.* Bärenreiter, Germany: Deutscher Taschenbuch Verlag; 1988.

In German. Covers modes, chord changes, structure, and quality, pentatonic scales, blues, substitutions, and applications of concepts to jazz. Numerous musical examples drawn from standard repertoire.

1982. Campbell, Gary. *Triad Pairs for Jazz.* Miami: Warner Brothers; 2000.

Teaches a person to improvise by using triad pairs as the basis of your solos. Contains numerous three-, four-, six-, and eight-note patterns. Also includes triad variations, and a guide on how to apply them when improvising.

1983. _____. *Expansions.* Lebanon, Ind.: Houston Publishing Incorporated; 1991.

Discusses methods of developing improvisational ideas for jazz fusion performers. There are numerous examples that focus on developing ideas for music in contemporary America. Michael and Randy Brecker, John Abercrombie, and Bob Mintzer endorse the book.

1984. Carubia, Mike. *The Sound of Improvisation.* Sherman Oaks, Calif.: Alfred Music; 1975.

Designed to instruct individuals, combos, jazz bands, and concert bands in a comprehensive method of improvisation. A play-along cassette features the Thad Jones-Mel Lewis rhythm section while the tunes feature ii–V7 progressions and require some knowledge of major, minor and Mixolydian scales/mode. Good for high school and early college students (1981).

1985. Clarke, Bruce. *Jazz Studies I.* Melbourne, Australia: Allaus; 1987.

A pedagogical approach to improvisation that includes comments on jazz styles and periods, instrumental genealogy, and solo transcriptions. The book is divided into four major sections: the first section covers the basic elements of harmony, including ii–V–I progressions; the second section examines tonality in cycles and progressions; the third section relates tonality to different types of blues, and the fourth section examines a myriad of jazz scales, including pentatonic, Lydian dominant, multi-dimensional blues, and diminished.

1986. Coker, Jerry. *Drones for Improvisation.* New York: Columbia Pictures Publications; 1985.

The first method to use a drone as an adjunct when practicing scales and patterns. He varies the pitches selected for each drone, thereby allowing a person to choose more than one drone for each keystone. The drone approach is excellent for ear training.

1987. _____. *Elements of the Jazz Language for the Developing Improviser.* Miami, Fla.: CPP/Belwin; 1991.

Draws upon the musical practices of several jazz greats (John Coltrane, Bill Evans, Charles Parker, Phil Woods, and others) to address improvisational devices. He discusses what students should learn in order for them to speak the jazz language. Tape and computer disk (Macintosh) included. He discusses running changes, 7–3 resolution, 3–b9, bebop scales, sequences, enclosure, tritone substitutions, and more.

1988. _____. *How to Practice Jazz.* New Albany, Ind.: Jamey Aebersold; 1990.

Includes a list of play-along tunes and exercises. He suggests several areas of practice, including chord arpeggios, fermata practice, intervals, patterns, tone quality, chromaticism, chord changes and substitutions, transcribed solos, and much more. He offers suggestions on how to structure practice time, including ear training, play-alongs, four-track tape recorder, and more. The appendix lists several play-along tunes from many series.

1989. _____. *Improvising Jazz.* Englewood Cliffs, N.J.: Prentice Hall; 1964.

Gives the beginning performer with some technical ability and knowledge of key signatures and scales a sequential approach to improvisation. He discusses blues, melody, and rhythm, after which he proceeds to more advanced concepts like chord progressions, functional harmony, and extended chords. There are numerous musical examples, including chord progressions and left-hand chord voicings. He also categorizes a select group of tunes by their chord progressions.

1990. _____. *The Jazz Idiom.* Englewood Cliffs, N.J.: Prentice-Hall; 1975.

Primarily a pedagogical guide for jazz performers. Included are concise histories of jazz, and suggestions on transcription, developing one's ear, arranging, keyboard, and improvisation skills. Users should supplement this book with individual approaches.

1991. Coker, Jerry, Jimmy Casale, Gary Campbell, and Jerry Greene. *Patterns for Jazz.* Lebanon, Ind.: Studio P/R; 1970.

Contains a total of 326 patterns constructed for use in major through chromatic scales. This book is designed for performers. The patterns are organized by scales, including diminished, melodic minor, and whole tone (addition to 1981).

1992. Collier, Tom. *Jazz Improvisation.* New York: Music Minus One; 1983.

Covers basic harmonic, melodic, and rhythmic elements in jazz. Specific coverage of jazz and rock rhythm dictation, blues, bass diction, and several scales (major pentatonic, diminished, and whole tone). The method is available in either nine LP recordings or five cassettes.

1993. Crook, Hal. *How to Improvise: An Approach to Practicing Improvisation.* New Albany, Ind.: Advance Music; 1991.

Addresses harmony, melody, and rhythm. The book is organized into sections dealing with chords, phrasing, scales, time, rhythms, and theory. A basic background knowledge of jazz improvisational styles is recommended before using this book. A pedagogical approach.

1994. Dean, Roger T. *New Structures in Jazz and Improvised Music Since 1960.* Bristol, Pa.: Open University Press; 1992.

The author examines improvisatory music of the second half of the twentieth century, regardless of genre or style. He discusses numerous applications of improvisation, whether they are generated from an aesthetic, cultural, psychological, psychometric, or a myriad of other perspectives. His study covers 1960 to the early 1990s; however, because there is no paradigm of pre-1960 improvisation, or coverage of performers who utilized those approaches in their post-1960 performances, for example, Sonny Rollins and John Lewis, the book is not useful as a tool of comparison. There are five appendices: analysis of improvised music; references (articles and books); references (printed musical scores); references (films and recordings); and a core collection of improvised music and how to obtain it. Index.

1995. Deutsch, Maury. *Lexicon of Symmetric Scales and Tonal Patterns.* New York: Charles Colin; 1962.

Contains a wealth of information on scales and melodic patterns designed to expand one's harmonic facility. Scales are treated in categories such as polyharmonic, polytonality, polyrhythm, microfrequency, and polymodality. The book is well-organized and scholarly (1981).

1996. DiBlasio, Dennis. *DiBlasio's Bop Shop: Getting Started in Improvisation, Volumes I & II.* Delevan, N.Y.: Kendor Music; 1986.

Geared to beginning students, the author begins with blues, after which he focuses on three chord types and their corresponding scales. He also discusses diminished chords and scales. Volume 2 focuses on ear training, jazz compositions, patterns, and transcribing, and contains suggestions on learning tunes.

1997. Dunlap, Larry. *Great Moments in Jazz.* Petaluma, Calif.: Sher Music Company; 1991.

Contains over 500 transcribed improvisational phrases by artists such as Clifford Brown, Michael Brecker, John Coltrane, Miles Davis, Bill Evans, Herbie Hancock, Sonny Rollins, and Wayne Shorter. The phrases are organized into two groups; characteristic and unique. The user is encouraged to listen as well as play along with the accompanying cassette.

1998. Evans, Lee. *Improvise by Learning How to Compose.* New York: Piano Plus, Inc.; 1986.

Introduces basic compositional and improvisational techniques with specific emphasis on melodic development and reference in improvisation. Also offers realizations and answers for the assignments and exercises in the appendix.

1999. _____. *Modes and Their Use in Jazz.* New York: Piano Plus, International; 1986.

Presents comprehensive coverage of diatonic modes, focusing on how they may be identified, and developing knowledge of their qualities, sounds, and function in both jazz and nonjazz contexts. Suggestions are given for their use in jazz composition and improvisation. There are numerous exercises and several compositions written in specific modes.

2000. Feldstein, Sandy. *Practical Music Theory.* Six discs and three textbooks. Van Nuys, Calif.: Alfred Publishing; 1982.

Uses Apple computers to teach music theory from the notes and staff, to nonharmonic tones, four-part harmony, composition, and transposition. There are 84 lessons in three workbooks, each lesson designed to reinforce the material covered in the three previous lessons.

2001. Freeman, Steve. *Jazz-Rock.* Milwaukee: REH/Music Dispatch (Distributor); 1991.

Focuses on single note improvising over either one-chord vamps or basic chord changes. He advocates a funky blues, jazz-rock feel (George Benson, John Scofield, Mike Stern). Includes a cassette tape.

2002. Gornston, David. *Fun with Swing: For Clarinet, Trumpet, Vibes, Saxophone, Accordion, Piano, Violin, and Theory Students.* New York: Sam Fox; 1978.

Uses three chords in three keys. Good for beginners, the book moves through phrasing to passing tones and first embellishments (1981).

2003. Green, Bunky. *Jazz in a Nutshell.* New Albany, Ind.: Jamey Aebersold; 1985.

Offers alternative approaches to learning ii–V–I chord progressions. He covers rhythmic vitality, half- and double-time feels, hybridization, and substitutes. There are 80 ii–V–I patterns covering all diatonic keys. One of the few methods to recognize rhythm as an important vehicle when performing ii–V–I patterns.

2004. Grove, Dick. *Applied Modal Improvisation Set.* Studio City, Calif.: Dick Grove Publications; 1983.

A multimedia approach for beginning and intermediate improvisers. He covers the dorian, phrygian, mixolydian, and lydian modes. Each set contains a text, workbook, and a play-along cassette. The set is available for different instruments in different keys.

2005. Haerle, Dan. *The Jazz Language.* Lebanon, Ind.: Studio P/R; 1980.

Designed to assist persons in teaching jazz improvisation and theory. The chapters are organized sequentially, with a set of study questions and several musical examples. He focuses on scales, chords, and their applications.

2006. _____. *The Jazz Language.* Milwaukee: Hal Leonard; 1986.

Covers chords, scales, progressions, interpretation, and more.

2007. _____. *The Jazz Sound: A Guide to Tune Analysis and Chord/Scale Choices for Improvisation.* Milwaukee: Hal Leonard; 1987.

Haerle addresses the function of melody and context in determining appropriate choices in improvisation. He covers the gamut of chord/scale choices, including lydian dominant and diminished.

2008. _____. *The Jazz Sound.* Milwaukee: Hal Leonard Publishing; 1989.

Focuses on composition, analysis, and chord/scale choices for improvisation. He discusses how melody and context dictate scale choice by addressing: (1) What are the key areas of the piece, (2) What are the specifics of the chord symbols, (3) What are the implications of the melody and what tones are shared by the chord/scales? There are numerous musical examples. Appendix of scales and chord symbols.

2009. Haerle, Dan, Jack Petersen, and Rich Matteson. *Jazz Tunes for Improvisation.* Lebanon, Ind.: Studio P/R Inc.; 1982.

The objective is to compile a list of tunes for the study of improvisation, either individually or in class situations. The tunes are based on common chord progressions in addition to some that present specific harmonic problems.

2010. Haerle, Dan. *Scales for Jazz Improvisation.* Lebanon, Ind.: Studio P/R; 1975.

Presents the scales used in jazz improvisation in bass and treble clefs. The text treats modes generated by the major scale (e.g., ionian, dorian, phrygian); modes generated by the ascending melodic minor scale (e.g., lydian augmented); symmetric altered scales, and others (1981).

2011. _____. *Scales for Jazz Improvisation.* New York: CPP/Belwin; 1979.

An encyclopedia of scales and modes and how they function in a jazz context. Each scale is discussed in relation to the chord in which it best works. The scales and modes are presented in all keys in both treble and bass clefs.

2012. Higgins, Dan. *The ii–V7–I Progression in Solo Form.* Two volumes. Wailuko, Hawaii: Aquarian Enterprises; 1978.

Contains an extended solo based on a popular chord progression in the first text. The second text contains 120 blues choruses in all keys.

2013. Jatt, Andrew. *Jazz Theory.* Dubuque, Iowa: William C. Brown Company; 1983.

Covers many jazz theory topics, including cadences, chord progressions, modulations, tritone substitutions, reharmonization, and quartal harmony, with many musical examples. Also included are analyses of "But Not For Me," "Chelsea Bridge," and "Giant Steps."

2014. Jennings, Paul. *Jenson Jazz Lab Improvisation Method.* Two volumes. New York: Jenson Publications; 1982.

A method for beginning improvisers. Jennings suggests warm-up drills, ear training exercises, combo tunes, and big band tunes. He begins with a discussion of scales, chord exercises, and sequences. Includes teacher's guides.

2015. Kynaston, Trent, and Robert J. Ricci. *Jazz Improvisation.* Englewood Cliffs, N.J.: Prentice-Hall; 1978.

Designed for both the classical musician entering the world of jazz and the jazz musician seeking a detailed harmonic and melodic approach to improvisation. The book covers jazz chords and chord charts, jazz scales and scale charts, chord-function-scale charts, patterns, progressions, and more. The book is well-written and geared to the student with some knowledge of the basics in music (1981).

2016. LaPorta, John. *Tonal Organization of Improvisational Techniques.* Delevan, N.Y.: Kendor Music; 1976.

Offers a comprehensive jazz improvisation method for all levels of study from beginning to advanced. Written for C treble, C bass, and E♭ and B♭ instruments with a supplemental piano "comping" book and four 12-inch LP records. The text is well-organized and logically presented and thorough (1981).

2017. Liebman, David. *A Chromatic Approach to Jazz Harmony and Melody.* New Albany, Ind.: Jamey Aebersold (Distributor); 1991.

Focuses on developing chromatic approaches to harmony, melody, and improvisation. Two broad approaches, theoretical concepts and musical examples, are taken from jazz and classical music. He discusses form, tension and release, and ways of using chromaticism to increase expressive outlets. Includes numerous examples of chromaticism drawn from the music of J. S. Bach, Chick Corea, John Coltrane, Miles Davis, Herbie Hancock, Charles Ives, Arnold Schoenberg, Wayne Shorter, and others. A scholarly discussion of the topic.

2018. Lenten, Lance. *Creative Jazz Exercises, Volume I and II.* New York: Charles Colin; 1986.

Demonstrates how scales and rhythm patterns can aid improvisation. He uses blues, modes, and rhythm progressions to realize his objective. Volume 1 covers blues, fourths, and several scales (pentatonic, diminished, chromatic, modes, and more). Volume 2 covers chord substitution, color tones and color scale exercises, superimposed chords, and more. Several improvised solos are used to demonstrate the discussed concepts.

2019. Levey, Joseph. *Basic Jazz Improvisation.* Delaware Gap, Pa.: Shawnee; 1971.

Covers different chord types geared to the beginning improviser. Includes some exercises and a limited treatment of harmony (addition to 1981).

2020. Lindsay, Martin. *Teach Yourself Jazz.* London: English University Press; 1958.

Comments generally on topics ranging from articulation to progressions. This do-it-yourself guide does not treat any topic in depth. The coverage is limited and surface in its treatment (addition to 1981).

2021. Marshall, Wolf. *101 Must Know Jazz Licks.* Milwaukee: Hal Leonard; 2001.

Groups short, self contained musical phrases into swing, bebop, hard bop, modal jazz, soul jazz, and other classifications. The CD provides helpful suggestions regarding how to use the musical phrases.

2022. Mymit, Chuck. *A Beginner's Approach to Jazz Improvisation.* New York: Chappel; 1973.

Covers the study of chords, a basic review of scales, ii–V7 progressions, and the application of chord scales to compositions (1981).

2023. Phillips, Alan. *Jazz Improvisation and Harmony.* New York: Robbins Music; 1973.

Explains methods for creating and developing individual styles of playing, moving from elementary improvisational and harmonic concepts to the advanced levels. The text treats such topics as scales, basic chords, modes and ragas, the complete fifteenth chord, mystic chords, harmonizing with the isolated minor scale, and polytonality. This book is useful for musicians, arrangers, composers, and students of all instruments (1981).

2024. Pickens, Harry. *Guides Imagery For Jazz Mastery.* New Albany, Ind.: Jamey Aebersold; 2001.

A collection of mediations, and self-affirmations that are accompanied by a clam, and hypnotic soundtrack to build a sense of confidence and relaxation. He believes the aforementioned is necessary before one can bring chords, harmonies, and melodies into one's music. In short, he espouses that one must achieve harmony in life before it can be accomplished in music.

2025. Poole, Carl. *Jazz for Juniors: 15 Progressive Duets Designed to Develop Interpretation of Dance Music.* New York: Henry Adler; 1961.

Designed for beginning jazz players, with valuable tips on jazz articulation and phrasing. The duets do not cover all scales used in jazz (addition to 1981).

2026. Progris, Jim. *Go for Baroque with That Jazz Feeling.* New York: Charles Hansen; 1974.

Comprised of melodies from Bach, Schein, Handel, Corelli. Rameau, and others, arranged with the original melody above a jazz interpretation. Instructions on jazz interpretation and articulation are outlined and chord symbols are provided (1981).

2027. _____. *Virtuoso Jazz Stylings.* New York: Hansen House; 1982.

Contains 35 compositions covering blues, Dixieland, swing, bebop, jazz-rock, funk, and avant-garde. The compositions include an improvised solo, historical comments, ii–V progressions, diminished seventh and dominant ninth chords, and more.

2028. Ricker, Ramon. *Pentatonic Scales for Jazz Improvisation.* Lebanon, Ind.: Studio P/R; 1975.

Acquaints the advanced high school or college improviser with the vast resource of melodic material available through the use of pentatonic scales. This is not a complete method of improvisation but does cover the application of pentatonic scales to various chord types, altered pentatonic, improvised solos, and ii–V–I exercises (1981).

2029. _____. *The Ramon Ricker Improvisation Series.* Five volumes. Lebanon, Ind.: Studio P/R; 1979.

Presents blues in all keys for all instruments. Volume 1 covers the beginning improviser; volume 2, the developing improviser; volume 3, all blues;

volume 4, ii–V–I progressions; and volume 5, Jerome Kerns's great jazz songs. Each volume is accompanied by a rhythm section (1981).

2030. _____. *Technique Development in Fourths for Jazz Improvisations.* Lebanon, Ind.: Studio P/R; 1976.

Designed for the advanced player, the book covers application of fourths to chord changes and contains a short discography of performers using fourths in their improvisations. Exercises are included (1981).

2031. Rizzo, Phil. *Scale Variations.* Palisades, Calif.: Palisades Publishing; 1960.

Helps students learn how to embellish scales for jazz improvisation. The book is somewhat outdated as it does not contain exercises on the modes or other scales used in jazz since 1960 (1981).

2032. Russell, George. *The Lydian Chromatic Concept of Tonal Organization for Improvisation.* New York: Concept Publishing; 1959.

In one of the most important theoretical additions to the literature, the author demonstrates the relationship between chords and scales. This book is geared to the musician with a good knowledge of chord quality, scales, and jazz literature. The author uses his experience as a jazz composer and pianist to frame his theory. A significant contribution, it uses jazz practice to evolve a theory rather than theory to evolve a practice. Selected discography.

2033. Sabina, Leslie M. *Jazz Arranging and Orchestration: A Concise Introduction with Interactive CD-Rom.* New York: Thomson/Schirmer; 2002.

Intended as an introductory course at four-year schools. Generally requires two years of music theory, and knowledge comparable to Jazz Arranging I. She uses a step-by-step approach through the basics of arranging for a big band. The book contains over 200 musical examples that are geared to support the theory discussed in the text. The examples appear in two formats with synthesizer sound: locked finale files for analysis, and unlocked standard MIDI formula files that allow students to experiment with sound technique as they change the musical example.

2034. Shneidman, Jack. *1001 Jazz Licks.* New York: Cherry Lane Music Company; 1999.

A comprehensive listing of jazz licks divided into three main categories: "Essential Licks," "Stylistic Licks," and "Licks over Standard Type Progressions." Useful for all improvisers.

2035. Smith, Hale. *Progressive Jazz Patterns.* New York: Charles Colin; 1976.

Gives examples of jazz phrases set to chords in both root position and inversions. The text also contains blank paper for students to write out their solos. The jazz phrases follow several harmonic progressions, including ii–V–I (addition to 1981).

2036. Spera, Dominic. *Learning Unlimited Jazz Improvisation: Making the Changes.* Milwaukee: Hal Leonard; 1977.

Fully covers ii–V7 patterns and instrumental and vocal techniques. There are also brief sections on tempo, the language of jazz, and more. A cassette is included (1981).

2037. Spitzer, Peter. *Jazz Theory Handbook.* Pacific, Mo.: Mel Bay; 2001.

A thorough examination of major and minor scales, basic chord voicing, some bebop chord progressions, and a few lead-sheet interpretations. Permeated with exercises, pattern diagrams, and more. A CD is included.

2038. Stanton, Kenneth. *Introduction to Jazz Theory.* Boston: Crescendo; 1971.

Discusses the entire range of jazz theory, moving from the basics (e.g., chord structures), to progressions and substitutions. This text represents adequate coverage of these topics to 1971; however, new practices in voicing, progressions, and substitutions have emerged since this book was published (addition to 1981).

2039. Stuart, Walter. *Create Your Own Jazz Phrases.* New York: Charles Colin; 1978.

Coordinates chord symbols with one- and two-measure phrases. This is a step-by-step approach for all instruments that requires in-depth musical knowledge.

2040. _____. *Jazz Scales.* New York: Charles Colin; 1974.

Written for all treble instruments and contains 12 jazz versions of major and minor scales. Somewhat limited in that he does not cover the myriad scales used in jazz that are not major or minor.

2041. _____. *Jazz Soloist: For All Instruments.* New York: Charles Colin; 1972.

Discusses topics such as rhythm and transposition with exercises included (1981).

2042. _____. *Rhythm and Syncopation in Modern Jazz.* New York: Charles Colin; 1974.

Features 4/4, 3/4, and 2/4, covering numerous additional rhythm and syncopation situations (1981).

2043. Swayzee, Tom, Jr. *Scales and Etudes for Modern Musicians.* Memphis: Franton Music; 1987.

Designed for heterogeneous instruments and covers scale patterns, major and minor pentatonics, diminished, blues, whole-tone scales, and turnbacks.

2044. Tarto, Joe. *Basic Rhythms and the Art of Jazz Improvisation.* New York: Charles Colin; 1973.

Instruct beginning players in performing syncopated rhythms for jazz band and improvisations. Exercises do not contain separate parts for treble clef instruments but are designed for one or more players.

2045. Tilles, Bob. *Practical Improvisation.* Rockville Centre, N.Y.: Belwin Mills; 1967.

Treats a wide range of topics pertinent to jazz improvisation, from intervals to the cycle of fourths. The author presents some particularly interesting ideas concerning how to comprise blues using major, minor, augmented fifth, dominant seventh, and diminished seventh chords (1981).

2046. Toch, Ernest. *Shaping Forces in Music.* New York: Criterion Music Corporation; 1991.

Discusses harmony, melody, counterpoint, and form. He covers ii–V patterns, tritone substitutions, extended harmonies, and methods of use in constructing melodies and counterpoint.

2047. Tranchina, Joseph. *Linear and Structural Improvisation.* New York: Charles Colin; 1983.

Challenges most of the boundaries of tertian tonality. The author uses both linear melodic concepts and structural harmonic improvisational ideas combined with an overtone scale to introduce many new ideas. He uses undertones to demonstrate how overtones will affect ear training. There are numerous musical examples of pentatonic patterns.

2048. Weiskopf, Walt, and Ramon Ricker. *Coltrane: A Player's Guide to His Harmony.* New Albany, Ind.: Jamey Aebersold; 1993.

Focuses on two Coltrane classics, examining the harmonic structure of "Giant Steps" and "Countdown" in detail. Contains practice exercises, solos, and suggestions on how to use Coltrane's harmonic style with standard harmonies.

2049. White, Leon. *Modern Improvising: A Guide to Jazz Scale Soloing.* Studio City, Calif.: Professional Music Products; 1978.

Introduces the student with some musical background to the sounds of modern improvising through the study of the sources, organization, and application of various scales. The author offers some interesting ideas on improvising and argues that modes are a complicated and unnecessary approach to learning jazz. Numerous exercises and explanations are included (1981).

2050. Wise, Les. *Inner Jazz.* Milwaukee: REH/Music Dispatch (Distributor); 1992.

Focuses on tension and release and cadential playing. He demonstrates these concepts with arpeggios and scales. Includes demonstrations on cassette tape.

2051. _____. *Bebop Bible.* New York: REH Publications/Columbia Pictures Publications; 1982.

Focuses on ii–V melodic ideas organized as major and minor ideas, dominate 7th ideas, ii–V ideas, one-measure phrases, turnarounds, and substitutions. The book contains over 800 patterns by Dizzy Gillespie, Charles Parker, Bud Powell, Fats Navarro, Thelonious Monk, and others.

2052. Wolking, Henry. *Jazz.* North Vancouver, British Columbia Canada (P.O. Box 86011): Touch of Brass Music Corporation; 1987.

A collection of etudes and exercises that are designed to facilitate jazz improvisation. He covers major, minor, and dominant seventh chords, ii–V progressions, augmented chords, and more. The exercises are designed to aid the hearing of harmonic progressions.

Bands

2053. Baker, David N. *Jazz Pedagogy: A Comprehensive Method of Jazz Education for Teachers and Students.* Chicago: Maher, 1979; Van Nuys, Calif.: Alfred Publishers, 1988.

A comprehensive book addressing topics such as methods of teaching, improvisation, ear training, rehearsing/organizing combos and big bands, developing course content, and issues in jazz education. One of the earliest and best attempts to address these issues. Baker also includes a selected bibliography and discography.

2054. Eisenhauer, William. *Contemporary Concepts for Stage Band.* New York: Bourne; 1974.

Teaches sight reading in the jazz medium. The book contains patterns that illustrate articulation, phrasing, and much more that is useful. Good for beginning jazz students (1981).

2055. Grove, Dick. *Dick Grove Stage Band Reading Method.* Los Angeles: Dick Grove Publications; 1980.

Designed to teach jazz band reading techniques. He covers articulation, melodic shape, ghost notes, and more. Grove uses 12 compositions to evoke the interpretation concepts presented. He discusses rhythmic interpretation, particularly swing. Great for beginning jazz band directors.

2056. LaPorta, John. *Developing Sight Reading Skills in the Jazz Idiom.* Boston: Berklee; 1967.

Offers a programmed method for C instruments designed to aid students in improving their musical conception of the stage band idiom and developing their awareness of solo, duet, and group techniques. Each example is composed of one or two musical ideas and/or rhythmic units repeated and varied melodically (1981).

2057. Lawn, Richard. *The Jazz Ensemble Director's Manual.* Oskaloosa, Iowa: C.L. Barnhouse Company; 1983.

Discusses techniques of building and maintaining a jazz ensemble program. There are 12 chapters, including "Starting a Jazz Ensemble Program," "The Jazz Ensemble Conductor," "Understanding Chord Notation," and "Teaching Basic Jazz Improvisation." A recording reinforces the chapters on "Phrasing and Articulation," and "The Rhythm Section." Good for beginning and advanced jazz ensemble directors.

2058. Perkins, Charles R. *Jazz Improvisation for Stage Band.* New York: Charles R. Perkins; 1985.

Provides ideas for teaching jazz improvisation to big bands. He systematically covers pentatonic scales, non-chord tones, riffs, syncopation, and blues. There are general lessons and improvisation and rhythm studies. A practice tape is included.

2059. _____. *Jazz I Improvisation: An Intermediate Collection.* New York: Charles R. Perkins; 1987.

A follow-up to *Jazz I Improvisation for Stage Band,* this book applies the concepts discussed in the first book to additional keys and harmonic progressions. He also includes six original compositions written in two different keys.

2060. Spear, Sammy, Robert Stein, and Nicholas Lamitola. *Basic Syncopation: A Practical Approach to Stage Band Reading, Interpretation, and Articulation.* Westbury, N.Y.: Pro Art; 1967.

Provides lessons in reading, interpretation, and articulation for trumpet, saxophone, and trombone (1981).

2061. Wiskirchen, George. *Developmental Techniques for the School Dance Band Musician.* Boston: Berklee; 1961.

Designed for beginning jazz instrumentalists or high school jazz band directors. In one of the first books written on this topic, the author offers good ideas on the teaching of jazz articulation and phrasing and includes appropriate exercises (1981).

Bass

2062. Bredice, Vincent, and Charles Hansen. *Basic Impulse Bass Guitar.* New York: Charles Hansen; 1975.

Aimed at the beginning electric bassist, Bredice and Vincent cover the basics such as chord structures and progressions (1981).

2063. Carrol, Frank. *Easy Electric Bass.* New York: Warner; 1978.

Contains some valuable information on how to build a bass line, boogaloo patterns, and etudes in all major and most minor keys (1981).

2064. Carter, Ron. *Building a Jazz Bassline.* New York: Charles Hansen; 1971.

Shows the student how to build a bass line through knowledge of chord structures and harmony. The information proceeds from the simple to the complex (1981).

2065. Carter, Ron, and Charles Hansen. *Comprehensive Bass Method.* New York: Charles Hansen; 1977.

Useful for both acoustic and electric bassists, offering materials ranging from chord functions to progressions. The book also has several exercises for each position discussed (1981).

2066. Clayton, John. *Big Band Bass.* Lebanon, Ind.: Studio P/R; 1978.

Discusses the essentials of becoming a big band bassist. The text includes information on building bass lines, chord function, and much more. An excellent and comprehensive text for both double and electric basses (1981).

2067. Dewitt, John, and Charles Hansen. *Rhythmic Figures for Bassists.* Two volumes. New York: Charles Hansen; 1977.

Designed to acquaint the intermediate to advanced bassist with contemporary bass lines. The bass lines in both volumes proceed from the simple to the complex. Includes information on fills and double stop patterns, and transcribed solos. Good illustrations (1981).

2068. Filiberto, Roger. *Play Electric Bass from Chord Symbols.* Pacific, Mo.: Mel Bay; 1978.

Suggests a detailed method for reading chord symbols. The explanations are clear and concise (1981).

2069. Goldsby, John. *Bowing Techniques for the Improvising Bassist.* Long Island City, N.Y. (P.O. Box 6616): Bass Lion Enterprise; 1990.

Designed for all bassists who aspire to develop bowing techniques. He covers arpeggios, scales (bebop, diatonic, chromatic, diminished, whole-tone, and more), slurs, vibrato, and jazz rhythms. There are seven transcribed solos, including three versions each of choruses by Jimmy Blanton, Paul Chambers, Eddie Gomez, Slam Stewart, and John Goldsby.

2070. Hammick, Valda. *Electric Bass Technique.* Hollywood, Calif.: Solena; 1977.

Thoroughly covers left-hand technique, ranging from fingering position to bass patterns. The most advanced text on the subject.

2071. Kaye, Carol. *Contemporary Bass Lines.* New York: Warner; 1976.

Contains bass lines indicative of several styles of rock that can be analyzed for their rhythmic and harmonic content. The bass patterns might be useful for jazz bassists playing fusion-style jazz (1981).

2072. Montgomery, Monk. *The Monk Montgomery Electric Bass Method.* Lebanon, Ind.: Studio P/R; 1978.

Provides a complete method, from the basics to challenging solo and ensemble work. The information on bass lines and bass patterns is especially helpful (1981).

2073. Pastorius, Jaco, and Jerry Jemmott. *Jaco Pastorius Modern Electric Bass.* New York: Manhattan Music Publications (Distributed by DCI); 1985; 1990

This is a transcription of the interview comments made by Pastorius on his DCI video, *Jaco Pastorius: Modern Electric Bass.* Pastorius analyzes his solos from the video. He also covers scale-chord applications.

2074. Progris, James. *Basic Electric Bass.* Five volumes. New York: Sam Fox; 1978.

The first four volumes cover the spectrum of bass playing, including chord structure, chord functions, walking bass patterns, and etudes. The fifth volume consists of 140 basic rhythmic patterns, chord progressions, walking jazz patterns, and etudes at an advanced level. The text also covers meters/feels not commonly used in jazz, for example, 6/4, 7/4, 7/8, and 9/8.

2075. Reid, Rufus. *The Evolving Bassist.* Chicago: Myriad; 1974.

Geared toward developing a total musical concept for the double bass and for the four- and six-stringed electric bass. Good for classical and jazz bassists (1981).

2076. Stuart, Walter. *Jazz Improvising for All Bass Instruments.* New York: Charles Colin; 1973.

Explains specific components of jazz improvisation, along with exercises and chord symbols. Requires some knowledge of music (1981).

Bass Clef Instruments

2077. Most, Abe. *Jazz Improvisation for Bass Clef Instruments.* Sherman Oaks, Calif.: Gwyn; 1976.

Serves as the counterpart to the treble edition (1981).

B♭, C, and E♭ Instruments

2078. Konitz, Lee. *Jazz Lines.* New York: William H. Bauer; 1959.

Consists of 11 tunes with chord symbols for B♭ instruments. Some of the tunes are written for two instruments (1981).

2079. LaPorta, John. *A Guide to Jazz Phrasing and Improvisation.* Two volumes. Boston: Berklee; 1972.

Contains duets for C and E♭ instruments representative of a broad range of jazz performances from 1952 to 1972. Each volume contains 14 duets varying from intermediate to advanced levels along with a recording. The second half of each composition is written as a counterpoint to the first (A section), so that two students can play it as a duet. Individual students can also play along with the recording (1981).

Clarinet

2080. Goodman, Benny. *Benny Goodman's Clarinet Method.* Milwaukee: Goodman/Hal Leonard; 1987.

A reprint of a book written by Benny Goodman that is geared to beginning students. He discusses clarinet tone, style, technique, and musicianship. He also discusses assembling and tuning the clarinet, hand position, scales, and expression. There are several exercises, compositions, and a biography of his career to 1940.

Drums/Percussion

2081. Bellson, Louis, Hank Bellson, and Dave Black. *Contemporary Brush Techniques.* Van Nuys, Calif.: Alfred Publishing Company; 1985.

Covers the basics as well as wire brush techniques. In addition to general drumming concepts, he covers Latin, rock, swing, soloing, special effects, and more. The cassette features Bellson performing exercises, commenting, and playing an extended solo.

2082. Branch, Harold. *Practical Cha-Cha and Merengue Figures.* Plainview, N.Y.: Harold Branch; 1976.

Designed to acquaint one with rhythms that are not commonly used in jazz. The book is also designed to provide some insight into the structure of Latin musical styles. The exercises are in three-part harmony and are organized by chord progressions (1981).

2083. Chesky, David. *Advanced Jazz/Rock Rhythms: For All Treble Clef Instruments.* New York: Charles Colin; 1978.

Encompasses contemporary jazz-rock rhythmic and melodic devices, including accents, fills, bass drum techniques, swing concepts, and more (addition to 1981).

2084. Cusatis, Joe. *Rudimental Patterns for the Modern Drummer.* Melville, N.Y.: Belwin/Mills; 1968.

Covers the basic patterns and techniques necessary to become a good drummer. The book is good for beginning drummers regardless of style preference (1981).

2085. Dawson, Alan, and Don DeMichael. *A Manual for the Modern Drummer.* Boston, Berklee: 1975.

Geared to the beginning or intermediate drummer able to read music. The text is divided into three sections: fundamentals of drum set playing, dance band drumming, and jazz. Also included are chapters on playing drum solos and transcribed solo excerpts of famous jazz drummers (1981).

2086. DeJohnette, Jack, and Charlie Perry. *The Art of Modern Jazz Drumming.* New York: Drum Center Publications; 1986.

Deals with principles, techniques, rhythms, and concepts of jazz drumming. Among the topics they cover are "Improvisation," "Interaction of Parts," "Meter Within Meter Phrasing," "Cymbal Patterns," "Triplet Performance Patterns," "Independence Performance Patterns," and more.

2087. DeMearle, Les. *Jazz-Rock Fusion Revised.* Milwaukee: Drum Center Publications/Hal Leonard (Distributor); 1989

Among the topics covered are sixteenth note feels, double time feels, melodic scales, fusion high-hat patterns, odd time signatures, paradiddle jazz inversions, independence, funk in 7/4, variations in 7/8, the bass drum, and open high-hat work. Includes several drum transcriptions.

2088. Dentato, Johnny. *The All New Louis Bellson Drummer's Guide.* New York: Camerica; 1979.

Contains notated rhythms including salsa, rock, jazz, reggae, and batucada (1981).

2089. Erskine, Peter. *Drum Concepts and Techniques.* Studio City, Calif.: 21st Century Publications; 1990.

The author is a renowned jazz-fusion drummer. In this book, he covers the concepts and techniques that he uses in his drumming including drum setup, beats, brushes, phrasing, reading, and more. A complete discography of Erskine's performances on record is also included.

2090. Grossman, Norman. *Drum Styles.* New York: Amsco Music Publishers; 1972.

Addresses the rhythmic basis of jazz, rock, disco, and reggae. Specifically, the author discusses interpretation, techniques for fills, and influences on the previously mentioned styles. There are numerous musical examples.

2091. Houghton, Steve. *A Guide for the Modern Jazz Rhythm Section.* Oskaloosa, Iowa: C.L. BarnHouse Company; 1983.

There are chapters on setup, rhythm section styles, functions, and concepts. In addition, the section on musical interpretation includes individual rhythm section parts for six different big band arrangements. A play-along recording accompanies the text.

2092. Houghton, Steve, and Tom Warrington. *Essential Styles for the Drummer and Bassist.* Van Nuys, Calif.: Alfred Publishing; 1990.

Focuses on comping techniques on the 30 recorded tracks. They cover funk, Afro-Cuban, ballads, Basie swing, bossa nova, up-tempo blues, reggae, rhythm and blues, rock and roll, vamps, and more. The bass and drums are recorded on different channels, thereby allowing users to turn down one or the other channel and substitute their own playing. Included are a chart for each track and suggestions for listening/performance.

2093. Mater, Hans. *An Introduction to Latin Percussion.* Milwaukee: IMP/Music Dispatch (Distributor); 1990.

Suited for private and group study. Discusses performance techniques of Latin American drummers and other instrumentalists, especially in rhythm (salsa, son, rumba, mambo, and more). Demonstrates how to integrate respective rhythms into a rhythm section and also provides useful notes on equipment and maintenance.

2094. Moreira, Airto. *Airto—The Spirit of Percussion.* Studio City, Calif.: 21st Century Publications; 1985.

Primarily a journey into Airto's philosophy and techniques of playing music. Of special note are the insights that he provides on the multiple percussion instruments that he plays.

2095. Morello, Joe. *Joe Morello: Master Studies.* New York: Modern Drummer Books; 1989.

Focuses on hand development and drumstick control. He discusses accent studies, buzz-roll exercises, simple and double-stroke patterns, control studies, flam patterns, dynamic development, endurance studies, meter exercises, and more.

2096. Morton, James. *Killer-Fillers.* Pacific, Mo.: Mel Bay; 1980.

Includes a cassette tape of all exercises. The author focuses on fundamentals (hand-foot coordination, paradiddles, and strokes), as well as swing concepts. The book is permeated with fill concepts.

2097. Norine, Jr., William. *4-Way Fusion for the Modern Drummer.* Boston: Berklee Productions; 1991.

A comprehensive compilation of exercises and extended solos in four-way coordination for the jazz/rock drummer. There are 900 exercises covering a variety of meters (3/4, 4/4, 5/4, 7/4, 7/8), and several solos that entail inherent performance problems. Good for four-way coordination/independence study.

2098. Sims, Rodman. *Fundamentals of Jazz Drumming, Volumes 1 and 2.* Milwaukee: Centerstream Publications/Hal Leonard (Distributor); 1990.

Volume 1 is designed to improve a player's skill from the beginning to the intermediate level. Topics covered include time, dexterity, speed, note groupings (eighth, sixteenth, triplets), jazz interpretation of eighth notes, and more. A cassette tape contains demonstrations of the exercises. Volume 2 is designed to improve a player's skills to an advanced level. Topics covered include "Eighth Note Patterns Between the Snare and Bass Drum," "Triplet Patterns Between the Snare and Bass Drum," and techniques dealing with interpretation.

2099. Sulesbruck, Birger. *Latin American Percussion.* New Albany, Ind.: Jamey Aebersold (Distributor); 1982.

A detailed coverage of rhythms and rhythm instruments; 25 instruments are covered. The book is divided into two major parts. part one focuses on Brazilian and Cuban rhythm instruments, and part two deals with rhythms from Cuba, Brazil, and Trinidad (the Calypso). The three cassette tapes contain examples of Cuban and Brazilian instruments and rhythms. There is a discography as well as numerous photographs and references.

2100. Ulano, Sam. *Drummer's System, Parts 1, 2, 3, and 4.* Radio City Station, New York (P.O. Box 576): Solomon P. Ulano/Sam Ulano; 1991.

Discusses methods and problems of performing in jazz ensembles. He covers cutting with the band, fills, phrasing, shading, solos, and more. The book is permeated with pedagogical suggestions on each concept discussed.

2101. _____. *Simplified Coordination System.* New York: Almo; 1974.

Provides information on the essential coordination skills needed for contemporary drumming. This intermediate-level text concentrates on developing hand independence in six different stages: jazz, Latin, rock, double bass drum reading, two lines, and polyrhythms.

Flute

2102. Dentato, John. *How to Play Jazz Flute.* New York: Charles Hansen; 1975.

Includes 16 jazz standards and originals, many written with jazz variations as well as the original version, with special tips and instructions on playing jazz flute (1981).

Guitar

2103. de Mause, Alan. *How to Play Jazz Guitar: For Group or Individual Instruction.* New York: Acorn Music; 1978.

Progresses from singing, playing and learning jazz styles, to jazz rhythm, harmony, dynamics, structure, and basic improvisation. To use this book effectively the student should be familiar with the first four frets on the guitar (first position). Treatment of these topics is not too thorough (1981).

2104. DiMeola, Al. *Al DiMeola's Picking Techniques.* Milwaukee: 21st Century Publications/Music Dispatch (Distributor); 1991.

Describes his personal approach to guitar playing. He uses excerpts and exercises from his music to advocate a systematic approach to improving one's performance ability.

2105. Diorio, Joe. *Jazz: Joe Diorio.* Milwaukee: REH/Music Dispatch (Distributor); 1989.

Contains a discussion of scales including major, minor, altered, as well as ii–V–I's, and turnarounds. These working concepts are combined in a solo and are demonstrated on a cassette tape.

2106. Dunbar, Ted. *The Inter-relationship of Chords, Scales, and Fingerboard of Each One of the 12 Tonalities of the Guitar.* Kendall Park, N.J.: Dante Publishing Company; 1981.

A new system of breaking down the 20-fret neck into 12 separate fingerboards. The purpose is to allow the student to see each tonality separately, with all of its corresponding scales and chords, for understanding finger-ings, the entire tonal connection for each key, and the performance of ideas.

2107. Kessel, Barney. *The Guitar.* Lebanon, Ind.: Studio P/R; 1975.

Helps guitarists with varying degrees of experience. The book covers topics from fingering patterns to chord progressions and substitutions. This is primarily an all-purpose, how-to book (1981).

2108. Leavitt, William G. *Melodic Rhythms for Guitar.* Boston: Berklee; 1975.

Presents 42 exercises and 92 harmonized etudes, with chord symbols given for each example. The text is geared to the guitarist with some knowledge of the basics of music and is particularly good for sight-reading and jazz patterns (1981).

2109. Lee, Ronny, and Charles Hansen. *Jazz Guitar.* Two volumes. New York: Charles Hansen; 1975.

Includes 10 theory lessons, jazz solo lessons, and assignments in Volume 1. Volume 2 contains 42 jazz solo lessons, several musical examples, and some information on voicing (1981).

2110. Matson, Rod. *Basic Jazz/Rock Improvisation for All Treble Clef Instruments Including Guitar.* Westbury, N.Y.: Pro Art; 1974.

Surveys the fundamentals of music theory (scales, key, intervals, chords), in the first part, and offer a step-by-step approach to the construction of original improvised solos in the second (1981).

2111. McKee, Pat. *Jazz Harmonies: The System.* Milwaukee: Hal Leonard; 1991.

A method designed to accentuate the learning of chord voicing. Discusses four-string chord voicing in all major and minor keys, provides 288 chord voicings, and presents a method of understanding chord construction and functions.

2112. Middlebrook, Ron. *Scales and Modes in the Beginning (updated).* Milwaukee: Centerstream Publications/Music Dispatch (Distributor); 1991.

A comprehensive scale book written for the guitar. The book is divided into four sections: fretboard visualization, the breaking down of the whole into parts; scale terminology, which focuses on whole and half steps, scale degrees, intervals; scale and mode, with applications and exercises; and four-scale, which discusses chord/scale relationships. Includes tablature.

2113. Nunes, Warren. *Jazz Guitar Series.* Five volumes. New York: Charles Hansen; 1976.

Covers the entire range of guitar playing from the basics of chord construction to chord progressions, substitutions, fingering patterns, and much more. Volume 1 covers rhythm and background chords; volume 2 covers the blues; volume 3, guitar solos; volume 4, solo patterns; and volume 5, jazz guitar portfolio.

2114. Pass, Joe. *Joe Pass Guitar Method.* Milwaukee: Hal Leonard; 1990.

Discusses how to develop an individual approach to improvisation by learning chords, scales, and practice patterns. He uses transcriptions and original compositions to develop individual skills.

2115. Roberts, Howard, and James Stewart. *The Howard Roberts Guitar Book.* North Hollywood, Ca.; Playback Music; 1971.

Contains five sections dealing with topics ranging from the fingerboard and licks to improvising, comping, and chord solo playing. Requires some knowledge of music (1981).

2116. Roberts, Howard. *Howard Robert's Guitar Manual Sight Reading.* North Hollywood, Ca.: Playback Music; 1972.

Covers subjects such as sight reading on single and combined strings, linear reading, and ledger lines. Helpful in developing an awareness of problems confronting guitarists (1981).

2117. Roberts, Howard. *Super Chops: Jazz Guitar Techniques in 20 Weeks.* North Hollywood, Ca.: Playback Music; 1978.

Gives the improvising guitarist a regimented program of weekly-programmed project lessons. The author recommends practice of 50 minutes per day, six days per week. Previous musical background is necessary (1981).

2118. Smith, Johnny. *The Johnny Smith Approach to the Guitar.* Two volumes. Pacific, Mo.: Mel Bay; 1976.

Focuses on the harmonic aspects of guitar playing. The explanations of chord symbols and types, voicing alternatives, tonal perspectives, progressions, and other supporting materials are excellent.

2119. Strum, Harvey, and Harold Branch. *Improvising Jazz and Blues Guitar.* Plainview, N.Y.: Harold Branch; 1977.

Deals with blues fundamentals in beginning improvisational instruction. The students write out and play their improvisations to gain skill in reading and notating music.

2120. Volpe, Harry, and Jimmy Dale. *Jazz Improvisation on 1000 Chords.* Three volumes. New York: Clef Music; 1974.

Deals with both beginning and advanced levels and covers the entire range of chords and chord functions. For each of the 1,000 chords presented there are from three to five inversions, patterns, scales, functions, and guitar fingerings given (1981).

2121. Wise, Les. *The Ultimate Lick System.* Milwaukee: REH/Music Dispatch (Distributor); 1991.

A course designed to teach the guitar styles and theoretical concepts of selected jazz artists. Lesson one covers arpeggio substitutions in the styles of Wes Montgomery, J. Smith, and Jimmy Raney; lesson two discusses scale substitutions in the styles of Tal Farlow, Joe Pass, Herb Ellis, and Jim Hall; lesson three focuses on tension and resolution in the styles of Pat Martino, George Benson, and Wes Montgomery; lesson four covers jazz blues in the styles of George Benson, Wes Montgomery, Tal Farlow, and Joe Pass; lesson five describes chord soloing in the styles of Barney Kessel, Kenny Burrell, Wes Montgomery, and D. Blickert; and lesson six covers virtuoso guitar concepts in the styles of Joe Pass, Barney Kessel, and J. Smith.

Keyboard

2122. Butler, Artie. *Creative Keyboard Sounds.* Sherman Oaks, Calif.: Gwyn; 1976.

Acquaints keyboard players with basic rock, boogaloo, gospel, and Latin rock. Exercises and explanations for each style are included (1981).

2123. Delp, Ron. *Vibraphone Technique: Four Mallet Chord Voicing.* Boston: Berklee Publications; 1992.

Provides information on chord voicing, both in comping and chord melodies. He uses numerous musical examples, exercises, phrases, and tunes to sequentially demonstrate modern chord voicing techniques. Specific topics covered include tensions, guide tones, background comping, harmonic rhythm, voicing with the melody, and more.

2124. Dobbins, Bill. *The Contemporary Jazz Pianist.* Two volumes. Jamestown, R.I.: GAMT Music Press; 1978.

Comprehensively treats the entire range of jazz piano playing, covering topics from the basics of improvisation to a wide variety of scales (modes, progressions, substitution, and much more). (1981)

2125. Fisher, Clare. *Harmonic Exercises for Piano.* New York: Warner; 1973.

Contains 15 types of harmonic exercises for piano designed to be performed in several different keys. The book is intended for the advanced jazz theory student interested in new voicing and harmonic sequences (1981).

2126. Friedman, David. *Vibraphone Technique: Dampening and Pedaling.* Boston: Berklee; 1992.

Deals in depth with new dampening and pedaling techniques. The techniques are designed to increase flexibility both in phrasing and in multiline performing, thereby expanding the expressive freedom of the performer. There are 27 etudes demonstrating his theories.

2127. LaPorta, John. *Functional Piano for the Improviser.* DeLevan, N.Y.: Kendor Music; 1969.

Based on learning the harmonic rhythm of a tune through its application and analysis at the keyboard. Seventy-two tunes with voicing for all chords are included for this purpose. Very thorough.

2128. Mance, Junior, and Charles Hansen. *How to Play Blues Piano.* New York: Charles Hansen; 1975.

Introduces the beginning jazz student to piano blues techniques and the basic sounds of the blues.

2129. Mehegan, John. *Jazz Improvisation.* Four volumes; 1958–1965. New York: Watson-Guptill; 1965.

Although geared to the pianist, this collection is permeated with useful information for all jazz instrumentalists. The four volumes are organized as follows: volume 1, *Tonal and Rhythmic Principles,* covers the basic elements (chord, scales, articulation); volume 2, *Jazz Rhythm and the Improvised Line,* focuses on the importance of rhythm and development of improvisational lines, illustrated with numerous transcriptions; volume 3, *Swing and the Early Progressive Piano Styles,* analyzes the styles of Bud Powell, George Shearing, Horace Silver, Art Tatum, and Teddy Wilson; volume 4, *Contemporary Piano Styles,* uses Oscar Peterson as a model, and discusses technical aspects of jazz improvisation, articulation, phrasing, extended chords, and more.

2130. Peterson, Oscar. *Jazz Exercises and Pieces for the Young Pianist. No 1, No. 2, and No. 3.* New York: Charles Hansen; 1975.

Offers excellent original exercises and tunes to strengthen the fingers and teach vocabulary, phrasing, and technique to the young jazz pianist (1981).

2131. Sandole, Adolph. *Jazz Piano Left Hand.* New York: Sandole; 1978.

Deals usefully with progressions, comping, and varying chords. Contains several musical examples (1981).

2132. Schwartz, S. *Jazz Patterns Made Easier. Jazz Beginnings Made Easier. Jazz Improvisation Made Easier. Boogie Basics Theory. Jazz Instructor (Step by Step). Erroll Garner Jazz Stylings. Midnight Sun. Fats Waller Jazz Stylings. Country Blues.* 1974–1977. New York: Charles Hansen; 1977.

Presents detailed lessons for the average pianist on blues, the walking bass, the voicing of chords, improvisation, syncopation, suspensions, inner voices, and more. Also included are numerous arrangements of popular songs in jazz style as well as pieces, which illustrate jazz style and concepts.

2133. Southern, Jeri. *Interpreting Popular Music at the Keyboard.* Lebanon, Ind.: Studio P/R; 1978.

Discusses how to transform printed symbols into contemporary sounds, moving from the simple to the more complex application of chords. This is primarily a piano voicing text not intended for beginners.

2134. Storeman, Win. *Jazz Piano: Ragtime to Rock Jazz.* New York: Arco; 1975.

Covers the basics of several jazz styles with several musical examples for intermediate-level pianists.

2135. Sudnow, David. *Ways of the Hand: The Organization of Improvised Conduct.* Cambridge, Mass.: Harvard University Press; 1978.

The author is an ethnographer, sociologist, and amateur jazz pianist. In this book, he discusses how he learned to play improvised jazz. The book is divided into three parts: "Beginnings," "Going for the Sounds," and "Going for the Jazz." He uses semiotic techniques to aid the reader in seeing, hearing, and thinking along with him. There are photographs and descriptions of keyboard fingers and some musical analysis.

2136. Tillis, Frederick. *Jazz Theory and Improvisation.* New York: Charles Hansen; 1975.

Presents materials ranging from basic harmonic concepts and ii–V7 progressions to substitute chords and quartal and secundal harmony. All musical examples are written for the piano (1981).

2137. Wheaton, Jack. *Basic Modal Improvisation Techniques for Keyboard Instruments.* Studio City, Calif.: Dick Grove; 1983.

Presents the 12 basic modes or scales that are used in improvisation. He treats each mode regarding structure, usage, and some of the most common progressions associated with it.

Phrasing

2138. Brown, Marshall. *Duets in Jazz Phrasing.* New York: Charles Colin; 1961.

Covers numerous topics such as shakes, natural fall-off, bends, and false fingering. Good for beginning players working on jazz phrasing on treble clef instruments (1981).

2139. Giuffre, Jimmy. *Jazz Phrasing and Interpretation for C Instruments.* New York: Associated Music; 1969.

Acquaints students, either in classroom or private study, with principles of jazz phrasing that they can apply to actual pieces in performance. The author examines each area of phrasing, outlining some general practices, then examines specific exercises (e.g., uneven eighths, slide-slur, short pickup), pointing out what is needed to make a jazz passage. Good approach to the topic (1981).

2140. Rothmans, Joel. *Reading with Jazz Interpretation.* New York: JR Publications; 1965.

Aims at helping musicians attain the correct jazz articulation and phrasing. He includes musical exercises (addition to 1981).

Rhythm

2141. Coker, Jerry. *Figured Reading Series: Rhythmic Studies of Today's Music.* New York: Columbia Pictures Publications; 1988.

Discusses how to interpret rhythms that are found in contemporary jazz and commercial music. The two cassettes contain numerous vocal and instrumental demonstrations of rhythmic inflections of musical lines. The text covers several different styles, including swing, funk-rock, rock, and Latin.

2142. Colin, Charles, and Bugs Bower. *Rhythms Complete. Vol. I.* New York: Charles Colin; 1975.

Represents the entire range of rhythmic problems in 238 melodies. For treble clef instruments only but good for improving sight reading for all musicians (1981).

2143. _____. *Rhythms: for All Instruments. Vol. 2.* New York: Charles Colin; 1976.

Designed to improve sight reading. The studies cover a myriad of rhythmic problems (1981).

Saxophone

2144. Cooper, Bob. *Jazz Development for the Saxophonist.* Pacific, Mo.: Mel Bay; 1983.

Designed to aid the understanding of harmony, theory, phrasing, and articulation. The author offers suggestions on how to use chord progressions, melodic patterns, and scales. Among the scales/harmonic concepts covered are diminished, whole-tone, and pentatonic scales, and nonharmonic and ii–V7 patterns. Number exercises and several solos are included.

2145. Harris, Eddie. *Jazz Cliché Capers.* Hollywood: Highland Music; 1978.

Deals with jazz licks, or the short, popular phrases played by most soloists during several jazz eras. In the introduction, the author suggests eight ways modern jazz saxophonists play cliché effects. Recommended for all jazz saxophonists (1981).

2146. Herman, Woody. *Sax Scales, Chords, and Solos.* New York: Charles Hansen; 1974.

Presents in 48 pages a complete method for saxophonists interested in scales and other studies. Six Woody Herman solos are included (1981).

2147. Nash, Ted. *Ted Nash's Studies in High Harmonics for Tenor and Alto Saxophone.* Milwaukee: MCA/Hal Leonard; 1987.

A book of fingering charts, exercises, and solos. Primarily concerned with procedures and techniques one uses to make so-called "False Notes."

2148. Niehaus, Lennie. *Basic Jazz Conception for Saxophone.* Hollywood, Ca.: TRY; 1964.

Designed for beginning students interested in jazz rhythms, articulations, and phrasings. The first section contains 12 exercises emphasizing various rhythmic patterns developed through a melodic-song approach. The second section contains 10 tunes, which incorporate all of the material presented in the exercises. The author phrases all materials (1981).

2149. Niehaus, Lennie. *Intermediate Jazz Conception for Saxophone.* Hollywood, Ca.: TRY; 1966.

Stresses the fundamental rhythms, articulations, and phrasings commonly used by jazz groups. The book is divided into two sections—the first consists of 20 exercises on various rhythmic patterns; the second consists of 25 etudes that utilizes all the material presented in the exercises. In both exercises and etudes care is taken to phrase all the materials. This is a good book for students with some background in jazz (1981).

2150. _____. *Jazz Conception for Saxophone.* Hollywood, Ca.: TRY; 1964.

Focuses on rhythmic patterns for more advanced students. Twenty etudes in 3/4 and 5/4 meter cover several keys with a phrasing section included (1981).

2151. Seckler, Stan. *Take the Lead.* Lebanon, Ind.: Houston Publishing, Incorporated; 1991.

Discusses the role and techniques that a lead alto saxophonist is often called on to play in a performance. Balancing the section, rehearsal suggestions, and section phrasing are addressed.

2152. Viola, Joseph. *The Technique of the Saxophone.* Three volumes. Boston: Berklee and Hal Leonard; 1979.

Designed to facilitate the technical and musical development of the saxophone student. Through exercises and solos he teaches harmony, improvisation, and melodic and rhythmic techniques. The volumes are organized as follows: volume 1 covers all major scales and related modes with 210 exercises enabling the student to perform any major scale beginning on any scale tone; volume 2 continues and expands techniques covered in volume 1 and focuses on chordal concepts with exercises built on basic and extended chords; volume 3 deals with rhythms found in contemporary music, containing duet exercises for rhythms in simple meter and solo exercises in compound time signatures. In addition, there are 15 advanced etudes utilizing diverse rhythmic concepts.

2153. White, Andrew. *Improvisation.* Washington, D.C.: Andrew's Music; 1981.

Provides suggestions on learning how to improvise from a personal viewpoint. He covers techniques that he uses in his improvisations.

2154. Yellin, Peter. *Jazz Saxophone.* New York: Charles Colin; 1982.

A beginning method for interpreting jazz rhythms and articulations. There are 19 etudes organized by styles (swing, rock, ballad, Latin, and others), each preceded by an explanation of the style. He also provides several examples of the alignment of chord symbols and notated rhythms.

Treble Clef Instruments

2155. Applebaum, Stan. *Encyclopedia of Progressive Duets.* New York: Charles Colin; 1973.

Treats progressive duets for treble instruments with chord symbols and different tempo markings included in the first section. The second section, "Duets in the Modern Jazz Idiom," contains 10 original duets by Irving

Bush. The third section, "Duet Inventions," has works compiled and edited by Constance Weldon with several duets in keys that have no more than three flats. These duets, as those in the previous section, might be more helpful to pop rather than jazz performers (1981).

2156. Baker, David N. *Advanced Improvisation.* Chicago: Maher Publication; 1974.

The third volume in the trilogy after *Jazz Improvisation* (1969) and *Techniques of Improvisation* (1968–1970). This book is designed by content and concept to provide all information needed to implement the universal concepts and techniques necessary for written and improvised composition regardless of idiom. He covers a myriad of improvisational facets including rhythmic and metric materials, pitch materials, and related topics such as "Psychological Approach to Communication Through an Improvised Solo," "Drama in Music," "Idiomatic Devices for Trombone," "Twelve-Tone Techniques," and more. In the discussion of "Pitch Materials," he covers numerous scales, including composite, bitonal, and polytonal. There are numerous examples, a "Suggested Listening and Study" discography (classical and jazz), organized by composer, complete with a selected list of concepts that are inherent in the composition. Very thorough.

2157. Branch, Harold. *Improvising 2-Bar Jazz Licks.* West Babylon, N.Y.: Harold Branch; 1979.

Based on harmony (C, D, E♭, F, G, A, B♭), with over 50 improvised licks included. The licks are preceded by an outline of the major scale, chord, passing tones, and changing tones. For treble clef instruments, however, they can be transposed (1981).

2158. Most, Abe. *Jazz Improvisation for Treble Clef Instruments.* Sherman Oaks, Calif.: Gwyn; 1975.

Contains 25 etudes broken down into jazz phrases. At the beginning of each exercise is a phrase or musical idea. The student is to learn the exercise in all keys by using the circle of fifths (1981).

Trombone

2159. Baker, David N. *Contemporary Techniques for the Trombone: A Revolutionary Approach to the Problems of Music in the Twentieth Century. Vols. 1 and 2.* New York: Charles Colin; 1974.

Addresses itself to the teacher, student, amateur, or professional trombonist interested in master techniques of trombone performance (jazz and non-jazz), in twentieth-century music. The coverage ranges from exercises in developing skills with angular lines to some advanced concepts in jazz playing. The second volume begins with polymeric music and continues with information on metric modulations. Profiles on two contemporary trombonists (Jim Fulkerson and Stuart Dempster), and suggested listening and study lists are included. These are thorough volumes recommended for serious trombonists (1981).

2160. Johnson, J. J. *Exercises and Etudes for the Jazz Instrumentalist.* New Albany, Ind.: Jamey Aebersold; 1998.

A collection of original piece for trombone that feature common and uncommon time signatures and keys, and stylistic pieces from bebop and ballads to funk.

2161. Van Lier, Bart. *Coordination Training Program for Trombone.* New Albany, Ind.: Jamey Aebersold; 2001.

Not limited to jazz trombonists, but offers good suggestions on three elements of playing: air, lips, and tongue. Provides numerous musical examples to solve the aforementioned issues.

2162. Waltrous, Bill, and Alan Ralph. *Trombonisms.* New Albany, Ind.: Jamey Aebersold; 1998.

A book and CD that goes beyond the introduction of standard techniques to introduce new concepts like sound production. Numerous exercises and examples.

Trumpet

2163. Farmer, Art. *The Art of Art Farmer.* New Albany, Ind.: Jamey Aebersold; 2000.

Addresses the technical demands of the beginning improviser, and includes chapters on daily warmups, mouthpiece practice, lip/tongue slurs, pedal points, and essential jazz scales.

2164. Harbison, Pat. *20 Authentic Bebop Solos.* New Albany, Ind.: Jamey Aebersold; 2000.

The solos are based on standards often performed during the era. The solos accentuate the articulations and phrasings heard during the era, and can be played with the Jamey Aebersold Play-A-Long volumes 6, 14, and 36. A rhythm section accompanies the solos.

2165. _____. *Technical Studies for Modern Trumpet.* New Albany, Ind.: Jamey Aebersold; 1999.

Designed to develop technical fluency and ear training. Also incorporates modern jazz scales, and a series of daily studies.

2166. McNeil, John. *The Art of Jazz Trumpet.* New Albany, Ind.: Jamey Aebersold; 2001.

A book and CD, his former two volume series has been revised and now includes a play-along CD. The chapters cover articulation, multiple tonguing, wide interval improvisation, alternate fingerings, circular breathing, microphone techniques, and more.

2167. _____. *Jazz Trumpet Techniques for Developing Articulation and Fast Fingers.* Lebanon, Ind.: Studio P/R; 1976.

Discusses how to improve technique and articulation. Exercises, examples, and methods of practice designed to help the jazz performer are provided (1981).

2168. Mintzer, Bob. *14 Blues and Funk Etudes for Trumpet.* New Albany, Ind.: Jamey Aebersold; 2001.

A book and two CDs that contains solo-from etude with theoretical explanations, performance suggestions, and practice tips. One CD is a Play-along and the other features members of the *Yellow Jackets* performing the etudes.

2169. Sandoval, Arturo. *Playing Techniques and Performance Studies for Trumpet.* Three volumes. New Albany, Ind.: Jamey Aebersold; 2001.

The three volumes cover basic, intermediate, and advanced levels, and cover issues and concepts such as daily routines, interpretation exercises, developing technical expertise, and more. He includes a CD of him playing many of the exercises.

2170. Shew, Bobby. *Exercises and Etudes for Jazz and Classical Players.* New Albany, Ind.: Jamey Aebersold; 2000.

Designed to enhance the technical ability coupled with harmonic awareness and facility.

Instrument-Specific Approaches to Improvisation

Bass

2171. Doherty, Steve, and Warren Nunes. *Solo Improvisation Techniques for the Jazz Bass.* New York: Hansen House; 1981.

One of a series of four books; the others are for flute, saxophone, and piano. There are several exercises, which use chords and melodic motifs as a basis for improvisation. Tonality and scales (harmonic and melodic minor, diminished, and whole-tone) are also addressed.

2172. Drew, Lucas. *Basic Electric Bass.* New York: Sam Fox; 1977.

Includes several solos and duets for electric bass. The solos, though not complex, lend themselves to harmonic analysis (1981).

Flute

2173. Dentato, John. *How to Play Jazz Flute No. 2.* New York: Charles Hansen; 1976.

Features 18 jazz standards and originals arranged with the original melody and chord symbols plus a jazz variation (1981).

2174. _____. *Jazz Flute for Christmas.* New York: Charles Hansen; 1977.

Contains 17 Christmas standards and carols arranged with the original version facing a new jazz version (1981).

2175. Doherty, Steve, and Warren Nunes. *Solo Improvisation Techniques for Jazz Flute.* New York: Hansen House; 1981.

Another book in the *Solo Improvisation Techniques Series.* Like the other methods, this book contains several exercises designed to facilitate one's ability to play chord changes. He uses chords, motifs, harmonic and melodic minor, and diminished and whole-tone scales to build solos.

Guitar

2176. Baione, Larry. *Berklee Practice Method: Guitar.* Boston: Berklee Press; 2000.

Dedicated to preparing one for live performances. Covers specifics like sharpening your comping, soloing, practical skills, and overall musicianship on stage. Begins with how to hold a guitar pick, and covers issues like swinging eight notes, following a chart, soloing in different keys, and more. The CD teaches one how to trade fours, and how to practice call and response patterns.

2177. Baker, Mickey. *Jazz and Rhythm 'n' Blues Guitar.* New York: Amsco Music; 1969.

Contains 14 solos and duets, in jazz and rhythm and blues styles, for guitar. Requires good reading skills (1981).

2178. Boukas, Richard. *Jazz Riffs for Guitar.* New York: Music Sales; 1978.

Presents guitar riffs in the styles of Django Reinhardt, Charlie Christian, Joe Pass, Wes Montgomery, and Tal Farlow. Arranged in order of difficulty, each riff is presented with alternate fingerings for easy playing in difficult keys. A solo at the end of the book combines short and long phrases into a complete piece. A discography is included (1981).

2179. Bredice, Vincent. *Guitar Improvisation.* Pacific, Mo.: Mel Bay; 1976.

Includes a wide range of information on guitar improvisation, including the harmonic aspects of bass line construction. Although this book is geared to the beginning student, it should be supplemented with other materials (1981).

2180. Christiansen, Corey. *Jazz Scales for Guitar.* Pacific, Mo.: Mel Bay; 2000.

A book for beginners that proceeds from the difference between whole and half steps to common modes and some jazz sales. Includes many notated examples and some suggestions for performing.

2181. Diorio, Joe. *Intervallic Designs for Jazz Guitar.* Milwaukee: Hal Leonard; 2000.

The author breaks away from the rigid and systematic approach to playing jazz, and advocates an imaginative approach that draws from intuitive reasoning. His lines and examples weave in and out of conventional harmonies and altered chords, thereby creating a sense of exploration. A CD is included.

2182. Fowler, William. *Guitar Patterns for Improvisation.* Chicago: Downbeat Publishing; 1974.

Deals with the guitar fingerboard as well as chords, structures, progressions, melodic materials, ii–V patterns, chord-scale relationships, chord quality, and much more (1981).

2183. Greene, Ted. *Jazz Guitar: Single Note Soloing. Vols. I and 2.* Westlake Village, Calif.: Dale Zdenek; 1978.

Covers in the first volume the basics of chord structures, progressions, and so on. Volume 2 is more advanced, covering playing through changes, chromatic tones, basing solos on a given melody, and altered scales (1981).

2184. Grossel, Jack. *Jazz Rhythm Guitar.* Milwaukee: Hal Leonard; 2001.

Teaches basic chord construction, syncopated rhythms, and standard comping techniques for the beginning guitarist. Contains several diagrams, practice tips, and technical suggestions to compliment the numerous exercises. A CD is included.

2185. Ingram, Adrian. *Jazz Guitar Greats.* Pacific, Mo.: Mel Bay; 2001.

Geared to immediate to advanced-level guitarists who wish to emulate the styles of Kenny Burrell, Pat Martino, Wes Montgomery, Johnny Smith, and Joe Pass. Includes historical information before the exercises on chord substitutions, "Minorisation," and altered tension, chord/scale relationships, comping, pedals and octave playing.

2186. Kessell, Barney. *The Guitar.* Hackensack, N.J.: Wehman Brothers; 1967.

Covers the gamut from selecting a teacher and guitar to becoming a professional player. The 15 chapters focus on topics such as transposition, technique, chords and voicing, substitutions, improvisation, and accompanying. Recommended for beginning and advanced guitarists.

2187. Lucas, Paul. *Jazz Improvisation for the Rock/Blues Guitarist.* Lebanon, Ind.: Studio P/R; 1978.

Puts forth a comprehensive method from the basics to chord voicing, blues progressions, and blues scales. (1981).

2188. Martino, Pat. *Jazz: Pat Martino.* Milwaukee: REH Hotline Series/Music Dispatch (Distributor); 1991.

Martino discusses and demonstrates his improvisational techniques and philosophies. Includes a cassette demonstration tape.

2189. Savage, Ron, and Casey Scheuerall. *Berklee Practice Method: Drum Set.* Boston: Berklee Press; 1998.

Proceeds from how to grip a pair of drum sticks to suggestions regarding accompanying, and how to play different styles. Also covers how to follow a chart, develop stage awareness, and the "stop time" break for drums.

2190. Sokolow, Fred. *Fretboard Road Maps: Jazz Guitar.* Milwaukee: Hal Leonard; 2000.

Teaches on how to navigate the guitar fretboard, and to discern the patterns that characterize complicated jazz solos. He author uses logical reasoning to explain his approach, and musical exercises, diagrams, and charts to demonstrate them.

Keyboard

2191. Amadle, Jimmy. *Jazz Improvisation: How to Play It and Teach It.* New Albany, Ind.: Jamey Aebersold; 2000.

Uses the concept of tension and release and cadences, and also covers basic harmonic progressions, blues, bitonality, and modal practices.

2192. Adler, Wilfred, and Mel Bay. *Piano Improvisation.* Pacific, Mo.: Mel Bay; 1978.

Designed to help the traditionally trained pianist learn to improvise. This text, which is good for advanced performers, contains materials in all keys with harmonic and melodic materials used in jazz emphasized (1981).

2193. Denke, Debbie. *The Aspiring Jazz Pianist.* Santa Barbara, Calif.: Wingspan; 1991.

A method for developing improvisational skills, Denke covers three-note chords, major sevenths, dominant sevenths, minor sevenths, ii–V progressions, half and full diminished seventh chords, rhythm problems, and more. There is a play-along cassette that demonstrates the concepts covered in the book.

2194. Doherty, Steve, and Warren Nunes. *Solo Improvisation Techniques for the Jazz Piano.* New York: Hansen House; 1981.

Unlike the other three books in this series, this book contains numerous comping (chords and voicing), exercises. They also present chords, scales, and motifs as devices for use in building improvised solos.

2195. Haerle, Dan. *Pocket Guide to Jazz Improvisation.* New Albany, Ind.: Jamey Aebersold; 2003.

Focused on the theory and methods necessary to improvise jazz. He includes chapters on chords, chord symbols, voicing, blues ii/V/Is, guide tones and more.

2196. _____. *Scales for Jazz Improvisation.* New Albany, Ind.: Jamey Aebersold; 1998.

A syllabus of 21 different scales used by jazz improvisers, including major, minor, modal, and scales like the Lydian Dominant and more.

2197. _____. *Jazz Improvisation for Keyboard Players.* Three volumes. Lebanon, Ind.: Studio P/R; 1977.

Volume 1—*Basic Concepts*—deal with creating melodies using the left hand, pianistic approaches to improvising, and chord progressions. Volume 2—*Intermediate Concepts*—deals with developing melodies, further use of the left hand, and scale choices for improvisation. Volume 3—*Advanced Concepts*—deals with advanced factors affecting scale choice and approaches to harmonic conception. A useful, well-presented series.

2198. Harvey, Eddie. *Jazz Piano.* London: English Universities Press; 1974.

An introduction to the fundamentals of piano improvisation, Harvey addresses scale and chord relationships and blues and gives several musical examples of ideas that can be used. He incorporates some standard jazz tunes as models for improvisation.

2199. Kerper, Mitch. *Jazz Riffs for Piano.* New York: Mitch Sales; 1978.

Consists of riffs and phrases in the styles of Bud Powell, Herbie Hancock, and McCoy Tyner, for the intermediate jazz pianist. A series of solos combines short and long riffs into complete pieces. Arrangement is from simple to moderately complex. A discography is included with this extremely useful and practical book (1981).

2200. Kroepel, Bob, and Mel Bay. *Piano Rhythm Patterns.* Pacific, Mo.: Mel Bay; 1978.

Contains a wide variety of accompaniment patterns for the left hand in jazz, gospel, and rhythm and blues styles (1981).

2201. Olmstead, Neil. *Solo Jazz Piano.* New Albany, Ind.: Jamey Aebersold; 2001.

Focuses on the improvisational techniques of Dave McKenna and Lennie Tristano, and begins with a review of chord symbols, bass line development, and how to perform several melodic lines simultaneously. Demonstrates how to develop solo lines that embellish and support the melody, and how to use lead sheets to develop your own improvisational ideas. The 21 lessons focus on practice exercises and compositions based on jazz standards. There are transcriptions of improvisations, and the CD enables the student to hear the improvisational ideas in practice.

Saxophone

2202. Bay, Mel. *Saxophone Improvising Workbook.* Pacific, Mo.: Mel Bay; 1979.

Studies the theory that guides improvisation in depth. Chordal, scalar, and harmonic approaches are covered (1981).

2203. Fazio, Dean, and Warren Nunes. *Solo Improvisation Techniques for the Jazz Saxes.* New York: Hansen House; 1981.

Addresses ways of developing improvisations. They use chords, motifs, several scales, and triads as devices in building improvised solos. There are several written and recorded examples.

2204. Gerard, Charley. *Improvising Jazz Sax.* New Albany, Ind.: Jamey Aebersold; 2000.

For performers with little or no improvisation experience. He covers scales, sample licks, different chord patterns, blues, and transcribed solos.

2205. Jones, Thad. *Lead Sax Book.* New Albany, Ind.: Jamey Aebersold; 1997.

A compilation of advice and suggestions to play the lead alto, flute, and soprano parts of tunes recorded on his Consummation Album. Includes the following tunes: "Dedication," "It Only Happens Every Time," "A Child is Born," "Us," "Ahunk Ahunk," "Fingers," and "Consummation."

2206. Lateef, Yusef. *123 Duets.* New Albany, Ind.: Jamey Aebersold; 2000.

Can be used for saxophone and other treble clef instruments. Very creative, and contains interesting harmonic, melodic, and rhythmic turns.

2207. Luckey, Robert. *Sax Altissmo-High Note Development for the Contemporary Player.* Second edition. New Albany, Ind.: Jamey Aebersold; 2001.

In this revised edition, the author includes separate fingerings for alto, baritone, tenor, and soprano saxophones, as well as excerpts from famous saxophone pieces. The special etude section can be performed with the rhythm tracks in volume 43 of the Aebersold Play-A-Long series.

2208. McGhee, Andy. *Improvisation for Saxophone: The Scale-Mode Approach.* Boston: Berklee Press Publications. (Distributed by Hal Leonard Publishing Corporation); 1974.

A method designed to develop the technique and chord-scale-mode relationships necessary to improvise. Exercises use modes and scales (harmonic and melodic minor, diminished, and whole-tone), and include chord symbols for rhythm accompaniment. Five solos, based on discussed concepts, are included. Each of 15 chapters begins with a short explanation of the mode or scale.

2209. _____. *Modal Studies for Saxophone: A Scale-Mode Approach.* Boston: Berklee Press Publications. (Distributed by Hal Leonard Publishing Corporation); 1991.

According to the author, "The objective of this study method is to help you develop familiarity with the 'sounds' and 'shapes' of those melodic patterns which are used in traditional and contemporary improvisational styles" (foreword). There are 13 sections covering all modes, and minor, diminished, and augmented scales. Each section follows an identical format; pentatonic segments implying the modality of the phrase; chordal arpeggios with the same modal relationship; and melodic variations based on the modal scale or combining different modal scales. There are no articulations or tempos indicated.

2210. Miedema, Harry. *Jazz Styles and Analysis: Alto Sax.* Chicago: Maher; 1975.

Approaches the history of the jazz alto saxophone through recorded solos that are transcribed and annotated. The book also includes profiles of each musician whose solo is transcribed. The coverage of alto saxophonists is wide and the transcriptions are good (1981).

2211. Niehaus, Lennie. *Jazz Improvisation for Saxophone.* New Albany, Ind.: Jamey Aebersold; 1999.

Uses a variety of chord changes, duets, etudes, and solos to teach improvisation.

2212. _____. *Jazz Conception for the Saxophone*. New Albany, Ind.: Jamey Aebersold; 1999.

A six volume series that follows a step-by-step process to teach the student the essential concepts of jazz style/concept. The series focuses on concepts like articulating, phrasing, sound, and much more.

2213. _____. *Six Jazz Duets*. New Albany, Ind.: Jamey Aebersold; 2001.

Two volumes designed to develop jazz articulation, phrasing, and style concepts. The duets are also available for other saxophones.

2214. _____. *Lennie Niehaus Plays the Blues in All Keys*. New Albany, Ind.: Jamey Aebersold; 2000.

A book and CD that features the author performing the transcribed solos that are related to volume 42 of the Aebersold Play-A-Long series.

Strings

2215. Baker, David N. *Jazz Expressions and Explorations for Strings*. New Albany, Ind.: Jamey Aebersold; 2001.

Includes string specific technical information, and includes a systematic approach to jazz expression for string performers. He suggests ways and means for performers to become more musical in their articulations, phrasings, and feelings. The book is permeated with patterns and phrases to illustrate the concept being discussed.

2216. Bardfeld, Sam. *Latin Violin: How to Play Salsa, Charanga, and Latin Jazz Violin*. New Albany, Ind.: Jamey Aebersold; 2001.

A book and CD that includes chapters such as "A Brief History of Charanga", "How the Violin Was Afro-Cubanized," "How the Music Works," and "Solo Transcriptions and Analysis (Miguel Barbon, José Silva, okAlfredo De La Fe," Lewis Kahn, Rob Thomas, and others). The CD includes famous Afro-Cuban solos, and an extended play-along session featuring John Almendra, Mongo Santamaria, and Willie Colon.

2217. _____. *A Complete Improvisation Method for Stringed Instruments*. New Albany, Ind.: Jamey Aebersold; 2002. Two volumes.

This two-volume method covers topics ranging from the nature and terminology of improvisation to basic approaches and annotated solos. The reference charts illustrate cycles, multiple stops, progressions, patterns, scales, and more. Volume 1 is devoted to violin and viola and volume 2 to cello and bass viol.

2218. Glaser, Mett, and Stephané Grapelli. *Jazz Violin.* New York: Oak; 1981.

An insightful and scholarly assessment of the role and function of the violin in jazz. The insider perspectives of Grapelli, Jean-Luc Ponty, Stuff Smith, and Joe Venuti aid the book. Also includes solo transcriptions, analysis of styles, and references to recordings. Selected discography.

2219. Lowinger, Gene. *Jazz Violin.* New York: George Schirmer; 1981.

Contains many musical examples and a synopsis of the styles of several blues/jazz/fusion violinists. Among the artists covered are Papa John Creach, Don "Sugarcane" Harris, Stephané Grappelli, Eddie South, Stuff Smith, Michael Urbaniak, and Jean-Luc Ponty.

2220. Snidero, Jim. *Easy Jazz Conception for Strings.* New Albany, Indiana; Jamey Aebersold; 2001.

A book and CD that contains 15 easy etudes in a variety of styles and feels by famous jazz string players. The student is able to play-along with the string player, and is accompanied by a rhythm section.

Treble Instruments

2221. Gerard, Charley. *Jazz Riffs for Flute, Saxophone, Trumpet, and Other Treble Instruments.* New York: Music Sales; 1978.

Offers riffs and patterns in the styles of Charlie Parker and John Coltrane. Special sections cover minor, major, whole-tone, and non-Western scales, ii–V patterns, and soul and rock. Each riff is transposed four times. Chord chart and discography are included (1981).

2222. Paisner, Ben. *19 Swing Etudes for Saxophone, Clarinet, Xylophone, Violin, or Guitar.* New York: Sam Fox; 1977.

Contains tunes with chord symbols and articulation markings (1981).

Vocalists

2223. Breck, Alan. *The Art of Body Singing: Volume I.* New York: Breck Alan Music/Snacky Time Records; 2001.

Includes anatomical drawings and posture to demonstrate this unique approach to vocal mechanics. He treats singing as a body art rather than solely as a throat activity. He includes torso diagrams, wavelength charts, full-body stretches to accompany one's daily vocal calathetics.

2224. Clayton, Jay. *Jazz Vocal Practice Series.* Volumes 1 and 2. New Albany, Ind.: Jamey Aebersold; 2001.

Books and CDs that evolve from warming-up exercises, breathe control, widening of vocal range, improving accuracy, and intonation. The second volume, *Vamps and Blues,* focuses on hearing ideas and developing solos. The CD includes eight piano vamps using a variety of chord progressions and feels.

2225. Coker, Patty. *The Singer's Jam Session.* Lebanon, Ind.: Columbia Pictures Publications/Studio P/R; 1984.

Contains suggestions for beginning vocalists, practice materials, and a summary of concepts one should elicit from the sing-along tracks. The two-cassette improvisations cover several styles including blues, ballads, bebop, modal rock, and more.

2226. Coker, Patty, and David Baker N. *Vocal Improvisation: An Instrumental Approach.* New Albany, Ind.: Studio P/R; 1981.

Focuses on the psychology of the singer, reacting to musical sound, vocalizing, tune acquisition, melodic development, beginning jazz keyboard, internalizing a tune, and more. The instrumental approach includes coverage of bebop scales, rules, blues, developing instrumental techniques, and more. Includes a play-along tape, numerous references, and correlation to other writings on specific topics.

2227. DiBlasio, Dennis. *Guide for Jazz and Scat Vocalists.* Cassette. New Albany, Ind.: Jamey Aebersold; 1991.

Chapters cover chord voicing, jargon, ear training, chords and scales, scat singing, and use of the pitch pipe. There is a demonstration tape, which includes compositions for scat singing. The "Happy Birthday" demonstration includes how Ella Fitzgerald, Dizzy Gillespie, and Al Jarreau would have performed it. There is a discography of recordings of Eddie Jefferson, Ella Fitzgerald, Bobby McFerrin, Clark Terry, Lambert, Hendricks, Ross, and several others.

2228. Fredson, Scott. *Scat Singing Method.* New York: Alfred Publications; 1998.

The method is designed to assist vocal jazz instructors beginning a program without jazz experience. He begins with an awareness of syllables, melodic, and rhythmic changes with the goal to combine the three into a useable format. Lots of examples of jazz articulations and phrasing.

2229. Johnson, Ellen. *Vocal Warm Up.* New Albany, Ind.: Jamey Aebersold; 2001.

Although the book and CD is not specifically designed to teach improvisation, it does contain important exercises to prepare one to perform. In addition to the warmup exercises, she includes information on basic ear training. There are male and female editions of the book.

2230. Shaw, Kirby. *Vocal Jazz Style.* Milwaukee: Hal Leonard; 1975.

Presents a good method for vocalists and instrumentalists. This book, designed primarily for reading jazz articulations (e.g., accents, flips, fall-offs, shakes), has clear explanations and illustrations (1981).

2231. Stoloff, Bob. *Scat! Vocal Improvisation Techniques.* New Albany, Ind.: Jamey Aebersold; 2000.

Includes rhythmic and melodic exercises, transcribed solos, vocal bass lines, and drum grooves. Also covers syllable articulations, etudes, and more, The CD includes call and response exercises, solos by the author, and sing-along chord patters in various styles.

2232. Swain, Alan. *Scat.* New York: Jasmine Music Publishers; 1985.

A sequential approach that proceeds from beginning to advanced concepts. He begins with basic blues changes, and proceeds to melody, rhythm, and more sophisticated blues changes. There are performance suggestions accompanying each musical example; vocal examples are sung.

2233. _____. *Scat II.* New York: Jasmine Music Publishers; 1986.

Expands concepts covered in the first book, from ear training and performance of chords to intervals, chord progressions, and specific tunes. A sing-along tape is provided and covers both ear training and compositions. Don Shelton sings the vocal examples.

2234. Weir, Michele. *Vocal Improvisation.* New Albany, Ind.: Jamey Aebersold; 2000.

A book and CD that presents techniques, concepts, and exercises appropriate for all levels of experience. Also includes information on jazz theory and keyboard information. One of the best features of the book is the information provided by Dee Dee Bridgewater, Jay Vlayton, Jon Hendricks, Bobby McFerrin, Mark Murphy, and others.

2235. Zegree, Stephen Dr. *Complete Guide to Teaching Vocal Jazz.* New Albany, Ind.: Jamey Aebersold; 2001.

Addresses generic problems of teaching jazz, pop, and show tunes. Covers topics like styles, ballad singing, theory, rhythmic issues, style, and interpretation. The CD includes 27 sing-along tracks.

Improvisation Materials for Bass and Treble Instruments

Jamey Aebersold Play-A-Long Series

2236. Aebersold, Jamey. *A New Approach to Jazz Improvisation.* (Recordings and Related Books). New Albany, Ind.: Jamey Aebersold; 1970–1993.

Includes 57 play-along books and recordings (CD and cassettes) in this series. Each book contains parts for all instruments, complete with melodies and chord progressions matching the accompaniment on the recordings. In addition, stereo separation allows for bass and drums on the left channel and piano, guitar, and drums on the right. The play-along recordings feature some of the best rhythm section performers in jazz.

2237. Volume 1—*Jazz: How to Play and Improvise* (revised 6th edition).

Chapters on scales/chords, developing creativity, improvisation fundamentals, 12 blues scales, bebop scales, pentatonic scales and usage, time and feeling, melodic development, ii–V7s, related scales and modes, practical exercises/patterns and licks, dominant seventh tree of scale choices, nomenclature, chromaticism, a scale syllabus, cycles, and more. The rhythm section features Jamey Aebersold (piano), Rufus Reid (bass), and Jonathan Higgins (drums). Recorded tracks include blues in B♭ and F, Dorian Minor tracks, cycle of dominants, four-measure cadences, 24-measure song, and ii–V7 patterns in all keys. He recommends Volume 24 *Major and Minor,* and two publications, Rufus Reid's *Rufus Reid Bass Lines,* and *Transcribed Piano Voicings from Volume I,* by Jamey Aebersold, as prerequisites and related publications.

2238. Volume 2—*Nothin' but Blues.*

Presents 12 blues in several keys, moods, and tempos, from slow to rock. The recorded tracks are "Mr. Super Hip," "68 Modal Blues," "Slow Blues in G," "Fast Blues in F," "Minor Blues in C," and "Bird Blues" (in F with changes from *Blues for Alice*). The rhythm section features Dan Haerle (piano), Mike Hyman (drums), and Rufus Reid (bass). Suggested prerequisites are Volume 1 *Jazz: How to Play and Improvise;* Volume 21 *Getting It Together;* and Volume 24 *Major and Minor.*

2239. Volume 3—*The ii–V7-I Progression.*

There are eight recorded tracks covering ii–V7–I patterns in all major keys; ii–V7 random progressions; V7+9–I in all keys; V7+9–I in all minor keys; G minor Blues; bebop tune (covers all keys); ii–V7–I in three keys, and F blues with an eight-bar bridge. In addition, the needed scales and chords, numerous written patterns (can be performed with selected tracks on the recording), a scale syllabus, and numerous chord voicings that correspond to the recorded tracks. The rhythm section has Dan Haerle (piano), Rufus

Reid (bass), and Charlie Craig (drums). Suggested prerequisites and related publications are Volume 2 *Nothin' but Blues* and Volume 1 *Jazz: How to Play and Improvise,* and Rufus Reid's *Rufus Reid Bass Lines* and Bunky Green's *Jazz in a Nutshell.*

2240. Volume 4—*Movin' On.*

Includes nine original compositions by Jamey Aebersold and Dan Haerle. The melody and chord/scale progressions are provided for all instruments; there are transposed parts. The compositions, tempo, and mood are as follows: "Magic Morning (light bossa nova)"; "Five 8-bar Phrases (up-tempo swing)"; "Agitation (medium up-tempo Latin)"; "Scotter (up-tempo swing)"; "Once Remembered (medium-tempo Latin)"; "Ballad Waltz (slow 3/4)"; "Quickie (up-tempo samba)"; "All Things Unfinished (alternates between 3/4 and 4/4)"; and "7/4–3/4" (alternates between 7/4 and 3/4)." Dan Haerle (piano), Rufus Reid (bass), and Charlie Craig (drums), constitute the rhythm section.

2241. Volume 5—*Time to Play Music.*

Designed to facilitate the transition from learning scales and chords to performing melodies and improvising on chord progressions. The compositions and objectives are: "Groovitis C Medium-Tempo Groove-Type Song" based on the chords to "Sugar" (Stanley Turrentine); "Modal Voyage" (contains four-bar minor scale phrases similar to Herbie Hancock's "Maiden Voyage"); "Killer Pete" (similar groove and feels as Benny Golson's "Killer Joe"); "Essence" (rock feel/Dan Haerle); "Beatitude" (a Latin feel with objective to work on major scales); "Bebopish" (medium tempo, based on the changes to "Lady Bird"); "Freddieish" (slow bossa nova feel); and "Snap, Crackle and Pop" (rock tune based on one scale). Rhythm section has Dan Haerle (piano), Rufus Reid (bass), and Jonathan Higgins (drums). Suggested prerequisites are Volumes 1, 3, and 24. Related publication is David Baker's *Jazz Solos* (also correlated to Volume 6).

2242. Volume 6—*Charlie Parker—"All Bird."*

The objective is to both learn and teach selected compositions by Charles Parker. The recorded compositions, feel or style, and tempos are: "Now's the Time" and "Billie's Bounce" (both are blues in F); "Yardbird Suite" (medium, 32-bar bebop feel); "Confirmation" (energetic, medium up-tempo); "Dewey Square" (32-bar swing feel); "Donna Lee" (based on the contrafact—"Indiana"); "My Little Suede Shoes" (Latin feel); "Ornithology" (based on the contrafact—"How High the Moon"); "Scrapple from the Apple" (up-tempo, energetic); and "Thriving from a Riff" (based on rhythm changes [contrafact] in B♭, up tempo). The professional rhythm section features Ron Carter (bass), Kenny Barron (piano), and Ben Riley (drums). Recommended publications are Ron Carter's *Ron Carter Bass Lines* and David Baker's *Jazz Solos.*

2243. Volume 7—*Miles Davis.*

Contains eight originals by Miles Davis, compositions that have become standards in the jazz repertoire. The compositions and concepts entailed are as follows: "Four" (32-bar form, medium tempo); "Tune Up" (based on ii–V–I progressions and related scales); "Vierd Blues" (slow tempo in B♭); "The Theme" (based on the contrafact—"I've Got Rhythm" changes in B♭); "Solar" (12 bars in minor); "Dig" (based on the contrafact—"Sweet Georgia Brown," medium up-tempo); "Milestones" (various changes); and "Serpent's Tooth" (based on rhythm changes with alterations). The rhythm section features Dan Haerle (piano), Rufus Reid (bass), and Jonathan Higgins (drums). Suggested related publications are *Miles Davis Solos,* and Volume 50, *Magic of Miles.*

2244. Volume 8—*Sonny Rollins.*

Features several originals by an outstanding tenor saxophonist. The compositions vary in difficulty and tempos, and include: "Doxy" (16-bar form); "St. Thomas" (calypso and swing feel); "Blue Seven" (medium tempo blues); "Valse Hot" (a 3/4 tune); "Tenor Madness" and "Solid" (medium up-tempo blues); "Pent-Up House" (features ii–V7–I patterns); "Airegin" (challenging changes, up-tempo); and "Oleo" (based on rhythm changes). A rhythm section of Dan Haerle (piano), Rufus Reid (bass), and Jonathan Higgins (drums).

2245. Volume 9—*Woody Shaw.*

Offers original compositions by Woody Shaw that contain melodies and jazz progressions that often vary from the typical ii–V–I, or iii–VI–ii–V–I patterns often heard in bebop. The compositions and feel/tempo are: "Little Red's Fantasy" (bossa nova in 4/4); "Katrina Ballerina" (very melodic in 3/4); "Blues for Wood" (minor blues with a Coltrane feel); "Moontrane" (energetic, up-tempo); "In Case You Haven't Heard" (bossa nova and swing); "Tomorrow's Destiny" (Latin and swing); "Beyond All Limits" (bossa nova and slow); and "Beyond All Limits" (swing and up-tempo). The expanded rhythm section features Ronnie Mathews and James Williams (piano), Jamey Aebersold and Stafford James (bass), and Louis Hayes and Mike Hyman (drums).

2246. Volume 10—*David Baker.*

There are eight original compositions covering diverse styles and tempos. The compositions are "Aulil" (medium, bossa nova); "LeRoi" (up-tempo 4/4 and 3/3); "Kentucky Oysters" (3/4 blues); "Passion" (ballad); "Black

Thursday" (medium-tempo groove with moving chords); "Bossa Belle" (bossa nova); "Soleil d'Altamira" (bossa nova in 4/4 and 3/4). and "Le Miroir Noir" (rock tune based on diminished scales). The rhythm section features two drummers, Charlie Craig and Jonathan Higgins, Dan Haerle (piano), and Rufus Reid (bass). The recommended related publication is David Baker's *Bebop Jazz Solos*.

2247. Volume 11—*Herbie Hancock.*

Includes eight original compositions by Herbie Hancock, covering rock, modal, and swing works. They range from blues to funk to swing styles, including "Cantaloupe Island" (funky, repetitious, three chords), "Maiden Voyage" (modal, with repeated melody), "And What If I Don't" (shuffle, blues-based melody), "Dolphin Dance" (uses creative chord progression and scales), "Jessica" (3/4 meter), "Toys" (swing feel), and "Eye of the Hurricane" (F minor, up-tempo blues). The rhythm section features Kenny Barron (piano), Ron Carter (bass), and Billy Hart (drums).

2248. Volume 12—*Duke Ellington.*

Covers original compositions ranging from ballads to swing. This volume is designed to promote standards that every jazz performer should know. The compositions include "Satin Doll," "Take The 'A' Train" (composed by Billy Strayhorn), "Mood Indigo," "Perdido" (composed by Juan Tizol), "In a Sentimental Mood," "I Let a Song Go Out of My Heart," "Solitude," "Sophisticated Lady," and "Prelude to a Kiss." The rhythm section consists of Kenny Barron (piano), Ron Carter (bass), and Ben Riley (drums). Suggested related play-along, Volume 48 *In A Mellow Tone.*

2249. Volume 13—*Cannonball Adderley.*

A collection of diverse compositions focusing primarily on blues. The compositions are "Work Song" (16 bars in a minor key); "Del Sasser" (features ii–V–I patterns, written by Sam Jones); "Scotch and Water" (blues with an 8-bar bridge, composed by Joe Zawinul); "Saudade" (Book's bossa) (bossa nova written by Walter Booker); "Unit 7" (blues, bridge in C, composed by Sam Jones); "This Here" (3/4 funky blues by Bobby Timmons); "Sack of Woe" (blues in F); and "Jeannine" (composed by Duke Pearson, 56 bars in A♭). The rhythm section features former Cannonball Adderley sidemen: Ronnie Mathews (piano), Sam Jones (bass), and Louis Hayes (drums). Suggested related publications are David Baker's *Bebop Jazz Solos* and *Jazz Solos* by David Baker.

2250. Volume 14—*Benny Golson.*

This volume was produced by Benny Golson, and includes several of his most famous compositions. Among the compositions are "Killer Joe" (moderate melody with syncopated comping); "Ease Away Walk" (features recurring turnaround patterns in C minor); "I Remember Clifford" (a ballad in memory of Clifford Brown, which uses diminished and diminished whole tone scales); and "Stablemates" (lots of ii–V7 patterns). Other compositions ranging from blues to moderate swing tunes with interesting chord progressions are "Along Came Betty," "Are You Real," "Whisper Not," and "Blues March." All were first introduced by Art Blakey and the Jazz Messengers, a group Golson previously performed with. The rhythm section contains Patrice Rushen (piano), Bob Magnusson (bass), and Roy McCurdy (drums).

2251. Volume 15—*Payin' Dues.*

A series of original compositions by Jamey Aebersold that are based on chord progressions of standards like "Stella by Starlight," "Body and Soul," "Cherokee," "I'll Remember April," "There Will Never Be Another You," "What Is This Thing Called Love," "It's You or No One," and "The Song Is You." Aebersold believes that by learning many standard compositions, jazz harmonies, and root movements (contrafacts), one can quickly expand their jazz repertoire. The Aebersold-composed originals, based on the aforementioned chord progressions, are "Another Yew," "Stella," "Flesh and Spirit," "What Is This?," "It's You," "You're the Song," "April," and "Share-A-Key." "Another Yew" is played in both fast and slow tempos. The rhythm section is Kenny Barron (piano), Ron Carter (bass), and Grady Tate (drums). Suggested related publication is Ron Carter's *Ron Carter Bass Lines.*

2252. Volume 16—*Turnarounds, Cycles, and ii–V7's.*

A continuation of volume 3 but more comprehensive. The tracks on this volume are: "Turnaround Tracks"; "6 Cycle Tracks"; "Coltrane Blues"; "Some of the Things I Am" (substitute ii–V7s); "Joy Spring" (contains ii–Vs); "Six ii–V7 Tracks"; "Coltrane Changes in Twelve Keys"; "B♭ Rhythm Changes" (based on "I've Got Rhythm"); and "Guess What Key I'm In." The strength of the volume is that it explores all keys and offers ii–V patterns with standards like "Joy Spring" and "I've Got Rhythm" as well as exercises. The rhythm section features Jamey Aebersold (piano), John Clayton (bass), and Mike Hyman (drums).

2253. Volume 17—*Horace Silver.*

Includes several of Silver's most popular compositions. The compositions and selected characteristics are: "Song for My Father" (24 bars, minor key); "The Preacher" (catchy, repetitive melody); "The Jody Grind" (minor blues with an ostinato bass throughout, based on lydian dominant scales); "Sister Sadie" (32-bars, based on dominant chords, shuffle rhythmic feel); "Gregory

Is Here" (bossa nova); and "Peace" (ballad). Kenny Barron (piano), Ron Carter (bass), and Al Foster (drums) constitute the rhythm section.

2254. Volume 18—*Horace Silver.*

A continuation of Volume 17, includes several excellent, relatively unknown Silver compositions including "Strollin'" (in D♭, slow swing); "Summer in Central Park" (3/4, very creative harmonically); "Room 608" (Rhythm changes with an altered bridge); "Nica's Dream" (permeated with ii–Vs and the use of melodic minor scales); "Ecaroh" (features Latin and swing rhythmic feel); "Mayreh" (energetic, swinging); "Barbara" (contains several diminished scales, in 6/4), and "QuickSilver" (extremely fast, swinging tempo). The rhythm section is the same as in Volume 17.

2255. Volume 19—*David Liebman.*

A departure from the ii–V compositions that permeate the other volumes. The absence of ii–V patterns forces the performer to think and perform with noncliché harmonic progressions, thereby improving their ability as an improviser. The compositions and characteristics are: "Picadilly Lilly" (frequent movements); "Slumber" (Coltrane influenced); "Oasis" (minor altered blues); "Loft Dance" (features Lydian and other scales); "Brite Piece" (uses major, Lydian, and Lydian dominant scales, swings); "Bonnie's Blues" (variation of blues changes); "Tomorrow's Expectations" (ballad with contemporary harmonies and voicing); and "Lookout Farm" (8- and 16-bar phrases, pedal point modality center on "C"). These compositions expand one's improvisational awareness beyond bebop. The rhythm section is Richie Bierach (piano), Frank Tusa (bass), and Al Foster (drums).

2256. Volume 20—*Jimmy Raney.*

Covers 10 transcribed solos written and performed by Raney. The chord progressions are based on standards, thereby enabling users to apply them to other situations. The compositions and the standards they are based on are "'Bout You and Me" ("How About You"); "Autumn" ("Autumn Leaves"); "Hotel Grande" ("There's a Small Hotel"); "B♭ Blues for Wes, Friends" ("Just Friends"); "Nowhere" ("Out of Nowhere"); "Rhythm in B♭" ("I Got Rhythm"); "Like Somebody" ("Like Someone In Love"); and "Groove Blues in F." All solos were composed by Raney and are notated in the booklet. Raney (guitar) is accompanied by Steve Rodby (bass) and Mike Hyman (drums).

2257. Volume 21—*Gettin' It Together.*

It is suggested that this volume be used in conjunction with Volume 1. Aebersold believes the two will enable one to successfully challenge any jazz situation. The scales cover all 12 keys and include major, minor,

Dorian, harmonic and melodic minor, dominant seventh, half-diminished, Lydian, and sus4. The two slow blues are notated in F and B♭ respectively. The booklet contains information on practicing, ear training, nomenclature, chromaticism, digital patterns, cycle exercises, fourth exercises, double-time passages, suggestions for band directors, and more. Designed for instrumentalists and vocalists.

2258. Volume 22—*13 Favorite Standards* (with text).

Play-along set with book and text. There are 13 standards and two versions of "Lover" (3/4 and 4/4). The single versions are: "Stella By Starlight," "My Old Flame," "My Ideal," "Easy Living," "The Nearness of You," "Wives-Lovers," "Soon," "If I Should Lose You," "It Could Happen to You," "Out of Nowhere," "Tangerine," and "I Remember You." This volume is recommended along with Volumes 12, 23, 25, 31, 32, 34, 36, 38, 39, 40, 41, 44, 46, 48, 49, 51, 52, and 55 as a way of improving one's jazz repertoire and musical growth. Dan Haerle (piano), Todd Coolman (bass), and Ed Soph (drums) form the rhythm section.

2259. Volume 23—*One Dozen Standards* (with text).

Another play-along set with book and text. Includes compositions recorded by numerous artists. They are: "Angel Eyes," "But Beautiful," "Everything Happens to Me," "Here's That Rainy Day," "I Should Care," "Imagination," "Like Someone in Love," "Polka Dots and Moonbeams," "Violets for Your Eyes," "Will You Still Be Mine," "You Say You Care," and "Personality." The rhythm section is Michael Weiss (piano), John Goldsby (bass), and Jonathan Higgins (drums). Melodies are transposed for all instruments.

2260. Volume 24—*Major and Minor.*

Focuses on beginners and advanced players and contains numerous exercises designed to improve major and minor skills. Jamey Aebersold performs exercises and solos on alto saxophone; all exercises and saxophone solos on the demonstration record are transcribed and notated in the booklet. Features Jamey Aebersold (piano and saxophone), John Goldsby (bass), and Charlie Craig (drums). Recommended with Volume 1.

2261. Volume 25—*All-Time Standards* (with text).

Continuation of the play-along sets with book and text. The compositions are "Summertime," "Speak Low," "September Song," "Old Devil Moon," "The Party's Over," "My Funny Valentine," "My Favorite Things," "Our Love Is Here to Stay," "I've Grown Accustomed to Your Face," "It Might As Well Be Spring," "I Love You," "I Could Write," "I Can't Get Started," "Have You Met Miss Jones," "Foolish Heart," "Come Rain or Come Shine," and "A Foggy Day." Melodies are transposed for all instruments. The Phil Woods rhythm section (at the time of the recording) is featured; Hal Galper (piano), Steve Gilmore (bass), and Bill Goodwin (drums). Recommended related publication is Steve Gilmore's *Steve Gilmore Bass Lines to Volume 25.*

2262. Volume 26—*Scale Syllabus.*

Recommended for all levels, instrumentalists, and vocalists. Features David Liebman (soprano saxophone), and Jamey Aebersold (piano). Liebman's solos on two versions (slow and fast) of each scale in his scale syllabus. His *David Liebman Scale Syllabus Solos* is the recommended related publication. In addition, a list of piano voicings is provided in the supplement. Stereo separation allows users to either practice or solo with Liebman or Aebersold.

2263. Volume 27—*John Coltrane.*

Play-along tunes include "Mr. P.C." (dedicated to Paul Chambers); "Some Other Blues" (blues in F); "Naima" (dedicated to Coltrane's wife); "Like Sonny" (adapted from a motif of Sonny Rollins); "Spiritual" (religious flavor); "Blues Minor" (minor blues, no V chord); "Crescent" (relatively unknown, energetic rhythm, and atypical form); and "The Promise" (uses dorian mode and two chord changes). The rhythm section consists of Harold Mabern (piano), Ron Carter (bass), and Adam Nussbaum (drums). Recommended related publication is *David Liebman Scale Syllabus Solos.*

2264. Volume 28—*Giant Steps—John Coltrane.*

Features the same rhythm section as volume 27 and contains both some of Coltrane's most endearing and least known compositions. The compositions are "Impressions" (slow and fast versions); "Giant Steps" (root movement in thirds, fourths, and tritones); "26–2" (draws harmonically on Charlie Parker's "Confirmation," but uses the "Giant Steps" harmonic movement); "Up Against the Wall" (blues in A♭); "Dear Lord" (strong diatonic melody); "A Love Supreme" (F-minor melody); "Mr. Day" (blues in F♯); and "Countdown" (like "Giant Steps," features two-beat chord changes at a fast tempo). Recommended related publications are David Liebman's *David Liebman Plays* and Walt Weiskopf and Ramon Ricker's *Coltrane: A Player's Guide to His Harmony.*

2265. Volume 29—*Play Duets with Jimmy Raney.*

For all artists, especially guitarists and rhythm section players. The duets are written in C with chord progressions transposed for B♭ and E♭ instruments. Raney comps on one channel and solos on the other. In addition, there are 10 original compositions based on standard chord changes, covering different meters, and feels. Recommended related publication is *Jimmy Raney Solos.*

2266. Volume 30A and 30B—*Rhythm Section "Work-Out."*

30A is for keyboardists and/or guitarists, and 30B is for bassists and drummers. The booklet contains chapters by Aebersold and the other rhythm section players on the role and function of respective instruments in the rhythm section. There are transcribed solos by Dan Haerle (piano), Jack Petersen (bass), and Todd Coolman (bass), piano and guitar voicings, bass lines and information on bass line construction, and drum information. Volume 30 allows the user to turn off the drums, the first volume in the Aebersold series to allow this opportunity for drummers.

2267. Volume 31—*Bossa Novas* (with text).

Contains melodies, chords, and text, along with transposed parts for other instruments. The compositions are "Girl from Ipanema," "Desafinado," "So Nice," "How Insensitive," "Quiet Night," "One Note Samba," "Meditation," "Little Boat," and "Once I Loved." The rhythm section is Hal Galper (piano), Steve Gilmore (bass), and Bill Goodwin (drums).

2268. Volume 32—*Ballads* (with text).

The compositions are "Lover Man," "You Don't Know What Love Is," "Skylark," "You've Changed," "Soul Eyes," "Chelsea Bridge," "Lush Life," and "Ballad Blues." The same rhythm section as Volume 31.

2269. Volume 33—*Wayne Shorter.*

A collection of original compositions by this outstanding jazz composer and saxophonist. The compositions are "Infant Eyes," "Witch Hunt," "Footprints," "E.S.P.," "Nefertiti," "Speak No Evil," "Children of the Night," "Virgo," "Miyako," "Wild Flower," "Yes and No," "Ju-Ju," "Adam's Apple," "El Gaucho," "Black Nile," and "This Is for Albert." The compositions are permeated with interesting and challenging harmonic and melodic movements and were recorded with the Art Blakey and Miles Davis groups. A rhythm section of Kenny Barron (piano), Ron Carter (bass), and Adam Nussbaum (drums). Recommended related publication is David Liebman's *Dave Liebman Plays.*

2270. Volume 34—*Jam Session* (with text).

Contains 19 compositions including "The Shadow of Your Smile," "Stompin' at the Savoy," "On Green Dolphin Street," "On the Trail," "Without a Song," "You Stepped Out of a Dream," "Spring Is Here," "Once In a While," "Over the Rainbow," "Don't Blame Me," "Blue Moon," "Laura," "Just Friends," "No Greater Love," "I Left My Heart In San

Francisco," "Star Eyes," "Invitation," and "My Secret Love." Recommended related publication is Steve Gilmore's *'Jam Session' Bass Lines*. Rhythm section features Hal Galper (piano), Steve Gilmore (bass), and Bill Goodwin (drums).

2271. Volume 35—*Cedar Walton*.

Features Cedar Walton (piano), Ron Carter (bass), and Billy Higgins (drums). The compositions are "Cedar's Blues," "Bolivia," "Clockwise," "Firm Roots," "Maestro," "Fantasy in D," "Midnight Waltz," "Hand In Glove," and "Ojos De Rojo." Harmony parts are included with some compositions. Recommended related publication is *Ron Carter Transcribed Bass Lines*.

2272. Volume 36—*Bebop and Beyond*.

Contains some of the best bebop and postbebop compositions. The compositions are "Ladybird" (Tadd Dameron); "Prince Albert" (Kenny Dorham); "Ruby Me Dear" (Thelonious Monk); "Ray's Idea" (Ray Brown and W. Fuller); "Freight Trance" (Tommy Flanagan); "Robbin's Nest" (Sir Charles Thompson and Illinois Jacquet); "Theme For Ernie" (Fred Lacey); and "I Mean You" (Thelonious Monk). The rhythm section consists of Ronnie Mathews (piano), Ray Drummond (bass), and Marvin Smith (drums).

2273. Volume 37—*Sammy Nestico*.

A volume of one of the best jazz composer's compositions. Although Nestico is best known for big band writing (he wrote several compositions for the Count Basie Band), these compositions are arranged for combos. The compositions are "Switch In Time," "Hay Burner," "Basie-Straight Ahead," "Warm Breeze," "88 Basie Street," "Samantha," "Wind Machine" (slow and fast versions) "Lonely Street," and "Ya Gotta Try." The rhythm section is Dan Haerle (piano), Todd Coolman (bass), and Ed Soph (drums). Recommended related publication is *Todd Coolman Bass Lines*.

2274. Volume 38—*Blue Note*.

Seventeen jazz classics recorded by several artists on the Blue Note jazz label. The compositions cover different moods, and harmonic and melodic spectrums. Among the composers are Chick Corea, John Coltrane, Joe Henderson, Freddie Hubbard, Lee Morgan, Hank Mobley, Wayne Shorter, Stanley Turrentine, and more. The compositions are "This I Dig of You," "El Toro," "Blue Train," "Lazy Bird," "Moment's Notice," "Locomotion," "Home at Last," "Crisis," "Chick's Tune," "Recorda-Me," "One for Daddy-O," "Shirley," "Inner Urge," "Blue Bossa," "Isotope," "Marie Antoinette," and "Ceora." Some compositions contain harmony parts. Rhythm section includes Hal Galper (piano), Steve Gilmore (bass), and Steve Goodwin (drums).

2275. Volume 39—*Swing, Swing, Swing* (with text).

Eight swing-era standards, long important components of the jazz repertoire. The standards are "Oh, Lady Be Good," "Sweet Georgia Brown," "Bye Bye Blackbird," "Avalon," "Blue Room," "Poor Butterfly," "Indian Summer," and "Too Marvelous for Words." A rhythm section of Hal Galper (piano), Steve Gilmore (bass), and Bill Goodwin (drums).

2276. Volume 40—*'Round Midnight* (with text).

A compilation of some of the most recorded compositions in jazz. They include "'Round Midnight" (haunting melody in C-minor); "Love for Sale" (often recorded, popular harmonic progression); "Early Autumn" (rich chords, Stan Kentonian); "Lullaby of Birdland" (easy swinging melody); "Softly, As in a Morning Sunrise" (in C-minor); "You Got to My Head" (40-bar bebop style); and popular favorites such as "A Time for Love," "Days of Wine and Roses," "I Cover the Waterfront," "September in the Rain," "Nancy," "Namely You," "I Know That You Know," and "If I Love Again." Same rhythm section as volume 39.

2277. Volume 41—*Body and Soul* (with text).

Another collection of standards, featuring a rhythm section of Dan Haerle (piano), John Goldsby (bass), and Ed Soph (drums). The 17 standards are "Misty," "What's New," "Body and Soul," "Alone Together," "What Is This Thing Called Love," "Time After Time," "Lover, Come Back to Me," "Yours Is My Heart Alone," "You and the Night and the Music," "Teach Me Tonight," "You're My Everything," "The Very Thought of You," "That's All," "Fools Rush In," "I'm an Old Cowhand," "When Your Lover Has Gone," and "I Thought About You."

2278. Volume 42—*"Blues" in All Keys*.

Covers blues in all keys at slow tempos. Each key has a different melody and two compatible chord/scale progressions. A rhythm section of James Williams (piano), Bob Cranshaw (bass), and Mickey Roker (drums). Recommended related publication is Volume 42 *Bass Lines*.

2279. Volume 43—*"Groovin' High."*

There are six bebop compositions and two standards. The compositions are "Groovin' High" and "A Night in Tunisia" (Dizzy Gillespie); "All the Things You Are" (contains Gillespie's introduction); "West Coast Blues" (3/4 blues by Wes Montgomery); "I'll Remember April" (swing and Latin flavor); "Bluesette" (jazz waltz); "An Afternoon in Paris" (lots of ii–V patterns); and "High Fly" (Randy Weston's composition, 12/8 feel). A rhythm section of Dan Haerle (piano), Todd Coleman (bass), and Steve Davis (drums).

2280. Volume 44—*Autumn Leaves* (with text).

Includes "Autumn Leaves," "My Shining Hour," "Tenderly," "After You're Gone," "Stormy Weather," "S'Posin," "There Will Never Be Another You," "Witchcraft" (ABCDA form), and "All or Nothing at All." A discography of recordings of each composition. The rhythm section features Niels Lan Doxy (piano), Christian Daly (bass), and Billy Hart (drums).

2281. Volume 45—*Bill Evans*.

A volume of selected compositions by one of the best composers/performers in jazz. The compositions are "Waltz for Debby," "Laurie," "Peri's Scope," "Very Early" "Time Remembered," "Walkin' Up," "Turn out the Stars," "Funkallero," and "Interplay." Dan Haerle (piano), Todd Coolman (bass), and Steve Davis (drums) constitute the rhythm section.

2282. Volume 46—*Out of This World* (with text).

Nine standards that span different jazz styles and periods. The compositions are "If I Were a Bell," "Mr. Sandman," "Out of This World," "Ill Wind," "Basin Street Blues," "Weaver of Dreams," "Prisoner of Love," "I'm Glad There Is You," and "Four Brothers" (lots of ii–V's and turnarounds). Includes a rhythm section of Mulgrew Miller (piano), Connie Plaxico (bass), and Ronnie Burrage (drums).

2283. Volume 47—*I Got Rhythm*.

Performs "I Got Rhythm" ("rhythm" changes), in all keys. There is a written melody and solo section for each key, including slow tracks to help the user to hear and understand the changes. The book contains instructions on approaching and practicing rhythm changes, as well as use the blues, diminished, pentatonic, and other scales with rhythm changes. An excellent play-along because numerous tunes, especially bebop and several Charles Parker tunes are based on the contrafact ("I Got Rhythm"). A rhythm section of Jim McNeely (piano), Todd Coolman (bass), and Steve Davis (drums).

2284. Volume 48—*In A Mellow Tone—Duke Ellington* (with text).

Nine Ellington classics arranged for combos. The compositions are "In a Mellow Tone," "I Got It Bad," "Do Nothing Till You Hear from Me," "C Jam Blues," "I Didn't Know About You," "Don't Get Around Much Anymore," "Warm Valley," "Cottontail," and "Just Squeeze Me." Text is provided for several compositions. Rhythm section is Dan Haerle (piano), John Goldsby (bass), and Steve Davis (drums).

2285. Volume 49—*"Feels Good": Sugar* (with text).

Features Frank Marr and Jimmy Rupp on a Hammond B-3 Organ. The compositions are blues flavored and include "Sugar," "Sunny," "Flamingo," "Misty," "Georgia on My Mind," "Stranger in Paradise," "When Sunny Gets Blue," "On the Sunny Side of the Street," and "Blues in F." Stereo separation of parts.

2286. Volume 50—*The Magic of Miles.*

Draws from several classic compositions of the 1957 to 1964 period. The compositions are "All Blues," "So What," "Freddie the Freeloader," "Milestones," "Nardis," "Seven Steps to Heaven," "Eighty-One," "Joshua," and "Blue in Green" (Bill Evans). The rhythm section contains Mark Levine (piano), Todd Coolman (bass), and Steve Davis (drums). Suggested related publication recommendation is Volume 50 *Transcribed Piano Comping* and Volume 7 *Miles Davis.*

2287. Volume 51—*Night and Day* (with text).

Contains several standards by composers such as George Gershwin, Cole Porter, and Richard Rogers. The compositions are "Embraceable You," "The Man I Love," "How Long Has This Been Going on," "I Got Rhythm," "Night and Day," "Just One of Those Things," "You Do Something to Me," "I Get a Kick out of You," "Tea for Tea," "With a Song in My Heart," "Three Little Words," "I'm a Fool to Want You," and "My One and Only Love." Features a rhythm section of Jim McNeely (piano), Steve Gilmore (bass), and Bill Goodwin (drums).

2288. Volume 52—*Collector's Items* (with text).

This collection focuses on melody, and contains several of the most recognizable standards in the jazz repertoire. Included are "I'm Getting Sentimental over You," "Sweet Lorraine," "Ghost of a Chance," "Stars Fell on Alabama," "When Lights Are Low," "Easy Living," "Serenata," "The Night Has a Thousand Eyes," "Too Young to Go Steady," and "Mr. Lucky." Swinging rhythm section of Rob Schneiderman (piano), Rufus Reid (bass), and Akira Tana (drums).

2289. Volume 53—*Clifford Brown.*

Twelve compositions by this outstanding jazz composer and trumpeter. The compositions have been recorded by several artists/groups, including Sonny Rollins and the Jazz Messengers. Includes "Sandu," "Joy Spring," "Daahoud," "Larve," "Tiny Capers," "Sweet Clifford," "Gerkin for Perkin,"

"Minor Mood," "Jordu," "Swingin,'" and "The Blues Walk." The rhythm section features two different pianists, bassists, and drummers. Pianists are Jim McNeely and Jamey Aebersold; bassists are John Goldsby and Tyrone Wheeler; and drummers are Jonathan Higgins and Steve Davis.

2290. Volume 54—*Maiden Voyage.*

A potpourri of jazz compositions covering several composers, styles, and moods. Improvisation suggestions are provided for each composition, and scales are suggested for each chord change. The compositions are "Summertime," "Blue Bossa," "Maiden Voyage," "Doxy," "Song for My Father," "Satin Doll," "Footprints," "B♭ Shuffle Blues," "Impressions," "Watermelon Man," "Autumn Leaves," "Cantaloupe Island," "Blues in F," and iii–VI7 and ii–V7 progressions. A rhythm section of Jamey Aebersold (piano), Tyrone Wheeler (bass), and Steve Davis (drums). Suggested related publication recommendation is Volume 54 *Transcribed Piano Voicings, Bass Lines and Drum Tracks.*

2291. Volume 55—*Yesterdays—Jerome Kern's Jazz Classics.*

Eleven standards by one of the most recorded nonjazz composers. Jazz artists dating back to the 1940s have recorded Kern's compositions. The standards are "All The Things You Are" (fast and slow), "The Song Is You," "Yesterdays," "I'm Old Fashioned," "Dearly Beloved," "The Way You Look Tonight," "Smoke Gets in Your Eyes," "Long Ago and Far Away," "Why Do I Love You," and "Pick Yourself Up." Hal Galper (piano), John Goldsby (bass), and Steve Davis (drums), form the rhythm section. Recommended related publication is *Hal Galper's Transcribed Comping.*

2292. Volume 56—*Thelonious Monk.*

Contains several jazz classics by one of the greatest composers/performers in jazz history. Contains "In Walked Bud," "Ruby My Dear," "Epistrophy," "Monk's Mood," "Well You Needn't," "Off Minor," "Inspiration," "Round Midnight," "I Mean You," and "Thelonious and Monkish" (original by Jamey Aebersold). The Monkish performing rhythm section features Mark Levine (piano), Todd Coleman (bass), and Ed Soph (drums).

2293. Volume 57—*Minor Blues in All Keys.*

Minor blues in all keys, with various approaches to either vertical or horizontal playing. Rhythm section of Rob Schneiderman (piano), Rufus Reid (bass), and Akira Tana (drums). Suggested prerequisites are Volumes 2 and 42.

2294. Volume 58—*Unforgettable.*

Includes lyrics and is accompanied by Hal Galper, Wayne Dockery, and Steve Ellington. Among the numerous tunes in this Play-A-Long series are

"Let's Fall in Love," "Unforgettable," "I'll Take Romance," "Imagination," "Gone with the wind," "I Hadn't Anyone Till You," "Like Someone in Love," "Lullaby of the Leaves," "Someday My Prince Will Come," "I'm Confessing That I Love You," and several more.

2295. Volume 59—*Invitation.*

A play-along with the B-3 organ that includes lyrics and features Steve Davis on drums and Hank Marr on the B-3 organ. The tunes are recorded in nice grooves, and allow the parts to be separated. Among the transcriptions are "Invitation," "Moonbeams," "Caravan," "Ceora," "Easy Living," "Star Eyes," "Stella By Starlight," "Out of Nowhere," "On Green Dolphin Street," "Shadow of Your Smile," "The Nearness of You," and several more.

2296. Volume 60—*Freddie Hubbard.*

Accompanied by a rhythm section of Dan Haerle or Mark Levine on piano, Todd Coolman or John Goldsby on bass, and Ed Soph or Barry Ries on drums. The book and CD are geared to intermediate/advanced students. The transcriptions are "Little Sunflower," "Coral Keys," "Crisis," "Red Clay," "Pensativa," "Dear John," "Sky Dive," "Gibralter," "Up Jumped Spring," "Lament for Booker," and "Birdlike."

2297. Volume 61—*Burnin: Up-Tempo Jazz Standards.*

For advanced students, the tempos are very fast. The volume features a rhythm section of Dan Haerle or Mark Levine on piano, Todd Coolman or John Goldsby on bass, and Ed Soph or Barry Ries on drums. A special feature of the volume is the performing of "Cherokee" in all 12 keys. There are transcriptions of "Indiana," "Secret Love," "Blues with Bridge," "Keep It Up," "It's You or No One," "Lover, Lover Come Back to Me," "Cherokee," "The Third Rail," and "The Way You Look Tonight."

2298. Volume 62—*Wes Montgomery Jazz Standards.*

Contains 11 transcriptions that capture the groove and feel of this great artist. The rhythm section features Hal Galper on piano, John Goldsby on bass, and Barry Ries on drums. The transcriptions are "Cariba," "Four on Six," "Road Song," "Jingles, West Coast Blues," "Leila," "Angel," "D Natural Blues," "Doujia," "Full House," and "Far *Wes.*"

2299. Volume 63—*Tom Harrell Jazz Originals.*

There are 12 transcriptions that are imbued with both traditional and contemporary musical features. Dan Haerle on piano, Todd Coolman on bass, and Ed Soph on drums accompany the tunes. The transcriptions are "Little Dancer," "April Mist," "Buffalo Wings," "Sail Away," "The Water's Edge,"

"Train Shuffle," "Glass Mystery," "Hope Street," "Angel," "Moon Alley," "Suspended View," and "Scene."

2300. Volume 64—*Salsa/Latin Jazz Classics.*

A book and CD of 13 transcriptions of salsa/Latin compositions that are permeated with the bass figures, syncopations, and voicing of the style(s). There is no drum set; however, the Latin American rhythm section features Mark Levine on piano, David Belove on bass, John Santos on timbales and other percussion, and Harold Muniz on congas and other instruments. The transcriptions are "Sabor," "Linda Chicana," "Mambo Inn," "ii–V7–I Cha Cha," "ii–V7–I Bolero," "Afro Blue," "Come Candela," "Delirio," "Manteca," "Curacao," "Philly Mambo," "Mindanao," and "Picadillo."

2301. Volume 65—*Four and More: Organ and Drums.*

A swinging book and two CDs that feature Hank Marr on the B-S organ and Steve Davis on drums. Among the 22 transcriptions are "Four," "Jeannine," "Giant Steps," "Confirmation," "Nica's Dream," "Tune Up," "Oleo," "Blues For Alice," "Good Bait," "Perdido," "September Song," "Fly Me to the Moon," and several more.

2302. Volume 66—*Billy Strayhorn: Lush Life.*

A chance to experience the uniqueness of Strayhorn's compositional style. The book and CD features a rhythm section of Hal Galper on piano, Lynn Seaton on bass, and Steve Davis on drums. The 12 transcriptions are "Lush Life," "Satin Doll," "Take the 'A' Train," "A Flower Is a Lovesome Thing," "Rain Check," "My Little Brown Book," "Blood Count," "Isfahan," "Drawing Room Blues," "Chelsea Bridge," "Johnny Come Lately," and "UMMG."

2303. Volume 67—*Tune Up.*

An intermediate book and CD that features the seven transcriptions in all 12 keys. The first chorus for each tune is in the original key and followed by improvisations in the other 11 keys. The rhythm section features Dan Haerle on piano, Todd Coolman on bass, and Ed Soph on drums. The transcriptions are "Sweet Georgia Brown," "Tune Up," "Autumn Leaves," "Solar Flair," "Perdido," "Four," and "Rhythm Changes."

2304. Volume 68—*Giant Steps.*

Geared to the advanced level student, and performed in all of the 12 keys. Each tune is first performed in the original key followed by improvisations in the other 11 keys. The book is supplemented with a CD, which features a rhythm section of Mark Levine on piano, Lynn Seaton on bass, and Barry Ries on drums. Among the transcriptions are "Confirmation," "Stella By

Starlight," "All the Things You Are," "Giant Steps," "It's You or No One," and several more.

2305. Volume 69—*Bird Goes Latin: Charlie Parker Originals.*

The book and CD explores a little known feature of Parker's infatuation with so-called Latin jazz. The rhythm section features Mark Levine on piano, David Belove on bass, John Santos on timbales and other instruments, and Harold Muniz on congas and other instruments. The transcriptions are "Barbados," "Marmaduke," "Buzzy," "Dewey Square," "Yardbird Suite," "Ornithology," "Laird Baird," "Moose the Mooche," "My Little Suede Shoes," "Bird Gets the Worm," "Scrapple from the apple," "Donna Lee," and "Confirmation."

2306. Item deleted.

2307. Volume 70—*Killer Joe.*

The book and CD is accompanied by the same rhythm section found on Volume 54: Jamey Aebersold on piano, Tyrone Wheeler on bass, and Steve Davis on drums. The compositions feature slow-to-moderate tempos, and easy chord changes. The transcriptions are "Killer Joe," "Blue Moon," "Sweet Georgia Brown," "Sugar, Misty," "Stop-Time Blues," "Girl from Ipanema," "B♭ New Orleans Blues," "You Stepped Out of a Dream," "Mr. PC," "Ladybird," "Afternoon in Paris," and "3/4 Blues. "

2308. Volume 71—*East of the Sun Famous Standards.*

A book and CD with 12 transcriptions. The play-along rhythm section features Dan Haerle on piano, Todd Coolman on bass, and Ed Soph on drums. The transcribed compositions are "The Boy Next Door," "East of the Sun," "Falling in Love with Love," "Honey Suckle Rose," "I Wish I Knew, Just Squeeze Me," "Melancholy Baby," "My Heart Stood Still," "Old Folks," "One O'clock Jump," and a ballad and swing version of "The Second Time Around."

2309. Volume 72—*Street of Dreams.*

Another set of standards in book and CD form. Mark Levine on piano, Tyrone Wheeler on bass, and Barry Ries on drums accompany the 12 transcriptions. The transcriptions are "Every Thing I Have Is Yours," "If You Could See Me Now," "I'm in the Mood for Love," "I'm Through with Love," "Jitterburg Waltz," "Just You, Just Me," "The Lamp Is Low," "Poinciana, Street of Dreams," "That Old Feeling," "The Touch of Your Lips," and "Try a Little Tenderness."

2310. Volume 73—*Stolen Moments Oliver Nelson's Favorites.*

Contains 11 transcriptions by Nelson in a book and accompanied by a rhythm section on CD. The rhythm section features Andy Laverne on piano, Lynn Seaton on bass, and Steve Davis on drums. Featured transcriptions are "Stolen Moments," "Alto-Itis," "Elegy for a Duck in Passing," "Black, Brown, and Beautiful," "Latino," "I Remember April," "Patterns, Six and Four," "The Meeting," "Straight Ahead," and "Teenie's Blues."

2311. Volume 74—*Latin Jazz.*

Contains 12 of the most popular Latin jazz standards. Offers another approach that contrasts with the typical swing and bossa nova styles that permeate most repertoires. The transcription are "St. Thomas," "West Coast Blues," "Soul Eyes," "Body and Soul," "Forest Flower," "Have You Met Miss Jones," "Desafinado," "What is This Thing Called Love," "What's New," "Don't Blame Me," "Opus de Funk," and "I Can't Get Started." The rhythm section features Mark Levine on piano, David Belove on bass, and Harold Muniz and John Santos on various percussion.

2312. Volume 75—*Countdown to Giant Steps.*

An interesting and informative book and two CDs by Andy LaVerne that includes a systematic approach to learning the harmonies of "Giant Steps" and "Countdown", and how to substitute those chord changes for standard chord changes on selected standards. The second CD breaks the "Giant Steps" harmony down into easy segments and moderate tempos. He also includes several standards with "Giant Steps" harmony substituted for the original harmony. The transcriptions are "Countdown," "Giant Steps," "Satellite," "26–2," "Body and Soul," "Exotica," "Central Park West," "Fifth House," "Night Has a Thousand Eyes," "Step by Step," and "But Not for Me." A second CD includes 17 primer tracks. The rhythm section features Andy LaVerne on piano, John Patitucci on bass, and Steve Davis on drums.

2313. Volume 76—*How to Learn Tunes.*

A book supplemented with a CD by David Baker. He focuses on how to memorize harmonies and melodies. The CD contains listening/learning play-along tracks, and the book contains exercises, practice tips, and information on how chord changes work.

2314. Volume 77—*Paquito D'Rivera: Latin, Brazilian, Caribbean, Jazz and Beyond.*

A book and CD that includes 13 Latin jazz classics by the saxophonist and his band. Includes are "A Night in Englewood," "Guataca City," "La Dama y Elvagabundo," "Christmas Without You," "Lorenzo Wings," "Memories,"

"Chucho," "Bluellespie," "El Cura," "Gdansk," "South of the Waltz," "Chick," and "Wapango." The band includes Daniel Freiberg on piano, Oscar Stagnaro on bass, Mark Walker on drums, and Parnell Saturnino on percussion.

2315. Volume 78—*Jazz Holiday Classics.*

A book and CD that features a rhythm section of Andy LaVerne on piano, Lynn Seaton on bass, and Steve Davis on drums. The holiday classics are "We Three Kings," "Have Yourself a Merry Christmas," "I Saw Mommy Kissing Santa Claus," "Santa Claus is Coming to Town," "Silent Night," "Winter Wonderland," "I'll Be Home for Christmas," "Let It Snow," "Sleigh Ride," "Rudolph the Red Nose Reindeer," "Auld Lang Syne," and several more.

2316. Volume 79—*Avalon.*

The 12 transcriptions are in book form, and accompanied by a rhythm section on a CD. The rhythm section features Dan Haerle on piano, Lynn Seaton on bass, and Ed Soph on drums. Among the transcriptions are "Avalon," "Ja-Da," "Three O'clock in the Morning," "Toot Toot Tootsie," "Bill Bailey Won't You Please Come Home," "You Made Me Love You," "After You've Gone," and "Margie."

2317. Volume 80—*Indiana.*

Includes 12 standards that are similar in mode to Volume 79. Important because some of the tunes function as harmonic contrafacts to many bebop compositions. Among the transcriptions are "Look for the Silver Lining," "Baby Won't You Please Come Home," "I Hear a Rhapsody," "Poor Butterfly," "Indiana," "My Melancholy Baby," "Billy Boy," and "Some of These Days."

2318. Volume 81—*Contemporary Standards and Originals with the David Liebman Group.*

Presents new interpretations of old standards, and features challenging and creative arrangements. He includes originals as well as new harmonizations of old standards to create a new musical expression. The arrangements include "Dancing in the Dark," "All Blues," "Green Dolphin Street," "Nica's Dream," "Maiden Voyage," and many more.

2319. Volume 82—*Dexter Gordon.*

Transcriptions of several of the compositions that characterized the big, hard driving, and swinging sound of this giant. Accompanied by a rhythm section of George Cables on piano, Rufus Reid on bass, and Victor Lewis on drums. Among the 13 transcriptions are "Fried Bananas," "Sticky

Wicky," "Montmartre," "Apple Jump," "Soul Sister," "Boston Bernie," "I Want More," "Dexology," and "For Regulars Only."

2320. Volume 83—*The Brecker Brothers.*

Produced by George Whitty and imbued with electronic sounds and contemporary rhythms, there are 10 funk/fusion transcriptions in this book and on CD. The transcriptions are "Skunk Funk," "Above and Below," "And Then She Wept," "Funk See, Funk Do," "Inside Out," "Slang," "Song For Barry," "Sponge," "Straphangin'," and "African Skys."

2321. Volume 84—*Dominant Seventh Workout.*

Explores the nature of the dominant seventh, and describes different ways jazz artists have used it for color and texture. Includes numerous patterns on the two CD tracks for practice, developing technique, and for understanding the myriad of ways and means the chord can be used in jazz contexts. A rhythm section of Jamey Aebersold on piano, Tyrone Wheeler on bass, and Steve Davis on drums accompany the exercise.

2322. Volume 85—*Tunes You Though: Reharmonized Standards.*

A special play-along designed by Andy Laverne that includes new harmonies for many old standards. Laverne is accompanied by Rufus Reid on bass and Steve Davis on drums. Among the transcriptions are "Cantaloupe Island," "I Hear a Rhapsody," "Maiden Voyage," "On Green Dolphin Street," "Smoke Gets in Your Eyes," "Watermelon Man," "Song for My Father," "Stella by Starlight," "Dream," and "Yesterdays."

2323. Volume 86—*Horace Silver: Shoutin' Out.*

A representation of a variety of Silver's style, tempos, and uses of harmony. These songs can be combined with the classics covered in Volumes 17 and 18 to give the student a comprehensive knowledge of the composer's approaches and style. Mark Levine on piano, Lynn Seaton on bass, and Adam Nussbaum on drums accompany the CD. the transcriptions are "Doodlin'," "Juicy Lucy," "Jungle Juice," "Mary Lou Moon Rays," "Penny," "Pretty Eyes," "Senor Blues," "Serenade to a Soul Sister," "Shoutin' Out," "The Hardbop Grandpop," and "Tokyo Blues."

2324. Volume 87—*Benny Carter: When the Lights Are Low.*

A good collection of compositions that represent Carter's fine harmonic and melodic gifts. Harry Pickens on piano, Tyrone Wheeler on bass, and Steve Davis on drums accompany the 12 transcriptions. Among the transcriptions are "All That Jazz," "Another Time," "Another Place," "Doozy," "Summer Serenade," "When Lights Are Low," "You, Only You," and "The Romp."

2325. Volume 88—*Millennium Blues.*

The 14 transcriptions include both originals and tunes by some giants of jazz. In addition, the book and CD cover diverse keys, forms, and meters. Among the 14 transcriptions are "Solar," "Dance of the Infidels," "Slow 12/8 Blues," "C Minor Blues," "Bossa Nova Blues in F Minor," "16 Bar Blues," "The Real McCoy," "Stop-Time Blues in F," and more. The compositions are accompanied by John Stetch on piano, Rufus Reid on bass, and Akira Ttana on drums.

2326. Volume 89—*Darn That Dream.*

The book and CD contain 12 of the most performed standards accompanied by Mark Levine on piano, Lynn Seaton on bass, and Steve Davis on drums. Among the transcriptions are "Can't We Be Friends," "Darn That Dream," "Gentle Rain," a slow and fast version of "I Can't Give You Anything But Love," "No More Blues," "This Can't Be Love," and "Who Can I Turn To."

2327. Volume 90—*Odd Times: Unusual Time Signatures.*

This volume contains a collection of compositions in meters that are not common in jazz. Accompanied by Andy Laverne on piano, John Goldsby on bass, and John Riley on drums, there are 10 transcriptions in the collection. The transcriptions are "First Step," "Girl From Ipanema," "Guido Rides Again," "Latin Minor Blues," "Major Scales," "My Favorite Things," "On Green Dolphin Street," "Seven for Twelve," "Shuffle Blues," and "Take Five."

2328. Volume 91—*Player's Choice: Favorites From Maters of the Craft.*

Another collection of compositions that are popular among jazz performers. Among the favorites are "A Child Is Born," "Azule Serape," "Beatrice," "Bernie's Tune," "Dear Old Stockholm," "Our Delight," "Slow Boat to China," and several more. The rhythm section features Mark Levine on piano, Rufus Reid on bass, and Barry Ries on drums.

2329. Volume 92—*Lennie Niehaus.*

A book and CD personally assembled by the composer, arranger, and recording artist. Enables the student to explore his compositional and improvisational techniques. The songs include a variety of styles such as swing, bossa, waltz, minor blues, 5/4, blues, and several more. The rhythm section has Lynn Arriale on piano, Tyrone Wheeler on bass, and Steve Davis on drums.

2330. Volume 93—*What's New: Guitar Trio.*

This is the first collection of songs in the Aebersold Play-A-Long series to feature a guitar trio. The trio consists of Dave Stryker on guitar, Bill

Moring on bass, and Tim Horner on drums. The songs include "Autumn in New York," "Body and Soul," "On Green Dolphin Street," "Ornithology," "The End of a Love Affair," "There Will Never Be Another You," "What's New," and "Stella by Starlight."

2331. Volume 94—*Hot House.*

A book and CD of bebop standards that features James Williams on piano, Christian McBride on bass, and Jeff Watts on drums. The classics are "All or Nothing at All," "As Time Goes By," "Blue and Sentimental," "Chi Chi," "Close Your Eyes," "Crazy Rhythm," "Estate," "Good-Bye," "Hot House," and "The Old Country."

2332. Volume 95—*Five Hundred Miles.*

A collection of jazz standards in book form and on a CD. A rhythm section of David Hazeltine on piano, Dennis Irwin on bass, and Tony Reedus on drums is featured. Among the compositions are "500 Miles High," "All of Me," "Only Trust Your Heart," "The Talk of the Town," and "Windows."

2333. Volume 96—*Latin Quarter: Dave Samuels and the Caribbean Project.*

Features Dave Samuels on vibes, Steve Kahn on guitar, Dario Eskenazi on piano, Ruben Rodriquez and Oscar Stagnaro on bass, Mark Walker and Robbie Ameen on drums, and Richie Flores on percussion. The transcriptions include "One Stop Ahead," "Paco and Dave," "Latin Quarter," "Sadie's Dance," "Jamboree," "Ivory Coast," and "Rain Forest."

2334. Volume 97—*Standards With Strings.*

The 10 arrangements by Lennie Niehaus include many of the popular favorites recorded by several jazz artists. The arrangements include "I Cover the Waterfront," "Fools Rush In," "You Go to My Head," "You're My Everything," "Autumn in New York," and "Lover Come Back to Me." Steve Allee accompanies the arrangements on piano, Tyrone Wheeler on bass, Steve Davis on drums, Peter McHugh on violin, and Alan Oldfield on synthesized strings.

2335. Volume 98—*Antonio Carlos Jobim Authentic Brazilian Bossa Novas.*

Dave Stryker accompanies the compositions on nylon string guitar, Bill Mooring on bass, and Duduka Da Fonseca on drums and percussion. The compositions are "Once I Loved," "Corcovado," "Wave," "So Danco Samba," "O Grande Amor," "Trista," "Mediation," "One Note Samba," "Desafinado," "Girl From Ipanema," "How Insensitive," and "No More Blues."

2336. Volume 99—*Soultrane.*

This collection features the music of Tadd Dameron, one of the first great arranger and composers of the bebop era. The often performed compositions are "Ladybird," "Good Bait," "Soultrane," "Super Jet," "Hot House," "Our Delight," "Mating Call," "You're A Joy," "Tadd's Delight," "On a Misty Night," "The Scene Is Clean," and "If You Could See Me Now." The rhythm section consists of Andy Laverne on piano, Rufus Reid on bass, and John Riley on drums.

2337. Volume 100—*St. Louis Blues: Dixieland Classics.*

Accompanied by Steve Allee on piano, John Goldsby on bass, and Rob Rawsthorne on drums, this play-along includes 18 songs. Among the songs are "After You've Gone," "Alexander's Ragtime Band," "Bill Bailey Won't You Come Home," "Indiana," "Royal Garden Blues," "Tiger Rag," Way Down Yonder in New Orleans, "When the Saints Go Marching In," and several more.

2338. Volume 101—*Secret of the Andes: Andy Laverne Tunes.*

A compilation of the tunes of the pianist and composer, a frequent accompanist on the Aebersold play-along recordings. Offers a sampling of his favorites and demonstrates his chord substitution style. The compositions are *"Subject to Change," "Gone Forever," "Bilbao," "Anticipointment," "A Loan to Gather," "Secret of the Andes," "Process of Illumination," "Walking Off the Moon," "There's No There There,"* and several more. In addition to Laverne on piano, the rhythm section features Rufus Reid on bass and John Riley on drums.

2339. Volume 102—*Jerry Bergonzi: Sound Advice.*

The compositions have been previously recorded on CDs and represent some of the best work of this former Dave Brubeck tenor saxophonist. Featured are "Out House," "Red's Blues," "The Ray," "Sound Advice," "Wind Print," "Inside Out," "Con Brio," "Simultaneous Looks," "Different Places," and several more. The rhythm section includes Renato Chicco on piano, Dave Santuro on bass, and Adam Nussbaum on drums.

2340. Volume 103—*David Sanborn.*

A collection of fusion compositions written by Sanborn and Marcus Miller. This is an electronic play-along arranged by George White, and includes "Snake," "Chicago Song," "Corners," "Imogene," "Run For Cover," "Straight to the Heart," "Lisa," "Hideaway," "Full House," and "As We Speak."

2341. Volume 104—*Kenny Werner: Free Play.*

This play-along features Kenny Werner on piano, Jahannes Weidenmueller on bass, and Ari Hoenig on drums. He breaks all the traditional boundaries of harmony, melody, and rhythm, and also includes a blank canvas of sounds, pulses, and colors for the budding free improviser to generate their own conceptual ideas. They perform "Random Sequence Piece," "Just Sound Piece," "Short Note Piece," "Harmony Piece," "Time, No Changes," "A Prayer in C Minor," and "Unaccompanied Pieces for Bass, Drums, and Piano."

2342. Volume 105—*Dave Brubeck: In Your Own Sweet Way.*

Features several Brubeck favorities, and in addition to Brubeck on piano and Michael Moore on bass, Randy Jones is the drummer. The transcriptions are "All My Love," "Basie," "Broadway Bossa Nova," "Here Comes McBride," "In Your Own Sweet Way," "Take Five," "Waltzing," "Why Not," and several more.

2343. Volume 106—*Lee Morgan: Sidewinder.*

Contains some of his most important compositions, tunes that greatly influenced hard bop. The compositions include "Ceora," "Gigolo," "Koza's Waltz," "Morgan the Pirate," "Sidewinder," "Speedball," "Stop Short," "Totem Pole," "Zambia," and several more. The rhythm section features Steve Allee on piano, Tyrone Wheeler on bass, and Jonathan Higgins on drums.

2344. Volume 107—*It Had To Be You: Standards in Female Singer's Keys.*

A collection of 24 compositions in book form and on two CDs. The play-along CDs feature a sensitive rhythm sections that consists of Steve Allee on piano, Tyrone Wheeler on bass, and Jonathan Higgins on drums. Among the compositions are "A Foggy Day," "Alone Together," "Body and Soul," "But Not for Me," "Bye Bye Blackbird," "Misty," "My Funny Valentine," "Skylark," "Stardust," "Summertime," "What's New," "What Is This Thing Called Love," and several more.

2345. Volume 108—*Joe Henderson.*

The 15 songs display his compositional genius, and serves as a vehicle for producing the type of soundscapes that are indicative of Henderson's compositions and improvisations. Among the compositions are "Black Narcissus," "Granted," "Home Stretch," "Mo' Joe," "Inner Urge," "Mamacita," "Punjab," "Serenity," "A Shade of Jade," "The Kicker," and several more.

Aebersold for Bass

2346a. Aebersold, Jamey. *Transcribed Bass Lines* (Jamey Aebersold Play-a-Long Series).

A series of nine companion books to accompany selected Jamey Aebersold Play-A-Long recordings. The books focus on professional bass line construction with chord symbols above each measure.

2346. Carter, Ron. *"Charlie Parker" Bass Lines* (Volume 6, Aebersold Play-A-Long Series). New Albany, Ind.: Jamey Aebersold; 1972.

The transcribed bass lines that the author used on volume 6 of the Aebersold Play-A-Long Series. The compositions are "Billie's Bounce," "Confirmation," "Dewey Square," "Donna Lee," "My Little Suede Shoes," "Now's the Time," "Ornithology," "Scrapple from the Apple," "Thriving from a Riff," and "Yardbird Suite."

2347. _____. *Volume 15 "Payin' Dues" Bass Lines.* New Albany, Ind.: Jamey Aebersold; 1977.

The author transcribes the bass lines that he used on volume 15 of the Aebersold Play-A-Long Series. Bass lines to "Body and Soul," "Cherokee," "I'll Remember April," "It's You or No One," "Stella by Starlight," "There Will Never Be Another You," "The Song Is You," and "What Is This Thing Called Love."

2348. _____. *Volume 35 "Cedar Walton" Bass Lines.* New Albany, Ind.: Jamey Aebersold; 1979.

The third in the trilogy of bass lines books transcribed from an Aebersold Play-A-Long recording. Contains "Bolivia," "Cedar's Blues," "Clockwise," "Fantasy in D," "Hand in Glove," "Maestro," "Midnight Waltz," and "Ojos De Rojo."

2349. Coolman, Todd. *Volume 37 "Sammy Nestico" Bass Lines.* New Albany, Ind.: Jamey Aebersold; 1983.

Contains Coolman's bass lines on "88 Basie Street," "Basie-Straight Ahead," "Hay Burner," "Lonely Street," "Samantha," "Switch in Time," "Warm Breeze," "Wind Machine," and "Ya Gotta Try."

2350. _____. *The Bottom Line.* New Albany, Ind.: Jamey Aebersold; 1993.

The 23 chapters cover topics like bass line construction, sound production, practicing, special effects, blues, slow/fast tempos, and time/feel. There are exercises for each chapter.

2351. Cranshaw, Bob. *Volume 42 "Blues in All Keys" Bass Lines.* New Albany, Ind.: Jamey Aebersold; 1984.

Transcriptions of the electric walking bass lines the author performed on volume 42 of the Aebersold Play-A-Long Series. There are several choruses of two different blues progressions in all 12 keys.

2352. Davis, Steve. *Jazz Drum Play-a-Long CD.* New Albany, Ind.: Jamey Aebersold; 1993.

Play-along tracks from Volume 54 *Maiden Voyage* of the Aebersold Play-A-Long Series. The compositions represent various forms, feels, and tempos. A companion to volume 54. Book and CD.

2353. Gilmore, Steve. *Volume 25 "All-Time Standards" Bass Lines.* New Albany, Ind.: Jamey Aebersold; 1981.

Transcriptions of the author's bass lines on Volume 25 of the Aebersold Play-A-Long Series. Compositions are "A Foggy Day," "Come Rain or Come Shine," "Have You Met Miss Jones," "I Can't Get Started," "If I Could Write a Book," "I Love You," "It Might As Well Be Spring," "I've Grown Accustomed to Her Face," "My Funny Valentine," "Old Devil Moon," "Our Love Is Here to Stay," "September Song," "Speak Low," "Summertime," and "The Party's Over."

2354. _____. *Volume 34 "Jam Session" Bass Lines.* New Albany, Ind.: Jamey Aebersold; 1982.

The author's bass lines to "Blue Moon," "Don't Blame Me," "I Left My Heart in San Francisco," "Invitation," "Just Friends," "Laura," "My Secret Love," "No Greater Love," "On the Trail," "On Green Dolphin Street," "Once in a While," "Over the Rainbow," "Spring Is Here," "Star Eyes," "Stompin' at the Savoy," "The Shadow of Your Smile," "You Stepped out of a Dream," and "Without a Song."

2355. Goldsby, John. *Bass Notes.* New Albany, Ind.: Jamey Aebersold; 1990.

Goldsby's bass lines from volumes 41, 48, and 53 of the Aebersold Play-A-Long Series. Includes lines from "Alone Together," "What's New," "Do Nothin' Till You Hear from Me," "Sandu," "Joy Spring," and more. Analysis is offered for each composition. He also covers bass line construction and the role and function of the bass in combos. Book and cassette.

2356. Reid, Rufus. *Volumes I and 3 Bass Lines.* New Albany, Ind.: Jamey Aebersold; 1970

Transcriptions of the walking bass lines used in the two different volumes of the Aebersold Play-A-Long Series. Covers blues, Dorian minor, cycle of dominants, ii–V7 in all major keys, V7+9–I in minor keys, and more.

2357. Wheeler, Tyrone. *Volume 54 "Maiden Voyage" Bass Lines.* New Albany, Ind.: Jamey Aebersold; 1982.

Contains transcriptions of the bass lines the author used on volume 54 of the Aebersold Play-A-Long Series. The bass lines cover "Autumn Leaves," "B♭ Shuffle Blues," "Blue Bossa," "Cantaloupe Island," "Doxy," "F Blues," "Footprints," "Impressions," "Maiden Voyage," "Satin Doll," "Song for My Father," "Summertime," "Watermelon Man," and "iii–VI7 and ii–V7" progressions.

2358. _____. *Volume 54 Jazz Drum Style and Analysis.* New Albany, Ind.: Jamey Aebersold; 1993.

Contains comments on and transcriptions of the volume 54 *Maiden Voyage* play-along recording.

Aebersold for Piano

2359. Aebersold, Jamey. *Piano Voicings Transcribed from Volume 1* (Aebersold Play-A-Long Series). New Albany, Ind.: Jamey Aebersold; 1986.

Transcriptions of the chords, passing chords, voicing and pedal markings used by Aebersold on volume 1 (*Jazz: How to Play and Improvise*) of his Play-A-Long Series.

2360. _____. *Volume 54 Jazz Piano Voicings.* New Albany, Ind.: Jamey Aebersold; 1993.

A companion to Volume 54 *Maiden Voyage,* contains transcriptions of the voicings used by Aebersold on that recording.

2361. Galper, Hal. *Volume 55 "Jerome Kern."* New Albany, Ind.: Jamey Aebersold; 1993.

Uses digital transcribing to notate his melodic and rhythmic approaches. This book contains the techniques used on the *Jerome Kern* play-along recording (Jamey Aebersold).

2362. Levine, Mark. *Volume 56 "Thelonious Monk."* New Albany, Ind.: Jamey Aebersold; 1993.

Levine's use of Monkish comping, lead in, and harmonic concepts are transcribed in this book. The transcriptions can be used to follow volume 56, *Thelonious Monk,* of the Aebersold Play-A-Long Series.

2363. _____. *Volume 50 "Magic of Miles."* New Albany, Ind.: Jamey Aebersold; 1993.

Transcriptions of the comping and harmonic sequences the author used on volume 50 of the Aebersold Play-A-Long Series.

X

Transcriptions

Individual

Cannonball Adderley

2364. *The Cannonball Adderley Collection.* New Albany, Ind.: Jamey Aebersold; 2000.

Includes performance notes and an introduction to the artist, and 25 transcriptions of Adderley's classic solos. Among the transcriptions are "All Blues," "Dat Dere," "Freddie the Freeloader," "Love for Sale," "Jeanine," and more. Also included is an interview with Nat Adderley.

2365. Baker, David N. *The Jazz Style of Cannonball Adderley.* New York: CPP/Belwin; 1979.

Includes a biographical sketch, a musical genealogy chart, selected bibliography and discography, and worksheets. Among the transcribed solos are "Corcovado," "Green Dolphin Street," "The Weaver," "The Way You Look Tonight," "Straight, No Chaser," and more. ii–V harmonic tendencies are also discussed.

2366. Butler, Hunt (transcribed). *Cannonball Adderley.* New Albany, Ind.: Jamey Aebersold; 1990.

Contains 20 transcriptions of Adderley's solos. The solos were selected because (1) they would help to improve articulations, phrasing, style, and rhythm, and (2) they represent several contexts (ballads, blues, bossa novas, modal blues, and 32-bar standards). Nine of the solos are derived from *Cannonball Adderley Takes Charge.* Among the transcriptions are "If This Isn't Love," "I Guess I'll Hang My Tears out to Dry," "Stars Fell on Alabama," "Milestones," "Freddie the Freeloader," and "All Blues."

Herb Albert and Hugh Masekela

2367. Alpert, Herb, and Hugh Masekela. *Herb Alpert and Masekela: Jazz Transcriptions for Flugel Horn, Trumpet and Small Ensemble.* New York: Almo; 1978.

Presents short biomusical sketches on both performers along with such tunes as "African Summer," "Lobo," "I'll Be There for You," and "Skokian" (1981).

Louis Armstrong

2368. Armstrong, Louis. *125 Jazz Breaks for Trumpet—Louis Armstrong.* New York: Charles Hansen; 1977.

Compiles two-bar breaks in all keys from recordings of Louis Armstrong (1981).

2369. _____. *The Armstrong Treasury—Louis' Song Book/Trumpet Edition.* New York: Charles Hansen; 1976.

Contains over 30 songs associated with Louis and a special 16-page picture portfolio (1981).

2370. _____. *Jazz Giants—Louis Armstrong Dixieland Style Trumpet.* New York: Charles Hansen; 1975.

Features over 50 transcribed solos of Louis Armstrong, including "Tin Roof Blues," "High Society," "Doctor Jazz," "Copenhagen," "Chicago Breakdown," "New Orleans Stomp," "Wolverine Blues," and "Milenberg Joys" (1981).

2371. _____. *Jazz Giants: Louis Armstrong Dixieland Style Trumpet.* Milwaukee: MPL/Frank/Hal Leonard; 1977.

A collection of 51 solos transcribed from a myriad of Armstrong recordings. The solos include "Chattanooga Stomp," "Dixieland Blues," "Maple Leaf Rag," "Panama Blues," "Tin Roof Blues," "Wolverine Blues," "Gut Bucket Blues," "Heebie Jeebies," "Butter and Egg Man," "Struttin' with Some Barbecue," and more.

2372. _____. *Louis Armstrong's 44 Trumpet Solos and 125 Jazz Breaks.* New York: Charles Hansen; 1976.

Collects breaks and trumpet solos from the original "Fifty Hot Choruses of Armstrong" (1981).

2373. Schiff, Ronny (editor). *Louis Armstrong: A Jazz Master.* Milwaukee: MCA Music Publishing; 1961.

Begins with a concise biographical profile and continues with analytical comments on each transcription. The transcribed solos include "Butter and Egg Man," "Come Back Sweet Papa," "Cornet Chop Suey," "Gut Bucket Blues," "Heebie Jeebies," "Hotter Than That," "Potato Head Blues," "Struttin' with Some Barbecue," "Tight Like This," and several more.

George Benson

2374. Rubin, Dave. *The Guitar Style of George Benson,* Milwaukee: Hal Leonard; 2000.

In addition to the concise biographical profile, the book contains 13 transcriptions of Benson's improvisations. Included are "Billie's Bounce," "Gentle Rain," "Song for My Father," and 10 more. The author also provides helpful hints regarding how to develop a musical style like that of George Benson.

Bob Berg

2375. Berg, Bob. *Bob Berg: More Tenor Solos.* New Albany, Ind.: Jamey Aebersold; 2001.

There are two volumes to this series. There are 11 transcriptions in volume 2, including "Kwirk," "Autumn Leaves," "Silverado," "Walkie Talkie," "Upside Downside," "Bruze," "Night Hawks," "Words" and four more.

Art Blakey

2376. *Jazz Repertory Transcription Series.* New York: Second Floor Music; 1983.

Transcriptions of several compositions from Art Blakey and the Jazz Messengers recordings. The transcribed tunes are "Weirdo-o," "E.T.A.," "Ms. B. C.," "What Do You Say Dr. J.," and "Mr. Timmons." The transcriptions are for combos and are exact duplications of each part from the original. There are rehearsal notes and a conductor's score.

Michael Brecker

2377. No Author. *Michael Brecker Collection.* New Albany, Ind.: Jamey Aebersold; 2000.

The transcriptions are from his *Tales From the Hudson* and *Two Blocks From the Edge* albums. Among the transcriptions are "African Skies,"

"Cabin Fever," "Delta City Blues," "Impressions," "Slings and Arrows," and several more.

2378. Coan, Carl. *Michael Brecker Solos.* New Albany, Ind.: Jamey Aebersold; 2000.

Contains a concise biography and a discussion of his use of alternate fingerings, split-tones, and multiphonic playing. There are 19 transcriptions.

Clifford Brown

2379. Baker, David N. *The Jazz Style of Clifford Brown.* New York: CPP/Belwin; 1982.

In addition to the biographical sketch, a musical genealogy chart, selected bibliography and discography, and worksheets are included. Among the transcribed solos are "Joy Spring," "I'll Remember April," "All the Things You Are," "What Is This Thing Called Love," and more. The author also discusses harmonic tendencies, and provides a summary of ii–V patterns.

2380. Lewis, Marc. *Clifford Brown Complete Transcriptions.* New Albany, Ind.: Jamey Aebersold; 2001.

The 70 transcriptions cover nearly every recording made by Brown, including many from the Clifford Brown-Max Roach recordings. Among the numerous transcriptions are "Blues Walk," "Kiss and Run," "I'll Remember April," "Dahoud," "Gertrude Bounce," "All the Things You Are," "Joy Spring," and many more.

2381. Slone, Ken. *Clifford Brown Trumpet Solos.* Louisville, Kentucky: Ducknob Music; 1981.

In addition to the concise biographical sketch and selected discography (personnel, label, recording date, venue, and year), there are 16 transcriptions. The transcriptions are "Cherokee," "Daahoud," "Gertrude's Bounce," "If I Love Again," "I'll Remember April," "Jordu," "Joy Spring," "Kiss and Run," "Pent-Up House," "Sandu," "The Scene Is Clean," "The Song Is You," "Stompin' at the Savoy," "Tiny Capers," "What Is This Thing Called Love," and "Take the 'A' Train."

Dave Brubeck

2382. No Author. *Seriously Brubeck.* New Albany, Ind.: Jamey Aebersold; 2002.

Showcases Brubeck's classical-influenced jazz compositions. The transcriptions include "Glances," "Overture," "Blue Aria," "Struttin,'" "Doing the Charleston," "Points on Jazz," "Prelude," "Scherzo," "Blues," "Fugue,"

"Rag," "Chorale," "A La Turk," "Chromatic Fantasy Sonata," "Allegro," "Chorale," "Chaconne," "Fugue," and "Tritonis."

Benny Carter

2383. Carter, Benny. *Benny Carter Plays Standards.* New Albany, Ind.: Jamey Aebersold; 2000.

In addition to the concise essay on the man and his musical career, the collection includes several transcriptions of his improvisations. Included are "Misty," "I Can't Get Started," "Lover Man," and more.

Charlie Christian

2384. Ayeroff, Stan. *Charlie Christian.* New York: Amsco Publications; 1980.

Provides a musical profile, selected discography, and several transcriptions. Among the transcriptions are "Honeysuckle Rose," "Stardust," "Dinah," "Swing to Bop," "I Can't Give You Anything but Love," and more.

2385. No Author. *Charlie Christian the Definitive Collection.* New Albany, Ind.: Jamey Aebersold; 2000.

In addition to the biographical sketch, the collection contains 15 transcriptions. The transcriptions are "Air Mail Special," "Flying Home," "Gone With What Wind," "Grand Slam," "Honeysuckle Rose," "Rose Room," "Seven Come Eleven," "Shivers," "Six Appeal," "Solo Flight," "Stardust," "Stompin' at the Savoy," "Swing to Bop," "Till Tom Special," and "Wholly Cats."

John Coates, Jr.

2386. Dobbins, Bill (transcribed). *The Jazz Compositions of John Coates Jr.* Delaware Water Gap, Pa.: Shawnee Press Inc.; 1983.

Included are 12 compositions for jazz pianists. Heads are included but not improvised sections. The compositions are permeated with creative harmonic, melodic, and rhythmic ideas. John Coates originally recorded the compositions on Omnisound N-1004 and N-1015. Five of the compositions are labeled folk-rock; however, swinging and rubato movements are also provided. Coates deemphasized counterpoint but accentuated harmony and tonal concepts.

John Coltrane

2387. No Author. *John Coltrane.* New Albany, Ind.: Jamey Aebersold; 2000.

Includes transcriptions of "Blue Train," "Moment's Notice," "Lazy Bird," "Omicron," "We Six," "Nita," "Just for Love," and "Locomotion." Also includes the trumpet parts for "Omicron," "Moment's Notice," and "Lazy Bird." An introduction, chord changes, discography, and special notation also included.

2388. Baker, David N. *The Jazz Style of John Coltrane*. New York: CPP/Belwin; 1978.

Features a biographical profile, a musical genealogy chart, selected bibliography and discography, and worksheets. The transcribed solos include "Countdown," "Giant Steps," "Little Melonae," "Milestones," "Straight, No Chaser," and more. A discussion of ii–V tendencies is also included.

2389. Coan, Carl. *John Coltrane Transcriptions*. New Albany, Ind.: Jamey Aebersold; 2000.

Includes 27 soprano and tenor saxophone transcriptions. Includes "All Blues," "Blue Train," "Countdown," "Cousin Mary," "Giant Steps," "Grand Central," "My Favorite Things," "So What," "Oleo," and several more.

2390. Coltrane, John. *John Coltrane Plays Coltrane Changes*. New Albany, Ind.: Jamey Aebersold; 2002.

The book focuses on an exploration of Coltrane's harmonic changes, "Giant Steps" and "Countdown," by studying 13 of his improvisations. He espouses that each improvisation contains Coltrane's unique harmonic formula. The transcriptions include "Body and Soul," "But Not for Me," "Central Park West," "Countdown," "Fifth House," "Giant Steps," "Summertime," "The Night Has a Thousand Eyes," and more.

2391. *Coltrane Plays Standards*. Milwaukee: Hal Leonard; 2000.

Contains 14 transcriptions of standards played and popularized by John Coltrane. Begins with a concise biographical portrait followed by Coltrane's improvisations on "All or Nothing at All," "My Favorite Things," "My One and Only Love," and 11 more.

2392. Isacoff, Stuart. *The Music of John Coltrane*. Milwaukee: Hal Leonard Publishing Company; 1991.

A collection of 100 tunes composed by Coltrane. There is a biography of Coltrane, and tunes such as "Blue Train," "Cousin Mary," "Giant Steps," "Lazy Bird," "A Love Supreme," and 95 more. Alice Coltrane supplies chord suggestions. The discography lists the specific recording of each tune.

2393. Sickler, Don. *John Coltrane Improvised Solos*. Miami, Florida: CPP/Belwin, Inc.; 1986.

A biography, discography, and extensive notes on John Coltrane's style are included with the eight transcriptions. Three transcriptions include a trumpet melody. The other transcriptions are "Nita," "Just For Love," "We Six," "Blue Train," and "Locomotion." Chord symbols and articulation markings are included.

2394. White, Andrew. *John Coltrane Transcriptions.* Washington, D.C.: Andrew's Music; 1993.

The author has transcribed over 400 Coltrane solos. The titles, recordings, and dates are detailed in a catalogue available from the author. White is a scholar and an outstanding oboist/tenor saxophonist.

Chick Corea

2395. *Chick Corea: Inside Out.* Milwaukee: Hal Leonard; 1990.

There is a foreword by Corea, an explanation of his chord symbols, and several photographs. The six transcriptions are "Inside-Out," "Make a Wish," "Stretch It," "Kicker," "Child's Play," and "Tale of Daring."

2396. Novello, John; foreword by Chick Corea. *The Contemporary Keyboardist.* Los Angeles: Source Productions; 1986.

Covers philosophy, mechanics, business, and interviews. Among the philosophical issues discussed are "what makes a magical performance," "communication with music," and "objective self-criticism"; mechanical issues include ear training, comping, voicing, transposition, modes, blues, and improvisation. Business topics are concerned with surviving in the music world, including travel, lawyers, managers, public relations, and career decisions. The section on interviews includes the personal and probing beliefs, insights, and opinions of Chick Corea, Herbie Hancock, Keith Emerson, Michael Boddicker, Henry Mancini, and others.

2397. Sprague, Peter. *The Jazz Solos of Chick Corea.* Petaluma, Calif.: Sher Music Company (P.O. Box 445); 1992.

A collection of 23 pieces transcribed by an excellent guitarist. In addition to the transcriptions, the author recommends that students first listen to the tune and the solo before attempting to emulate the style. Among the transcribed solos are "Friends," "Litha," "500 Miles High," "Spain," and more.

Bob Cranshaw

2398. Boaden, Fred. *Bob Cranshaw Bass Lines.* New Albany, Ind.: Jamey Aebersold; 1988.

Transcriptions of 12 tracks of blues from Jamey Aebersold's "Blues in All Keys." A short discussion of blues changes and turnarounds is also included.

Miles Davis

2399. No Author. *Miles Davis: Standards, Volume I.* Milwaukee: Hal Leonard; 2000.

Highlights transcriptions from three recordings Davis made between 1955 and 1956. Begins with a short biography, and editor notes to the songs. Among the classics are "Bye Bye Blackbird," "My Funny Valentine," "Surrey with the Fringe on Top," and 18 more.

2400. _____. *Miles Davis Originals.* Volumes 1 and 2. New Albany, Ind.: Jamey Aeberold; 2000.

There are 15 transcriptions in volume 1, including "Agitation," "Circle," "Freddie the Freeloader," "Green Haze," "Miles," "Milestones," "Sid's Ahead," "All Blues," "Theme," "Blue in Green," "Flamenco," "Sketches," "Half Nelson," "So What," "Solar," and "Tune Up." Volume 2 contains 14 transcriptions, including "Agitation," "All Blues," "Bitches Brew," "Country Son," "Eighty One," "Filles De Kilimanjaro," "Four," "Miles," "Miles Run the Voodoo Down," "No Blues," "Petits Machins," "Seven Steps to Heaven," "So What," and "Spanish Key."

2401. _____. *Miles Davis: Kind of Blue.* New Albany, Ind.: Jamey Aebersold; 2000.

Complete transcriptions of all tunes on this famous album. Includes many piano voicings and bass lines, and the solos of Miles Davis, John Coltrane, Cannonball Adderley, and Bill Evans. Among the transcriptions are "All Blues," "Freddie the Freeloader," "Blue in Green," "So What," and several more.

2402. Baker, David N. *The Jazz Style of Miles Davis.* New York: CPP/Belwin; 1977.

Includes a biographical sketch, a musical genealogy chart, selected bibliography and discography, and worksheets. Transcribed solos include "So What," "Straight, No Chaser," "Tune Up," "Freedom Jazz Dance," and several more. ii–V patterns are also summarized.

2403. Brown, John Robert (transcribed). *Jazz Trumpet 2.* New York: Warner Brothers; 1987.

A collection of 21 Miles Davis solos, dating from his 1949 *Birth of the Cool* album to "Tutu." Among the transcriptions are "All Blues," "Boplicity," "E.S.P.," "Freddie the Freeloader," "The Maids of Cadiz," "So What," and more. There are comments to accompany each transcription.

2404. Edmonds, Hank. *More of Miles Davis for All Instruments.* New York: Charles Colin; 1958.

Contains some tunes for piano, accordion, guitar, and vibes (e.g., "Ruby and Garnet"), and others for trumpet-tenor sax-clarinet (e.g., "Amethyst"), or alto sax-bass sax and trombone (1981).

2405. Isacoff, Stuart. *Jazz Masters: Miles Davis.* New York: Consolidated Music Publishers; 1979.

An overview of his styles, 11 transcriptions and a selected discography. The transcribed solos are "Groovin High," "Dig," "Airegin," "I'll Remember April," "Doxy," "Oleo," "Tune Up," "All of Me," "Four," "Stella by Starlight," and "I Waited for You." The selected discography is limited to recordings where the tunes were first recorded.

2406. Washburn, Dick, and Pat Harbison. *Miles Davis.* New Albany, Ind.: Jamey Aebersold; 1980.

Begins with a short introduction and an analysis of each of the 10 transcriptions. The transcriptions are "Dig," "Serpent's Tooth," "Tune Up" (May 19, 1953), "Miles Ahead," "Solar," "Miles' Theme," "Vierd Blues," "Oleo," "Airegin," and "Tune Up" (October 26, 1956). Prestige records between October 1951 and October 1956.

2407. Item deleted.

Nathan Davis

2408. Davis, Nathan. *Flute Improvisation.* New York: Armstrong, Edu-tainment; 1975.

Presents 17 original flute solos representing various jazz styles as well as six exercises based on fourths, half steps, and the diminished modal style of John Coltrane (1981).

Paul Desmond

2409. Desmond, Paul. *Paul Desmond Jazz Saxophone Solos.* New York: Almo; 1978.

Includes tunes such as "Alianca," "Desmond Blues," "Late Lament," "Take Ten," and "Uberely." Chords in parentheses are in concert key for accompaniment by C instruments. A short biomusical essay appears at the beginning of the book (1981).

Al DiMeola, John McLaughlin, Paco DeLucia

2410. DiMeola, Al, John McLaughlin, and Paco DeLucia. *Friday Night in San Francisco.* Milwaukee: 21st Century Publications/Music Dispatch; 1991.

A matching folio to the Grammy Award–winning album recorded at a live concert in San Francisco. There are transcriptions of each tune, including "Short Tales of the Black Forest," "Mediterranean Sundance/Rio Ancho," "Fantasia Suite," and more.

2411. DiMeola, Al. *Music, Words, Pictures.* Milwaukee: 21st Century Publications/Music Dispatch (Distributor); 1991.

A collection of tunes transcribed from his solo recordings, a biography, selected discography, and a description of his techniques. Among the transcriptions are "Egyptian Danza," "Elegant Gypsy Suite," "Land of the Midnight Sun," and more.

Eric Dolphy

2412. No Author. *Eric Dolphy Collection.* New Albany, Ind.: Jamey Aebersold; 2000.

Introduces the student to the man and his music, and includes 16 transcriptions. The transcriptions include "God Bless the Child," "Serene, Stormy Weather," "The Way You Look Tonight," and "You Don't Know What Love is."

2413. White, Andrew. *Eric Dolphy Transcriptions.* Washington, D.C.: Andrew's Music; 1993.

Several alto and flute transcriptions organized by recording and date. The specific titles are listed in the author's comprehensive catalogue, available upon request.

Roy Eldridge

2414. No Author. *The Artistry of Roy Eldridge.* New Albany, Ind.: Jamey Aebersold; 2000.

The 14 transcriptions include "Body and Soul," "Stardust," "Undecided," "Wild Man Blue," and ten more. Also includes a concise biography of this celebrated trumpeter.

Duke Ellington

2415. *Duke Ellington for Jazz Guitar: 15 Sensational Songs.* Milwaukee: Hal Leonard; 2000.

Arranges 15 Ellington classics for solo guitar. The book contains compositions such as "Take the 'A' Train" and "It Don't Mean a Thing if It Ain't Got That Swing," traditional big band compositions, which led the arranger to imbue the compositions with blues and swing feels to make them palatable to solo guitar.

Bill Evans

2416. Evans, Bill. *Bill Evans; The Trio, Volumes 1–4.* New Albany, Ind.: Jamey Aebersold; 2002–2003.

Includes piano, bass, and drum transcriptions of eight tunes by Bill Evans, Scott LaFaro, and Paul Motian. Volume 1 includes "Alice in Wonderland," "Autumn Leaves," "How Deep is the Ocean," "Nardis," "Peri's Scope," "Solar," "Waltz for Debby," and "When I Fall in Love." Volume 2 features Evans, Chuck Israels, and Larry Bunker, and Paul Motian. The eight transcriptions are "Come Rain or Come Shine," "How My Heart Sing," "Isn't it Romantic," "Israel," "Re: Person I knew," "Show-Type Tune," "Stella by Starlight," and "34 Skidoo". The 1968–1974 trio transcriptions feature Evans, Eddie Gomez, and drummers Marty Morrell, Philly Joe Jones, and Jack DeJohnette on volume 3. The transcriptions are "Alfie," "Emily," "Funkallero," "Round Midnight," "A Sleepin'Bee," "Some Day My Prince Will Come," "The Touch of Your Lips," "Who Can I Turn To." In the fourth volume, featuring Evans, Marc Johnson, and Joe LaBarbera, there are seven transcriptions. The Transcriptions are "Bill's Hit Tune," "But Beautiful," "For All We Know," "Like Someone in Love," "My Foolish Heart," "My Romance," and "The Two Lonely People." Volume 4 contains a discography.

2417. *Bill Evans Signature Licks.* New Albany, Ind.: Jamey Aebersold; 2002.

A book and CD that discusses the playing style of Bill Evans. The book/CD uses musical excerpts from a dozen of Evan's best improvisations, including "Five," "One for Helen," "The Opener," "Peace Piece," "Peri's Scope," "Quiet Now," "Re: Person I Knew," "34 Skidoo," "Time Remembered," "Turn Out the Stars," "Very Early," and "Waltz for Debby." "

2418. *Bill Evans: Piano Themes.* New York: TRO; 1986.

Six compositions recorded by Evans with symphony orchestra on Verde Records: "Blue Interlude," "Elegia" (Elegy), "Valse," "Prelude," "Pavana," and "Granados."

2419. *Bill Evans: The 1970's.* New York: TRO; 1984.

Eight original compositions arranged for solo piano: "B Minor Waltz," "For Nenette," "Laurie," "Maxine," "Remembering the Rain," "Song for Helen," "We Will Meet Again," and "Your Story."

2420. *Bill Evans: The 50's and 60's.* New York: TRO; 1982.

There are 31 original compositions in lead sheet format (five contain lyrics), first recording information, and a selected discography. Compositions include "Children's Play Song," "Displacement," "Funny Man," "Interplay," "No Cover No Minimum," "A Simple Matter of Conviction," "Time Remembered," "The Two Lonely People," "Very Early," and "Waltz for Debby."

2421. *Bill Evans: The Last Compositions.* New York: TRO; 1988.

Piano solos and lead sheets, a selected discography and 10 transcriptions. The transcriptions are "Bill's Hit Tune," "Knit for Mary F.," "Letter to Evan," "Since We Met," "Tiffany," "The Two Lonely People," "Yet Ne'er Broken," "In April (for Nenette)", "It's Love," "It's Christmas," "Laurie (The Dream)."

2422. *Bill Evans Piano Solos.* New York: TRO; 1979.

Contains six piano compositions: "Fudgesickle Built for Four," "Interplay," "My Bells," "Time Remembered," "Very Early," and "Waltz for Debby."

2423. *Bill Evans Plays.* New York: TRO; 1981.

Includes a biography, several photographs, and five transcriptions: "Who Can I Turn To," "Funny Man," "One for Helen," "Only Child," "Orbit," and "Turn Out the Stars."

2424. *Bill Evans: Symbiosis.* New York: TRO; 1985.

Contains the first and second movements as recorded with the Claus Ogerman Orchestra on MPS records.

2425. LeVerne, Andy. *Bill Evans.* New York: Trio Music; 1998.

Andy LeVerne, a former student of Bill Evans, arranged the 19 transcriptions. Among the transcriptions are "Time Remembered," "Turn Out the Stars," "Re: Person I Knew," "Waltz for Debbie," and several more. The lengthy foreword is permeated with insightful observations and comments about Evans's life and music.

Maynard Ferguson

2426. Ferguson, Maynard. *The Jazz Styles of Maynard Ferguson.* New York: Warner; 1978.

Among the tunes transcribed for trumpet and piano included are "Chameleon," "Gospel John," "Maria," and "Primal Scream." A short biographical sketch is included (1981).

Frank Gambale

2427. Gambale, Frank. *Frank Gambale.* Milwaukee: Hal Leonard; 1991.

The transcriptions include a blend of melodic lines for guitarists and horn players, voicing for keyboard players, and bass lines. Transcriptions include "High 5," "Jet Ray," "Obsessed for Life," "Mr. Hollywood Line," and more. Gambale is a member of Chick Corea's Elektric Band.

Stan Getz

2428. No Author. *Stan Getz Tenor Solos.* New Albany, Ind.: Jamey Aebersold; 2000.

Includes a biographical sketch and the transcriptions of 20 Getz improvisations recorded from 1948 to 1990. The transcriptions include "All the Things You Are," "Body and Soul," "Cuba," "Girl From Ipanema," and "Yesterdays." The transcriptions are analyzed.

2429. Fishman, Greg. *Stan Getz Standards.* Milwaukee: Hal Leonard; 1999.

Begins with an introduction to the artists, and includes 18 transcriptions. Among the transcriptions are "Everything Happens to Me," "Indian Summer," "Moonlight in Vermont," "The Way You Look Tonight," "The Song is You," "Pennies from Heaven," "There Will Never be Another You," "Stella by Starlight," "Willow Weep for Me," and more.

Dizzy Gillespie

2430. No Author. *Dizzy Gillespie: The Collection.* New Albany, Ind.: Jamey Aebersold; 2000.

In addition to the short biographical essay, the collection includes numerous transcriptions. Included are transcriptions of "A Night in Tunisia," "Anthropology," "Blue 'N Boogie," "Con Alma," "Dizzy Atmosphere," "Dizzy Meets Sonny," "I Can't Get Started With You," "It Don't Mean a Thing if It Ain't Got That Swing," "Jambo," "Jersey Bounce," "Manteca," "Rose Room," "Salt Peanuts," "Sophisticated Lady," "Stardust," "Stella by Starlight," "Tin Tin Deo," "Tour De Force," and "Woodyn' You."

2431. Isacoff, Stuart. *Dizzy Gillespie: A Jazz Master.* Milwaukee: MCA/Hal Leonard; 1990.

Fourteen transcriptions including "Bebop," "Dizzy Atmosphere," "Hollywood and Vine," "Hothouse," "Groovin' High," and "Salt Peanuts." Also contains a musical profile and selected discography.

2432. Paparelli, Frank. *Dizzy Gillespie—A Jazz Master.* New York: MCA Music; 1961.

Transcribes tunes such as "Bebop," "Blue 'n Boogie," "Dizzy Atmosphere," "52nd Street," and "Salt Peanuts" for Bb and C instruments with piano accompaniment (1981).

Benny Goodman

2433. Goodman, Benny. *Benny Goodman: Composer/Artist.* Milwaukee: Goodman/Hal Leonard; 1987.

Contains 25 clarinet solos, separately and with piano accompaniment. Among the solos are "Sing Sing Sing," "Flying Home," "Tuxedo Junction," "Zing Went the String of My Heart," and more.

2434. _____. *Benny Goodman: Swing Classics.* Milwaukee: Leonard; 1988.

Features six transcribed solos, including "Airmail Special," "Flying Home," and "Mission to Moscow." A pullout piano accompaniment section is also included.

2435. _____. *Jazz Giants—Clarinet Solos.* New York: Charles Hansen; 1975.

Collects a variety of jazz tunes, with piano accompaniment, such as "Rosette," "Why Don't You Do Right," "Mahogany," "Hall Stomp," and "Bugle Call Rag."

2436. Goodman, Benny, and Woody Herman. *Jazz Studies/Solos.* New York: Charles Hansen; 1974.

Woody Herman deals in part one with improvisation through chord studies in all keys. Part two consists of solos by Benny Goodman, including "King Porter Stomp" and "Tin Roof Blues." Part three provides the piano accompaniment to part two (1981).

2437. Isacoff, Stuart. *Benny Goodman.* New York: Music Sales; 1989.

Contains transcriptions of "Farewell Blues," "King Porter Stomp," "After You've Gone," "Sugarfoot Stomp," "Honeysuckle Rose," and several more. A musical profile and selected discography are included.

Dexter Gordon

2438. Niehaus, Lennie (transcriber). *Dexter Gordon: Jazz Saxophone Solos.* Milwaukee: Hal Leonard Publishing Corporation; 1989.

The biomusical portrait is followed by 22 transcriptions. Each transcription contains the title of the LP where the tune was first recorded. Among the transcriptions are "The Apartment," "Apple Jump," "Back Stairs," "Cheesecake," "Dexter Digs in," "For Regulars Only," "Fried Bananas," "Montmartre," "Setting the Pace," and "Stanley the Steamer."

Wardell Gray

2439. No Author. *Wardell Gray Tenor Solos.* New Albany, Ind.: Jamey Aebersold; 1999.

The nine transcriptions include "Bernie's Tune," "Donna Lee," "Pennies from Heaven," "Jackie," and more.

Grant Green

2440. No Author. *The Best of Grant Green.* New Albany, Ind.: Jamey Aebersold; 2001.

A discussion of the guitar style and technique of this unsung giant. In addition to a concise biography, several transcriptions are explained and analyzed. Wolf Marshall performs the transcriptions on a CD.

Jim Hall

2441. Hall, Jim. *Exploring Jazz Guitar.* Milwaukee: Hal Leonard; 1991.

In addition to 10 transcriptions of Hall's compositions, there are performance suggestions for each work and additional information on preparation and performance techniques.

Sir Roland Hanna

2442. Sir Roland Hanna Collection. New York: Cherry Lane Music Company; 2000?

Hanna is known for his acute sense of timing, solid left hand, and the over 400 compositions he has composed. This collection contains nine transcriptions of improvisations, including "Century Rag," "A Child is Born," "A Night in Tunisia," "Yesterdays," and more. Also included are Hanna's insights and thoughts on composing and performing.

Tom Harrell

2443. No Author. *Tom Harrell Trumpet Transcriptions.* New Albany, Ind.: Jamey Aebersold; 2001.

In addition to the concise biography, there are 17 transcriptions. The transcriptions include "Joy Spring," "April Mist," "Buffalo Wings," "Brazilian Song," "My Funny Valentine," and 12 more. Many of the songs can be performed with the Jamey Aebersold Play-A-Long volume 63 as an accompaniment.

Gene Harris

2444. *The Gene Harris Collection.* Milwaukee: Hal Leonard; Two volumes; 2000.

Includes transcriptions of "Blues for Basie," "This Little Light of Mine," "Scotch and Soda," "I Remember You," and more. Contains a concise biography, many of his favorite licks, and is reflective of his eclectic approach to piano improvisation.

Joe Henderson

2445. No Author. *The Best of Joe Henderson.* New Albany, Ind.: Jamey Aebersold; 2000.

The 16 transcriptions include "Afro-Centric," "Black Narcissus," "El Barrio," "Home Stretch," "If," "Inner Urge," "Isotope," "The Kicker," "Mo' Joe," "Power to the People," "Punjab," "Recorda-Me," "A Shade of Jade," "Tetragon," and more.

2446. _____. *Joe Henderson Solos.* New Albany, Ind.: Jamey Aebersold; 2000.

The 12 transcriptions are from his *Lush Life* and *So Near, So Far* albums. Included are "Lush Life," "Miles Ahead," "Take the 'A' Train," "Milestones," and several more.

2447. Sickler, Don (transcribed). *Joe Henderson Improvised Saxophone Solos.* Miami, Fla.: CPP/Belwin Inc.; 1978.

Begins with a biographical sketch, selected discography, overview of his Blue Note recordings from the 1960s, and an explanation of notational symbols and devices used in the transcriptions. The transcriptions are "Home Stretch," "Recorda-Me," "Jinriksha," "Out of the Night," "In 'n Out," "Punjab" (also with trumpet melody), and "Serenity" (also with trumpet melody). The transcriptions contain chord symbols and numerous articulation markings.

Scott Henderson

2448. Henderson, Scott. *Scott Henderson Guitar Book.* Milwaukee: Hal Leonard; 1992.

Presents his music complete with an introduction and performance notes for each composition. Also contains guitar and bass lines. Among the 10 transcriptions are "Elvis at the Top," "Nomad," and "Big Girl."

Al Hirt

2449. Hirt, Al. *Jazz Giants—Al Hirt Trumpet.* New York: Charles Hansen; 1974.

Transcribes eight of Hirt's solos for trumpet with piano accompaniment: "Sugar Lips," "Cotton Candy," "Java," "Holiday for Trumpet," "When the Saints Go Marching In," "Easy Street," "Too Late," and "Carnival in Venice" (1981).

Johnny Hodges

2450. Hodges, Johnny. *Six Originals.* New York: Charles Hansen; 1973.

Provides five solos arranged for alto saxophone with piano accompaniment. Included are "Spruce and Juice," "Two-Button Suit," "Butterfly Bounce," "Parachute Jump," and "Uptown Blues" (1981).

Freddie Hubbard

2451. No Author. *Freddie Hubbard.* Milwaukee: Hal Leonard; 1986.

Transcriptions of 24 compositions and solos, an analysis of his improvisational style in the foreword, and an interview. The transcriptions include "Intrepid Fox," "Little Sunflower," "Red Clay," "Sweet Sioux," "Thermo," and "Up Jumped Spring."

Harry James

2452. James, Harry. *Jazz Giants—Harry James Blues, Rhapsodies, and Concerti.* New York: Charles Hansen; 1976.

Contains the complete series of trumpet solos with piano accompaniment, including "Carnival in Venice," "Concerto in A-Minor," "Concerto in Bb-Minor," "Concerto for Trumpet," "Flight of the Bumblebee," "Trumpet Blues," "Cantabile," and "Trumpet Rhapsody" (1981).

Quincy Jones

2453. Jones, Quincy. *Quincy Jones Mellow Flute.* New York: Charles Hansen; 1975.

Features the music of two of Quincy's albums with chord symbols. The tunes include: "Along Came Betty," "Mellow Madness," "Boogie Joe the Grinder," "Is It Love That We're Missin'," and "Soul Saga." A special illustrated biography of Quincy is also included (1981).

Barney Kessel

2454. Kessel, Barney. *The Jazz Guitar of Barney Kessel.* Milwaukee: Ashley Mark Publishing Company/Music Dispatch (Distributor); 1989.

A collection of some of Kessel's best guitar compositions, including fingerings. Compositions include "Blue Boy," "Brazilian Beat," "Jelly Beans," "New Blues," "Blazin," "You're the One for Me," "Mermaid," "Minor Mood," and several more.

Diana Krall

2455. Krall, Diana. *Diana Krall: Live in Paris.* New Albany, Ind.: Jamey Aebersold; 2001.

Although not transcriptions per say, lyrics and chord changes are added to the piano lines. The collection includes "I Love Being with You," "Let's Fall in Love," "Deed I Do," "The Look of Love," "East of the Sun," "I've Got You Under My Skin," "Devil May Care," "Maybe You'll Be There," "So Wonderful," "Fly Me to the Moon," "A Case of You," and "Just the Way You Are."

Scot LaFaro

2456. Palombi, Phil. *Scot LaFaro Solos.* New Albany, Ind.: Jamey Aebersold; 2001.

The transcriptions of LaFaro's parts are from Bill Evan's *Sunday at the Village* and *Waltz for Debby* albums. The 15 transcriptions are analyzed and contain chord changes. See the Bill Evans citations.

Hubert Laws

2457. Laws, Hubert. *Flute Improvisation.* New York: Armstrong/Edu-tainment; 1975.

Collects four of Law's solos transcribed from some of his most popular albums. The solos contain lip trills, growls, pitch bending, flutter tonguing, and much more (1981).

Dave Liebman

2458. Liebman, Dave. *David Liebman Tenor Solos.* New Albany, Ind.: Jamey Aebersold; 1986.

Cassette and book of Liebman's solos on the eight songs recorded for volume 19 (David Liebman), of the Aebersold Play-A-Long Series. Six of the solos are notated in the accompanying book.

2459. _____. *David Liebman Plays with Coltrane and Shorter Play-A-Longs.* New Albany, Ind.: Jamey Aebersold; 1985.

Contains the original 1982 and 1985 tracks recorded to complement volumes 28 and 33 of the Aebersold Play-A-Long Series. There are six Coltrane and five Shorter tunes.

2460. _____. *Scale Syllabus Solos.* New Albany, Ind.: Jamey Aebersold; 1984.

Transcriptions of all solos and examples performed on volume 26 of the Aebersold Play-A-Long Series. Performed on soprano saxophone.

Pat Martino

2461. No Author. *The Best of Pat Martino.* New Albany, Ind.: Jamey Aebersold; 2002.

A book and CD that are permeated with the riffs, compositions, and improvisations of Martino. Among the 14 transcriptions are "All Blues," "Along Came Betty," "Blue in Green," "Nefertiti," "Oleo," "Road Song," "Stone Blue," "The Visit," and six more.

Pat Metheny

2462. No Author. *Pat Metheny: Bright Size Life.* New Albany, Ind.: Jamey Aebersold; 2001.

The eight transcriptions were approved by Metheny and include eight songs from his 1975 debut, which also features Jaco Pastorius. The transcriptions include "Bright Size Life," "Unity Village," "Missouri Uncompromised," "Mid-western Nights Dream," "Uniquity Road," "Omaha Celebration," and "Round Trip/Broadway Blues."

2463. _____. *Pat Metheny: Question and Answer.* New Albany, Ind.: Jamey Aebersold: 2001.

The transcriptions were supervised by Metheny and include all the songs from his 1989 album. The transcriptions are "Solar," "Question and Answer," "H&H," "Never too Far," "Law Years," "Change of Heart," "All the Things You Are," "Old Folks," and "Flights Up."

Charles Mingus

2464. *Charles Mingus: More Than a Fake Book.* Milwaukee: Hal Leonard; 1991.

Profiles his life and career, and contains 55 compositions. There are musical analyses by Andrew Homzy of each composition. Also, there are anecdotes and stories about each composition along with a selected discography.

2465. Wilkins, Jack. *5 Guitars Play Mingus.* Milwaukee: Hal Leonard; 2000.

Wilkins, a guitarist and musical partner of Buddy Rich, arranged five Mingus originals for guitar quintet, accompanied by piano, bass, and drums. In addition to a concise biographical profile of Mingus, the collection includes "Boogie Stop Shuffle," "Diane," "Nostalgia in Times Square," "O.P.," and "Peggy's Blue Skylight."

Bob Mintzer

2466. Osland, Miles. *The Music of Bob Mintzer.* Miami: Warner Brothers Publications; 2000.

The 12 compositions and transcribed solos are designed to supply improvisational ideas to other tenor saxophonists. The accompanying CD combines moments of improvisation with moments of analytical discussion by Mintzer and Osland. The discussion focuses on what was played, and relate it back to the text. There are written exercises and audio samples.

Blue Mitchell

2467. Bunnell, Jeff. *Blue Mitchell Solos.* New Albany, Ind.: Jamey Aebersold; 2000.

A collection of 24 solos, including "True Blue," "The Song Is You," "I Can't Get Started," "A Night in Tunisia," "Spanish Gypsy," and "Up Jumped Spring." A concise biographical portrait of Mitchell is also included.

Hank Mobley

2468. Campbell, Gary. *Hank Mobley Transcribed Solos.* Lebanon, Ind.: Houston Publishing, Incorporated; 1991.

Contains eight solos by Mobley, as well as a complete analysis section that explores passing tones, scales, ii–V progressions, and other devices used by Mobley.

Thelonious Monk

2469. Isacoff, Stuart (editor). *Jazz Masters: Thelonious Monk.* New York: Consolidated Music Publishers; 1978.

Includes a musical overview, eight transcriptions, and a selected discography of tunes, album titles, labels, and numbers. The transcriptions are "Off Minor," "I Mean You," "Ruby My Dear," "In Walked Bud," "Monk's Mood," "Thelonious," "Epistrophy," and "Introspection."

James Moody

2470. No Author. *James Moody Collection.* New Albany, Ind.: Jamey Aebersold; 1999.

The 15 transcriptions include "Be-Bop," "Groovin' High," "Indiana," "It Might As Well Be Spring," "Parker's Mood," "Polka Dots and Moonbeams," "Wave," "Feelin' Low," and more.

Wes Montgomery

2471. No Author. *Wes Montgomery Guitar Transcriptions.* Milwaukee: Hal Leonard; 1987, 2000.

Provides an analysis of Montgomery's playing concepts and techniques, and 15 transcriptions. Included are "Boss City," "Four on Six," "Movin' Wes Part I & II," "Serene," "The Thumb," "Twisted Blues," and several more. Includes a biographical profile, discussion of chords and single-note lines, and a technical breakdown of his style. Requires a knowledge of chords, and other musical elements.

2472. _____. *The Best of Wes Montgomery.* New Albany, Ind.: Jamey Aebersold; 1998.

A transcription of the heads of 12 of Montgomery's most popular tunes. Includes "Missile Blues," "Yesterdays," "West Coast Blues," "Cariba," "I've Grown Accustomed to Her Face," "Besame Mucho," "Fried Pies," "Mi Cosa," "Four on Six," "Misty," "Sundown," and "OGD." Wolf Marshall performs the solos on the CD.

2473. Kahn, Steve. *Wes Montgomery Guitar Folio.* New Albany, Ind.: Jamey Aebersold; 1999.

A collection of 25 solos with guitar chords and voicings. Among the transcriptions are "West Coast Blues," "Canadian Sunset," "Fried Pies," "Sundown," "Angel Eyes," "Besame Mucha," "Cariba," "Days of Wine and Roses," "Four on Six," "Freddie Freeloader," "Tear It Down," "The Trick Bag," "Up and at It," "D Natural Blues," and several more. Four of the solos can be played with the Jamey Aebersold Play-A-Long volume 63.

Frank Morgan

2474. _____. *The Frank Morgan Collection.* Milwaukee: Hal Leonard; 1999.

The biographical profile covers his infatuation with Charles Parker, the 20 years spent in prison, and his successful return to jazz in the 1980s. Includes 14 transcriptions, including "How Deep is the Ocean," "Mood Indigo," "A Night in Tunisia," and the title track transcription from *Easy Living,* an album recorded after his release from prison.

Lee Morgan

2475. No Author. *Lee Morgan Solos.* New Albany, Ind.: Jamey Aebersold; 2000.

The 18 classic improvisations, including "The Sidewinder," "Ceora," "Speed Ball," "Lazy Bird," "Moments Notice," "Blue Train," and "Candy."

Jelly Roll Morton

2476. Dapogny, James. *Ferdinand "Jelly Roll" Morton: The Collected Piano Music.* Washington, D.C.: Smithsonian Institution Press; 1982.

A comprehensive collection that is concerned with describing the technical problems in the music. He begins with informative insights into Morton as a composer and pianist and provides a profile of his life. There is a chronology of compositions and a section on "Notes on the Music and Editorial Procedures." Among the 40 compositions are "New Orleans Blues," "Grandpa's Spells," "Mr. Jelly Lord," "Black Bottom Stomp," "Wildman Blues," "Seattle Hunch," "Kansas City Stomp," "Jelly Roll Blues," "Mister Joe," "King Porter Stomp," and several more. Each composition is preceded by copyright information, date(s) of recordings, and musical/historical insights. After each composition, a list of Morton performance concepts and/or idioms is addressed. An excellent collection.

Gerry Mulligan

2477. Ricker, Ramon. *Gerry Mulligan (Volume 6); Great Jazz Standards (Volume 7); Great Jazz Standards (Volume 8); and Great Jazz Standards (Volume 9).* Lebanon, Ind.: Studio P/R, Columbia Pictures Publications; 1981.

Continues the Ramon Ricker series of improvisational materials. These volumes are designed to teach jazz standards, including "Alfie," "Lime-Light," "Lover," "Moon River," "I Remember You," "Suddenly It's Spring," "Stella by Starlight," and more. The book contains suggestions for improving on the tunes, including how to use guide tones and how to play over chord changes. An LP accompanies each book.

Fats Navarro

2478. Baker, David N. *The Jazz Style of Fats Navarro.* New York: CPP/Belwin; 1982.

A concise biographical sketch, musical genealogy chart, selected bibliography and discography, and worksheets are provided. Included in the 15 transcriptions are "Fats Blows," "Ladybird," "Lady Be Good," "Ornithology," and "Wail." Navarro's ii–V tendencies are also outlined.

2479. Shoemake, Charlie. *Fats Navarro.* Bulle Sisse/Schweiz, Switzerland: Editions Bim; 1989.

Begins with English, French, and German translations of an essay devoted to Fats Navarro (the music, his harmonic approach, relating the proper scales to the chords, and practicing the solos). Each of the 13 transcriptions is prefaced by a concise musical analysis of the composition. The transcribed solos are "The Squirrel," "Double Talk," "The Chase," "Bouncing with Bud," "Dameronia," "Wail," "The Skunk," "Our Delight," "52nd St. Theme," "Lady Bird," "Dance of the Infidels," "Symphonette," and "Jahbero."

Charlie Parker

2480. Baker, David N. *Charlie Parker.* New York: Shattinger International Music Corporation; 1978.

Includes a chart on the relationship of chord to scales, a biographical sketch, a music genealogy, Parker tendencies, original compositions, and a selected bibliography and discography. There are four transcriptions: "Out of Nowhere," "Now's the Time," "Hot House," and "Perdido." The transcriptions are followed by a discussion of ii–V and melodic patterns.

2481. Christiansen, Corey. *Essential Jazz Lives: The Style of Charles Parker.* Pacific, Mo.: Mel Bay; 1999.

A compilation of exercises that are designed to help its users to understand and appreciate the improvisations of Parker. The volume includes a CD, and is available in the key of C, B flat, E flat, bass clef, and guitar editions. Requires practice and patience to master the difficult exercises.

2482. *Charlie Parker For Piano.* New York: Criterion; 1988

Notates Parker's solos for piano; volume 1 contains 13 compositions including "Confirmation," "Ornithology," and "Yardbird Suite"; volume 2 includes "LeapFrog," "Scrapple from the Apple," and 11 more; and among the transcriptions in volume 3 are "Donna Lee," "Now's the Time," and 10 more.

2483. *Charlie Parker Omnibook.* New York: Atlantic Music Corporation; 1978.

Contains 60 transcriptions, a biography, and scale syllabus (Jamey Aebersold). Among the transcriptions are "Confirmation," "Anthropology," "Billie's Bounce," "Card Board," "Chasing the Bird," "Donna Lee," "Koko," "Parker's Mood," "Scrapple from the Apple," "Yardbird Suite," and many more. Most of the solos were transcribed from his Savoy and Verve recordings. There are no articulations, only metronome markings.

2484. Isacoff, Stuart. *Charlie Parker, A Jazz Master.* Milwaukee: MCA/Hal Leonard; 1989.

Transcriptions of nine solos for Bb and C instruments with piano accompaniment. Among the transcriptions are "Hootie Blues," "Lover Man," "A Night in Tunisia," "Bird of Paradise," "52nd Street Theme," "I'll Remember April," "Oop Bop Sh-bam," "That's Earl, Brother," and more. Selected discography and a musical overview also included.

2485. Voelpel, Mark. *Charlie Parker for Guitar.* Milwaukee: Hal Leonard; 1999.

Contains 18 transcriptions of Parker's recordings, and a biographical profile of the saxophonist. Among the transcriptions are "Blues for Alice," "Ko Ko," "Ornithology," "Parker's Mood," and 14 more. Each transcription includes advice on how to play falls, scoops, ghost notes, and other performance concepts. Also included are performance note, and other information germane to performing Parker's compositions.

2486. White, Andrew. *Charles Parker Transcriptions.* Washington, D.C.: Andrew's Music; 1993.

Over 300 transcriptions organized into Savoy Sessions, Dial Sessions, Verve Sessions, and Live Sessions. A complete listing is available on request.

Joe Pass

2487. Christiansen, Corey. *Essential Jazz Lives: The Style of Joe Pass.* Pacific, Missouri: Mel Bay; 2000.

Emphasizes understanding both the harmonic and melodic underpinnings of Pass's guitar lines. The book is permeated with exercises, including one-measure minor seventh material, and two-measure ii–V patterns that enable the student to learn improvisational lines that fit specific harmonies.

Oscar Peterson

2488. *Oscar Peterson: Jazz Piano Playbook Volume IA.* New York: Tomi; 1990.

Five Peterson compositions complete with performance suggestions by Peterson. The compositions are "The Gentle Waltz," "He Has Gone," "Love Ballade," "Sushi," and "The Cakewalk."

Michael Petrucciani

2489. *Michael Petrucciani.* Milwaukee: Hal Leonard; 1991.

Seven original transcriptions by this renowned French jazz pianist, they are "Beautiful but Why," "Big Sur," "Big On," "Cold Blues," "Hommage a Enelram," "Atenig," "Juste Un Moment," "Mike P.," and "To Erlinda."

Bud Powell

2490. Isacoff, Stuart. *Bud Powell.* New York: Musical Scales; 1987.

Begins with a musical profile and contains six transcriptions and a selected discography. The transcriptions include "Celia," "A Night in Tunisia," "Hallucinations," "Strictly Confidential," and "Tempus Fugit."

Tito Puenté

2491. Puenté Tito, and Jim Payne. *Tito Puenté's Drumming with the Mambo King.* New York: Hudson Music; 2001.

Covers Latin jazz drumming with photos, drum charts, and exercises that teach the methods that Puenté uses in his Afro-Cuban rhythms. The 75-minute CD features Puenté in dialogue, jamming some examples cite in the text, six Timbale' solos, and 12 recordings that are representative of his distinguished career. A concise biographical profile of Puenté is also included.

Jimmy Raney

2492. Raney, Jimmy. *Jimmy Raney Solos.* New Albany, Ind.: Jamey Aebersold; 1989.

Compliments volume 29, *Playing Duets with Jimmy Raney,* of the Aebersold Play-A-Long Series. Transcriptions of all solos.

2493. Redman, Joshua. *The Music of Joshua Redman.* New Albany, Ind.: Jamey Aebersold; 2000.

Includes a concise biography of Redman, and transcriptions of "Got You," "Blues on Sunday," "Moose the Mooche," "Faith," "My One and Only Love," "Herbs and Roots," and "Home Fries."

Django Reinhardt

2494. Ayeroff, Stan. *Django Reinhardt.* New York: Amsco; 1987.

A musical profile, selected discography, and several transcriptions are included. The transcriptions include "Dinah," "Georgia on My Mind," "Nuages," "You Rascal You," "Shine," "In a Sentimental Mood," "After You've Gone," "Chasing a Rainbow," and more. Also included are comments on the transcriptions and a discussion of tools of the improviser.

2495. Peters, Mike. *Django Reinhardt Anthology* (The Goodman Group). Milwaukee: Hal Leonard; 1990.

Includes 70 Reinhardt classics, date of recording, and other pertinent information related to individual compositions and recording sessions.

2496. Reinhardt, Django. *The Genius of Django Reinhardt.* New York: Jewel Music; 1978.

Presents a short biographical sketch, plus a rare picture of the Django Reinhardt Quintet. Among the tunes included are "Anounman," "Belleville," "Daphne," "Minor Swing," "Swing 42," "Tears," and several others.

Lee Ritenour

2497. Carter, Rich (editor). *The Lee Ritenour Book.* Studio City, Calif.: Professional Music Products; 1979.

Presents songs illustrative of the many and diverse facets of Ritenour's music. In some cases, the second guitar, piano, and bass parts are included. Among the tunes selected is "Sugar Leaf Express," "What Do You Want," and "The Captain's Journey."

2498. Ritenour, Lee. *Lee Ritenour.* Milwaukee: Hal Leonard; 1990.

Contains a biography, discography, and 19 of his compositions, including "Captain Fingers," "Mr. Briefcase," "Dolphin Dreams," "Waiting for You," and several more.

Red Rodney

2499. No Author. *Red Rodney Solos Then and Now.* New Albany, Ind.: Jamey Aebersold; 2000.

The biography covers his life and musical career, and is supplemented with 10 transcriptions. The transcriptions include "Confirmation," "Congo Blues," "Little Suede Shoes," and seven more.

Sonny Rollins

2500. No Author. *Sonny Rollins Collection.* New Albany, Ind.: Jamey Aebersold; 2000.

A collection of 10 transcriptions and a concise biographical sketch of the composer/performer. The transcriptions include "Allison," "Biji," "Duke of Iron," "Echo-Side Blue," "Hear What I'm Saying," "Hear's to the People," "Sonny Moon for Two," "Times Slimes," and "Wynton."

2501. Baker, David N. *The Jazz Style of Sonny Rollins.* New York: CPP/Belwin; 1982.

Follows the precedent of the other five books in this series (Cannonball Adderley, Clifford Brown, John Coltrane, Miles Davis, and Fats Navarro), by providing a biographical sketch, musical genealogy chart, selected bibliography and discography, and worksheets. Among the nine transcribed solos are "Vierd Blues," "Doxy," "Airegin," "Tune Up," "Slow Boat to China," "Tenor Madness," and "Hold 'em Joe." A discussion of ii–V patterns is also included.

2502. Isacoff, Stuart. *Sonny Rollins.* New York: Music Sales; 1988.

Transcriptions of "God Bless the Child," "East Broadway Run Down," "On Impulse," "Alfie's Theme," "You Don't Know What Love Is," and more. A musical overview and selected discography is also included.

Joe Sample

2503. *Joe Sample: Ashes to Ashes.* Milwaukee: Hal Leonard Publishing Corporation; 1991.

A collection of nine piano transcriptions, a biographical profile, and a selected discography.

David Sanborn

2504. *The David Sanborn Collection: Artist Transcriptions.* Milwaukee: Hal Leonard; 1988.

A collection of 15 transcriptions, a biographical profile, selected discography, and comments regarding the compositions. Among the compositions are "A Change of Heart," "Hideaway," and "Straight to the Heart."

Woody Shaw

2505. Carley, Dale. *Woody Shaw Jazz Trumpet Solos: Transcriptions from the Original Recordings.* New York: Almo; 1979; *Woody Shaw Jazz Trumpet Solos;* edited by Ronny S. Schiff. Milwaukee: Hal Leonard Publishing Corporation; 1989.

The transcriptions include "In a Capricornian Way," "In Case You Haven't Heard," "Katrina Ballerina," "Little Red's Fantasy," "The Organ Grinder," "Rahsaan's Run," "Rosewood," "Stepping Stone," "There for Maxine," "To Kill a Brick," "Tomorrow's Destiny," "Woody I: On the Path," "Woody II: Other Paths," and "Woody III: New Offerings."

Wayne Shorter

2506. Marten, Stanford. *Wayne Shorter.* Milwaukee: Hal Leonard Publishing Corporation; 1990.

Begins with a biographical profile and a discography of the transcriptions, followed by 25 transcriptions. Among the transcriptions are "Adam's Apple," "E.S.P.," "Footprints," "Juju," "Lester Left Town," "Miyako," "Nefertiti," "Speak No Evil," "Virgo," and "Witch Hunt." A summary interview with Shorter concludes the book.

Horace Silver

2506a. Silver, Horace. *Horace Silver Collection.* Milwaukee: Hal Leonard; 2001.

Sixteen note-for-note transcriptions by Silver. The collection includes "Filthy McNasty" "Come on Home," "Home Cookin," "Nica's Dream," "Nutville," "Senor Blues," "Sister Sadie," "Song for My Father," and more.

2506b. _____. *The Art of Small Combo Playing.* Milwaukee: Hal Leonard; 2000.

Outlines the art of combo playing, group and solo playing, composing and arranging, the music business, discusses jazz philosophy, and more. The eight compositions are "Blowin the Blues Away," "Filthy McNasty," "I Surrender," "Nica's Dream," "Peace," "Sister Sadie," "Song for My Father," and "The Tokyo Blues."

Mike Stern

2507. Stern, Mike. *The Mike Stern Guitar Book.* Milwaukee: Hal Leonard; 1991.

Transcriptions of several of his most popular solos, including "After All," "Before You Go," "Little Shoes," "Upside Downside," and several more.

Sonny Stitt

2508. Keller, Gary. *Sonny Stitt's Greatest Transcribed Solos* (alto saxophone). Lebanon, Ind.: Houston Publishing Inc.; 1991.

Contains nine of Sonny Stitt's improvisations, covering tunes such as "Cherokee," "Tangerine," and "There Is No Greater Love." There is an analysis of ii–V patterns, and a group of melodic motifs, which best address a particular technique being used. There is a concise biographical sketch and a selected discography.

2509. Sickler, Don. *Sonny Stitt Improvised Solos.* Miami, Fla.: CPP/Belwin, Inc.; 1988.

Includes a biographical profile, selected discography, and performance tips. There are five transcriptions: "It Could Be You," "Just You Just Me," "On Green Dolphin Street," "Over the Rainbow," and "Stella by Starlight." There are chord symbols and articulation markings.

Billy Strayhorn

2510. Nicholas, John (arranger). *Billy Strayhorn: An American Master.* New York: Cherry Lane Music Company; 2000.

The 17 arrangements are edited by Milton Okun, and focus on Strayhorn's compositional style removed from Duke Ellington's shadow. The arrangements include "Chelsea Bridge," "Johnny Come Lately," "Take the 'A' Train," "Satin Doll," and 13 more. The biographical profile covers both his musical life and contributions to jazz.

Lew Tabackin

2511. *The Lew Tabackin Collection.* Milwaukee: Hal Leonard; 2000.

The collection contains some of the best improvisations done by this 1960s and after postbebopper. The 12 transcriptions include "Broken Dreams," "Chasin' the Carrot," "Dig," "Isfahan," "Easy Living," "I'll Be Seeing You," "Pyramid," and more. The concise biographical profile is informative regarding his career and style.

Art Tatum

2512. Distler, Jed. *Jazz Masters/Art Tatum: Volume 85;* Music for Millions Series. New York: Consolidated Music Publishers; 1981.

Contains several transcriptions from records still in print (early 1980s). Transcriptions include "Ain't Misbehavin," "Fine and Dandy,"

"Moon glow," "I Surrender Dear," and two versions of "Sweet Lorraine." Also included is a biographical profile, analysis of the transcriptions, and notes on Tatum's improvisational techniques. Selected discography.

2513. Isacoff, Stuart. *Art Tatum.* New York: Music Sales; 1988. Following the musical overview, several transcriptions are provided. Among the transcriptions are "Ain't Misbehavin'," "Fine and Dandy," "Moonglow," "Sweet Lorraine," "Shacked," "I Surrender Dear," and several more. A selected discography is also included.

Teddy Wilson

2514. *The Teddy Wilson Collection.* Milwaukee: Hal Leonard; 2000.

This collection has 12 of Wilson's improvisations, and covers his life and musical career as both a sideman with Benny Goodman, and his swing-based piano stylings. Among the transcriptions are "Ain't Misbehavin'," "Body and Soul," "Cheek to Cheek," "Moonglow," and eight more.

Eugene Wright

2515. Wright, Eugene. *Jazz Giants/Modern Music for Bass.* New York: Charles Hansen; 1977.

Contains 27 compositions arranged for piano and bass with chord symbols. Recommended for the advanced bassist.

Collective

2516. Aebersold, Jamey. *Bebop Jazz Solos.* New Albany, Ind.: Jamey Aebersold; 1981.

Part of a series of etude books that are designed to be used with play-along recordings. Covers diminished, diminished-whole tone, Lydian dominant, pentatonic fourths, blues, ii–V patterns, whole-tone scales, and more. The scales are used within exercises and are replete with musical ideas for solo use.

2517. Baker, David N. *Dixieland Giants—Trombone.* New York: Charles Hansen; 1974.

Offers 25 Dixieland standards arranged for solo trombone and piano accompaniment (1981).

2518. _____. *Jazz Styles and Analysis: Trombone in Recorded Solos, Transcribed and Annotated.* Chicago: Downbeat Publishing; 1973.

Contains annotations of 247 transcribed solos by 191 trombonists. Among the trombonists represented are J. J. Johnson, Kai Winding, Jimmy Cleveland, Kid Ory, Jack Teagarden, Curtis Fuller, and many more. Each solo is annotated with comments on style, context, and history.

2519. Baron, Art. *Jazz Riffs for Trombone.* New York: Music Sales; 1978.

Includes a discography and jazz riffs from easy to advanced in the styles of musicians such as J. J. Johnson, Jim Robinson, and Roswell Rudd (1981).

2520. Candoli, Conte. *World's Greatest Jazz Solos: Trumpet.* New York: Almo; 1978.

Presents transcribed solos such as "Bernie's Tune," "Four," "Giant Steps," "Moody's Mood," "So What," "Oleo," and "Night in Tunisia," as well as short biographical sketches. This volume contains the same tunes as the other collections of world's greatest jazz solos (1981).

2521. Dunlap, Larry. *Great Moments in Jazz.* Petaluma, Calif.: Sher Music Company; 1991.

Contains over 500 transcribed improvisational phrases by numerous jazz greats. Among the represented artists are Clifford Brown, Michael Brecker, John Coltrane, Miles Davis, Bill Evans, Herbie Hancock, Sonny Rollins, Wayne Shorter, and many more. The phrases are organized into two groups: characteristic and unique. The user is encouraged to listen as well as play along with the accompanying cassette.

2522. Harbison, Pat. *"Authentic" Bebop Jazz Solos.* New Albany, Ind.: Jamey Aebersold; 1989.

Several practice solos that were taken from selected play-along recordings by Jamey Aebersold. The compositions include "Confirmation," "Dewey Square," "Donna Lee," "Ornithology," and more. There are no phrasing or articulation marks, thereby allowing the student to be creative. Harbison also provides album title and track number for each solo.

2523. Isacoff, Stuart. *Solos for Tenor Sax.* New York: Carl Fisher; 1985.

Contains transcribed solos by John Coltrane, Stan Getz, Coleman Hawkins, Oliver Nelson, and Sonny Rollins. The solos are "Epistrophy," "Stella by Starlight," "Round Midnight," "Giant Steps," and "Good Bait" by John Coltrane; "Desafinado" by Stan Getz; "Body and Soul" by Coleman Hawkins; "Stolen Moments" by Oliver Nelson; and "Dig" by Sonny Rollins. Each transcription is preceded by an excellent discussion of improvisational style and a catalogue of phrases (musical examples). A catalogue of V–I and ii–V–I phrases of all performers of the transcribed solos and a selected discography are also included.

2524. Kupferman, Meyer. *Jazz Etudes for Clarinet.* New York: Charles Hansen; 1977.

Contains tunes for the advanced clarinetist such as "I Don't Care if the Sun Don't Shine," "Let's Get Lost," "Stella by Starlight," "Penthouse Serenade," and "Buttons and Bows" (1981).

2525. Kynaston, Trent (transcribed and edited). *The Blues: Jazz Tenor Solos.* Kalamazoo, Mich. (?): Corybant Productions; 1988.

The eight transcriptions are "Straight, No Chaser" (John Coltrane); "Tenor Madness" (Dexter Gordon); "Snakes" (Bob Berg); "Blue Monk" (Johnny Griffin); "Blue Walk" (James Moody); "Wheat Leigh Hall" (Sonny Rollins); "Footprints" (Wayne Shorter); and "I'll Drink to That" (Stanley Turrentine). Includes chord symbols, tempo markings, album title, and the label of the recording.

2526. Lee, Edward. *Jazz: An Introduction.* London: Kahn and Averhill, 1972; New York: Crescendo, 1977.

Although the title implies an introduction, this book is filled with analyses of selected compositions and artists. Analyses include "Struttin' with Some Barbeque," "Such Sweet Thunder," "Honeysuckle Rose," "Salute to Fats," "Billie's Bounce," "Perhaps," and "Freddie the Freeloader." There are several musical examples and solo transcriptions of Miles Davis, Coleman Hawkins, and Lester Young. Bibliography and selected discography.

2527. Mairants, Ivor. *Jazz Guitar Solos.* Milwaukee: Hal Leonard; 1991.

Ten jazz guitar solos as played and recorded by Charlie Christian, Charlie Byrd, George Benson, Ivor Mairants, Wes Montgomery, and Joe Pass. The transcriptions include "Night and Day," "Willow Weep for Me," and eight others.

2528. Niehaus, Lennie. *World's Greatest Jazz Solos: Piano.* New York: Almo; 1978.

Contains transcriptions for piano of several solos from great artists. Included are: "Four" (Miles Davis); "Giant Steps" (John Coltrane); "Maiden Voyage" (Herbie Hancock); "Monk's Dream" (Thelonious Monk); "Oleo" (Sonny Rollins); and "Yardbird Suite" (Charlie Parker). Also included are short biomusical sketches of the composers.

2529. Slone, Ken (transcriber). *28 Modern Jazz Trumpet Solos.* Miami, Florida: Studio 224/CPP/Belwin; 1980; *28 Modern Jazz Trumpet Solos; edited by Jamey Aebersold.* Hialeah, Fla.: Studio 224; 1983.

Transcriptions of selected solos of Chet Baker, Randy Brecker, Clifford Brown, Kenny Dorham, Dizzy Gillespie, Tom Harrell, Freddie Hubbard, Booker Little, Blue Mitchell, Lee Morgan, Fats Navarro, Woody Shaw, and Louis Smith. Among the transcribed solos are "Tangerine" (Baker); "Falling in Love with Love" (Brecker); "All the Things You Are" (Brown); "Ecaroh" (Byrd); "Seven Steps to Heaven" (Davis); "The Preacher" (Dorham); "Perdido" (Gillespie); "All the Things You Are" (Harrell); "Dolphin Dance" (Hubbard); "Old Milestones" (Little); "Strollin'" (Mitchell); "Blue Train" (Morgan); "Barry's Bop No. I (What Is This Thing)" (Navarro); "Fenja (Gettin' Sentimental)" (Shaw); and "There Will Never Be Another You" (Smith).

2530. Snell, Howard. *Jazz Giants—Flute Yesterday and Today.* New York: Charles Hansen; 1975.

Composed of solos, with some exercises, arranged for flute with chord symbols. The text includes examples of the music of Dave Brubeck, Duke Ellington, Horace Silver, Jelly Roll Morton, and others (1981).

2531. No Author. *Solos for Jazz Guitar.* New Albany, Ind.: Jamey Aebersold; 1999.

Transcriptions of George Benson, Larry Coryell, Charlie Christian, Tal Farlow, Barney Kessel, John McLaughlin, Wes Montgomery, Les Paul, and Django Reinhardt. Among the transcriptions are "Four on Six," "Birds of Fire," "So This Is Love," and many more.

2532. _____. *Solos for Jazz Piano.* New Albany, Ind.: Jamey Aebersold; 2001.

Includes transcriptions of improvisations by Dave Brubeck, Chick Corea, Bill Evans, Errol Garner, Herbie Hancock, Ahmad Jamal, Oscar Peterson, Bud Powell, Art Tatum, and Fats Waller. Among the transcriptions are "Spain," "Nardis," "All the Things You Are," and many more.

2533. _____. *Solos for Jazz Alto Sax.* New Albany, Ind.: Jamey Aebersold; 2001.

Includes transcriptions of improvisations of some of the most prominent alto saxophonists in jazz history. There are transcriptions of Cannonball Adderley, Paul Desmond, Eric Dolphy, Johnny Hodge, and Charles Parker. The transcriptions include "On Green Dolphin Street," "Summertime," and many more.

2534. _____. *Solos for Jazz Tenor Saxophone.* New Albany, Ind.: Jamey Aebersold; 2001.

Includes transcriptions of "Body and Soul," "Giant Steps," "Dig," "Desafinado," "Stolen Moments," and many more. Also includes numerous transcriptions of artists such as John Coltrane, Stan Getz, Coleman Hawkins, Oliver Nelson, and Sonny Rollins.

2535. _____. *Solos for Jazz Trumpet.* New Albany, Ind.: Jamey Aebersold; 1999.

Transcriptions of Louis Armstrong, Miles Davis, Dizzy Gillespie, Freddie Hubbard, and Lee Morgan. Among the transcriptions are "The Sidewinder," "My Funny Valentine," "Blue Moon," and many more.

2536. _____. *Solos for Jazz Flute.* New Albany, Ind.: Jamey Aebersold; 2001.

Transcriptions of Herbie Mann, Sam Most, Eric Dolphy, James Moody, Paul Horn, Hubert Laws, Joe Farrell, James Newton, and many others.

2537. White, Andrew. *Transcription.* Washington, D.C.: Andrew's Music; 1981.

Contains suggestions for transcribing, especially methods that the author has used to transcribe numerous John Coltrane, Eric Dolphy, and Charles Parker solos.

XI

Jazz Videos/DVDs

Individuals and Groups

Toshiko Akiyoshi

2538. *Jazz Is My Native Language;* produced by Kino International. New York: Kino International Corporation (Distributor); 1989.

Details the life and music of Toshiko Akiyoshi from Japan to New York. The video also focuses on her charts being performed by the Akiyoshi/ Tabackin Big Band. The band performs "Son of Road Time," "Feast in Milano," "Village," "Tales of a Courtesan," "Minamata," "Remembering Bud," "Count Your Blessings," and more. 60 minutes.

Ernie Andrews

2539. *Ernie Andrews: Blues for Central Avenue;* produced by Kino International. New York: Kino International Corporation; 1989.

Also features Buddy Collette and Harry "Sweets" Edison. Documents the history and events that transpired on Central Avenue (Los Angeles) in the 1930s and 1940s. Includes anecdotes and recollections. 60 minutes.

Louis Armstrong

2540. *Satchmo: Louis Armstrong;* produced by CBS Music Video. New York: CBS Music Video Enterprises; 1990.

This portrait of Armstrong includes performances of "West End Blues," "Potato Head Blues," "Weather Bird," "On the Sunny Side of the Street," "When You're Smiling," "Mack the Knife," and more. 87 minutes.

2541. *Jazz Concert I: Louis Armstrong and Duke Ellington;* produced by Goodyear. Reseda, Calif.: Glenn Video Vistas LTD (Distributor); 1961.

Features performances by Louis Armstrong and Duke Ellington. Armstrong plays his theme and is accompanied by Jewel Brown, Trummy Young, Billy Kyle, Joe Darensbourg, Danny Barcelona, and Billy Cronk. Ellington features Harry Carney, Russell Procope, Ray Nance, Johnny Hodges, Jimmy Hamilton, Paul Gonsalves, Cat Anderson, Lawrence Brown, Sam Woodyard, Aaron Bell, and Shorty Baker. They perform "Take the 'A' Train" and many more. 54 minutes, B&W.

2542. *Louis Armstrong;* produced for the American Insights Series by Hearst Metrotone News. Philadelphia: Counselor Films (Distributor); 1972.

An insight into the life and music of Armstrong. 13 minutes.

2543. *Louis Armstrong: The Gentle Giant of Jazz;* produced by Comco Productions. Van Nuys, Calif.: Aims Media Inc.; 1988.

Covers Armstrong's life from New Orleans to his achievement of worldwide fame. 24 minutes.

2544. *Louis Armstrong-Chicago Style;* produced by Stonehenge/Charles Fries Productions. New York: World Vision Home Video; 1975.

Chronicles how he was able to deal with the Chicago mob in the 1930s. 74 minutes.

2545. *Louis Armstrong;* produced by WGBH (Boston). New York: King Features Entertainment; 1983.

The music of Louis Armstrong along with interviews of Armstrong, Al Hibbler, Peggy Lee, and Billy Taylor. 13 minutes.

2546. *Louis Armstrong;* produced by Drew Archive. Los Angeles: Direct Cinema (Distributor); 1968.

Focuses on his personality and music. 58 minutes.

2547. *Goodyear Jazz Concert with Louis Armstrong;* produced by Mike Bryan, Goodyear. Sandy Hook, Conn.: Video Yesteryear (Distributor); 1961.

Assisted by Trummy Young, Joe Darensbourg, Billy Kyle, Billy Cronk, Danny Barcelona, and Jewell Brown. A studio performance of "When It's Sleepy Time Down South," "C'est Si Bon," "Someday You'll Be Sorry,"

"Jerry," "Nobody Knows the Trouble I've Seen," and "When the Saints Go Marching In." 27 minutes.

2548. *Louis Armstrong and His Orchestra, 1942–1965;* produced by Soundies Corporation. Rathway, N.J.: Audio Fidelity Enterprises; 1986.

This is one of the earliest soundies and it features Armstrong and his orchestra performing several compositions. Among the featured personnel are Buster Bailey, Buddy Catlett, Sidney Catlett, Velma Middleton, Louis Russell, and George Washington. They perform "Sleepy Time Down South," "Solo TV," "Shine," "Swingin' on Nothin," and "You Rascal You." 33 minutes.

Art Ensemble of Chicago

2549. *Art Ensemble of Chicago, Live from the Jazz Showcase;* produced by Susan Markel. Chicago: University of Illinois; 1982.

The ensemble, fully dressed in African garb, performs a variety of jazz styles, including early New Orleans, bebop, rock, and avant-garde in this live 1981 performance. The ensemble's personnel include Lester Bowie, Joseph Jarman, Malachi Favors Maghostut, Roscoe Mitchell, and Famoudou Don Moye. They evoke images of African American antebellum folk music in their rendition of "The Song of the Volga Boatman." 45 minutes.

Chet Baker

2550. *Chet Baker: Candy;* produced by Sony Video. New York: Sony Video Softward; 1978.

A look at Baker's practice sessions in Stockholm, Sweden. He performs "Candy," "Love for Sale," and "My Romance." 30 minutes.

2551. *Chet Baker, Let's Get Lost;* produced by Bruce Webster. Chicago: Facets Video (Distributor); 1989.

Details the life and music of this vocalist/trumpeter from his early influences, involvement with drugs, to his later years. Included are interviews of Baker, musical associates, and family. The video is permeated with performance footage. 119 minutes.

2552. _____. *Chet Baker: Live at Ronnie Scott's.* New Albany, Ind.: Jamey Aebersold; 1986.

The 58-minute film is available on VHS and DVD, and was made two years before his death. Among the tracks are *Ellen David, Just Friends, Sifting Down,* and seven more. Elvis Costello and Van Morrison accompany him.

Gato Barbieri

2553. Barbieri, Gato. *Gato Barbieri: Live from the Latin Quarter.* New Albany, Ind.: Jamey Aebersold; 1999?

This New York concert features Frank Colon, Robbie Gonzalez, Mario Rodriquez, and Mark Soskin in a passionate display of Latin-infused jazz. The tunes include *Mystica, Women on the Lake, Liamerito y Tango, Last Tango in Paris, Europa, 1812,* and *Via Emiliano Zapata.* DVD.

Count Basie

2554. *Count Basie and Friends;* produced by Universal Pictures. Rathway, N.J.: Audio Fidelity; 1986.

Contains old footage of Count Basie, his orchestra, and septet in four shorts: "Band Parade" (1943); "Basie's Conversation"; "Basie Boogie"; and Sugar Chile Robinson, Billie Holiday, and Count Basie shots from 1950. Helen Humes sings "If I Could Be with You One Hour Tonight," and Billie Holiday sings "God Bless the Child." 37 minutes, B&W.

2555. *Count Basie, Born to Swing;* produced by Rhapsody Videos. New York: Rhapsody Videos; 1986.

Directed by John Jeremy, and presents a portrait of the Count Basie Band as revealed by alumni and associates. John Hammond, Andy Kirk, Gene Krupa, Cootie Williams, Eddie Durham, Snub Mosley, Tommy Flanagan, Joe Newman, Jo Jones, Buck Clayton, and several others provide the anecdotes and recollections. There are performances featuring Eddie Durham, Tommy Flanagan, Snub Mosley, and Gene Ramsey. 50 minutes.

2556. *Count Basie in England.* Upper Montclair, N.J.: The Jazz Store; 1965

A performance of the great 1960s Count Basie Band. The band featured Al Gray, Eddie "Lockjaw" Davis, Marshall Royal, and many other stars. The arrangements were by Quincy Jones and Neal Hefti, and include "Flight of the Foo Birds," "Lil Darlin," "April in Paris," "The Midnight Sun Never Sets," and several more. 45 minutes in B&W.

2557. *Count Basie, Swinging the Blues.* Upper Montclair, N.J.: The Jazz Store; 1986.

The performances are from the late 1930s, and include rare photograph and interviews with many of his sidemen and other significant artists of the time. The interviews include comments and perceptions by Harry "Sweets" Edison, Earle Warren, Jay McShann, and Joe Williams. The tunes include "Take Me Back Baby," "Strike up the Band," and several others. The film is from the American Masters Series.

2558. *Count Basie Live at the Hollywood Palladium;* produced by VCL Home Video. Los Angeles: VCL Home Video; 1984.

One of Basie's last concerts, taped at the Hollywood Palladium, includes performances of "Shiny Stockings," "Big Stuff," "Splanky," and many more. 60 minutes.

Louis Bellson

2559. *Louis Bellson: The Musical Drummer;* produced by DCI Music Video. New York: DCI Music Video; 1984.

A demonstration tape of Bellson performing in several idioms including samba, swing, shuffle, and rock. 60 minutes.

2560. *Louis Bellson and His Big Band;* produced by Stanley Dorfman. New York: V.I.E.W. Video (Distributor); 1983.

Bellson's big band features jazz stars such as Herb Geller, Michael Brecker, Randy Brecker, Lew Soloff, and Benny Bailey. They perform "The Death Squad," "Samantha," "Blues for Freddy," "Niles Ahead," "Explosion," and "We've Come a Long Way Together." A swinging set. 55 minutes.

Tony Bennett

2561. *A Tony Bennett Songbook;* produced by Dennie H. Paget. Burbank, Calif.: RCA VideoDiscs (Distributor); 1981.

Taped in a nightclub setting, Bennett sings a Duke Ellington medley, "I Left My Heart in San Francisco," and many more. 94 minutes.

George Benson

2562. Benson, George. *George Benson: Absolutely Live.* New Albany, Ind.: Jamey Aebersold; 2000.

The concert was filmed May 28, 2000, at the Belfast Waterfront Hall in Belfast. The 90-minute concert features 17 tracks including "Moody's Mood," "The Masquerade is Over," "Lately, Danny Boy," "All of Me Broadway," and many others. The concert includes a guest appearance by Joe Sample. DVD.

Jerry Bergonzi

2563. Bergonzi, Jerry. *Inside Improvisation.* New Albany, Ind.: Jamey Aebersold; 2001.

In this 62-minute video, the author and former tenor saxophonist with Dave Brubeck demonstrates theoretical ideas and concepts that one can use in jazz, Latin, fusion, and rock improvisation.

Art Blakey

2564. *Art Blakey: Jazz Messenger;* produced by Kino International. New York: Kino International; 1989.

Details Blakey's past contributions and his continuing commitment to the future of jazz. Includes contributions by Walter Davis, Jr., Dizzy Gillespie, and Ray Haynes. 78 minutes.

2565. *Art Blakey;* produced by Adler Entertainment. New York: Sony Software; 1982.

Features Branford and Wynton Marsalis in a concert at the Smithsonian. 60 minutes.

2566. *Art Blakey and the Jazz Messengers: The Jazz Life;* producer N.A. Chicago: Facets Video (Distributor); 1992.

Performs "Fuller Love," "Littleman," "My Ship," "New York," "Gypsy Folktales," and "The Theme." The concert was recorded at Seventh Avenue South. 55 minutes.

2567. *Art Blakey* (Smithsonian Jazz Series); produced by the Smithsonian Institution. Chicago: Facets Video (Distributor); 1981.

Features Branford and Wynton Marsalis in a concert at the Smithsonian. A highlight is Wynton Marsalis's solo on Kurt Weill's "My Ship." 60 minutes.

2568. *Art Blakey/Richie Cole: Modern Jazz at the Village Vanguard.* New Albany, Ind.: Jamey Aebersold; 1982.

The concert featured past and present members of the Jazz Messengers playing some of the most popular bebop tunes of the day. Included among the personnel were Donald Brown, Richie Cole, Bobby Enriquez, Charles Fambrough, Bruce Forman, Marshall Hawkins, Branford and Wynton Marsalis, Scott Morris, and Billy Pierce. 55 minutes, DVD.

Brecker Brothers

2569. *Return of the Brecker Brothers;* produced by Allen Kelman for GRP Records and Pioneer LDC.: UNI Distribution (Distributors); 1992.

Recorded at the Palav De La Musica Catalon in Barcelona, Spain, and features the Brecker's Fusion Band. The band performs "Above and Below," "Inside Out," "Some Skunk Funk," "Song for Barry," and "Spherical."

Dee Dee Bridgewater

2570. *Dee Dee Bridgewater and Her Big Sisters.* Princeton, N.J.: Films for the Sciences and Humanities; 2000.

This documentary focuses on her ability to interpret the music of Billie Holiday, Ella Fitzgerald, Bessie Smith, Sarah Vaughan, and Dinah Washington. In addition, she discusses blues, scat singing, swing, and her life as a jazz performer.

Dave Brubeck

2571. *Dave Brubeck;* produced by TLF. Paramus, N.J.: Time-Life Film and Video (Distributor); 1978.

Profiles Dave Brubeck by reviewing his contributions to modern jazz, and by showing how he continues to grow and expand as both a musician and man. Also included is footage of the Dave Brubeck Quartet (Paul Desmond, Joe Morello, and Gene Wright) and of Brubeck performing with his sons. 52 minutes.

Dave Bruceck and Darius Milhaud

2572. *A Visit with Darius Milhaud;* produced by Audio Brandon Films (Macmillan). Chicago: Films Incorporated; 1958.

Included because it shows Milhaud with his former student (Dave Brubeck), in an informal jazz session at his home. Also shows Milhaud composing a sonatina for violin and cello. 31 minutes.

Gary Burton

2573. Burton, Gary. *Gary Burton Live.* New Albany, Ind.: Jamey Aebersold; 1987.

A companion to the Ahmad Jamal video because both Burton and Jamal appeared on the same concert. The two-set concert is 60 minutes. DVD.

Charlie Byrd

2574. *The Charlie Byrd Trio: Live in New Orleans;* produced by John Shoup. St. Paul (2): Leisure Video; 1991.

This session also features Joe Byrd and Chuck Redd. The concert was recorded at Duke's Place in New Orleans in 1984. They perform "Corcovado," "Wave," "Satin Doll," "Jive at Five," "Someone to Watch Over Me," and "How Long Has This Been Going On." 60 minutes.

John Carter and Bobby Bradford

2575. *New Music: John Carter and Bobby Bradford;* produced by Peter Bull and Alex Gibney. New York: Rhapsody Films (Distributor); 1980.

Provides penetrating insights into the aesthetics and philosophy of their music. They also perform several of their compositions. 29 minutes.

Benny Carter

2576. *Benny Carter;* produced by Adler Entertainment. New York: Sony Video Software (Distributor); 1982.

Carter performs "Take The 'A' Train," "Honeysuckle Rose," "Autumn Leaves," and many more. 57 minutes.

Ron Carter

2577. *Ron Carter Live: Double Bass;* producer N.A. Chicago: Facets Video (Distributor); 1988.

A live performance at NHK 101 Studio in New York, recorded in digital sound and high-definition video. He performs "Double-Bass," "Waltz," "Blues for D.P.," "The Third Plane," "Eight," and "Sometimes I Feel Like a Motherless Child." 55 minutes.

Ron Carter and Art Farmer

2578. *Ron Carter and Art Farmer: Live at Sunset Basil with Billy Higgins and Cedar Walton;* produced by View Video. New York: V.I.E.W. Video (Distributor); 1990.

Features several original compositions composed for the event, including Ron Carter's "Its About Time" and an arrangement of "My Funny Valentine." 60 minutes.

Buck Clayton

2579. *Buck Clayton All Stars.* Upper Montclair, N.J.: The Jazz Store; 1961.

This concert was recorded in a Brussels, Belgium, studio in 1961 and features Emmet Berry, Buddy Tate, Gene Ramey, Earle Warren, and Jimmy Witherspoon as sidemen. The performed tunes include "Stompin' at the Savoy," "Blue and Sentimental," "Night Train," "Ain't Nobody's Business," and several others. The film is in B&W and is 60 minutes.

Billy Cobham and Louis Bellson

2580. *Cobham Meets Bellson;* produced by Stanley Dorfman. New York: V.I.E.W. (Distributor); 1983.

Features both Billy Cobham and Louis Bellson with the Louis Bellson big band. The concert was taped in Switzerland.

Nat "King" Cole, The Mills Brothers, the Delta Rhythm Boys

2581. *Nat "King" Cole/the Mills Brothers/the Delta Rhythm Boys;* produced by Snador Telescriptions. Rathway, N.J.: Audio Fidelity Enterprises (Distributor); 1986.

Fifteen soundies and telescriptions. Songs performed include "You Call It Madness," "Home," "I'm an Errand Boy for Rhythm (Cole)," "Paper Doll," "Lazy River," and "You Always Hurt the One You Love (Mills Brothers)," "Take the 'A' Train," and "Never Underestimate the Power of a Woman (Delta Rhythm Boys)."

Ornette Coleman and David Moffett

2582. *Ornette Coleman, David Moffett, Ornette Coleman;* produced by Kino International. New York: Kino International (Distributor); 1966.

Details the frustration of recording the soundtrack for a Living Theatre project in Paris, France, 1966. In addition to Coleman and Moffett, David Izenzon (bass) is also featured. Coleman performs one of his most introspective ballads, "Sadness," as well as other music. 26 minutes in B&W.

John Coltrane

2583. *John Coltrane.* Princeton, N.J.: Films for the Humanities and Sciences; 2000.

Explores Coltrane's artistic legacy, integrity, and universality through his performances with Miles Davis, his own quartet, and as a solo performer. 56 minutes and in color.

2584. *John Coltrane: The Coltrane Legacy;* produced by Jazz Images (Burrill, Crohn, and David Chertok). New York: Jazz Images, 1985; Great Falls, Mont.: Video Artists International, 1987.

Contains rare footage of the Coltrane quartet (Elvin Jones, Jimmy Garrison, and McCoy Tyner) in rehearsal. Also features extended comments by Elvin Jones on the significance of Coltrane. A clip of Coltrane performing with Miles Davis ("So What," 1959) is also featured. 58 minutes.

2585. *A Tribute to John Coltrane.* Newport, R.I.: Media for the Arts (Distributor); 1989.

A session that features Richie Beirach, Jack DeJohnette, Eddie Gomez, Dave Liebman, and Wayne Shorter.

2586. *John Coltrane: The World According To.* New Albany, Ind.: Jamey Aebersold; 1987?

A multifaceted portrait of this legend's music, life, associates, and influence. Includes footage of Coltrane playing alto saxophone in 1946, and previously unreleased footage of his last group. 59 minutes, color, and available on VHS and DVD.

Eddie Condon

2587. *Goodyear Jazz Concert with Eddie Condon;* produced by Mike Bryan, Goodyear. Sandy Hook, Conn.: Video Yesteryear (Distributor); 1961.

A rare film portrait of Eddie Condon and several of his musical associates: Cutty Cutshall, Wild Bill Davidson, Buzzy Drootin, Peanuts Hucko, Johnny Varro, and Joe Williams. The musicians perform Chicago/New Orleans style traditional jazz in this 1961 concert. He performs "Big Ben Blues," "Blue and Brokenhearted," "Little Ben Blues," "Muskrat Ramble," "Royal Garden Blues," "Stealin' Apples," and several more. 28 minutes.

Eddie Condon and Bobby Hackett

2588. *Jazz Concert 2: Bobby Hackett and Eddie Condon;* produced by Goodyear. Reseda, Calif.: Glenn Video Vistas LTD (Distributor); 1961.

Hackett is accompanied by Urbie Green, Bob Wilbur, Morey Feld, Dave McKenna, and Nabil Totah. They perform "Swing That Music," and several more. Wild Bill Davidson, Peanuts Hucko, Cutty Cutshall, Buzzy Drootin, Johnny Varro, and Joe Williams accompany Condon. Among the tunes they perform are "Stealin' Apples" and "Blue and Broken Hearted." 51 minutes, B&W.

Chick Corea and Gary Burton

2589. *Chick Corea and Gary Burton Live in Tokyo;* produced by Pacific Arts Video (Chick Corea and Gary Burton). Pacific Arts Video: Pioneer Artists (Distributor); 1985.

Performed live at Yuhbin Chokin Hall in Tokyo, they perform "La Fiesta," "Senor Mouse," "Children's Songs," and more. 60 minutes.

Chick Corea

2590. *Chick Corea: Electric Workshop;* produced by DCI Music Video. New York: DCI Music Video (Distributor); 1988.

A lesson on how to create sounds and use them in music by layering them to create new textures. 60 minutes.

2591. *Chick Corea "Keyboard Workshop";* produced by DCI Music Video. New York: DCI Music Video (Distributor); 1988.

A demonstration video that presents his views on practicing, composing, and improvising. 60 minutes.

2592. *Chick Corea;* produced by BBC. Wilmette, Ill.: Verve Films (Distributor); 1976.

A live concert in which he performs several tunes including "Spain." 40 minutes.

2593. *Chick Corea;* produced by Sony Video. New York: Sony Video Software; 1980.

A reunion with "Return to Forever" and performances of several tunes, including "500 Miles High," "Guernica," and "L's Bop," and more.

Larry Coryell

2594. *The Jazz Guitarist—A Man and His Music (Larry Coryell);* Upon Reflection Series (University of Washington). Seattle: University of Washington (Distributor); 1987.

Al Page interviews Larry Coryell, a former University of Washington student. Coryell gives his view of the origin of jazz and demonstrates various jazz styles on his guitar. 28 minutes.

The Crusaders

2595. *The Crusaders Live;* produced by MCA Home Video. Universal City: MCA Home Video; 1984.

Features Wilton Felder, Stix Hooper, and Joe Sample performing jazz-fusion tunes. 52 minutes.

Eddie "Lockjaw" Davis

2596. *Eddie "Lockjaw" Davis.* New Albany, Ind.: Jamey Aebersold; 1985.

There are two concerts performed in 1985, one in Denver, Colorado, and the other in Tivoli Gardens, Copenhagan, Denmark. The Denver concert features Davis with Ed Thigpen and others performing "Take the 'A' Train," "Just Friends," "Shadow of Your Smile," and several others. The Denmark concert features "So Wonderful," "Shinny Stockings," "Meditation," "I Can't Get Started," and "Don't Get Around Much Anymore."

2597. *Eddie "Lockjaw" Davis Quartet: Live in Europe, 1985.* New Albany, Ind.: Jamey Aebersold; 1985.

This concert was recorded at the Jazzhus Slukefter Club, Copenhagen, Denmark, in 1985. In addition to Davis, the concert featured Niles Jorgen Steen on piano, Jesper Lungaard on bass, and Ed Thigpen on drums. The quartet performed "Take the 'A' Train," "Just Friends," "Out of Nowhere," "The Shadow of Your Smile," "If I Had You," "Light and Lovely," "So Wonderful," "Shinny Stockings," "Meditation," "I Can't Get Started," and "Don't Get Around Much Anymore." 88 minutes, DVD.

Miles Davis

2598. *Miles Ahead: The Music of Miles Davis;* produced by Mark Obenhaus and Yvonne Smith. New York: WNET/Thirteen and Obenhaus Films in association with Channel 4 Television, London (Distributor); 1986.

Filmed on location at the Saenger Theatre (1986) in conjunction with the New Orleans Jazz and Heritage Festival. The video is narrated by Oscar Brown, Jr., and contains personal assessments of Davis from Dizzy Gillespie, George Benson, Gil Evans, Herbie Hancock, Bill Cosby, Tony Williams, and Robben Ford. Also, there are comments from Miles Davis. Footage of his 1959 and 1967 quintets as well as his 1986 group are included. Excellent.

2599. *Miles Davis and Friends;* produced by JVC. New York: JVC (Distributor); 1991.

Taped at a concert at La Grand Halle in Paris in 1991, the concert features past and present Miles Davis sidemen. Among his present personnel were Kenny Garrett, G. McCleary, Deron Johnson, and Ricky Wellman; past personnel included Al Foster, Bill Evans, Chick Corea, Joe Zawinul, Dave Holland, Steve Grossman, Wayne Shorter, Darryl Jones, John Scofield, John McLaughlin, and Herbie Hancock. Davis, Garrett, and his friends handled the solos. Among the compositions performed were "In a Silent Way," "Peace Piece," and "Watermelon Man."

2600. *Miles in Paris;* produced by Rhapsody Videos. New York: Rhapsody Videos (Distributor); 1990.

Taped at the November 3, 1989, Paris Jazz Festival, featuring both a concert and an interview with Miles Davis. The band features Kenny Garrett on alto saxophone and flute and performances of "Tutu," "Amandela," and more. 60 minutes. VHS and DVD.

2601. *Miles Davis: The Story.* New Albany, Ind.: Jamey Aebersold; 2001.

Filmmaker Mike Dibb directed the 120-minute documentary. The file contains footage from all eras of his career including with John Coltrane, Wayne Shorter, Keith Jarrett, and others. Also included are interviews with Ron Carter, Herbie Hancock, Keith Jarrett, Clark Terry, Joe Zawinul, and several others. In addition, the film contains a biography from Francis Davis and album profiles of nearly all of Miles important recordings. VHA and DVD.

Eric Dolphy

2602. *Eric Dolphy, Last Date.* Upper Montclair, N.J.: The Jazz Store; 1964.

Portrays his final recording session in Hilverson on June 2, 1964. Includes information on his youth in Watts and Los Angeles, success in New York, and the insights of several musicians who knew and performed with him. Among the insights are the views of Buddy Collette, Ted Curson, Jaki Byard, and Richard Davis. The 92-minute B&W film includes footage from his performances with John Coltrane and his Scandinavian appearance with Charles Mingus.

Kenny Drew

2603. *Kenny Drew: Live at the Brewhouse.* New Albany, Ind.: Jamey Aebersold; 1992.

Niels-Henning Orsted Pedersen accompanies Drew on bass and Alvin Queen on drums. This 52 minute live DVD was recorded at the Brewhouse in London in 1992. The trio performs "My Shining Hour," "You Don't Know What Love Is," "Oleo," "Bluesology," "In Your Own Sweet Way," "All Blues," and "Blues in the Closet." 52 minutes.

Duke Ellington

2604. *A Duke Named Ellington;* produced by Jerry Carter. New York: WNET (American Masters—Distributor); 1988.

This two-part video is one of the most complete and probing assessments on the market. The videos are permeated with informative insider assessments of Ellington from musicians such as Herb Jeffries, Herbie Hancock, Clark Terry, Russell Procope, Leonard Feather, Cootie Williams, and Willie "The Lion" Smith. A film clip of Irving Mills is also included. Additionally, Alvin Ailey comments on his use of Ellington's "The River" and "Night Creature" for his choreography, and Alice Babs recounts her experience of working with Ellington (*Sacred Concerts*). Among the compositions performed are "Take the 'A' Train," "Mood Indigo" (different versions), "Eighth Veil," "Diminuendo and Crescendo in Blue" (featuring Paul Gonsalves), and "Happy Reunion," also featuring Paul Gonsalves. Excellent. Two parts, 120 minutes.

2605. *On the Road with Duke Ellington;* produced by Drew Associates: Direct Cinema Limited Incorporated; 1980.

A penetrating portrait, with comments from Ellington, of a rehearsal of "Satin Doll" and the band traveling across the country. 58 minutes, VHS and DVD.

2606. *Duke Ellington: Memories of Duke;* produced by View Video. New York: V.I.E.W. Video (Distributor); 1973.

Documents his life and includes early historical footage and interviews with Cootie Williams and Russell Procope. The 1968 performance features Ellington performing "Satin Doll," "Take the 'A' Train," "Mood Indigo," and the premier of "Mexican Suite." 85 minutes, color and B&W, VHS and DVD.

2607. *Jazz and Jive;* produced by Paramount. Commerce, Calif.: Blackhawk Films (Distributor); 1933.

Duke Ellington provides early jazz background in "Black and Tan," his first movie. The movie includes dance numbers for Dewey Brown ("Toot the Trumpet") and Major Bowles ("Radio Rebels"). 60 minutes, B&W.

2608. *Black and Tan;* produced by RKO. Davenport, Iowa: Blackhawk Films (Distributor); 1929.

A film version of Duke Ellington's "Black and Tan Fantasy."

2609. *Symphony in Black;* produced by Reel. Hollywood: Reel (Distributor); 1935.

Features Duke Ellington and his orchestra with Billie Holiday performing "Big City Blues."

2610. *Duke Ellington and His Orchestra, 1924–1952;* produced by Vitaphone. Rathway, N.J.: Audio Fidelity Enterprises; 1986.

Features Ellington's bands and musical associates via rare film footage. In addition to his bands, Billie Holiday, Ivie Anderson, Snakehips Tucker, and Fredi Washington are featured. Among the performed compositions are "Black and Tan Fantasy," "Caravan," "Sophisticated Lady," "Solitude," and "Symphony in Black." 40 minutes.

2611. *Goodyear Jazz Concert with Duke Ellington;* produced by Goodyear. Sandy Hook, Conn.: Video Yesteryear (Distributor); 1962.

Features performances of several of Ellington's popular hits, including "In a Sentimental Mood," "Sophisticated Lady," and "Take the 'A' Train." Solos by Cat Anderson, Harry Carney, Jimmy Hamilton, Johnny Hodges, Paul Gonsalves, Ray Nance, and Russell Procope. 27 minutes.

Bill Evans

2612. *The Universal Mind of Bill Evans;* produced by Helen Keane. New York: Rhapsody Films; 1966.

An excellent restoration and expansion of *Bill Evans: On the Creative Process,* featuring Evans discussing with his brother (Harry Evans, a composer) the aesthetics of jazz creativity. The video is punctuated with piano illustrations by Bill Evans and is significant because Evans seldom communicated his ideas on either music or creativity. 20 minutes.

Gil Evans

2613. *Gil Evans and His Orchestra;* produced in Switzerland. New York: V.I.E.W. (Distributor); 1983.

Composer/pianist Evans performs with his jazz orchestra the works of George Gershwin, Jimi Hendrix, Charles Mingus, and Thelonious Monk. The band includes Randy and Michael Brecker, Herb Geller, Howard Johnson, and Billy Cobham. 57 minutes.

2614. *Gil Evans.* Princeton, N.J.: Films for the Sciences and Humanities; 1999.

Covers his life from his early years in Canada to his friendships with Miles Davis, John Lewis, Gerry Mulligan, and Charles Parker. Footage from his *Porgy and Bess* album is discussed and acknowledged as one of the highlights of his career.

Tal Farlow

2615. *Talmage Farlow;* producer Lorenzo DeStefano. New York: Rhapsody Films, also Festival Films, and New Jersey Network; 1977.

Details his life and music including his influences. He performs several compositions, accompanied by Red Mitchell and Tommy Flanagan. 51 minutes.

Art Farmer

2616. *Art Farmer;* produced by Adler Entertainment. New York: Sony Video Software (Distributor); 1980.

A look at the life and music of Farmer. 58 minutes.

2617. *Art Farmer Qartet I.* New Albany, Ind.: Jamey Aebersold; 1964.

The B&W video was recorded in 1964 in a BBC concert. Jim Hall accompanied Farmer on guitar, Steve Swallow on bass, and Pete LaRocca on drums. Among the tunes performed in the 32-minute concert were "Some-time Ago," "Bilbao Song," "Darn That Dream," "Valse Hot," and "Blues Concept."

2618. _____. *Art Farmer Quartet II.* New Albany, Ind.: Jamey Aebersold; 1964.

This concert was recorded June, 6, 1964, for the BBC, and includes the same personnel cited on Quartet I. The 37-minute B&W concert features "So In Love," "Getting Sentimental Over You," "Petite Belle," "Bag's Groove," and "Funny Valentine."

Ella Fitzgerald

2619. *Ella Fitzgerald: The Singer, Not the Song.* Princeton, N.J.: Films for the Humanities and Sciences; 2001.

Examines her captivating talent and musicianship within the context of her life. Traces her career from an amateur contest at the Apollo to eventual stardom. Also discusses why her recordings continue to enchant both jazz artists and others today. 30 minutes and in color.

Ella Fitzgerald and Oscar Peterson

2620. *The Tender Game;* produced by AFBC. Stanford: Stanford University (Distributor); 1958.

Uses semiabstract animation of the song "Tenderly" as performed by Ella Fitzgerald and the Oscar Peterson Trio. The story is about a girl and boy falling in love. 6 minutes.

Stan Getz

2621. *Stan Getz: A Musical Odyssey;* produced by Faye Ginsburg and Lily Kharraz. City not available: Jewish Media Service (Distributor); 1977.

Stan Getz jams with local musicians during a concert tour of Israel. 27 minutes.

2622. *Stan Getz: Vintage Getz;* produced by View Video. Two videos. New York: V.I.E.W. Video (Distributor); 1983.

Accompanied by Jim McNeeley, Marc Johnson, and Victor Lewis, the first video features "Over the Edge," "From the Heart," "Spring Can Really Hang," "Tempus Fugit," and more; Video two features performances of "Lush Life," "Desafinado," "Girl from Ipanema," "Alone Together," and more. The concerts were filmed in 1982. Video one is 56 minutes and Video two is 52 minutes in length.

Dizzy Gillespie

2623. *Dizzy Gillespie;* produced by Les Blank. El Cerrito, Calif.: Flower Films; 1965.

Gillespie discusses his beginnings and theories of music. 20 minutes, B&W.

Dizzy Gillespie: Bop and Bent Trumpet. Princeton, N.J.: Films for the Humanities and Sciences; 1999.

Examines his life and musical contributions from his roots in Cheraw, North Carolina, to his status as a founder of modern jazz. Also covers his travels, and includes performances against the backdrop of his life.

2624. *Dizzy Gillespie, A Night in Tunisia;* produced by Bryan Elsom, A King Fisher Production for V.I.E.W. Video. New York: V.I.E.W. Video; 1992.

Leonard Feather narrates Gillespie's evolution as a jazz innovator through the creation and development of one of his most famous tunes, "A Night in Tunisia." There is a 1979 performance of the tune that features Tommy Campbell, Mike Howell, and Ed Cherry. Gillespie discusses his affection for harmony, how the main theme of "Tunisia" evolved, and the eventual completion of the composition. There are comments from Jon Faddis and Leonard Feather. 28 minutes.

2625. *Dizzy Gillespie;* producer N.A. Montvale, N.J.: Pioneer Artists; 1989.

Uses a laser disc format, Gillespie is assisted in this concert by Jon Faddis, Slide Hampton, Freddy Hubbard, Carmen McRae, James Moody, J. J. Johnson, Airto Moriera, and many more. 60 minutes.

2626. *Dizzy Gillespie's Dream Band;* produced by Jazz America Limited. New York: Sony Video Software (Distributor); 1981.

Gillespie is accompanied by an all-star band of his alumni performing tunes such as "Groovin' High," "Hot House," and "A Night in Tunisia." 16 minutes.

2627. *Dizzy Gillespie, Jivin' in Bebop 1947;* produced by Amvest Video. New Albany, Ind.: Jamey Aebersold (Distributor); 1979.

Features "A Night in Tunisia," "Oop Bop Shi Bam," "Salt Peanuts," and several more. Ralph Brown, Sahji, Freddie Carter, Helen Humes, and Ray Sneed. 60 minutes, B&W.

2628. *Dizzy Gillespie;* produced by Jazz America. New York: Sony Video Software; 1981.

Features Gillespie in concert performing tunes such as "Be-Bop," "Birk's Works," and more. 19 minutes.

2629. *Date with Dizzy;* produced by Hubley Studio. Chicago: Texture Films (Distributor); 1962.

A spoof about a director attempting to convince Gillespie to compose music for a commercial; however, Gillespie chooses to engage in a jam session. 11 minutes.

2630. *Dizzy's Dream Band.* New Albany, Ind.; Jamey Aebersold; 1999?

An all-star concert that features 25 of the most important musicians of the day. The 89-minute concert includes Pepper Adams, Jon Faddis, Curtis Fuller, Jimmy Heath, Milt Jackson, Paquito D'Rivera, Max Roach, and Gerry Mulligan.

2631. *Dizzy Gillespie in London.* New Albany, Ind.: Jamey Aebersold; 1990?

A live set at the Royal Festival Hall with a 13-piece all-star band. The band includes Flora Purim, James Moody, Slide Hampton, and Paquito D'Rivera performing 11 songs. 91 minutes and in color.

2632. *Dizzy Gillespie: Live in Montreal.* New Albany, Ind.: Jamey Aebersold; 1981.

Gillespie performs on trumpet, scats, croons, and dances in this excellent performance. The songs include "The Truth," "A Night in Tunisia," and "Dizzy's Blues." Ed Cherry on guitar, Michael Howell on bass, and Thomas Campbell on drums accompany Gillespie. 57 minutes and in color.

2633. *Dizzy Gillespie: And the U.N. Orchestra.* New Albany, Ind.: Jamey Aebersold; 1989.

Recorded live at London's Royal Festival Hall and featured both bebop standards and Latin tunes like "Manteca," and others. The orchestra included Arturo Sandoval, Paquito D'Rivera, Mario Rivera, Flora Purim, and others. VHS and DVD.

2634. *Dizzy Gillespie: A Night in Tunisia.* New Albany, Ind.: Jamey Aebersold; 1981?

An important video because it features Gillespie performing and telling his life story. The film begins with Gillespie rehearsing his first band, after which he recounts the story of him writing "A Night in Tunisia." He also discusses how the song affected jazz. A live concert concludes the video.

Benny Goodman

2635. Goodman, Benny. *Benny Goodman: Adventures in Swing.* New Albany, Ind.: Jamey Aebersold; N.D.

This 60-minute DVD covers his life and musical career, and includes footage from the 1920s, 1930s, and 1950s. Includes information on his famous quartet, relationship with specific musicians, and the importance of Fletcher Henderson to his success.

Dexter Gordon

2636. *Dexter Gordon and McCoy Tyner Cool Summer.* New Albany, Ind.: Jamey Aebersold; 1998?

Recorded live at the Harvest Jazz Festival at the Paul Masson Vineyards in central California. The DVD includes interviews, and the tunes by Gordon include "Cheesecake," "Skylark," "Backstage," and "At the Village." The second set features McCoy Tyne performing "Habana Sol," "Walk Spirit Talk Spirit," and "The Seeker" with Bobby Hutcherson.

2637. *Dexter Gordon: Round Midnight.* New Albany, Ind.: Jamey Aebersold; 1999?

In his first acting performance, Gordon produced an authentic and gripping performance of a drug-addicted American jazz artist living in Paris. The story depicts his struggle to defeat his drug habit and to go straight. He performs and is accompanied by Herbie Hancock and other musicians. Available in VHS and DVD.

2638. *Dexter Gordon Quartet: Live at the Maintenance Shop.* New Albany, Ind.: Jamey Aebersold; 1997?

The DVD includes "On Green Dolphin Street," "Polka Dots and Moonbeams," and "Tany—The Girl Next Door," and others. 60 minutes and in color.

2639. *Dexter Gordon: More Than You Know.* New Albany, Ind.: Jamey Aebersold; 1987?

Covers his career from his Los Angeles beginnings and as a sideman with Billy Eckstine and Lionel Hampton in the 1940s to his rise to stardom in jazz. Also covers his self-imposed exile in the 1960s, his return in the 1970s, and the making of *Round Midnight* in 1985. Gordon narrates and performs. 52 minutes.

Johnny Griffin/Richie Cole Group

2640. *Johnny Griffin Quartet and the Richie Cole Group.* New Albany, Ind.: Jamey Aebersold; 1981.

The Griffin group features Ronnie Matthews, Ray Drummond, and Kenny Washington performing "Opening," "Blues for Gonzo," "A Monk's Dream,"

"56," and "Closing." The Cole group features Bruce Forman, Marshall Hawkins, Bobby Enriquez, and Scott Morris performing seven tracks.

Spyro Gyra

2641. *Spyro Gyra;* produced by Hawk Productions. Burbank, Calif.: Warner Home Video; 1980.

The group performs their pop-jazz tunes and responds to interview questions. 56 minutes.

Bobby Hackett

2642. *Goodyear Jazz Concert with Bobby Hackett;* produced by Goodyear. Sandy Hook, Conn.: Video Yesteryear (Distributor); 1961.

A 1961 concert that featured traditional jazz by his sextet including Morey Feld, Urbie Green, Dave McKenna, Nabil Totah, and Bob Wilbur. He performs "Deed I Do," "Sentimental Blues," "The Saints," "Bill Bailey," "Struttin' with Some Barbecue," "Swing That Music," and more. 24 minutes.

Jim Hall

2643. *Jim Hall: A Life in Progress.* New Albany, Ind.: Jamey Aebersold; 2000.

Hall narrates his own life, and the film focuses on his trio, which consisted of Scott Colley and Terry Clarke. String and brass ensembles accompany the trio and the compositions are from his *By Arrangement* album. Guest artists include Tom Harrell, Joe Lavano, Pat Metheny, Greg Osby, and others.

Chico Hamilton

2644. *Chico Hamilton;* produced on Sony Video. New York: Sony Video Software (Distributor); 1982.

Performed at the Village Vanguard (New York); tunes include "Encore," "Sweet Dreams Too Soon," "First Light," and "Erika."

Lionel Hampton

2645. *Lionel Hampton's One Night Stand;* produced by Evart Enterprises. New York: Independent United Distributors; 1977.

Hampton performs with his band and guests include B. B. King, Johnny Mercer, Buddy Rich, and Mel Tormé. 50 minutes.

2646. *Lionel Hampton Live: Volume 1;* produced by Wesley Ruggles, Jr., and Gary Reber. New York: Sony Video LP; 1982.

This concert was taped at Paul Anka's Jubilation Club in Las Vegas and features Hampton's big band. They perform "Air Mail Special," "Hamp's Boogie Woogie," and "Smooth Sailin.'" 24 minutes.

Herbie Hancock

2647. *Herbie Hancock: The Jazz Channel Presents.* New Albany, Ind.: Jamey Aebersold; 1997.

Features a live performance on the *Jazz Central Program.* Contains a performance of "Fascinating Rhythm," "St. Louis Blues," "Cotton Tail," "Cantaloupe Island," "Maiden Voyage," and several others. The concert is 105 minutes and available on VHS and DVD.

2648. *Herbie Hancock: Future to Future.* New Albany, Ind.: Jamey Aebersold; 2000.

Presents a performance at the Los Angeles Knitting Factory that marked Hancock's return to the funk sound of the 1970s. The band features Darrell Diaz, Terri Lynn Carrington, Matthew Garrison, Wallace Roney, and DJ Disk. He performs standards as well as his repertoire of funk tunes.

2649. *Herbie Hancock and the Rockit Band;* produced by CBS Records. New York: CBS/Fox Video (Distributor); 1984.

Filmed at the Hammersmith Odeon and Camden Hall in London, England. This concert features multimedia presentations of break dancing, scratch music, robots, and a light show. The band plays "Rockit" and other tunes. 70 minutes.

2650. *Herbie Hancock Trio: Hurricane;* produced by View Video. New York: V.I.E.W. Video; 1979.

With Ron Carter and Billy Cobham, this concert, recorded in Switzerland, features among others, "Dolphin Dance," "Eye of the Hurricane," and "Willow Weep for Me." 60 minutes.

Hampton Hawes

2651. *Hampton Hawes All Stars;* producer N.A. Chicago: Facets Video (Distributor); 1979.

Hawes is accompanied by Leroy Vinnegar (bass), Bobby Thompson (bass), Joe Turner (vocals), Harry "Sweets" Edison (trumpet), Sonny Criss (saxophone), and Toddy Edwards (saxophone). They perform "Memory Lane

Blues," "Feeling Happy," "Shake, Rattle and Roll," and "Teddy's Blues."
28 minutes.

Coleman Hawkins and Roy Eldridge

2652. *After Hours: Coleman Hawkins and Roy Eldridge;* produced by Rhapsody
Films. New Albany, Ind.: Jamey Aebersold (Distributor); 1989.

Assisted by Cozy Cole, Johnny Guarneirl, and Milt Hinton. They perform
"Lover Man," "Taking a Chance on Love," "Sunday," and "Just You, Just
Me." There is some rare footage from a jam session at the After Hours
Club. 60 minutes.

Gil Scott Heron

2653. *Gil Scott Heron: Black Wax;* producer N.A. Chicago: Facets Video (Distributor); 1983.

Performs "Storm Music," "Washington, D.C.," "Paint It Black," "Waiting for the Axe to Fall," "Billy Green Is Dead," "Angel Dust," "Fun,"
"Winter in America," "Whitey on the Moon," "Alien," "Black History,"
"Johannesburg," and "Bemove." 80 minutes.

Earl "Fatha" Hines and Coleman Hawkins

2654. *Jazz: Earl Hines and Coleman Hawkins;* produced by Kino International.
New York: Kino International (Distributor); 1965.

This historic collaboration features Hines (piano and vocals) and Hawkins
performing "But Not for Me," "I'm a Little Brown Bird Looking for a
Blue Bird," "Fine and Dandy," "One More Choice," and "Crazy Rhythm."
Oliver Jackson and George Tucker assist them. 28 minutes, B&W.

Art Hodes

2655. *After Hours with Art Hodes, Program 1, featuring Wingy Manone;* produced
by Northwest Teleproductions. Bloomington: Indiana University Audio
Visual Center; 1979.

Includes Art Hodes, Herb Hall, Benny Morgan, Truck Parkham, and Red
Maddock. They perform "I Wish I Could Shimmy Like My Sister Kate,"
"How Come You Do Me Like You Do," "Corrine, Corrine," and "Good
Morning Blues." 29 minutes.

2656. *After Hours with Art Hodes, Program 2, featuring Little Brother Montgomery;* produced by Northwest Teleproductions. Bloomington: Indiana
University Audio Visual Center; 1979.

Features Montgomery, Truck Parkham, and Hilliard Brown. They perform "Mule Face Rag," "First Time I Met the Blues," "Cow Cow Blues," "Gonna Move on the Outskirts of Town," and "Blues." 29 minutes.

2657. *After Hours with Art Hodes, Program 3, featuring Kenny Dorham;* produced by Northwest Teleproductions. Bloomington: Indiana University Audio Visual Center; 1979.

In addition to Davern, Art Hodes, Truck Parkham, and Red Maddock are featured. Among the compositions performed are "CC Rider," "My Blue Heaven," "Apex," "Wild Man," and "That's Plenty." 29 minutes.

2658. *After Hours with Art Hodes, Program 4, Jam No. 1;* produced by Northwest Teleproductions. Bloomington: Indiana University Audio Visual Center; 1979.

This program features Art Hodes, Herb Hall, Kenny Davern, Butch Thompson, Bill Price, Benny Morton, Truck Parkham, Hilliard Brown, and Red Maddock. They perform "Tin Roof Blues," "Just a Closer Walk," "Kansas City Blues," "When the Saints Go Marching in," and "Creole Love Song." 29 minutes.

2659. *After Hours with Art Hodes, Program 5, Jam No. 2;* produced by Northwest Teleproductions. Bloomington: Indiana University Audio Visual Center; 1979.

The final program in this series features Art Hodes, Herb Hall, Kenny Davern, Butch Thompson, Bill Price, Benny Morton, Truck Parkham, and Hilliard Brown. They perform "Let That Man Go," "Hesitation Blues," "Lady Be Good," "Plain Corduroy Blues," "Just a Closer Walk," and "High Society." 29 minutes.

Billie Holiday

2660. *Lady Day, the Many Faces of Billie Holiday;* producer N.A. West Long Beach, N.J.: Kultur (Distributor); 1988.

Contains recollections by Harry "Sweets" Edison, Milt Gabler, Carmen McRae, and Mal Waldron; Ruby Dee reads passages from her autobiography *Lady Sings the Blues.* The rare film footage includes Billie singing "Fine and Mellow," "Lover Man," "God Bless the Child," "Strange Fruit," and "The Blues and Bluin." 60 minutes, B&W, and color.

2661. *Billie Holiday: The Life and Artistry of Lady Day.* New Albany, Ind.: Jamey Aebersold; 1997?

A thorough presentation of her historical performances, biography, discography, lyrics, compositions, and a bibliography. Includes rare and seminal film clips, and demonstrates the emotional content of her lyrics. B&W white, DVD.

Freddie Hubbard

2662. *Freddie Hubbard;* produced by Audio Visual Images. New York: Sony Video Software (Distributor); 1981.

Freddie Hubbard performs many standards.

Alberta Hunter

2663. *Alberta Hunter: Jazz at the Smithsonian;* produced and Directed by Clark Santee and Delia Gravel Santee. West Long Beach, N.J.: Kultur International Films; 1982.

Recorded two years before her death in 1984 at the age of 89. Hunter provides anecdotes, recollections, and wit, along with her superb interpretation of several songs: "Handyman," "Darktown Strutter's Ball," "Rough and Ready Man," "Blackman," "Remember My Name," "Without a Song," and "When You're Smiling." She also delineates between singing the blues and singing a ballad. Gerald Cook and Jimmy Lewis assist her. 60 minutes.

International Sweethearts of Rhythm

2664. *International Sweethearts of Rhythm;* produced by Cinema Guild. New York: Cinema Guild; 1986.

The International Sweethearts of Rhythm were an integrated band of female musicians of the 1940s. They were stationed primarily in the South, and this program places the group in historical context by focusing on the gender and racial issues affecting women and African Americans of that time. Oral history interviews with surviving members of the band are interwoven with rare film footage of the group in performance, photographs, and memorabilia from public collections. 30 minutes.

Milt Jackson

2665. *Club Date: Milt Jackson;* produced by KPBS (San Diego State University). San Diego: San Diego State University; 1977.

Jackson performs several compositions from his *Montreaux Festival '77* album at a concert at SDSU. Among the tunes he performs are "Sandra's Blues," "Mean to Me," "Bag's Groove," "You Are My Sunshine," and more. 30 minutes.

Ahmad Jamal/Gary Burton

2666. *Ahmad Jamal With Gary Burton.* New Albany, Ind.: Jamey Aebersold; 1998?

A 60-minute DVD that features Jamal's trio in the first half and the trio with Gary Burton's quartet in the second half. Features many of the songs for which the respective groups are known.

Bob James

2667. *Bob James Live;* produced by View Video. New York: V.I.E.W. Video; 1985.

Filmed at the 1985 Queen Mary Jazz Festival, he is accompanied by Kirk Whalum, Alexander Zonjic, David Brown, Gary King, Yogi Horton, and Leonard "Doc" Gibbs. They perform "Taxi Theme," "Zebra Man," "Unicorn," and "Ruby, Ruby." 56 minutes.

Al Jarreau

2668. *Al Jarreau in London;* produced by Warner Reprise Video. Warner Reprise Video; 1985.

A live concert at Wembley Arena, he performs nine songs, including "Take Five." 54 minutes.

Keith Jarrett

2669. *Keith Jarrett Trio: The Opening Theater East 1993.* New Albany, Ind.: Jamey Aebersold; 1993.

The trio includes Jack DeJohnette and Garry Peacock performing "In Your Own Sweet Way," "Basin' Street Blues," "If I Were a Bell," "Bye Bye Blackbird," "I Thought About You," and four more.

2670. *Keith Jarrett Solo Tribute;* produced by Sony Video. New York: Sony Video (Distributor); 1987.

A sterling solo piano performance recorded at Suntory Hall in Tokyo in 1987. Among the tunes performed is "The Night We Called It a Day," "Things Ain't What They Used to Be," "Do Nothing Till You Hear from Me," and "Summertime." 102 minutes, VHS and DVD.

2671. *Keith Jarrett: Last Solo;* produced by Sony Video. New York: Sony Video (Distributor); 1984.

A live concert at the Kan-i Hoken Hall in Tokyo. 92 minutes. DVD.

2672. *Standards: Keith Jarrett, Gary Peacock and Jack DeJohnette;* produced by Hisao Ebine and Masafumi Yamamoto for Video Arts Japan. Chicago: Home Vision Films; 1991.

Taped in 1985 at Tokyo's Koseinene-Kin Hall. Jarrett performs "I Wish I Knew," "If I Should Lose You," "Stella by Starlight," and "God Bless the Child." He performs on acoustic piano.

2673. *Standards II: Keith Jarrett;* produced by Sony Video. New York: Sony Video (Distributor); 1986.

Trio recorded in Tokyo in 1986, which includes Jack DeJohnette and Gary Peacock. Among the 11 tunes performed are "You Don't Know What Love Is," "With a Song in My Heart," "Georgia on My Mind," "When I Fall in Love," "On Green Dolphin Street," "All of You," "Blame It on My Youth," and more. 91 minutes.

Eddie Jefferson

2674. *Eddie Jefferson Live from Jazz Showcase;* producer Rhapsody Videos. Chicago: Facets Video (Distributor); 1985.

Accompanied by Richie Cole's quartet, Jefferson performs "Moody's Mood for Love," "I Cover the Waterfront," "Night in Tunisia," "How High the Moon," "Jeannine," and more.

J. J. Johnson

2675. Johnson, J. J. *J. J. Johnson in Concert.* New Albany, Ind.: Jamey Aebersold; 1991.

The concert was recorded February 1, 1991, at Kansas State University. He is accompanied by Jamey Aebersold on tenor, Phil DeGreg on piano, Tyrone Wheeler on bass, and Art Gore on drums. The set includes "My Funny Valentine," "Confirmation," "When the Saints Go Marching In," "I Can't Get Started," "Just Friends," "Misty," and many more. The concerts last for more than two hours. VHS and DVD.

Elvin Jones

2676. *Different Drummer: Elvin Jones;* produced by Edward Grey. Franklin Lakes, N.J.: Edward Grey Films; 1979.

This 28-minute film discusses his brothers (Hank and Thad), his roots in the African American church, and his early career in postwar Detroit, Michigan. Jones discusses his experiences with Miles Davis, Charles

Mingus, and Bud Powell. There is a clip of Jones in performance with the John Coltrane Quartet.

Louis Jordan

2677. *Louis Jordan and the Tympany Five.* Upper Montclair, N.J.: The Jazz Store; 1983.

A confluence of entertainment, performance, and vocal "soundies" that is indicative of his style. He performs duets with some of the great entertainers of the day including "Shine" with Louis Armstrong, "Call of the Jitterbug" with Cab Calloway, and "Boogie Woogie" with Sammy Davis, Jr., and other tunes. 48 minutes.

2678. *Louis Jordan and His Tympany Five: Five Guys Name Moe.* Upper Montclair, N.J.: The Jazz Store; 1994?

A compilation of many of his hit songs performed with his usual mix of energetic horn lines, entertainment, and vocals. Among the 21 tunes are "Caldonia," "Saturday Night Fish Fry," "Is You Is or Is You Ain't," and many more. The "soundies" cover the 1942 to 1960 time period.

2679. *Louis Jordan and Friends.* Upper Montclair, N.J.: The Jazz Store; 1986.

His friends include Maxine Sullivan, Nat Cole, Meade Lux Lewis, Una Mae Carlisle, Joe Turner, Ruby Richards, Maurice Rocco, Hilda Rogers, Dudley Dickerson, Slim and Sweets, and Sam Pheard. The tunes performed include "Caldonia," "Boogie Woogie," "Ration Blues," "Fuzzy Wuzzy," and several more. 46 minutes.

Rahsaan Roland Kirk

2680. *Rahsaan Roland Kirk and John Cage, Sound?* Upper Montclair, N.J.: The Jazz Store; 1995.

Although the two musicians never met or collaborated, they share their visions of the endless possibilities of music. In the film, Kirk plays three saxophones simultaneously, switches to flute, and plays a tape of birds backwards. He also involves the audience in accompanying him on whistles. Among the tunes performed are "When Nightingales Sang in Berkeley Square" and his suite "Rip, Rag, and Panic," and several more.

Lee Konitz

2681. *Konitz: Portrait of Artist;* producer N.A. Chicago: Facets Video (Distributor); 1983.

A documentary that features both his music and conversations with Konitz. He performs "Stella by Starlight," "Subconscious Lee," "She's Wild as Springtime," and more. 83 minutes.

Steve Lacy

2682. *Lift the Bandstand: Steve Lacy;* produced by Rhapsody Videos. New York: Rhapsody Videos; 1990.

Profiles Lacy and includes film clips of several musicians who influenced his playing, including Sidney Bechet, John Coltrane, Gil Evans, and Thelonious Monk.

Hank Levy

2683. Levy, Henry J. *A Head of Time: Henry J.C. Levy.* New York: Studio Visual Artists Productions; 2000.

Consists primarily of a warm tribute to Levy by an assortment of people who knew and respected him. The interviews include the perspectives of Peter Erskine, Maynard Ferguson, Clem DeRosa, Milcho Leviev, many former students, local musicians, and some of his neighbors. Also includes representative samples of his rehearsals and performances. Two hours.

Mel Lewis

2684. *Mel Lewis and His Big Band;* produced by Tel Ad. New York: V.I.E.W. Video (Distributor); 1983.

A concert of big band music that also features Lynn Roberts (vocalist). The concert was taped at the Jerusalem Theater. The band features Phil Markowitz, Dick Oatts, Billy Drews, and Lynn Roberts. Compositions include "Little Pixie," "I'm Getting Sentimental over You," and "Ding Dong Ding." 38 minutes.

2685. *Mel Lewis;* produced by Adler Entertainment and Sony. New York: Sony Video Software (Distributor); 1984.

Lewis performs at the Smithsonian Institution, compositions including "One Finger Snap," "Dolphin Dance," "Make Me Smile," and "Eye of the Hurricane." 55 minutes.

Abbey Lincoln

2686. *Abbey Lincoln, You Gotta Pay the Band;* producer N.A. Chicago: Facets Video (Distributor); 1986.

A broad coverage of Lincoln's musical style and an assessment of her significance by both writers and musicians. The video includes scenes from a live performance at the Promenade Theater (New York) in 1991 as well as scenes from recording sessions with Stan Getz, Charlie Haden, Hank Jones, Marc Johnson, and Max Roach. Tony Bennett, Ruth Brown, Stanley Crouch, Stan Getz, Dan Morgenstern, and Max Roach provide the assessments. Among the tunes performed are "Brother Can You Spare a Dime," "I'm in Love," "Winter Dreams," "Summer Wishes," and "You Gotta Pay the Band." 58 minutes.

Machito

2687. *Machito: A Latin Jazz Legacy;* produced by Carlos Ortiz. New York: American Federation of Arts; 1987.

Includes a biographical profile of this outstanding musician and documentary coverage of the growth of Latin jazz in America. 58 minutes.

Manhattan Transfer

2688. *The Manhattan Transfer Live;* produced by View Video. New York: V.I.E.W. Video (Distributor); 1991.

Taped in Tokyo. Among the 19 songs performed are "Boy from New York City," "Birdland," "Meet Benny Bailey," "Gloria," "How High the Moon," and "Duke of Dubuque." 80 minutes.

2689. *Manhattan Transfer in Concert;* produced by Ken Erlich. Montvale, N.J.: Pioneer Artist Inc.; 1983.

Performs a diverse concert including "Four Brothers," "Gloria," "Operator," and other jazz, pop, and soul tunes. 58 minutes.

Shelly Manne

2690. *The Shelly Manne Quartet;* produced by Euro-Films. New York: Rhapsody Films; 1986.

In addition to Manne, Ray Brown, Bob Cooper, and Hampton Hawkes are featured. The concert took place at Shelly's Manne Hole Club. They perform "Blues in the Basement," "Milestones," and "Stella by Starlight." 28 minutes.

Branford Marsalis

2691. *Branford Marsalis: Steep;* producer N.A. Chicago: Facets Video (Distributor); 1988.

An interview and performance featuring compositions such as "Giant Steps," "Lament," "Crescent City," "Swingin' at the Heaven," and more. 89 minutes.

Wynton Marsalis

2692. *Wynton Marsalis, Blues and Swing;* producer N.A. Chicago: Facets Video (Distributor); 1985.

Contains introspective comments from Marsalis given at the Duke Ellington School of Music and Harvard. Among the several topics discussed are aesthetics and his views of jazz. His quartet performs several tunes from his first solo album including "Knozz Moe King," "Caravan," "Big Butter and Egg Man," "Cherokee," and several more. 79 minutes.

2693. *Marsalis on Music.* New Albany, Ind.: Jamey Aebersold; 1999.

A discussion of different composer and forms by a consummate musician He emphasizes structure and form, and explains how to identify forms of music from Duke Ellington to Prokofiev, Gershwin, Ives, and others. The approach is geared to music appreciation.

Rob McConnell

2694. *Rob McConnell and the Boss Brass: Volume I;* produced by Wesley Ruggles, Jr., and Gary Rebner. New York: Sony Video LP; 1981.

A swinging set performed at Howard Rumsey's Concerts by the Sea (Redondo Beach, California). They perform "The Waltz I Blew for You," "My Man Bill," and "Street of Dreams." 25 minutes.

Bobby McFerrin

2695. *Bobby McFerrin: Spontaneous Inventions;* produced by View Video. New York: V.I.E.W. Video (Distributor); 1988.

Performs originals and compositions by the Beatles, James Brown, George Gershwin, and Charles Parker. Includes "Bwee-Dop," "Scrapple from the Apple," "I Got the Feelin'," and "Blackbird." 48 minutes.

Jackie McLean

2696. *Jackie McLean on Mars;* producer/director Ken Lewis. New York: Rhapsody Films; 1979.

Features McLean discussing sociopolitical issues, racism, and drug addiction. There are several compositions performed featuring Woody Shaw.

There are scenes of his teaching and of McLean improvising on changes to "April in Paris." McLean explicitly presents new insights into the obstacles that African American musicians experienced in the 1950s.

Carmen McRae

2697. *Carmen McRae Live;* producer N.A. Newport, R.I.: Media for the Arts (Distributor); 1989.

Contains old film clips and personal insights from McRae. Although the focus is on her life and musical style there are 21 vocals featured. Among these are "That Old Black Magic," "I Get Along Without You Very Well," "Thou Swell," "But Not for Me," and 17 more. 90 minutes.

Jay McShann

2698. *Confessin' the Blues: The Music of Jay McShann;* produced and directed by W. Stinson McClendon. New York(?): MT Productions (Distributor); 1987.

McShann profiles his roots from Muskogee, Oklahoma, to Kansas City, and his present stature. The video features interviews of McShann, Billy Taylor, Frank Driggs, Claude "Fiddler" Williams, and James F. Condell. He performs "Hello, Little Girl," "Confessin' the Blues," and, with Jeannie Cheatham, "Embraceable You." 35 minutes.

Mabel Mercer

2699. *Mabel Mercer: A Singer's Singer;* produced by Lou Tyrell. New York: V.I.E.W. Video; 1981.

A concert of 17 songs taped at Cleo's in New York (her last performance). She performs "Clouds," "Isn't He Adorable," "If Love Were All," and "Some Fine Day." 42 minutes.

2700. *Mabel Mercer;* produced by WCBS (New York), Camera Three. New York: New York State Education Department; 1963.

A concert of standards. 30 minutes.

2701. *Mabel Mercer: Cabaret Artist Forever and Always;* produced by View Video. New York: V.I.E.W. Video (Distributor); 1985.

This classic cabaret artist performs compositions by Cole Porter, Cy Coleman, Jerry Herman, Stephen Sondheim, and others. Compositions include "I'm Watching You," "Time Heals Everything," and "Down in the Depths." 58 minutes.

Kid "Punch" Miller

2702. *New Orleans: Didn't He Ramble: Till the Butcher Cut Him Down;* Kino International. New York: Kino International Corporation; 1971.

Profiles the life and music of Kid "Punch" Miller. Covered are his musical life, the difference between jazz and raggin' a tune, and his influence on Louis Armstrong. 53 minutes.

Marcus Miller

2703. *Marcus Miller in Concert.* New Albany, Ind.: Jamey Aebersold; 1994.

The 1994 concert was performed in Stuggart, Germany, and features Miller and band performing "Ju Ju," "Panther," "Tutu," "Steveland," "Scoop," and several more. The video is 60 minutes and available on DVD.

Charles Mingus

2704. *Mingus 1968;* producer N.A. New York: Rhapsody Films; 1968.

A probing assessment of the man and his music. There are scenes with him performing at a live concert accompanied by Walter Bishop, John Gilmore, Charles McPherson, and Dannie Richmond. Also included in this penetrating assessment are scenes of Mingus conducting his band, composing, singing, and reciting his own poetry. 58 minutes, B&W.

2705. *Charles Mingus: Triumph of the Underdog.* New Albany, Ind.: Jamey Aebersold; 2001?

The film focuses on the many faces of this complex and creative musician. Includes footage from his performances, opinions of artists who worked with him, musical achievements, and legacy. Available in both VHS and DVD.

Modern Jazz Quartet

2706. *Modern Jazz Quartet and the Julliard String Quartet;* produced by WCBS (New York), and Camera Three. New York: New York State Education Department (Distributor); 1974.

The quartets play separately and together. MJQ plays "Third Stream," "Da Capo," and more. 30 minutes.

2707. *Modern Jazz Quartet, The;* produced by WCBS (New York), and Camera Three. New York: New York State Education Department (Distributor); 1973.

MJQ performs five original compositions.

2709. *40 Years of the Modern Jazz Quartet.* New Albany, Ind.: Jamey Aebersold; 1999.

Features Bach and other classically influenced compositions, blues, and tunes representing the standard jazz repertoire. The video is based on a live concert.

Thelonious Monk

2710. *Thelonious Monk: Playful Keys.* Princeton, N.J.: Films for the Sciences and Humanities; 2000.

Covers his musical language and idiosyncratic style by tracing his musical career. Also examines his search for a style, gradual acceptance by the public, critical acclaim, and his decline into mental illness. 30 minutes.

2711. *Thelonious Sphere Monk: Celebrating a Jazz Master;* produced by Pioneer Artists. New York: Pioneer Artists; 1979.

A performance by and profile of Thelonious Monk. He performs "Round Midnight," "Just You, Just Me," "Ruby, My Dear," "Little Waltz," "Blue Monk," "Straight No Chaser," and more. 90 minutes.

2712. *Thelonious Monk: Jazz Master;* producer N.A. Montvale, N.J.: Pioneer Artists; 1989.

Uses a laser disc format. Ron Carter, Herbie Hancock, Dizzy Gillespie, Branford and Wynton Marsalis, Jon Hendricks, Billy Taylor, Urszula Dudziak, and others accompany Monk. 90 minutes.

2713. *Thelonious Monk, Straight No Chaser;* produced by Clint Eastwood. Burbank, Calif.: Warner Home Video; 1989.

Contains interviews with Monk's son, friends, and musical associates, plus rare performance footage. Among the 25 tunes performed are "Straight No Chaser," "Ask Me Know," "Round Midnight," "Epistrophy," and "Ruby My Dear." 89 minutes, and available on VHS and DVD.

2714. *Thelonious Monk American Composer.* New Albany, Ind.: Jamey Aebersold; 1997?

The 60-minute video is available on VHA and DVD, and covers his musical career. The emphasis is on the uniqueness of Monk as a composer and performer, and includes insights from former sidemen and family members. The performance clips include "Straight No Chaser," "Blue Monk," "Mysterioso," and others.

2715. *Thelonious Monk in Olso.* Upper Montclair, N.J.: The Jazz Store; 1966.

The concert features his quartet of Larry Gales on bass, Ben Riley on drums, and Charlie Rouse on tenor saxophone. Offers specific insight into his one-finger and cross-handed improvisational style, hand span, and shuffling of his right foot and use of the pedal with the left foot. The tunes include "Blue Monk," "Criss Cross," "LuLu's Back in Town," "Mysterioso," "Round Midnight," and several more.

Wes Montgomery

2716. *Wes Montgomery: Belgium 1965.* New Albany, Ind.: Jamey Aebersold; 1965.

The video is from the 1965 Belgian Jazz Prisma session, and confirms Montgomery as an emerging star in jazz. The video offers a glimpse into his unique guitar style and reasons why he is respected as both a guitarist and composer. Among the tunes performed are "Impressions," "Twisted Blues," "Here's That Rainy Day," "Jingles," and "The Boy Next Door." 25 minutes.

Gerry Mulligan

2717. *Gerry Mulligan;* produced by Jazz America Limited. New York: Sony Video Software (Distributor); 1981.

Features Mulligan performing his compositions including "K4 Pacific" and "North Atlantic Run." 18 minutes.

2718. *Gerry Mulligan.* Princeton, N.J.: Films for the Sciences and Humanities; 2000.

Pays homage to his musical talent, friends, and fellow musicians. Also discusses his commitment to jazz, and the nuances of his smooth, and sultry saxophone style. 52 minutes and in color.

Charlie Parker

2719. *Celebrating Bird: The Triumph of Charlie Parker;* produced by Sony Video Software. New York: Sony Video Software (Distributor); 1987.

This is the counterpart to Gary Giddins's book, *Celebrating Bird: The Triumph of Charlie Parker,* and Giddins here is one of the directors and the writer. The video is substantial as it contains interviews of Rebecca Parker Davis (his first wife), Leonard Feather, Dizzy Gillespie, Roy Haynes, Frank Morgan, Jay McShann, Chan Parker, and Roy Parker. In addition there are several musical excerpts of musical associates including Jay McShann, Billy Eckstine, Coleman Hawkins, Thelonious Monk, Lester Young, and more. An excellent video. 58 minutes.

2720. Eastwood, Clint. *Bird.* New Albany, Ind.: Jamey Aebersold; 1998.

This 2-hour-40-minute film presents a comprehensive assessment of the man, his music, influences, successes, and failures. The film features Forrest Whitaker in the role of Parker, and provides factual insight into his drug addiction, relationship with Chan, Gillespie, and other musicians, rise to fame, eventual downfall, as well as his struggles to cope with the endemic changes in his life.

Airto and Flora Purim

2721. *Airto and Flora Purim;* produced by V.I.E.W. Video. New York: V.I.E.W. (Distributor); 1985.

A concert taped at the Queen Mary Jazz Festival featuring Joe Farrell and the Batucaje Dance Troupe. 60 minutes.

Oscar Peterson

2722. *Begone Dull Care;* produced by McLaren Film Series. Chicago: International Film Bureau; 1949.

McLaren uses animation to interpret a modern jazz composition performed by the Oscar Peterson Trio. The composition offers tempo contrasts. 8 minutes.

2723. *Oscar Peterson: The Life of a Legend.* New Albany, Ind.: Jamey Aebersold; 1996?

Tells the life story of Peterson from growing up in Canada to his recognition as a giant in jazz. We hear his fight against racism and struggle to balance family life and travel, and witness his reunion with his children. Important because his children express their love and admiration of their father. Also contains vintage footage of past and contemporary performances.

Sun Ra

2724. *Sun Ra: A Joyful Noise;* produced by Robert Mugge and Rhapsody Films. Los Angeles: Direct Cinema Limited (Distributor); 1980.

Profiles the mysticism, philosophy, and music of Sun Ra. His Arkestra performs his music.

2725. *Sun Ra and His Arkestra, Mystery Mr. Ra;* producer N.A. New York: Rhapsody Films (Distributor); 1989.

Focuses on Sun Ra as a musician, bandleader, commune leader, psychic, philosopher, and shaman. This video was shot in France in 1984.

Compositions performed include "Love in Outer Space," "Nuclear War," and "1984." 51 minutes.

Lou Rawls

2726. *Lou Rawls Show with Duke Ellington;* produced by View Video. New York: V.I.E.W. Vidco (Distributor); 1971.

A powerful rendition of blues, ballads, and gospels. Duke Ellington performs "Satin Doll" and "Sophisticated Lady," and Lou Rawls and Freda Payne perform "Oh Happy Day."

Django Reinhardt

2727. *Gypsy Guitar: The Legacy of Django Reinhardt;* producer N.A. Chicago: Facets Video (Distributor); 1983.

Considers his impact, stylistic innovations, and influences on venues from a Parisian guitar shop, sites in Holland, and Somois-Sur-Seine, to the French village where he spent his final years. He is accompanied by Babik Reinhardt (son), Birele Lagrene, Gary Potter, and the Gypsy Kids. 60 minutes.

Lee Ritenour

2728. *Lee Ritenour and Dave Grusin: Live from the Record Plant.* New Albany, Ind.: Jamey Aebersold; 1985.

This 55-minute DVD was recorded August 14, 1985, and features both Ritenour and Grusin. Eight tracks are filmed, including "Power Wave," "Harlequin," "St. Elsewhere," "The Island," and more. Abe Laboriel, Ivan Lin, Carlos Vega, and Larry Williams. DVD accompany the artists.

2729. *Lee Ritenour: RIT Special.* New Albany, Ind.: Jamey Aebersold; 1984.

This 75-minute DVD was recorded June 29, 1984, at the Concord Pavillion in California. The band performs 12 tunes.

Max Roach

2730. *Sit Down and Listen: The Story of Max Roach;* produced as part of the RePercussion Series: A Celebration of African American Series. Chicago: Home Vision (Division of Films Incorporated) (Distributor); 1986.

Focuses on a family reunion, as well as his views of postwar East Coast jazz. Roach is featured both in musical situations (performing and teaching), and in reflections upon jazz past and present. Includes footage of the his roles as bandleader, performer, and professor, in the studio, on tour, and behind the podium. Additional performers include Cecil Bridgewater, Odean Pope, Tyrone Brown, the all-star M'Boom ensemble, and the Swedenborg String Quartet, which features his daughter. 60 minutes and in color.

2731. *Max Roach.* Princeton, N.J.: Films for the Science and Humanities; 1999?

Examines his stature, career, role as a civil rights activist in the 1960s and 1970s, and influence on other musicians. Covers his musical career from his early years with Dizzy Gillespie and Charles Parker to his role and function as a bandleader and musical director of M'Boom.

2732. *Max Roach: In Concert/In Session;* produced by Axis Video. New York: DCI Music Video (Distributor); 1985.

Roach demonstrates his drumming technique followed by a performance of his quintet at the 1982 Kool Jazz Festival. 60 minutes.

2733. *Max Roach;* produced by Jazz America Limited. New York: Sony Video Software; 1981.

Features several of Roach's compositions including "Six Bits," "Blues," and "Effie." 19 minutes.

Sonny Rollins

2734. *Saxophone Colossus: Sonny Rollins;* produced by Robert Mugge, Sony. New York: Sony Video Software; 1986.

Features an interview, rehearsal shots, a concert with his group, and a solo with the Yomuri Nippon Symphony Orchestra. Rollins group includes Clifford Anderson, Mark Soskin, Bob Cranshaw, and Marvin "Smitty" Smith. Rollins and his group perform "G-Man," "Tenor Saxophone Solo" (unaccompanied), "Saxophone Colossus," and with the Yomuri Nippon Symphony, "Concerto for Tenor Saxophone and Orchestra." A revealing portrait of this great artist.

2735. *Sonny Rollins Live;* produced by TCB. New York: Time-Life Video (Distributor); 1979.

Bob Cranshaw, Walter Davis Jr., MaSuo, and David Lee support Rollins. They perform "There Is No Greater Love," "Don't Stop the Carnival," "Alfie," "St. Thomas," and more. 36 minutes.

David Sanborn

2736. *David Sanborn the Super Session.* New Albany, Ind.: Jamey Aebersold; 2000?

A confluence of several popular musicians and Sanborn performing several popular songs. Among the performers and their recordings are Boz Scaggs, "Mary Don't Take Me on a Bad Trip" and "Low Down"; Isaac Hayes, "Spooky"; and Lou Reed and Isaac Hayes, "St. James Infirmary." The David Sanborn band performs the main theme.

George Shearing

2737. *George Shearing, Lullaby of Birdland;* produced by View Video. New York: V.I.E.W. Video (Distributor); 1993.

Features Shearing and bassist Neil Swainson in a 1991 concert at the Paul Masson Winery in California. He plays a combination of ballads and bebop including "Donna Lee," "Freedom Jazz Dance," "Lullaby of Birdland," "Isn't It Romantic," "Freedom Jazz Dance," "Donna Lee," and "Why Did I Choose You?" 55 minutes.

Jack Sheldon

2738. *Jack Sheldon in New Orleans;* produced by John Shoup. New Orleans, La.: Liesure Video; 1989.

Sheldon performs a concert at LuLu White's Mahoghany Hall. Among the many compositions performed are "I Was Ready," "Corcovado," "No Mama," "The Joint Is Jumpin," "The One I Love Belongs to Someone Else," and more. Sheldon also adds recollections of Chet Baker, Stan Kenton, Charles Parker, and today's young players.

Archie Shepp

2739. *Archie Shepp: I Am Jazz—It's My Life;* produced by Rhapsody Videos (Frank Cassenti). New York: Rhapsody Videos; 1984.

Contains Shepp's views on sociopolitical issues affecting jazz as well as examples of his music, poetry, and drama. He discusses the African origins and revolutionary purpose of jazz, the invisibility of African Americans, and more. He is accompanied by Siegfried Kessler (piano), Wilbur Little (bass), Don Mumford and Clifford Jarvis (drums), and Cheikh Tidiane Fall (percussion). 52 minutes.

Diane Schuur and Count Basie Orchestra

2740. *Diane Schuur and the Count Basie Orchestra;* produced by Pioneer Artists. New York: Pioneer Artists; 1990.

Schuur sings "Travelin' Light," "Only You," "I Loves You Porgy," "We'll Be Together Again," and more. 51 minutes.

Bobby Short

2741. *Bobby Short at the Cafe Carlyle;* produced by Lea Lou Productions. New York: V.I.E.W. Video; 1979.

Another concert of his favorite show tunes and standards. 65 minutes.

2742. *Bobby Short and Friends;* produced by MGM/UA. MGM/UA Home Video; 1986.

Short performs several show tunes at New York's Cafe Carlyle. 60 minutes.

Zoot Sims

2743. *The Zoot Sims Quartet;* produced by Euro-Film Corporation. New York: Rhapsody Films; 1988.

Roger Fellaway, Larry Bunker, and Chuck Berghofer assist Sims. The concert was filmed at Dante's in Los Angeles and features "Zoot's Piece," "My Old Flame," "On the Trail," and "Motoring Along." 28 minutes.

Clark Terry

2744. *Clark Terry: Live in Concert.* New Albany, Ind.: Jamey Aebersold; 2001.

Includes an interview with Terry and his performance in an all-star concert. Donald Harrison, Anthony Wonsey, Curtis Lundy, and Victor Lewis accompany Terry. Among the songs performed are "Quicksand," "Elijah," "Moten Swing," "Love Love Love," "St. Lucia Vlies," "All Blues," "My Gal," "Take the 'A' Train," and "Bye Bye Blackbird." VHS and DVD, 84 minutes and in color.

2745. *Clark Terry Quartet: Copenhagen Live.* New Albany, Ind.: Jamey Aebersold; 1985.

The concert was recorded April 4, 1985, at Copenhagen's Club Montmartre, and Duke Jordan, Jimmy Woods, and Sven Norregaard accompanied Terry. Among the songs performed are "Mellow Tone," "Mood Indigo," "Just Squeeze Me," "God Bless the Child," "Satin Doll," and "Lady Be Good."

Clark Terry/Duke Jordan

2746. *The Duke Jordan Trio with Clark Terry.* New Albany, Ind.: Jamey Aebersold; 1985.

This concert was held at the Copenhagen Montmartre Jazzhus, and was a special tribute to Ben Webster. The concert featured both the Duke Jordan trio, which was recorded as the Duke Jordan Trio, at the club Montmartre, Copenhagen, April 7, 1985, and featured Jesper Lundgaard, and Age

Tandgaard. The trio with Clark Terry was recorded on the same date, and featured Jimmy Woode on bass, and Svend E. Norregaard on drums. Among the tunes performed were "In a Mellow Tone," "Mood Indigo," "Just Squeeze Me," "God Bless the Child," "Satin Doll," Oh Lady Be Good," and several more. 75 minutes and DVD.

Cal Tjader

2747. *Club Date: Cal Tjader;* produced by KPBS Television (San Diego State University). San Diego: San Diego State University; 1977.

Tjader performs at SDSU. Tunes include "Green Dolphin Street," "Tangerine," "Black Orpheus," "Soul Source," and more. 50 minutes.

Mel Tormé

2748. *Mel Tormé;* produced by One Pass Production. New York: Sony Video Software (Distributor); 1983.

Tormé sings some of his most significant hits, including "New York State of Mind," "Born in the Night," "Down for Double," and more.

2749. *Mel Tormé and Della Reese in Concert;* produced by ITV. Universal City, Calif.: MCA Home Video (Distributor); 1981.

A concert recorded live at the Jubilee Auditorium in Edmonton, Canada. Tormé performs "Bluesette" and more. 45 minutes.

2750. *Mel Tormé Special;* produced by One Pass Productions. New York: Sony Software (Distributor); 1983.

Sings "Bluesette," "New York State of Mind," and several more. 53 minutes.

Lennie Tristano

2751. *Lennie Tristano: The Copenhagen Concert.* New Albany, Ind.: Jamey Aebersold; 1965.

This solo performance was recorded on October 31, 1996, in the Tivoli Gardens Concert Hall. Among the performed tunes are "Darn That Dream," "Lullaby of the Leaves," "Expressions," "You Don't Know What Love Is," "Tivoli Gardens Swing," "Ghost of a Chance," "It's You or No One," "Imagination," and "Tangerine."

Stanley Turrentine

2752. *Stanley Turrentine;* producer N.A. West Long Beach, N.J.: Kultur (Distributor); 1989.

Turrentine discusses his career, which spans styles from bebop to funk, and performs in this concert filmed at the Village Gate (New York) in 1990. Among several tunes performed are "My Romance," "Impressions," "Salt Song," and "Sugar." 60 minutes, color.

2753. *Stanley Turrentine: In Concert;* producer N.A. Chicago: Facets Video (Distributor); 1984.

Recorded at New York's Village Gate. Turrentine discusses his career and performs several of his most popular recordings including "Don't Mess with Mister T." 60 minutes.

Sarah Vaughan

2754. *Sarah Vaughan: The Divine One;* produced by Hisao Ebine, Susan Lacy, and Kirk D'Amico. New York: WNET/American Masters Series; 1991.

Replete with comments from Vaughan as well as personal/musical assessments of her by Paris Vaughan (daughter), her mother, George Gaffney, Marty Paich, Roy Haynes, Joe Williams, and especially Billy Eckstine. She performs "London Town," "Misty," "Tenderly," "Over the Rainbow," "Send in the Clowns," and more. Dan Morgenstern wrote the videotext. 60 minutes.

2755. *Sass and Brass: A Jazz Session;* producer HBO Video.: BO Video; 1988.

Features Sarah Vaughan, Dizzy Gillespie, Chuck Mangione, Maynard Ferguson, Al Hirt, Don Cherry, and Herbie Hancock. Vaughan sings "Alfie," "Tenderly," and more. 60 minutes.

2756. *Sarah Vaughan and Friends;* produced by View Video. New York: V.I.E.W. Video (Distributor); 1988.

Previously titled "Sass and Brass," this historic concert also features Ron Carter, Don Cherry, Chuck Mangione, Maynard Ferguson, Dizzy Gillespie, and Freddie Hubbard. Among numerous songs performed are "Round Midnight," "Take the 'A' Train," "You'd Be So Nice to Come Home To," and several more. 60 minutes.

Fats Waller

2757. *Fats Waller: An American Original;* produced by Camera Three Series. Boston: WGBH TV (Distributor); 1979.

A documentary biography of Waller, which includes rare footage of Waller in performance, photographs, recordings, and performance of some of his standard works from "Ain't Misbehavin." 30 minutes.

2758. *Fats Waller and Friends, 1941–46;* produced by Amvest Video. New Albany, Ind.: Jamey Aebersold (Distributor); 1987.

A 1945 soundie that features Waller and several of his musical friends and associates, including Dorothy Dandridge, Tiny Grimes, Mabel Lee, Dusty Brooks and his Four Tones, and the Three Chefs. Compositions performed are "Ain't Misbehavin,'" "Honeysuckle Rose," "Your Feets Too Big," "Moo Cow Boogie-Woogie," "Tiny Grimes Boogie-Woogie," "She's Too Hot to Handle," "Shout Brother Shout," "Chicken Shack Shuffle," "Breakfast in Rhythm," and "The Joint Is Jumpin.'" 29 minutes.

Grover Washington

2759. *Grover Washington, Jr. In Concert;* producer View Video. New York: V.I.E.W. Video; 1991.

Accompanied by Steve Gadd, Eric Gale, and Richard Tee in a 1981 performance. He performs "Let It Flow," "Just the Two of Us," "Mister Magic," and more. 60 minutes.

Ben Webster

2760. *Ben Webster: The Brute and the Beautiful;* producer N.A. Chicago: Facets Video (Distributor); 1974.

Traces his style from his origins in Kansas City in the 1920s through his collaborations with Duke Ellington, Benny Carter, Teddy Wilson, Gerry Mulligan, and Jimmy Witherspoon to his European exile and final performance in Holland in 1973. 60 minutes.

2761. *Ben Webster in Europe;* produced by Johan Van der Keujen. New York: Rhapsody Videos; 1967.

Interviews Webster in Europe. His musical performance includes "My Romance," "Perdido," "You'd Be So Nice to Come Home To," and several more. 31 minutes, B&W.

Tim Weisberg

2762. *Club Date: Tim Weisberg;* produced by KPBS (San Diego State University). San Diego: San Diego State University; 1977.

A concert at SDSU in which Weisberg and his band perform several tunes from his *Dream Speaker* album. Among the compositions performed are "Scrabble," "Tibetan Silver," "Because of Rain," and more. 30 minutes.

Joe Williams

2763. *Joe Williams: Jazz at the Smithsonian.* Upper Montclair, N.J.: The Jazz Store; 1982.

In this 1982 concert, Keeter Betts, Kirk Stuart, and Steve Williams accompanied Williams. The concert was 58 minutes and includes "Everyday I Sing the Blues," "Once in a While," "Everything Must Change," "Who She Do," "Well Alright-Ok You Win," "Stella by Starlight," and five others.

Joe Williams and George Shearing

2764. *Joe Williams with George Shearing, a Song Is Born;* produced by View Video. New York: V.I.E.W. Video (Distributor); 1993.

Like the George Shearing *Lullaby of Birdland* video, this concert was filmed at the 1991 Paul Masson Winery in California. Williams is assisted by George Shearing, Neil Swainson, and Paul Humphrey, and performs "A Child Is Born," "Just Friends," "Little Girl Blue," "I Let a Song Go out of My Heart," "Who She Do," "Shake, Rattle and Roll," "Tenderly," and several more. 57 minutes.

2765. *Joe Williams;* produced by Adler Enterprises. New York: Sony Video Software (Distributor); 1984.

Among the songs performed are "Everyday I Have the Blues," "Once in a While," "Who She Do," "Save That Time for Me," and others. 58 minutes.

Mary Lou Williams

2766. *Mary Lou's Mass;* produced by New Jersey Network. Trenton: New Jersey Network (Distributor); 1977.

A filmed performance of Mary Lou Williams's jazz interpretation of the Roman Catholic Mass. 60 minutes.

2767. *Mary Lou Williams;* produced by Gene Bunge, Henry Morgan/Nebraska ETV Network, and the Mid-American Arts Alliance—Lincoln. Mid-American Arts Alliance and the University of Nebraska Educational Television (Distributor): 1981.

Narrated by Billy Taylor, the video contains Williams's comments on how she began playing jazz, how to play good jazz, her orchestration of "Walkin' and Swingin,'" and other compositions. She performs in a trio setting. Informative. 30 minutes.

Nancy Wilson

2768. *Nancy Wilson at Carnegie Hall;* produced by V.I.E.W. New York: V.I.E.W. Video; 1989.

A performance at the JVC Festival in New York.

2769. *Nancy Wilson at Carnegie Hall;* produced by View Video. New York: V.I.E.W. Video (Distributor); 1987.

Features highlights from the New York City 1987 JVC Jazz Festival. Includes "First Time on a Ferris Wheel," "Forbidden Lover," and more.

2770. *Nancy Wilson;* produced by Sony Video. New York: Sony Video Software (Distributor); 1982.

Wilson is joined by several former Return to Forever members to perform "I Want to Be Happy," "But Not for Me," "Round Midnight," and several more. 60 minutes.

Phil Woods

2771. *Phil Woods in Concert;* produced by V.I.E.W. Video. New York: V.I.E.W. (Distributor); 1986.

Woods performs with Joe Sudler's Swing Machine in this 1986 concert from the Chestnut Cabaret in Philadelphia. He performs "Body and Soul," "Groovin' High," "Watch What Happens," and "Willow Weep for Me." 67 minutes.

Collective Jazz Performances

2772. *Jazz Miami Celebration of Latin Jazz.* New Albany, Ind.: Jamey Aebersold; 2001.

A celebration and tribute to the Latin jazz heritage. The concert was held at the Jackie Gleason Theater in Miami, and featured highly energized performances from Chick Corea, Pete Escovedo, Oscar D'Leon, Hilton Ruiz, Pancho Sanchez, Arturo Sandoval, Dave Valentine, Ray Vega, and several more.

2773. *Four Tenors: John Coltrane, Charles Lloyd, Sonny Rollins and Ben Webster.* New Albany, Ind.: Jamey Aebersold; 1962, 1963, 1968.

A 103-minute DVD that is a collection of four separate television performances from the 1960s. It features the 1963 quartet of John Coltrane (McCoy Tyner, Jimmy Garrison, and Elvin Jones); The Ben Webster quartet of Vince Guaraldi, Monty Budwig, Colin Bailey, along with Jimmy Witherspoon; Sonny Rollins quartet of Jim Hall, Bob Cranshaw, and Ben Riley, and the Charles Lloyd quartet of Keith Jarrett, Ron McLure, and Jack DeJohnette. The DVD is in B&W.

2774. *Great Performances: Lester Young, Charles Parker, and Miles Davis.* New Albany, Ind.: Jamey Aebersold; 1950, 1959.

A collection of the known footage of Charles Parker appearing with Illinois Jacquet, Lester Young, and other significant artists. The DVD features the *Sound of Miles Davis,* an excellent television program that featured the Miles Davis quintet of John Coltrane, Wynton Kelly, Paul Chambers, and Jimmy Cobb with the Gil Evans Orchestra. A concert of the *Jazz at the Philharmonic,* from early September 1950 that featured Ray Brown, Harry Edison, Ella Fitzgerald, Colman Hawkins, Hank Jones, Charles Parker, Flip Phillips, Lester Young, and others. Also included is the performance of the April 2, 1959, *Sound of Miles Davis* (same personnel as the previously mentioned concert) performing "So What," "The Duke," "Blues for Pablo," and "New Rhumba." The DVD also includes "Jammin the Blues," and performances of "Sweet Georgia Brown," "If I Could Be With You One Hour Tonight," and "Blues for Marvin."

2775. *Greatest Jazz Films Ever.* New Albany, Ind.: Jamey Aebersold; 1944, 1950, 1952, and 1959.

A two-DVD set of an hour and a half collection of performances by John Coltrane, Miles Davis, Billie Holiday, Charles Parke, and Lester Young. Included are the following films: disc one, *Jammin the Blues,* performed in Hollywood, California, August–September 1944. The concert featured Harry Edison, Barney Kessel, Illinois Jacquet, and Lester Young. It also includes *Charlie Parker: TV Stage Entrance Show,* February 24, 1952, in New York. In addition to Parker, Dizzy Gillespie, Dick Hyman, and several other artists are featured. The *Jazz at the Philharmonic* concert from early September 1950 that featured Ray Brown, Harry Edison, Bill Harris, Coleman Hawkins, Hank Jones, Ella Fitzgerald, Charles Parker, Buddy Rich, Lester Young, and others. Disc one ends with a performance from *The Sound of Miles Davis* concert that was performed April 2, 1959, in New York City. In addition to the Miles Davis quintet, 15 other artists were featured.

Disc two contains *The Sound of Jazz: Count Basie All-Star Orchestra,* the complete big band with soloists Count Basie, Coleman Hawkins, Gerry Mulligan, Joe Newman, and Dickie Wells; The Red Allen All-Star Orchestra, a concert that featured Allen Coleman Hawkins, and others; The Thelonious Monk Trio of Ahmed Abdul Malik, and Ossie Johnson perform several songs; The Count Basie All-Star Orchestra with Jimmy Rushing (includes the same personnel as above) with Jimmy Rushing perform several blues; Billie Holiday with the Mal Waldron and the Count Basie All-Star Orchestra, perform several songs; Jimmy Giuffre Three, and with his quintet and Pee Wee Russell, accompanied by Jim Hall, Jim Atlas, Milt Hinton, and Jo Jones. The Ahmad Jamal Trio with Israel Crosby and Vernell Fournier, and the Ben Webster Sextet of 1959 that featured Buck Clayton, Vic Dickenson, and Hank Jones ends disc two.

2776. *The Ladies Sing the Blues.* Chicago: Clearvue/EAV; 2000?

Although labeled blues, the 60-minute video also includes jazz singers. The black-and-white video contains footage of Billie Holiday, Lena Horn, Peggy Lee, Dinah Washington, and Sarah Vaughan. DVD.

2777. *Monterey Jazz Festival, 1975.* New Albany, Ind.: Jamey Aebersold; 1975.

The 60-minute DVD features numerous performances at the festival. Among the artists featured are the Akiyoshi Big Band, Bobby Blue Bland, Blood Sweet and Tears, Bill Evans, Paul Desmond, Dizzy Gillespie, Etta James, John Lewis, Chuck Mangione, Marian McPartland, Clark Terry, and several more.

2778. *Saxophone Salute: Roots.* New Albany, Ind.: Jamey Aebersold; 1996.

Recorded live at the Brewhouse Theater, this 55-minute DVD features Arthur Blythe on alto saxophone, Chico Freeman on tenor and soprano, and Nathan Davis on alto, tenor, and soprano saxophones. In addition, Don Pullen on piano, Santi Debriano on bass, and Idris Muhammad on drums round out the group. They salute saxophone greats by performing six compositions.

2779. *The Sound of Jazz.* New Albany, Ind.: Jamey Aebersold; 1957.

Originally broadcasted on CBS in December 1957, the video features a confluence of musicians and styles. Among the musicians appearing in the video are Red Allen and His All Stars, Count Basie and Jimmy Rushing, Billie Holiday, Thelonious Monk, Jimmy Giuffre, and the Pee Wee Russell-Jimmy Giuffre Ontet. VHS and DVD, 58 minutes.

2780. *The Story of Jazz: Masters of American Music.* New Albany: Jamey Aebersold; 1997?

Permeated with comments, historical insights, and performances from early New Orleans to modern jazz. Includes performance by Louis Armstrong, Count Basie, John Coltrane, Miles Davis, Duke Ellington, Ella Fitzgerald, Dizzy Gillespie, Charles Mingus, Thelonious Monk, and several others.

2781. *Trumpet Kings.* New Albany, Ind.: Jamey Aebersold; 1984.

The 25 performances are hosted by Wynton Marsalis, and feature trumpeters covering styles from New Orleans to the mid-1980s. The performances include Louis Armstrong, Dizzy Gillespie, Miles Davis, Roy Eldridge, Fats Navarro, and many more.

From 1983 to 1992, KPBS and Elario's Restaurant and Night Club in San Diego, California, produced a series of concerts entitled "Club Date." All concerts were taped live at Elario's. The concerts are not for sale or distribution; however, performers and scholars may contact the programming office at KPBS (San Diego State University) to determine the date of the next airing of a particular concert. These concerts are included because they represent some of the best performances of past and contemporary jazz. Artist in alphabetical order in the preceding section lists "Club Dates" before 1983. The following "Club Dates" are organized by year.

2782. *Club Date: The Larry Vuckovich Quartet* (#105), produced by KPBS (S.D.S.U.), San Diego; KPBS (Distributor); 1983.

Contemporary jazz pianist Larry Vuckovich, who occasionally blends the Balkan folk music of his native Yugoslavia with blues, bop, and jazz, appears here in a program the *New York Times* called "well worth tuning in for" and "a fine sampling" of Vuckovich's talents. He is joined by Tom Harrell, trumpet; John Heard, bass; and Sherman Ferguson, drum, for such numbers as "Village Voices," "Lush Life," and "Blues News." Saxophonist Charles McPherson sits in for the final blues classic, "After Hours."

2783. *Club Date: The Peter Sprague Trio* (#106), produced by KPBS (S.D.S.U.), San Diego; KPBS (Distributor); 1987.

Critically acclaimed young jazz guitarist Peter Sprague, who has played alongside the likes of Chick Corea and Hubert Laws, is accompanied by Bob Magnusson, bass; Tripp Sprague, flute and saxophone; and Duncan Moore, drums. The program features several of Sprague's own compositions, including "Ensenada," "Seattle Stomp," "Maya," and "Musica Del Mar," as well as the standard ballad "It Could Happen to You." This particular Club Date won two Emmy Awards (Best Entertainment Program and Best Directing) in 1988 from the San Diego Chapter of the National Academy of Television Arts and Sciences.

2784. *Club Date: Papa John Creach* (#107), produced by KPBS (S.D.S.U.), San Diego; KPBS (Distributor); 1988.

Mike Wofford on piano and Bob Magnusson accompany the 73-year-old violinist Papa John Creach, who also tried his hand at rock in the 1960s and 1970s with the Jefferson Airplane and Jefferson Starship, on bass, and Jim Plank on drums. Featured numbers include "Exactly Like You," "Georgia on My Mind," "Git Fiddler," and "Movin.'"

2785. *Club Date: Freddie Hubbard* (#108), produced by KPBS (S.D.S.U.), San Diego; KPBS (Distributor); 1989.

Jazz "superstar" Freddie Hubbard, recently voted the best trumpet player in the world in the *Down Beat Magazine* reader's poll, is joined by drummer

Sherman Ferguson, pianist William Cantos, Chris Conner on bass, and Doug Webb on tenor saxophone.

2786. *Club Date: Barney Kessel* (#201), produced by KPBS (S.D.S.U.), San Diego; KPBS (Distributor); 1988.

World-renowned jazz guitarist Barney Kessel was a member of the Oscar Peterson Trio until 1953 and was music director for the Bob Crosby TV show in 1954. Kessel was the winner of the *Down Beat Magazine* reader's poll from 1956 through 1959 and the *Playboy* poll from 1957 through 1960. He has appeared on record albums with Lionel Hampton, Red Norvo, Billie Holiday, Ben Webster, and Woody Herman and has been called "the most rhythmically vital guitarist in modern jazz." Kessel performs on Club Date with Bob Magnusson on bass and Sherman Ferguson on drums. He is joined on the final two selections by special guest Herb Ellis, his longtime friend and fellow guitarist. The selections performed are: "Wave," "I've Grown Accustomed to Your Face," "Brazil Medley," "Body and Soul," and "Flintstones."

2787. *Club Date: Bud Shank* (#202), produced by KPBS (S.D.S.U.), San Diego; KPBS (Distributor); 1988.

Jazz alto saxophonist Bud Shank first came to prominence in the big bands of Charlie Barnet and Stan Kenton during the late 1940s. Throughout the 1950s, he had a long tenure with Howard Rumsey's Lighthouse Allstars and with trumpeter Shorty Rogers. A charter member of the cool "West Coast sound," Shank has worked more recently with the world-renowned LA Four, where he helped popularize the field of chamber jazz. Shank appears on Club Date with Mike Wofford on piano, Bob Magnusson on bass, and Jim Plank on drums. Selections performed are: "The Doctor Is In," "Sea Flowers," "Softly as in a Morning Sunrise," "Emily," "Tomorrow's Rainbow," and "Bud's Theme."

2788. *Club Date: Laurindo Almeida* (#203), produced by KPBS (S.D.S.U.), San Diego; KPBS (Distributor); 1988.

Jazz guitarist Laurindo Almeida is a multiple Grammy nominee and winner. He first gained prominence as a member of the Stan Kenton Orchestra in the 1950s. Since that time, he has been featured with smaller groups and most recently as a member of the LA Four. Attributed with popularizing Brazilian or bossa nova jazz in the United States, Almeida continues to blend samba rhythms with jazz and classical guitar themes. Appearing with him on Club Date are bassist Bob Magnusson and drummer Jim Plank. Selections performed are "Samba De Breck," "Artistry in Rhythm," "Inquetacao," "Busy Bee," and Almeida's famous arrangement of "One Note Samba."

2789. *Club Date: Buddy DeFranco/Terry Gibbs* (#204), produced by KPBS (S.D.S.U.), San Diego; KPBS (Distributor); 1989.

Jazz clarinetist Buddy DeFranco teams up with vibraharpist Terry Gibbs for a spirited Club Date session of bebop. Each has been a respected leader/soloist on the jazz scene for over 40 years. They joined forces in 1980 and have been touring together ever since. "What Benny Goodman and Lionel Hampton were to the swing era, these two are to a latter generation" (Leonard Feather, *LA Times*). The quintet also features Robert Hamilton, piano; Chris Conner, bass; and Terry's son Gerry Gibbs on drums. Selections include "The Carioca," "I Thought About You," "Sister Sadie," "What's New," "Love for Sale," and "Blues for Brodie."

2790. *Club Date: James Moody* (#205), produced by KPBS (S.D.S.U.), San Diego; KPBS (Distributor); 1989.

Jazz saxophonist James Moody gained prominence as a member of Dizzy Gillespie's big bebop band of the late 1940s. His improvisational solo of "I'm in the Mood for Love," recorded in Sweden in 1949, is now a classic and has been immortalized in vocal versions retitled "Moody's Mood for Love." Equally adept on alto or tenor sax, Moody is one of the pioneers of jazz flute, at which he is a master. Moody appears on Club Date with pianist Rob Schneiderman, bassist Bob Magnusson, and drummer Chuck McPherson. Selections include "Anthropology," "Loverman," "Moody's Mood for Love," and "Wave."

2791. *Club Date: Herb Ellis* (#206), produced by KPBS (S.D.S.U.), San Diego; KPBS (Distributor); 1989.

Premier jazz guitarist Herb Ellis replaced Barney Kessel in the Oscar Peterson Trio in 1953 and remained with that group until November of 1958. In 1959, he played with Ella Fitzgerald. He has been primarily involved with studio bands for the Steve Allen, Danny Kaye, Joey Bishop, and Merv Griffin shows. "Ellis is one of the great modern jazz guitarists, swinging effortlessly and warmly at all tempos and to exceptionally moving effect on the blues," noted one critic. Ellis performs on Club Date with bassist Bob Magnusson and drummer Sherman Ferguson and is joined on the final two selections by his long-time friend and fellow guitarist Barney Kessel. The selections performed are "I Love You," "Detour Ahead," "Things Ain't What They Used to Be," "Lover Man," and "The Sheik of Arabie."

2792. *Club Date: Mose Allison* (#302), produced by KPBS (S.D.S.U.), San Diego; KPBS (Distributor); 1989.

Jazz/blues singer, songwriter, piano player Mose Allison is the featured artist on Club Date. Born in Mississippi in 1927, Mose's unconventional style of singing and playing along with his distinct rhythmic way of putting words and music together have built him a loyal following of fans who buy his albums and seek out his performances. Mose was nominated for a Grammy award in 1983 and nominated for Best Jazz Album, 1988 New York Music Awards. Selections performed include "Swingin' Machine," "No Special Place," "You Are My Sunshine," "Your Mind Is on Vacation," "Gettin' There," and "You Can Count on Me to Do My Part." Appearing with Allison is saxophonist Gary Lefebvre, bassist Gunnar Biggs, and drummer Dave Coleman.

2793. *Club Date: Hank Crawford & Jimmy McGriff* (#303), produced by KPBS (S.D.S.U.), San Diego; KPBS (Distributor); 1989.

Alto saxophonist Hank Crawford and organist Jimmy McGriff perform their own special mix of jazz/blues before an enthusiastic audience on Club Date. Crawford, who got his basic training in the blues with Ray Charles—serving as Charles's musical director for three years—and McGriff, who studied at Julliard and privately with famed jazz organist Jimmy Smith, teamed up in 1986 and have been performing and recording together to rave reviews ever since. Selections include: "Everyday I Have the Blues," "You Send Me," "Frim Fram Sauce," "Frame for the Blues," and "Vickie." Guitarist Bob Devos and drummer Jimmy Smith round out the quartet.

2794. *Club Date: Harry "Sweets" Edison* (#304), produced by KPBS (S.D.S.U.), San Diego; KPBS (Distributor); 1989.

Born in Columbus, Ohio, in 1915, Harry "Sweets" Edison is one of the living legends of jazz. He is considered one of the most gifted and distinctive trumpet stylists the world has produced. Edison first came to prominence as the principal soloist for the Count Basie Orchestra between 1937 and 1950. Harry's "sweet-sour" muted sounds became the trademark for the Basie band and earned him the nickname "Sweets." Edison subsequently toured with Jazz at the Philharmonic, the Buddy Rich Orchestra, and later with singer Frank Sinatra. Selections include "Out of Nowhere," "I Want Something to Live for," "The Days of Wine and Roses," "Wave," and "Centerpiece." Internationally known concert and recording artist Clifford Jordan is featured on the tenor saxophone. Pianist Mike Wofford, bassist Bob Magnusson, and drummer Jim Plank round out the quintet.

2795. *Club Date: Jimmy Witherspoon* (#305), produced by KPBS (S.D.S.U.), San Diego; KPBS (Distributor); 1990.

Renowned blues singing legend Jimmy Witherspoon performs with his trio on Club Date. Born in Arkansas in 1923, Witherspoon had no formal training in music and like so many blues singers learned to sing in church.

He is considered to be one of the most compelling blues singers of our time. His first big hit record in the early 1950s was "Ain't Nobody's Business," which is included along with "Cherry Red" and "C.C. Rider" on this Club Date concert. Performing with Witherspoon is Roy Alexander on the organ, Gene Edwards on guitar, and Maurice Simon, Jr., on drums.

2796. *Club Date: The Art Farmer Quintet* (#306), produced by KPBS (S.D.S.U.), San Diego; KPBS (Distributor); 1990.

Stellar flugelhornist Art Farmer and saxophonist Clifford Jordan began performing together back in 1957 in Horace Silver's band during the heyday of the bebop era. Over the years, each was acknowledged as a master soloist, yet both still found the time to record and perform together often as a quintet—almost anywhere in the world. Before their stint on Club Date, they were performing to sellout crowds at Sweet Basil in New York. "Their playing reflects both a profound respect for their musical roots and an uncommon dedication to their elegant craft"—Jim Kelton, *The Herald*. Performing with Farmer and Jordan are Mike Wofford on piano, Bob Magnusson on bass, and Jim Plank on drums. Selections include "Summer Serenade," "Warm Valley," "Ph.D.," and "Blue Wail."

2797. *Club Date: The Red Rodney Quintet* (#401), produced by KPBS (S.D.S.U.), San Diego; KPBS (Distributor); 1990.

Legendary trumpeter Red Rodney began his career at age 15 with the big bands of the 1940s. It was Dizzy Gillespie who brought Red (at age 18) to New York to meet his idol Charlie Parker. Rodney's years as Parker's sideman on-stage and sidekick off-stage were chronicled in the movie *Bird*. Actor Mike Zelnicker portrayed Red, and Rodney himself played trumpet for the soundtrack. Other members of the quintet for Club Date are Gary Lefebvre on saxophone, Frank Strazzeri on piano, Bob Magnusson on bass, and Jim Plank on drums. Selections performed include: "In Case of Fire," "For You," "The Red Snapper," "Ev'ry Time We Say Goodbye," "Monday's Dance," and "Shuffle, Shuffle."

2798. *Club Date: Kenny Barron Trio* (#402), produced by KPBS (S.D.S.U.), San Diego; KPBS (Distributor); 1990.

Jazz pianist Kenny Barron's versatile career has spanned more than a quarter of a century. An original member of the renowned Dizzy Gillespie Quintet from 1962 to 1966, Kenny went on to perform with such jazz greats as Freddie Hubbard, James Moody, Stan Getz, Buddy Rich, and Joe Henderson. He eventually recorded over 26 albums as a leader. Special guest artist alto saxophonist Charles McPherson sits in with Kenny and the trio consisting of Bob Magnusson on bass and Jim Plank on drums.

Selections include: "Voyage," "Lullabye," "The Only One," "Joanne Julia," "Star Eyes," and "Billie's Bounce."

2799. *Club Date: Anita O'Day* (#403), produced by KPBS (S.D.S.U.), San Diego; KPBS (Distributor); 1990.

Born and raised in Chicago, jazz vocalist Anita O'Day was discovered by drummer Gene Krupa singing in a tavern. She eventually joined Krupa resulting in a teaming with trumpeter Roy Eldridge and a string of hit records. In 1944 she joined the Stan Kenton band establishing her own unique and new vocal style. "The O'Day sound, a distinctive element in jazz for four decades, remains entirely her own" (Leonard Feather, *Variety*). Now in her 70s, O'Day's career continues to flourish in clubs, theaters, and at jazz festivals throughout the world. Appearing on Club Date with Anita O'Day is Gordon Brisker on saxophone, Randy Porter on piano, Bob Magnusson on bass, and Jim Plank on drums. Selections included "Wave," "You'd Be So Nice to Come Home To," "S'Wonderful," "They Can't Take That Away from Me," "Honeysuckle Rose," "Let Me Off Uptown," and "Boogie Blues."

2800. *Club Date: Kenny Burrell* (#404), produced by KPBS (S.D.S.U.), San Diego; KPBS (Distributor); 1990.

Kenny Burrell has been called "the master of the mellow guitar." Getting his start in Detroit, he performed with such jazz artists as Tommy Flanagan, Barry Harris, and Thad Jones. Kenny's big break came in 1955 when he replaced Herb Ellis in the Oscar Peterson Trio. Soon Burrell became a star on his own, touring and recording albums under his own name. Bob Magnusson accompanies him on Club Date on bass and Sherman Ferguson on drums. Selections include "Jeannine," "Listen to the Dawn," "Moon and Sand," "Spring Can Really Hang You up the Most," "All Blues," and "Do What You Want to Do."

2801. *Club Date: The Cedar Walton Trio* (#405), produced by KPBS (S.D.S.U.), San Diego; KPBS (Distributor); 1990.

Jazz pianist Cedar Walton performs with his trio featuring Billy Higgins on the drums and Tony Dumas on bass. Long considered among the finest jazz pianists in the idiom, Walton moved from Denver to New York in the early 1960s to perform and record with the Art Farmer/Benny Golson Jazztet and Art Blakey's Jazz Messengers. More recently he has teamed up with legendary drummer Billy Higgins, acknowledged as the most consistently innovative of the postbop drummers. Selections include "Bremond's Blues," "Lament," "Bolivia," "Strayhorn Medley," and "Satin Doll."

2802. *Club Date: Charles McPherson* (#406), produced by KPBS (S.D.S.U.), San Diego; KPBS (Distributor); 1990.

Born in Mississippi, Charles McPherson has earned an international reputation as one of the most accomplished jazz saxophonists in the world. He has recorded over 15 solo albums and recorded and played with numerous world-class groups. Critics have described his work as "brilliant" and "masterful." Clint Eastwood honored McPherson by selecting him to perform the Charlie Parker solos in the movie *Bird*. Selections performed include "Illusions in Blue," "Crazyology," "Body and Soul," and "Tenor Madness." Joining McPherson is Randy Porter on Piano, Gunnar Biggs on bass, and Chuck McPherson (Charles's son) on drums. Special guest artist Kenny Barron sits in at the piano later in the set.

2803. *Club Date: Frank Morgan* (#501), produced by KPBS (S.D.S.U.), San Diego; KPBS (Distributor); 1990.

Critics have called Frank Morgan the greatest jazz saxophonist alive. Long considered the heir apparent to Charles Parker, Morgan's career got off to a whirlwind start in 1948 when at the tender age of 15 he took over the Johnny Hodges chair in the Duke Ellington Orchestra. Frank began appearing on jazz recordings and at the age of 22 cut his first solo album. But then his young brilliant career took an all-too-familiar turn. His next steady gig was with the Warden's Band in San Quentin. Frank's bouts with drugs and crime kept him pretty much a regular in that band until his release in 1985. Determined to put all of that behind him Morgan has accomplished much since his release from prison. His New York performances at the Village Vanguard and Birdland were sold out standing-room-only triumphs. His hit album *Mood Indigo* remained on the Top Five jazz charts for 30 weeks. More important, Morgan has earned the respect and admiration of his jazz colleagues. "There is no one around who is better on the alto saxophone"—Wynton Marsalis. The all-star group performing with Frank Morgan includes George Cables on piano, Andy Simpkins on bass, and "Tootie" Heath on drums. Selections include "Night in Tunisia," "Helen's Song," "Flower Is a Lovesome Thing," and "Footprints."

2804. *Club Date: The Hank Jones Trio* (#502), produced by KPBS (S.D.S.U.), San Diego; KPBS (Distributor); 1990.

Born in 1918, raised in Pontiac, Michigan, jazz pianist Hank Jones began playing "gigs" before entering high school. In 1943 his career took him to New York where, in two years, he became a member of Billy Eckstine's Big Band. From 1947 to 1951, Jones toured the world with Jazz at the Philharmonic joining such jazz greats as Charlie Parker, Ray Brown, Roy Eldridge, Max Roach, Joe Jones, and Buddy Rich. Hank was accompanist for Ella Fitzgerald for over four years, toured Russia with Benny Goodman, and later joined the staff at CBS where he remained for 17 years. During that period, he became the first pianist for the Thad Jones/Mel

Lewis Band. (Thad is Hank's brother.) Considered the "dean" of jazz pianists, Hank Jones appears on Club Date with Bob Magnusson on bass and Jim Plank on drums. The trio performs "On Green Dolphin Street," "Interface," "Lazy Afternoon," "Scrapple from the Apple," "Recorda Me," and "Blue Monk."

2805. *Club Date: Rob Mullins* (#503), produced by KPBS (S.D.S.U.), San Diego; KPBS (Distributor); 1991.

Keyboard whiz Rob Mullins is one of the brightest new artists to arrive on the jazz scene. His trademark is funky, synthesized jazz-fusion, though he is equally adept at playing in a straight ahead acoustic piano trio. A good example of this is his highly successful album *Jazz* that rose to number six on Billboard's jazz chart. On Club Date, Rob performs a variety of his own compositions, including "Making Love," which received a Grammy nomination. Other songs are: "Shroeder Meets Basie," "Breakthrough," "Tokyo Nights," and "Rocking at the Regas." Performing with Mullins are Wilton Felder on saxophone, Joel Taylor on drums, and Dave Carpenter on bass.

2806. *Club Date: The Buddy Collette Quartet* (#504), produced by KPBS (S.D.S.U.), San Diego; KPBS (Distributor); 1991.

Multireedman Buddy Collette has been an influential figure on the West Coast music scene since the early 1940s. He first came to prominence in the orchestras of Louis Jordan, Benny Carter, and Gerald Wilson. Best known as a key member of the original Chico Hamilton Quintet, Collette has recorded over 30 albums as leader and currently divides his time between leading his own band, teaching, composing, and performing for feature films and television. His studio activities have included stints with Duke Ellington, Ella Fitzgerald, Frank Sinatra, and Nelson Riddle. The quartet also features Larry Nash on piano, Richard Reid on bass, and Mel Lee on drums. The quartet performs "Hunt and Peck," "Someone I Never Know," "Emaline's Theme," "Magali," and "Andre."

2807. *Club Date: The Ray Anderson Quartet* (#505), produced by KPBS (S.D.S.U.), San Diego; KPBS (Distributor); 1991.

Born in Chicago in 1953, jazz virtuoso Ray Anderson was voted number one trombonist in *Down Beat* magazine's international critics poll for four consecutive years. "An exuberant performer who carries the more rough-and-tumble sounds of Dixieland brass into experimental territory, Mr. Anderson commands a formidable arsenal of expressive instrumental growls, moans and cries"(*New York Times,* April 10, 1991). Ray Anderson's unique trombone style and sense of humor and his Louis Armstrong type speaking and singing voice combine to make highly entertaining sets. Appearing with Ray Anderson is his recording group consisting of Funio Itabashi on piano, Mark Helias on bass and Dion Parsons on drums. The selections include "Ahsoca," "The Gohtooze," "Comes Along Love," and "Alligatory Crocodile."

2808. *Club Date: The Mundell Lowe Allstars* (#506), produced by KPBS (S.D.S.U.), San Diego; KPBS (Distributor); 1990.

Mundell Lowe has been an internationally acclaimed guitarist since he first came to prominence in the 1940s performing with the Red Norvo and Ray McKinley bands. Lowe wrote music for many years as a staff musician at NBC in New York, and remained active as a jazz artist playing with such artists as Benny Goodman and Charlie Parker. He came west in 1965 to work for the "studios." He has recorded albums with Sarah Vaughan and Carmen McRae, among others, and served as Peggy Lee's music supervisor. During the 1980s Lowe appeared at the White House and toured Japan with Benny Carter. Most recently, Lowe has been recording and making concert appearances with Ray Brown as part of the Andre Previn Trio. The all stars appearing with Mundell Lowe are former Kenton Band tenor man Bob Cooper, legendary bassist Monty Budwig, and standout drummer Roy McCurdy. Selections include: "Have You Met Miss Jones," "If You Could See Me Now," "Lime House Blues," "You're My Everything," and "Like Someone in Love."

2809. *Club Date: The Vuckovich/Harrell Quintet* (#601), produced by KPBS (S.D.S.U.), San Diego; KPBS (Distributor); 1991.

Leader Larry Vuckovich has developed a solid reputation on both coasts, listed among the best on jazz piano. With five albums under his own name, Larry's album titled *City Sounds/Village Voices* earned a five-star review from *Down Beat* magazine. Vuckovich has played with jazz luminaries such as Dexter Gordon, Elvin Jones, Bobby McFerrin, Gerry Mulligan, Mel Tormé, Joe Williams, Mel Lewis, Red Norvo, and Jon Hendricks. Harrell has appeared on scores of albums and toured with some of the world's finest jazz artists, including the Phil Woods Quintet. Escovedo is considered one of the best Latin/jazz percussionists in the world. He has recorded and performed with Herbie Hancock, Mongo Santo Maria, Cal Tjader, Carlos Santana, Tito Puente, Anita Baker, and Woody Herman, and his own daughter Sheila E. Rounding out the quintet is Harold Mason on drums and Al Obidinski on bass. The selections performed include "Dancero," "Historia de un Amor," "Serenade in Blue," "Locomotion," and "Serbo-Afro."

2810. *Club Date: The Holly Hoffman/Bobby Shew Quintet* (#602), produced by KPBS (S.D.S.U.), San Diego; KPBS (Distributor); 1991.

Holly Hoffman's classical training and natural jazz ability has made her one of the most talked-about jazz flutists in the United States. Leonard Feather describes her as one of the most outstanding and rapidly rising flutists in the world. She has shared the stage with jazz veterans such as Mundell Lowe, Cedar Walton, James Moody, Leroy Vinnegar, Kenny Barron, and Bobby Shew. Her debut solo recording "Take Note" received four our of five possible stars in *Down Beat* magazine. Bobby Shew has spent the better part of his career playing lead trumpet for big bands such as Woody Herman, Buddy Rich, Terry Gibbs, Bill Holman, Neal Hefti, Maynard Ferguson, and Benny Goodman. More recently, Shew has concentrated on playing with small groups, recording and touring the jazz club circuit worldwide. His album *Outstanding in His Field* was a Grammy nominee in 1980. Selections performed include "Cabu," "Little Dancer," "In Your Own Sweet Way," "We'll Be Together Again," and "Dancin' Feet." Rounding out the quintet are Mike Wofford on piano, Bob Magnusson on bass, and Sherman Ferguson on drums.

2811. *Club Date: The Les McCann Quintet* (#603), produced by KPBS (S.D.S.U.), San Diego; KPBS (Distributor); 1991.

Often called "The Father of Fusion," pianist/singer Les McCann has revolutionized jazz. His music cannot be categorized into a single type, since he has fused many different forms into his own style. He assisted in starting such careers as those of Roberta Flack and Lou Rawls by producing Roberta's first album and coproducing Lou Rawls's first album. Performing with Les McCann is Jeff Elliott on trumpet, Richard Taylor on bass, and Tony St. James on drums. Selections include: "Cold Duck Time," "Young and Foolish," "Right Here and Now," and "Compared to What."

2812. *Club Date: Sue Raney* (#604), produced by KPBS (S.D.S.U.), San Diego; KPBS (Distributor); 1992.

Sue Raney, one of the most respected vocalists of our time, began her professional career singing on her own television show in Albuquerque when she was 14 years old. At age 16, she made her national radio debut. She signed with Capitol Records, has recorded over a dozen successful albums and has had four Grammy nominations. She has performed in venues from New York and Paris to Australia and Peru. Nightclub appearances have ranged from the Las Vegas Sahara with Don Rickles to headlining at the Puerto Rico Hilton. Her television credits include "The Tonight Show," "The Dean Martin Show," "The Bob Hope Show," and a PBS tribute to Henry Mancini. "Sue Raney's style, timbre, phrasing, accompaniment, choice and pacing of material are all perfect ... a stunning, sophisticated lady who radiates sweetness, wit, tenderness, and rhythmic sensitivity" (Leonard Feather, *Los Angeles Times*). Joining Sue Raney on Club Date will be Mike Wofford on piano, Bob Magnusson on bass, and Jim Plank on drums. Selections include: "Ridin' High," "Let's Eat Home," "Skylark," "Poor Butterfly," "There Will Never Be Another You," and "No More Blues."

2813. *Club Date: Shorty Rogers and the Giants* (#605), produced by KPBS (S.D.S.U.), San Diego; KPBS (Distributor); 1992.

Shorty Rogers joined the Woody Herman Band during World War II and later became a key member of the Stan Kenton Orchestra, writing, arranging, and playing as a member of the trumpet section. He is best known for his work with the smaller ensembles he formed from members of the Kenton groups and Hollywood studio musicians. His groups recorded and performed West Coast "cool" jazz, a style that contrasted with the hot, hard driving bebop derivations coming from the East Coast. Performing with Rogers on Club Date is former Kenton colleague Bob Cooper on tenor sax, Joe Romano on alto sax, Lou Levy on piano, Larance Marable on drums, and Bob Magnusson on bass. Selections include: "It's Sand Man," "Have You Hugged a Martian Today?," "We'll Be Together Again," and "Eight Brothers."

2814. *Club Date: Jazz Messengers Tribute* (#606), produced by KPBS (S.D.S.U.), San Diego; KPBS (Distributor); 1992.

The Jazz Messengers, led by the late Art Blakey, have long been considered one of the most significant, innovative jazz ensembles ever assembled. Recently, a group of former Jazz Messengers was reunited to perform, tour, record, and to pay tribute to this legendary jazz institution and its renowned drummer. The Jazz Messengers features an all-star assemblage of jazz greats from both coasts, which includes Phil Harper (of the Harper Brothers) on trumpet, Essiet Essiet on bass, and Ralph Penland on drums. Selections include "Whisper Not," "Moaning," "You've Changed," and "Blues March."

Artists, Concerts, Groups, Tributes

2815. *Black Jazz and Blues;* produced by RKO. New York: Video Goodyear (Distributor); 1938.

Three different programs from 1929, 1935, and 1945, which focus on: *St. Louis Blues,* featuring Fletcher Henderson, James P. Johnson, and Bessie Smith; *Symphony in Black,* which details different aspects of the African American experience, featuring Duke Ellington and his orchestra, and an appearance by Billie Holiday; and *Caledonia,* which focuses on Louis

632 Jazz Scholarship and Pedagogy, Third Edition

Jordan and his Tympany Five. There are comedy routines, tap dancing, and rhythm and blues songs. 44 minutes.

2816. *Buddy Rich Memorial Scholarship Concert;* produced by DCI. New York: DCI Music Video; 1989.

Features several drummers in concert at the Wilshire Theatre in Los Angeles in a concert dedicated to the memory of Buddy Rich. 120 minutes.

2817. *Buddy Rich Memorial Scholarship Concert.* New York: DCI Music Videos; 1991.

Features solos by several of Rich's alumni including Marvin Smith, Steve Smith, and Neil Peart. 73 minutes.

2818. *Implosions;* producer N.A. Chicago: Facets Video (Distributor); 1990.

Features an eclectic group of artists, including Randy Brecker, Stanley Clarke, Peter Erskine, Eric Gale, Frank Morgan, McCoy Tyner, and Ernie Watts. Among the performed compositions are "All the Things You Are," "Green Dolphin Street," "Loverman," and "Skylark." The concert was recorded at the Wiltern Theatre, Los Angeles. 60 minutes.

2819. *Jazz: The Intimate Art;* produced by Drew Associates. Los Angeles: Direct Cinema Limited (Distributors); 1980.

Profiles four musicians representing different styles of jazz: Louis Armstrong, Dave Brubeck, Dizzy Gillespie, and Charles Lloyd. 55 minutes.

2820. *Jazz Ball;* produced by NTA: Hal Roach. New York: Video Goodyear (Distributor); 1956.

Songs, footage, and performances by several jazz artists of the 1930s and 1940s. There are performances by Louis Armstrong, Cab Calloway, Duke Ellington, Betty Hutton, Gene Krupa, Peggy Lee, and Buddy Rich. 60 minutes, B&W.

2821. *Jazz Concert #3;* produced by Vitaphone. Reseda, Calif.: Glenn Video Vistas Limited; 1933.

Features clips of Louis Armstrong, Eubie Blake, Cab Calloway, Duke Ellington, and Don Redman. 60 minutes, B&W.

2822. *Jazz in America;* produced by Dick Reed and Paul Rosen. Beverly Hills: Nelson Entertainment (Distributor); 1981.

The second of two concerts in this series; this concert focuses on the appreciation and performance of contemporary jazz. Featured artists are Harold Danko, Billy Hart, Frank Luther, and Gerry Mulligan. 60 minutes.

2823. *Jazz in America;* produced by Bill Hancock. Beverly Hills: Nelson Entertainment (Distributor); 1981.

One of two concerts that feature a tribute to bebop by Dizzy Gillespie and His All Stars, Pepper Adams, Gerry Mulligan, Candido, and Max Roach. 90 minutes.

2824. *Jazz in Exile;* produced by Chuck France. New York: Rhapsody Films Festival Films (Distributor); 1982.

Profiles several American artists who have spent much of their careers as expatriates. Included artists are Richard Davis, Dexter Gordon, Randy Weston, and Phil Woods. 58 minutes.

2825. *Jazz Is Our Religion;* produced by Kino International. New York: Kino International (Distributor); 1972.

Features narration by Val Wilmer and provides a penetrating assessment of the lives and music of several jazz artists. The focus is Art Blakey, Dizzy Gillespie, Johnny Griffin, Jo Jones, Ted Jones, and Sunny Murray. 50 minutes, B&W.

2826. *Jazz Is Our Religion;* produced by Valerie Wilmer. Chicago: Facets Video (Distributor); 1985.

Looks at the lifestyles and attitudes of jazz musicians through the photographs and research of Valerie Wilmer. Contains anecdotes and music presented by Ted Jones, Jo Jones, Dizzy Gillespie, Sunny Murray, Art Blakey, Johnny Griffin, and several drummers. 50 minutes.

2827. *Jazz Legends: Part Three;* produced by Tom Pelissero for A K-Twin and Bob DeFlores. Montvale, N.J.: Pioneer Artists; 1987.

This video features Billie Holiday accompanied by Coleman Hawkins, Ben Webster, Lester Young, Gerry Mulligan, Vic Dickenson, and Roy Eldridge, singing, "Fine and Mellow" (1957); Dizzy Gillespie and His Orchestra performing "Salt Peanuts"; Thelonious Monk, "Blue Monk" (1957); the John Coltrane Quartet, "Alabama"; Count Basie, "Cherry Point"; Gene Krupa and His Orchestra with Anita O'Day and Roy Eldridge, "Thanks for the Boogie Ride"; Mike Bryan with Georgia Auld, "Seven Come Eleven"; Woody Herman and His Herd, "Your Father's Moustache"; Louis Jordan and His Band with Dinah Washington, "What a Difference a Day Makes" and "Makin Woopee"; and Bud Freeman, Jimmy McPartland, Gene Krupa, Bobby Haggart, Jack Teagarden, Pee Wee Russell, and Joe Sullivan performing "China Boy." The other two programs feature John Coltrane and Thelonious Monk. 52 minutes.

2828. *Jazz Masters: Vintage Collection, Volume One;* produced by View Video. New York: V.I.E.W. Video (Distributor); 1959.

Includes performances by The Count Basie Orchestra, Billie Holiday, Jimmy Guiffre, Thelonious Monk Trio, Lester Young, Coleman Hawkins, Gerry Mulligan, and Ben Webster. Contains lengthy rare footage. 50 minutes, B&W.

2829. *Jazz Masters: Vintage Collection, Volume Two, 1960–61;* produced by View Video. New York: V.I.E.W. Video (Distributor); 1961.

Rare footage of the Miles Davis Quintet, John Coltrane, Ahmad Jamal, Ben Webster, and the Gil Evans Big Band. 45 minutes, B&W.

2830. *The Ladies Sing the Blues;* producer N. A. New York: V.I.E.W. Video (Distributor); 1986?

A tribute to great blues singers featuring Connie Boswell, Lena Horne, Helen Humes, Peggy Lee, Sarah Vaughan, Dinah Washington, and Ethel Waters. The video also features rare black-and-white footage of Billie Holiday and Bessie Smith. 60 minutes.

2831. *The Last of the Blue Devils;* producer/director Bruce Ricker. New York: Rhapsody Films; 1979.

Features Count Basie and His Orchestra, Big Joe Turner, and Jay McShann. This video recounts both the Blue Devils and Kansas City history of the 1930s. It traces the Blue Devils through the Benny Moten band to Count Basie. Among the other artists covered briefly in the video are Jo Jones, Budd Johnson, Baby Lovett, Charles McPherson, Gene Ramey, Jimmy Forrest, Claude "Fiddler" Williams, and Paul Quinichette. They perform "Dickie's Dream," "Moten Swing," "Night Train," "Jumpin' at the Woodside," "Shake, Rattle, and Roll," and more. 90 minutes.

2832. *The Leaders: Jazz in Paris, 1988;* producer N.A. Chicago: Facets Video (Distributor); 1988.

The group of Arthur Blythe, Lester Bowie, Cecil McBee, Kirk Lightsey, Chico Freeman, and Don Moye constitute the Leaders, a group that describes its music as "Schizo Music." They perform seven songs. 54 minutes.

2833. *Live From The Village Vanguard; produced by Video Artist International.* New York: Video Artist International (Distributor); 1984–89.

A collection of six concerts held at the Village Vanguard (New York).

Volume 1—Freddie Hubbard, Ron Carter, Cedar Walton, and Lenny White. 59 minutes.
Volume 2—The Michael Petrucciani Trio with Jim Hall. 59 minutes.

Volume 3—John Abercrombie, Michael Brecker, Marc Johnson, and Peter Erskine. 58 minutes.

Volume 4—Mal Waldron, Woody Shaw, Charles Rouse, Reggie Workman, and Ed Blackwell. 60 minutes.

Volume 5—Lee Konitz, Roland Hanna, George Mraz, and Mel Lewis. Performances of "Max," "Dream Stepper," and "A Story Often Told," among others. 60 minutes.

Volume 6—David Murray, John Hicks, Fred Hopkins, and Ed Blackwell. "Off Season," "Lovers," "Morning Star," and others. 60 minutes.

2834. *Moscow Sax Quintet: The Jazznost Tour;* produced by View Video. New York: V.I.E.W. (Distributor); 1991.

One of Russia's foremost jazz groups performs compositions by the Beatles, George Gershwin, Fats Waller, and Charles Parker. They perform several Parker solos in five-part harmony at very fast tempos. 62 minutes.

2835. *Musicians in Exile;* producer N.A. New York: Rhapsody Films (Distributor); 1990.

Features the music of Daniel Pouce, Hugh Masekela, Paquito Riviera, and Quilapayun. 78 minutes.

2837. *Newport Jazz Festival;* producer N.A. New York: CBS / Fox Video; 1962.

Features the music of Count Basie, Ruby Braff, Duke Ellington, Roland Kirk, Lambert-Hendricks-Bavan, Pee Wee Russell, Joe Williams, the Oscar Peterson Trio with Ray Brown, and more. 60 minutes.

2838. *Outside in Sight: Music of the United Front;* produced by G. Chapnick and S. Woods. Chicago: Facets Video (Distributor); 1986.

Profiles the San Francisco jazz group United Front, which features Anthony Brown (percussion), Mark Izu (bass), Lewis Jordan (saxophone), and George Sims (trumpet).

2839. *Paris Reunion Band;* producer N.A. Chicago: Facets Video (Distributor); 1978.

A concert dedicated to the memory of Kenny Clarke by a collection of musicians who called themselves the Paris Reunion Band for this live Stuttgart, Germany, taping. Featured musicians are Nat Adderley, Nathan Davis, Curtis Fuller, Joe Henderson, Idris Muhammad, Walter Bishop, Jr., Woody Shaw, and Jimmy Woode. 57 minutes.

2840. *Piano Legends;* producer N.A. New York: Val Jazz Video.

In this video, Chick Corea narrates a tribute to Count Basie, Duke Ellington, Bill Evans, Thelonious Monk, Oscar Peterson, Art Tatum, Cecil Taylor, McCoy Tyner, and Mary Lou Williams.

2841. *Playboy Jazz Festival, Volume 2;* produced by Playboy Productions. Burbank, Calif.: RCA/Columbia Pictures Home Video (Distributor); 1984.

Hosted by Bill Cosby, this festival featured numerous diverse groups including Dave Brubeck and Sarah Vaughan. 90 minutes.

2842. *Prime Cuts-Jazz and Beyond;* produced by CBS Music Video Enterprises. New York: CBS / Fox Video; 1985.

Features one tune each from Miles Davis, Al Dimeola, Clark/Duke Project, Herbie Hancock, Chuck Mangione, Hiroshima, Weather Report, and Andres Wollenweider. 35 minutes.

2843. *Reed Royalty;* produced/directed by Burrill Crohn for Jazz Images. New York: VAI Video; 1992.

Hosted by Branford Marsalis and packaged as a way of paying tribute to his musical elders, the focus is on clarinetists and alto, baritone, and soprano saxophones. There are clips of each instrument; the clarinet clips feature Benny Goodman, Woody Herman, Pee Wee Russell, Artie Shaw, Omer Simeon, and former Ellington sidemen, Harry Carney, Jimmy Hamilton, and Russell Procope. Among the saxophonists represented are Sidney Bechet, John Coltrane, Jimmy Dorsey, Benny Carter, Phil Woods, Cannonball Adderley, Harry Carney, Gerry Mulligan, Jane Ira Bloom, and others. 58 minutes.

2844. *Rhythmstick;* produced by View Video. New York: V.I.E.W. Video (Distributor); 1990.

Features 17 artists in a concert salute to Dizzy Gillespie. Among the featured artists are Bob Berg, Airto, Flora Purim, Art Farmer, Dizzy Gillespie, Jimmy McGriff, John Scofield, Phil Woods, and several more. Benny Golson arranged the standards and originals. A testimony to his impact and exploration of crosscultural influences in jazz. They perform compositions by Sigmund Romberg, Charles Parker, and others.

2845. *Swing: Best of Big Bands; Volumes I, II, III, IV;* producer New York: Val Jazz Video (Distributor); 1986

Volume 1: Tommy Dorsey, "Opus One"; Rosemary Clooney and Tony Pastor, "Movie Tonight"; Billie Holiday, "God Bless the Child"; Duke Ellington, "Frankie and Johnny," as well as performances by Ray Anthony, Benny Carter, Harry James, Charlie Barnet, and Gene Krupa. 50 minutes.

Volume 2: 20 performances including The Dorsey Brothers, "Yes, Indeed"; Nat King Cole, "Route 66"; Woody Herman, "Caledonia"; Sarah Vaughan, "Don't Blame Me," as well as performances by Charlie Barnet, Lionel Hampton, Ralph Materie, Gene Krupa, Stan Kenton, Tex Benecke, and the Glenn Miller Orchestra. 50 minutes.

Volume 3: 19 performances including Count Basie, "Red Bank Boogie"; Gene Krupa, "Stompin' at the Savoy"; The Ink Spots, "If I Didn't Care"; Harry James, "Brave Bulls" as well as performances by Jimmy Dorsey, Les Brown, Duke Ellington, Teresa Brewer, and Charlie Barnet. 50 minutes.

Volume 4: 18 performances including Tex Benecke and Glenn Miller, "Little Brown Jug"; The Mills Brothers, "Paper Magic"; Buddy Rich, "Burn," and performances by Count Basie, Ray Anthony, Jimmy Dorsey, the Skylarks, and Ray Kenton.

2846. *Swing: The Best of the Big Bands.* Four Volumes; producer N.A. Los Angeles: Universal; 1983?

These four volumes are based on rare footage from the Universal archives. The focus is on big bands, ensembles, and vocalists.

Volume 1 features Charlie Barnet, Ray Anthony, Rosemary Clooney, Benny Carter, Tommy Dorsey, Duke Ellington, Billie Holiday, the Hi-Los, Harry James, Gene Krupa, and Tony Pastor; volume 2 includes performances by Charlie Barnet, Tex Benecke, Tommy and Jimmy Dorsey, Nat King Cole, Woody Herman, Lionel Hampton, Ralph Materie, Stan Kenton, and Glenn Miller; volume 3 features Count Basie, Harry James, Gene Krupa, Harry James, and the ink Spots; and volume 4 contains performances by Ray Anthony, Count Basie, Tex Benecke, Jimmy Dorsey, Stan Kenton, Glenn Miller, the Mills Brothers, and the Skylarks. The videos average 60 minutes each and are in B&W.

2847. *Tenor Titans;* producer N.A. New York: VAI Jazz Video; 1986.

Hosted by Branford Marsalis, this video covers the history of jazz tenor saxophonists from Coleman Hawkins to the present. Includes footage of Coleman Hawkins, Sonny Rollins, John Coltrane, Wayne Shorter, and several rhythm and blues saxophonists. Marsalis begins and ends the program with a tenor solo. 60 minutes.

2848. *Trumpet Kings;* producer N.A. New York: VAI Jazz Video; 1988.

Hosted by Wynton Marsalis, this video contains footage of Louis Armstrong, Miles Davis, Dizzy Gillespie, Harry James, Freddie Hubbard, Clifford Brown, and others. Marsalis also performs. 60 minutes.

History and Influence

2849. *America's Music, Chicago and All That Jazz;* produced by Sandra Turbow. Glenside, Pa.: Around the World in Sight and Sound (Distributor); 1984.

Hosted by Gary Moore, this video focuses on Chicago style jazz from the early 1900s to the 1930s. The video features jazz and selected non-jazz soloists/groups. Among the featured musicians are the Chicagoans (J. McPartland, J. Teagarden, P. Russell, B. Freeman, J. Sullivan, E. Condon, B. Haggert, and Gene Krupa). Clips of the Original Dixieland Jazz Band, Eddie Condon and the NBC Orchestra, and soloists like Mae Barnes, Meade Lux Lewis, and Leon James are also featured. This video was first featured as a Dupont Show of the Week in 1961. 58 minutes.

2850. *A Great Day in Harlem.* Upper Montclair, N.J.: The Jazz Store; 1995.

This documentary film follows the making of the famous Art Kane photograph of 58 legendary jazz artists in Harlem in 1958 for *Esquire* magazine. The film includes interviews that offer important insights into the artists and their music. Among the interviewees are Art Blakey, Dizzy Gillespie, Art Farmer, Milt Hinton, Marian McPartland, Sonny Rollins, and many more.

2851. *Black Music in America: From Then Till Now;* produced by Black Music Association. Deerfield, Ill.: Learning Corporation of America; 1971.

Covers the history of African American music. There are performances by Louis Armstrong, Count Basie, Duke Ellington, Nina Simone, and Bessie Smith. 28 minutes.

2852. *Bones;* produced by Carol Munday Lawrence. Evanston, Ill.: Beacon Films (Distributor); 1975.

Introduces John Henry Nobles of Beaumont, Texas, who creates percussive rhythm for jazz with dried beef bones held between his fingers. Nobles devised this unique method because he could not afford a musical instrument. 29 minutes.

2853. *Conjunto Nuestro: Latin Jazz;* produced by Luis Alonso. Trenton: New Jersey Network; 1983.

The Conjunto Nuestro Orchestra plays salsa. 30 minutes.

2854. *Country;* produced by Filmaus. New York: Film Australia-Australian Consulate; 1971.

Presents some of Australia's leading jazz musicians performing at an annual event in an Australian town. 11 minutes.

2855. *Discovering Jazz;* produced as part of the Discovering Music Series by BFA Educational Media, Division of CBS. New York: Phoenix/BFA Films and Video Inc.; 1969.

Presents an historical overview of jazz as an American art form. Discusses the acculturation of African rhythms and European harmony into Dixieland and blues. Traces the evolution of jazz from Dixieland to the funk and electronic influences of the late 1960s.

2856. Dobbins, Bill. *The Evolution of Solo Jazz Piano.* New Albany, Ind.: Jamey Aebersold (Distributor); 1990.

A study of the solo piano styles of 24 distinguished pianists, 1900 to the present. Dobbins composed a melody based on the changes of "All of Me," after which he performs the theme in the styles of the 24 artists. Part one represents the styles of Earl "Fatha'" Hines, James P. Johnson, Duke Ellington, Jelly Roll Morton, Willie "The Lion" Smith, Fats Waller, Art Tatum, and others. Among the styles/individuals represented in part two are Bill Evans, Erroll Garner, Thelonious Monk, Oscar Peterson, Bud Powell, Lennie Tristano, and several more. The subtle differences are fully covered. 60 minutes.

2857. *Early Jazz* (captioned edition); produced as part of *Jump Street: A Story of Black Music Series.* Washington, D.C.: WETA-TV; 1980.

Illustrates the musical characteristics of ragtime and early jazz, their relationship, and the musical cultures from which they evolved. Alvin Alcorn and Roy Eldridge demonstrate the sound of a jazz combo. 30 minutes.

2858. *The EAV History of Jazz;* produced by Educational Audio Visual. Pleasantville, New York: Educational Audio Visual; 1986.

Traces the evolution of jazz from cries and hollers to the avant-garde movement. The presentation is narrated by Billy Taylor and is replete with information on the role and function of jazz in the African American community, the influence of the civil rights movement, and the impact of technology. Rare footage of Dave Brubeck, Paul Desmond, Charles Parker, and Bessie Smith is also included. Taylor, assisted by Curtis Boyd and Victor Gaskin, demonstrates styles and elements. 49 minutes.

2859. *Echoes of Jazz;* produced by USA: Dance Series. Bloomington: Indiana University Audio Visual Center; 1966.

Traces the development of America's jazz dance from tap dancing through the theatrical forms of the 1900s, orchestrated jazz of the 1930s, to the abstract forms of the 1960s. There are demonstrations of tap dance performed by Honi Coles. There are several choreographed dances: Paula Felly,

Dudley Williams, and William Luther dance to "Storyville, New Orleans"; Grover Dale and Michel Harty dance to "Idiom 59"; and John Butler, Mary Hinkson, and Buzz Miller dance to Gunther Schuller's variations on a theme by John Lewis, "Django." 30 minutes.

2860. *Introduction to Jazz;* produced by UCLA. Los Angeles: UCLA; 1952.

Traces the development of jazz from the New Orleans period to the early 1950s. The narration is in blank verse and is supported by original recordings by jazz composers and performers. 112 minutes, B&W.

2861. *Jazz: A Multimedia History;* produced by E Book, Inc. Louisville, Kentucky: ZTEK Company; 1992.

Discusses jazz history with extensive examples of music in audio, MIDI, and standard notation form. Narrated by Lewis Porter.

2862. *Jazz: An American Classic—New Orleans Traditional;* produced by the University of Minnesota. Lincoln: Great Plains Instructional TV, University of Nebraska (Distributor); 1980.

A second program in this series, this program focuses on the early history and development of jazz by focusing on its roots in antebellum New Orleans and slave music. Also, there is a discussion of the synthesis of selected elements into the New Orleans style. 29 minutes.

2863. *Jazz: An American Classic-Born in America;* produced by the University of Minnesota. Lincoln: Great Plains Instructional TV, University of Nebraska; 1980.

Discusses jazz styles, elements, and improvisation. Also discusses the African and European roots and influences. 29 minutes.

2864. *The Jazz Channel Presents.* Chicago: Clearvue/EAV; 2000.

A series of 13 videos and DVDs that highlight performances on Black Entertainment Television. Each program features the artist performing some of their popular songs. Among the jazz and jazz-related videos are the Earl Klugh, Herbie Hancock, Keiko Matsui, Kenny Rankin, Lou Rawls, and Marl Whitefield. Each video/DVD average 75 minutes and are in color.

2865. *Jazz Legend Series* Chicago Clearvue/EAV; 2001.

A series of four compact discs that feature rare song cuts, historic photographs, detailed accompanying notes, and remastered sound.

Disc one, *Artie Shaw His First Three Bands, 1936–1940.* This CD showcases the talent of this clarinetist who performed in the shadow of Benny Goodman.

Disc two, *Art Tatum: The Incredible Tatum, 1933–1949,* features this great pianist performing boogie-woogie, stride, and swing along with many standards of the period.

Disc three features *Jelly Roll Morton: Pioneer of Jazz 1923–1939,* and shares the many and diverse talents of the composer, pianist, and entertainer. Focuses on his ability to write songs and his creative arranging and composing.

Disc four, *Jazz Legends: The Birth of Bebop, 1937–1945,* includes the compositions and performances of Dizzy Gillespie, Charles Parker, Bud Powell, and other significant artists of the era. In addition, the video highlights the chordal improvisations, individual solos, drumming concepts, and innovative piano playing of the period.

2866. *Jazz Parade: Feet Don't Fail Me Now;* produced by Alan Lomax. Chicago: Facets Video (Distributor); 1939.

Jelly Roll Morton, the Preservation Hall Jazz Band, the Dirty Dozen Brass Band, and more, in New Orleans, join Lomax. 60 minutes.

2867. *Jazz People* (captioned edition); produced by *Jumpstreet: A Story of Black Music Series.* Washington, D.C.: WETA-TV (Distributors); 1980.

Explores the social and environmental factors within African American culture that lead to the development of modern jazz. Uses film clips and photographs to identify numerous individuals and groups that were key contributors to various jazz genres. 30 minutes.

2868. *Jazz Summit;* produced by Jackie Ochs. New York: Icarus Films (Distributor); 1987.

Life on the road with the Gamelin Trio, considered by many to be Russia's leading free jazz group. 20 minutes.

2869. *Jazz Vocalists;* produced by *Jumpstreet: A Story of Black Music Series.* Washington, D.C.: WETA-TV (Distributor); 1980.

Demonstrates the influence of West African music and language on African American vocal jazz, focusing particularly on the jazz vocalist's use of improvisation and the relationship between jazz vocal and instrumental music. There are vocal renditions by Carmen McRae, Al Jarreau, and Oscar Brown, Jr. 50 minutes.

2870. *On the Downbeat—A Jazz Heritage;* produced by David Derkacy. Bloomington: Indiana University Audio Visual Center (Distributor); 1982.

A review of the history of jazz in Indiana from the beginnings of ragtime at the turn of the century, through bebop to the early 1980s. Jazz scholars

David Baker and Duncan Scheidt recall the contributions of Jesse Crump, Russell Smith, and Julia Niebergall along with renowned artists such as Freddie Hubbard, Virgil Jones, and Wes Montgomery.

Pedagogy

2871. Abercrombie, John. *Jazz Guitar Improvisation with John Abercrombie.* New Albany, Ind.: Jamey Aebersold; 1997?

He uses several exercises playing on one string, created half-note and quarter-note phrases by using two notes per phrase. He uses standards to demonstrate his concepts and view that a myriad of possibilities exist for improvising guitarists.

2872. Aebersold, Jamey. *Anyone Can Improvise;* produced by Jamey Aebersold. New Albany, Ind.: Jamey Aebersold (Distributor); 1993.

This two-hour video covers scales, patterns such as ii–V, chord-scale relationships, chord construction, and much more. The focus is on the fundamentals of improvisation.

2873. Argersinger, Charles. *Masterpiece Series: Approaches to Improvisation.* Chicago: Charles Argersinger, 1872; N. Clybourne (Chicago, Illinois 60604).

Discusses concepts that should be taught in a beginning improvisation class. He covers basic harmony, chord/scale types, nonharmonic scales, exotic scales, and chord progressions. Musical notation performed on the piano is displayed on the screen. 50 minutes.

2874. Barranco, Steve. *Jazz Improvisation I, II, III.* Newport Beach, Calif.: Vignette Video; 1987.

A video instruction course on jazz improvisation that covers the subject from beginning through advanced levels. There is a study guide for each tape. He covers topics ranging from blues and ii–V applications to linear concepts.

2875. Bellson, Louis. *Beginner's Drum Course;* produced by Backstage Pass. New Albany, Ind.: Jamey Aebersold (Distributor); 1989.

Begins with hand positions, followed by basic techniques and suggestions for reading charts. Bellson discusses the role and function of the drum set as well as performance and improvisation. 60 minutes.

2876. _____. *The Musical Drummer;* produced by DCI Music Video. New York: DCI Music Video (Distributor); 1990.

Focuses on the pedagogy of drumming, covering the role and function of drums in several different contexts and genres. Bellson demonstrates desirable techniques of performing swing, shuffle, bossa nova, samba, funk/rock, bebop, and more. He also covers techniques of comping, double bass drum, and wire brushes. A book accompanies the video. 60 minutes.

2877. Berrios, Steve. *Latin Rhythms Applied to the Drum Set;* produced by Alchemy Pictures. Queens, New York: Alchemy Pictures; 1993.

Berrios has performed with Hilton Ruiz, Gerry Gonzalez, Mongo Santamaria, Tito Puente, Eddie Palmerie, and others. He discusses Latin rhythms, including salsa, conga, mambo, and rhumba, in a band setting. After performing the rhythms, he discusses their origin, uses, and functions. 60 minutes.

2878. Cyrill, Andrew. *Jazz Methodology in Drum Music;* produced by Alchemy Pictures. Queens, New York: Alchemy Pictures; 1993.

Cyrill has performed with Muhal Richard Abrams, Anthony Braxton, Coleman Hawkins, Freddie Hubbard, and many more leading jazz artists. In this video, he covers table of time exercises, on-screen notation, brush techniques, long- and short-note techniques, free time, sound, and effects with percussion. Cyrill also discusses several original compositions that are performed with Fred Hopkins and Jon Stubblefield. 90 minutes.

2879. DiMeola, Al. *Al DiMeola;* produced by REH Video. Milwaukee: Music Dispatch (Distributor); 1990.

DiMeola shares concepts and techniques that have proven successful for him. He demonstrates his scale choices for soloing over chords and techniques for picking. The accompanying booklet contains several examples of his melodic lines, licks, rhythm patterns, and solos. He performs throughout the video, on compositions such as "Cielo e Terra" and "Orient Blue." 75 minutes.

2880. Dobbins, Bill. *The Evolution of Solo Jazz Piano.* New Albany, Ind.: Advance Music (Jamey Aebersold); 1992.

A two-part video that focuses on solo piano styles developed by 24 significant pianists from 1924 to the present. Dobbins used a theme that he composed to address the stylistic approaches of each pianist. Part one is devoted to traditional styles, and features the styles of Scott Joplin, Jelly Roll Morton, James P. Johnson, Willie "The Lion" Smith, Earl "Fatha" Hines, Thomas "Fats" Waller, Teddy Wilson, Duke Ellington, Art Tatum, Meade Lux Lewis, Pete Johnson, and Jimmy Yancey. Part two addresses the styles of Thelonious Monk, Bud Powell, Oscar Peterson, Erroll Garner, Lennie Tristano, Bill Evans, Clare Fisher, Jimmy Rowles, Cecil Taylor, Chick Corea, Keith Jarrett, and Richie Beirach. By using the same theme to elicit stylistic differences, one becomes more aware of the subtle yet significant differences that exist between these great pianists.

2881. *The Drum Set: A Musical Approach,* Featuring Ed. Soph and Horace Arnold; produced by Quasi Productions for Yamaha by DCI Music Video. New York: DCI Music Video; 1985.

John Scofield, Bob Quaranta, and Tom Barney assist Soph and Arnold. Soph does most of the narration and gives lessons on several aspects of drumming, including brush, stick, and pedal techniques, as well as an overview of New Orleans, swing, bebop, Afro-Cuban, fusion, and R&B styles. 120 minutes.

2882. Ellis, Herb. *Swing Jazz: Soloing and Comping;* produced by REH Video. Milwaukee: Music Dispatch (Distributor); 1990.

In this video, Ellis uses the 12-bar blues progression as background while he discusses and demonstrates some of his favorite lines. He also discusses chord formations, tunings, comping, picking, scales, melodic ideas, and equipment. 60 minutes.

2883. Fonesca, Duduka Da, and Bob Weiner. *Brazilian Rhythms for Drumset.* New York: DCI Music Video; 1991.

Focuses on samba, bossa nova, baiao, popular music, religious music and ritual, and processional music. The perspective is that of pedagogy. Includes a book filled with exercises. Bibliography, discography, and glossary.

2884. *George Duke: Keyboard Vocal Accompaniment;* produced by DCI. New York: DCI Music Video; 1988.

Discusses chord construction, voice leading, phrasing, and how to use these concepts effectively when accompanying. 60 minutes.

2885. Gonzalez, Gerry. *Learn Conga Drumming from a Master;* produced by Alchemy Pictures. Queens, New York: Alchemy Pictures; 1992.

Gonzalez has performed with Dizzy Gillespie, Freddie Hubbard, Tito Puente, Woody Shaw, McCoy Tyner, and others. He proceeds from hand techniques and exercises to Tumbador, Tres Golpes, and Quinto patterns as applied to different Afro-Caribbean rhythms. There are performances in ensemble settings.

2886. Henderson, Scott. *Jazz Fusion Improvisation;* produced by REH Video. Milwaukee: Music Dispatch (Distributor); 1990.

Discusses his approach to improvising over chords that are used in jazz fusion. He demonstrates his use of major, pentatonic, melodic minor, diminished, and whole-tone scales, as well as arpeggios and triads. Additional coverage includes a discussion of melodic and rhythmic phrasing, and the art of "outside" playing. On-screen music. 60 minutes.

2887. *Jazz in the Concert Hall;* produced by CBS. Carlsbad, Calif.: MCGN/CRM Films Distributor; 1964.

Leonard Bernstein discusses what he considers to be excellent examples of jazz in the concert hall. He uses Gunther Schuller's "A Journey into Jazz," Aaron Copland's "Concerto for Piano and Orchestra," and Larry Austin's "Improvisation for Orchestra" and "Jazz Soloist" to discuss his views. 51 minutes, B&W.

2888. *Jazz Masters Vintage Collection;* produced by View Video. New York: V.I.E.W. Video (Distributor); 1959.

Features jazz and jazz artists from the 1950s and 1960s.

Volume 1—1958–59, features Count Basie, the Thelonious Monk Trio, Jimmy Rushing with John Lee Hooker, Billie Holiday, and the Jimmy Guiffre Trio.

Volume 2—1960–61, features Ahmad Jamal, Miles Davis with Gil Evans's big band, and the Ben Webster Sextet.

The quality is very poor. 45 minutes each, B&W.

2889. Kaye, Carol. *Carol Kaye Electric Bass.* Littleton, Colo.: Gywn Publications; 1986.

Covers electric bass technique, theory, cycles of chords, scales, ii–V progressions, passing chords, rhythm patterns, tuning, how to groove, reading, how to get inside a progression with chord substitutions, and more. A booklet accompanies the video and contains anecdotes and stories about her musical peers and experiences. 2 hours and 15 minutes.

2890. *Legends of Jazz Drumming.* Upper, Montclair, N.J.: The Jazz Store; 1998?

A two-part series hosted by historian and drummer Kenny Washington that traces the history of drumming from the 1920s to the 1990s. Part one, 1920–1950, includes performances by Baby Dodds, Chick Webb, Max Roach, Buddy Rich, and Gene Krupa. Part two, 1950–present (when the video was made) features Elvin Jones, Peter Erskine, Joe Morello, and Steve Gadd.

2891. *Legends of Jazz Guitar.* Three volumes. New Albany, Ind.: Jamey Aebersold; 1999–2001.

A rich collection of tributes to guitar greats of the past and the time the videos were made.

Volume 1 features Wes Montgomery playing "Twisted Blues," "Jingles," and "Yesterdays"; Joe Pass performing "Original Blues in G" and "Do Nothin' Till You Hear From Me"; Barney Kessel performing "Basie's Blue" and "The Shadow of Your Smile"; Herb Ellis performing "It Might as Well Be Spring," "Things Ain't What They Used to Be," and "Sweet Georgia Brown," and more.

Volume 2 features Barney Kessel, Kenny Burrell, and Grant Green playing "Blue Mist"; Wes Montgomery performing "Full House" and "Round Midnight"; Joe Pass performing "Original Blues in A" and "Prelude to a Kiss"; Kenny Burrell performing "Lover Man" and "My Ship"; Barney Kessel performing "BBC Blues" and Charlie Byrd performing "Jitterburg Waltz" and "Isn't It a Lovely Day."

Volume 3 includes Jim Hall performing "I'm Getting Sentimental Over You," "Valse Hot," and "My Funny Valentine"; Barney kessel performing "Manha De Carnival" and "Samba De Orfeu"; Tal Farlow performing "Fascinating Rhythm"; Barney Kessel and Herb Ellis performing "Oh Lady Be Good" and "The Flintstones"; Pat Martino performing "Do You Have A Name"; Barney Kessel, Herb Ellis, and Charlie Byrd performing "Nuages," "Goin' Out Of My Head," and "Flying Home." The volumes are available on VHS and DVD.

2892. Liebman, Dave. *The Improviser's Guide to Transcription;* produced by Caris Music Services. Stroudsburg, Pa.: VHS Video; 1991.

Demonstrates how to transcribe a solo by using ear training, notation, instrumental technique, music analysis, and how to make a solo into your own creative product. He covers exercises, methods of analysis, play-along concepts, ii–V lines, and more. Overall, he demonstrates how one can use transcriptions as a way and means of developing a personal voice.

2893. *Listening to Jazz;* produced/written by Steven D. Gyrb for Prentice-Hall. Englewood Cliffs, N.J.: Prentice Hall; 1992.

Focuses on instruments, roles and functions, and combining elements. The material is presented in a module format (drums, piano and synthesizers, comping, stop-time, and more). The rhythm includes some of the former, as well as ballad, Latin, contemporary, and more. Good for students with little or no knowledge of jazz. 60 minutes.

2894. Pass, Joe. *Joe Pass Jazz Lines;* produced by REH Video. Milwaukee: Music Dispatch (Distributor); 1989.

Discusses the scales and arpeggios he uses when improvising. In the accompaning book, there are notated examples of major seventh, minor seventh, static and altered dominant seventh chord types, plus a section devoted to turnarounds. Provides insights into his thinking while improvising. 60 minutes.

2895. Radd, John. *Radd on Jazz Piano.* Madison: University of Wisconsin; 1990.

A jazz video that addresses three broad areas: fundamentals (chord symbols, harmony, and voicings); advanced voicing, scales, and suggestions for practices; and application of theoretical concepts. 108 minutes.

2896. Scofield, John. *On Improvisation.* New York: DCI Music Video; 1986.

Explains playing technique, performance and practice tips, written exercises. Includes performance segments with group accompaniment. 60 minutes.

2897. *The Subject Is Jazz;* produced by New Jersey Network. Trenton: New Jersey Network (Distributor); 1983.

Hosted by Ben Sidran, this video features Chico Mendoza, and the William Peterson College Latin Jazz Band, describing the language and music of Latin jazz. 30 minutes.

2898. Vizzutti, Allen. *Steps to Excellence: Allen Vizzutti.* New York: Yamaha International Corporation; 1984.

An approach to trumpet playing that covers three broad areas: practicing for profits, endurance and technique, and developing styles. The approaches are geared to both jazz and nonjazz performers. Specific topics covered are embouchure, practicing tips, pacing, breath control, controlled air stream, double and triple tonguing, range and endurance, and more. 60 minutes.

Jazz Film

2899. Hippenmeyer, Jean Roland. *Jazz sur films, ou 55 années de rapports jazz-cinema vis à trouvers plus de 800 films tournés entre 1917 et 1972.* Paris: Editions de la thiele; 1973.

Contains a comprehensive filmography for the years 1917 to 1972 as well as an introductory essay on jazz in motion pictures. The book contains films on people or jazz topics, as well as some films that feature jazz as background music (addition to 1981). Index.

2900. Meeker, David. *Jazz in Movies: A Tentative Index to the Work of Jazz Musicians for the Cinema.* London: British Film Institute; 1972.

Identifies 2,239 films about jazz and blues including those in which jazz and blues artists appear as well as feature films of famous jazz musicians.

The entries are annotated, including identifying musicians on the soundtrack, composers or conductors, other personnel, title, director, country, and duration (addition to 1981).

2901. Whannel, Paddy. *Jazz on Film.* London: British Film Institute; 1961.

Lists 61 feature-length films and shorts with annotations on the jazz musicians featured. The entries also contain details of country, date, director, duration, and distributor. There are no entries in which jazz is featured solely as background music.

XII

Harlequin Collection of Jazz and Hot Dance

This section contains concise annotations of each volume, based on the liner notes provided by the respective writers. This collection is included because it provides important information for scholars interested in the dissemination of African American culture, and jazz in particular, on a global basis. The annotations are restricted primarily to information about dissemination and cultural context.

2902. *Jazz and Hot Dance in Argentina (1915–1950).* HQ 2010.

According to Willy Oliver and Tomás Mooney, the diffusion of jazz to Argentina began with the 1903 Carnival when the cakewalk was popular at Buenos Aires society balls. Thereafter, several African American and Anglo-American ragtime troupes appeared at music halls and popular groups added this genre to their repertoire. Rags were recorded (1902–20) by a variety of groups. Beginning in 1918, Victor Records of Argentina distributed "jazz" recordings of the Original Dixieland Jazz Band and Earl Fuller. Recordings by Louis Armstrong, Bix Beiderbecke, Jelly Roll Morton, McKinney's Cotton Pickers, and others soon followed. Eleuterio Yribarrens was, in 1922, the first Argentina jazz band to record jazz. The notes continue with pertinent facts about influence(s), diffusion, and style characteristics to 1950.

2903. *Jazz and Hot Dance in Switzerland (1921–1952).* HQ 2011.

In liner notes provided by Rainer F. Lotz, several significant points are made about musical contact, acceptance, influences, and distribution. Lotz asserts that "Chronologically speaking, the prehistory of jazz in Switzerland starts in the 1860's, although Afro-American performers, singers, dancers, and instrumentalists visited the country noticeably less frequently than any of the neighboring countries. Art forms such as the cakewalk, ragtime, or spirituals—although occasionally demonstrated in the more metropolitan centers such as Geneva and Zürich—hardly left any impression on the public in general and musicians in particular." He reveals that the musical-box companies of the St. Croix area began recording African American songs and dances around 1890. The first formal contact took place in 1926 when Francesco Guarente bought his group, "World Known Georgians" to Europe. African American troupes began touring Switzerland in 1926. Two of the first groups were "Chocolate Kiddies," with music by Sam Wooding's Club Alabam Orchestra," and "Black People," directed by Louis Douglass and featuring Sidney Bechet. According to Lotz, the "Lanigiros" was the first Swiss jazz group to make a "conscious effort to play jazz." He continues by concisely documenting the continuing evolution of out-side influence on Swiss jazz. There are 15 tracks, dating from 1921 to 1952.

2904. *Jazz and Hot Dance in Russia (1910–1963).* HQ 2012.

Rainer E. Lotz begins his notes with a concise historical account of African American musicians touring Russia in the second half of the nineteenth-century: "The pre-history of jazz in Russia can be traced back to the second half of the 19th century, when Afro-American entertainers toured the country—singers, instrumentalists, and dancers. There was a regular theatre circuit covering not only St. Petersburg, the capital, but also all townships up-country between Buchara and Nishni Novgorod, Archangel, and Ivanovo Vollnosensk. From 1900 onwards a veritable wave of black performers toured Russia. To pick a few names at random, banjoist Edgar Jones performed around the turn-of-the-century, the uncrowned cakewalk champions Johnson and Dean gave repeated demonstrations between 1907–1911, (and) Garlands Opera Troupe presented 'A Trip to Coontown' in 1910. Visits by Sam Wooding's Chocolate Kiddies and Benny Peyton's Jazz Kings (featuring Sidney Bechet and Frank Withers), were made in 1926." John Philip Sousa's introduced "orchestral ragtime" to Russia in 1905. Lotz provides informative comments about the recordings, covering style, influences, the impact of the German invasion (1941), and more. There are 15 tracks, covering genres ranging from tangos and waltzes to jazz. As Lotz correctly notes, the term "jazz" refers more to instrumentations than to the type of music performed.

2905. *Jazz and Hot Dance in India (1926–1944).* HQ 2013.

Not available.

2906. *Jazz and Hot Dance in Austria (1910–1949).* HQ 2014.

In his liner notes, Klaus Schultz provides evidence of African American contact with the Austro-Hungarian monarchy in 1903. He reports: "Tishy's Negro Dance Troupe performed at the Vienna Ronacher Variety Theatre for 30 days in 1903; and in 1905 the Cake Walk was first demonstrated in Vienna by another troupe of 30 Afro-Americans." According to Schultz, several groups visited Vienna in subsequent years. The Syncopated Orchestra performed at the Vienna "Prater" amusement park in 1922; Arthur Briggs's Savoy Syncops Orchestra 1925–26; The Seven Michigan Jazz (featuring Abdullio Villa on clarinet), in 1926–27; Sam Wooding's Orchestra with the Chocolate Kiddies (featuring Tommy Ladnier, Herb Fleming, and Gene Sedric), in 1925; Leon Abbey, Eddie South, Teddy Sinclair's Original Orpheus Band (featuring Frank Guarente on trumpet) in 1927, and Bobby Hind and his London Sonora Band, Babe Egan's Hollywood Redheards, and the Weintraubs Syncopators from Germany also visited in the late 1920s. The influences of Jack Hylton and Paul Whiteman are alluded to, followed by additional historical comments and remarks concerning the 16 tracks.

2907. *Jazz and Hot Dance in Hungary (1912–1949).* HQ 2015.

According to Attila Csányi and Géza Gábor Simon, the diffusion of African American culture to Hungary probably dates to the 1860s when the first minstrel troupes toured the Austro-Hungarian monarchy. By the 1890s, Jackson and Joseph, Brooks and Duncan, and the Ethiopian Serenaders had performed in Hungary. The visits continued and in the 1920s Sam Wooding's Chocolate Kiddies (1925), the Palm Beach Five, Billy Arnold, Herb Fleming, and Benny Peyton visited, as well as groups from England and Germany. Information on the emergence of Chapry (Jeno Orlay-Obendorfer), the first publication of ragtime compositions, and notes about the 16 recordings are also provided.

2908. *Jazz and Hot Dance in Trinidad (1912–1939).* HQ 2016.

The music of Trinidad is a synthesis of African, English, French, Spanish, and African American influences. This volume includes recordings dating from Lovey's Trinidad String band of 1912 to a piano solo by George Cabral in 1939. The degree of jazz influence was summarized by Rainer E. Lotz: "The early performing ensembles were string groups frequently augmented by flute or clarinet, the latter being the older Albert-style instruments which produced that distinctive Franco-Creole tone heard throughout the Caribbean to New Orleans. By the 1920s, New York's Harlem population had witnessed the emigration of West Indians from many islands. With the general opening of the record industry to black artists, Trinidadians began to bring their music to the studios on a regular basis. Occasionally, jazz elements would be borrowed, but the émigrés never incorporated jazz wholesale. Even the last cut on this album, made in 1938 by clarinetist George Felix, transforms a current Johnny Mercer hit into an island paseo devoid of any jazz-like embellishment or improvisation." The four recordings cover paseo- and waltz-influenced waltzes, calypsos, and the jazz-influenced recordings of Jack Celestain and His Caribbean Stompers, and the Harmony Kings Orchestra of British Guiana.

2909. *Jazz and Hot Dance in Finland (1929–1950).* HQ 2017.

When African American entertainers, dancers, and singers traveled from Oslo, Norway, to St. Petersburg, Russia, some would add Helsinki, Finland, to their itinerary. According to Pekka Gronow, among the many artists who performed in Finland were Miss Flowers and Geo Jackson (1892), Sir Issacs de St. Vincent and Henry Parris (1893), Edgar Jones (1904), and a performance of "A Trip to Coontown" by the Negro Operetta Troupe (1913). Gronow reveals that jazz arrived after World War I, and although it might be properly labeled pseudojazz, it remained popular with a Finnish-American dance band in 1926. Thereafter, with the influence of three members of the Finnish American who remained in Finland, the diffusion of jazz was in full force. In the concise liner notes Gronow also dates the first jazz recording and provides biomusical comments on the groups and recordings. There are 16 tracks.

2910. *Jazz and Hot Dance in Martinique (1929–1950).* HQ 2018.

In his liner notes, Alain Boulanger reveals that "Recording studios were not established on the French Antilees until the 1950's." He feels the lack of earlier recordings is unfortunate because the music of St. Pierre and Martinique was similar to that of New Orleans. According to Boulanger: "The unique musical form of the beguine, geographically limited to Martinique and its sister island Guadeloupe, emerged roughly the same time as jazz in the USA, the paseo in Trinidad, the tango in Argentina, and the danzón in Cuba, i.e., around the turn of the century." In addition, he reveals that the pioneer of Créole music in Paris was a clarinetist from Martinique, Alexandre Stellio, that Felix Valvert is credited with the first recordings around 1930, and that Robert Mavounzy is the "Grand Old Man" of Antillais jazz. Of particular note to jazz scholars is the work of Sidney Bechet (soprano sax) and Willie "The Lion" Smith (piano) on the 1939 recordings of Sous Les Palmiers. There are comments on each of the 16 tracks.

2911. *Jazz and Hot Dance in Czechoslovakia (1910–1946).* HQ 2019.

American entertainers since the 1880s have been regularly visiting Prague, Czechoslovakia. By the 1890s, both African American and Anglo-American groups were common. Among the most significant traveling groups was the Texas Jack Wild West Show (1895), which included, according to Vladimir Kaiser and Rainer E. Lotz, American plantation scenes, song, dance, and instrumental solos by the National Quintette of Real American Negroes (Billy Watson, Richard Thompson, A.A. Anderson, Edward Cole, and Harry Neuman). In 1899, the Carters, the Rosebuds, James and Arabella Fields, the Anderson Sisters, and Anglo-American groups in black-face (the Harwood Brothers, Wood and Sheppard), performed in Prague. Recordings were not made until the late 1920s. Thereafter, recordings from America, England, and Germany became available. After World War I, jazz proliferated with the organization and recordings of numerous bands. The authors assert that the theoretical knowledge and technical ability necessary to improvise jazz are not realized until the 1930s. Among the additional informative points mentioned: the Czech label Esta devoted much of its output to jazz; after 1918 "jazz instrumentation" included banjos, saxophones, vilonophones, flexatones, and drums, and the Nazis allowed the inmates of the Theresienstadt concentration camp to organize a jazz band. Includes historical comments about each of the 16 tracks.

2912. *Township Jazz—Black Jazz and Hot Dance in South Africa (1946–1959).* HQ 2020.

Explores jazz-related music in the African townships of South Africa, particularly Johannesburg. African American cultural forms, performed by African and Anglo Americans, date as far back as 1862, the year that Joe Brown, a jig dancer, toured the area as a member of Nish's Christy Minstrels (1883). Burt Shepard (1898), the Fisk Jubilee Singers, John Philip Sousa's Band (1911), and England's banjo ragtime king Olly Oakley (1915) all completed performance tours. Horst Bergmeier provides a concise history of the sociocultural conditions that nurtured the growth and development of the music as well as notes on the music. Specifically, he relates that "The imported 1930's recordings of American swing bands and close-harmony vocal groups had a strong bearing on the emerging local black jazz scene." The 16 tracks are permeated with Western influences, including instrumentations, scales, harmonies, and improvisations. These recordings date from 1946, however Bergmeier relates that "the music of the Shebeens and the first generation of township jazz went unrecorded."

2913. *Jazz and Hot Dance in Australia (1925–1950).* HQ 2021.

According to Mike Sutcliffe, African American minstrel groups, including the Fisk Jubilee Singers and the Georgia Minstrels, toured Australia from around 1876. He believes that the many entertainers who were touring Australia at the time transmitted ragtime between 1900 and 1914. With the distribution of the ODJB recordings around 1918 and the visits of groups like the Frank Ellis Californians and the Bert Ralton Savoy Havana Band in 1923 the dissemination of American jazz was in full force. The earliest recording (1925), on the World Record Company label, was Ray Tellier's San Francisco Orchestra. Sutcliffe provides information on the groups, personnel, soloists, and date and time period of each recording. There are 16 tracks.

2914. *Jazz and Hot Dance in Canada (1916–1949).* HQ 2023.

The notes provided by Jack Litchfield are replete with vignettes regarding the impact and evolution of jazz in Canada. He reveals that African American musicians were in Canada, having escaped from slavery in the United States, as early as 1775. Dating from the eighteenth century, African American music included folk and sacred music, and beginning in the late nineteenth century, ragtime. Among the earliest Anglo-Canadians who recorded in a jazz or ragtime style were Willie Eckstein, Vera Guilaroff, Harry Thomas, and Luis Waizman. Several combos and big bands recorded between 1910 and 1920, and Guy Lombardo organized his first orchestra in London, Ontario, in 1921. Litchfield continues by detailing the evolution of Canadian jazz, discussing selected personnel, giving dates of recordings, influences, and relating the bebop achievements of Harold "Stepp" Wade. He also includes two recordings by Oscar Peterson. There is no mention of George Shearing. There are 17 tracks.

2915. *Jazz and Hot Dance in Denmark (1909–1953).* HQ 2024.

Denmark has long been one of the favorite venues of jazz musicians. According to Erik Wiedemann, "Most foreign bands visiting Scandinavia at least played in Denmark, and during the period 1928–31—until foreign musicians were denied working permits by the German authorities—several Danish musicians played and even had their own bands in Germany and neighboring countries." He continues by stating that John Philip Sousa introduced the saxophone to Denmark in 1903 and that contact with African American music dates to at least the 1860s. The Black Opera visited in 1891–92; Cunningham's San Francisco Minstrels Orchestra in 1894; the Fisk Jubilee Singers in 1895; an African American Orchestra in 1899; and the American Black Troubadours in 1900. Thereafter, he lists other musicians who visited, including Louis Armstrong (1933), Coleman Hawkins (1935), Benny Carter (1936), Edgar Hayes and Fats Waller (1938), and

Duke Ellington (1939), to name a few. A concise discussion of recordings, personnel, and dates is also provided. Important to scholars is the author's reference to his doctoral dissertation, which covers the history of jazz in Denmark before 1950, *Jazz: Denmark Ityveme, Trediveme og iyrreme* (two volumes, plus three cassette tapes).

2916. *Hot Dance Music in Cuba (1901–1937).* HQ 2035.

This album features the accumulated genres that developed in Cuba rather than the North American music referred to as jazz. Crisóbal Diaz Ayala and Richard Spottswood begin their notes with references to the Euro-Islamic-African musical hegemony of Cuba, which, in turn, has produced the danzón, son, rumba, mambo, and others. They continue by presenting a historical musical overview of the danzon and son. In addition, musical-historical notes are provided on each of the 13 tracks complete with references to dates, personnel, instrumentation, and meaning.

2917. *Jazz and Hot Dance in Spain (1919–1949).* HQ 2026.

Rainer E. Lotz maintains that in spite of resentment of anything American, the ragtime craze reached Spain around the same time that it reached the rest of Europe, and that African American "Song and Dance teams such as Mister Johnson & Miss Bertha exhibited the 'Original Cake Walk' in 1905 at Barcelona's Circo Alegria." Furthermore, he asserts that Barcelona and Catalonia held no ill feelings toward America, and as a result, the acceptance of jazz became a symbol of their quest for independence. During the 1910s and 1920s two recording bands emerged, and beginning with the late 1920s, with visits by African American and French jazz musicians, we see the adaptation of jazz and jazz-related genres by numerous Spanish musicians. According to Lotz: "The major impact was undoubtedly the visit of Sam Wooding and His Chocolate Kiddies Orchestra." He continues by stating: Robert Martin (not Tommy Ladnier), is the trumpeter on a hitherto unissued take of "Blake's Blues," a composition by reedman Jerry (in Spanish: Jacinto) Blake. The issued take was labeled "Sweet-Black Blues," subtitled in brackets (Jacinto Blues), with composer credits to Jacinto Blake. The impact of political events on the history and evolution of Spanish jazz, notes on personnel, soloists, and important dates and venues are also discussed. There are 15 tracks, including one that features Don Byas.

2918. *Jazz and Hot Dance in Belgium (1910–1952).* HQ 2027.

Belgians attempting to emulate African American cultural traditions might have began with their contact with minstrel acts. According to Robert Pemet, "Some of the better known acts were Mr. Berleur Negro Virtuoso (1878); The American Negro Scene (1881); Howard Baker (1892); Sam

Anderson (1895); Cantrell and Williams (1896); The Elks (1903); Freddy and Rudy Walker (1904–1905); The Georgia Piccaninnies (1904–1906); The Black Troubadours (1906), and The Alabama Minstrels (1910)." The impact of ragtime, the varied meaning of the word jazz, and the impact of American recordings upon the evolution of jazz are also concisely discussed. Pemet continues by providing notes of the soloists, personnel information, historical vignettes, and date of recording for each of the 16 tracks. Oran "Hot Lips" Page is featured on the 1952 recording "Keep on Chumin' (till the Butler Comes)."

2919. *Jazz and Hot Dance in Thailand (1956–1967).* HQ 2028.

Contact between a Western musician and Thailand dates to the nineteenth century when Jakob Reit of Trier, a German Kapellmeister, emigrated to Siam. According to Rainer E. Lotz, both Jakob Reit and his son taught European notation techniques and trained the musicians of the Royal Orchestra in brass music. He reveals that Misses Florrie and Violet, members of the Harnston's Grand Circus, demonstrated the cakewalk in 1904. Thereafter, the Lindström Company (Beka), and the International Talking Machine Company (Odeon), began to record local artists, however the first discernible transmission of jazz occurred around the time of Benny Goodman's visit in the mid-1950s. In addition to this contact, the presence of American military personnel in Thailand in the 1960s also fueled the thirst for jazz and soul music. The 9 tracks include Thailand concerts by Benny Goodman, Jack Teagarden, and Lionel Hampton; Goodman teams with members of the Prasarn Mitr Band on one recording, and performs six tracks with his orchestra in the Voice of America concert held at the American Pavillion, Constitution Fair Grounds, Bangkok, Thailand, December 10, 1956.

2920. *Jazz and Hot Dance in Norway (1920–1946).* HQ 2029.

Jan Evensmo and Bjørn Stendahl provide concise, historically significant information on the transmission of African American culture to Norway. They state: "As early as 1897, the instructor of I Brigade's Brass Band, Oscar Borg, introduced Kerry Mills at a Georgia Camp Meeting in an arrangement called 'Georgia Cakewalk'". In 1906, the melody was entered in Pathe's catalogue for phonograph rolls, in a piccolo-flute version. Following this, modern dances like the two-step, foxtrot, tango, fishwalk, and one-step were introduced, until 1919 offered the newest of the new: "Jazz Dance." Traveling African American troupes introduced minstrels, spirituals, and ragtime as early as 1897 in Christiania (later renamed Oslo). The influence of ODJB and Paul Whiteman was significant because their recordings were available from around 1919. The author advises that "The first Norwegian group generally accepted as a 'jazz band' was led by violinist Lavritz Stang in 1920." They also discuss the concept of "Clover Jazz" as exhibited by Roy Eldridge, Chu Berry, and Teddy Wilson. The liner notes focus more on contact, dissemination, and evolution, than on discussions of the 16 tracks.

2921. *Jali Music Bolu Koi (Gambia) (1984).*

Notes from this anthology are not included because there is no proven connection between Jali music and jazz. The aforementioned conclusion was made in spite of research done by Paul Oliver and Samuel Charters (blues), and Alfons Dauer and Ernest Bornemann (jazz).

2922. *Jazz and Hot Dance in Sweden (1899–1969).* HQ 2065.

According to Rainer E. Lotz, African American music was first introduced to Sweden in 1895 when the Fisk Jubilee Singers introduced spirituals and other genres. Beginnings in the early twentieth-century Swedish shops were offering stock arrangements of American popular music including the cakewalk, ragtime, and accordion and brass band music. He continues by providing insights into the first Swedish contact with jazz: "The word jazz was new in the Swedish language in 1919, soon after W.W.I, important music people and also the Musician's Union condemned jazz and wanted the government to forbid the import of the 'infectious disease'— without success—jazz came to stay. Pianist Sven Runo headed one of the earliest Swedish 'jazz bands' on record, but the music sounded far from New Orleans (black New Orleans musicians were first recorded in 1923, the same year as Runo's recordings)." Anyhow, the band included the black banjoist Russell Jones, who arrived with an English group around 1914. Jones settled in Sweden, and his obbligato playing makes this recording (A/2) especially interesting as traces of early ad-lib improvisation appeared in the late 1920s. Hàkan von Eichwald organized the first big band in 1930. Lotz relates that the 1933 Louis Armstrong visit, the 1935 appearance of Coleman Hawkins, and the 1936 appearance of Benny Carter lead Swedish jazz musicians to prefer the "real stuff." He continues by providing details of soloists, personnel, compositions, and important dates. There are 16 tracks.

2923. *Jazz and Hot Dance in Italy (1919–1948).* HQ 2078.

Raffaele Borretti admits that he was selective when including artists who helped to disseminate jazz in Italy. He reveals that the first American people/groups to visit Italy were the Will Marion Cook Orchestra (featuring Sidney Bechet and Arthur Briggs), the Original Dixieland Jazz Band, Art Hickman, Vincent Lopez, Adrian Rollini, Paul Whiteman, and more. Even though jazz was not welcomed in the late 1930s, the music continued to spread because their listening influenced Italian musicians and travel experiences. Borretti asserts: From 1915, Italian dance bands began furtively to play foxtrots and other rhythmic music, introducing instruments like the banjo and drums: It's very interesting to note that until recently in Italy, in provincial places at least, the word "jazz" designated the drums. Rome and Milan, with their many theatres, dance halls, "Cafe-Chantants," and big audiences were the first centers where jazz saw the light. Thereafter he chronicles the deeds of some of Italy's early groups, the influence of American artists like Red Nichols, the Dorsey's, Venuti-Lang, and the impact of musicians like Sam Wooding, Claude Hopkins, Mitchell's Jazz Kings, Louis Armstrong, and others. Musical-historical notes on personnel, date, and soloists on some of the 16 tracks, and style influence(s) are also provided.

XIII

Selected Recordings: Anthologies and Collections

2924. *Art of the Jam Session: Montreux '77–0.*

Oscar Peterson, Dizzy Gillespie, Clark Terry, Lockjaw Davis, NHOP, Milt Jackson, Ray Brown, Monty Alexander, Ronnie Scott, Joe Pass, Count Basie, Al Grey, Vic Dickenson, Zoot Sims, Roy Eldridge, Benny Carter. 8-Pablo L. 2620106.

2925. *Atlantic Jazz*—A 141 track retrospective, recorded 1947–1986, in 12 volumes (3 double and 9 single albums or 12 compact discs) compiled according to style. All recordings are digitally remastered.

The Avant-Garde—selections by Roland Kirk, Charles Mingus, Ornette Coleman, John Coltrane, the Art Ensemble of Chicago. Atlantic 81709–2; 81709–4

Bebop—selections by Dizzy Gillespie, Art Blakey & the Jazz Messengers with Thelonious Monk, John Coltrane, Sonny Stitt, Philly Joe Jones, Max Roach. Atlantic 81702–2; 81702–4.

Fusion—selections by Miroslav Vitous, Les McCann, Billy Cobham, Larry Coryell with Alphonse Mouzon, Passport, Jean-Luc Ponty. Atlantic 81711–2; 81711–4.

Introspection—selections by Hubert Laws, Chick Corea, Charles Lloyd, Joe Zawinul, Keith Jarrett, Gary Burton. Atlantic 81710–2; 81710–4.

Kansas City—selections by Joe Turner, Vic Dickenson, Jay McShann, Buster Smith, T-Bone Walker. Atlantic 817701–2; 81701–4.

Mainstream—selections by Tony Fruscella, Ray Charles, Coleman Hawkins & Milt Jackson, the MJQ, Stephane Grappelli, Duke Ellington, Art Farmer, Woody Herman, Ira Sullivan, the Clarke-Boland Big Band. Atlantic 81704–2; 81704–4.

New Orleans—selections by Paul Barbarin, George Lewis, Jim Robinson, Wilbur de Paris, Turk Murphy, the Eureka Brass Band, Ernest "Punch" Miller, Joseph "De De" Pierce. Atlantic 81700–2; 81700–4.

Piano—selections by Erroll Garner, Mary Lou Williams, Lennie Tristano, Phineas Newborn, Ray Charles, Thelonious Monk with Art Blakey and the Jazz Messengers, John Lewis, Billy Taylor, Roland Hanna, McCoy Tyner, Bill Evans with Herbie Mann, Randy Weston, Dwike Mitchell, Joe Zawinul, Junior Mance, Herbie Hancock, Ray Bryant, Keith Jarrett, Dave Brubeck, Don Pullen, Ahmad Jamal. Atlantic 81707–2; 81707–4.

Post-Bop—selections by the Teddy Charles Tenet, Lee Konitz, the MJQ with Sonny Rollins, the Jazz Modes, John Coltrane, the Slide Hampton Octet, Von Freeman, Freddie Hubbard, Gil Evans. Atlantic 81705–2; 81705–4.

Singers—selections by Ray Charles, Joe Turner, Jimmy Witherspoon with Wilbur de Paris, Joe Mooney, Lavern Baker, Ruth Brown, Helen Merrill, Lurlean Hunter, Ann Richards, Mose Allison, Chris Connor, Mel Tormé, Nancy Harrow, Joao Gilberto, Betty Carter, Vi Redd, Esther Phillips, Earl Coleman, Carmen McRae, Al Hibbler with Roland Kirk, Aretha Franklin, Peggy Lee, Sarah Vaughan, Sylvia Syms, the Manhattan Transfer. Atlantic 81706–2; 81706–4.

Soul—selections by Leo Wright, Shirley Scott, Johnny Griffin, Clarence Wheeler, Brother Jack McDuff, Ray Charles, Herbie Mann, Yusef Lateef, Les McCann, Eddie Harris, Hank Crawford, Nat Adderley, Joe Zawinul, King Curtis. Atlantic 81708–2; 81708–4.

West Coast—selections by Eddie Safranski, Shorty Rogers, Jack Montrosa, Conte Candoli, Jimmy Giuffre, Red Mitchell & Harold Land, Shelly Manne. Atlantic 81703–2; 81703–4.

2926. *Atlantic Records: Great Moments in Jazz.*

Selections by Shorty Rogers, Jimmy Giuffre, the Modern Jazz Quartet, Milt Jackson, Charles Mingus, Art Blakey & Thelonious Monk, John Coltrane, Ornette Coleman, Herbie Mann, Mel Tormé, Carmen McRae,

Rahsaan Roland Kirk, David Newman, Hank Crawford, Mose Allison, Eddie Harris, Yusef Lateef, Les McCann & Eddie Harris, Freddie Hubbard, Billy Cobham, Jean Luc-Ponty, the Manhattan Transfer, Passport, Gerald Albright, Ahmad Jamal. Atlantic 2- 81907–2; 2- 81907–4.

2927. *The Bass.*

Blanton, Pettiford, Brown, Mingus, Chambers, Lafaro, Hinton, Duvivier, Garrison, Grimes, Haden, Sirone, Workman, Carter, Clarke, Davis, Izenson, McBee. 3-Impulse 9284.

2928. *Bebop Revisited.*

Volume 1, with Dexter Gordon, Earl Coleman, Fats Navarro, Chubby Jackson, Terry Gibbs. Xanadu 120.

Volume 2, with Oscar Pettiford, Dizzy Gillespie, Rubberlegs Williams, Roy Stevens, Kai Winding, Karl George, J. J. Johnson, Aaron Sachs, Terry Gibbs (rec. 1945–46). Xanadu 124.

Volume 3, with Tony Fruscella, Sam Most, Kai Winding, Warne Marsh, Billy Taylor, Jack Lesberg, Charlie Perry, Melvin Moore (vocals), (rec. 1951, 1953). Xanadu 172.

Volume 4, with James Moody, Bennie Green, Ernie Royal, Davie Burns, Bud Johnson, Roy Haynes, Babs Gonzales (rec. 1948–1950). Xanadu 197.

Volume 5, with Kenny Dorham/Conte Candoli: Side 1—Dorham (trumpet), w. Barry Harris, Julian Euell, Al Heath (rec. live in NYC, 1964); Side 2— Candoli (trumpet) with Richie Kamuca, Dick Shreve, Red Mitchell, Stan Levy (rec. live in L.A., 1957). Xanadu 205.

Volume 6, with Frankie Socolow, John Hardee, Eddie "Lockjaw" Davis, Paul Quinichette, Freddy Webster, Bud Powell, Al Haig, Kenny Drew, John Collins, Freddie Green, Leonard Gaskin, Clyde Lombardi, Gene Ramey, Irv Kluger, Norman "Tiny" Kahn, Denzil Best, Gus Johnson (rec. 1945, 1947, 1948 & 1952). Xanadu 208.

2929. *The Bebop Revolution.*

Dizzy Gillespie, 52nd Street All-Stars, Kenny Clarke and His 52nd Street Boys, Lucky Thompson and His Lucky Seven, Coleman Hawkins (rec. 1946–1949). Bluebird 2177–2-RB; 2177–4-RB.

2930. *Best of the Big Bands.*

Charlie Barnet, Count Basie, Louis Bellson, Duke Ellington, Benny Goodman, Lionel Hampton, Woody Herman, Harry James, Gene Krupa ("Walkman Jazz/Compact Jazz" series). Verve 833281–2; 833281–4.

2931. *The Best of Blue Note.*

Volume 1—selections by John Coltrane, Herbie Hancock, Donald Byrd, Art Blakey and the Jazz Messengers, Lou Donaldson, Horace Silver, Jimmy Smith, Kenny Burrell, Lee Morgan. Blue Note B21Y-96110; B41F-96110.

2932. *The Best of Bossa Nova.*

Laurindo Almeida, Charlie Byrd, Stan Getz, Astrud Gilberto, Joao Gilberto, Luiz Henrique, Antonio Carlos Jobim, Gary McFarland Orchestra, Baden Powell, Walter Wanderley ("Walkman Jazz/Compact Jazz" series). Verve 833289–2; 833289–4.

2933. *The Best of Chess Jazz.*

James Moody & His Orchestra, Gene Ammons Sextet, Clark Terry, Zoot Sims Quartet, Ahmad Jamal, Benny Goodman & Orchestra, Sonny Stitt, Art Farmer/Benny Golson Jazztet, Kenny Burrell Trio, Ramsey Lewis, Ray Bryant, Roland Kirk & Ira Sullivan, Art Blakey & the Jazz Messengers, Oliver Nelson, Budd Johnson Quartet, Jack McDuff, Illinois Jacquet, John Klemmer. Chess CHD-6025.

2934. *The Best of Dixieland* ("Walkman Jazz/Compact Jazz" series).

Kid Ory, George Lewis, Louis Armstrong, Henry Red Allen, Max Kaminsky, Eddie Condon, Jack Teagarden, Original Tuxedo Jass' Band, Dejan's Original Olympia Brass Band, Ken Colyer, Alex Welsh, Monty Sunshine, Mr. Acker Bilk, Terry Lightfoot, Chris Barber, Humphrey Lyttleton. Verve 831375–2; 831375–4.

2935. *Big Band Jazz: Tulsa to Harlem (1949–1953).*

Cab Calloway, Ernie Fields & Jimmy Hamilton. Delmark DL-439; DC-439.

2936. *Big Bands of the Swingin' Years.*

Selections by Woody Herman, Benny Goodman, Charlie Barnet, Tommy Dorsey, Artie Shaw, Johnny Long, Louis Armstrong, Larry Clinton, Count Basie, Russ Morgan, Tony Pastor, Duke Ellington, Billy Daniels, Jimmy Dorsey, Billie Holiday, Glenn Miller. Quicksilver QSCD-1018; QS-5–1018.

2937. *Big Bands of the Singing Years.*

Volume 1—Woody Herman, Artie Shaw, Benny Goodman, Duke Ellington, Charlie Barnet, Louis Armstrong, Jimmy Dorsey, Count Basie, Tommy Dorsey, Chick Webb with Ella Fitzgerald. Collectables COL-5096; COLCD-5096; COLC-5096.

Volume 2—Glenn Miller, Duke Ellington, Tony Pastor, Artie Shaw with Kitty Kallen, Chick Webb with Ella Fitzgerald, Louis Armstrong with Jack

Teagarden, Woody Herman, Jimmy Lunceford with Trummy Young, Jimmy Dorsey, Charlie Barnet. Collectables COL-5097; COLCD-5097; COLC-5097.

2938. *Big Bands Greatest Hits.*

Volume 2—Hampton, Spivak, Brown, Ellington, Thornhill, Kyser, Pastor, Bradley, Busse, Martin, Noble, James, Kaye, Gray, Herman, Lombardo. Col. CG-31213; CGA-31213.

2939. *Big Band Jazz: From the Beginnings to the Fifties:* Smithsonian Press.

Eighty performances covering Louis Armstrong, Fletcher Henderson, Benny Goodman, Count Basie, Tommy Dorsey, Artie Shaw, Dizzy Gillespie, Stan Kenton, and many more. A 52-page listening guide is included.

2940. *Black California.*

Volume 1—Sonny Criss, Slim Galliard, Roy Porter Big Band with Eric Dolphy, Helen Humes, Harold Land, Hampton Hawes, Art Pepper. Savoy Jazz 2 SJL-2215.

Volume 2—Helen Humes, Slim Galliard, Wardell Gray, Russell Jacquet, Kenny Clarke with Milt Jackson, Percy Heath, et al. (rec. 1946–1954). Savoy Jazz 2 SJL-2242.

2941. *Black Swing Tradition.*

Fletcher Henderson, Mary Lou Williams, Buster Bailey, Stuff Smith, Coleman Hawkins, Hot Lips Page, Don Byas, Slam Stewart, Benny Carter, Red Norvo, et al. (rec. 1931–1944). Savoy Jazz.

2942. *Black Giants.*

J. J. Johnson, J. Lewis, M. Davis, H. Silver, T. Monk, C. Mingus, Bud Powell, C. Hawkins, C. Terry, A. Blakey, R. Lewis, L. Armstrong, D. Ellington, D. Gillespie, E. Garner, Q. Jones, C. Basie, A. Tatum, J. Coltrane, C. Adderley. 2-Col. PG-33402.

2943. *Early Black Swing: The Birth of Big Band Jazz.*

Henry Red Allen, Louis Armstrong, Duke Ellington, Fletcher Henderson, Earl Hines, Charlie Johnson's Paradise Ten, Jimmie Lunceford, McKinney's Cotton Pickers, the Missourians, Bennie Moten's Kansas City Orchestra. Bluebird 9583–2; 9583–4.

2944. *Blue Note 50th Anniversary Collection.*

(Five volumes—six hours of music—documents every period of jazz during the last 50 years. All five volumes also available as a limited edition box set.)

Volume 1—"From Boogie to Bop, 1939–1956"—Albert Ammons, Meade Lux Lewis, Sidney Bechet, Thelonious Monk, Bud Powell, Horace Silver, et al. Blue Note: B12L-92465; B21S-92465; B42L-92465.

Volume 2—"The Jazz Message, 1956–1965"—John Coltrane, Julian "Cannonball" Adderley, Wayne Shorter, Herbie Hancock, Bobby Hutcherson. Blue Note: B12L-92468; B21S-92468; B42L-92468.

Volume 3—"Funk and Blues, 1956–1967"—Horace Silver, Jimmie Smith, et al. Blue Note: B12L-92471; B21S-92471; B42L-92471.

Volume 4—"Outside in, 1964–1989"—Eric Dolphy, Ornette Coleman, McCoy Tyner, Andrew Hill, et al. Blue Note: B12L-92474; B21S-92474; B42L-92474.

Volume 5—"Lighting the Fuse, 1970–1989"—artists not specified. Blue Note: B12L-92477; B21S-92477; B42L-92477.

2945. *Bop City.*

Evidence—Jaki Byard & Roland Kirk, George Russell & Eric Dolphy, Booker Ervin, Mal Waldron, Bill Evans, Thelonious Monk. Boplicity: BOPM-12.

Midnight—Wes Montgomery, Milt Jackson, Miles Davis, Ben Webster, Jackie McLean, Sonny Rollins, Thelonious Monk. Boplicity: BOPM-9.

Straight Ahead—Art Blakey and the Jazz Messengers, Miles Davis, Oliver Nelson, Donald Byrd & Art Farmer, John Coltrane, Sonny Rollins. Boplicity: BOPM-10.

Things Are Getting Better—Cannonball Adderley, Bobby Timmons, Wes Montgomery & Johnny Griffin, Gene Ammons, Bobby Timmons & Blue Mitchell, Oliver Nelson. Boplicity: BOPM-11.

2946. *Brass Fever.*

Rosolino, Winding, G. Brown, Bohanon, Brashear, Marcus (arr.) Implulse 9308 (Q).

2947. *Les Chanteurs de Jazz: 1925–1939.*

Selections by Perry Bradford's Jazz Phools, Jelly Roll Morton and His Red Hot Peppers, Pinetop Smith, Will Johnson with Henry "Red' Allen and His Orchestra, Louis Armstrong and His Sebastian New Cotton Club Orchestra, Don Redman and His Orchestra, Harlan Lattimore with Fletcher Henderson and His Orchestra, Cab Calloway and His Orchestra, Wilson Myers with the New Orleans Feetwarmers, the Mills Brothers with Duke Ellington and His Orchestra, the Spirits of Rhythm, Louis Bacon with Duke Ellington and His Orchestra, Taft Jordan with Chick Webb and His Orchestra, Stuff Smith with Jonah Jones, Fats Waller and His Rhythm, Jimmy Rushing with Count Basie and His Orchestra, Slim and Slam, Hot Lips Page and His Band, Trummy Young with Jimmy Lunceford and His Orchestra, Dan Grissom with Jimmie Lunceford and His Orchestra, Joe Turner with Pete Johnson and His Boogie Woogie Boys. L'Art Vocal 8 (AAD).

2948. *Les Chanteuses de Jazz: 1921–1939.*

Selections by Katie Crippen with Henderson's Novelty Orchestra, Lena Wilson with Porter Grainger, Eva Taylor with Clarence Williams Blue Five, Edmonia Henderson, Bertha "Chipie" Hill with Louis Armstrong, Alberta Hunter with Fats Waller, Adelaide Hall with Duke Ellington and His Orchestra, Baby Cox with Duke Ellington and His Orchestra, Bessie Smith, Victoria Spivey with Luis Russell Orchestra, Ivie Anderson with Duke Ellington and His Orchestra, Gladys Palmer with Roy Eldridge and His Orchestra, Billie Holiday with Teddy Wilson and His Orchestra, Ella Fitzgerald with Chick Webb and His Orchestra, Trixie Smith with Sidney Bechet, Valaida Snow, Nan Wynn with Teddy Wilson and His Orchestra, Lil Armstrong and Her Orchestra, Helen Humes with Count Basie and His Orchestra, Ethel Waters, Thelma Carpenter with Coleman Hawkins and His Orchestra, Laurel Watson with Roy Eldridge and His Orchestra. L'Art Vocal 7 (AAD).

2949. *Charlie Parker Memorial.*

Dexter Gordon, Lee Konitz, Hayes, Eddie Jefferson, Dorham, Ray Nance, Howard McGhee, Red Rodney, Philly Joe Jones, Muhal R. Abrams. 2-Chess 60002.

2950. *Charlie Parker, 10th Memorial Concert.*

Gillespie, Konitz, Moody, Eldridge, Hawkins, Dave Lambert, Billy Taylor, Dorham, Kenny Barron Trio. 5510; 8T5510.

2951. *The Charlie Parker Memorial Concert.* Recorded North Park Hotel, Chicago, August 1970.

Featuring Red Rodney, Dexter Gordon, Von Freeman, Jodie Christian, Rufus Reid, Roy Haynes, Kenny Dorham, Ray Nance, Joe Daley, Richard Abrams, Wilbur Campbell, Arthur Hoyle, Lee Konitz, John Young, Philly Joe Jones, Eddie Jefferson, Howard McGhee, Vi Redd. Vogue: VG-600188.

2952. *Charlie Parker 10th Memorial Concert.*

Five performances from "A Tribute to Charlie Parker" Carnegie Hall concert, rec. 3/27/65: featuring Dizzy Gillespie, James Moody, Kenny Barron, et al. Limelight 826985–2.

2953. *Chicago Volume 2.* (Robert Parker series).

Selections by Jelly Roll Morton, Benny Goodman, King Oliver, Eddie Condon, Ma Rainey, Louis Armstrong, et al. ABC Music: 836–181–2.

2954. *Chicago Jazz, 1923–29.*

Clarence Jones, Young's Creole Band, J.C. Johnson's Five Hot Sparks, Sammy Stewart's Ten Knights of Syncopation, Wades' Moulin Rouge Orchestra. Biograph 12005.

2955. *Chicago Jazz Volume 2, 1925–1929.*

Love Austin's Blues Serenaders, Preston Jackson's Uptown Band, John Williams's Syncho Jazzers, Charles Pierce's Orch., Richard M. Jones Jazz Wizards, Jimmy Bythe's Ragmuffins, Windy Rhythm Kings, Kansas City Frank's Foot Warmers. Biograph 12043.

2956. *Chicago Jazz Summit.*

Featuring Frank Chase with Vince Giordano & the Nighthawks, Kenny Davern, Wild Bill Davison, Barrett Deems, Milt Hinton, Art Hodes, Clarence Hutchenrider, Franz Jackson, Max Kaminsky, Hank Lawson, Jimmy McPartland, Marian McPartland, George Masso, Eddie Miller, Truck Parkham, Ikey Robinson, George Wein (rec. at New York's Town Hall during the 1986 JVC Jazz Festival). Atlantic Jazz 81844–2; 81844–4.

2957. *At the Jazz Band Ball: Chicago/New York Dixieland.*

Eddie Condon's Hot Spots, Mugsy Spanier and His Ragtime Band, Bud Freeman and His Summa Cum Laude Orchestra; vocals George Brunies, Jack Teagarden. Bluebird 6752–2.

2958. *Chocolate Dandies 1928–1933.*

Benny Carter, Don Redman, J.C. Higginbotham, Fats Waller, Rex Stewart, Coleman Hawkins, Lonnie Johnson, Teddy Wilson, with vocals by George Thomas, Benny Carter, Jimmy Harrison, Don Redman. Swing CDSW-8448.

2959. *Classic Jazz Piano (1927–1957).*

Count Basie, Duke Ellington, Bill Evans, Erroll Garner, Earl Hines, James P. Johnson, Meade Lux Lewis, Jelly Roll Morton, Oscar Peterson, Bud Powell, Jess Stacy, Art Tatum, Lennie Tristano, Fats Waller, Mary Lou Williams, Teddy Wilson, Jimmy Yancey, Willie "The Lion" Smith, Billy Strayhorn. Bluebird 6754–2-RB; 6754–2-RB.

2960. *Classic Pianos.*

Erroll Garner, Earl Hines, Art Hodes, James P. Johnson. Signature: AK-38851; FAT-38851.

2961. *Classic Pianos.*

Erroll Garner, Earl Hines, James P. Johnson, Ray Bryant, Nat Jaffe, Hazel Scott, Art Hodes, Page Cavanaugh. EPM: FDC-5010.

2962. *Classic Tenors: 1944–1952.*

Four selections each by Don Byas (rec. 1946), Eddie "Lockjaw" Davis (rec. 1944), Paul Quinichette (rec. 1952), Ben Webster (rec. 1944). EPM: FDC-5170.

2963. *Concord Jazz Guitar Collection.* Vol. 1 & 2.

Laurindo Almeida, George Barnes, Kenny Burrell, Charlie Byrd, Cal Collins, Eddie Duran, Herb Ellis, Tal Farlow, Freddie Green, Duncan James, Barney Kessel, Remo Palmier, Joe Pass, Howard Roberts (rec. 1973–1980). Concord Jazz: CJ-160; CCD-4160; CJ-160.

2964. *CTI Summer Jazz in the Hollywood Bowl.*

Deodato, Hammond, Bob James, Ron Carter, DeJohnette, Benson, Airto, Crawford, Farrell, Turrentine, G. Washington, Hubbard, Laws, Milt Jackson. (Rec. 7/72)—Live One CTI 7076; 8–7076; C-7076. Live Two CTI 7077; 9–7077; C-7077. Live Three CTI 7078; 8–7078; C-7078 W.E. Phillips.

2965. *CTI Masters of the Guitar.*

Selections by Joe Beck, George Benson, Kenny Burrell, Eric Gale, Grant Green, Jim Hall, John McLaughlin, Gabor Szabo, Phil Upchurch (rec. 1971–75). CTI/CBS Associated: ZK-44176; FZT-44176.

2966. *CTI Masters of the Keyboard.*

Chick Corea, Deodato, Don Grolnick, Dave Grusin, Bob James, Keith Jarrett (11/89). CTI/CBS Associated: ZK-45218; FZT-45218.

2967. *CTI Masters of the Saxophone.*

Selections by Hank Crawford, Joe Farrell, Joe Henderson, David Sanborn, Stanley Turrentine, Grover Washington, Jr. (rec. 1970–75). CTI/CBS Associated: ZK-44187; FZT-44187.

2968. *Cylinder Jazz.*

NY Military Band, Louisiana Five, Harry Raderman's Jazz Orchestra, Duke Yellman and His Orchestra, the Merry Sparklers, Billy Wynne's Greenwich

Village Orchestra, Clyde Doerr and His Orchestra, Earl Oliver's Jazz Babies, Frisco Jazz Band, Tennessee Happy Boys, Paul Victorin's Orchestra (from Edison cylinders; rec. 1913–27). Saydisc 334: CDSDL-334.

2969. *Decade of Jazz, 1959–1969. Vol. 3.*

J. Smith, Quebec, Burrell, D. Byrd, Morgan, Dolphy, Silver, Turrentine, O. Coleman, Donaldson. Impulse 99.

2970. *Definitive Jazz Scene, Volume 1 (9–64).*

Volume 2—Charles, Scott, Hampton, Nelson, J. J. Johnson, Coltrane, Tyner, Albam, Flanagan. (3–65) Impulse 100.

Volume 3—Coltrane, Shepp, Nelson, Tyner, Hamilton, Russian Jazz Quartet, Scott E. Jones. (1–66) Impulse 9101.

2971. *The Drums.*

Blakey, Roach, Clarke, Philly Joe Jones, Sid Catlett, Jo Jones, Connie Kay, Haynes, Richmond, Bellson, Manne, Hamilton, Purdie, E. Jones, Rashied Ali, Milford Graves, Baby Dodds, J. Chambers, Beaver Harris, N. Connors, E. Blackwell, Sunny Murray, Mouzon, Paul Motian, B. Altschul. 3-Impulse 9272.

2972. *Encyclopedia of Jazz in the 70's.*

Leonard Feather presents L. L. Smith, Manne, Tapscott, Gil Evans, Barbieri, Dankworth, Cleo Laine, Akiyoshi and Tabackin, Amram, Simone, Groove Holmes, Rich, Jazz Piano Quartet, O. Nelson, B. Mitchell, Ellington. 2-RCA APL2–1984.

2973. *Greatest Jazz Concert in the World.*

Ellington and Orchestra, Fitzgerald, Peterson, Benny Carter, Hawkins, Z. Sims, C. Terry, T-Bone Walker. (JATP) 4-Pablo 2625704 S25704.

2974. *Impulsively.*

Barbieri, Jarrett, White, Mel Brown, Klemmer, Saracho, Haden, Redman, Marion Brown, Sun Ra, J. Coltrane, Rivers. 2-Impulse 9266 (Q); 8027–9266H.

2975. *Jam Sessions at Montreux '77.*

Basie, Gillespie, Milt Jackson, Ray Brown, O. Peterson, Benny Carter, Sims, Lockjaw Davis, C. Terry, Faddis, Eldridge, Al Grey, Vic Dickenson. NHOP 2-Pablo L. 2620105; S20105; K201105.

2976. *Jazz for a Sunday Afternoon, Volumes 1 & 2.*

Adams, Corea, R. Davis, Gillespie, E. Jones, M. Lewis, Nance/Adams, G. Brown, Corea, R. Davis, Gillespie, Lewis. (4/68) 2-Solid 18027/8. Vol. 3—Bryant, H. Edison. Solid 18037.

2977. *A Jazz Piano Anthology.*

Blake, J. P. Johnson, Waller, Yancey, Hines, Tatum, Wilson, Ammons, M. L. Lewis, P. Johnson, M. L. Williams, Basie, Ellington, Monk, Powell, Garner, J. Lewis, Silver, B. Evans, C. Taylor, and others. 2-Col PG-32355.

2978. *Jazz Years—25th Anniversary.*

Rogers, Tristano, Charles, Giuffre, M. Jackson, Modern Jazz Quartet, Blakey, Newman, Mingus, Coltrane, Coleman, Mitchell-Ruff Trio, Allison, B. and G. Lewis, Crawford, Lloyd, Hubbard, Kirk, Mann, Lateef, McCann and Harris. 2-At. 2–316; TP-2–316; CS-2–316.

2979. *The Esquire All-American Jazz Concert.* (January 18, 1944, Metropolitan Opera House, New York City).

Featuring Louis Armstrong, Roy Eldridge, Jack Teagarden, Barney Bigard, Benny Goodman, Coleman Hawkins, Red Norvo, Lionel Hampton, Art Tatum, Jess Stacy, Teddy Wilson, Al Casey, Oscar Pettiford, Sid Weiss, Sidney Catlett, Morey Feld, Mildred Bailey (four vocals), Billie Holiday (three vocals) (6/89). EPM 2: FCD-25118.

2980. *The Essential Keynote Collection.* (on Mercury Label).

The Complete Benny Carter on Keynote

The Complete Coleman Hawkins on Keynote

The Complete Lenny Tristano on Keynote

The Complete Lester Young on Keynote Early Bebop

The Fabulous Ellingtonians Improvisations (Red Norvo)

The Keynoters With Nat King Cole—(13 tracks): Charlie Shavers, Jonah Jones, Budd Johnson, Johnny Guarnieri, Milt Hinton, J. C. Heard, (rec. New York, 1944); Willie Smith, Nat King Cole, Red Callendar, Jackie Mills, (rec. Los Angeles, 1946) (11/87). Mercury 830967–2.

2981. *Famous Jazz Singers.* Volume 1.

Selections by Ivie Anderson with Duke Ellington and His Orchestra, Ethel Waters, Connie Boswell with the Dorsey Brothers Orchestra, Anita O'Day with Gene Krupa and His Orchestra, Mildred Bailey, Dolores Hawkins, Betty Carter, Billie Holiday with Mal Waldron's All Stars, Sarah Vaughan with George Treadwell and His All Stars, Midge Williams and Her Jazz

Jesters, Boswell Sisters, Ella Fitzgerald with Teddy Wilson and His Orchestra, Peggy Lee with Benny Goodman and His Sextet, Sarah Vaughan, Maxine Sullivan with John Kirby and His Orchestra, Betty Roche with Duke Ellington and His Orchestra (12/90). Bellaphon 625.50.003; Columbia FCT-37972.

2982. *From the Newport Jazz Festival Tribute to Charlie Parker.*

Sonny Stitt, J. J. Johnson, Howard McGhee, Max Roach, Jackie McLean, Harold Mabern, Arthur Harper, Jr., Lamont Johnson, Scott Holt, Billy Higgins (4/88). Bluebird 6457–2-RB.

2983. *From Spirituals to Swing.*

Thirty-one selections by Benny Goodman Sextet, Helen Humes with Count Basie and His Band, Hot Lips Page with the Basie Band, Kansas City Six, Basie/ Jones/Page, Basie/Young/Clayton/Page, James P. Johnson, the New Orleans Footwarmers, Golden Gate Gospel Quartet, Ida Cox with James P. Johnson, et al., Jam Session, Sonny Terry, Joe Turner with Pete Johnson, Lewis/ Ammons/Page/Jones, Broonzy/Ammons/Page/Jones, Mitchell's Christian Singers. Vanguard: VCD2–47/48.

2984. *Fun on the Frets: Early Jazz Guitar.*

Carl Kress, Dick McDonough, Tony Mottola, George Van Eps. Yazoo: 1061: C-1061.

2985. *Gems of Jazz: All Star Jazz Artists.*

Selections by Joe Williams, Clark Terry, Art Blakey, Bobby Hutcherson, Bunky Green, Jimmy & Stacy Rowles, Bobby Shew & Chuck Findley (2–91). Delos 13491–3507-2.

2986. *Giants of Blues Tenor Sax.*

Arnett Cobb, Eddie "Lockjaw" Davis, Frank Foster, Illinois Jacquet, Al Sears, Buddy Tate (rec. 1958–1969). Prestige: P-24101.

2987. *Giants of the Blues Tenor Sax/Giants of the Funk Tenor Sax.*

Buddy Tate, Jimmy Forrest, Coleman Hawkins, Arnett Cobb, Eddie "Lockjaw" Davis, Arnett Cobb/Eddie "Lockjaw" Davis/Coleman Hawkins/ Buddy Tate, Hal Singer, Al Sears, Illinois Jacquet/Frank Foster, Jimmy Forrest/King Curtis/Oliver Nelson, Gene Ammons, Sonny Stitt, Rusty Bryant/Seldon Powell, Willis Jackson, Houston Person/Babe Clarke, Johnny Griffin/Edwin Williams, Stanley Turrentine, Houston Person, Rusty Bryant, Gene Ammons/Richard Landry (6/90). Prestige: PCD-2302-2.

2988. *Giants of Jazz.*

Dizzy Gillespie, Thelonious Monk, Kai Winding, Sonny Stitt, Al McKibbon, Art Blakey (rec. live in London, 1972). George W.: GW-3004; CCD-43004; 3004.

2989. *The Giants of Jazz.*

In Berlin '71: Dizzy Gillespie, Sonny Stitt, Kai Winding, Thelonious Monk, Al McKibbon (9–88). EmArcy 834567–2.

2990. *Giants of Small Band Swing.*

Volume 1—Billy Kyle's Big Eight, Russell Procope's Big Six, Sandy Williams's Big Eight, Dicky Wells's Big Seven, Jimmy Jones's Big Four (rec. 1946) (previously Riverside 143) (reissue 10–90). Fantasy/OJC: OJC-1723: OJCCD-1723–2.

Volume 2—Dicky Wells's Big Seven, Sandy Williams's Big Eight, Joe Thomas's Big Six, J.D. Higginbotham's Big Eight, Jimmy Jones's Big Four (rec. 1945 & 1946) (previously Riverside 145) (reissue 10–90). Fantasy/OJC: OJC-1724; OJCCD-1724–2.

2991. *Giants of Traditional Jazz.*

Various bands, with Mutt Carey, Sidney Bechet, Wild Bill Davison, Joe Marsala, Edmond Hall, Jack Teagarden, Bobby Hacket (rec. in NY, London, Boston & L.A., 1944–1952). Savoy Jazz: SJL-2251.

2992. *The Great Jazz Album.*

Volume 1—various artists Project 3 2-PRC2–6009.

Volume 2—various artists Project 3 2-PRC2–6023.

2993. *Great Jazz Pianists: 1938–1970.*

Selections by Erroll Garner (rec. 1945), Earl Hines (rec. 1941–1970), Jess Stacy (rec. 1938), Art Tatum (rec. 1938 & 1948). Zeta: ZET-725.

2994. *Great Ladies of Jazz.*

Sarah Vaughan, June Christy, Dakota Staton, Billie Holiday, Anita O'Day, Gloria Lynne, Peggy Lee, Nancy Wilson, Dinah Washington, Ketty Lester, Carmen McRae. K-Tel 539–2; 539–4.

2995. *Great Ladies of Jazz II.*

Selections by Ella Fitzgerald, Peggy Lee, Sarah Vaughan, Anita O'Day, Carmen McRae, Julie London, Dinah Washington, Billie Holiday, Morgana King, Nancy Wilson (10/91). K-Tel 6023–2; 6023–4.

2996. *Great Saxophones: 1943–1946.*

Selections by Coleman Hawkins (rec. 1943), Ben Webster (rec. 1946), Lester Young with Dickie Wells and His Orchestra (rec. 1943). Zeta: ZET-721.

2997. *Great Trumpets. (Classic Jazz to Swing).*

Henry "Red" Allen, Louis Armstrong, Bix Beiderbecke, Bunny Berigan, Buck Clayton, Roy Eldridge, Harry James, Bunk Johnson, Tommy Ladnier, Red Nichols, King Oliver, "Hot Lips" Page, Muggsy Spanier, Rex Stewart, Cootie Williams, Lee Collins, Sidney DeParis, Wingy Malone, Max Kaminsky, Ziggy Elman, Frankie Newton (rec. 1927–1946). Bluebird 6753–2-RB; 6753–4-RB.

2998. *Folkways Jazz.*

Volume 2: The Blues—W. Johnson, Jefferson, Oliver, Rainey, Armstrong, Morton, Yancy, Smith. Folkways 2802.

Volume 3: New Orleans—Armstrong, Dodds, Red Onion. Folkways 2803.

Volume 4: Jazz Singers—Armstrong, Cox, Thomas, Morton, Anderson, Fitzgerald, Rushing, O'Connell, Watson, Gillespie, Holiday, Waller, Carlisle, Smith, Rainey, Loften, Hill, Terry, Dupree. Folkways 2804.

Volume 8: Big Bands Before 1935—Henderson, Moten, C. Johnson, Ellington, Russell, McKinney, Little Chocolate Dandies, Pollack, Charleston Chasers, Lunceford. Folkways 2808.

Volume 9: Piano—Dixie Four, Morton, Hines, Sullivan, Stacy, Armstrong, J.P. Johnson, Waller, Chocolate Dandies, Lewis, Dupree, M.L. Williams, Tristano. Folkways 2809.

2999. *Jazz Africa.*

Featuring Herbie Hancock, Foday Musa Suso, Armando Peraza (10–90). Verve 847145–2; 847145–4.

3000. *The Jazz Age: New York in the Twenties.*

Selections by Red Nichols, Benny Goodman, Tommy Dorsey, Jimmy McPartland, Joe Venuti, Eddie Lang. Bluebird 3136–2-RB; 3136–4-RB.

3001. *The Jazz Arranger.*

Volume 1: 1928–1940—19 original recordings by Blue Rhythm Band, Cab Calloway, the Dorsey Brothers, Duke Ellington, Benny Goodman, Joe Haymes, Fletcher Henderson, Teddy Hill, Earl Hines, Claude Hopkins,

Harlan Lattimore, Jimmie Lunceford, Ben Pollack, Joe Venuti, Chick Webb (11–89). Columbia Jazz Masterpieces CK-45143; CJT-45143.

Volume 2: 1946–1963—performances by Al Cohn, Woody Herman and His Orchestra, Chubby Jackson and His Orchestra, Gene Krupa and His Orchestra, Elliott Lawrence and His Orchestra, John Lewis, Gerry Mulligan and His Orchestra, Oliver Nelson, George Russell, Bill Russo Orchestra, Carol Sloane, Claude Thornhill and His Orchestra (2–90). Columbia Jazz Masterpieces CK-45445; CT45445.

3002. *Jazz at the Opera House. Conrad Silvert Presents.*

Toshiko Akiyoshi, Charlie Haden, Herbie Hancock, Wynton Marsalis, Bobby Hutcherson, Wayne Shorter, Denny Zeitlin, others. Columbia: C2–38430.

3003. *Jazz at the Philharmonic.*

Hartford, 1953. Pablo Live 2308–240; PACD-2308–240–2; 52308–240. In Tokyo, 1953 (At the Nichigeki Theater). Pablo Live: PACD-2620–104–2. In Tokyo, 1983 ("Return to Happiness")—Ella Fitzgerald, Oscar Peterson, Zoot Sims, et al. Pablo Live: 2620–117; PACD-2620–117; 52620–117.

JATP All-Stars, 1983—Eddie "Lockjaw" Davis, Harry Edison, Al Grey, et al. Pablo 52310–882.

London, 1969: Louis Bellson, Benny Carter, Bob Cranshaw, Dizzy Gillespie, Coleman Hawkins, James Moody, Zoot Sims, Clark Terry, T-Bone Walker, Teddy Wilson (12–89). Pablo: 2620–119; PACD-2620–119–2; 52620–119. Montreux '75. Pablo: PACD-2310–748–2.

Stockholm '55: The Exciting Battle. Pablo: PACD-2310–713–2.

3004. *Jazz at the Philharmonic: Bird & Pres, the '46 Concerts.*

Charlie Parker, Lester Young, Dizzy Gillespie, Willie Smith, Charlie Ventura, Mel Powell, Al Kilian, Howard McGhee, Coleman Hawkins, Buck Clayton, Buddy Rich. Verve 833565–4.

3005. *Jazz Classics of New Orleans.*

Selections by Teddy Buckner, Russell Moore, Claude Luter, Sidney Bechet, Albert Nicholas, Peanuts Holland (6–91). Vogue: VG-670021.

3006. *Jazz Club.*

Alto Saxophone (15 tracks)—Charlie Parker, Bud Shank, Art Pepper, Phil Woods, Cannonball Adderley, Charlie Parker/Johnny Hodges/Benny Carter, Charlie Mariano, Paul Desmond, Sonny Stitt, Jackie McLean, Lee Konitz,

Gigi Gryce, Eric Dolphy, Herb Geller, Lee Konitz/"Pony" Poindexter/Phil Woods/Leo Wright. (1–90). Verve 840036–2; 840036–4.

Bass (15 tracks)—Slam Stewart, Chubby Jackson, Charles Mingus, Ray Brown, Oscar Pettiford, Percy Heath, Eddie Safranski, Paul Chambers, Red Mitchell, Sam Jones, Ron Carter, Neils-Henning Orsted-Pederson, Richard Davis, Jaco Pastorius, Stanley Clarke (1–90). Verve 840037–2; 840037–4.

Big Band—Benny Goodman, Woody Herman, Gene Krupa, Harry James, Lionel Hampton, Count Basie, Buddy Rich, Johnny Hodges, Dizzy Gillespie, Maynard Ferguson, Terry Gibbs, Pete Rugolo, Quincy Jones, Gerry Mulligan, Gil Evans, Oliver Nelson. Verve 840030–2; 840030–4.

Drums—Art Blakey, Jo Jones, Kenny Clarke, Max Roach, Shelly Manne, Elvin Jones, Philly Joe Jones, Billy Higgins, Dannie Richmond, Billy Cobham, Alphonse Mouzon, Gene Krupa, Buddy Rich, Tony Williams, Louis Bellson, Paul Humphrey, Willie Bobo. Verve 840033–2; 840033–4.

Guitar (17 tracks)—Les Paul, Chuck Wayne, Billy Bauer, Herb Ellis, Barney Kessel, Jimmy Raney, Tal Farlow, Wes Montgomery, Kenny Burrell, Joe Pass, Baden Powell, George Benson, Charlie Byrd, John McLaughlin, Larry Coryell and Philip Catherine, Jim Hall, Grant Green (1–90). Verve 840035–2; 840035–4.

Piano—Bud Powell, Thelonious Monk, Dodo Marmarosa, George Shearing, Lennie Tristano, Red Garland, John Lewis, Bill Evans, Erroll Garner, Oscar Peterson, Hank Jones, Tommy Flanagan, Horace Silver, Chick Corea, Herbie Hancock, Cecil Taylor, Keith Jarrett. Verve 840032–2; 840032–4.

Tenor Sax—Lester Young, Don Byas, Ben Webster, Dexter Gordon, Gene Ammons, Sonny Stitt, Johnny Griffin, Eddie "Lockjaw" Davis, Sonny Rollins, Al Cohn, Zoot Sims, Hank Mobley, Wardell Gray, Stan Getz, Wayne Shorter, John Coltrane, Joe Farrell, Booker Ervin, Yusef Lateef, Joe Henderson, Coleman Hawkins. Verve 840031–2; 840031–4.

Trombone (15 tracks)—Bill Harris, J.J. Johnson, Kai Winding, Melba Liston/Jimmy Cleveland/Frank Rehak/Slide Hampton, Jimmy Knepper, Bob Brookmeyer, Urbie Green, Jimmy Cleveland, Melba Liston/Bennie Green/Al Grey/Benny Powell, Curtis Fuller, Frank Rosolino, Grachan Moncur III, Slide Hampton/Albert Mangelsdorff/Aake Persson/J. Wigham, Julius Watkins, Don Elliott. Verve 840040–2; 840040–4.

Trumpet (15 tracks)—Louis Armstrong, Dizzy Gillespie, Miles Davis, Kenny Dorham, Clifford Brown, Lee Morgan, Clark Terry/Maynard Ferguson/Clifford Brown, Chet Baker, Nat Adderley, Thad Jones, Donald Byrd, Freddie Hubbard, Don Ellis, Roy Eldridge (1–90). Verve 840038–2; 840038–4.

Vibraphone—Red Norvo, Lionel Hampton, Lem Winchester, Milt Jackson, Terry Gibbs, Gary Burton, Victor Feldman, Cal Tjader, Bobby Hutcherson, Gary McFarland, Don Elliott, Marjorie Hyams, Dave Pike. Verve 840034–2; 840034–4.

Violin (10 tracks)—Joe Venuti, Stuff Smith, Ray Nance, Stephane Grappelli, Svend Asmussen and Stuff Smith, Jean-Luc Ponty, Don "Sugarcane" Harris, Didier Lockwood, Zbigniew Seifert, Michael Urbaniak (1–90). Verve 840039–2; 840039–4.

Vocal—Ella Fitzgerald, Billie Holiday, Sarah Vaughan, Anita O'Day, Dinah Washington, Astrud Gilberto, Nina Simone, Carmen McRae, Louis Armstrong, Jack Teagarden, Jimmy Rushing, Mel Tormé, Joe Williams, Billy Eckstine, Jon Hendricks, Dave Lambert. Verve 840029–2; 840029–4.

3007. *Jazz Club Mainstream.*

Alto Sax, Clarinet, & Flute—various artists. Polydor 845145–2; 845145–4.

Big Bands—various artists. Polydor 845153–2; 845153–4.

Dixieland—various artists. Polydor 845149–2; 845149–4.

Drums—various artists. Polydor 845148–2; 845148–4.

Guitar and Bass—various artists. Polydor 845150–2; 845150–4.

Piano—various artists. Polydor 845147–2; 845147–4.

Tenor and Baritone Sax—various artists. Polydor 845146–2; 845146–4.

Trombone—various artists. Polydor 845144–2; 845144–4.

Trumpet—various artists. Polydor 845151–2; 845151–4.

Vocal—various artists. Polydor 845152–2; 845152–4.

3008. *Jazz '84: Highlights for the IXth Moscow Jazz Festival.*

V. Budarin, V. Konovaltsev, V. Karminsky, G. Garanyan, M. Yuldybayev, et al. (10–88). Mobile Fidelity: MFCD-21–00894; MFSL-60–00894.

3009. *Jazz from Famous Door.*

Sharkey & Kings of Dixieland, Pecora & N.O. Jazz Band, Girard & N.O. 5. GHB 116.

3010. *Jazz from the USSR.*

Oleg Lundstrem, David Azarian Trio, Retro Quartet, Allegro Jazz Ensemble, Valery Mysovsky Trio, Leonid Chizhik, et al. (4–88). Mobile Fidelity: MFCD-21–00890.

3011. *Jazz in a Vertical Groove, 1926–28.*

Red Nichols, Miff Mole, Phil Napoleon, Jimmy Dorsey, Tommy Dorsey, et al. Biograph 12057.

3012. *Jazz in the Thirties.*

Forty original recordings by Benny Goodman, Joe Venuti, Eddie Lang, Gene Krupa, Bud Freeman, et al. Swing: CDSW-8457–58.

3013. *The Jazz Life.*

Features Charles Mingus, Max Roach, Booker Little, Kenny Dorham, Lucky Thompson, Kenny Clarke, Eric Dolphy, Tommy Flanagan, Roy Eldridge, Booker Ervin, Benny Bailey, Jimmy Knepper, Ted Curson, Julian Priester, Cecil Payne, Martial Solal, Jo Jones, Dannie Richmond, Walter Benton, Cal Massey, Lightnin' Hopkins, Julius Watkins, Hugh Brodie, Patti Brown, Jimmy Garrison, G.T. Hogan, Peter Trunk, Lonnie Hillyer, Charles McPherson, Nico Bunick, John "Peck" Morrison. (5–91). Candid: CCD-79019.

3014. *Jazz Piano Essential Series. Concord Records Series.*

This is a select series of thematic compact disc collections featuring the most essential recorded performances by some of the finest pianists in jazz.

The Music of Thelonious Monk.

Features Kenny Barron, Fred Hersch, Hank Jones, George Shearing, and many more. CD 4908.

The Music of Richard Rodgers.

Features Richie Beirach, JoAnne Brackeen, Gene Harris, Cedar Walton, and many more. CD 4909.

The Music of Cole Porter.

Features Kenny Drew, Jr., Dick Hyman, Dave McKenna, Denny Zeitlin, and several others. CD 4910.

The Music of George Gershwin.

Features George Cables, Sir Roland Hanna, Gene Harris, Jessica Williams, and others. CD 4911.

The Music of Jerome Kern.

Features Richie Beirach, Marian McPartland, Ralph Sutton, Cedar Walton, and many others. CD 4912.

The Music of Duke Ellington.

Features Toshiko Akiyoshi, Roger Kellaway, Dave McKenna, Marian McPartland, and several others. CD 4913.

3015. *Jazz Piano, Smithsonian Recordings.*

Sixty-nine performances of piano greats, including Jelly Roll Morton, Nat King Cole, Duke Ellington, Art Tatum, Oscar Peterson, Keith Jarrett, and many more.

Volume 1—Jelly Roll Morton, James P. Johnson, Willie "The Lion" Smith, Fats Waller, Earl Hines, Teddy Wilson, Jimmy Yancey, Meade "Lux" Lewis, Pete Johnson, Avery Parrish with Erskine Hawkins, Count Basie, Billy Kyle (rec. 1924–1970). Smithsonian Collection: RD-0391.

Volume 2—Mary Lou Williams, Art Tatum, Duke Ellington, Jess Stacy, King Cole Trio, Erroll Garner, Jimmy Jones, Bud Powell Trio, Lennie Tristano Trio (rec. 1939–1955). Smithsonian Collection: RD-0392.

Volume 3—Dodo Marmarosa Trio, Ellis Larkins, Dave McKenna, Al Haig, Oscar Peterson Trio, Jimmy Rowles, Thelonious Monk Quintet, Thelonious Monk, Phineas Newborn, Jr., Horace Silver, Martial Solal Trio, Herbie Nichols Trio, Hank Jones, Tommy Flanagan and Hank Jones, Tommy Flanagan Trio (rec. 1946–1978). Smithsonian Collection: RD-0393.

Volume 4—John Lewis, Randy Weston, Ray Bryant, Bill Evans Trio, Bill Evans, McCoy Tyner, Chick Corea, Keith Jarrett, Herbie Hancock (rec. 1955–1972). Smithsonian Collection: RD-0394.

3016. *Jazz Record Story, Volume 1.*

Art Hodes, Duke DuVal, George Bruines, Rod Cless, Joe Grauso (trans. from 78s; rec. date unknown) Jazzology 82.

3017. *The Jazz Singers.*

Bessie Smith, Louis Armstrong, Fats Waller, Mildred Bailey, Ivie Anderson, Billie Holiday, Sarah Vaughan, Billy Eckstine, King Pleasure, Annie Ross, Joe Carrol, Ray Charles, Mose Allison, Ella Fitzgerald, Dinah Washington, Jimmy Rushing, Lambert/Hendricks/Ross, Abbey Lincoln, Aretha Franklin, Mark Murphy, Eddie Jefferson, Joe Williams, Flora Purim (rec. 1927–1975). Prestige: P-24113; 5P-24113.

3018. *The Jazz Singers: Vocals by Great Instrumentalists.*

Selections by Louis Armstrong, Fats Waller, Jack Teagarden, Dizzy Gillespie, Bunny Berigan, Jelly Roll Morton, et al. (10–91). Bluebird 3137–2-RB; 3137–4-RB.

3019. *Jazz and Slows: 1940–1984.*

Selections by Count Basie, Julian Dash, Duke Ellington, Mercer Ellington, Erroll Garner, Stephane Grappelli, Earl Hines, Billie Holiday, Thad Jones, Sonny Rollins, Ben Webster. EPM: FDC-5701.

3020. *Jazz Trumpet Volume 2.*

Modern Time: Dizzy Gillespie, Fats Navarro, Miles Davis, Kenny Dorham, Clifford Brown, Thad Jones, Donald Byrd, Lee Morgan, Chet Baker, Nat Adderley, Freddie Hubbard (rec. 1948–1980). Prestige: P-24112.

3021. *Jazz Trumpet Volumes 1 & 2.*

Classic Jazz to Modern Swing Times (6–90). Prestige: PCD-2301–2.

3022. *The Jazzology Poll Winners 1964.*

Kid Thomas Valentine, George Lewis, "Big" Jim Robinson, Don Ewell, et al. (3–86). GHB 200.

3023. *Jelly Roll Morton. Smithsonian Recordings. Three Volumes.*

Volume 1—The best of his 1923–26 solo piano recordings.

Volume 2—19 of his compositions for New Orleans-style jazz bands.

Volume 3—The late 1920s and early 1930s, and samples from the end of his career.

3024. *Morton, Ferdinand "Jelly Roll."*

Blues and Stomps from Rare Piano Rolls. (rec. 1983–85) Biograph BCD-111.

Chicago Days, Vol. 1 (with his Red Hot Peppers). (rec. 1926–27) EPM FDC 5108.

The Complete Piano Solos 1923–1939.

Music Memoria 34000.

Great Original Performances 1926–1934. ABC Music 836–199–2.

The Greatest Ragtime of the Century (three piano rolls) Immortal Milestone M-2003.

Jelly Roll Morton with Roy Palmer, Wilson Townes, Charles Harris, Jasper Taylor, Jack Russell, Boyd Senter, Ray Bowling, Clay Jefferson, King Oliver (rec. 1923–26) Milestone M-47018; MCD-47018–2.

Jelly Roll Morton, Vol. 1 (1923–24) Masters of Jazz MJCD-3019.

Jelly Roll Morton, Vol. 2 (1924–26) Masters of Jazz MJCD-3020.

The Jelly Roll Morton Centennial: His Complete Victor Recordings (5 cassette, 5 CD set, 111 performances from 1926–30 and 1939) Bluebird 6588–2-RB; 6588–4-R.

The Library of Congress Recordings, Volume One. Solo Art SACD-11.

Mr. Jelly Lord. Tomato R2–70384. (1923–24) Milestone 2–47018; MCD-47018–2.

1923–24, w. Bernie Young, Wilson Townes, Charles Harris, Jasper Taylor, Matty Dominique, Zue Robertson, Horace Eubanks, Boyd Senter, W. E. Burton, Jack Russell, Russell Senter. Classics 584.

1923–27, with Lammar Wright, Harry Cooper, Ed Lewis, Paul Webster, Thamon Hayes, Woody Walder, Sam Tall, LaForest Dent, Leroy Berry, Willie Hall, Willie McWashington, Harlan Leonard, Vernon Page, Jack Washington. Classics 549.

The Pianist & Composer:

Volume 1: with Joe "King" Oliver, Voltaire de Faut, et al. (rec. 1923–26). Smithsonian Collection of Recordings CDRD-043.

Volume 2: From Chicago to New York 1927–28, with George Mitchell, Gerald Reeves, Johnny Dodds, Stump Evans, Bud Scott, Quinn Wilson, Baby Dodds, Edwin Swayze, Louis Taylor, Walter Thomas, Leslie Corley, Hayes Alvis, Wallace Bishop, Frances Hereford, Johnny Dunn, Herb Fleming, Garvin Bushell, Harry Hull, Mort Perry, Ward Pinkett, Geechie Fields, Omer Simeon, Lee Blair, Bill Benford, Tommy Benford. EPM 982202.

Volume 3: Piano Creole 1926–39. EPM 982212.

3025. *The Kings of Swing.*

Sixteen big band selections by Benny Goodman, Harry James, Tex Beneke, Bob Crosby, Les Brown, Charlie Barnet. Bridge (Switzerland) 100.017–2.

3026. *The Kings of Swing Volumes 1–5.*

Volume 1—Benny Goodman, Woody Herman, Harry James. Master Digital CD-19901.

Volume 2—Jimmie Lunceford, Glenn Miller, Artie Shaw. Master Digital CD-19902.

Volume 3—Count Basie, Duke Ellington, Baby Cox & the Ellington Orchestra, Cab Calloway, Lena Horne. Master Digital CD-19903.

Volume 4—Tommy Dorsey, Ella Fitzgerald, Teddy Wilson. Master Digital CD-19904.

Volume 5—"Live Concert of New York City" (Armstrong, Teagarden, Holiday, Tatum, Pettiford, Norvo, Eldridge, et al.). Master Digital CD-19905.

Volumes 1–5 (boxed set of above). Master Digital CD-19900.

3027. *Laughter from the Hip: 24 Jazz Comedy Classics.*

Sidney Bechet and His New Orleans Footwarmers, Hoagy Carmichael and His Orchestra, Ethel Waters and Her Ebony Four, Don Redman and His Orchestra, Wingy Malone and His Orchestra, Red Allen and His Orchestra, Eight Squares and a Critic (Bud Freeman), Bud Freeman and His V-Disc Jumpers, Charlie Shavers with Tommy Dorsey and His Orchestra, George Lewis Band, Eddie Johnson's Crackerjacks, Harry Roy and His Bat Club Boys, McKinney's Cotton Pickers, the Three Keys, the Slim Gaillard Trio, John Kirby and His Orchestra, Clarence Williams' Novelty Band, Ted Nichols and His Five Pennies, the Washboard Rhythm Kings, Woody Herman and His Orchestra (the Band That Plays the Blues), Fats Waller and His Rhythm, Ted Weems and His Orchestra, with Perry Como & Gary Moore, Leo Watson and His Orchestra, Louis Armstrong and His Orchestra. Jazz: J-CD-20.

3028. *Legendary Black Jazz Stars in Their First Films, 1929–34.*

Bessie Smith, Louis Armstrong, Cab Calloway, et al. Biograph M-3.

3029. *Lennie Tristano Memorial Concert, Town Hall, New York City, January 28, 1979.*

Record 1—Connie Crothers; Liz Gorrill; Fran Canisius; Fran Canisius & Liz Gorrill; Lloyd Lifton & Murray Wall.

Record 2—Sheila Jordan with Harold Danko, Cameron Brown & Lou Grassi; Virg Dzurinko; Larry Meyer.

Record 3—Lenny Popkin, Peter Scattaretico & Stan Fortuna; Sal Mosca.

Record 4—Nomi Rosen; Nomi Rosen & Connie Crothers; Warne Marsh, Eddie Gomez & Peter Scattaretico.

Record 5—Lynn Anderson, Liz Gorrill; Max Roach. JR-3.

3030. *The Legends of Jazz Guitar, Volumes 1 & 2.*

Volume 1—Frankie Trumbauer & His Orchestra with featured guitarist Eddie Lang, the Kansas City Six with featured guitarists Eddie Durham & Freddie Green, Jack Teagarden & His Orchestra with featured guitarist Allan Reuss, George Barnes, Charlie Christian, the Cat & the Fiddle with featured guitarist Tiny Grimes, Charlie Parker Septet with featured guitarist Barney Kessel, Laurindo Almeida Quartet, Tal Farlow, Howard Roberts, Wes Montgomery, Lenny Breau, Lenny Tristano w. Featured Guitarist: Billy Bauer, Larry Coryell w. Featured Guitarists: Larry Coryell & John McLaughlin, Jim Hall, Derek Bailey, John Scofield (10–90). Rhino R21S-70717; R41H-70717.

Volume 2—selections by Carl Kress & Dick McDonough, Charlie Barnet & His Orchestra (Bus Etri), the King Cole Trio (Oscar Moore), Johnny Smith Quintet (Johnny Smith), Django Reinhardt, the Oscar Peterson Trio (Herb Ellis), Kenny Burrell with John Coltrane, Return to Forever Featuring Chick Corea (Bill Connors), Joe Pass, Jim Hall Trio, Pat Methany Group, Ralph Towner, Art Tatum & His Band (John Collins), Mary Lou Williams; Girl Stars (Mary Osbornbe), Stanley Jordan (3–91). Rhino R21S-70722; R41H-70722.

3031. *Marian McPartland Piano Jazz Series. Concord Records Series.*

The Piano Jazz Series was selected from the Peabody award-winning National Public Radio show, hosted by Marian McPartland, and featuring performances and insightful conversations with some of jazz's most important artists.

Mary Lou Williams and Marian McPartland.

Mary Lou was the last to be recorded in this important series. Discusses her pioneering efforts to help women in jazz and several other issues. CD 12045.

Lionel Hampton and Marian McPartland.

Hampton enlivens the program with his effusive personality and knowledge. He jams on vibraphone with Marian McPartland on "Teach Me Tonight" and his own classic "Flying Home." Hampton also plays the piano on and sings on "Sweet Georgia Brown" and "Mack The Knife." In addition, he talks candidly and insightfully about his life in jazz, including the first time the vibraphone appeared on a jazz recording and the beginnings of the Benny Goodman Quartet. CD12046.

Dave Brubeck and Marian McPartland.

McPartland engages Brubeck in conversation and reveals deep insight into his music. The two play solos and duets, and cover several of Brubeck's time-honored compositions, including "Summer Song" and "The Duke." CD 12043.

Rosemary Clooney and Marian McPartland.

McPartland engages Clooney in conversation about her career and the early days with her sister, Betty. Offers insight into the business of music and professional interpretation of songs. CD 12041.

Chick Corea and Marian McPartland.

Corea engages McPartland in conversation about his approach to improvisation, piano playing, and his musical influences that range from Thelonious Monk to Wolfgang Amadeus Mozart. He performs standards as well as some of his classic compositions. CD 12040.

Bill Evans and Marian McPartland.

Offers deep insight into Evans's music, aesthetics, and philosophy. McPartland provides historical insight into the man and his artistry, and the two of them engage in wonderful interpretation of several tunes. CD 12038.

Dizzy Gillespie and Marian McPartland.

Gillespie discusses his relationship with artists such as Duke Ellington, Thelonious Monk, Chano Pozo, and Charles Parker. He also shares his musical philosophy, and plays his trumpet in both solo contexts and with McPartland accompanying. CD 12042.

Carmen McRae and Marian McPartland.

A program of duet performances and conversation. In addition, McRae sings and accompanies herself on piano, and reveals the many musical influences that shaped her career and style. CD 12039.

Oscar Peterson and Marian McPartland.

Between candid conversations about his approach and musical philosophy, Peterson demonstrates his impeccable musical lines, phrasing, touch, feel, and virtuosity. A highlight of the recoding is Peterson playing both his own compositions and tunes such as "Take the 'A' Train" in time, and as a duet with McPartland. CD 12033.

3032. *Master Jazz Piano.*

Hines, S. White, C. Jackson, C. Hopkins, McShann. Mas. J. 8105.

Vol. 3—T. Wilson, Hines, Hearn, S. White, Dunham. Mas. J. 8105.

Vol. 4—McShann, Hines, Hearn, Smalls, C. Jackson. Mas. J. 8129.

3033. *Masters of the Modern Piano.*

Bud Powell, Cecil Taylor, Mary Lou Williams, Paul Bley, Wynton Kelly, Bill Evans (rec. '55–'56) 2-Verve 2514; 8T2–2514; CT-2–2514.

3034. Garrod, Charles. *The A Jazz Glenn Miller Lives Series Companion.* Zephyrhills, Fla.: Joyce Music Publications.

A cassette tape series. Accompanied by a book, which lists the titles contained on each cassette. The series contains 43 volumes, covering broadcasts from numerous venues, on different dates, from June 1938 to November 1944. The broadcasts are as follows:

C– 2101 Volume 1–June, 1938: Paradise Rest, New York

C–2102 Volume 2–June 27, 1938–January 18, 1939

C–2103 Volume 3–January 18, 1939–March 26, 1939

C–2104 Volume 4–March 31, 1939–April 18, 1939, Meadowbrook

C–2105 Volume 5–April 18, 1939, Meadowbrook–June 30, 1939, Glen Island

C–2106 Volume 6–June 10, 1939, New York–August 4, 1939, Glen Island

C–2107 Volume 7–August 4, 1939, Flen Island–October 6, 1939, Carnegie Hall

C–2108 Volume 8–October 6, 1939, Carnegie Hall–November 24, 1939, Meadowbrook

C–2109 Volume 9–November 25, 1939–January 4, 1940

C–2110 Volume 10–January 4, 1940–January 10, 1940

C–2111 Volume 11–January 11, 1940–February 26, 1940

C–2112 Volume 12–February 26, 1940–April 3, 1940

C–2113 Volume 13–April 4, 1940–April 25, 1940

C–2114 Volume 14–April 30, 1940–May 28, 1940

C–2115 Volume 15–May 28, 1940–June 13, 1940

C–2116 Volume 16–June 30, 1940–July 16, 1940

C–2117 Volume 17–July 16, 1940–July 30, 1940

C–2118 Volume 18–July 30, 1940–August 14, 1940

C–2119 Volume 19–August 14, 1940–September 11, 1940

C–2120 Volume 20–September 11, 1940–October 8, 1940

C–2121 Volume 21–October 9, 1940–November 4, 1940

C–2122 Volume 22–November 6, 1940–November 18, 1940

C–2123 Volume 23–November 18, 1940–November 28, 1940

C–2124 Volume 24–December 4, 1940–January 1, 1941

C–2125 Volume 25–January 7, 1941–March 25, 1941

C–2126 Volume 26–February 20, 1941–May 7, 1941

C–2127 Volume 27–May 8, 1941–July 31, 1941

C–2128 Volume 28–August 13, 1941–September 3, 1941

C–2129 Volume 29–September 3, 1941–November 8, 1941

C–2130 Volume 30–November 8, 1941–November 15, 1941

C–2131 Volume 31–November 29, 1941–December 27, 1941

C–2132 Volume 32–December 27, 1941–February 17, 1942

C–2133 Volume 33–February 24, 1942–May 6, 1942

C–2134 Volume 34–May 6, 1942–June 23, 1942

C–2135 Volume 35–June 23, 1942–July 14, 1942

C–2136 Volume 36–July 15, 1942–August 25, 1942

C–2137 Volume 37–September 9, 1943

C–2138 Volume 38–Late 1943

C–2139 Volume 39–September, 1943–December 11, 1943

C–2140 Volume 40–December 11, 1943–June, 1944

C–2141 Volume 41–November, 1944 BBC Propaganda Broadcast with Ilsa (in German)

C–2142 Volume 42–November, 1944 BBC 2nd Propaganda Broadcast

C–2143 Volume 43–November, 1944 BBC Propaganda Broadcasts continued plus air checks

3035. *The Modern Art of Jazz.*

Selections by Hank Jones/Oscar Pettiford/Charlie Smith, Julius Watkins/ Joe Puma/Mat Matthews/Oscar Pettiford/Kenny Clarke, Herbie Mann/Joe Puma/Mat Matthews/Oscar Pettiford/Kenny Clarke, Dick Katz/Art Farmer/ Gigi Gryce/Mat Matthews/Oscar Pettiford/Kenny Clarke, Milt Hinton/ Zoot Sims/Bob Brookmeyer/Gus Johnson/John Williams, Milt Hinton/ Hank Jones/Al Cohn/Frank Rehak/Osie Johnson (8–91). Biograph: BCD-120.

3036. *Modern Jazz Piano Album.*

Bud Powell, Lennie Tristano, Herbie Nichols, Dodo Marmarosa, George Wallington, Horace Silver with Sonny Stitt, Kenny Dorham (rec. 1946–1956). Savoy Jazz 2-SJL-2247; ZDS-4425; SJK-2247.

3037. *Montreux Collection.*

Basie, J. Griffin, M. Jackson, Eldridge, J. Pass, O. Peterson, E. Peterson, E. Fitzgerald, Gillespie, and others (rec. '75) 2-Pablo 2625707; S25707.

3038. *New American Music Volume 1.*

Gil Evans, Milford Graves, M. L. Williams, S. Rivers, S. Murray. Folk 33901.

3039. *New Music: Second Waves.*

Paul Bley, Bill Dixon, Bob Pozar, Archie Shepp, Marzette Watts (rec. 1962–68). Savoy Jazz 2- SJL-2235.

3040. *The New New Orleans Music.*

Jump Jazz: Ed Frank Quintet/Ramsey McLean & the Survivors (rec. 1988). Rounder 2065; CD-2065; C-2065. New Music Jazz: New Orleans Saxophone Ensemble/Improvising Arts Ensemble (rel. 1988). Rounder 2066; CD-2066; C-2066.

Vocal Jazz: Germaine Bazzle & Friends/Lady BJ, with Ellis Marsalis Quartet (rel. 1988). Rounder 2067; CD-2067; C-2067.

3041. *On the Edge: Progressive Music Pushing the Boundaries.*

Selections by Ronald Shannon Jackson, Steve Kahn, Anthony Braxton, Courtney Pine, Paranoise, Startled Insects, Ornette Coleman, Marc Ribot, Gary Windo, Defunkt, Power Tools (1–91). Antilles 422–848210–2; 422–848210–4.

3042. *One Night with Blue Note Preserved.*

Volume 1 (10–85). Blue Note B21Y-46147.

Volume 2 (10–85). Blue Note B21Y-46148.

Volume 3 (10–85). Blue Note B21Y-46149.

Volume 4 (10–85). Blue Note B21Y-46150.

3043. *One O'Clock Jump: Swing Classics of the Golden Era by the Bands That Made Them Famous.*

Tommy Dorsey and His Orchestra, Bunny Berigan and His Orchestra, Count Basie and His Orchestra, Bob Crosby and His Orchestra, Duke Ellington and His Orchestra, Teddy Wilson and His Orchestra, Artie Shaw and His Orchestra, Ziggy Elman and His Orchestra, Jimmy Lunceford and

His Orchestra, the All-Star Band, Gene Krupa and His Orchestra, Glenn Miller and His Orchestra, Hal Kemp and His Orchestra, Woody Herman and His Orchestra, Benny Goodman and His Orchestra, Lionel Hampton and His Orchestra, Jack Teagarden and His Orchestra. Seville LPSVL-211; CDSVL-211; CSVL-211.

3044. *Open Boundaries.*

Compositions by Paul Schoenfield, Mary Ellen Childs, Leslie B. Dunner, Lloyd Ultan, Arthur Campbell; performed by Young-Nam Kim, Peter Howard, Paul Schoenfield, Relache Ensemble: (Wesley Hall, Chuck Holdeman, Guy Klucebsek, Barbara Noska, Marshall Taylor, Jerry Tanenbaum), Carol Sebron, Leslie B. Dunner, Jerry Rubino, Tamas Strasser, Robert Thompson. Innova: CDMN-108; CMN-108.

3045. *Piano Giants.*

Ellington, Hines, Tatum, Garner, Monk, Powell, Tristano, Haig, Shearing, Lewis, Silver, Hawes, Timmons, Peterson, Newborn, Jamal, Garland, Kelly, Hancock, Zawinul, Corea, Jarrett, Tyner. Prestige 2- P-24052.

3046. *Piano One.*

Solo piano performances by Ryuichi Sakamoto, Eddie Jobson, Joachim Kuhn, Eric Watson (8–66). Private Music 2004–1-P; 2004–2-P; 2004–4-P.

3047. *The Piano Players.*

Dolo Coker, Kenny Drew, Barry Harris, Duke Jordan, Lou Levy, Jimmy Rowles, Mickey Tucker, Cedar Walton (rec. 1975–78). Xanadu 171.

3048. *Piano Two.*

Yanni, Suzanne Ciani, Michael Reisman, Joachim Kuhn (1–88). Private Music 2027–1-P; 2027–2-P; 2027–4-P.

3049. *Pioneers of the Jazz Guitar.*

Eddie Lang, Lonnie Johnson, Carl Kress, Dick McDonough, Nick Lucas, John Cali, Tony Gottuso. Yazoo 1057; C-1057.

3050. *Prestige All-Stars.*

Earthy, with Kenny Burrell, Al Cohn, Art Farmer, Hal McKusick, Mal Waldron, Teddy Koick, Ed Thigpen (previously Prestige 7102) (reissue 12–85). Fantasy/OJC: OJC-1707. Roots, with Idrees Sulieman, Pepper Adams, Cecil Payne, Frank Rehak, Jimmy Cleveland, Bill Evans, Tommy Flanagan, Doug Watkins, Louis Hayes, Elvin Jones (rec. 1957) (previously Prestige 8202). Fantasy/OJC: OJC-062.

3051. *Prestige Soul Masterpieces.*

Selections by Charles Earland, Billy Butler, Jack McDuff & Gene Ammons, Charles Kynard, Oliver Nelson with King Curtis & Jimmy Forest, Rusty Bryant, Shirley Scott & Stanley Turrentine, Willis Jackson Quintet, Houston Person, Harold Mabern, Eddie "Lockjaw" Davis Quintet, Red Hollow, Jack McDuff, Arnett Cobb, Richard "Groove" Holmes (8–88). Fantasy/OJC: OJC-1201.

3052. *Progressive Records All Star Tenor Sax Spectacular.*

Scott Hamilton, Peter Loeb, Flip Phillips, Frank Sokolow, Ray Turner, Bennie Wallace, with Derek Smith, Howie Collins, George Mraz, Ronnie Bedford (rec. 1977). Progressive: PRO-7019; PROC-7109.

3053. *Progressive Records All Star Trombone Spectacular.*

Art Baron, Sam Burtis, Gerry Chamberlain, Mickey Gravine, Jimmy Knepper, Rod Levitt, Sonny Russo, with Roland Hanna, Bucky Pizzarelli, Earl May, Ronnie Bedford (rec. 1977). Progressive: PRO-7018; PROC-7018.

3054. *Progressive Records All Star Trumpet Spectacular.*

Volume 1—Harold Lieberman, Markie Markowitz, Howard McGhee, Hannibal Marvin Peterson, Lou Soloff, Danny Stiles, with Derek Smith, Bucky Pizzarelli, Richard Davis, Ronnie Bedford (rec. 1977). Progressive: PRO-7015; PROC-7015.

Volume 2—John Dearth, John Eckert, Tom Harrell, Danny Hayes, Mike Lawrence, Danny Moore, Waymon Reed, with Jimmy Rowles, Michael Moore, Ronnie Bedford (rec. 1977). Progressive: PRO-7017; PROC-7107.

3055. *The Riverside History of Classic Jazz.*

Selections by Blind Lemon Jefferson, Rev. J. M. Gates, Sodero's Military Band, Fred Van Eps, Scott Joplin, James Scott, Joseph Lamb, Jelly Roll Morton, Cow Cow Davenport, Ma Rainey, Bessie Smith, Ida Cox, Chippie Hill, Big Bill Broonzy, King Oliver's Creole Jazz Band, New Orleans Rhythm Kings, Original Memphis Melody Boys, Red Onion Jazz Babies, Wesley Wallace, Jimmy Yancey, Cripple Clarence Lofton, Meade Lux Lewis, Art Hodes, Pete Johnson, Johnny Dodds, Tiny Parham, Freddie Keppard's Jazz Cardinals, Barrelhouse Five, State Street Ramblers, Lovie Austin's Blues Serenades, Doc Cook's Dreamland Orchestra, Muggsy Spanier's Stomp Six, Bix Beiderbecke, the Wolverines, the Original Wolverines, Charles Pierce Orchestra, Jungle Kings, Wingy Manone, James P. Johnson, Fats Waller, Cliff Jackson, Clarence Williams, Duke Ellington's

Washingtonians, Fletcher Henderson Orchestra, Original Memphis Five, California Ramblers, Red and Miff's Stompers, Wild Bill Davison, Hank Lawson, Kid Ory, Bunk Johnson, George Lewis, Lu Watter's Yerba Buena Jazz Band, Bob Helm's Riverside Roustabouts, Dixieland Rhythm Kings. Riverside 5-: RB-005.

3056. *The Smithsonian Collection of Classic Jazz.*

Volume 1—selections by Scott Joplin, Jelly Roll Morton, Bessie Smith, King Oliver, Sidney Bechet, James P. Johnson, Louis Armstrong, Frankie Trumbauer, Bix Beiderbecke, Jimmie Noone (rec. 1916–1944) (10–91). Smithsonian CDRD-033–1.

Volume 2—selections by Fletcher Henderson, Red Nichols, Bennie Moten, Fats Waller, Meade "Lux" Lewis, Coleman Hawkins, Billie Holiday, Ella Fitzgerald, Art Tatum, Jimmie Lunceford, Gene Krupa, Chocolate Dandies, Hot Club of France, Count Basie, Benny Goodman (rec. 1926–1953) (10–91). Smithsonian CDRD-033–2.

Volume 3—selections by Duke Ellington, Slam Stewart, Dizzy Gillespie, Charlie Parker, Erroll Garner, Bud Powell, Dexter Gordon, Todd Dameron (rec. 1927–1951) (10–91). Smithsonian CDRD-033–3.

Volume 4—selections by Miles Davis, Lennie Tristano, Sarah Vaughan, Thelonious Monk, Horace Silver, Charles Mingus, Modern Jazz Quartet, Sonny Rollins (rec. 1948–1973) (10–91). Smithsonian CDRD-033–4.

Volume 5—selections by Sonny Rollins, Wes Montgomery, Miles Davis, Bill Evans, John Coltrane, Ornette Coleman, World Saxophone Quartet (rec. 1956–1981) (10–91). Smithsonian CDRD-033–5.

3057. *The Smithsonian Collection of Jazz Piano.*

Volume 1—selections by Jelly Roll Morton, James P. Johnson, Willie "The Lion" Smith, Fats Waller, Earl Hines, Teddy Wilson, Jimmy Yancey, Meade "Lux" Lewis, Pete Johnson, Avery Parrish (10–91). Smithsonian CDRD-039–1.

Volume 2—selections by Mary Lou Williams, Art Tatum, Duke Ellington, Jess Stacy, Nat King Cole, Erroll Garner, Jimmy Jones, Bud Powell, Lennie Tristano (10–91). Smithsonian CDRD-039–2.

Volume 3—selections by Dodo Marmarosa, Dave McKenna, Al Haig, Oscar Peterson, Thelonious Monk, Phineas Newborn, Jr., Horace Silver, Herbie Nichols, Hank Jones, Tommy Flanagan (10–91). Smithsonian CDRD-039–3.

Volume 4—selections by John Lewis, Randy Weston, Ray Bryant, Bill Evans, McCoy Tyner, Chick Corea, Keith Jarrett, Herbie Hancock (10–91). Smithsonian CDRD-039-4.

3058. *Columbia Jazz Masterpieces.*

The 1930's: Big Bands—16 selections by Goodman, Ellington, Basie, Cab Calloway, et al. Columbia Jazz Masterpieces: CK-40651; CJT-40651.

The 1930's: The Singers—Henry Allen, Louis Armstrong, Mildred Bailey, Connie Boswell, the Boswell Sisters, Chick Bullock, Bing Crosby & the Mills Brothers, Duke Ellington, Ted Lewis, Louis Prima, Don Redman, Spirits of Rhythm, Jack Teagarden, Ethel Waters, Midge Williams, Teddy Wilson (1–88). Columbia Jazz Masterpieces: CK-40847; CJT-40847.

The 1930's: Small Combos—Jack Purvis, the Chocolate Dandies, the Rhythmakers, Henry Allen, Wingie Manone, Red Norvo, Jones-Smith Inc., Stuff Smith, Teddy Wilson, Roy Eldridge, Cootie Williams, the Gotham Stompers, Frankie Newton, Sidney Bechet, Chu Berry, John Kirby (10–87). Columbia Jazz Masterpieces: CK-40833; CJT-40833.

The 1940's: The Singers—16 selections by Billie Holiday, Anita O'Day, Peggy Lee, Cab Calloway, et al. Columbia Jazz Masterpieces: CK-40652; CJT-40652.

The 1940's: The Small Groups: New Directions—Woody Herman & His Woodchoppers, Gene Krupa Jazz Trio, Harry James & His Sextet (rec. 1945–47) (7–88). Columbia Jazz Masterpieces: CK-44222.

1944: Esquire Jazz All-Stars—Art Tatum, Oscar Pettiford, Sid Catlett, Coleman Hawkins, Roy Eldridge, Billie Holiday, (rec. Jan. 16 & 18 during live broadcasts). Air check 27.

The 1950's: The Singers—selections by Billie Holiday, Louis Armstrong, Jimmy Rushing, Sarah Vaughan, Joe Williams, Betty Carter, Lambert Hendricks & Ross, et al. Columbia Jazz Masterpieces: CK-40799; CJT-40799.

3059. *Swing That Music: The Singers, The Soloists, and The Big Bands 1929–1956. Smithsonian Recordings.*

Ninety-four performances. Booklet contains comments on the artists, music, and bands. Includes Duke Ellington, Louis Armstrong, Mildred Bailey, Chris Connor, and many more.

3060. *The Women: Classic Female Jazz Artists 1939–1952.*

Mary Lou Williams's Girl Stars, Beryl Booker Trio, Vivian Garry Quintet, Una Mae Carlisle, International Sweethearts of Rhythm, Hazel Scott with the Sextet of the Rhythm Club of London, Alberta Hunter, Mildred Bailey, Helen Ward with Gene Krupa and His Swing Band, Barbara Carrol Trio, Kay Davis with Duke Ellington and His Orchestra. Bluebird 6755–2-RB; 6755–4-RB.

XIV

Jazz Journals: Domestic and Foreign

3061. *ASCAP Jazz Notes.* New York: Lynn Farnol Group, 1963– vol. l–. Issued à 12.

3062. *L'actualité; revue du jazz international et du spectacle.* Bruxelles: 1944–. Issued à 12.

3063. *L'actuel jazz; musique contemporaine, théatre, poésie.* Paris: Claude Delcoo; Plessis-Robinson.

3064. *American Jazz Monthly.* Flushing: American Jazz Club, fl. ca. 1944. Superseded by *American Jazz Review.*

3065. *American Jazz Review.* Flushing: American Jazz Club, 1945–1947, vl-3n4. Issued à 12. Superseded American Jazz Monthly.

3066. *Annual Review of Jazz Studies.* Newark, N.J.: Rutgers University.

3067. Arbeitsgemeinschaaft Norddeutscher Jazz Club. *Mitteilungsblatt.* Hamburg: Jazz Club Itzehoe, 1956–. Supersedes *Jazzfreund.*

3068. *Berlin Jazz.* Berlin: Jazz Club Berlin, 1955–1958, vol. l–[4?].

3069. *Bielefelder Katalog; Verzeichnis der Jazz-Schallplatten.* Bielefeld: Bielefelder Verlagsanstalt, 1960–. Issued à 1.

3070. *Black Music and Jazz Review.* London: fl. 1978. Issued à 12.

3071. *Black Music Research Journal.* Chicago: Center for Black Music Research, Columbia College Chicago.

3072. Bremen Radio, Bremen. *Jazzbrief.* Bremen: 1966–. Issued à 12.

3073. British Institute of Jazz Studies. *Newsletter.* London?: 1966–.

3074. *Cadence; the American Review of Jazz and Blues.* Redwood, N.Y.: Bob Rusch, 197?–. Issued à 12.

3075. *Coda; Canada's Jazz Magazine.* Toronto: John Norris, 1958–, vol. 1–. Issued à 12.

3076. *Collana di musica jazz.* Milano: Messaggierie Musicale, 1960–, vol. 1–. Also known as *Collezione di musica jazz.*

3077. *Current Musicology: A Special Commemorative Festschrift in Honor of Mark Tucker.* New York: Columbia University Music Department; 2001–2002.

3078. *Dance Band and Jazz Musician.* Ponders End: Tots & Woolf, 1961–, vol. 1–. Issued à 7.

3079. *Decca Complete Catalogue.* London: Decca Record Co., 1967–. Issued à 1. RILM 70/210.

3080. *Different Drummer; the Magazine for Jazz Listeners.* Rochester: BOAPW, 1973-, vol. 1–. Issued à 12.

3081. *Discography for the Jazz Student.* London: 1942–1947. Issued à 26 (1942–1944), irregularly. Merged with *Jazz Music.*

3082. *Doctor Jazz; contactblad voor liefhebbers en versamelaars van classic jazz, blues en verwante volksmuziek.* Wageningen: J. Nijland, 1963–, no. 1–. Issued à 6.

3083. *Down Beat.* Chicago: Maher Publications, 1934–, vol. 1–. Issued à 26. Subtitle varies: *Music news from coast to coast (1934) and Ballroom, café, radio, studio, symphony, theatre.* Not printed: vol. 31 no. 19–31 no. 23.

3084. *Down Beat Music ...* Chicago: Maher Publications, 1956–, vol. 1–. Issued à 1. Title ends with year of issue, as *Down Beat Music '67.* Alternate titles: *Yearbook, Down Beat's Music, Music.*

3085. *Down Beat Music Directory.* Chicago: Maher Publications, 1969–, vol. 1–. Issued à 4.

3086. *Down Beat Jazz Record Reviews.* Chicago: Maher Publications, 1957–1967, vol. 1–7.

3087. *Down Beat's Yearbook of Swing.* Chicago: Maher Publications, 1939–, vol. 1–. Issued à 1. Former title: *Miller's Yearbook of Popular Music* (to 1943).

3088. *L'echo des sociétiés musicales; harmonies, fanfares, symphonies, chorales, jazz, accordéon.* Bruxelles: J. Buyst, 1946–1948.

3089. European Jazz Federation. *Swinging Newsletter.* Wien: European Jazz Federation, 1972–. Issued irregularly.

3090. *European Jazz Newsletter.* Berne: Lance Tschannen.

3091. *Hip; the Jazz Record Digest.* Milwaukee [etc.]: 1962–1967, vol. 1–5 no. 5; 1967–1971, ns vol. 1-10n6. Issued à 12. Superseded by *Jazz Digest.* Microfilm reprint by Greenwood Press (XJAZ 24).

3092. *Hot Jazz Club.* Santa Fé, Argentina: 1944–. Issued à 4.

3093. *Hot Jazz Information.* Offenbach: Gesellschaft für Förderung des New Orleans Jazz, fl. 1978. Issued à 12.

3094. *Hot Revue; revue mensuelle de jazz hot.* Lausanne: Editions de l'Echiquier J. F. Chastellain, 1945–1947, vol. 1–2 no. 7. Issued à 12. Merged with *Jazz Hot.*

3095. Howard University, Washington, D.C., Department of Jazz Studies. *Liner Notes.* Washington, D.C.: Howard University, 1972–.

3096. International Arts of Jazz. *Newsletter.* Stony Brook: State University of New York, c. 1974–. Issued à 12.

3097. *Internationales Jazz-Podium.* Stuttgart: Verlag Jazz Podium. Issued à 12.

3098. *Jazz; a Quarterly of American Music.* Berkeley: 1958–1960, nl-5. Issued à 4. LC 67–33137. Microfilm reprint by Greenwood Press (XJAZ 5).

3099. *Jazz; nederlandsche uitgave.* Bruxelles: J.W. Genin, 1945–1946, no. 1–13. Issued à 6. Supersedes *Hot Club Magazine.*

3100. *Jazz.* Forest Hills: 1942–1943, vol. 1 no. 1–1 no. 10. Issued irregularly. Superseded by *Jazz Magazine.* Microfilm reprint by Greenwood Press (XJAZ 17).

3101. *Jazz.* Frankfurt am Main: Hoedt, 1949.

3102. *Jazz; miesiecznik ilustrawny.* Gdansk: Gdanskie Wydawnictwo Prasowe RSW Prasa, 19??– (1960), no. 1–(53).

3103. *Jazz; tidning for jazzmusik.* Göteborg: Brod. Weiss (vol. 1 no. 1–2), Västan (vol. 1 no. 3–), 19??, vol. 1–. Issued à 12.

3104. *Jazz.* København: E. Pedersen, 1934–1938. Issued à 12. Former title: *Jazz Avisen.*

3105. *Jazz.* Lisboa: Clube Universitário de Jazz, 1958–. Issued à 9, à 10.

3106. *Il Jazz.* Milano: Ottavio Fabri, Robert Leydi, 1968–1969, no. 1–97. Issued with phono-discs. LC 72–300791.

3107. *Jazz.* New York: Jazz Press, fl. 1944. Issued à 12.

3108. *Jazz: list venovany jazzu a moderni hudbé.* Praha: Gramoklub Praha, Melody Club Praha, 1947–1948, vol. 1–. Issued à 12.

3109. *Jazz Service Organization.* Washington, D.C. (P.O. Box 50152).

3110. *Jazz.* Stockholm: Abe Nyblom & Co., 1934–1936, vl-3.

3111. *Jazz.* Warszawa: 1956–, vol. 1–. Issued à 12. Published in Danzig, 1956–1958.

3112. *Jazz; International Jazz Magazine, deutsche Ausgabe.* Zürich: fl. 1935.

3113. *Jazz, Blues & Co.* Paris: Jazz, Blues & Co., fl. 1978. Issued à 12.

3114. *Jazz and Blues.* London: Hanover Books, 1970–, vol. 1–. Issued à 12. Absorbs *Jazz.* Absorbed by *Jazz Journal.*

3115. *Jazz and Pop.* New York: Jazz Press, 1962–1971, vol. 1–6. Issued à 12. Former title: *Jazz* (vol. 1–6 no. 7).

3116. *Jazz aus Stuttgart; Mitteilungsblatt.* Stuttgart: Club zur Pflege Progressiver Musik, 1956–.

3117. *Jazz Bazaar.* Rotterheide: Hans W. Ewert. Issued à 12.

3118. *Jazz Beat.* London?: 1956–1966. Issued à 52. Former title: *Jazz News.* LC 64–55548.

3119. *Jazz Bücherei; Lebensbeschreibungen für alle Freunde der Jazz.* Wetzlar: Pegasus-Verlag, 1959–, vol. 1–.

3120. *Jazz-Bulletin.* Pilzen: Föderation der CSSR-Jazz Clubs in Prag und Pilsen, fl. 1967. Issued à 6.

3121. *Jazz Catalog; Katalof der Jazzschallplatten; eine nahezu lückenlose Uebersicht über alle in Deutschland erscheinenen JazzPlatten.* Bielefeld: Bielefelder Verlagsanstalt, 1959–, vol. 1–. Issued à 1.

3122. *Jazz Catalogue.* London: Jazz Journal, 1960–, vol. 1–.

3123. *Jazz Circle News.* Manchester, England: Jazz Circle, fl. 1978. Issued à 12.

3124. *Jazz Club News.* Frankfurt am Main: 1945–1948. Issued à 12.

3125. *Jazz Commentary.* Dalbeattie: 1944–1945.

3126. *Jazz di ieri e di oggi.* Milano: G. Spinello, 1959–, vol. 1–. Issued à 4, à 12.

3127. *Jazz Digest.* McLean: E. Steane, 1972–1974, vl-3n6. Issued à 12. *Supersedes Hip; the Jazz Record Digest.*

3128. *Jazz-Echo; ständige Gondel-Beilage für die Jazzfreunde.* Hamburg: Gondel, 1949–. Supplement to *Gondel-Magazin.*

3129. *Jazz-Echo.* New York: International Jazz Federation, fl. 1978. Issued à 5, irregularly.

3130. *Jazz Forum; quarterly review of jazz and literature.* Fordingbridge Ontario: Delphic Press, 1946–1947, no. 1–5. Issued à 4.

3131. *Jazz Forum.* Warszawa: Polska Federacja Jazzova & Polskie Stawarzysznie Jazzowe, 1967–, vol. 1–. Issued à 4.

3132. *Jazz Guide.* London: Chris Wellard, 1964–.

3133. *Jazz hip; revue d'information.* Marseille: Jazz-Club du Sud-Est, 1956–1961, vol. 1–5.

3134. *Jazz Home.* Frankfurt am Main: The Two-Beat Friends, 1949.

3135. *Jazz Hot.* Bruxelles: 1948. Merged with *Jazz Hot* [Paris] in 1948.

3136. *Jazz Hot; la revue internationale du jazz.* Paris: Montmartre, 1935–1939, 1945–, no. 1–32, ns no. 1–. Issued à 11. Issued by Fédération Internationale des Hot Clubs (1947–1956), Fédération Internationale des Hot Clubs Francais (1947–1956). Former title: *Revue* (or *Bulletin*) *Hot Club de France.* Supplemented by Annuaire du jazz. Absorbed same title, issued from Bruxelles, in 1948. Microfilm reprint by Greenwood Press (XJAZ 8).

3137. *Jazz Hot Club Bulletin.* Tokyo: Hot Club of Japan.

Jazz Improvisation. Jenkintown, Pa.: E.S. Proteus.

3138. *Jazz Index; bibliography of jazz literature in periodicals and collections.* Dreieich: Buchdrückerei Schäfer, 1977–, vol. 1–. Issued à 4.

3139. *Jazz Information.* New York: 1939–1941, vol. 1–2 no. 16. Issued à 52 (1939), à 26 (1940–1941). Microfilm reprint by Greenwood Press (XJAZ 6).

3140. *Jazz Journal.* Halle: Arbeitsgemeinschaft für Jazz in der FDJ, Organization der Martin-Luther-Universität, 1955–1956, no. 1–2 no. 3.

3141. *Jazz Journal International.* London: Novello, 1948–, vol. 1–. Issued à 4, à 12. Absorbs *Jazz and Blues* (1975, vol. 28). Former titles: *Jazz Journal and Jazz and Blues, Jazz Journal* (to 1977, vol. 29).

3142. *Jazz Kalender.* Munchen: Nymphenburger Verlag, 1956–, vol. 1–.

3143. *Jazz Letter.* New York: Jazz Arts Society, 1960–. Issued à 12.

3144. *Jazz Magazine.* Buenos Aires: 1945–1946. Issued à 12.

3145. *Jazz Magazine.* Chilwell: Jazz Appreciation Society, 1943–.

3146. *Jazz Magazine.* Northport, N.Y.: Jazz Magazine, 1976–. Issued à 4.

3147. *Jazz Magazine.* Paris: Del Duca, 1954–, vol. 1–. Issued à 12, à 6. Microfilm reprint by Greenwood Press (XJAZ 2).

3148. *Jazz Moderne.* Wien: Hot Club de Vienna, 1953–1954, no. 1–3.

3149. *Jazz Monographs.* StanhopeEngland: Walter C. Allen, 1955–, vol. 1–. Issued irregularly.

3150. *Jazz Monthly.* TruroEngland: Pennare House, 1954–. Issued à 12.

3151. *Jazz Music: The International Jazz Magazine.* London: Jazz Sociological Society, 1942–1943, 1046–1960. Issued à 6, à 12. Absorbs *Jazz Tempo, Discography,* and *Hot News.* Superseded by *Jazz Times.*

3152. *Jazz Music, U.S.A.: The Metronome Yearbook.* New York: Metronome, 1950–1951, 1953–1956.

3153. *Jazz News; revue mensuelle.* Paris: Blue Star Revue, 1948–. Issued à 12.

3154. *Jazz News.* Zürich: Hot Club of Zürich, 1940–1942. Issued à 6, irregularly.

3155. *Jazz Note Bulletin.* Lyon: Hot Club de Lyon, 1953–.

3156. *Jazz Notes.* Adelaide: 1941–, vol. 1–. Issued à 12. Former title: *Jazz Notes and Blue Rhythm.*

3157. *Jazz Notes.* Indianapolis: Indianapolis Jazz Club. Issued à 12.

3158. *Jazz nu: Maandblad voor aktuele geimproviseerde muziek.* Tilburg: Jazz Nu, fl. 1978. Issued à 12.

3159. *Jazz Nytt.* Oslo, Norway.

3160. *Jazz-Nytt fran SJR.* Stockholm: Svenska Jazzriksforbundet, 1965–, vol. 1–. Issued à 6.

3161. *Jazz Panorama.* Toronto: 1946–1948. Issued à 12, irregularly.

3162. *Jazz Podium.* München: Deutsche Jazz Föderation, 1952–, vol. 1–. Former titles: *Das Internationale Jazz-Podium* (vol. 1–3), *Deutsche-Jazz-Foderation Mitteilungsblatt.*

3163. *Jazz (Pop) Music Mirror.* London: 1954–. Former title: *Music Mirror* (1954–1956). Supersedes *Music.*

3164. *Jazz Publications.* Basel: Jazz Publications, 1957–, vol. 1–. [Schweizerische Landesbibliothek, Bern, cites run of 1961–1962, vol. 1–6].

3165. *Jazz Quarterly.* Chicago: Jazz Quarterly Society, 1942–, vol. 1–2 no. 4. Issued à 4. Microfilm reprint by Greenwood Press (XJAZ 18).

3166. *Jazz Rapporter.* Copenhagen: Frantz Christtreus Bogtrukkeri, 1943–1946. Issued à 12.

3167. *The Jazz Record.* New York: 1943–1947, no. 1–60. Issued à 26 (no. 1–9), à 12 (no. 10–60). Microfilm reprint by Greenwood Press (XJAZ 19).

3168. *Jazz Record.* Newark, England: 1943–1944.

3169. *Jazz Report.* Ventura, Calif.: Paul Affeldt, 1958–, vol. 1–. Issued à 6. Also known as *Jazz Report U.S.A.*

3170. *Jazz Review.* London: Jazz Music Books, 1948–. Issued à 12.

3171. *Jazz Review.* New York: 1958–1961, vol. 1–4 no. 1. Reprinted by Kraus Reprint in 1973 (vols. 1–3, lacking vol. 4 no. 1).

3172. *Jazz Revue: Monatsschrift der Interessengemeinschraft.* Berlin: German Jazz Collectors, 1950–1954, vol. 1–5. Supplement to *Vier Viertel.*

3173. *Jazz, Rhythm and Blues: Schweizerische Jazz-Aeitschrift.* Zürich: Jazz Zeitschrift, 1968, vol. 1.

3174. *Jazz Riffs.* Antwerpen: Antwerpse Jazz Club, 1940, 1946–1948, no. 1–2, ns no. 1–28. Issued à 12.

3175. *Jazz rytm i piosenka.* Warszawa. Issued à 12.

3176. *Jazz-Scene.* Birsfelden: Hot Club Basel, 1952–1961, vol. 1–10, nl-92. Former title: *Jazz-Bulletin* (vol. 1–9). Supplemented by *Jazz-Statistics* and *Who's Who; Discograph.*

3177. *Jazz Scene.* London: 1962–, vol. 1–. Issued à 12.

3178. *Jazz Session.* Chicago: Hot Club of Chicago, 1944–1946, no. 1–13. Issued à 6, à 12. Microfilm reprint by Greenwood Press (XJAZ 20).

3179. *Jazz Shop; a bimonthly magazine for collectors.* Milano? Issued à 6.

3180. *Jazz-Statistics.* Basel: Hot Club Basel, 1952–1963. Issued à 6. Supplement to *Jazz-Scene.* Supplemented by *Swiss Jazz Notes.*

3181. *Jazz Studies.* Chinnor: British Institute of Jazz Studies, 1967.

3182. *Jazz tango; revue mensuelle de la musique et des orchestras de danse.* Paris: 1930–1936. Issued à 12. Merged with *L'orchestre* to form *L'orchestre et jazz tango réunis.*

3183. *Jazz Tempo.* Hollywood, Calif.: 1946–. Issued à 12.

3184. *Jazz Tempo: Zeitschrift der Freunde des Jazz.* Kassel: 1951.

3185. *Jazz Tempo.* London: 1943–1944. Issued à 12. Merged with *Jazz Music.*

3186. *Jazz Times.* London: West London Jazz Society, British Jazz Society, 1964–(1967), vol. 1–. Issued à 12. Supersedes *Jazz Music.*

3187. *Jazz Times Bulletin.* Hempel: Society for Jazz Appreciation in the Younger Generation.

3188. *Jazz Up.* Buenos Aires: Ediciones Floryland, 1965–, vol. 1–.

3189. *Jazz Wax.* Birmingham, England 1940–(1948?), no. 1–3.

3190. *Jazz Wereld.* Hilversum: International Musicales, fl. 1965. Issued à 6.

3191. *Jazzbeat.* London: Kemps International Publications, 1956–, vol. 1–. Former title: *Jazz News and Review* (1956–1962).

3192. *Jazzette.* Boston: Boston Jazz League, 1944–, vol. 1–.

3193. *Jazzforschung; jazz research.* Graz: Hochschule für Musik und Darstellende Kunst, Institute für Jazzforschung, International Society for Jazz Research, Universal Edition, 1969–, vol. 1–. Issued à 1.

3194. *Jazzfreund: Mitteilungsblatt des Jazz Club Itzehoe.* Itzehoe, Germany: Jazz Club Itzehoe, 1953–1955, vol. 1–3. Superseded by *Arbeitsgemeinschart Norddeutscher Jazz Club Mitteilungsblatt.*

3195. *Der Jazzfreund: Mitteilungsblatt für Jazzfreunde in Ost und West.* Menden: 1945(?)–1968, vol. 1–10, also fl. 1978? Issued à 4.

3196. *Jazzinformation: Tribune.* København: Selandia Bogtrykeri, 1945–1946. Former title: *Tribune: Tidsskrift for moderne dansemusik* (1945).

3197. *Jazzkalender.* Stockholm: Wenneberg, 1955–. Former title: *Ungdomens Jazzkalender* (1955).

3198. *Jazzmen News.* London: 1945.

3199. *Jazznytt.* Molde Norway: Norsk Jazzforbund, fl. 1978. Issued à 5.

3200. *Jazzology.* London: Corthall Press, 1944–1947. Issued à 12.

3201. *Le Jazzophone.* Paris: Le Jazzophone, fl. 1978. Issued à 4.

3202. *JazzTimes.* P.O. Box 99050, Collingswood, New Jersey 08108–0613.

3203. *Jazztimes.* Stockholm: Svenska Jazz Klubbarnas Riksförbund, fl. 1955.

3204. *Jazzways: A Yearbook of Hot Music.* Cincinnatti: 1946–1947, vol. 1–2.

3205. *Journal of Jazz Discography.* Newport, England Chris Evans, fl. 1978. Issued à 2, irregularly.

3206. *Journal of Jazz Studies.* New Brunswick, N.J.: Rutgers Institute of Jazz Studies. 1973–, vol. l–. Issued à 2. Incorporates *Studies in Jazz Discography* LC 74–641997.

3207. *Latin Beat.* Gardenia, California.

3208. *Maitres du jazz.* Paris: Editions du Belvedère, 1949, vol. l.

3209. *Matrix: Jazz Record Research Magazine.* Madeley [etc.]: Bernard Holland & Gary Charsley, 1954–1975, no. l–107/108. Issued à 6. Absorbed *Discophile* in 1959. Microfilm reprint by Greenwood Press (XJAZ 12).

3210. *Mecca: The Magazine of Traditional Jazz.* New Orleans: 1974–1975, vl-2. Issued à 12.

3211. *Memory Lane: Dance Band, Vocal and Jazz Review.* Leigh-on-Sea, England: fl. 1978. Issued à 4.

3212. *Mitteilungen für Jazz-Interessen.* Berlin: 1943, no. l–3.

3213. *Modern Jazz.* Bologna: Ruggero Stiassi, fl. 1967. Issued à 12. In English.

3214. *Music: Le magazine du jazz.* Bruxelles: 1924–1930. Issued à 12.

3215. *Music Memories and Jazz Report.* Birmingham, England: Great: 1954–. Issued à 4. Absorbed *Jazz Report* in 1961.

3216. *Musica Jazz.* Milano: Messaggerie Musicali, 1945–, vol. l–. Issued à 11.

3217. *Musik revue: Tidsskrift for jazzmusik.* København: 1954–1956, nl-8. Subtitle varies: *Jazz, pop, klassik.*

3218. *Musique variété, musette, jazz, ciinémas, chansons.* Vilvorde: Belgium Notes Distributions, 1958–, no. l–. Issued à 2, irregularly. Title concludes with year of issue, as *Musique 58.*

3219. *NOJC News.* Tiburon: New Orleans Jazz Club of Northern California, 1971–, vol. l–. Issued à 12.

3220. National Association of Jazz Educators. *NAJE Educator.* Manhattan, KS: National Association of Jazz Educators, 1968–, vol. l–. Issued à 5. Former title: its *Newsletter* (vol. l–2 no. l). Microfilm reprint by Greenwood Press (XJAZ 14).

3221. New Jazz Club, Zürich. *Mitteilungsblatt.* Zürich: New Jazz Club, 1956–.

3222. *Nicopia Jazz.* Nyköping: Nicopia Jazz Club, 1958–, vol. l–.

3223. *Opus.* Gävle: Gävle Jazzklub, 1966–, vol. l–.

3224. *Orkester Journalen.* Stockholm: 1933–, vol. l–. Issued à 12. Also known as *OJ: Tidskrift för jazzmusik.* Subtitle varies: *Aktuelle för modern* *dansmusik* (1933–1935), *Aktuelle för jazzmusik,* and *Tidskrift för modern dansmusik.*

3225. *PL Yearbook of Jazz.* London: 1946–, vol. 1–.

3226. *Perfectly Frank: The Magazine for the Connoisseur of Popular Jazz Music.* London. Issued à 6.

3227. *Pieces of Jazz.* Kent, England. Issued à 4.

3228. *Playback.* New Orleans: Orin Blackstone, 1948–1952, vol. 1–4 no. 29. Issued and numbered irregularly. Former title: *Jazzfinder* (1948–1949). Microfilm reprint by Greenwood Press (XJAZ 11).

3229. *Le Point du Jazz.* Bruxelles: fl. 1973.

3230. *Radio Free Jazz.* Washington, D.C.: fl. 1978. Issued à 12.

3231. *Le revue de jazz.* Paris: Hot Club de France, 1949–1950, 1952.

3232. *Schlagzeug; das Jazz-Magazin.* Berlin: Aquator Verlag, 1956–1959, vol. 1–4. Issued à 12.

3233. *The Second Line.* New Orleans: New Orleans Jazz Club, New Orleans Jazz Museum and Archives, 1950–, vol. 1–. Issued and numbered irregularly. Microfilm reprint by Greenwood Press (XJAZ 4).

3234. Sheffield University. Jazz Club. *Magazine.* Sheffield: 1966–.

3235. *Studies in Jazz Discography.* New Brunswick, N.J.: Institute of Jazz Studies, Rutgers University, 1971–, vol. 1–. Absorbed by *Journal of Jazz Studies.* Reprint by Greenwood Press in 1978.

3236. *Swing: Tidskrift for ungdom modern musik, sport och dans.* Stockholm: 1944–, vol. 1–.

3237. *Tradjazz-nytt: Organ för trad jazz.* Stockholm: 1973–. Issued à 6.

3238. *Universal Jazz.* Reading: 1946–. Issued à 12.

3239. *VJM: Vintage Jazz Mart.* London: Trevor Benwell. Issued à 6, irregularly.

3240. *Vibrations: The Sound of the Jazz Community.* New York: 1967–, vol. 1–. Issued à 12.

3241. *Vier-Viertel: Musik-Magazin für Schlager-, Film, Jazz- und Schallplatten-freunde.* Berlin: Capriccio (1947–1954), Finanz-Verlag (1955–1956), 1947–1956, vol. 1–10. Issued à 24. Subtitle varies: *Halbmonatsschrift für Musik und Tanz.* Supplemented by *Jazz Revue* (1950–1959) and *Jazz Courier* (1955–1956).

3242. *Vieux Carré Courier: What's New and To Do in these Fabled Environs.* New Orleans: New Orleans Jazzfest International, 1968–, vol. 1–. Also known as *Jazzfest International.*

3243. *Westjazz: Jazz-Nachrichten aus Westdeutschland.* Dortmund: Wulff (1955), Herschenbach (1956–), 1955–, vol. 1–. Former title: *HCD Bulletin* (vol. 1).

XV

Jazz Research Libraries

3244. Berklee College of Music—Library. 1140 Boylston Street: Boston, Massachusetts 02215.

Contains an extensive collection of recording, scores, periodicals, and books.

3245. Detroit Public Library—Music and Performing Arts Department. 5201 Woodward Avenue: Detroit, Michigan 48201.

In addition to books and periodicals, the library contains materials on Detroit and Detroit-area jazz artists and other musicians.

Special Collections: E. Azalia Hackley Collection (Blacks in the Performing Arts). Contains some materials of potential interest to jazz scholars.

3246. Indiana University—Black Music Center—Library. 244 Sycamore Hall: Bloomington, Indiana 47401.

Includes numerous recordings of jazz and other African American musical styles, scores, periodicals, and books.

3247. New Orleans Jazz Club—New Orleans Jazz Museum—Library. 340 Bourbon Street: New Orleans, Louisiana 70116.

Subjects: jazz, swing, ragtime, boogie-woogie, bop, minstrelsy, progressive jazz.

Special Collections: Music of Africa, Haiti, and early Louisiana.

Holdings: over 600 books; 20 bound periodicals, volumes, 5 vertical file drawers of archival material dealing with jazz and its prehistory; photographs, tapes, sheet music, and records.

3248. New Orleans Public Library—Art and Music Division. 219 Loyola Avenue: New Orleans, Louisiana 70140.

Special Collections: Souchan jazz collection (recordings); early U.S. sheet music; Fischer collection of early vocal recordings.

Holdings: Over 28,000 books; 1,212 bound periodical volumes; 4 vertical file drawers of film catalogs; 4 vertical file drawers of pamphlets; 45,276 mounted pictures; 19,273 phonograph records; 800 framed art prints.

3249. New York Public Library—Arthur Alfonso Schomburg Collection. 515 Lenox Avenue: New York, New York 10037.

Special Collections: International in scope and interest. Includes more than 58,000 volumes (all areas of black music) along with phonograph records, tape recordings, promos, posters, paintings, sculptures, clippings, periodicals, pamphlets, sheet music, and newspapers as well as large holdings of manuscript and archival records. Much of the collection is of jazz.

3250. Rutgers, The State University of New Jersey—Institute of Jazz Studies. Newark, New Jersey.

Holdings: More than 6,000 books; 5,000 bound periodical volumes; records and collections, manuscripts, piano rolls, photographs, jazz magazines, music, instruments, and sculptures. Library open to public by appointment only.

3251. Tulane University of Louisiana—Archive of New Orleans Jazz. Howard-Tilton Memorial Library: New Orleans, Louisiana 70118.

Subjects: New Orleans jazz, with related background material and a limited amount of material pertaining to later developments in jazz.

Special Collections: Nick La Rocca collection (2644 items); Al Rose collection (902 items); John Robichaux collection (7219 items); Herbert A. Otto collection (20 tapes).

Holdings: Over 1,200 books; 6 reels of microfilm; 32 motion picture reels; 7,415 periodicals; 5,456 photographs; 56 piano rolls; 8,617 records; 2,046 reels of tape recorded music and interviews. Open to researchers.

3252. UCLA Oral History Program. Los Angeles, California 90095.

Contains many interviews that relate to the history of jazz in Los Angeles. Among the many interviews are those of Ernie Andrews, Clora Bryant,

Buddy Collette, William Green, Jack Kelson, Horace Tapscott, Gerald Wilson, Marl Young, and many others. In addition, the program includes a wealth of materials that deal with the history and evolution of jazz on Central Avenue (Los Angeles).

3253. University of Miami—School of Music—Albert Pick Music Library. Coral Gables, Florida 33124.

Subjects: Music scores and recordings.

Special Collections: Autographed recordings (composers and performers); ethnic recordings, especially African, Latin American, American Indian, and jazz. Holdings: over 12,000 music scores and 8,000 phonograph recordings.

3254. U.S. Navy—School of Music—Reference Library. NAVPHI base, Little Creek: Norfolk, Virginia 23521.

Subjects: Analysis, conducting, composition, counterpoint, harmony, instruments, jazz, military music, and theory of music.

3255. Yale University—Beinecke Library, 120 High Street: New Haven, Connecticut 06520. James Weldon Johnson Collection of Negro Arts and Letters.

Founded by Carl Van Vechten in 1961. Concentrates on the achievements of blacks in the United States in the twentieth century in the fine arts. It contains extensive holdings of original recordings of black performers, for example, Bessie Smith, Clara Smith, and W. C. Handy. Also included are some original manuscripts of black musicians.

Yale University Music Library, 98 Wall Street: New Haven, Connecticut 05620.

Holdings: 1,500 Benny Goodman arrangements, plus his photographs, scrapbooks, programs, and publicity materials; Stanley Dance and Helen Oakley Dance archives includes photographs of jazz performers, jazz periodicals, and miscellaneous papers; jazz band collections by Red Norvo; jazz arrangements and personal papers of Slam Stewart; Eddie Sauter jazz arrangements and orchestrations for films and musicals.

Index

A

Aasland, Benny, 1283
ABC, 1838, 2953, 3024
Abercrombie, John, 895, 922, 1983, 2833, 2871
Aboucaya, Jacques, 1095
Abrams, Max, 204, 736, 887, 937, 1097, 2878, 2949, 2951
Adams, Pepper, 812, 887, 2630, 2823, 2976, 3050
Adderley
    Cannonball, 167, 888, 915, 1518, 1541, 1549, 2249, 2364–2366, 2401, 2501, 2533, 2843, 3006
    Nat, 2364, 2839, 2925, 3006, 3020
Adler, Wilfred, 2025, 2192, 2565, 2576, 2616, 2685, 2765
Aebersold, Jamey, 1760, 1817, 1819, 1827–1828, 1830, 1843, 1847, 1852, 1859, 1867, 1869–1873, 1875–1884, 1887–1888, 1891, 1893–1896, 1898–1900, 1903–1904, 1913, 1919, 1923, 1926–1927, 1929, 1933–1934, 1940, 1942, 1944, 1948–1950, 1953–1954, 1963, 1977–1978, 1988, 2003, 2017, 2024, 2048, 2099, 2160–2166, 2168–2170, 2191, 2195–2196, 2201, 2204–2207, 2211–2217, 2220, 2224, 2227, 2229, 2231, 2234–2237, 2240, 2245, 2251–2252, 2257, 2260, 2262, 2266, 2289–2290, 2292, 2307, 2321, 2330, 2338, 2345–2364, 2366, 2375, 2377–2378, 2380, 2382–2383, 2385, 2387, 2389–2390, 2398, 2401, 2406, 2412, 2414, 2416–2417, 2428, 2430, 2439–2440, 2443, 2445–2446, 2455–2456, 2458–2463, 2467, 2470, 2472–2473, 2475, 2483, 2492–2493, 2499–2500, 2516, 2522, 2529, 2531–2536, 2552–2553, 2562–2563, 2568, 2573, 2586, 2596–2597, 2601, 2603, 2617–2618, 2627, 2630–2640, 2643, 2647–2648, 2652, 2661, 2666, 2669, 2675, 2693, 2703, 2705, 2709, 2714, 2716, 2720, 2723, 2728–2729, 2736, 2744–2746, 2751, 2758, 2772–2775, 2777–2781, 2856, 2871–2872, 2875, 2880, 2891
Aebersold for bass, 2346a
Aebersold for piano, 2359
Aesthetics, 1–84
    dissertations/theses on, 1638
Africa, 100, 136, 237, 241, 246, 433, 976, 1017, 1021, 1031, 1034, 1055, 1521, 1523, 1654, 1811, 2912, 2999, 3247
African influences, 235–246
African roots, 8, 233, 241, 977, 1764, 1766
Afro-Cuban, 235–236, 238, 576, 645, 648–650, 1017, 1109, 1487, 1706, 1886, 1897, 1904, 2092, 2216, 2491, 2881
Afro-Cuban influence, 235–246
After Hours Club, 2652
Agostinelli, Anthony J., 1, 645
Ahola, Sylvester, 366
Airto, 243, 734, 2094, 2625, 2721, 2844, 2964
Aitken, Allen, 1037, 1725
Ake, David, 3, 301, 1638
Akiyoshi, Toshiko, 837, 857–858, 902, 934, 2538, 2777, 2972, 3002, 3014
Aladdin, 1492
Albert, Don, 367
Alcorn, Alvin, 2857
Alexander, Van, 356, 738, 1273, 1798, 1813, 2667, 2795, 2924
All-Stars, 2929, 3003, 3050
Allee, Andy, 2334, 2337, 2343–2344
Allen, Daniel, 85
Allen, George Edward, 1802
Allen, Red, 368, 836, 899, 939, 1212, 1444–1445, 2775, 2779, 2934, 2943, 3026
Allen, Walter, 606, 1222, 1366
Almeida, Laurindo, 2788, 2932, 2963, 3030
Alpert, Herb, 2367